Personal Property Law

For TK-D

Personal Property Law

by

Simon Gleeson

Partner,
Richards Bulter

LAW & TAX

© Pearson Professional 1997

Simon Gleeson has asserted his rights under the Copyright Designs and Patents Act 1988 to be identified as the author of this work.

ISBN 0752 002848

Published by
FT Law and Tax
21–27 Lamb's Conduit Street
London WC1N 3NJ

http://www.ftlawandtax.com

A Division of Pearson Professional Limited

Associated offices
Australia, Belgium, Canada, Hong Kong, India, Japan, Luxembourg,
Singapore, Spain, USA

A CIP catalogue record for this book is available from the British Library.

Printed and bound by Biddles, Guildford

Contents

Preface

It is possible that as late as the beginning of this century the law of property could be divided into the law of ownership and seisin of land and the law of ownership and possession of goods. This produced books on land law, which emphasised the doctrines of conveyancing, and a small number of books on personal property which discussed the law relating to transfers of goods. In the modern world the division is trifurcate, into land, goods and financial assets. The class of financial assets has grown to overtop all others in terms of total value and importance in commercial transactions, but the law has not moved as fast as perhaps it might have to address the issues which arise out of the separate existence of these assets as property. In this book I have almost disregarded the classical law relating to the transfer of goods, on the basis that this subject is already dealt with exceptionally well in existing works both on property and on sale of goods. What I have sought to do here is to elucidate a law of personal property which is focused on financial assets. This has led me into a number of choices as to content, the most regrettable being the exclusion of the law relating to intellectual property rights. The decision is defensible on the grounds that these rights are already sufficiently well treated in existing works that I cannot believe that there would have been anything of value to say here, whereas large proportions of the law relating to property interests in financial assets are precariously balanced upon the back of some *obiter dicta* (as it is not unreasonable to call them) of the twin atlases of the subject, Roy Goode and Philip Wood.

Currency has always been a special type of property, being not a thing but the measure of all things, and in particular it has the unique property that perfect title to it is created anew in the hands of any transferee for value. It may be said that the law of title to goods is based upon the maxim that *nemo dat quod non habet*, the law of currency is based upon the maxim that *omnes possunt dare quod non habent*. This 'negotiability' of currency in the form of coinage was mimicked by merchants with their bills and banks with their notes, and these documents acquired over time an almost identical characteristic of negotiability. Around this core there grew a class of intangible property which, although not negotiable, had many of the characteristics of negotiability, and around that again there grew further classes of intangible property—shares, bonds, certificates of deposit, letters of credit and suchlike. All of these financial assets, clearly not being goods, tend to be treated at law as being quasi-land, regardless of the fact that they are in all respects completely unlike land.

The problem here is not the baroque splendour of eighteenth- and nineteenth-century conveyancing. Classical land law is a rigorous logical construct and its propositions, rigorously applied, would deal satisfactorily with many of these issues. The problems arise from two sources. One is that the primary distinction between land and property is that property is fungible, land is not. There is nothing that a person who has wrongfully obtained seisin of land can do to improve his title to it. The person who has wrongfully obtained possession of goods, and to an even greater extent the person who has wrongfully obtained the indicia of title to a financial asset, can render his title unchallengeable by simply mixing that property with other identical property of his own. The second is that the remedial, equitable element of the system relied upon the extraordinary width of the concept of constructive notice, such that the class of those who could resist the claims of a prior owner on the basis that they were purchasers for value without notice was confined within narrow limits. In the case of financial assets every transferee is a purchaser for value without notice until the contrary be proved. What is being attempted in the field of financial assets is to apply nineteenth century common law without recourse to nineteenth century equity, and the result is neither pretty nor logically satisfactory. It is this dysfunction which has led to the explosion of activity in the field of restitution, where some of the best minds of our generation are trying to find a common law mechanism which will overcome the problem.

The primary distinction in the categorisation of property wrongs is as between those wrongs which do not result in title to property passing, and those wrongs which do result in title to property passing. The first class may be summarised as 'theft', the second as 'fraud'. The first category is massively the larger class in terms of the number of acts which the judicial system is required to deal with. However, the consequences of these wrongs are not much considered by civil lawyers. Stolen property was (and is) seldom recovered by litigation since the wrong is usually patent and only the location of the goods is in doubt. Where the goods can be identified in the hands of the wrongdoer, their return to the original owner tends to be an administrative process, entered into on the underlying assumption that *nemo dat quod non habet*. If the goods are not in the hands of the wrongdoer the owner does not acquire any right against the other property of the wrongdoer. There is a small and rare exception to this latter rule where the thief has in his hands property which, although it is not the stolen property, is clearly and identifiably property which is wholly the exchange product of the stolen property. The interference with property rights which this involves is serious, and the remedy is only available in a very few cases. This is the remedy which is known as common law tracing, and it is a remedy which arises in the cases only of wrongs which do not pass title.

Financial assets cannot be stolen, in the sense that any misappropriation tends to result in a passing of title. Thus the remedies for wrongs involving the misappropriation of financial assets tend to be found exclusively in the sphere of the second class: that of remedies for wrongs which do pass title. In these cases the remedy involves an offence against the principles of certainty of title and quiet possession. Commerce requires a faith in the ability to transfer property; and entry into any transaction of sale and purchase requires a fundamental certainty that the property transfer bargained for is not arbitrarily reversible. The confinement of the availability of this remedy to wrongs which constitute breaches of 'fiduciary relationships' has been bitterly criticised as contrary to the most fundamental principles of justice. This criticism is fully justified. However, certainty of title is also contrary to the most fundamental principles of justice, if what is meant by that term is the doing of complete equity between man and man. It may well be that we now know that the market itself is inimical to the doing of complete equity between man and man, but if this is the case then we also know that attempts to overthrow the market in the interests of that perfect equity result in real oppression, starvation and mortality without any appreciable increase in the overall level of equity done. Some limitation on the proprietary remedy available for wrongfully induced transfers of title is essential, and the confinement to fiduciaries, although arbitrary, is probably the widest limit which can be set.

The conclusion to which we are drawn is that the orthodox rules of property law do not deal satisfactorily with the issues which are raised by wrongs committed in relation to financial assets, and that the solution here is, in the long term, either the development of a distinct and separate common law of title to financial assets or statutory intervention. The prospect of legislation seems firmly closed in this country for the moment, although in the United States the adoption of the new Article 8 of the Uniform Commercial Code has gone a long way towards effecting a wholesale modernisation of property law which appears to address, if not completely solve, most of the problems which are outlined above. The bold experiment effected by Article 9 of the same code, which dispenses with the ordinary doctrines of property law in the field of security, replacing them with a single statutory security interest, should have been effected in this country. It may be that the disastrous implementation of the first phase of the Crowther Committee programme in the Consumer Credit Act 1974 cured the Department of Trade and Industry for all time of the desire to intervene in this area, and the chances of such action are not enhanced by the fact that it is generally reckoned that any future improvement of the law of security should encompass a restructuring of the Consumer Credit Act, an act which has been described as the worst possible implementation of the best possible conceptual structure for the regulation of the provision of credit. The work of the Crowther and Diamond Committees has demonstrated beyond a shadow of doubt both the need and the mechanism by which the need may be filled, but implementation seems to have been postponed *sine die*. As far as the development of the common law system is concerned, the process of creating new proprietary remedies is, through the development of the law of restitution, very far advanced. However what is not done, and possibly cannot be done, is the execution of existing proprietary rights, and the continuing controversy as to the legal position of those whose business is the provision of custodianship of financial assets illustrates very clearly the difficulties of denying proprietary remedies in clearly proprietary situations, even to those who neither request nor require them.

My interest in the area of personal property law was sparked partly by a long-standing interest in the law of restitution and of tracing, partly by my daytime work as a solicitor taking security over property. The second convinced me that the principles of property law were poorly understood outside the field of land law, and the first that these principles were not always rigorously applied by those in hot pursuit of justice. I eventually came to understand that, because of the way in which the law has developed, personal property law has been a Cinderella for a number of other disciplines, and that it was so rarely given centre-stage that in order to uncover underlying principles it is necessary to collect fragments from each of these disciplines and to piece them together into a coherent whole. This is what I have endeavoured to do in this book. Rereading it in its final form I am tempted to feel that its epigraph should be that seldom in the field of legal scholarship has one person written in one book on so many areas in which he is so far from expert. I cannot deny this charge, but I can plead in mitigation that the work may make up in breadth what it lacks in depth, and I am not unhopeful that the process of refuting some of the conjectures advanced herein may benefit others as well as myself in terms of concentrating attention on some fundamental foundations of our law which, having been neglected for some time, may stand in need of a little maintenance.

The ideas and concepts which are developed in this book are very much my own, and I do not wish to besmirch the good name of any of my friends or colleagues with them, although I cannot resist mentioning the stance taken by Tracy Kingsley-Daniells, who maintained throughout that it was a harebrained scheme best left unattempted (at least by me). This is probably the proper wifely response to any attempt by husbands to write books, and I should like to record my gratitude that her threats of divorce remain unconsummated. I should also like to acknowledge a debt of gratitude to three professors. Peter Birks, Regius Professor of Civil Law at the University of Oxford, provided me, as so many others, with both a conceptual framework for the law of restitution and a target to aim at in the form of his beautifully lucid prose. David Hayton, Professor of Law at Kings College London, has shaped our understanding of equity for many years and shown so many students (including myself) that difficult points of law could also be the most tremendous fun. Finally Anthony Levi, who was, when I first met him, Buchannan Professor of French Language and Literature at the University of St Andrews, to whom I am more grateful for support intellectual, spiritual and personal than I can ever say. I must also record a tremendous debt to the two people who perhaps looked forward most to seeing this book in print. Joseph Gleeson and Ivan Kingsley-Daniells will be remembered by all who knew them for long after the book has been forgotten.

Simon Gleeson
Richards Butler

10 November 1997

Table of Cases

Table of Statutes

Table of Statutory Instruments and Conventions

Section 1

The Legal Nature of Property

Contents

Chapter 1

The Legal Nature of Property

Property has been famously defined as the residue of legal rights in an asset remaining in a person, or persons concurrently, after specific rights in the asset have been granted to others[1]. This is probably incorrect. The exclusive analysis of law in terms of rights and obligations which has dominated jurisprudence in the recent past has left little room for any concept of property other than as a 'bundle of rights'[2]; yet it is clear that where a person untrained in the law thinks of his property, he thinks not of his relations with other persons but, initially at least, of a relationship with the thing itself. Recent work is beginning to explore the idea that the property relationship is more than a simple bundle of rights, and it is beginning to be asserted that even in jurisprudential terms it may be necessary to consider the 'thinghood' of property as well as the rights which make up the incidents of property[3]. This book endeavors to catalogue some of the things which are capable of being the subject of property rights, and to discuss some of the rights and liabilities which may arise from different transactions in relation thereto. The orientation towards types of property rather than types of rights is an essential component to property law, and it is interesting (and may be significant) that a descent from the abstract to the day-to-day in the context of legal analysis necessitates the adoption of such a 'thing-based' perspective.

The things which are 'property' may be defined as things which have actual existence and are capable of being owned. Some things have existence but cannot be owned; these are not property[4]. Equally, some things have no incidents of existence aside from their ownership[5]; these are nonetheless property. Something which is owned but cannot be transferred under any circumstances is not property. Natural or human rights, if they may be said to exist, are not a species of intangible property for this reason. However, a distinction must be drawn between property which could be transferred were it not for a prohibition upon such transfer[6] (which is property despite its untransferrability),

---

[1] A M Honoré, 'Ownership' in *Oxford Essays in Jurisprudence* (ed A G Guest), p 126; R W M Dias, *Jurisprudence*, 4th edn, p 405.

[2] J E Penner 'The "Bundle of Rights" Picture of Property', 43 UCLA Law Review 711.

[3] See J E Penner, *The Idea of Property in Law* (OUP, 1997), especially at Chap 5, 'The Objects of Property: the Separability Thesis'.

[4] For example, at common law a dead body cannot be owned (3 Co Inst 110 at 203; *Haynes' Case* (1614) 12 Co Rep 113, *Handyside's Case* (1750) 2 East PC 652; *Doodeward v Spence* (1908) 6 CLR 406, in which a corpse was described as *nullius in rebus*).

[5] For example, an advowson (a right of presentment), although these are incorporeal hereditaments: Co Litt 17b.

[6] For example, profits from an office held under the Crown (*see* pp 130–3 *below*).

and property which is logically incapable of vesting in any person other than the transferor (eg a 'right' to free speech). Where something can be owned and can be transferred, it is property whether or not it has physical existence, and for this purpose a thing can be transferred whether or not the transferor or the transferee has any say in or influence over its transfer[7].

Land and other property

The distinguishing characteristic of the English law of property is a bifurcation between the law relating to land and the law relating to other property which, driven originally by the imperatives of feudal administration, has ripened into a complex—and at times baffling—system in which apparently identical rules can produce radically different results depending on the class of property concerned[8]. The object of this book is not to separate the two, for the concepts, although nominally separate, are in reality closely intertwined.

The rules of English property law grew in an era where wealth was land and land was wealth, and the rules relating to non-land were confined to a small part of law's empire. Maitland's jest that 'not even in the feudal age did men eat or drink land'[9] is valid to the extent that it emphasises that at all times and in all places there must have been a law of personal property. However, the relative unimportance of that law in the courts of England at the time[10] may be simply explained by considering the relative proportions of the wealth of the country which was embodied in land on the one hand and in goods on the other.

This division of wealth has been turned on its head in the living past. The bulk of the wealth of the globe, let alone England, is today held in the form of that subdivision of personal property known as intangible assets—bonds, shares, money obligations of every kind. This area of economic activity dwarfs the aggregate value of transactions in goods which formed the major part of the law of property as recently as a century ago, and the aggregate value of those transactions in goods in turn dwarfs the total value of the land of most of the countries to which that trade relates.

Land and goods are relatively easily identifiable in the outside world, and are not always easily distinguishable. Intangible property, by contrast, is usually identifiable and exists (when it does exist) entirely within the legal system[11]. Intangible property may exist in three forms: as a claim either to land, to goods, or to money. A claim to money may loosely be called a 'pure' intan-

---

[7] Thus entailed property, which passes from one to another upon death without the voluntary act of either party, is nonetheless property. Thus, so is a gift subject to condition subsequent. Penner (*see* fn 3 *above*) begins the analysis with renounceability, deriving an ability to transfer from the possibility of abandonment. However, this approach is open to question since it may not deal satisfactorily with cases of involuntary transfer.

[8] For example, the question of whether a purchaser of property is bound by agreements concerning the property with third parties has radically different answers depending on whether the property is characterised as real or personal—(*see* pp 20–4*below*).

[9] Pollock & Maitland, *History of English Law*, 2nd edn (Cambridge University Press,1968), p 149.

[10] The idea that there was a flourishing jurisprudence of personal property in courts merchant whose records are unfortunately lost is currently under sustained attack—see J S Rogers, *The Early History of Bills & Notes* (Cambridge University Press, 1995), pp 12–20.

gible. In pure theory a distinction should be drawn between a claim to land or goods and a property right in land or goods.

This categorisation has substantive consequences for the rights and liabilities which can be created in or attached to property. It is therefore necessary to delineate the boundary between real and personal property[12].

Origins of the distinction between real and personal property

The distinction between real and personal property was first developed in the law of succession. Government in all ages has endeavored to control the distribution of wealth between its subjects, and it is unsurprising that the primary legacy of a millennium in which the most important component of the country's wealth was its own soil has been a complex system of law concerning that soil. Succession to the ownership of things, by contrast, seems not to have been given the same importance.

This division became reinforced within the structure of the court system by the fact that claims relating to goods seem to have been dealt with largely outside the King's courts. This is more likely to have been the result of accident than of policy. Courts whose primary role is the hearing of long and complex actions concerning historical title to land would not have reacted favourably to being confronted with short, pithy points of mercantile practice between parties who had hours or days to decide their cases. If the merchants were not prepared to take title seriously, the early courts may then have felt, they should take their disputes elsewhere.

Not that the King's courts would have then been idle. The rules governing the transmission of title to land are simple in no system, and the policing of government regulation as to who might pass title to land to whom would have been sufficient for a substantial schedule of hearings. To this must be added the administrative burden of policing the power structures of the feudal system, which was itself (viewed in one light) an incident of the law of real property. The primary necessity was to identify which property was and which property was not real property, and to apply the primary feudal doctrine of impartible succession to the heir at law[13]. A man might do what he would with his other goods, but continuation of the unity of his fief was a matter of public policy. As Pollock and Maitland observe[14]:

---

[11] In the field of intangibles it must never be forgotten that where a man owes me money or a duty, the question of whether I own an asset depends entirely on how effectively I can compel him to pay the money or perform the duty. Leaving aside extra-legal enforcement, this in turn is a question of the operation of the law. If the law certainly compels him, then I have an asset. If the law may compel him depending on the fall of external (ie non-legal) factors, then I have a lottery ticket. If the law does not compel, then I have nothing.

[12] As mentioned below the intermediate class of chattels real, although contributing largely to the development of English law, is in this era best discarded.

[13] Ie the person whom the law designated as the rightful heir, as opposed to some irritating interloper whose sole claim was that the deceased had wished him to be his heir.

[14] Pollock & Maitland (*see* fn 9 *above*), vol II, p 262. In this case administrative law and land law are indivisible—from a king who is also a seigneur only the most theoretical of constitutional lawyers can truly distinguish a rent and a tax.

It is in the highest and the lowest of the social strata that impartible succession first appears. The great fief which is both property and office must, if it be inherited at all, descend as an integral whole; the more or less precarious rights which the unfree peasant has in a tenement must, if they be transmissible at all, pass to one person.

However, in a society based entirely on landholding it was clear that this related only to land. Personal property, the peripheral residue of landholding, neither required nor warranted such protection, and those items which, not being land, were still essential to the exercise of power or authority were deemed to be land (as 'heirlooms').

This principle, which created across Europe the unnatural rule of primogeniture (although the rule was that the succession was impartible rather than primogenital; there are examples of impartible succession by the youngest rather than the eldest son), required as a necessary corollary a rule for the identification of what was and what was not an integral part of the succession. The popularity of the last will and testament leaving substantial bequests to the church led to continual and substantial dispute over which assets might and which might not be granted away upon death, and these arguments merged imperceptibly into those about what might and might not be granted away during life. This is the paradox that a man who could claim the whole of his ancestor's estate upon his death might not prevent that ancestor granting away the whole of his patrimony whilst still alive—the problem that *nemo est heres viventis*[15]. Glanville described a complex series of rules by which a landowner might not alienate land without the expectant heir's consent. These rules were swept away in his lifetime[16] and Bracton does not deign to notice them[17]. This effected a dramatic division between the structure of the law of property in England and its continental counterparts. In the continental countries the right of the heir to defeat a gift by his ancestor lingered on to bedevil conveyancers and purchasers alike. In England, by contrast, the position was simplified to a symmetry: during his life the landowner might do any thing; upon his death his estate passed strictly according to law to the one true heir.

The rule thus crystallized that only personal property might be disposed of by will. Initially even personal property might not be freely disposed of, and dispositions were restricted in the way similar to that still found in continental legal systems that a testator may dispose of only one-third of his estate, the remaining two-thirds standing as a statutory bequest to his wife and children respectively[18]. This rule endured curiously long; indeed in London it was only formally abolished in 1725[19]. However, as a general rule there were never substantial restrictions on the free transferability of personalty upon death.

---

[15] Although the status of heir was a peculiar one—as Glanville said, only God can make an heir (Pollock & Maitland (*see* fn 9 *above*), vol II, p 325).
[16] Pollock & Maitland (*see* fn 9 *above*), vol II, p 308.
[17] Bracton, fn 17.
[18] Pollock & Maitland (*see* fn 9 *above*), vol II, p 348.
[19] By 1 Geo I, c 18, 1724, ss 17 and 18.

Restrictions on bequests of land, however, took longer to clear. Technically they were defeated by the device of enfeoffment to use during the life of the testator, and the belief that the Statute of Uses 1535 took effect to interfere with this method of achieving free testamentary disposition of land resulted in the passing of the Statute of Wills in 1540 in order specifically to authorise limited devises of land. In effect, the Tenures Abolition Act 1660 had the effect of making all land freely devisable by will, but the old system endured in the case of intestacy, and prior to 1925 the position on intestacy remained that real property owned by the deceased at the time of his death passed to the (single) heir at law, whilst personalty passed to the next of kin in equal shares[20].

In terms of individual testamentary succession, the distinction was preserved long after the end of its useful life in the Administration of Estates Act 1925, where different provisions relate to the treatment of real and personal property. There are still circumstances in which the characterisation of property as real or personal may affect its treatment by the executor.

Distinguishing real and personal property

Having seen why the distinction between real and other property became of such great importance, it is easier to understand the mechanisms by which the distinction was made. As might be expected, the fact that land is relatively easily identifiable did not exhaust the possibilities. Because of the policy and other considerations which underlay the division there were a number of cases in which the question of what was and what was not land might be answered only by the application of an advanced legal calculus. Of this calculus only three propositions remain of importance; these are the rules relating to a leasehold interest in land, to incorporeal hereditaments, and the doctrine of conversion.

The lease of land

The lease of land has conventionally been treated as a type of property *sui generis*, lying halfway between real and personal property. The suggested explanation is that the leasehold, being a contractual arrangement governing the occupation of land, was a structure repugnant to the feudal doctrines of tenure, and that the feudal rules which laid down the doctrine of succession to real property could not embrace it. However, to treat a leaseholder in occupation as having no proprietary interest in the land (as, in effect, holding no more than a contractual licence protected only by an action for money compensation) was an idea repugnant to the courts and to their ideas of rights to land, and the leasehold tenant troubled the structure of English law for some time until a means was found to accommodate him.

The way in which the leaseholder passed from being a person with a per-

---

[20] Fuller details can be found in Megarry & Wade, *The Law of Real Property*, 5th edn (Stevens, 1984), pp 539–48.

sonal right to damages under a contract to being a person with a proprietary right in land is here briefly summarised. First, and most important, is the question of the action by which a leaseholder might protect his interest in the land which he held on lease. Because the early law regarded the leaseholder as not having a property right in his tenement it denied him the ordinary landowners' remedy of the *novel disseisin*. An action therefore developed on the writ *quare eiecit infra terminum* which might be brought against a landlord who ejected a leaseholder[21]. This action was in fact a personal rather than a proprietary action, since it provided no remedy against the purchaser of the tenement from the lessor who subsequently ejected the lessee. The oppressed lessee therefore turned to the writ of trespass *quare clausum fregit*. The writ of trespass was in its origins a criminal action, and initially operated not to defend property, but to restrain wrongdoing. The form of the action was therefore focused on an act complained of rather than a property right infringed, and the rules for who might bring it were deliberately made as wide as possible.

The rule was that any person might have the writ of trespass *quare clausum fregit* who had possession of the property upon which the trespass was committed at the time of the trespass. This writ, which protected neither seisin nor title but actual presence, turned out to answer perfectly to the lessee's needs, and eventually became his primary remedy. The lessee's writ of trespass was eventually refined into the writ *de eiectione firmae* which could be used to claim not only damages, but also the readmission of the lessee to the leasehold land.

This assimilation of leasehold interest with property interest led to the designation of leaseholds as a separate class of property, 'chattels real', having some of the characteristics of real property but being properly described as personal property.

Chattels real

The intermediate class of chattels real turned out to be a valuable concept. In particular some of the most valuable forms of mediæval property, rights of marriage and of wardship, fell within it. The best way for the modern lawyer to regard the right of marriage or wardship (to the extent that he does not regard it as a gross breach of fundamental human rights) is as a situation in which the woman or child concerned becomes a sort of negotiable instrument embodying title to the lands with which he is enfeoffed. Thus the right was not only intensely valuable but also correctly categorised as an indirect right in land.

It is clear from the above that rights to chattels real, not being rights in land directly, were not bound by the rules of impartible succession and might therefore be devised by will. To those bound by rules intended to prevent the devolution of land on death to any but the legally designated heir, such freedom was highly prized, and it is clear that in at least the early stages of its development this intermediate category was aggressively developed by landowners

---

[21] Bracton, fn 220.

anxious to retain as full a control as they could over their property. The concept of chattels real endured until the legislation of 1925 removed its *raison d'être*. At that date the class contained only the lease of land. Since the lease of land is now an integral part of the discipline of real property law, we may now for practical purposes declare the class of chattels real closed.

Incorporeal hereditaments

An incorporeal hereditament is a chose in action, usually contractual but occasionally otherwise, which is treated by law as a piece of real property. 'This classification of rights and things as if they were similar has been ridiculed on theoretical grounds ... but in reality is the inevitable outcome of having two separate systems of property law.'[22] The origins of this doctrine are found in the pre-1925 laws of succession, whereby upon an intestacy land might vest in the heir whilst a contractual right essential to occupation of that land—for example, a right to drain the land through a neighbouring ditch—would, if treated as personal property, have passed to the next of kin in equal shares. The rights which have this characteristic are as follows:

(1) *Titles of honour*, in other words peerages. This is clearly part of the concept of impartible inheritance, that with estates should go power and authority. Baronetcies, although a modern honour having no territorial designation, also have this characteristic[23].

(2) *Offices*   The concept behind this is to be found in circumstances where an office (ie any office from Marshall of England or Chamberlain of the Exchequer to steward of a manor, constable, bedell, parker, falconer or master of hounds) is remunerated by a grant of land. The office then runs with the land as would a peerage. It is probable that even a grant of a modern office for a term longer than the life of the incumbent creates heritable property[24].

(3) *Advowsons and tithes*   An advowson is the right to present a curate to a vacant living. Advowsons have had the character of property rights from the earliest times, and the creation of the petty assize of *darrein presentment* protecting the right of the owner of the advowson was one of the fundamental reforms of Henry II.

(4) *Rentcharges,* ie a right to a stream of income derived from the property of another. These are, if it can be believed, anomalous incorporeal hereditaments, in that they are in fact personal rights charged on realty, and as such have less in common with a right to land than a lease. Since no new rentcharge has been capable of being created since 1977[25] we may leave this improbability in peace.

---

[22] Megarry & Wade (*see* fn 20 *above*), p 814.
[23] *Re Rivett-Carnac's Will* (1885) 30 Ch D 136.
[24] See D W Logan (1945) 61 LQR 249–53 in connection with dispositions of modern civil service appointments.
[25] Rentcharges Act 1977, s 2.

(5) *Annuities and corrodies* An annuity is similar to a rentcharge, save that it is not charged on land. A corrody is a grant equivalent to an annuity save that it is paid in kind rather than in coin. Again, the reasons why these rights were treated as real rather than personal in nature be consigned to the wallet which time keeps at his back.

(6) *Profits à pendre* Rights to take from another's land fish, game or other things.

(7) *Easements* The right to pass over or do something to or on the land of another.

Only (6) and (7) are of any importance in the field even of land law, but they form together a mighty corpus of doctrine whose intricacies provide meat and drink to the inhabitants of Lincoln's Inn. Fortunately, they may now be dismissed from our study as belonging wholly to the area of real property law.

Conversion

The equitable doctrine of conversion is based on the maxim that 'equity looks on as done that which ought to be done'[26]. In the days when it mattered tremendously whether a given piece of property constituted real or personal property, the courts were prepared to look to any obligations with which the property holders were bound to comply, and treat the property concerned as if those obligations had already been performed. The reasoning behind this doctrine was that it seemed unfair to allow the accident of the testator's date of death to determine the distribution of his assets in the face of his express instructions. However, it also had the potential to turn an intestacy into a battleground between the heir and the next of kin, a development which it can be imagined took little provocation.

The issue arose in different guises, but the *locus classicus* of the action in conversion was the case where a trustee holds a fund of money with directions to invest it in land. Upon the beneficiary's death, the interest was deemed to be an interest in land and passed to the heir at law, despite the fact that at all material times the trustee held only money[27]. Conversely, in the case of the old statutory trust for sale, where the trustees held real property upon trust for sale with a power to postpone the sale, the trust property was deemed to be money rather than land.

The doctrine of conversion has been largely neutralised by the Trusts of Land and Appointment of Trustees Act 1996. This Act abolishes the old rules relating to trusts of land and replaces them with a single, simple trust of land. The abolition of the old rules relating to trusts of land is a development which is warmly welcomed. In particular, for a person wishing to create successive interests for different persons in a piece of property (classically, by will for a spouse during their lifetime and for children thereafter), the only way of avoiding the operation of the Settled Land Act 1925 was to settle land upon 'an immediate binding trust for sale'[28]. However, since it was never intended by

---

[26] *Snell's Equity*, 29th edn, 40.
[27] *Fletcher v Ashburner* (1779) 1 Bro CC 497.
[28] Settled Land Act 1925, s 1(7).

anyone that the land should be actually sold, the trustees were given by statute[29] a power to postpone sale[30].

Viewed in the context of the doctrine of conversion, this form of settlement created a trust of money, not land, as the obligation to sell is deemed to have been carried out. However, it had the unfortunate side effect of denying to the beneficiaries under such a trust any proprietary interest in the land itself. This point manifested itself in its full complexity in a series of matrimonial cases, in which the courts sought to hold that where the matrimonial home was held by a husband upon trust for sale for himself and his wife jointly, although the wife had notionally no interest in the land, she should be treated at law as though she had[31]. The Trusts of Land and Appointment of Trustees Act 1996 now applies so that henceforward a beneficiary of a trust which holds land on trust for sale is treated as having a beneficial interest in land.

The doctrine of conversion itself, however, is not abolished and manifests itself in a number of other situations. For example the assets of a partnership are collectively the partner's personal property. This includes land held jointly by the partners. Section 22 of the Partnership Act 1890 effects a statutory conversion for this purpose, such that land which has become partnership property is part of the partner's personal estate. It is notable that the draftsmen of the Partnership Act clearly did not think that the matter was relevant in any terms other than the law of succession, for this statutory conversion is only effected as against the executors or administrators of the partners' estates. Further, a person who binds himself by contract to sell land is under an obligation to convey it to the purchaser, and where the obligation is specifically enforceable, then if title to the land is still vested in him at the time of his death he is deemed by equity to have fulfilled his obligation. The value of the land in his hands is therefore deemed to be personal rather than real property[32]. This is equally true where the obligation arises by virtue of a court order. Thus where a court orders that land be sold, conversion is effected at the moment of the giving of the order[33].

The doctrine of conversion applies only to conversions which ought to be made. Thus where there is a countervailing obligation not to convert, the obligations are weighed accordingly. The beneficiaries of a trust acting together can in effect compel a trustee not to exercise a power to sell, and in this circumstance there is a deemed reconversion[34]. Such a direction can be implied from the beneficiary's passive acquiescence in the failure by a trustee to per-

---

[29] Law of Property Act 1925, s 25(1). This power is deemed into all trusts for sale unless the instrument contains an express intention that the land be actually sold.

[30] This is why any trustee could compel sale, since the trustees could only exercise their power to postpone sale if they acted unanimously.

[31] *Williams & Glyn's Bank v Boland* [1979] Ch 312, upheld [1981] AC 487.

[32] *Hillingdon Estates v Stonefield Estates* [1952] Ch 627, and see generally Oakley, *Constructive Trusts* (1996), Ch 6.

[33] *Steed v Preece* (1874) LR 18 Eq 192; *Fauntleroy v Beebe* [1911] 2 Ch 257; *Re Silva* [1929] 2 Ch 198. Note that some statutes provide that a court can make such an order without effecting a conversion—eg Mental Health Act 1983, s 101.

[34] See *Seeley v Jago* (1717) 1 P Wms 389.

form an obligation to sell[35], but more usually springs from an express direction. It is suggested that a reconversion can be created by the majority of the beneficiaries acting together[36]. The reconversion is also effected by the death of one of a pair of equitable joint tenants who hold behind a trust for sale[37].

Moveable and immovable property

As is clear from the foregoing, the division at common law between real and personal property is not clear cut[38]. The English division has a number of incidents which are unique to the common law, and the precise dividing line between real and personal varies between different common law countries— what is real property in one jurisdiction may be personal property in another. To take an extreme example, the English courts have held that slaves on a Jamaican plantation were, for the purposes of Jamaican law, real property[39]. However, as a matter of private international law the most evident contrast is between the common law systems with their division between personal property and the civil law systems, which make for this purpose their primary distinction as between moveable and immovable property.

The English courts take the view that the real/personal distinction is a matter of municipal English law. With respect to problems arising out of the conflict of laws, even where a civil law system is not involved in the relevant conflict, they adopt the distinction between moveable and immovable property in order to resolve the conflict[40]. Thus it is a principle of English conflicts of law that the law applicable to a particular piece of property is determined by reference to whether that piece of property is moveable or immovable[41].

Thus where the question arises in front of an English court as to the law applicable to a particular asset, the court first determines the status of the asset as a moveable or an immovable. If the asset is an immovable, the law of the place of its *situs* is considered to determine the existence of any restrictions upon its transfer or transmission. For example an interest in a mortgage of land is not at English law an interest in land and is therefore personalty. However, it is categorised at English law, undoubtedly correctly, as immovable[42]. Thus, in the case of a person dying intestate in England leaving an

---

[35] *Crabtree v Bramble* (1747) 3 Atk 680; *Mutlow v Bigg* (1875) 1 Ch D 385.

[36] Bell, *The Modern Law of Personal Property in England and Ireland* (Butterworths, 1989), p 29, citing ss 26(3) and 30 of the Law of Property Act 1925; *Smith v Smith* (1975) 120 SJ 100.

[37] This fascinating problem creates the position where the surviving joint tenant and the executors of the deceased joint tenant are trustees of the legal estate for the surviving joint tenant absolutely. Thus the trustees continue to hold land subject to a trust for sale, but the duty to convert is unenforceable. See Bell *above*, p 30, fn 1 and cases cited therein.

[38] In fact it calls to mind the story of the perplexed Irish farmer who was unable to understand that his cows, his personal property, might eat only grass, his personal property, and yet defecate real property.

[39] *Ex p Rucker* (1834) 3 Dea & Ch 704.

[40] *Re Hoyles* [1911] 1 Ch 179, CA; *Re Berchtold* [1923] 1 Ch 192; *Macdonald v Macdonald*, 1932 SC(HL) 79.

[41] See Dicey & Morris, *The Conflict of Laws* (Collins, ed), 12th edn (Sweet & Maxwell, 1993), p 917, citing *Re Cutcliffe* [1940] Ch 565 and *Macdonald v Macdonald* 1932 SC(HL) 79, but *contra Re Hoyles* [1911] 1 Ch 179, CA.

interest in a mortgage on land in Erewhon, the English court first determines whether (by English rules) the asset is moveable or immovable. Having determined that it is an immovable sited in Erewhon, the English court then goes on to consider the application of the laws of Erewhon. If, however, the courts of Erewhon have different rules of identification from the English court as to what is moveable and what immovable, the English court hears evidence of what result the operation of those rules would produce. If the Erewhon courts regards the asset as immovable then the English court applies the laws of Erewhon in respect of intestate succession to immovables. If, however, the Erewhon court regards the asset as moveable then a species of renvoi is applied and the asset devolves according to the English rules of intestate succession to personal property.

There is no abstract English rule which governs the identification of an asset as moveable or immovable, only a series of decided cases. The most important category is that of the leasehold interest in land, which it is clear is an immovable for purposes of English law[43]. Rent charges[44], interests in mortgages of land[45], the interest of an unpaid vendor in land[46] and land held on trust for sale[47] are all immovables.

It seems that the doctrine of conversion will not be applied so as to convert a moveable into an immovable or vice versa[48]. This disapplication of the doctrines of conversion highlights an interesting aspect of the real/personal-moveable/immovable comparison, being that the two concepts are different in nature. The moveable/immovable distinction is a categorisation of things by reference to their properties. The real/personal distinction, by contrast, is a distinction between interests in things[49], and the two are therefore 'distinctions in different planes'[50]. As is frequently the case with comparative law exercises, this highlights an aspect of English law which is otherwise obscure. That is that systems which utilise the moveable/immovable distinction are systems in which a real action still has a flourishing existence, and in which it makes sense to speak of the law relating to a thing itself. In England the disappearance of the real action has meant that the whole of English jurisprudence consists of a scale of worse and better rights to things, and the distinction applied is therefore one of rights rather than of things.

---

[42] *Re Hoyles* [1911] 1 Ch 179, CA; *Re Dalrymple Estate* [1941] 3 WWR 605 (Sask CA); *Hogg v Provincial Tax Commissioner* [1941] 4 DLR. See also Dicey & Morris *above*, p 919, fn 21 and the authorities cited therein.

[43] *Freke v Carbery* (1873) LR 16 Eq 461; *Duncan v Lawson* (1889) 41 Ch D 394; *Pepin v Bruyère* [1900] 2 Ch 504; *Re Gentili* (1875) IR 9 Eq 541; *De Fogassieras v Duport* (1881) 11 LR Ir 123.

[44] *Chatfield v Berchtoldt* (1872) LR 7 Ch App 192.

[45] *Re Hoyles* [1911] 1 Ch 179, CA.

[46] *Re Burke* [1928] 1 DLR 318 and Dicey & Morris (*see* fn 41 *above*), p 919, *sed contra Re Hole* [1948] 4 DLR 419; *Haque v Haque (No 2)* (1965) 114 CLR 98.

[47] *Re Berchtold* [1923] 1 Ch 192.

[48] *Re Berchtold* at 206. The apparently conflicting decision in *Re Cutcliffe* [1940] Ch 565 is explained in Dicey & Morris (*see* fn 41 *above*), p 920; see also *Re Crook* (1936) 36 SRNSW 186, *Re Middleton's Settlement* [1947] Ch 583, CA.

[49] Dicey & Morris *above*, p 916.

[50] Cook in Dicey & Morris *above*, Ch 10.

Intangible property

The English rules of what is movable and what immovable are relatively basic, having being developed only through the medium of multi-jurisdictional testamentary and intestate disputes. As a general rule real property is immovable and tangible personal property is moveable. In relation to intangible property the learned editors of *Dicey & Morris* observe that[51]

> the distinction between moveables and immovables is not appropriate to intangible things, since a thing which cannot be touched cannot be moved. Logically, therefore, things should be classed as being (1) tangible things, which may be either (a) moveable or (b) immovable, and (2) intangible things.

This is made clear by the fact that the function of the rule as to moveables is to determine the appropriate *situs* of a thing[52], and the difficult status of intangible things in this context is demonstrated by the problems which arise when considering the ascription to intangible things of a *situs*. The former rule at common law was that a thing in action had no *situs*[53] (although the ecclesiastical courts had always ascribed *situs* to an intangible[54]). However, this rule produced undesirable tax consequences and was reversed by the House of Lords in *English, Scottish and Australian Bank v IRC*[55] Where a chose in action is not yet actionable it has been held that it has no *situs*[56], but there is authority for the contrary view[57].

As a matter of the logic of the law the attempt to ascribe *situs* to intangibles creates many more problems than it solves, and it may be ventured that were it not for the unfortunate equivalence of the concepts 'without situs' and 'not subject to tax' the problems which have been created by these decisions need not have troubled us. To the extent that it is considered rational to ascribe *situs* to an intangible then the ordinary rule is and must be that an intangible, being entirely a creature of law, must be sited in the jurisdiction whose rules give it life[58]. However this rule would also produce unfortunate tax consequences, and a complex regime of approximation has therefore been put in place in order to determine these rules. It is noticeable that the learned editors of *Dicey & Morris* begin their disquisition upon this subject with the words: 'The rules in the following paragraphs are thought to have general utility but they are not always applicable'[59].

---

[51] Dicey & Morris *above*, p 918, citing Falconbridge pp 506–8.

[52] Dicey & Morris *above*, rule 113.

[53] *Lee v Abdy* (1886) 17 QBD 309, 312; *Smelting Co of Australia v IRC* [1897] 1 QB 175, CA; *Danubian Sugar Factories v IRC* [1901] 1 QB 245, CA; *Velasques Ltd v IRC* [1914] 3 KB 458, CA.

[54] *A-G v Bouwens* (1838) 3 M & W 171.

[55] [1932] AC 238.

[56] *Re Helbert Wagg & Co's Claim* [1956] Ch 323 at 339–40.

[57] *Kwok Chi Leung Karl v Commr of Estate Duty* [1988] 1 WLR 1035, PC.

[58] *New York Life Insurance Co v Public Trustee* [1924] 2 Ch 101 at 109, CA; *Alloway v Phillips* [1980] 1 WLR 888 at 893–4, 897, CA.

[59] Dicey & Morris, *The Conflict of Laws*, Collins (ed), 12th edn (Sweet & Maxwell, 1993), p 924.

Section 2

Legal Title to Property

Contents

Chapter 2

Property Rights and Third Parties

In *National Provincial Bank v Ainsworth*[1], Lord Wilberforce explained that a property right is a right which is 'definable, identifiable by third parties, capable in its nature of assumption by third parties, and have some degree of permanence or stability'[2]. It has been pointed out[3] that this is almost completely circular. 'Definability' and 'permanence' are criteria of legal existence, and the point which His Lordship makes is nothing more than that a property right is a right which is transferable to and/or enforceable against third parties. However, this is an incomplete response. The characteristic distinction between a lease and a licence is that a lease confers a right of 'exclusive possession' which is transferable[4]. However, in the field of real property law it has been clear for some time that a right to exclude all persons—including the owner of property—is in practice indistinguishable from a proprietary right. In *Mafo v Adams*[5] Lord Widgery pointed out that the position of a tenant whose tenancy was protected under the Rent Acts was 'one of the most significant rights of property' which it was possible to have in land. A protected tenant might not be able to transfer his rights in land to a third party, but as between the tenant and the landlord it would be an abuse of language to say that the tenant did not have a powerful and immediate property right in the land.

It is also necessary to deal with the point made by Lord Denning in *Davis v Johnson*[6]. Lord Denning explained that:

> It is true that in the 19th century the law paid quite high regard to the rights of property. But this gave rise to such misgivings that in modern times the law has changed course. Social justice requires that personal rights should, in a proper case, be given priority over rights of property.

It is undoubtedly true that the reason that the issue of whether a right is a 'property' right is a question of so much moment is that 'property' rights are perceived as being 'stronger' than personal rights. However, there are also clearly cases in which a personal right is 'stronger' than a proprietary right.

---

[1] [1965] AC 1175.
[2] At 1247G–1248A.
[3] Gray, *Elements of Land Law*, 2nd edn (Butterworths, 1993), p 926; [1991] CLJ 252 at 292.
[4] *Street v Mountford* [1985] AC 809.
[5] [1970] 1 QB 548 at 557.
[6] [1979] AC 264.

For example, in the Domestic Violence and Matrimonial Proceedings Act 1976 the courts were given power to make an order ousting a person from property which he was otherwise entitled to occupy.

Property and obligation

The primary distinction between the law of property and the law of obligations is the idea that property rights are good against all the world, whereas an obligation is bipartite. Against a stranger to a transaction only title prevails, since the rule of privity takes effect to prevent a right created between A and B being enforced either by or against C. Where A, the original owner of a piece of property, has a valid contract with B conferring upon B rights to, over or concerning property, A has to some extent parted with his rights of absolute dominion over the property. Rights over property are themselves property, and the fact that what B received was a right does not necessarily make him any the less a transferee of property. What if A then purports to dispose of the whole title to the property to C? The issue which arises is whether the contract will affect C or, more accurately, whether B's rights will be affected by the transaction with C, and this in turn will be determined by answering the question of whether B has a contractual right against A or a property right in the property.

The rule is that all agreements create personal rights unless they are agreements which satisfy criteria as creating a property right. An obligation can always be created in any circumstances; a property right can only be created in certain circumstances.

The importance of the point is clear from the position of B in the above example. If what he has is a property right, then he may assert his right against C, the transferee, in the same way in which he could have asserted it against A, the transferor. Conversely, if what he has is a personal right against A, then his right in the property is extinguished by the transfer, although his right against A is unaffected by it.

Rights in property at common law

The best starting place for this analysis is the law of easements over real property. Throughout the recorded history of our law it has been possible for the owner of land to separate out specific rights, identified as property rights, and grant them away. Such rights, when disposed of, are capable of independent existence as property[7]. The question therefore arises as to which rights are capable of having such an independent existence. The answer to this question is provided in the case of land by the decision in *Re Ellenborough Park*[8], in

---

[7] The modern law of easements no longer distinguishes between rights appurtenant and rights in gross (*Hewlins v Shippam* (1826) 5 B & C 221 at 229) and it may safely be said that all easements are separate items of property rights.

[8] [1956] Ch 131.

which it was held that a right was capable of independent existence as an item of property if it satisfied four criteria:

(1) There must be a dominant and a servient tenement.

(2) The easement must accommodate the dominant tenement.

(3) The dominant and servient tenement must not be occupied by the same person at the moment of creation of the easement.

(4) The easement must be capable of forming the subject-matter of a grant.

Note that the first three of these rules are different in kind from the fourth. They are rules of practice which reflect the position that whereas in theory all easements were created by deed of grant[9], in reality contentious issues concerning easements almost invariably involve the assertion or denial of rights acquired by prescription and long user. These first three rules therefore constitute further criteria which require to be satisfied over and above the ordinary prescription criteria before an easement will be admitted as having existence.

The fourth, however, is a rule of substantive law. In addressing this issue the courts have been sensitive to the problem which would be created for conveyancers if the creation of independently existing property rights were to be left entirely to the whim of individual property owners. In *Hill v Tupper*[10] Pollock CB said[11]:

It is an old and well-established principle of our law that new estates cannot be created. New rights or incidents of property cannot be created, nor can a new species of burden be imposed upon land at the pleasure of the owners ... A grantor may bind himself by covenant to allow what rights he pleases over his property, but the law will not permit him to carve out his property so as to enable the grantee of such a limited right to sue a stranger in the way here contended for.

The common law has therefore developed rules of recognition in order to determine what interests can, and what cannot, be created by grant. This rule may be stated as that the right claimed must be within the general nature of rights capable of being created as easements.

This creates the expectation that there would be a finite list of rights capable of being easements, but, perhaps surprisingly, this is not the case. The reason was succinctly stated by Lord St Leonards in *Dyce v Lady James Hay*[12] as 'the category of servitudes and easements must alter and expand with the changes that take place in the circumstances of mankind'[13]. Thus although there are 'major' species of easement which are instantly recognisable as such— for example, rights of way, rights of water, right of air and rights of light—

---

[9] Easements which cannot be proved by the production of an existing grant may be proved by showing long user. However, the effect at common law of proving long user is to give rise to an irrebuttable presumption that the right concerned was initially granted by the owner of the legal estate by a deed which has subsequently been lost.

[10] (1863) 2 H & C 121.

[11] (1863) 2 H & C 121 at 127–8.

[12] (1852) 1 Macq 305.

[13] At 312, 313. The easement recognised in *Dowty Boulton Paul Ltd v Wolverhampton Corp (No 2)* [1976] Ch 13 to operate an airfield is perhaps the best example of this sort of development.

there is a myriad other rights which have been recognised as capable of being rights of property, including rights to use a washing line[14], a letter-box[15] and a lavatory[16].

Where a right which has been granted fulfills the criteria for an easement it is treated as a piece of property. This means that the easement holder may, as owner of a piece of property, bring actions of trespass against any person who interferes with his right of enjoyment of that property. Conversely, if the right which has been granted fails to satisfy the criteria for an easement, then it is a mere contractual permission, or licence, a personal right enforceable only against the landowner.

The effect of this distinction is clear. Where a landowner, having granted a right over his land, sells that land, then if the right which he has granted amounts to an easement then what he sells is the property interest which he has, that is, the whole title less the easement. The grantee of the easement may enforce the right against the new owner since, the easement being his property, he may enforce it against all the world. Conversely, if the right does not satisfy the criteria for recognition as a piece of property, then the purchaser of the land takes the whole estate. The holder of the right has a personal contractual action against the vendor, who has committed a breach of contract by putting it out of his power to honour his contractual obligation. However, the holder of the right has no action against the new owner of the land, since he has no property to protect nor any contractual relationship with the new owner[17].

This position is illustrated by the facts of *Hill v Tupper*[18]. In that case a landowner purported to grant to a leaseholder an exclusive right to rent out boats on a river running through the affected land. A rival operator appeared on the land and commenced to hire out boats in competition with the lease-holder. The leaseholder brought an action in his own name against the rival boat-hirer asserting his exclusive right. The issue before the court was one of whether what the leaseholder had received from the landlord was an absolute proprietary right, or merely licence. It was held that the right which the land-lord had purported to grant was not a recognisable grant in a form known to law, and must therefore be a mere licence sounding only in contract against the landlord personally.

Proprietary rights in personal property

It is clear from the foregoing that the rules of common law which give grants of interests in property the status of independent pieces of property in their own right are restricted to cases of rights to real property. In law this is be-

---

[14] *Drewell v Towler* (1832) 3 B & Ad 735.

[15] *Goldberg v Edwards* [1950] Ch 247.

[16] *Miller v Emcer Products Ltd* [1956] Ch 304.

[17] In the Roman system of law, in which the lessee of land acquires no proprietary right in the land, we find that this is indeed the case, and the lessee's only remedy against a third party is an action against his lessor to compel the lessor to act—D.9.2.11.9; 19.2.60.5.

[18] (1863) 2 H & C 121.

cause an easement properly so-called can only exist as between two parcels of land[19]. However, the true reason is that whereas at common law title to land has always been divisible, ownership of personal property is, at common law, indivisible. This principle is clear in the case of physical personal property—a man may not separate out and grant away part of his title to his car because that title is indivisible. It is harder to see in the context of intangibles, but it is still the case that having granted a right (for example, by promising to pay a certain amount of money on a certain date), the grantee cannot subsequently create a property right in that right.

The circumstance that proprietary rights in goods can be created only by absolute conveyance and not by grant of any lesser interest leads to the absolute rule of law that *emptio tollit locatum* —a subsequent sale defeats any prior interest in the property concerned, even the right to exclusive possession for a period created by a contract of hire which would, if it were a contract relating to land, unquestionably create a property right. No common law legal property interest other than absolute ownership may be created in respect of personal property. Another way to put this is that in the case of personal property there is at common law no equivalent to a lease of land, whereby a property interest may be spelt out of a contract for the grant of exclusive possession for a term at a rent.

It is clear that interests in personal property can arise in equity under a trust of personal property, and it is equally clear that personal property may in equity be charged, mortgaged and made subject to an equitable lien in the same way and with the same effect as real property. As indicated above, there is also a class of common law interests—that is, easements—which by their nature can exist in land but not in personal property. The issue which is addressed here is whether the equitable equivalent of the easement, the restrictive covenant, can exist in equity in personal property or whether it is, like the easement, confined to land.

The importance of this question is primarily in the context of the contract of hire. It is clear that at law a contract of hire is simply a contract and confers upon the hirer nothing but a contractual right. The hirer cannot resist the removal of the hired property from his hands by a purchaser of it, and by his hire he acquires no property interest in the property. In equity the analogous position has been in doubt for many years.

The *locus classicus* for this branch of equity is the decision in *Tulk v Moxhay*[20], and the best starting point is the facts of that case. This is primarily because in order to examine the ghost-like existence of the decision in the field of personal property it is necessary to be clear what was and was not decided in the field of real property law.

Tulk v Moxhay was in essence an action brought by a person owning property in Leicester Square, London to enforce a covenant that the square garden should not be built on. The defendant was a purchaser of the land with notice

---

[19] See eg *Mason v Shrewsbury and Hertford Rly* (1871) LR 6 QB 578 at 587.
[20] (1848) 2 Ph 774.

of the covenant. The plaintiff was the original covenantee[21]. The court's decision was to the effect that where a person purchased property with notice of a restrictive covenant validly created over the property, then the covenant would be enforced against such purchaser in equity. Stated as a wide general principle this is innovative bordering upon radical in the context of conveyancing law. The courts thereupon commenced a course of reduction until the rule in *Tulk v Moxhay* could be fitted more comfortably into the existing scheme of transfer of rights and obligations.

The first inroad was made by reducing the scope of the class of covenant which might benefit from the rule. Early cases after *Tulk v Moxhay* had held that the rule applied to any covenant[22], but in *Formby v Barker*[23] it was made clear that only rights which benefited one piece of land for the benefit of another could bind a purchaser with notice. This approximation of the new equitable doctrine to the old common law rules relating to easements requiring a dominant and a servient tenement produced a sigh of relief from the existing establishment, who in the person of Jessel MR promptly recategorised the new doctrine as no more than an equitable extension of the common law rule as to negative easements[24]. The doctrine laid down in *Tulk v Moxhay* was eventually recognized as a new equity in its own right[25], but the new equity had by then been reconfigured to comply with the existing rules of conveyancing of land.

In the context of the *Tulk v Moxhay* decision itself this recategorisation is correct. In finding the new equity to exist at all, Lord Cottenham had based his reasoning on the proposition that if such covenants did not run with the land 'it would be impossible for an owner of land to sell part of it without incurring the risk of rendering what he retains worthless'[26]. This is a neat illustration that at no point in the decision did their Lordships raise their eyes from questions of conveyancing of real property to consider whether they were enunciating a proposition of universal truth. However, the question remained at large as to whether the decision might not have been a manifestation of a larger undiscovered principle, such a principle being as applicable to other forms of property as to land.

In *De Mattos v Gibson*[27] it was argued that this was the case. In the Court of Appeal Knight-Bruce LJ issued the ringing declaration that[28]

Reason and justice seem to prescribe that, a least as a general rule, where a man, by gift or purchase, acquires property from another with knowlege of a previous

---

[21] Note that this is (probably) the very situation which s 56 of the Law of Property Act 1925 was passed to deal with. However the decision of the majority of the House of Lords in *Beswick v Beswick* [1968] AC 58 has rendered the section unreliable in the case of anything other than real property.

[22] *Catt v Tourle* (1869) 4 Ch App 654; *Luker v Dennis* (1877) 7 Ch D 227.

[23] [1903] 2 Ch 539.

[24] *London & South Western Rly v Gomm* (1882) 20 Ch D 562 at 583.

[25] *Re Nisbet & Potts' Contract* [1905] 1 Ch 391 at 396.

[26] *Tulk v Moxhay* at 777.

[27] (1858) 4 De G & J 276.

[28] Ibid at 282.

contract, lawfully and for valuable consideration made by him with a third person, to use and to employ the property for a particular purpose in a specified manner, the acquirer shall not, to the material damage of the third person, in opposition to the contract and inconsistently with it, use and employ the property in a manner not allowable to the giver or seller. This rule ... is applicable alike in general as I conceive to moveable and immovable property ...

This dictum, albeit spoken in the Court of Appeal, unfortunately cited no authority other than reason and justice. It therefore acquired the status of a sort of legal Banquo's ghost, appearing in a series of cases in which it was greeted with horror and rejected with vigour[29]. This continued until the Privy Council unexpectedly embraced the doctrine in *Lord Strathcona Steamship Co v Dominion Coal Co*[30], explicitly approving the dictum of Knight-Bruce LJ cited above as being of 'outstanding authority'[31].

The fate of the decision in the *Lord Strathcona* case is one of the more interesting studies in the doctrine of precedent. Decisions of the Privy Council are of merely persuasive force as far as the English courts are concerned, but are conventionally treated as quasi-binding. An English judge will not lightly disregard a Privy Council decision unless there are very good grounds for doing so. This is exactly the approach which was taken by Scrutton LJ in *Port Line Ltd v Ben Line Steamers*[32], where he held that he was free to disregard the decision in the *Strathcona* on the grounds that it was clearly wrong. This brave approach was based on the analysis that the Privy Council had come to its conclusion in the case by holding that the beneficiary of the covenant had thereby a 'plain interest' in the property. What, asked Scrutton, was the nature of this interest in property? Having asked the question he found himself unable to answer it, and went on to hold that there was no such proposition of English law as that which Knight-Bruce J had enunciated[33].

The views of Scrutton LJ in *Port Line* found widespread acceptance as a statement of the general law in relation to covenants affecting goods. However in the particular area of hire there have been revivals of the idea that a hirer acquires some form of equitable proprietary interest in the property which he hires. This controversy was reignited in 1990, when in *Bristol Airport plc v Powdrill*[34] Browne-Wilkinson V-C was called upon to decide whether an airplane hired by an airline was the airline's 'property'. He said[35]:

---

[29] *Taddy & Co v Sterious & Co* [1904] 1 Ch 354; *McGruther v Pitcher* [1904] 2 Ch 306; *Barker v Strickney* [1919] 1 KB 121.
[30] [1926] AC 108.
[31] Ibid at 118.
[32] [1958] 2 QB 146.
[33] There has been speculation that the words of Knight-Bruce LJ may be correct in that they represent a statement of the rule relating to the tort of interference with contract (see per Browne-Wilkinson J in *Swiss Bank Corp v Lloyds Bank Ltd* [1979] Ch 548). This is probably also incorrect (see Tettenborn [1982] CLJ 58 at 82–3; Gardner (1982) 98 LQR 279 at 289–93; Swadling, 'The Proprietary Effect of a Hire of Goods', *Interests in Goods* (Lloyds of London Press, 1993) pp 16–17).
[34] [1990] Ch 744.
[35] [1990] Ch 744 at 759.

Although the [lease] is a contract, it does not follow that no property interest is created in the chattel. The basic equitable principle is that if, under the contract, A has certain rights over property as against the legal owner, which rights are specifically enforceable in equity, A has an equitable interest in such property. I have no doubt that a court would order specific performance of a contract to lease an aircraft, since each aircraft has unique features peculiar to itself. Accordingly, in my judgment the 'lessee' has at least an equitable right of some kind in that aircraft which falls within the statutory definition as being some 'description of interest arising out of, or incidental to' that aircraft.

This dictum has been strongly criticised and Swadling[36] in particular has analysed in detail the possible support for and objections to it; concluding that that such an interest, were it to exist, would be *sui generis* and outside any of the existing categories of property rights, a conclusion which he holds offends against the *numerus clausus* principle identified above[37] in relation to easements existing at common law.

This conclusion is unquestionably correct, but it may be reached by a simpler route and without introducing doctrines of the common law into the sphere of equity. The specific performance which Browne-Wilkinson V-C referred to would in fact not be available *in respect of a contract of hire*. It is very probable that specific performance would be available in respect of a contract for the *purchase* of an aircraft[38], but in such a case the operation of equity would simply be to vest title to the asset in the purchaser. An order for specific performance of a contract of hire would be equivalent to an order for equitable possession, and there is no such thing as equitable possession[39]. Equity deals only with title, and at the fullest extent of performance of a contract of hire no title passes to the hirer. He does have (or may have) a right to an order for an injunction restraining interference with his possession (*see also* p 47 *below*). This order, however, has no proprietary base, and emanates simply from the equitable jurisdiction to compel the performance of legal obligations and restrain interference with the performance of such obligations.

Thus it appears that a hirer of property acquires no title, legal or equitable, to the hired property. He is entitled to the bailment upon terms of the property, and if such bailment is refused his remedy is in damages, but he has no claim to the property itself.

---

[36] Fn 33 *above*, at pp 11–13.
[37] At p 19.
[38] *Sed quaere* given *Société des Industries Metallurgiques SA v The Bronx Engineering Co Ltd* [1975] 1 Lloyd's Rep 465.
[39] *See* p 256 *below*, and see also Goode, *Commercial Law*, 2nd edn (Penguin, 1995), p 677.

Chapter 3

Possession

Although title is in essence a legal issue to be determined as a matter of law, possession appears to be an issue of fact. However, it is not. The question of whether a man possesses a thing is a complex legal issue in its own right, and the rules for determining it are far more complex than a simple assessment of relative location.

The basis of the matter of possession is the issue of the degree of physical proximity necessary to constitute possession. I possess my watch whilst I am wearing it. I continue to possess it if I put it down in order to wash my hands. Do I still possess it if one morning I decide not to wear it, and leave it in my bedroom? Such questions are of more than superficial interest; in *R v Purdy*[1] the validity of an arrest turned upon the issue of whether the policeman making the arrest was in 'possession' of the arrest warrant[2], which was at the relevant time inside a police car, parked 50 yards away[3].

It is virtually impossible to set fixed legal rules on the issue of how far a man's possession extends, since almost every case is an individual issue to be determined according to its own facts. However, there are some general principles which may be applied in the determination of this question.

(1) Where it is sought to reduce a thing to possession, the capture must be complete. This rule proceeds from cases involving wild animals. In *Young v Hichens*[4], a fisherman had almost surrounded a shoal of pilchards with a net when another fisherman rowed through the gap in the net and entrapped some of the fish for himself. In the subsequent hearing it was held that there was no trespass against the existing possession of the fish, since the fish had not been completely reduced to possession. Pursuit short of capture does not give rise to possession[5].

(2) Where it is sought to transfer possession of a thing from one person to another, the transfer must be complete. This is a variant of the rule mentioned above. It is illustrated *by Balmoral Supermarket Ltd v Bank of New Zealand*[6], a rare modern case on the interruption by a third party of a transfer. A bank customer, in the process of making a deposit at a branch of a bank, was in the process of counting out the cash to be deposited on the branch counter in front

---

[1] [1975] QB 288.
[2] Then required by s 102 of the Magistrates' Courts Act 1952.
[3] It was held that he was.
[4] (1844) 6 QB 606.
[5] Pollock & Wright, *An Essay on Possession in the Common Law* (Clarendon, 1888), p 39.
[6] [1974] 2 NZLR 155.

of the teller when robbers entered the bank. The robbers seized the cash from the counter and made off with it. The question was one of whether the loss occasioned by the theft should be borne by the customer or by the bank. The court held that until the transfer was completed to its utmost extent, then possession remained vested in the customer. The test which the court seems to have applied is that, whilst the customer was handling the money, he could at any time have required the return of those specific notes and coins. Upon completion of the transfer of possession the notes and coins became the bank's property. This case has a peculiarity in that the transfer of possession of money also effects a transfer of title, but it is submitted that the issue would have been decided in the same way had the customer been, for example, delivering a watch to a watchmaker for repair. The principle remains that delivery must be perfected in order for a bailment to take effect[7].

(3) Possession follows control. A man who rides in a taxi with his suitcase beside him retains possession of his suitcase. However if he allows the taxi-driver to take the suitcase from him and secure it about the taxi, then he has in effect ceded control of the suitcase and therefore transferred possession of the suitcase to the taxi-driver[8]. This rule raises a number of issues relating to shared control. These are most clearly illustrated in *Chowdhary v Gillot*[9], where a car-owner delivered his car to a factory for repairs, and then allowed a factory employee to drive him to the station in it. His clear intention to surrender control of the car upon delivery was sufficient to overcome the presumption that a man in his own car possesses it. However, the situation is otherwise where a man merely allows a friend to drive his car whilst he sits in the passenger seat, since there is no intention to surrender complete control over the vehicle.

(4) An occupier of land has possession of every thing on or attached to the land provided that he intends to exercise control over such things. This rule is helpful in situations in which property is left unattended but secured. A man is in possession of the goods in the house which he occupies, whether he be in it or not[10], and this principle extends to things left upon his land generally as long as he has the intention of controlling such things. In principle, an occupier of land does intend to exercise such control. Thus in *South Staffordshire Water Co v Sharman*[11] a water company was held to be the possessor of two gold rings which were found in the mud at the bottom of a pool on their land. Although they were not aware of the presence of the rings themselves, they did have a general intention to control all the things upon their own land. Equally, in *Hibbert v McKiernan*[12] a golf club was held to have the intention to control golf balls which lay lost upon the course which it occupied. Although the exertion of such control would have been an impossibility (if some-

---

[7] Palmer, *Bailment*, 2nd edn (Sweet & Maxwell, 1991), p 104, and see particularly the unreported cases cited in fn 32 thereto.
[8] *Hancock v Cunnain* (1886) 12 VLR 9.
[9] [1947] 2 All ER 541.
[10] Pollock & Wright (*see* fn 5 *above*), p 38.
[11] [1896] 2 QB 44.
[12] [1948] 2 KB 142.

thing is lost then I must find it before I may control it), the intention to control is sufficient.

By extending a general licence to enter upon his land, a man may lose the benefit of this presumption. In *Bridges v Hawkesworth*[13], a bundle of banknotes were found in the public part of a shop by a third party. The third party delivered the notes to the shopkeeper for the purpose of returning them to their true owner. It was held that, although the notes had clearly passed out of the owner's possession, the possession which they passed into was that of the finder, and the shopkeeper had no possession in respect of the notes merely by virtue of the fact that they were within his shop. The position would be otherwise had the notes been found in a part of the shop from which the public was barred[14]. In *Parker v British Airways Board*[15] a passenger found a gold bracelet in the international executive lounge at Heathrow airport. The occupier of the lounge itself was British Airways, which at all times had exercised its power to restrict entry to the lounge. The Court of Appeal[16] held that there was a distinction between the exercise of control over admission to premises and the exercise of control over goods lying on those premises. Unless British Airways manifested an intention actually to control such goods then it did not have possession of them. The court conceded that British Airways had the right to control such goods, but that the right to do a thing should not be confused with the doing of it. No control equals no possession.

Possession and custody

These rules are, taken together, capable of determining whether a person who wishes to possess an object has succeeded in doing so. However, there is a further and separate issue which must now be treated, which is the issue which is raised where a person having physical control of a thing renounces any intention to take control over it. For example, a customs officer inspecting a traveller's baggage may at any given moment have possession of the thing which he inspects, but it is not his intention to exercise control over it to the exclusion of the passenger[17]. The status of one who at the same time possesses and does not possess creates difficulties. The term which is conventionally used in this context is of a 'custodian' of the property.

The law of custody has been developed through the law of master and servant, since for many years the law was held to be that the servant who has

---

[13] (1851) 21 LJQB 75.
[14] This was not the view of the judges in the case itself; indeed there are *obiter* to exactly the opposite effect—per Patteson J (1851) 21 LJQB 75 at 78. However, the conclusion follows from the explanation of the *ratio* of the decision found in *Parker v British Airways Board* [1982] QB 1004.
[15] [1982] QB 1004.
[16] It is an interesting sidelight on the infrequency of possessory litigation that this appears to have been the first time that a case on the rights of finders had been heard by the Court of Appeal—per Donaldson LJ at 1008.
[17] Per the Canadian Court of Appeal in *Zien v The Queen* (1986) 26 DLR(4th) 121, upholding (1984) 15 DLR(4th) 283.

physical possession of his master's goods does not have legal possession thereof, but merely custody[18]. This may be explained by reference to the general principle—if my butler polishes my silver, he clearly has physical possession of my silver, but he has no intention of controlling it to my exclusion, and therefore does not satisfy the test of control.

The reason for the development of this principle is to be found in the state of the English criminal law prior to the Theft Act 1968. Under the old dispensation, larceny was an offence whose ingredients were a wrongful interference with the possession of goods accompanied by an *animus furandi*. It followed from this that in circumstances where there was no transfer of possession there was no theft[19]. This created the most tremendous difficulties in the case of felonious servants. Where a master entrusted his goods to a servant who subsequently misappropriated them, the idea that the servant had possession led inevitably to the conclusion that at the moment of the misappropriation there was no interference with possession, and thus no theft. This was not a workable conclusion in terms of public order, and the idea grew up that a servant should not be credited with possession of his master's goods.

Since possession is the basis of bailment there grew up a pure apposition—that a servant could never be a bailee, and a bailee could never be a servant[20]. Thus a servant owes none of the duties of a bailee towards the actual possessor, and if he damages the goods in his custody he is impeachable only under his contract of service or by reference to a general duty of care towards his master. This position becomes more complex still when the question of the status of third parties is introduced. If the positions of servant and master and bailor and bailee are mutually exclusive, then it follows that where a person is a bailee for another, then no vicarious liability may be ascribed to that other for the activities of the bailee[21].

The idea that a servant is always a custodian and never a bailee has never been absolute, and is currently under sustained attack. Pollock and Wright conceded that a master may create his servant a possessor of his goods by express language, but go on to observe that 'the law does not regard this as a

---

[18] Pollock & Wright, *An Essay on Possession in the Common Law* (1888) 57–60, Palmer, *Bailment*, 2nd edn, 456 (see the authorities cited in fn 1 thereto). Oliver Wendell Holmes purported to find the origin of this doctrine in the classical rule that a slave might not own or possess any property, so that all property in the possession of the slave was in fact in the possession of the master (*The Common Law* (1974) 226). It has been suggested that the effect of the decision in *R v Harding* (1929) 21 Cr App R 166 was to abolish this rule (see (1930) 46 LQR 135), but this view has not found favour.

[19] Hence the interesting conclusion that the illegitimate harvesting of the another's crops is not theft. The crop is not capable of being in possession whilst growing, since in that condition it is part of the real property. The cutting of the crop renders it capable of being possessed at the same time as the harvester acquires possession, so there is at no time an interference with possession (Pollock & Wright, *An Essay on Possession in the Common Law* (Clarendon, 1888), pp 230–1).

[20] *Hopkinson v Gibson* (1805) 2 Smith 202; *Wiebe v Lepp* (1974) 46 DLR(3rd) 441; *Associated Portland Cement Manufacturers (1900) Ltd v Ashton* [1915] 2 KB 1; *Gibson v O'Keeney* [1927] IR 66; *Ormrod v Crosville Motor Services Ltd* [1953] 1 WLR 1120; *France v Parkinson* [1954] 1 WLR 581.

[21] *Associated Portland Cement Manufacturers (1910) Ltd v Ashton* [1915] 2 KB 1.

normal state of things, and probably rather strict proof would be required.'[22].
Palmer[23] identifies some circumstances in which such a transaction might ordinarily be contemplated, but these examples all fall outside the normal ambit
of the relationship of master and servant. Palmer goes on to launch a masterly
and sustained assault upon the idea that the rigid distinction between the positions of servant and bailee is of any practical value[24], and it is not to be doubted
that in the fullness of time the English courts will accept the idea of a bailee
who is also a servant of his bailor. However, the point is still undecided.

Finally, although the category of custodians is composed almost entirely
of servants, as mentioned above there are other circumstances in which a person may possess a thing as a mere custodian.

The conclusion to be drawn from this analysis is that the question of whether
a man possesses a thing is as much a question of law as the question of whether
he has title to it—both issues being in truth of mixed law and fact.

Things which cannot be possessed

It has always been acknowledged that only some of the things which exist can
be possessed. The Romans had a class of *res extra commercium*[25] which by
their very nature could be neither possessed nor owned. However in the case
of modern English law it is difficult to identify such a class. Human beings,
both alive and dead, may not be owned. Live human beings have not been the
subject of bailment since the abolition of slavery[26], and there can be no property in a corpse[27]. Palmer[28] suggests that the reasons for this is that burial was
originally within the exclusive jurisdiction of the ecclesiastical courts[29]. In the
Australian case of *Doodeward v Spence*[30], involving a dead two-headed baby,
it was held that some corpses and parts of corpses might be possessed[31], and
the same must be true of a person's own body, since any unauthorized removal of any part of a person's person, so to speak, is a conversion[32]

---

[22] Pollock & Wright, *An Essay on Possession in the Common Law*, p 60.
[23] Palmer, *Bailment*, 2nd edn (Sweet & Maxwell, 1991), p 458.
[24] At pp 458–68.
[25] The full list of *res extra commercium* is (a) *res communes* (things common to all men (the sea, the air and, puzzlingly, the seashore)); (b) *res publicae* (public things (harbours and rivers)); (c) *res universitatis* (things belonging to a group of people and not alienable thereby, such as theatres and racecourses); (d) *res nullius* (things belonging to no-one, being (i) *res religiosae* (religious things such as graveyards), (ii) *res sacrae* (sacred things such as churches and church furniture), and (iii) *res sanctae* (things such as city walls and gates against which any offence is capital)).
[26] For a consideration of this aspect of law, see Stealey, 'Responsibilities and Liabilities of the Bailee of Slave Labour in Virginia' in *American Journal of Legal History* (1968) III, 336.
[27] 3 Co Inst 110 at 203, 215; *Haynes' Case* (1614) 12 Co Rep 113; 1 Hawkings PC 148; and see *Williams v Williams* (1882) 20 Ch D 659 at 663.
[28] Palmer, *Bailment*, p 9.
[29] (1926) 9 U Pa LR 404 at 405.
[30] (1908) 6 CLR 406.
[31] See Palmer *above*, pp 9–11 for a definitive analysis.
[32] *F N Moore v Regents of the University of California* 215 Cal App 3d 709 (1988); 793 P 2d 479 (1990).

Classically land can never be possessed, although if 'seisin is possession', as Pollock and Maitland taught, then the rule is no more than semantic. Perhaps more importantly, land is not the subject of bailment, since otherwise every tenancy of land whereby the tenant is granted exclusive possession would be a bailment, and this is not the case.

More important for our purposes is the Roman rule that intangible or incorporeal things—what we would call choses in action—also cannot be possessed. This is a rule of English law to this day. However in later Roman law this became 'an abstract dogma without practical significance'[33]. The reason why this came about almost exactly mirrors the development of seisin of land in England. At Roman law the usufructuary was in possession of land but had no title thereto. The only 'thing' which he 'owned' was his contractual claim against the landowner to remain in possession. However there seemed no reason in logic why of two neighbours, one occupying his land as an absolute owner and the other as usufructuary merely, the absolute owner should have better remedies against third parties despoiling his property. Thus to the usufructuary was extended juristic possession, or quasi-possession[34], in order to enable him to protect his land against third parties. However, where English law had stopped, Roman law continued, and the right to the interdicts by means of quasi-possession was extended to prædial servitudes, to inheritance and eventually to almost every incorporeal right in the Roman system, and at its full development it may be said that possession in the Roman system was divided into possession of tangibles and quasi-possession of intangibles, both giving rise to identical remedies. By contrast, at English law the rule that possession can only exist in tangible things remains fixed. '[A]ll personal things are either in possession or in action. The law knows no tertium quid between the two'[35], and a thing in possession is not a thing in action.

Constructive possession

Possession can be divided into actual and constructive possession. Actual possession is only very slightly more than physical possession: it is physical possession accompanied by an *animus domini*, or intention to control. Constructive possession is, in fact, no possession at all. Constructive possession arises where one person delivers to another a symbol of, or the means of control over, goods which are in fact stored in another place altogether[36]. This can be achieved in one of two ways. One is the transfer of a physical embodiment of control—classically, the key to a locked store-room in which the goods are kept[37]. The other is where the goods are in the custody of a third party bailee,

---

[33] R W Lee, *Elements of Roman Law*, 4th edn (Sweet & Maxwell, 1956), p 181. *See* pp 226–8 *below* for further details of the Roman law of possession.

[34] D.4.1.10, 5.

[35] Per Fry LJ in *Colonial Bank v Whinney* (1885) 30 Ch D 261, CA at 285.

[36] *Meyerstein v Barber* (1866) LR 2 CP 38; *Official Assignee of Madras v Mercantile Bank of India Ltd* [1935] AC 53 at 58–9.

[37] This can also be achieved by the delivery of a document of title; *see* Chapter 5 *below*.

and involves the immediate possessor instructing that bailee to make a statement to the transferee to the effect that henceforth he will hold the goods to
the order of the transferee. This is a delivery of possession by attornment. The
statement creates an estoppel against the bailee, who is from then on estopped
from denying the transferee's right to take immediate possession of the goods.
This has the same effect in law as the delivery of the key to a locked store-
room, in that it enables the transferee to take possession whenever he wishes,
and therefore the two methods of transferring possession should be regarded
as being similar.

It is important to distinguish constructive possession from a right to immediate possession, in that a person who has a mere right to immediate possession, although he has all the incidents of a possessor and may sue in conversion
on any interference with the goods, cannot pledge, bail or otherwise transfer
possession of the goods. However, a person who has constructive possession
of property can give another constructive possession.

The importance of possession

The primary importance of possession is that it is a root of title. A finder or a
person otherwise in possession of property is treated in law as absolute owner
against all the world except the rightful owner. This means that where no
person can show a better title to the property, the possessor is in effect the
owner. Secondary aspects of possession are that a possessor has the benefit of
various statutory provisions which have the effect of treating him in some
respects as if he had title. Additionally, and as part of the concept of possession as a root of title, possession gives a right to sue.

It is possible to imagine a legal system in which possession is all and title
is nothing—indeed some primitive systems work on exactly this basis. However once the two concepts have been independently admitted, the question
arises of how the law will deal with the three-cornered problem when possession and title are separated. Thus it is not at all uncommon that a person is in
possession, for whatever reason, of goods belonging to another. Where a third
party converts or otherwise interferes with those goods, the question arises
whether, in two-handed proceedings between the converter and the possessor,
the converter may be able to defend the action by arguing that his liability was
only to the owner, and not the possessor.

As mentioned above, the abandonment of the writ of right at early English
law meant that for a long time the English courts could deal with this question
very simply. The court's role was to determine the best right amongst those
before it, and the putative rights of non-parties were not to be considered.
However this simple system came under severe threat in the seventeenth century when defendants in actions of trover were allowed to plead the right of a
third party owner against a plaintiff possessor[38]. However, the protection of

---

[38] *Dockwray v Dickenson* (1679) Skin 640, although *per contra Armory v Delamirie* (1722) 1
Stra 505 and doubted in *Elliot v Kemp* (1840) 7 M & W 306 at 312 by Parke B.

possession remained of great importance, and in *Jeffries v Great Western Rly Co*[39] it was finally established that the possessor for the time being might sue on the basis of his possession alone, title to the goods being left out of the action.

The right to sue is not, however, the right to claim substantial damages. Until the mid-nineteenth century the action of the possessor was precarious, in that his action, although undoubtedly available, might be met with the reply that where goods in the bailee's possession were damaged by a third party without any negligence on the bailee's part, since the bailee was not liable in damage to the owner, then the quantum of damages which should be ordered against the third party was zero, otherwise the bailee would be unjustly enriched[40]. This dangerous argument was finally scotched by the Court of Appeal in *The Winkfield*[41], a case which has since been followed by the House of Lords[42].

Possession in common law and in civil law

The concept of possession as found in common law is different from the concept as usually encountered in civil law countries. The reason for this is the different perspectives of Roman and common law on the matter of possession. Roman law, and most of the systems which are based on it, classify possession as an idea not dissimilar to seisin. Possession belongs to the person with the right, not the person with the goods themselves. Equally a person who has goods pursuant to a contract which recognises another person's right to possess does not possess these goods. Thus in some cases the bailee does not have possession[43].

The reasoning behind this principle is largely structural.

---

[39] (1856) 5 El & Bl 802.

[40] *Claridge v South Staffordshire Tramway Co* [1892] 1 QB 422; *Brown v Hand-in-Hand Fire Insurance Society Ltd* (1895) 11 TLR 538.

[41] [1902] P 42. The bailee was the Postmaster-General in posession of mail, who was *ex officio* absolutely immune from suit in any event. The interesting point of when title to mail in the hands of the Post Office passes from sender to addressee was therefore not decided.

[42] *Morrison SS Co Ltd v Greystoke Castle (Cargo Owners)* [1947] AC 265; *The Jag Sharti* [1986] AC 337. For similar reasons, a bailee's insurable interest in an asset is equal to the full value of the asset and is not limited to the bailee's liability to the bailor. The reasons for this rule are discussed at length in *Petrofina (UK) Ltd v Magnaload Ltd* [1984] QB 127 at 135, and see *Hepburn v A Tomlinson (Hauliers) Ltd* [1966] AC 451 and *The Albazero* [1977] AC 774 at 846.

[43] Strictly speaking, Roman law does deal with actual possession under the name of natural possession. However the possession which is protected by the interdict (and therefore the possession which matters) is juristic possession, and natural possession is a mere foil for it (Dig 41 2. 3, 18; 20). There are five exceptions to this rule—the *emphyteuta* (or holder of a farming lease), the *pledgee*, the *superficarius* (or tenant with a long lease), the *precario tenens* (or tenant at will) and the *sequester* (or stakeholder)—all of whom may have the interdict. This is the view expressed by Savigny and is the consensus view. *Per contra* Ihering maintained that Roman law was based on natural possession, but limited the availability of the interdict to a sub-class of the total class of possessors.

A possessor is always thought of [at Roman law] as a possible defendant in a real action, and therefore one who is and will remain owner, unless the Plaintiff can oust him by proof of his title. All of this is quite alien to English law. English law does not think of the possessor as a defendant in a real action but as a plaintiff in an action of Trespass.[44]

---

[44] Buckland & McNair, *Roman Law and Common Law*, 2nd edn (Cambridge University Press,

Chapter 4

Bailment

Crossley Vaines observed that: 'It seems that the confusion in the law of bailment may be due to postulating a law of bailment'[1]. Winfield[2] famously pointed out that no mention of bailment was to be found in Bullen and Leake's *Precedents of Pleadings*, and hypothesised from this that bailment might be a portmanteau legal concept which could be completely anatomised into claims in contract and tort, and that the absence of a claim for 'breach of bailment' indicated that there might be no such thing as a law of bailment.

This is too easy. The bailor's action against a defaulting bailee is an action in 'breach of bailment' in exactly the same way in which a beneficiary's action against a defaulting trustee is an action in breach of trust. Bailment is the name of a bundle of rights and duties which arise where a person has possession of chattels owned by another, in the same way in which a trust is the name of a bundle of rights and duties as between trustee, beneficiary and the outside world. Both arise from the proprietary nature of the relationship in relation to the chattels bailed.

However, it is clearly true that a division of legal rights into those of contract and tort leaves little room for bailment as a concept. This is a pity, since the existence of bailment as a fact is too evident to be easily ignored, and it follows from this that the division into contract and tort is too neat. This has been clear for centuries—the actions in quasi-contract were developed expressly to deal with a world which obstinately refuses to conduct itself according to lawyers' paradigms, and the development of the law of restitution in our own time is another example of such. For those whose attachment to the modern forms of action is so great that they cannot easily conceive of a common law right which is neither tortious nor contractual, they may pacify themselves with the thought that the common law actions, both contractual and tortious, dealt only with obligations[3]. When we come to bailment we come to the common law's attempt to deal with property rights and its treatment thereof is, rightly, a different kind of action from that in either contract or tort.

---

[1] Crossley Vaines, *Personal Property* (Palmer, ed), 5th edn (Butterworths, 1973).

[2] *Province of the Law of Tort*, p 101.

[3] There is a continuing illusion that contract at common law deals with title. It does not. The most a common law contract can ever do is to give rise to an action for damages—for proprietary remedies the plaintiff must go to equity.

[4] 2nd edn (Sweet & Maxwell, 1991), p 3.

[5] There is in fact a US decision to the effect that 'it is the element of lawful possession, however created, and duty to account for the thing as the property of another that creates a bailment' (*Foulke v New York Consolidated RR* 228 NY 269, 127 NE 137 (1920)). However, the modern

The nature of bailment

Professor Palmer, in his monumental work *Bailment*, opines that a bailment arises in all cases where the separation of ownership and possession is the result of one person being knowingly and willingly in possession of goods which belong to another[4]. It is submitted that this is a correct statement of the nature of a bailment at English law.

It is necessarily true that where ownership and possession are unified there can be no bailment, since bailment necessitates the separation of possession and title. It is equally clearly true that not every separation of possession and title creates a bailment. These two propositions may well represent the limit of the consensus in this field[5].

Bailment and contract

In *R v Ashwell*, Lord Coleridge said that 'bailment is not a mere delivery on a contract, but a contract in itself ... the contract of bailment is not a mere loose and common phrase, but it is the accurate expression of a legal idea'[6]. However the weight of authority is that this is now, as Palmer says, 'outmoded ... and a bailment may arise in the absence of any contract obliging or entitling the bailee to take possession'[7]. This is clearly true on historical grounds; bailment was an established legal concept at a stage where the law of contract had barely begun to emerge from the general law of obligations, and is equally in line with the contention that, as Fifoot put it, 'bailment is *sui generis*—an elementary and unique transaction, the practical necessity of which is self-evident and self-explanatory'[8]. It may be useful to remember in this context that it was not until the decision in *Donoghue v Stevenson*[9] that it was clearly understood that there could be an action in negligence (as opposed to trespass) without a pre-existing contract.

Early views[10], dependent on the fallacy that bailment was a form of contractual relationship, rejected as bailments many agreements which are nowadays correctly so classified because of the lack of a contractual relationship between the parties. As the grip of contract law on English law weakened it became accepted that any consensus between bailor and bailee was capable of creating a bailment, and this is the view taken by Pollock and Wright[11].

This view is now also widely regarded as too restrictive, and it is accepted that a bailment may be created without mutual consent. For example, where a

---

US view is better reflected in *Berglund v Roosevelt University* 310 NE (2d) 773 (1974) at 775–6 that both knowlege and consent on the bailee's part are required.

[6] (1885) 16 QBD at 223.

[7] *Bailment* (*see* fn 4 *above*), p 19. The authorities are collected in that volume at p 19, fn 88, p 567, fn 54 and pp 1281–1366 *passim*.

[8] Fifoot, *History & Sources of the Common law* (1949), pp 24–5.

[9] [1932] AC 562.

[10] Tay argues that the earliest views of bailment were inclusive, and that the 'modern' widening of the doctrine is no more than a return to its original form ((1966) Syd LR 239, criticised in Palmer (*see* fn 4 *above*), pp 38–43).

[11] At 163, repeated by Winfield, *Province of the Law of Tort* (1931), Paton, *Bailment* (1936) and Stoljar (1955) 7 *Res Judicatae* 160.

person finds a thing belonging to another, he becomes a bailee of those goods from the moment of finding and is liable to the owner if he fails to exercise due care in relation to the thing found[12]. In these circumstances the owner is necessarily oblivious of the finding, but this is not fatal to the bailment. Equally, where a bailee has been ordered by his bailor not to sub-bail the goods and does so, the sub-bailee is an actual and existing sub-bailee of the bailor despite the fact that the original bailor not only did not consent to, but actively objected to, his appointment.

Bailment and tort

In a number of cases it has been held or assumed that where there is no contract governing a bailment, the bailee's duties to the bailor are the ordinary tortious duties[13]. Wingfield held that the obligations owed by a bailee to his bailor were not tortious in origin, but his analysis is flawed by its dependence upon the concept of bailment as a consensual relationship[14]. Palmer[15] has demonstrated the independence of the obligations which arise from bailment from those which arise out of the ordinary tort relationship, citing such principles of the law of bailment as the prohibition upon the bailee's denial of his bailor's title[16], the absolute vicarious liability for the act of a sub-bailee and the duty to guard the property against theft. All of these obligations exist in the case of a voluntary bailment, but do not arise out of the ordinary law of tort and cannot by definition arise from contract. Thus they must arise as an incident of the relationship of bailor and bailee constituted by the delivery of property independently of both contract and tort.

Requirements for a bailment

It seems to be universally accepted that an unknowing or involuntary posessor is, at least, not a bailee[17], and that the relation is created by the bailee acquiring actual or constructive possession of the chattel with the intention to possess it *as bailee*. The primary ingredient of a bailment is therefore the transfer of possession, and this topic has been dealt with at length in the previous chapter. The distinction between those transfers of possession which do, and those which do not, create bailments is therefore in the mental element of the recipient.

This qualification complicates matters considerably. The average bailee

---

[12] *Morris v C W Martin & Sons Ltd* [1966] 1 QB 716; *Gilchrist Watt and Sanderson Pty Ltd v York Products Pty Ltd* [1970] 3 All ER 825; *Parker v British Airways Board* [1982] 1 QB 1004.
[13] *Morris v C W Martin & Sons Ltd* [1966] 1 QB 716 at 738; *BWIA v Bart* (1966) 11 WLR 378.
[14] Winfield, *Province of the Law of Tort* (1931), pp 99–100.
[15] Palmer, *Bailment*, 2nd edn (Sweet & Maxwell), pp 44–49.
[16] Ibid, pp 262–85.
[17] Even Tay ((1966) 5 Syd LR 239 at 252–3) accepts this point, although there have been incidences (notably (1959) 12 Stan LR 264 at 266) of the absolute view that all separation of possession and ownership gives rise to a bailment. This is dealt with by Palmer at p 44, who instances purchasers for value who have unknowingly failed to obtain good title and persons upon whose land goods are lost as possessors without title who are clearly not bailees.

does not know the meaning of the word and cannot therefore consciously decide to act as one. When a watch is delivered to the watchmaker for mending, he does not say to himself 'I hereby constitute myself bailee of this watch', but accepts it with an intention to do a number of things. However this is to complicate matters unnecessarily. A watchmaker who accepts a watch with legitimate intentions other than as bailee would be in some difficulty as to exactly what it was that he did intend to do. The thought would occur only if he were to wish not to be a bailee.

Thus the rule may be inverted and stated as that the separation of possession and ownership gives rise to a bailment in all cases except those where the person acquiring possession either does so unknowingly or without willingness to become a bailee[18].

It follows from this that the modern bailment is in fact not a relation between persons but a relation between a person and a thing[19]. This gives rise to the next series of questions on the relationship between bailment and title.

The property which the bailee has in the bailed chattel is in many ways equivalent to an estate in land[20]. It is a package of rights against the goods which is independent of, and is neither extinguished nor affected by, a transfer of the title to the goods[21]. There is modern authority to the effect that what the bailor retains may properly be described as a 'reversionary interest'[22]. This proprietary status is to some extent concealed behind the older authorities, which adopt the obscure terminology that the bailor has a 'general' and the bailee a 'special' property in the chattel bailed[23].

Although a bailment is created by transfer of possession, redelivery of possession is not required. It has become accepted that a bailment may come into being in cases where neither side has the slightest intention that the goods concerned will be returned to the bailee—for example in conditional sale agreements[24].

Classes of bailment

In *Coggs v Bernard*[25], Lord Holt CJ set out a Roman classification of the types of bailment. The objective of his classification was to support his decision that 'If a man [makes] actual entry upon [a] thing, and taking the trust himself ... and it miscarries in the performance of his trust, an action will lie against him for that, though no other body could have compelled him to do the thing'. Against his Lordship was a formidable pile of authorities, largely exhibiting

[18] *The Captain Gregos (No 2)* [1990] 2 Lloyd's Rep 395; 2 Halsbury (4th edn) para 1501.
[19] Tay (1966) 5 Syd LR and see Palmer, p 36.
[20] *Australian Guarantee Corp v Ross* [1983] 2 VR 319.
[21] *Rich v Aldred* (1705) 6 Mod 216; *Franklin v Neate* (1844) 13 M & W 481.
[22] *Kwei Tek Chao v British Traders and Shippers Ltd* [1954] 2 QB 459 at 487; *The Playa Larga and the Marble Islands* [1983] 2 Lloyd's Rep 171 at 179; *The Mineral Transporter* [1986] AC 1 at 18.
[23] *Heydon v Smith* (1610) 13 Co Rep 67, 69, Crossley Vaines.
[24] *Karflex Ltd v Poole* [1933] 2 KB 251.
[25] (1703) 2 Ld Raym 909 at 912–3.

the confusion between proprietary and contractual rights identified above, which tended to the view that where there was no consideration there was no action on the bailment. The end of Lord Holt's judgment is an assertion of the identity of voluntary bailment with the Roman contract of *mandatum*, supported by Vinnius' commentaries upon Justinian. The only English authority in which this identity is asserted is Bracton (p 919), and His Lordship was therefore required to establish the authority of Bracton over the existing cases in order to maintain his point.

The defects in Lord Holt's Romanistic categorisations of bailment have long been apparent[26]. They encompass only consensual bailments, between two parties by transfer of actual possession, restrictions which the modern law of bailment has superseded. As Turner J said in the New Zealand case of *Motor Mart Ltd v Webb*[27],

> although the bailments known to Roman law were sufficient for Lord Holt CJ in 1703, I decline to assume that, under the pressures and stresses of modern legal necessity, some new mutation may not have burst into flower, of a quality to startle the author of the Institutes were he privileged to behold it. Such a sport may readily be seen in the bailment which is undoubtedly the product of the *Helby v Matthews* type of agreement ...

However, the fact that the categorisation is defective does not render it useless, and the concepts deployed at least define the various possibilities. They are:

    (a)   *depositum*—a bare deposit of goods to be kept for the use of the bailor;
    (b)   *commodatum*—a deposit of goods for use by the bailee, to be returned intact;
    (c)   *locatio conductio*—a commodatum for reward; the lender is the *locator*, the hirer the *conductor*;
    (d)   *vadium*—a pledge of goods as security for money borrowed;
    (e)   *locatio operis faciendi*—a delivery to carry for reward; the delivery may be to a private person or to a public servant;
    (f)   *mandatum*—an undertaking to do some act to or to carry the goods bailed without reward.

Bailee's obligations

The object of Lord Holt's classification was to establish limits to the old doctrine that a bailee was strictly liable for any damage done to the bailed property[28]. The effect of the decision in *Coggs v Bernard* was to establish a hierarchy of liabilities, such that the bailee in a case where the bailment was for the benefit of both parties—*locatio conductio*, *vadium* and *locatio operis faciendi*

---

[26] Palmer *above*, p 3.
[27] [1958] NZLR 773 at 784.
[28] *Southcot v Bennet* (1601) Cro Eliz 815. This strict liability was said to be the basis for the bailee's action in trespass 'because he is chargeable over' (*Heydon v Smith* (1610) 13 Co Rep 67 at 69.

in the above categorisation—would be liable for ordinary negligence but not otherwise. Where the bailment was exclusively for the bailor's benefit—*depositum* and *mandatum*—then the bailee's liability was reduced accordingly, and the standard of liability was said to be 'gross' negligence. Where the bailment was entirely for the bailee's benefit—*commodatum*—the bailee was to be under a greater legal burden, and to be liable even for slight negligence.

The difficulty which this approach created was that 'gross' negligence and 'slight' negligence had no independent existence, and proved in practice to be remarkably difficult to set; and it was this difficulty which led Rolfe B to explain that gross negligence is nothing but 'negligence with the addition of a vituperative epithet'[29], a sentiment which, no matter how incorrect at law, probably accurately captured the result in litigation of an attempt to establish the distinctions.

The modern approach to the bailee's liability is to say that 'the standard of care required is the standard demanded by the circumstances of each particular case'[30]. This standard of 'gross' negligence was accurately described by Willes J as follows[31]:

Confusion has arisen from regarding negligence as a positive instead of a negative word. It is really the absence of such care as it was the duty of a defendant to use. A bailee is only bound to use the ordinary care of a man, and so the absence of it is called gross negligence. A person who undertakes to do some work for reward to an article must exercise the care of a skilled workman, and the absence of such care in him is negligence. Gross, therefore, is a word of description and not of definition.

In respect of the liability for 'slight' negligence in the case of *commodatum*, or gratuitous bailment for use, Palmer has pointed out that there is really no English authority more recent than *Coggs v Bernard*[32], but that the trend of the common-law world is towards an homologation of the standard required from a gratuitous bailee towards the general standard of 'reasonable care'[33].

Bailor's rights

Where a bailee has a chattel for a period for reward, he has both possession and the right to possession. Thus only the bailee may sue a person who dam-

[29] *Wilson v Brett* (1843) 11 M & W 113. In *Armitage v Norse* (1997) *The Times*, 31 March, CA, Millet LJ pointed out that 'gross negligence' at English law is not a separately existing concept, and that the civil law concept that *culpa lata dolo aequiparetur* (sufficiently great negligence is equivalent to fraud) has no basis at English law. Consequently, he denies the existence of a separate category of 'gross' negligence.
[30] *Houghland v R R Low (Luxury Coaches) Ltd* [1962] 1 QB 694; *Port Swettenham Authority v T W Wu & Co (M) Sdn Bhd* [1979] AC 580 at 589.
[31] *Grill v General Iron Screw Collier Co* (1866) LR 1 CP 600 at 612.
[32] Palmer *above*, p 668.
[33] See the Canadian cases *Riverdale Garage v Barrett Bros* [1930] 4 DLR 429; *A R Williams Machinery Co v Muttart Builders Supplies (Winnipeg) Ltd* (1961) 30 DLR(3rd) 339; *Fairley and Stevens (1966) Ltd v Goldsworthy* (1973) 34 DLR(3rd) 554; *Jenkins v Smith* (1969) 6 DLR(3rd) 309.

ages the goods in conversion[34]. The bailor cannot compel the bailee to sue for damage to the goods[35], but the bailor may sue for damage to his reversionary interest[36]. Where the bailee does not have an enforceable right to retain the goods (ie is a bailee at will) the bailee has possession but the bailor has the right to immediate possession, and it is therefore the bailor who can sue for any interference with the goods[37].

The most complex problems in relation to the bailor's position arises where the bailee sub-bails the goods. If the sub-bailment is without consent, or is contrary to any express term of the bailment, the bailor may have an action against the sub-bailee in conversion as well as an action against the bailee in breach of bailment[38]. Where a bailee is not given express authority to sub-bail the goods, such authority may be implied either from trade usage or from the contemplated means of performance of the terms of the bailment[39].

In such a case the bailor can treat the sub-bailee in all respects as if he were his direct bailee. This means that the bailor may proceed directly against the sub-bailee for any failure of the sub-bailee in respect of the ordinary duties created by a bailment[40]. It seems that the sub-bailee's duties are assessed according to the nature of the sub-bailment. Thus, where the sub-bailment is for reward, the sub-bailee's duty is as a bailee for reward, even though the initial bailment may have been gratuitous[41]. The sub-bailee, however, will seek to argue that the sub-bailment was made by the bailee upon the bailor's ostensible authority—a plea which will enable him to take advantage of any limitation of liability provisions contained in the initial contract of bailment.

Particular types of bailment

Involuntary bailments

An involuntary bailment arises in any circumstances in which a person finds that, without any consent on his part, he has another's goods under his control[42]. There are a number of ways in which this can arise—possibly too many to be categorised—but in all cases Lord Holts' principles hold to the extent that the liability created is less than an ordinary liability in negligence. The modern statement of the liability of an involuntary bailee can be found in *Elvin & Powell Ltd v Plummer Roddis*[43], in which the liability was defined as

---

[34] *Gordon v Harper* (1796) 7 Term Rep 9; *Ferguson v Cristall* (1829) 5 Bing 305; *O'Sullivan v Williams* [1992] 3 All ER 385, CA.

[35] *Leigh & Sullivan v Aliakmon Shipping Co Ltd; The Aliakmon* [1986] AC 785; *Candlewood Navigation Corporation Ltd v Mitsui OSK Lines Ltd* [1986] AC 1, PC.

[36] *Mears v LSW Rly* (1862) 11 CB(NS) 850; *Dee Trading Co Pty Ltd v Baldwin* [1938] WLR 173; *Moukataff v BOAC* [1967] 1 Lloyd's Rep 396.

[37] *United States of America and Republic of France v Dollfus Mieg et Cie SA* [1952] AC 582.

[38] *Chitty on Contracts*, 27th edn (Sweet & Maxwell, 1994), para 32-013.

[39] *Learoyd Bros v Pope & Sons* [1966] 2 Lloyd's Rep 142.

[40] *The Pioneer Container* [1994] 3 WLR 1, PC.

[41] *The Pioneer Container* at 7–9.

[42] Eg *Heugh v LNW Rly* (1870) LR 5 Ex 51 (carrier when consignee refuses delivery); *Howard v Harris* (1884) Cab & El 253 (theatre manager sent a script of a play).

[43] (1933) 50 TLR 158.

that 'if persons were involuntary bailees and had done everything reasonable, they were not liable to pay damages if something which they did resulted in the loss of the property'. However, it seems that this lower level of liability pertains only as long as the involuntary bailee remains completely inert. If he does some act asserting control over the property he is judged on the ordinary standard[44].

The position of involuntary bailees has been improved by the enactment of the Unsolicited Goods and Services Act 1971. This Act was passed to deal with a brief (and almost inexplicable) craze for mail order selling by despatching goods at random, following up the despatch with threats unless the consignees paid either for the goods or for the (usually heavy) cost of returning them. The Act applies in any case where the goods were sent to a person 'with a view to his acquiring them', and takes effect so that the recipient becomes the absolute owner of the goods six months after their arrival or 30 days after the dispatch of a notice to the sender of the goods requesting their collection.

Even outside the Act a similar right avails under the common law, since there is authority that an involuntary bailee who writes to his bailor indicating an intention to dispose of the bailed goods may subsequently dispose of the goods with the bailor's implied consent[45]. Alternatively he can now apply for the exercise of the wide powers of sale conferred by ss 13 and 14 of the Torts (Interference with Goods) Act 1977.

Deposit

Deposit is the bailment of a chattel to be kept by the bailee without reward and to be returned upon demand. A bailee under a contract of deposit, under Lord Holt's principles, was liable only for gross negligence. The modern approach is to determine liability according to the facts, in particular the nature of the goods and the way in which they were kept[46]. The bailee may not use the goods at all; if he does he must account for any detriment suffered by them[47]; if his use is wholly inconsistent with the terms of the deposit then it is terminated immediately and the bailor may sue him in conversion[48].

A gratuitous bailee has the right to charge his bailor with any costs necessarily incurred in caring for the goods[49].

Mandate

Mandate is a gratuitous bailment of a specific chattel for a specific purpose. There are two types of mandate:

---

[44] *Summer v Challenor* (1926) 70 SJ 760; *Gilchrist, Watt and Sanderson Pty Ltd v York Products Pty Ltd* [1970] 1 WLR 1262.

[45] *Sachs v Miklos* [1948] 2 KB 23.

[46] *Giblin v McMullen* (1868) LR 2, PC.

[47] *Lilley v Doubleday* (1881) 7 QBD 510.

[48] *Fenn v Bittleston* (1851) 7 Exch 152; *North General Wagon and Finance Co Ltd v Graham* [1950] 2 KB 7.

[49] *China-Pacific SA v Food Corp of India; The Winson* [1981] 3 All ER 688, HL.

(a)   for the purpose of enabling an act to be done which could not be done
without the chattel, and
(b)   for enabling an act to be done to the chattel by the mandatory.

A mandatory is required to exercise reasonable care, despite the absence of
reward[50]. Where the ground for the mandate is the possession by the mandatory of a special skill, failure to exercise that skill constitutes a breach of the
mandate.

The mandatory is entitled to be reimbursed for the costs incurred in the
exercising of the mandate.

Commodatum

A commodatum is a gratuitous loan made to enable the borrower to utilise the
chattel bailed. Because the idea of the commodatum is that the chattel will be
used, the bailee is not liable for ordinary wear and tear of the chattel. He is,
however, liable for any damage resulting from failure to exercise reasonable
skill in using it[51], or for failure to exercise any special skill in reliance upon
his possession of which the bailor agreed to the bailment in the first place[52].
The bailee must also bear all the usual costs of use of the chattel[53].

A commodatum is always for a particular purpose, and the bailee may only
use the chattel for that specific purpose. Any deviation from the purpose is
actionable by the bailor, and the bailee will in such a case become an insurer,
responsible for all damage to the chattel howsoever caused[54].

Even though the commodatum is not for reward, by allowing the bailee to
have possession of the chattel the bailor acquires some obligations. In particular, if the chattel is old, out of condition, or has inherent or latent defects,
the bailor must notify the bailee of this, and is liable to the bailee for any loss
so caused if he does not do so[55].

Hire of goods

A *locatio conductio*, or hire of goods, is a commodatum for reward. A hirer of
goods is entitled during the hire period to undisturbed possession of the hired
goods, and may prevent the owner from interfering with the chattel against
his will in the same way as any other person[56].

At common law the hirer is obliged to take reasonable care of the chattel
hired, to return it at the stated time, and to pay the agreed hire charge. He is
bound to take reasonable care of the chattel hired, but is only liable for damage owing to his negligence, and is not liable if the chattel is damaged or lost
without fault on his part[57].

---

[50] *Houghland v R R Low (Luxury Coaches) Ltd* [1962] 1 QB 694.
[51] *Blakemore v Bristol & Exeter Rly* (1858) 8 E & B 1035.
[52] *Chaudry v Prabhakar* [1989] 1 WLR 29.
[53] *Handford v Palmer* (1820) 2 Brod & B 359.
[54] *Coggs v Bernard* (1703) 2 Ld Raym 909.
[55] *Coughlin v Gillison* [1899] 1 QB 145.
[56] *Lee v Atkinson & Brook* (1609) Yelv 172.
[57] *Sanderson v Collins* [1904] 1 KB 628.

As with commodatum, restrictions of the purpose of the hire must be strictly observed, and a person who uses a chattel for a purpose outside the purpose of the hire is liable both in contract and in tort for any resulting loss[58].

The hirer is not obliged to make repairs to the hired chattel save for such repairs as would ordinarily be required for use over a period equal to the hire period[59]. The repair of a hired chattel conventionally throws up the problem that a hirer is not permitted to allow a third party lien to arise on the hired goods, but the delivery of a chattel to a repairer for a repair almost inevitably creates such a lien[60]. The solution to this is that where the hire period is such that a maintenance obligation is implied, the owner's consent to the creation of a repairer's lien is also implied[61]. This gives the lien effect as against the owner as well as the hirer.

Note that 'consumer' hire agreements are subject to strict controls (on documentation, terms and restrictions on enforcement of those terms) through the Consumer Credit Act 1974. These terms are outside the scope of this work, and reference should be made to the authorities on consumer credit[62].

Custody

In reality the provision of custody services is the primary area of the law of bailment. Where a person hires himself out as a custodian, he incurs a series of obligations under contract, in tort and through the relationship of bailment.

The contract of custody is subject to the Unfair Contract Terms Act 1977, and any exclusion clause therein must satisfy the test laid down in ss 2 and 11 thereof. However, in addition to this the contract is subject to the Supply of Goods and Services Act 1982, which implies certain specified terms into all contracts for the supply of services. The Act permits these terms to be varied or abrogated by agreement between the parties or by custom. The relevant provisions are:

(a) 'In a contract for the supply of a service, where the supplier is acting in the course of a business, there is an implied term that the supplier will carry out the services with reasonable care and skill' (s 13);

(b) s 14(1) provides that where the contract does not fix a particular time, the time for performance of the contract will be within a reasonable time. By s 14(2) what is meant by this term is a question of fact to be determined in all the circumstances of the case.

(c) s 15(1) provides that where the price is not expressly provided, the customer must pay a reasonable price for the service.

The standard of care which must be exercised by a custodian for reward is 'reasonable care' as the term is commonly understood. Thus the bailee must

---

[58] *Burnard v Haggios* (1863) 14 CB(NS) 45.
[59] *Sutton v Temple* (1843) 12 M & W 52.
[60] *See* pp 247 *below*.
[61] *Albermarle Supply Co v Hind* [1928] 1 KB 307; *K Chellaram & Sons (London) Ltd v Butlers Warehousing & Distribution Ltd* [1977] 2 Lloyd's Rep 192.
[62] See especially Goode, *Consumer Credit Law* (Sweet & Maxwell, looseleaf) and Guest, *Encyclopædia of Consumer Credit Law*.

keep the goods in an appropriate place and in appropriate conditions[63], must protect the goods against any imminent danger[64] and must take all proper steps to preserve the goods against third party claims adverse to the title of his bailor[65], and to preserve the chattel from deliberate damage[66]. Whilst the bailee for reward remains in actual possession of the goods he is not an insurer, and is only liable for damages as a result of his own negligence[67]. However if he deals with the goods contrary to the terms of his bailment, such as by depositing them with an unauthorised sub-bailee, he becomes an insurer until such time as the goods have returned to his possession[68] unless he can show that the damage is caused entirely independently of his default[69].

If the chattel is damaged whilst in the bailee's hands, the onus of proof is on the bailee to show that the damage was not the result of his negligence[70]. However he need not prove the actual cause of the damage, but merely that no default by himself could have caused the damage alleged[71].

Custody for reward is an elastic concept, since it does not require a specific agreement and identifiable separate consideration. It has been held that the most general of contractual arrangements can constitute a person a bailee for reward, even where the bailee is only indirectly connected with the relevant contract[72]. For this reason a bank safe deposit arrangement constitutes a bailment for reward, the reward being spelt out of the general contract of banker and customer[73]. A bank which has care of a safe deposit box may not open the box, and does not have a lien on its contents.

[63] *Searle v Laverick* (1874) LR 9 QB 122.
[64] *Brabant & Co v King* [1895] AC 632.
[65] *Ranson v Platt* [1911] 2 KB 291.
[66] *Lockspeiser Aircraft Ltd v Brooklands Aircraft Co Ltd* [1990] CLY 250, and see Palmer, *Bailment*, 2nd edn (Sweet & Maxwell, 1991), pp 1677–9.
[67] *Searle v Laverick* (1874) LR 9 QB 122.
[68] *Jackson v Cochrane* [1989] 2 Qd R 23.
[69] *James Morrison & Co Ltd v Shaw Savill and Albion Ltd* [1916] 2 KB 783.
[70] *Coldman v Hill* [1919] 1 KB 443; *British Road Services Ltd v Arthur V Crutchley & Co Ltd* [1968] 1 All ER 811.
[71] *Bullen v Swann Electric Engraving Co* (1907) 23 TLR 258.
[72] *Andrews v Home Flats* (1945) 173 LT 408.
[73] *Chitty on Contracts*, 27th edn (Sweet & Maxwell, 1994), para 32-039.

Chapter 5

Documents of Title to Goods

A negotiable instrument may in some circumstances be correctly described as a document of title to a chose in action, although the two are so closely inter-twined that a distinction between them may seem otiose. A document of title to goods, on the other hand, is conceptually very difficult. In the case of a document of title the physical essence of one thing—the goods—becomes mystically bound up with the physical essence of a specific document. How, it will be asked, can two things be in law one thing.

Characteristics of a document of title

A document of title is a document which in some respects 'is' the goods which it represents. Delivery of possession of the document constitutes delivery of possession of the goods, and, in the same way that delivery of possession of goods with an intention to transfer title constitutes a transfer of title to goods, delivery of possession of a document of title to goods accompanied by an intention to transfer title constitutes a valid transfer of the title of those goods.

There is no doubt that the transferor and transferee of a document of title may, by agreement, contrive that title to the goods to which the bill relates will pass at the moment of transfer. It seems equally clear that they may by agreement contrive that title should not pass at that time[2]. However the question of the passage of title to goods is a matter between the parties to the transfer of the goods. In the case of the relationship between the goods' owner and the possessor, the relevance of the document of title is exclusively in the field of possession[3].

The effect of a transfer of a document of title is sometimes said to be that the transfer itself operates as an attornment by the carrier to the transferee. This cannot be right, since the mere transfer of the document of title itself cannot confer rights against the true possessor unless the parties to the trans-fer so intend[4].

The correct analysis of the effect of a transfer of a document of title under the existing law must therefore be that such a transfer may be effective to

---

[1] *See* pp 159–61 *below.*
[2] See Goode, *Commercial Law*, 2nd edn (Penguin, 1995), p 902.
[3] *The Delfini* [1990] 1 Lloyd's Rep 252 (except, that is, in the unlikely event that one wishes to transfer ownership of the goods to the carrier).
[4] *The Future Express* [1993] 2 Lloyd's Rep 542, CA, *affmg* [1992] 2 Lloyd's Rep 79.

transfer either title or possession or both, depending on the parties' intention[5].

The importance of the document of title from the perspective of the person in actual possession of the property is that it evinces an intention to be bound as attorney by a transfer of the document of title. It is probable that this obligation is related to, if not identical with, the concept of 'negotiability by estoppel' as illustrated in *Goodwin v Robarts*[6]. The possessor of the goods renders himself a bailee of the holder in due course of the document of title by virtue of the fact that, having issued the document of title himself (or having allowed it to be issued in his name) he is estopped from denying the title of any holder[7].

Part of the statutory magic of a bill of lading is that the transfer of the document effects an automatic quasi-novation of the contract of carriage which is said to be embodied in it. This is not necessarily the case with other documents of title.

What documents are documents of title?

The only documents which are inarguably documents of title in the sense given above are bills of lading, which are rendered such by s 2 of the Carriage of Goods by Sea Act 1992, and various dock warrants issued by bodies whose warrants have been rendered documents of title by specialist local Act of Parliament[8]. It is also accepted that trade custom can render a variety of other documents as documents of title[9], although such a custom may be more easily shown outside the UK[10].

It is suggested that the class of documents which may be treated as documents of title by trade custom is now in effect closed. Attempts to have new documents treated as documents of title have been unsuccessful[11], and in the last of the great title fights, *Official Assignee of Madras v Mercantile Bank of*

---

[5] *Sewell v Burdick* (1884) 10 App Cas 74 at 95–7.

[6] (1876) 1 App Cas 476 at 487.

[7] *Laurie & Morewood v Dudin & Sons* [1926] 1 KB 223; see also Palmer, *Bailment*, 2nd edn (Sweet & Maxwell, 1991), pp 1369–71.

[8] Mersey Dock Acts Consolidation Act 1858, s 200 (the Mersey Docks and Harbour Board); Trafford Park Act 1904 (Trafford Park Co); Liverpool Mineral and Metal Storage Co Ltd (Delivery Warrants) Act 1921; and the Port of London Act 1968. These statutes conventionally create a document similar to a bill of lading in that the right to the goods can pass by endorsement of the warrant.

[9] See *Merchant Banking Co of London v Phoenix Bessemer Steel Co* (1877) 5 Ch D 205, in which it was held that by custom of the iron trade a delivery warrant was not only a document of title but also negotiable. It seems most unlikely that this case would be decided the same way today.

[10] Because custom must be local—a custom of a place. It was on this ground that the Privy Council determined in *Kum v Wah Tat Bank Ltd* [1971] 1 Lloyd's Rep 439, PC that a mate's receipt was held to be a document of title in the trade between Sarawak and Singapore.

[11] *Gunn v Bolckow, Vaughan & Co* (1875) 10 Ch App 491 (delivery orders); *Britain & Overseas Trading (Bristles) Ltd v Brooks Wharf and Bull Wharf Ltd* [1967] 2 Lloyd's Rep 51 (delivery warrants); *Dublin City Distillery v Doherty* [1914] AC 823; *Laurie & Morewood v Dudin & Sons* [1926] 1 KB 223, CA (warehouse warrants).

India[12], it was held that a pledge of any document other than a bill of lading took effect as a delivery of the documents only and not of possession of the goods concerned[13]. Thus Goode has said that the only document of title currently existing at modern English law is the bill of lading and the various statutory warrants[14].

As a conclusion this is unexceptionable save for a conundrum. In the Factors Act 1889 various important provisons are keyed off the possession by a mercantile agent of a document of title. The Act therefore defines the term 'document of title' to include

> any bill of lading, dock warrant, warehouse-keeper's certificate, and warrant or order for the delivery of goods, and any other document used in the ordinary course of business as proof of the possession or control of goods, or authorising or purporting to authorise, either by endorsement or by delivery, the possessor of the document to transfer or receive goods thereby represented.

This list has puzzled lawyers for generations, since it encompasses a number of documents which could never be, and certainly have never been, accepted as 'documents of title' in the sense that their possession affects the legal status of the goods to which they relate. Since the hypothesis that the Factors Act was drafted by someone completely unfamiliar with the ordinary meaning of the term 'document of title' is unlikely, it is necessary to explain this apparently eccentric statutory usage.

The explanation is to be found in the work of Michael Bools on the early law of the bill of lading[15]. Bools explains that the decision in *Lickbarrow v Mason*[16] in 1787, widely treated as having established that a bill of lading is a document of title, in fact established nothing of the kind, and goes on to show that as late as 1820 a court could hold that a possessor of a bill of lading did not necessarily thereby acquire any possessory interest in the cargo to which the bill related[17]. Thus when the predecessor of s 3 of the Factors Act 1889 was enacted in 1842[18] the concept of a document of title operating as a substitute for the goods themselves was unknown at English law.

It therefore seems that the documents listed in s 1 of the Factors Act 1889 would indeed have been 'documents of title', as the term was understood in 1842 (ie in the context of title deeds to land). No-one ever suggested that the possession of title deeds to land conferred any interest in land. However, their possession or otherwise by the owner raised a series of evidential presumptions. Where a person claiming title to land was in possession of the title deeds to that land the fact of possession constitutes evidence of that title, but

---

[12] [1935] AC 53.
[13] Per Lord Wright at 59.
[14] Goode, *Commercial Law*, 2nd edn (Penguin, 1995), p 277.
[15] M A Bools, *The Bill of Lading; A Document of Title to Goods. An Anglo American Comparison* (Lloyds of London Press, 1997).
[16] (1787) 2 TR 63 at 69.
[17] *Sargent v Morris* (1820) 2 B & Ald 277; see also *Patten v Thompson* (1816) 5 M & S 350.
[18] Factors Act 1842, s 4.

no more than evidence[19]. Where such a person does not have title deeds, their absence raised a duty to enquire, but no more than that[20]. The effect of the Factors Act is no more than to raise this evidential presumption to the status of an irrebuttable presumption.

---

[19] *Peto v Hammond* (1861) 30 Beav 495; *Spencer v Clarke* (1878) 9 Ch D 137.
[20] *Plumb v Fluitt* (1791) 2 Anst 432; *Hewitt v Loosemore* (1851) 9 Hare 449; *Agra Bank Ltd v Barry* (1874) LR 7 HL 135. It is debateable how much effect these principles now have in respect to land since the Law of Property (Miscellaneous Provisions) Act 1989 has largely abolished the equitable mortgage by mere deposit of title deeds, since the conventional reason for the absence of the title deeds from the hands of the landowner being a ground for suspicion was the possibility of the existence of such a mortgage.

Chapter 6

Acquisition and Disposal of Title by Operation of Law—Occupation, Abandonment, Accession and Mixtures

Acquisition, disposal and mixtures are physical events or acts which have an impact upon legal title to property, and they can be considered together as the group of concepts by which legal title passes other than pursuant to a contract or a gift.

The creation of something from nothing being impossible, every creation involves the application (and sometimes consumption) of existing things, and therefore touches on the law of mixtures where the things employed are not all in the same ownership. Destruction clearly entails loss of ownership, but destruction can arise as easily by consumption in a process as by absolute destruction. Mixtures combine these characteristics; in at least some mixtures it can accurately be said that the goods which went into the mixture have ceased to exist, and a new thing has come into being (the classical example is the making of wine out of grapes). In all these cases title to the goods is affected by the act.

In questions such as this assistance may be gleaned from the precise categorisations of the various techniques of acquisition and mixture which characterised the work of the Roman lawyers. As with the Roman classifications of bailment, these distinctions do not fit perfectly into common law, but the ideas involved are sufficiently universal that they can never be unhelpful. The Romans considered the questions posed by the combination of things as falling within one of the following categories:

(1) *Occupatio* This involves taking possession of a thing which is unowned at the time of occupation—a *res nullius. Occupatio* arose both in the case of genuinely unowned things (the example being a new island arising out of the sea[1]) and in the case of the taking possession of things which have been abandoned. In practice the primary class of *res nullius* would have been composed of wild animals, as the taming of a wild animal, then as now, resulted in an *occupatio.*

(2) *Accessio* The process whereby a minor thing (the accessory) is added to another (the principal). In an *accessio* title to the accessory was extinguished, and title to the whole vested in the owner of the princi-

---

[1] At English law these belong to the Crown; see Bl Comm ii, 262. Islands formed in rivers are at Roman law treated as instances of *occupatio* rather than *accessio* (Inst II, i, 22).

pal. *Accessio* occurred only where there was a recognisable princi-pal—the textbook example being the addition of a hand to a mutilated statue—and no possibility of the recovery of the accessory. The most important instance of *accessio* for our purposes is building work, where the building necessarily accedes to the land. Roman law also allowed the owner of the accessory to retain a kind of 'ghost' title to his prop-erty, in that if it was subsequently separated from the principal, his title revived.

(3) *Specificatio*   The process of bringing into existence a thing of a new kind out of existing material. *Specificatio* does not necessarily involve a physical mixture; in that if I take your grapes and make wine out of them I have effected a *specificatio* which has the effect of creating a new thing, title to which is vested in me, even though the grapes may have been wholly yours. However upon examination it is clear that this is also a case of mixture in that I have mixed my work with your goods.

(4) *Commixtio*   The Romans distinguished between mixtures of solids and mixtures of liquids. A *commixtio* is an inseparable mixture of sol-ids—for example a mixture of grain belonging to two or more persons.

(5) *Confusio*   A *confusio* is an inseparable mixture of liquids or of things which mix in a liquid state, such as metals.

Note that with respect to *commixtio* and *confusio* it is the inseparability which gives rise to the mixture. Separable combinations are not mixtures for this purpose.

Occupation and abandonment

Occupatio cannot be practised in respect of a thing which is owned. Where a thing which is owned is occupied the occupier acquires a defeasible possessory title which is good against all the world except the true owner. In the case of a true *occupatio* of a *res nullius* the occupier acquires good absolute title.

Pollock & Wright[2] give five cases of acquisition by occupation at English law.

- Capture of wild animals[3]
- Appropriation of free natural elements such as water
- The collection of matter from the sea or seashore[4]
- Severance of a thing from the soil or from a tree or plant attached to the soil
- The finding of a thing which has been absolutely abandoned by or has become irrecoverably lost to its former possessor.

---

[2] *Possession in the Common Law* (Clarendon, 1888), p 124.

[3] It is accepted that an animal *ferae naturae* is not owned, but that the process involved in domes-ticating the animal has the effect at law of changing the animal's legal nature such that it be-comes *mansuetae naturae* and thus capable of ownership, such ownership vesting in the person who domesticates the animal.

[4] The seashore is the property of the Crown (Megarry & Wade, *The Law of Real Property*, 5th edn (Stevens, 1984), p 62.

The first three of these cases are self-explanatory. The fourth is incorrect as a matter of law. Where a thing is severed by a person who is not the owner of the soil, the suggestion that there is a valid *occupatio* rests on the analysis of Pollock & Wright; who reasoned that since criminal conversion was constituted by the taking of a chattel out of the possession of another, where A severed the crops of B from B's land, B never had possession of those crops as chattels but only as realty. Therefore A had not taken the crops from B's possession, and there was no criminal conversion. As a statement of the criminal law this is still accurate, both in theft[5] and in criminal damage[6]. However it was held in *Mills v Brooker*[7] that this argument is not relevant in the context of the tort of conversion, which is completed by an interference with a right to possession. When A severs B's crops, B has an immediate right to possession of the chattels as soon as they are severed, and if A deals with them contrary to B's right he is liable to B in conversion for the value of the chattels.

It is the fifth case which creates the greatest amount of difficulty, in that although it is not difficult to identify an assumption of property rights over a thing, the question of whether this act takes effect as an occupation or as a conversion depends on whether the thing concerned is indeed a *res nullius*, or unowned thing.

Unowned things

In addition to things which come into existence having the state of *res nullius*, a thing may become a *res nullius* by abandonment[8]. At English law abandonment occurs where an owner of a thing forms and exhibits an intention to disclaim any interest in that thing. There was dispute in classical times over when the divestment occurred—the Sabinians took the view that it occurred immediately upon the formation of the intent by the then owner, whereas the Proculians took the view that a man who had resolved to abandon a thing remained owner of it until it had been occupied by another person[9]. In England the latter view was accepted in the case of land.

The position for personal property is unclear. It has been denied that property can be abandoned[10], but there is both academic support[11] and judicial authority[12] for the proposition that at common law a thing is abandoned at the

---

[5] Theft Act 1968, s 4(3).
[6] Criminal Damage Act 1971, s 10(1)(*b*).
[7] [1919] 1 KB 555.
[8] As to abandonment generally, see A Hudson, 'Abandonment' in *Interests in Goods* (Palmer & McKendrick, eds) (Lloyds of London Press, 1993), p 424.
[9] Buckland, *A Textbook of Roman Law*, 3rd edn, 207.
[10] *Haynes' Case* (1614) Co Rep 113; see also Crossley Vaines, *Personal Property* (Palmer, ed), 5th edn (Butterworths, 1973), p 427.
[11] Hudson, 'Is Divesting Abandonment Possible in Common Law?' (1984) 100 LQR 110; Bell, *Modern Law of Personal Property in England and Ireland* (Butterworths, 1989), pp 51–3; Palmer, *Bailment*, 2nd edn (Sweet & Maxwell, 1991), p 1432, fn 64.
[12] *White v Crisp* (1854) 10 Ex 312; *Arrow Shipping Co v Tyne Improvement Commissioners; The Crystal* [1894] AC 508; *Pierce v Bemis; The Lusitania* [1986] QB 384.

time when the owner exhibits a clear intention to abandon it. For example in *Arrow Shipping Co v Tyne Improvement Commissioners; The Crystal*[13], the Tyne Improvement Commissioners had improved the Tyne by blowing up an abandoned ship. They then sought to recoup their costs from 'the owners', as they were entitled to do by statute. The owners had abandoned the ship some time previously and it had not been subsequently occupied. The House of Lords held that since owners had divested themselves of their ownership when they abandoned the ship they were no longer 'the owners' and therefore not liable for this cost. It does not appear that there is any requirement for notice to the outside world to be given of the intention. In *Simon v Taylor*[14], a Singapore case decided upon English authorities[15], it was held that very clear evidence of the formation of the intention to abandon would be required. It appears from this decision that notice to the outside world constitutes evidence of intention but is not an absolute requirement for abandonment.

Bona vacantia

The idea of abandonment interacts with the common law doctrine of *bona vacantia*; the idea that property which has no other owner vests in the Crown. The effect of the operation of the doctrine of *bona vacantia* is that there is a deemed *occupatio* by the Crown immediately upon abandonment. It is clear that the doctrine does not apply in all cases, since otherwise all property not immediately vested in some person would be vested in the Crown. It has been suggested that there is a general rule which determines what goods vest in the Crown *bona vacantia* and which continue as *res nullius*; the Crown takes *bona vacantia* where there is no possible owner[16]. However this distinction does not stand up to detailed scrutiny[17], and the better view is that property vests in the Crown *bona vacantia* in certain specific cases provided by common law. These may be listed as follows.

Intestacy

Everyone is somebody's relative, and as a matter of pure logic no-one should die without a successor no matter how distantly related that successor may be. However, the Administration of Estates Act 1925 governs the distribution of the estates of those who die either without wills or with wills which have become irrelevant. The Inheritance (Provision for Family and Dependants) Act 1975 also allows application to be made to the court for an order making provision for a dependant of any deceased out of the estate. If both of these

[13] [1894] AC 508.
[14] [1975] 2 Lloyd's Rep 338.
[15] In particular *Bradley v Newsome* [1919] AC 16.
[16] *Re Wells* [1933] Ch 29.
[17] Ing, *Bona Vacantia* (1971); A Bell, 'The General Law Relating to Bona Vacantia' in *Interests in Goods* (Palmer & McKendrick, eds) (Lloyds of London Press, 1992) 401 at p 406.

provisions fail, there is at law no heir and the property of the deceased vests *bona vacantia* in the Crown.

Dissolved companies

The dissolution of a registered company brings its legal existence to an end, and from the moment of its deletion from the Register of Companies it ceases to be a legal person. This may occur either upon the request of the company itself or through a decision of the Registrar of Companies that the company is defunct. In both cases, there may be property vested in the company at the time of its dissolution. Alternatively, and more usually, a contingent right held by the company at the time of its dissolution may mature into an asset. In either case an application may be made for the restoration of the company to the Register[18]. If such an application is not made the asset vests in the Crown.

Failure of a trust

This issue can arise where a valid purpose trust has been established and the purpose has been achieved without exhausting the fund. In these circumstances the conventional analysis is that the property is held on a resulting trust for the donors[19], but where the property has been given to the trustees absolutely (for example, by being placed in public collecting tins) then the possibility of a resulting trust is discarded and, unless the money can be applied *cy-pres*, it will go to the Crown.

Treasure trove[20]

Treasure trove is a peculiar manifestation of the rule of *bona vacantia*[21]. The rule is that: 'A man, that hides his treasure in a secret place, evidently does not mean to relinquish his property, but reserves a right to claiming it again, when he sees occasion: and, if he dies and the secret also dies with him, the law gives it to the king, in part of his royal revenue'[22] Treasure is rarely abandoned in the ordinary sense of the word, and the doctrine of treasure trove takes effect with respect to any chattels which satisfy the following criteria:
  (a) they are composed of gold or silver,
  (b) they have been deliberately concealed by someone who intended to return for it subsequently, and
  (c) there is no identifiable owner or successor in title to the owner.
In addition to these rights the Crown has residuary rights to certain ownerless property which has not been occupied—notably waifs (goods discarded by a

---

[18] Companies Act 1985, s 651.

[19] *Re Gillingham Bus Disaster Fund* [1958] Ch 300.

[20] It is clear that the doctrine of treasure trove is a manifestation of the law of bona vacantia (*Webb and Webb v Ireland and the Attorney-General* [1988] IRLM 565, SC at 583).

[21] *See* Hill, *Treasure Trove in Law and Practice* (1936); Law Commission, *Treasure Trove, Law Reform Issues* (Sept 1987); Palmer, 'Treasure Trove and Title to Discovered Antiquities' in *Interests in Goods* (*see* fn 17 *above*), p 305.

[22] Bl Comm 1, 295.

thief in flight) and estrays (tame animals found wandering without evidence of ownership).

Finding

Where an unowned thing does not fall within one of the classes listed above, it may be made the subject of an *occupatio* by finding. English law follows Roman law in that a person who comes across an unowned thing may have title to it by taking possession of it. However this can only occur in the case of things which are *res nullius* either from their origin or by abandonment. In the absence of abandonment there can be no *occupatio* by finding, even if the owner has lost possession and does not currently know the location of the property[23], and the person taking possession will acquire no title.

Because it is not possible to tell the state of legal title to a thing by examination of the thing itself, the finder cannot know at the moment of finding whether the thing itself is owned or not, and Palmer[24] suggests that the true status of a finder upon finding a thing is that he becomes a bailee *sans* bailor. Palmer explains that this is a reasonable conclusion in that, since it is now clear that bailment does not require agreement, there can be no objection to the idea of a non-consensual bailment. This is true, but it does not go far enough. Where an item has been abandoned, then the finder acquires absolute title by operation of law unless he takes possession without intending to take ownership[25]. Where the item has not been abandoned, the finder acquires a defeasible absolute title. This must be the case, as if the finder stands merely as bailee until such time as the owner appears, it is impossible to see how the finder can become the true owner, as, it is accepted, he does. The position of a holder of defeasible absolute title is not compatible with the status of bailee.

There are some special rules relating to finding at English law, such that the person who finds abandoned or lost property does not necessarily become entitled to it.

All chattels are found upon land, and, unless they are found on the seashore, the land will have an owner. The rule is that where property is abandoned on land belonging to X, X is entitled to that property. Where the finder is a leaseholder the terms of the lease will govern[26]. If they are inapplicable (as they usually are), title vests in the owner rather than the leaseholder. Where the finder has no interest in the land, the rights of the occupier of the land for the time being is preferred to the rights of the finder. The reasoning behind this is that the occupier must have been in possession of the property before the finder found it, since knowledge of the existence of a chattel is not necessary for possession of it[27]. However, in *Parker v British Airways Board*[28] the

---

[23] *Moffat v Kazana* [1969] 2 QB 152.

[24] Palmer, *Bailment*, 2nd edn (Sweet & Maxwell, 1991), p 1418–9.

[25] This is possible—a person finding an abandoned drum of chemical waste on the foreshore might take possession of it in order to take it to the authorities, but unless he assumes possession with a positive intention to take title (which is unlikely) then the law does not impose title upon him simply by virtue of his possession.

[26] *City of London Corp v Appleyard* [1963] 2 All ER 834.

Court of Appeal held that where the occupier of land permits public access to a part of it, things found on that part are not the property of the occupier unless the occupier has taken actual control of them[29]. The facts of *Parker*, which involved property found in a first-class departure lounge, indicate that merely restricting access to the property is insufficient to manifest control. Some support was also given in *Parker* to the proposition that the occupier's right would always take precedence over the rights of the individual finder where the finder was, at the time of the finding, a trespasser upon the land. It would therefore seem to follow that the outcome in *Parker* would have been different if Mr Parker had been the bearer of a business-class ticket and was illegitimately in the first-class lounge.

Another common difficulty arises where a person finds a thing in the course of his employment. In principle, an employee finder holds the goods which he finds for the benefit of his employer, and acquires no independent possession[30]. However this principle operates only in the case of a finding in the course of carrying out the employment. In the delightful Australian case of *Byron v Hour*[31] a policeman, who was on his way to direct traffic, found a gold ingot at the roadside. It was held that the finding was fortuitous and that he, rather than his employer, was entitled to retain the gold.

A further issue arises in the case of a finder who finds goods which are in the deemed possession of a non-owner. This is merely a case of consecutive possession, and the finder interferes with the possession of the prior possessor, and is liable in conversion[32].

Accession

The rule of *accessio* is that where a person owns a thing and that thing increases, then the increase does not affect the ownership right. In principle this seems obvious—to use an example beloved of Roman lawyers, where a river sweeps soil off my neighbour's land and deposits it on my own, the new land becomes mine at the moment of the accretion. This is also the rule at English law[33]. It is always difficult to distinguish *accessio* from simple mixture, as in both cases things are combined together[34]. However the general rule is that[35]

---

[27] *South Staffordshire Water Co v Sharman* [1896] 2 QB 44; *Hibbert v McKiernan* [1948] 2 KB 142 (lost golf balls property of the golf club); Palmer (*see* fn 24 *above*), Ch 6.

[28] [1982] QB 1004.

[29] Following *Bridges v Hawkesworth* (1851) 21 LJQB 75.

[30] *Hannah v Peel* [1945] 1 KB 509; *City of London Corp v Appleyard* [1963] 2 All ER 834.

[31] [1965] Qd R 135.

[32] *Cartwright v Green* (1803) 8 Ves 405; *Merry v Green* (1841) 7 M & W 623.

[33] Bracton, Book. 2, Ch 2, fn 9; Bl Comm ii, 262. The authorities on this recherché point are fully reviewed in *Southern Centre of Theosophy Inc v South Australia* [1982] AC 709.

[34] The special case of pregnancy of animals is dealt with at English law by the rule *partus sequitur ventrem*, for, as Blackstone says: 'Wherefore as her owner is the loser by her pregnancy, he ought to be the gainer by her brood' (Bl Comm 2, 390). This is not, however, the case with swans (*Case of Swans* (1592) 7 Co Rep 15b at 17a). Where animals are leased, it seems that title to the offspring of the leased animals vests in the lessee rather than the lessor (*Tucker v Farm and General Investment Trust* [1966] 2 All ER 508).

[35] Dig 41.1.26 pr (Walker's translation), a passage from Paulus citing Servius and Labeo.

if anything be added to substances *in which a special characteristic is kept in view*[36], the addition is merged with the whole, as a foot or a hand joined on to a statue, a base or a handle to a cup, a leg to a couch, a plank to a ship, a stone to a building, for the whole belongs to him who was previously owner.

It is clear that this is a different rule from the equivalent rule of land law. The reason for this difference is that land law relies on the easy identifiability of the components of *accessio*. *Quicquid plantatur solo, solo cedit* is not simply a statement of the rule of accession, it is also a directional rule relating to the question of which item accedes to which. No matter how bulky and volumi-nous the addition, or how meager or valueless the land, the combined result belongs entirely to the landowner.

Without such a directional rule it is extremely difficult to determine whether there has been an *accessio*. To extend the examples given in the *Digest*: how many planks may be added to a ship or stones to a building before the point is reached that the 'special characteristic' of the ship or building is lost or changed? To take an even more extreme example, the woodcutter who had used the same axe for 14 years, in which time it had had four new heads and seven new handles, presents the fascinating possibility of a series of *accessio* which can cumulatively change the mere essence of the thing acceded to whilst individually constituting individual accessions.

Principles of mixture[37]

In order to apply the special rules relating to title to mixtures it is necessary to be able to identify a mixture. A mixture may be described as an indissoluble combination. Soluble combinations are almost by definition unproblematic, since the rights of title affected by the mixture can be satisfied by disintegra-tion. The question of whether two things are indissolubly united is a relative one, the answer to which depends upon the amount of effort, time and ex-pense which it is proposed to expend upon the separation.

Mixtures are not confined to physical mixtures, but can also involve the mixture of the property of one person with the labour of another. Where I mix my property with yours and do work on the mixture, then the thing which I produce is my own. In cases in which one person does work on the property of another, the test which Justinian propounded was that the thing belonged to the maker unless it was (theoretically) possible to undo the work and reduce the components to their original state, in which case the thing belonged to the original owner of the materials. This had the unfortunate side effect that two separate rules developed for mixtures, such that some mixtures which were held to constitute natural *confusio* when mixed were classed as being revers-

---

[36] *In quibus propria qualitas expectaretur*—alternative translations are 'things with which what we look for is a thing answering some particular description' (Monro), and 'Objects which have a proper quality'(de Zulueta).

[37] This topic is treated at length by Prof P B H Birks, 'Mixtures' in *Interests in Goods* (Lloyds of London Press, 1993), pp 449–68, and I am heavily indebted to this essay for much of what follows.

ible for the purposes of determining ownership[38].

The instinctive legal response to mixture is co-ownership. The principle that where A's goods are combined with B's goods, the result is jointly owned by A and B seems in principle to be one of such dramatic good sense that it must surely provide a solution to every difficulty. Sadly, such is not the case. Blackstone, indeed, approached the matter in this way. Where two persons voluntarily intermixed their property, the result was co-ownership. Where the mixing was involuntary as to one part, he said that where 'one willfully intermixes' his property with that of another '[o]ur law, to guard against fraud, gives the entire property, without any account, to him whose original dominion is invaded, and endeavored to be rendered uncertain, without his own consent'[39].

Co-ownership

A co-owner of property owns an asset, being his share in that property. Like any other co-owner, he does not have any direct proprietary interest in any specific part of the property. Consequently, where a co-owner purports to sell the property of which he is a co-owner, title to the property cannot pass to the purchaser until the property itself has been divided up amongst the co-owners, since until that time the vendor has no title in the underlying property to transfer. A co-owner of a bulk of wheat can sell his proportionate share in the bulk; but if before the bulk is divided he purports to sell wheat then he is agreeing to sell something which he does not yet own[40].

The courts will not deem a purported sale of goods which are part of a bulk at the moment of sale to be a sale of a share in the bulk[41]. The reasons for this may be found in the different nature of the two contracts. Assume a bulk of wheat of 100 tonnes, to which A has contributed 20 tonnes. A is therefore a co-owner of the bulk to the extent of one-fifth of its mass. If A contracts to sell his co-ownership share to B, then what B is contracting to buy is one-fifth of the total bulk as delivered. This is probably not what either A or B intend. What B wants is to buy wheat—that is, he wants a commitment from A that he will deliver 20 tonnes of wheat, and if the shipment is short then it is up to A to make up the difference or pay damages. Conversely, if the bulk delivered is for some reason greater than 100 tonnes then A will wish to be entitled to the overdelivery greater than 20 tonnes.

In respect of mixtures created pursuant to the sale of goods the situation has now been affected by the Sale of Goods (Amendment) Act 1995. The

---

[38] Since the essence of *confusio* was some element of irreversibility, it can have done no good to have mixtures which were deemed irreversible for some purposes but not others.

[39] Bl Comm 2, 404–5. For examples of the operation of this rule see *Lupton v White* (1808) 15 Ves 342; *Warde v Aeyre* (1613) 2 Bulst 323. However in *Indian Oil Corp v Greenstone Shipping Company SA, The Ypatianna* [1987] 3 All ER 893, Staughton J said that the rule should only be applied where there were overwhelming evidential difficulties.

[40] Sale of Goods Act 1979, s 16. Note that this rule is not an abstract doctrine but a codification of existing property law.

[41] *Re Wait* [1927] 1 Ch 606.

effect of the Act is to give 'prepaying' purchasers both a claim to goods and a share in the co-ownership of the bulk. The scheme is that where a contract is made for purchase of part of a bulk, the purchaser under the contract acquires upon purchase both a right to the delivery of goods upon division of the bulk, and also a proportionate share in the bulk itself equal to the proportion which the goods which he has bought bear to the total bulk. The effect of this is that where a seller becomes insolvent before the goods have been divided, the purchaser can claim a proportion of the goods in satisfaction of the obligation to deliver[42].

Voluntary mixtures

Mixtures may be divided into those which do and those which do not result in the manufacture of a new thing. The mixture of grain and grain produces a bulk of grain, and the mixing of copper and tin without more produces a separable bulk. If the mixture is heated and worked upon, however, what is produced is brass. The question of the proprietary effects of such mixtures has been debated since Roman times. Justinian divides the possibilities as follows. In the case of segregated property—sheep, for example—if we agree to herd our sheep together then my sheep remain mine and your sheep remain yours; we have not mixed them. The situation is called *commixtio*. However, if we agree to mix our wine together in a single barrel, the nature of the property is such that it is not possible for our separate rights to exist, and we become co-owners of the bulk. This situation is called *confusio,* but for clarity is referred to as natural *confusio*, since *confusio* can also be artificial. If we agree to pool our flocks of sheep into a single economic unit and to treat that unit as indivisible, by doing so we may constitute ourselves co-owners of the whole flock and create an artificial *confusio*.

Artificial *confusio* requires the consent of all contributors. Where such a mixture is made without the consent of one or other of the parties then there is no co-ownership and each party retains its rights to its respective parts of the bulk—there is *commixtio*, not *confusio*.

Modern English law broadly follows these principles and in particular in accordance with the fundamental common law principle of the primacy of the parties' intention where two persons voluntarily mix their property then the bulk which is thereby created is a single piece of property held in co-ownership. However, the primary problem (at least, before the courts) is whether and in what circumstances a non-consensual mixing creates a co-owned bulk.

Involuntary mixtures

The development of English law on this point has been hampered by the 'penal rule' that where A mixes his goods with those of B without B's permission

---

[42] There are some extremely complex issues raised by this legislation which are yet to be resolved—for a good overview see Ulph, 'The Sale of Goods (Amendment) Act 1995: co-ownership and the rogue seller' in [1996] LMCLQ at 93.

or consent, ownership of the bulk as a whole is vested solely in B[43]. This rule provides a sufficiently simple means of dealing with the problems caused by involuntary mixture that it may be responsible for the long silence of the English courts. However, the rule is one of evidence designed primarily to avoid difficulties of proof, and this was recognised in *Indian Oil Corporation v Greenstone Shipping Company SA, the Ypatiannia*[44] in which Staughton J made it clear that the penal rule was in reality no more than an evidential presumption which could be displaced by clear evidence of the components of the mixture and the results of the mixing[45].

Fluid mixtures and confusio

These are mixtures which the Romans would have classified as natural *confusio*—that is to say, mixtures where the nature of the things mixed renders it practically impossible to separate them thereafter. The reason that these are known as fluid mixtures is to do with the nature of the mixing as much as of the thing mixed, and this applies to mixtures of any substance whilst in its molten state as well as mixtures of ordinary fluids and mixtures of gasses.

The Ypatianna[46] is clear authority that in the event of such a mixture, the resulting bulk is held in common by the original owners. The objection has been raised in respect of such a conclusion that to effect a co-ownership in such a case is to throw on the involuntary contributor the risk of subsequent loss[47]. Support for this position has been found in the argument that in *The Ypatianna*, Staughton J said that, although the bulk was indeed in co-ownership, the proportionate shares of the co-owners were not determinate, but that the share of the involuntary contributor was to be assessed as 'a quantity equal to that of his goods which went into the mixture …'[48], and it is argued that this is incompatible with the nature of co-ownership.

It is hard to see why this should be the case. In law there can be direct co-ownership of a chattel without the necessity of the intervening trust for sale which is required in the case of land. There is little authority on co-ownership at law, but I am not able to find any clear authority to the effect that an undivided share in a chattel must be expressed as a proportion of the whole. If it is possible to have a share whose measure is '40 tons out of the surviving bulk', then this objection is unsustainable.

Granular mixtures and commixtio

The case of a granular mixture is different from that of a fluid mixture in that in a granular mixture it is always possible for the individual items of property mixed to be separated. If my ten tonnes of wheat are mixed with your ten tonnes of barley in a silo it is physically possible to separate them out, though

---

[43] Blackstone, Book 2, 404–5; *Lupton v White* (1808) 15 Ves 342.
[44] [1987] 3 All ER 893.
[45] At 906–7.
[46] [1987] 3 All ER 893.
[47] See P Matthews, 'Proprietary Claims at Common Law for Mixed and Improved Goods' [1981] CLP 159.
[48] At 907–8.

in reality hopelessly impractical. Even if my ten tonnes of wheat are mixed with your ten tonnes of wheat in a silo, it is physically impossible but theoretically possible to separate the mixture grain by grain until the *status quo ante* has been achieved. The theoretical possibility of complete separation constitutes a *commixtio*, regardless of the practicality of the separation.

The Roman solution in the case of involuntary *commixtio* was that the individual property rights endured—in the above example, that my wheat remained vested in me and the fact of the mixing was denied at law. This idea has had support at English law[49], and it is clear that in some cases the mixture is so loose that the practical remedy of physical separation rather than the legal remedy of co-ownership is a more practical proposition. However, where any property has been mixed, the question of separability is one of practicality rather than one of law, and it is not clear how useful the idea of the perseverance of separate title actually is. In practice it results in the position in which no owner of any part of the mixture may deal with the bulk without committing a conversion against the goods of the other. The resulting paralysis of the goods is unlikely to be commercially or practically desirable.

In such cases (ie where division is practically impossible) co-ownership is the only practical solution. In *Spence v Union Marine Insurance Co Ltd*[50] the court was presented with a number of bales of cotton from which all the identifying markings had been obliterated. The identities of the bales' consignees was established, but it was impossible to say which bale was whose property. It was held that the consignees were co-owners of the bales, such that each was entitled to a proportionate share equal to his proportion of the total consignment. Bovill CJ held that the case was one where separation was 'impracticable', and that it was therefore on all fours with a case of fluid mixture.

The analysis employed by Bovill J seems to eliminate the concept of *commixtio* from English law. If the items are separable then there is no true mixture, and if they are not, then there is a *confusio*. This appears as an oversimplification only if the term 'mixture' is applied to separable combinations. It is submitted that this is an abuse of the term. It is further submitted that this is the correct and the most desirable result, since the question of a mixture's separability is of considerably more practical importance than the question of its material form.

If there is no *commixtio* of physical goods at English law then the consequences of physical mixtures may be explained entirely in terms of the law of co-ownership.

Mixtures of money

The relative simplicity of the conclusion reached above has been permitted by disregarding the authorities relating to mixtures of money. This may not be a permissible approach. Professor Birks maintains that 'no rational defence can

[49] *Smith v Torr* (1862) 3 F & F 505; *Colwill v Reeves* (1811) 2 Camp 575; *Wiles v Woodward* (1850) 5 Exch 557; *cf* also *Foster v Ward* (1882) 9 LR Ir 446.
[50] (1868) LR 3 CP 427.

be made of different rules for mixed money in a box and mixed corn or coal'[51]. It is therefore necessary to begin reviewing the cases on mixture of money by considering the legal nature of money and property rights therein.

Money is not a chose in action for the good reason that no action can be brought upon it. A coin is a symbol which has a value affixed to it by law[52], but what is symbolised is abstract value rather than any legal right. Consequently money in its purest form is not an object of property, and it is for this reason that it is correctly said that money is not an object of exchange, but a medium of exchange[53]. A coin is a symbol of the abstract value of the money which it represents.

The law relating to money is set out below in Chapter 16. Its most important aspect for this purpose is its negotiability. Negotiability is frequently, and erroneously, considered only as an attribute of bills of exchange. This is to get the cart well in advance of the horse. The character of negotiability which is attributed to bills by statute is nothing more than an attempt to have such bills treated as 'as good as currency'—ie as coins. All banknotes derive their negotiability from statute, but the coin is older than the note, and the aim of the note is no more than to replicate the coin. Thus the concepts of currency and negotiability are fundamental to the idea of money.

Currency, or negotiability, means that title passes when the item concerned is delivered for value. This rule has two aspects. The first is that coins and notes cannot be recovered back if they have been employed in a commercial transaction. The second, the mirror of the first, is that notes and coins can be recovered back if they have been transferred other than in a commercial transaction. Because the law provides a mechanism for transfer of title to these particular chattels, it to that extent disables other potential mechanisms, including mixture. This must to some extent be at root a policy distinction. In law notes and coins are treated as indistinguishable from each other, regardless of whether any physical distinction is in fact possible—so that any mixture of money is necessarily and inevitably an inseparable mixture. To allow that mixture of money effected a transfer of title to money would allow the thief to acquire title to stolen money simply by putting it in his wallet, and this is intolerable to a law one of whose strongest principles is that a thief acquires no title at all to stolen goods.

The leading case is *Jackson v Anderson*[54]. In that case a consignment of Spanish dollars packed in a barrel was dispatched by factors in South America to bankers in London. The bankers sold the whole barrel to the Bank of England. It was subsequently found that the barrel contained money belonging to the plaintiff, who sued the bank in conversion. It was held that the plaintiff had retained the right to his particular notes and coins throughout the transaction, and that no co-ownership had arisen in respect of the barrel as a whole.

The application of the ordinary rules given above on title to money indicates that this decision was correct. The title to the money in the barrel re-

---

[51] 'Mixtures' in *Interests in Goods* (Lloyds of London Press, 1993), p 465.
[52] *See* pp 143–5 *below*.
[53] *Moss v Hancock* [1899] 2 QB 111.
[54] (1811) 4 Taunt 24.

mained vested in the true owner thereof, as there had been no value given for the money and therefore no transfer of title. Title to money cannot be transferred other than by a transaction for value, so that in the absence of such a transaction the money remained mingled but unmixed. When the barrel was disposed of, there was an interference with identifiable property of the plaintiff (for money in a barrel is no less identifiable than money in a bag) which was at the time vested in the plaintiff, and the action was therefore successful. It will be seen that the case is an example of the satisfaction of the evidential burden identified above.

In the case of mixtures of money, therefore, the fact of mixture does not affect title, and what is produced is a *commixtio*. The logic of this can be illustrated in a number of ways. If a thief steals my £50 note it would be absurd if he could claim title to it by inserting it in his wallet with other money of his own and claiming to have acquired title to it. Additionally, it is conventionally supposed that there cannot be a mixture of bills of exchange, since each is identifiable. However, if they were indistinguishable (as are banknotes) the idea that title might be acquired to a bill by mixing it with others would be equally offensive. Wrongful taking of money has no effect upon the title to that money, and it is for this reason that a mixture of money has a completely different effect in law to the mixing of other goods[55].

The leading English authority for the proposition that a mixing of money has a proprietary effect is generally taken to be the speech of Lord Ellenborough in *Taylor v Plumer*[56]:

> ... the product of or substitute for [a] thing still follows the nature of the thing itself, so long as it can be ascertained to be such, and the right only ceases when the means of ascertainment fail, which is the case where the subject is turned into money, and mixed and confounded in a general mass of the same description. The difficulty which arises in such a case is a difficulty of fact and not of law, and the dictum that money has no ear-mark must be understood in the same way; ie, as predicated on an undivided and indistinguishable mass of current money. But money in a bag, or otherwise kept apart from other money, guineas, or other coin marked (if it were so) for the purpose of being distinguished, are so far ear-marked as to fall within the rule on this subject, which applies to every other description of personal property.

It seems clear that what His Lordship was talking about in the last part of his judgment is an evidential difficulty. The plaintiff must prove that his money remains his (ie that it has not passed into currency). As a matter of title to property, if I receive £100 from you, spend it and receive £100 from a differ-

---

[55] This view has been criticised as impractical and leading to undesirable consequences: Birks, 'Mixtures' in *Interests in Goods* (*see* fn 51 *above*), pp 449–68; Smith, *The Law of Tracing* (OUP, 1997), pp 71, 164, citing *Pennell v Deffell* (1853) 4 De GM & G 372, in which Knight-Bruce J said that the normal rules for mixing of goods apply to money, although at 382 of that report he appears to confirm the *commixtio* analysis of monetary mixtures.

[56] (1815) 3 M & S 562 at 575; see also *Re J Leslie Engineers & Co Ltd* [1976] 1 WLR 292; *Agip (Africa) Ltd v Jackson* [1991] Ch 547 at 564–5; *Lipkin Gorman (A Firm) v Karpnale Ltd* [1991] 2 AC 548.

ent source you have no property right in any money held by me. However, I need not defend my case by proving that this has happened; it is up to you to prove that it has not. If you can prove no more than that I received £100 of yours then you may have a claim for money had and received, but you have no property claim. Mere mixing of money does not and cannot affect title to individual notes and coins, but it may well turn the evidential burden upon a person who seeks to assert a proprietary right in those notes and coins into an inseparable obstacle. This, it is submitted, is the correct explanation of these words—they are an expression of rules about following (ie as to what can be done to an asset owned by A before A's title is extinguished) rather than about tracing (ie as to which assets in the hands of the defendant 'represent' assets of the plaintiff wrongfully dealt with by the defendant)[57]. They are not authority for the proposition that a mixture of money necessarily destroys title to that money.

---

[57] *Contra* Smith, *The Law of Tracing* (OUP, 1997), pp 163–4.

Section 3

Equitable Title to Property

Contents

Chapter 7

The Nature of Equitable Title

Equitable title is title to property in the same way in which legal title to property is title to property—both confer immediate property rights in a thing. The distinction is that a person who has title to property in equity does not have absolute dominion over it. Some of the rights which arise in respect of the ordinary package of rights embodied in the relationship of ownership are vested in another person, and an incident of equitable ownership is the right to compel such persons to exerise those rights for the benefit of and at the direction of the equitable owner.

The rules of equity apply to personal property in exactly the same way in which they apply to real property, except to the extent that particular rules of law modify the application of particular principles of equity in particular circumstances. Thus a trust may arise over personal property in exactly the same way as it arises over real property. However, the application of some of the proprietary rules of equity to personal property is unclear, in particular in the following cases:

(1) *Supervening rules of common law* In *Transport & General Credit Corp v Morgan*[1] it was held that the effect of the proprietary doctrines of equity—in particular the equitable lien—were displaced in the case of the sale of goods as the Sale of Goods Act was intended to be a complete code covering both legal and equitable rights. This doctrine has not been extended to any other enactment, and has been doubted even in the context of the sale of goods where the obligation to deliver goods is specifically performable.

(2) *Constructive notice* The equitable rule that an equitable proprietary right will persevere in property which is sold for value to a purchaser with actual or constructive notice of the right is modified in the case of personal property[2]. The extent of the modification is unclear, but it may be said that whereas in respect of land the purchaser will be afflicted with constructive notice of any fact which he could have found out, in respect of goods the purchaser is afflicted with notice only of facts which he would have found out had he acted according to the norms of ordinary commercial behaviour. Since inquiries into title do not form a substantial part of ordinary commercial behaviour, this rule goes a long way towards eliminating the doctrine of constructive no-

---

[1] [1939] Ch 531; see also *Re Wait* [1927] 1 Ch 606.
[2] *See* pp 278–80 *below*.

tice from commercial dealings.

(3) *Specific performance* It is said that the doctrines of equity are not applied to transactions where equity does not decree specific performance of the transaction. This is correct to the extent that equity does not assist in any transaction which savours of the nature of a gift. However, the rule that specific performance is not granted where damages would be an adequate remedy means that specific performance is almost never available in ordinary commercial contracts, and it has been argued that it follows from this that the doctrines of equity are not available to any contract which would not be susceptible to specific performance (ie any but a very few commercial transactions in goods). This point is considered in greater detail in Chapter 10 *below*.

This chapter endeavours to identify some of these areas.

Origin and nature of equitable title

The development of legal title as an interest in property is explained by the learned authors of *Snell's Equity* as follows[3]:

> When it would have been unconscionable for the legal owner of property to keep the property for himself, the Court of Chancery acted on his conscience and compelled him to hold the property for the benefit of another person. In their origin, therefore, equitable interests were merely rights in personam. However, in the fifteenth and sixteenth centuries the Chancellors began to enforce equitable interests not only against the person originally bound, but also against his heir, or a donee, or a purchaser who took without notice. Finally, equitable rights became enforceable against all except a purchaser without notice, and so it became possible to treat them as rights in rem, or proprietary rights ... What began as a mere personal equity has ended as a right of property.

There is much jurisprudence on whether legal and equitable title are different titles, different aspects of a single indivisible title, or whether equitable title is merely an application of the maxim that 'Equity looks upon as done that which ought to be done'[4]. However, this jurisprudence addresses itself primarily to an insoluble problem. This was identified and discussed in the Australian case of *Colbeam Palmer Ltd v Stock Affiliates*[5], in which the issue arose whether, because a right to a trade mark at common law might be protected by injunction, it therefore followed that the right was in equity a proprietary right. This question may be rephrased as 'which comes first, the right or the remedy?', and presents upon its face a jurisprudential mystery[6].

---

[3] *Snell's Equity* (P V Baker, ed), 29th edn, p 23.
[4] See for example Hart (1899) 15 LQR 294, Scott (1917) 17 Col LR 269; Stone (1917) 17 Col LR 467; Hanbury (1929) 45 LQR 198; Latham (1954) 32 Can BR 520; Waters (1967) 45 Can BR 219; *Baker v Archer-Shee* [1927] AC 844.
[5] 122 CLR 25 at 34.
[6] Per Kearney J in *Burns Philp Trustee Co v Viney* [1981] 2 NSWLR 261.

The mystery may be at least partially solved by reference to *Commissioner of Stamp Duties v Livingstone*[7], in which the nature of equitable proprietary interests was exhaustively analysed. The issue before the court was whether an interest in an unadministered estate constituted 'any beneficial interest in property'[8]. It was indisputable that the beneficiary under the will, a Mrs Coulson, had a right to one-third of the assets falling to be distributed on completion of the administration, and it was equally indisputable that the personal representatives held the assets of the estate on trust. The issue was therefore whether this package of rights rendered Mrs Coulson the owner of the property concerned.

The Privy Council held that it did not. Viscount Radcliffe was at pains to deny the proposition that where there is a legal owner there is necessarily an equitable owner, observing that it was not the case that[9]:

> for all purposes and at every moment of time the law requires the separate existence of two different kinds of estate or interests in property, the legal and the equitable ... Equity in fact calls into existence and protects equitable rights and interests in property only where their recognition has been found to be required in order to give effect to its doctrines.

The picture of a trustee holding property for no beneficiary is disturbing to those who think of equitable title as being synonymous with legal title. However this phenomenon is not as uncommon as may at first appear—the trustees of a charitable trust, for example, do not hold the property of the trust for any person but for a purpose. Attempts to locate the equitable title to such property are misleading and counterproductive—as long as there is a person capable of requiring the trustee to perform his duties, then there is no need for a designated equitable 'owner'. The same is also true of trustees who hold property on fully discretionary trusts, it is possible to locate a right to this property as held jointly among the class of persons who may receive the property, but this is nothing more than an explanatory device. In such cases there is no equitable title to the property, nor need there be.

This appears to explain the conundrum identified in *Colbeam Palmer*, for the conundrum is based on the premise that the existence of an effective equitable remedy implies the existence of equitable title. After *Commissioner of Stamp Duties v Livingstone* this is not a supportable proposition. Equitable remedies such as injunction and specific performance are available to protect proprietary rights, but there is no valid chain of reasoning which commences with the existence of an equitable remedy and proceeds to the existence of equitable title. *Ubi remedio, ibi jus* has never been a maxim of law or of equity. It follows from this that there should, therefore, be no symmetrical linkage between remedies and rights, and this is indeed the case. In another Australian case, *Burns Philp Trustee Co v Viney*[10], the court was asked to

---

[7] [1965] AC 694.
[8] Within the meaning of the Queensland Succession and Probate Duties Acts 1892–1955.
[9] *Commissioner for Stamp Duties (Queensland) v Livingstone* [1965] AC 694 at 712.
[10] [1981] 2 NSWLR 216.

decide whether a person who was barred by statute from obtaining any equitable remedy of any type therefore forfeited his equitable rights in trust property. The court held that enforceability was not a pre-condition of the existence of an equitable interest but a mere incident of it.

The fact that an equitable right is a right in property can be demonstrated in a number of ways, including the following. First a beneficiary's interest under a bare trust is an interest in the trust property itself. The alternative analysis—that the beneficiary has a personally enforceable right to require the trustee to transfer the trust property to him coupled with a personal right to recover such property from third parties—cannot survive the string of tax cases which identify beneficial ownership as true ownership[11]. Secondly, a contract for the sale of an equitable interest in land is classified as a sale of an interest in land for the purposes of s 2 of the Law of Property (Miscellaneous Provisions) Act 1989, which provides that: 'A contract for the sale or other disposition of an interest in land can only be made in writing ...'[12]. If what were being disposed of were no more than a personal right to require a trustee to perform his trust, then the disposition would not fall within this provision[13]. Thirdly, the writ of sequestration, the precursor of the modern receivership order, was in common use in the Court of Chancery as early as 1530[14]. This order had the effect of dispossessing a defendant of his property completely until he had performed the terms of the order against him. Had equity had the peculiarly personal characteristic ascribed to it, then it would have been impossible for the courts of equity to enforce such a remedy without bringing into action the courts of law.

For all these reasons we must conclude that when we speak of an equitable interest in property we do not mean simply a personal right against the legal owner of that property, but a right in that property.

Types of equitable title

Absolute equitable title

The primary instance of equitable title to property is, as we have seen, the case of the bare trust. In such a case it is clear that the beneficial owner of property has not only the right to call for the property to be vested in him at any time[15], but in the period prior to such a call being made has a property interest in whatever may be the subject-matter of the trust.

---

[11] See eg *Baker v Archer-Shee* [1927] AC 844. The view that tax cases are in some strange way outside the common law and may be disregarded for non-tax purposes is sometimes expressed in the fields of equity and private international law. It is wholly insupportable.

[12] Sub-section (6). The statute re-enacts with modifications s 40 of the Law of Property Act 1925 which in turn re-enacted the provisions of the Statute of Frauds 1677.

[13] *Cooper v Critchley* [1955] Ch 431; and see (1955) 71 LQR 178; [1955] CLJ 155. See also *Elias v Mitchell* [1972] Ch 652, in which it was held that a beneficiary of a trust of land was a 'person ... interested ... in land' and was therefore entitled to enter a caution against a registered title. The decision is analysed in 36 Conv(NS) 206 by Prof D J Hayton.

[14] Guy, *Career of More*, pp 58–9.

[15] *Saunders v Vautier* (1841) 4 Beav 115.

Collective equitable title

A more common case is where the beneficiary's right to the trust assets is less than absolute. The most common case of this is the testamentary bequest 'to A (usually the spouse of the testator) for the remainder of his/her life, and to my children in equal shares thereafter', but terms of years or conditional gifts all fall within this category. In this case the beneficiary has no right in the property individually, but together with the other beneficiaries can assert a collective entitlement. In such cases the beneficiaries acting together can compel transfer to themselves absolutely as if they had absolute title. It is important to note that there is no parallel with joint tenancy at common law. Each equitable interest in such a trust is absolutely independent of the other, and no act of one beneficiary can affect the position of any other.

Conditional equitable title

The settlor may impose restrictions on the equitable title of the beneficiary in the same way in which a donor might, prior to the reforms of the nineteenth century, limit the interest of the donee in land conveyed to him. The point in both cases is that a donor or settlor having absolute title may make his gift in any way in which he desires. Thus he can impose any condition which he pleases upon his gift. And, even if he has not provided a gift over upon the failure of the condition, any residue will result to him or his estate[16].

In cases of conditional title, the beneficiary has an interest which is capable of being brought to an end by an event. Again, the most common example is the bequest subject to a condition—'to my wife, until she shall marry again'—but the instances are legion. The nature of title in these particular circumstances depends upon a highly artificial calculus of whether the gift is an absolute gift subject to a condition subsequent, or whether the gift is a conditional gift subject to a condition precedent. If the former, the donee acquires equitable ownership subject to the possibility of divestment. If the latter, the donee acquires a contingent interest which may become absolute at some later stage.

Discretionary equitable title

The position of beneficiaries under a discretionary trust is more difficult. Discretionary trusts are conventionally created for tax purposes[17], although are commonly encountered in the wills of those who nurture forebodings about the industry of their offspring. In the true discretionary trust the trustee may apply the trust property as he thinks best within a series of conditions, relating primarily to the identity of the recipients of his beneficence but occasionally importing wholly extraneous criteria. He has a right against the trustee to

---

[16] *Re Vandervell's Trusts (No 2)* [1974] Ch 269.
[17] For example, the most familiar incarnation of the discretionary trust, the accumulation and maintenance trust, owes nothing to history and everything to Pt III of the Inheritance Tax Act 1984.

have the trustee administer the trust in accordance with the instrument creating the trust, a right which has been compared with the right of a creditor against a company subject to a winding-up order[18], but there is no titular nexus as between him and the trust assets. This does not, however, mean that such a beneficiary has no *claim* to the trust assets. In the same way that there is no property in a chose in action between the parties thereto, but property as between the plaintiff and a third party, so with the beneficiary; he has no right to the trust assets as against the trustee, but if the trust assets pass into the hands of a third party immediately the beneficiary's right to the trust assets revives.

The position was considered by the House of Lords in *Gartside v IRC*[19]. A person who had been one of the limited class of potential beneficiaries under a discretionary trust died, and the question before the court was whether he had had an 'interest' in the trust property which ceased on his death, thus giving rise to a charge to tax. Their Lordships held that although he clearly had a right to require the trust to be administered, and equally clearly a right to prevent improper disposition of trust property, these rights did not together constitute an equitable proprietary right in the trust property. The force of this decision was tested in *Re Weir's Settlement Trusts*[20], in which the Court of Appeal was prepared to agree that where there was a discretionary trust whose potential beneficiaries were two individuals, the death of one did not have the effect of causing any benefit to accrue to the other, a conclusion which can only be supported on the assumption that beneficiaries under discretionary trusts do not have under any circumstances a beneficial interest in the trust property.

Equitable charges

An equitable charge is an equitable interest which arises indirectly through entry into an enforceable obligation rather than through a direct grant of an interest. It arises where a person undertakes to pay a particular sum of money out of a particular fund in such a way as to grant the beneficiary a (specifically enforceable[21]) right to be paid that money out of that fund[22]. The fund may comprise money or property, the implication being in the case of property that the sum will be paid out of the rents of or the proceeds of sale of the property[23]. An excellent example is provided by the facts of *Swiss Bank Corp v Lloyds Bank*[24]. SBC had made a loan in Swiss Francs to Israel Finance Trust

---

[18] By D J Hayton in Hayton & Marshall, *Cases and Commentary on the Law of Trusts*, 9th edn (1991) 11; see also *Ayerst v C & K (Construction) Ltd* [1976] AC 167.

[19] [1968] AC 553.

[20] [1971] Ch 145.

[21] Strictly speaking specific performance is not available for a contract to pay money. However, this is another manifestation of the principle mentioned above that in this context references to specific performance are references to jurisdiction, not to rules of discretion.

[22] *Swiss Bank Corp v Lloyds Bank Ltd* [1982] AC 584.

[23] *Anders Utkilens Rederi A/S v O/Y Lovisa Stevedoring A/B, The Golfstraum* [1985] 2 All ER 669.

[24] [1982] AC 584.

(IFT) to purchase securities, and IFT had secured the loan by making an equal deposit of sterling with SBC. IFT had undertaken to repay the loan out of the dividends and sale proceeds of the securities. If the latter agreement was specifically enforceable then a charge would arise over the securities. It was held that in order to create a charge there must be a very clear intention exhibited that repayment should be charged upon specific property, and the circumstances of the case did not create sufficient certainty. However, it illustrates the mechanism by which a specifically enforceable obligation gives rise to an equitable interest.

Note that a charge on property which is equal in value to the whole of the property plus its proceeds indefinitely, without possibility of redemption, operates in equity as a transfer of the property.

Mere equities

The mere equity is one of the most troublesome components of the system of equity[25]. A mere equity does not give rise to an equitable interest, but to a right to have an equitable interest vested in the holder at some point in the future upon the doing of a particular act. Although equity treats as done that which ought to be done, it does not treat a right arising out of a mere equity as exercised, because the decision to exercise is vested in the equity holder. Thus, for example, where a person has the right to have a contract rescinded for misrepresentation, it is that party's decision whether or not to exercise his right, and until he does so equity does not interfere in the operation of the contract.

The paradigm case of the mere equity is the right to have a conveyance set aside for fraud[26]. The defrauded party has no interest in the property arising out of his equity, but does have the right to have the conveyance set aside. Before he exercises that right, the transferee under the conveyance has perfect title. When the defrauded party exercises his right, the court will avoid the conveyance as from its initial execution such that at law it is treated as never having been made, and the jurisdiction may be exercised to order delivery up and cancellation of the relevant documents so that no record of the transaction need survive. However, from the moment of execution of the conveyance to the moment of exercise of the equity, complete equitable title as well as legal title vests in the transferee, who can dispose of it to a third party, leaving the equity holder without a right to trace.

The mere equity is characteristic of a voidable transaction. The grounds which give rise to the equity are, in addition to fraud, undue influence[27] and mutual mistake[28]. Further, the power of a mortgagor to reopen a foreclosure is

---

[25] Discussion is to be found in [1955] CLJ at 160 (Wade); (195) 19 Conv(NS) 343 (F R Crane); (1957) 21 Conv(NS) at 201 (Delaney); 1970 40 Conv(NS) 209 (Everton).

[26] *Bowen v Evans* (1844) 1 Jo & lat 178 at 263, 264; *Phillips v Phillips* (1861) 4 De G F & J 208 at 218; *Ernest v Vivian* (1863) 33 LJ Ch 513; *Latec Investments Ltd v Hotel Terrigal Pty Ltd* (1965) 113 CLR 265.

[27] *Bainbrigge v Browne* (1881) 18 Ch D 188.

[28] *Garrard v Frankel* (1862) 30m Beav 445.

also such an equity[29]. The rights of a licensee of real property against that property have been said to give rise to an equity[30].

There is no authority which addresses the precise difference between an equity and an equitable interest is. It is said that mere equities which may affect a purchaser are essentially rights which are ancillary to or dependent upon some interest in the property which that purchaser takes[31]. However this does not progress the matter much further. It may be better to say that an equitable interest is a right to a thing whereas a mere equity is a right to have the benefit of a transfer of a thing, the latter being distinguished by its optional character.

Fiduciaries

Fiduciary relationships

Equity recognises all legal obligations, and the maxim that 'equity treats as done that which ought to be done' applies without differentiation to equitable obligations and common law contractual obligations. It is, however, clear that there is a class of obligation which has a favoured status in equity—that of fiduciary obligations. In equity the beneficiary of a fiduciary obligation is in a position not only to compel his fiduciary to do his duty, but also to restrain his fiduciary from doing any act whatsoever which might in any way conflict with or impede the doing of his fiduciary duty, and may recover any property which accrues to the fiduciary as a result of his fiduciary status. This should be compared with the position of the beneficiary of the mere common law obligation, who has a narrow right to compel the performance of the obligation but nothing more.

Why is there this distinction? In *Good Faith in Sales*[32] Reziya Harrison argues that the fiduciary obligation is a remnant of a previously existing requirement of good faith which was formerly universal in English law but withered completely at common law in the face of a tide of nineteenth-century literalism, surviving only in the remoter nooks and crannies of the Court of Chancery.

But this argument is based on a confusion between equitable fraud[33] and breach of fiduciary duty[34]. If there ever were a general duty of good faith at

---

[29] *Campbell v Holyland* (1877) 7 Ch D 166 at 172–5.

[30] *Westminster Bank Ltd v Lee* [1956] Ch 7 at 20.

[31] *National Provincial Bank Ltd v Ainsworth* [1965] AC 1175 at 1238, per Lord Upjohn.

[32] 1st edn (Sweet & Maxwell, 1997).

[33] The term 'equitable fraud' is sometimes criticised for embracing too many things which are not ordinarily categorised as 'frauds'. However the equitable usage is the older and the correct one, since prior to the decision in *Derry v Peek* (1889) 14 App Cas 337 it was also the usage in the common law courts; eg the term 'fraudulent' misrepresentation was used at common law to mean any representation which was not innocent (Spencer Bower & Turner, *Actionable Misrepresentation*, 3rd edn (Butterworths, 1974), p 113–29) . 'All Lincoln's Inn' thought *Derry v Peek* wrongly decided and it has deprived us of a term which embraces all wrongdoing short of negligence without providing a substitute. In equity, at least, we may therefore retain the somewhat archaic vocabulary of equitable fraud until the courts choose to provide us with another.

English law, and if such a duty may be said still to exist, as Harrison claims, it could well have given rise to the consequences which arise from equitable fraud, but it is hard to see that it could ever have given rise to those which flow from a finding of a fiduciary duty. A world in which every man is prevented from engaging in the components of equitable fraud—unconscionable dealings with the poor and ignorant, applying powers given for one purpose in pursuit of his own ends, and exercising undue influence over persons in a very unequal position—is perfectly compatible with ordinary trade. A world in which every man is the fiduciary of every other would make profit, and therefore trade, impossible. Since it seems improbable that the scope of the fiduciary obligation expanded at the very time at which it was withering, we must regretfully abandon any identification of the fiduciary duty as the residual category of a pre-existing general duty of good faith[35].

What is a fiduciary?

If the fiduciary is not simply a survivor then it must follow that his onerous duties were specifically imposed upon him for some particular purpose.

We can divide fiduciaries from non-fiduciaries in a number of ways. The minimum criteria for fiduciary status is that a fiduciary is one who does an act. The difference between a fiduciary actor and a non-fiduciary actor is that a fiduciary actor is someone who does something on my behalf, whereas a non-fiduciary actor is someone who does something at my behest. My taxi-driver is not my fiduciary, not because I do not place trust and confidence in him (for I must do that in order to enter the taxi in the first place), but because the transaction we are engaged in is a sale by him to me of his services. What I get is what I have bargained for, and as long as those services are not so deficient as to breach the terms of the contract between us, it is wrong that they should be treated differently in law than any other purchased commodity. My estate agent, by contrast, undertakes to do something in my own interest, to make my interest his interest. A taxi-driver who takes me to the wrong station is merely incompetent, but an estate agent who sells my house to the lower bidder is dishonest. Even if the sale is due to honest incompetence, he is still dishonest in that he undertakes to do something which only he can meas-

---

[34] Ibid at 328–9. Specific objections to this identification are set out in *Snell's Equity*, 29th edn, p 558), and are that one may be a fiduciary without being presumed to have exercised undue influence (*Re Coomber* [1911] 1 Ch 723) and vice versa (*Williams v Bayley* (1866) LR 1 HL 200); a transaction by a fiduciary may be set aside whether or not it is 'manifestly disadvantageous whereas this is a requirement for setting aside a transaction obtained by undue influence (*Bank of Credit and Commerce International v Aboody* [1990] QB 923 at 962–4; and that a gift from the beneficiary to the trustee of trust property is not in any way contrary to any fiduciary duty but raises a strong presumption of undue influence.

[35] Note that in Roman terms the *exceptio dolus*, which developed in the civil law jurisdictions into the general concept of good faith, resembled nothing so much as the ordinary common law doctrine of misrepresentation. Subsequent developments requiring eg exclusive negotiation are modern developments. The *actio quod metus causa*, the twin sister of the *exceptio dolus*, was the ancestor through the church courts of the equitable jurisdiction over unconscionable transactions: see generally Zimmermann, *The Law of Obligations; Roman Foundations of the Civilian Tradition*, 1st edn (OUP, 1997) at 651–77.

ure, and then he elects not to measure it.

It has been correctly said that the categorisation of fiduciary relationships is in fact an illusory oversimplification; fiduciary relationships arise from facts alone, although in certain cases the facts are sufficiently necessary to the nature of the relationship to permit the generalisation that 'all relationships of this form are fiduciary', this is a mere encapsulation of the fundamental rule that fiduciary relationships are fact-based rather than legal ideals[36]. The facts which are to be sought include:

(a)   an undertaking on the fiduciary's part to act on behalf or for the benefit of another person;

(b)   a discretion or power which affects the interest of that other person; and

(c)   the peculiar vulnerability of that other person to the fiduciary as shown by such factors as dependence upon advice, the existence of a relationship of confidence and the significance of a particular transaction for the parties[37].

The third criterion serves primarily to qualify the first two, which alone capture slightly too many situations for practical purposes.

Thus the reason for the restriction of the fiduciary is that he is his own policeman. It is unfair and unreasonable to expect a man to employ his discretion in weighing up his own interests against those of another. Equity therefore deprives him of the use of that discretion. Within broad limits he may do as he pleases, but thereafter he is strictly bound.

A fiduciary does not necessarily hold property on behalf of his beneficiary, but breach of his fiduciary obligation has an immediate property consequence. A fiduciary may be clothed in the authority of the person to whom he owes a duty in a number of ways—he may have a power to dispose of their property, or a right to execute a transaction on their behalf, or any manner of other powers or rights—but as soon as he exercises any of those powers outside the terms of his obligation, then any property which vests in him as a result of that breach is held for his principal. This was made clear by the Privy Council in *A-G for Hong Kong v Reid*[38], and although the decision has been criticised[39], it forms a coherent base for the liability; if the defaulting trustee's liability is anything other than to the utmost limit of the enrichment which has accrued to him as a result of his default then the policy object behind the imposition of the stricter liability is unsatisfied.

It is necessary to examine here the equitable concept of fiduciary. All trustees are fiduciaries, but many persons who are not trustees are still treated by equity as fiduciaries. A fiduciary relationship is one between persons, arising out of specific circumstances, in which equity imposes obligations upon one

---

[36] See *Hospital Products Ltd v United States Surgical Corporation* (1984–5) 156 CLR 41; *Lac Minerals Ltd v International Corona Resources Ltd* [1989] 2 SCR 574; Law Commission Consultation Paper No 124, *Fiduciary Duties and Regulatory Rules*.

[37] *Coleman v Myers* [1977] 2 NZLR 225, 325; *Re Chez Nico (Restaurants) Ltd* [1991] BCC 736.

[38] [1994] 1 AC 324.

[39] Crilley (in [1994] 2 RLR 57) uses the term 'Proprietary overkill'.

of the persons to act in the interest of the other. In *Hospital Products Ltd v United States Surgical Corp*[40] Mason J said:

> The accepted fiduciary relationships are sometimes referred to as relationships of trust and confidence or confidential relationships; cf. *Boardman v Phipps*[41]; *viz.* trustee and beneficiary, agent and principal, solicitor and client, employee and employer, director and company, and partners. The critical feature of these relationships is that the fiduciary undertakes or agrees to act on behalf of or in the interests of another person in the exercise of a power or discretion which will affect the interests of that other person in a legal or practical sense. The relationship between the parties is therefore one which gives the fiduciary a special opportunity to exercise the power or discretion to the detriment of that other person who is accordingly vulnerable to abuse by the fiduciary of his position. The expressions 'for', 'on behalf of' and 'in the interests of' signify that the fiduciary acts in a 'representative' character in the exercise of his responsibility.

The relationships listed above are the 'classical' fiduciary relationships, but it seems clear that the courts will find others[42]. A relationship may be fiduciary in some but not all aspects[43]. There is much Australian jurisprudence of when fiduciary relationships arise, much of it in respect to joint venture agreements[44]. Aside from concluding that the courts will be unwilling to find a fiduciary relationship between persons dealing with each other on a commercial basis, this body of authority is surprisingly unhelpful in identifying exactly who is and who is not a fiduciary. There are some clear negatives—a chargeor of a fund of property is not a fiduciary of the chargee[45], and a thief is not a fiduciary of the true owner of the stolen property[46].

The important point about the fiduciary is that he is treated in equity as if he were a trustee. Where property is in the hands of a fiduciary, then he must account to his principal for any increase in the value of that property, or any other benefit to him arising out of his possession of it, and the fiduciary will hold any such profit on constructive trust for his principal[47].

Any breach by the fiduciary of his fiduciary duty will be actionable by the person to whom the duty is owed. The action may be for the return of the relevant property, or may be a claim for damages to represent a loss suffered. The claim for equitable damages is assessed on a different basis from an ordinary claim in damages at common law, the primary distinctions being that no

---

[40] (1984) 156 CLR 41.

[41] [1967] 2 AC 46 at 127.

[42] For example, a company promoter was held to be a fiduciary of the company in *Erlanger v New Sombrero Phosphates* (1878) 3 App Cas 1218, and see generally *English v Dedham Vale Properties Ltd* [1978] 1 WLR 93 and *Lac Minerals Ltd v International Corona Resources Ltd* (1989) 61 DLR(4th) 14.

[43] *NZ Netherlands Society 'Oranje' Inc v Kuys* [1973] 2 All ER 1222.

[44] See Meagher, Gummow and Lehane, *Equity: Doctrines and Remedies*, 3rd edn, pp 132–3 for a review of the relevant authorities.

[45] *Halifax Building Society v Thomas* [1996] Ch 217.

[46] Although Browne-Wilkinson J cast doubt upon this proposition in *Westdeutche Landesbank Girozentrale v Islington LBC* [1996] AC 669.

[47] *Boardman v Phipps* [1967] 2 AC 46.

rule of remoteness or foreseeability is imposed in the interests of the fiduciary, who is thus in principle obliged to make good the whole of the loss suffered by the principal, including both actual loss and lost profits. The full rigour of this rule has recently been mitigated[48], but it remains true that in most cases a fiduciary who breaches his fiduciary duty may expect to pay heavier damages than those for which he would be liable if he had breached an identical contractual duty.

Fiduciaries and constructive trustees

The relationship between the statuses of fiduciary and constructive trustee is frequently misunderstood. Leaving aside for the moment the category of 'knowing assistance' constructive trusteeship[49], in principle a constructive trust is a property-based relationship which arises only when property which equity regards as rightfully belonging to one person is vested at common law in another. Where there is no separation of property interests there is no trust relationship. Fiduciary status, by contrast, arises out of the possession by one person of a power to deal with, or affect dealing with, the property of another. A fiduciary is recognised not be the fact that property is vested in him, but by the fact that he has power to affect the property of another which may remain at all times vested in that other.

It is probable that fiduciary relationships arise only in respect of powers concerning property, and not powers which may be exercised in any other way. When I travel by air I place in the airline, and in the pilot, a good deal more faith than I place in the discretionary manager of my portfolio of investments, but the latter is a fiduciary whereas the former is not. The difference is the power to affect property.

---

[48] *Target Holdings Ltd v Redferns* [1994] 1 WLR 1089.
[49] The reason that a 'knowing assistance' constructive trustee is a trustee is that he is deemed to have dealt with the trust property—to use an old term, that he has intermeddled with it. Since a fiduciary has an express power to intermeddle, he must be liable on a different basis from simply being alleged to have done so.

Chapter 8

Trusts

A trust is the relationship which arises wherever a person in whom property is vested at common law (called the trustee), whether real or personal, and whether by legal or equitable title, for the benefit of some persons (of whom he may be one and who are termed beneficiaries) or for some object permitted by law, in such a way that the benefit of the property accrues, not to the trustee, but to the beneficiaries or other objects of the trust'[1]. Trusts occur in two forms: express trusts, which are created by a deliberate act of settlement by a person, and implied trusts, which arise by operation of law consequent upon the doing of (or failure to do) some act by some person.

Express trusts

An express trust may be created by any person who is competent to own and dispose of property. A trust of personal property may be created without writing[2], since even where the declaration has the effect of vesting an equitable interest in another, the provisions of s 53(1)(c) of the Law of Property Act 1925 which require any disposition of an equitable interest in property to be in writing do not apply since the subsection applies only to 'subsisting' interests.

A trust may be created either by a person declaring himself trustee of property vested in him for the benefit of a third party, or by a person transferring property to another to hold as trustee for the benefit of the third party. The distinction is important. If what is intended is to create a trust by transfer to a trustee then, if the settlor fails to complete the transfer (or to make it at all), the trust will fail. Equity will not perfect an imperfect gift, and therefore the apparently obvious solution—that of treating the settlor as having declared himself trustee of the assets—will not be applied[3].

Where the trust is to be constituted by a transfer to a trustee, and the trust assets are shares in a UK company, the transfer by the settlor to the trustee is not entirely within the gift of the settlor, since the transfer will only take effect when the transfer's registration is approved by the company's directors[4]. In such a case, the trust is deemed to have been perfected when the settlor has

---

[1] Sheridan & Keeton, *The Law of Trusts*, 11th edn (1983), p 2.
[2] *M'Faden v Jenkyns* (1842) 1 Ph 153; *Paul v Constance* [1977] 1 WLR 527; *Re Kayford* [1975] 1 WLR 279.
[3] *Milroy v Lord* (1862) 4 De G F & J 264.
[4] *See* pp 198–9 *below.*

done everything in his power to divest himself of the property[5], and at that point the settlor is treated as holding the shares upon trust for the beneficiaries until the transfer is registered.

Where the trust is constituted by a declaration by the settlor of himself as trustee, no question of transfer of assets arises, and the difficulty is whether the settlor has created a trust at all. In a number of cases it has been held that words used to indicate to a person that he was to have an interest in the property of the owner were indications of an intention to give, such gift failing for want of actual transfer, and that therefore the rule against the completion of imperfect gifts prevented the court finding a trust[6]. However, a declaration of self as trustee may be implied by the court from conduct[7].

The test of whether a valid trust is created is by reference to the 'three certainties' which are required. These are as follows.

Certainty of intention

This point traditionally arose in the context of trusts created by wills, where property is transferred to A accompanied by a request that it be employed for the benefit of B. However its modern application is in the case of trusts created to 'shelter' property. In *Midland Bank v Wyatt*[8] a husband executed a deed of trust of the family home, settling it on his wife and daughter. The family continued occupying the house as their main home, the husband purporting to mortgage it to the bank in order to raise money for his business. When the business failed the husband sought to defeat the Bank's claim by relying on the trust. The court held that the trust was a sham since there had never been a real intention to create a trust.

Certainty of subject-matter

This arises in two forms. Where a person constitutes a trust by expressing himself to be trustee for another, then the trust will only be validly constituted if he indicates with sufficient accuracy which of his property will be the trust assets. Where the trust is constituted by a transfer to a trustee this issue does not arise. However the transfer must be complete before the trust can take effect. A trust cannot be declared of after-acquired property[9]; however, if the settlor enters into an enforceable agreement to settle after-acquired property, equitable title to the property passes to the beneficiaries as soon as legal title to the property vests in the settlor[10].

In *Re London Wine Shippers*[11] it was held that a declaration of trust of unspecified property would fail. The case concerned wine held as part of a larger bulk in a warehouse which had not been specified or ascertained. The

---

[5] *Re Rose* [1952] Ch 499.
[6] *Jones v Lock* (1865) 1 Ch App 25; *Richards v Delbridge* (1874) LR 18 Eq 11.
[7] As, for example, in *Paul v Constance* [1977] 1 WLR 527.
[8] [1995] 1 FLR 697.
[9] *Re Ralli's Will Trust* [1964] Ch 288; *Simpson v Simpson* [1992] 1 FLR 601.
[10] *Re Lind* [1915] 2 Ch 345.
[11] (1986) PCC 121.

rationale was that the property was not fungible, and the exact nature of the trust property could not be known until the separation was made. Where property had been segregated then a trust of it could be validly constituted[12]. This decision was upheld in *Re Goldcorp Exchange Ltd*[13] in respect of gold bullion. This rule apparently applies only to chattels which may differ each from the other—as, for example, wine which may be corked, or bullion which may be adulterated—but does not apply in the case of true fungibles—money, securities and the like[14].

Certainty of beneficiaries

Where a trust is created for a group of beneficiaries absolutely, they must all be individually identifiable[15], although as long as they are identifiable it does not matter if they cannot be found, for in such a case the share could be paid into court to await their appearance. However, where a discretionary trust is created and the trustees have discretion to pay the trust fund to any of the members of a class of persons, the trust is completely constituted if the class is designated in such a way that it can with certainty be said in the case of any individual that that individual either is or is not a member of the class of potential beneficiaries[16]. If this test can be satisfied then it does not matter that a list of potential beneficiaries cannot be drawn up.

Thus far we have concentrated on equitable title as created deliberately by settlors. However the express trust has all but disappeared from modern commercial life, although it maintains some outposts of empire in the fields of security and of tax law. The majority of trust questions which reach the courts arise out of implied trusts. Implied trusts are divided into resulting and constructive trusts.

Resulting trusts

The doctrine of resulting trusts is complicated by the fact that it is used to encompass two different types of action under the same conceptual umbrella. The conventional classification of these two is into 'presumed' and 'automatic' resulting trusts[17]. Their common denominator is that where a person voluntarily[18] transfers property to another the law holds that that other must hold the property on trust for the transferor *unless the contrary be shown.*

---

[12] *Re Stapylton Fletcher Ltd* [1994] 1 WLR 1181.

[13] [1995] 1 AC 74.

[14] *Hunter v Moss* [1994] 1 WLR 452, *sed quaere* given *Macjordan Construction Ltd v Brookmount Erostin Ltd* [1992] BCLC 350.

[15] Hanbury & Maudsley, 15th edn, 98, *sed contra* P Matthews [1984] Conv 22.

[16] *McPhail v Doulton* [1971] AC 424.

[17] Per Megarry J, at first instance in *Re Vandervell's Trusts (No 2)* [1974] Ch 269.

[18] It seems that the doctrine of resulting trusts has no application to involuntary transfer, because 'before any doctrine of resulting trust can come into play, there must be at least some effective … transfer … of interest in property' (per Megarry J in *Re Vandervell's Trusts*, above). An involuntary transfer does not usually transfer title.

This is a rule relating to the law of gifts, and is in fact no more than equity's rule of recognition for a valid gift—that the recipient should be able to prove some intention to give on the part of the donor and that the donor should have received no benefit as a result of the gift.

It is because the resulting trust arises only in respect of a gift that any transfer resulting from a contract is not subject to the doctrine of resulting trust[19]. However, the rule is brought into play in two very different classes of case.

Imperfect dispositions

The classical imperfect disposition occurs where a settlor, thinking that he has settled all of his property, in fact leaves an unadministered balance. In the absence of any rule such as that relating to resulting trusts such a balance would vest in the trustee absolutely—an outcome repugnant to equity. The resulting trust therefore arises, and the property left undisposed of is said to 'result' back to the settlor[20]. Since the creation of the trust will have involved vesting the trustee with absolute legal ownership, this means that the settlor in effect becomes one of the beneficiaries of the trust[21].

Drafting ineptitude is not the only way in which a settlement can fail. Uncertainty, lapse, disclaimer, perpetuity, illegality, failure to comply with formal requirements and a multitude of other equitable principles conspire to ensure that there is no shortage of ineffective equitable dispositions where the rule is applied. The most common is probably still the badly drafted will—'to my wife for the rest of her life, and then to my children for their lives' is a common example. In these circumstances the property would result back to the testator's estate and he distributed either in accordance with the residual bequest of the will or, if there is none and the whole will is incomplete, in accordance with the rules of intestate succession.

The rule produces approximate justice as far as the parties to the gift are concerned, by assuming that the settlor intends to retain that which was not expressly given, but breaks down a little in the 'disaster' cases in which money was subscribed by the general public for a fund to alleviate the effects of a particular disaster. The effects having been fully alleviated (in so far as money could do so), a surplus was found in the fund. In these cases the donors had made absolute gifts, and had no wish to see their money again. However the test applied by the courts disregards the donor's intentions. So repugnant is the concept of the property vesting in the trustee that the donor will be compelled to accept back his property over his own protestations[22]. This rule is, however, increasingly subject to the principle that the donor may validly aban-

---

[19] *Cunnack v Edwards* [1896] 2 Ch 679; *Re West Sussex Constabulary's Benevolent Fund Trusts* [1971] Ch 1.

[20] *Re Gillingham Bus Disaster Fund* [1958] Ch 300; *Re West* [1900] 1 Ch 84.

[21] For purposes of tax planning this outcome is a financial disaster, since income tax law treats as income of a settlor income of any trust in which he has a beneficial interest (*Re Vandervell's Trusts (No 2)* [1974] Ch 419. It is therefore extremely rare to find an express trust with this defect.

[22] *Re British Red Cross Balkan Fund* [1914] 2 Ch 419; *Re Welsh Hospital Fund* [1921] 1 Ch 655; *Re Houborn Aero Components Ltd's Air Raid Disaster Fund* [1946] Ch 194.

don his property to another, for example by placing money in a street collecting tin such that his identity may never be ascertained[23].

The rule simplifies the difficulty which is occasionally encountered in dealing with the property of unincorporated associations. Where persons have together subscribed money for the purchase of assets for the benefit of such an association, or even agreed to pay a subscription to such an association, it is argued from time to time that the persons in whom title to the association's property is vested hold such property on a resulting trust for the donors. However it is now clear that membership of an unincorporated association is a matter of contract[24], and that the club's property is held on trust for the members rather than on resulting trust for the donors[25]. The usual modern structure is to create either an express trust (avoiding the difficulty created by the perpetuity rule) or, more commonly, a limited company.

Gifts

It is fair to say that equity looks with great suspicion upon *inter vivos* gifts. The rule that equity will not assist a volunteer may be invoked where no doubt whatsoever arises over the intention to alienate. However, the effect of the rule is to give the donor a *locus poenitentiae* lasting from the time when he has declared his intention to give to the time where he effects the transfer of legal title. During that time the recipient remains dependent upon the donor's munificence, and has no action to compel the completion for the gift.

There are, however, cases where the imperfection appears not in the actual transfer of legal title but in the motivation of the transferor. As a general rule, equity presumes that where a person makes a transfer to another, he intends that the transferor should hold the property as bare trustee[26]. In such cases equity intervenes to measure the parties' true intention, and where there is no evident and complete intention to give, orders that legal title to the gift be transferred from the donee to the donor. In addition to gifts of property, this principle also arises where a purchase is made in the name of a person with money provided by another[27], where one person purchases property in the name of himself and another[28], and where two persons purchase property in the name of one only of them[29].

This is an evidential rule. Unless proceedings are commenced it has no application; thus a gift is a gift until challenged. When it is challenged, the burden is in principle upon the donee to prove that the donor intended a gift, unless the donor and the donee stand to each other in one of a series of specified relationships, in which any transfer of property is presumed to be a valid

---

[23] *Re Bucks Constabulary Fund Friendly Society (No 2)* [1979] 1 WLR 936.
[24] *Tierney v Tough* [1914] 1 IR 142; *Re St Andrews Allotment Association* [1969] 1 WLR 229; *Re William Denby Ltd's Sick Fund* [1971] 1 WLR 973; *Re West Sussex Constabulary's Benevolent Fund* [1971] Ch 1; *Re Sick & Funeral Society of St John's Sunday School, Golcar* [1973] Ch 51; *Re GKN Bolts and Nuts Ltd Sports and Social Club* [1982] 1 WLR 774.
[25] *Re Rechers Will Trusts* [1972] Ch 526; *Re Lipinski's Will Trusts* [1976] Ch 235.
[26] *Murless v Franklin* (1818) 1 Swans 13.
[27] *Dyer v Dyer* (1788) 2 Cox Eq Cas 92; *Wray v Steele* (1814) 2 Ves & B 388.
[28] *Benger v Drew* (1721) 1 P Wms 781; *Rider v Kidder* (1805) 10 Ves 360.
[29] *The Venture* [1908] P 128; *Bull v Bull* [1955] 1 QB 234.

gift unless the contrary be proved. The most important rule is that where the gift is to a child, or one to whom the purchaser then stood *in loco parentis*, the effect of the presumption is reversed and there is a 'presumption of advancement'[30]. The rule also applies as between spouses. The presumption of advancement has been described as a 'judicial investment of last resort'[31] and should not be relied on except in a very clear case.

The fact that this rule is one of evidence gives rise to various technicalities. The most important is as to the admissibility of relevant evidence. The primary evidence for such gifts is the parties' conduct, their declared intentions and their acts at the time of the gift. Thereafter, equity does not permit the donor to revoke his gift at a mere whim, and the donor's conduct subsequent to the gift tending to show that a gift was not (or was no longer) intended is not admissible. Conversely, the donee's conduct after the gift tending to show that he did not regard himself as being the absolute owner of the property is admissible against him, but evidence of intention to appropriate the property is not[32].

In the field of personal property, the most common manifestation of the phenomenon of purchase in the name of another is the joint bank account. A bank account is merely a chose in action for a sum of money which the account holders have against the bank. Where the account is a 'true' joint account (ie where both parties have the right to pay in and withdraw monies from the account) then the chose in action is jointly held and no effort will be made to divide it between the contributors[33]. However, where money is paid in by both parties but drawn out by one the position is more difficult. There is some doubt over whether property purchased with the proceeds of such withdrawal should be treated as being held on trust by the purchaser for the benefit of the account holders. The principle is that the joint legal ownership endures unless some equity displaces it[34], but such an equity may well arise if, for example, the monies are paid into the account by one joint tenant and extracted by another. It is also, presumably, possible to sever a joint tenancy of a joint account in the same way as it is possible to sever any other joint tenancy, such that the account holders will continue to be jointly entitled to the account balance but will hold it on trust for themselves in proportionate shares.

Where one person has exclusive access to and use of the account during his life, leaving the other with no interest beyond the bare right of the *jus accrescendi*, then it is debatable whether the joint account is held by the account holders on trust for the single contributor as beneficiary[35].

[30] Per Viscount Simonds, *Shephard v Cartwright* [1955] AC 431 at 445.

[31] *McGrath v Wallis* [1995] 2 FLR 114, and see *Tribe v Tribe* [1995] 4 All ER 236.

[32] *Pole v Pole* (1748) 1 Ves Sen 76; *Stock v McAvoy* (1872) LR 15 Eq 55; *Bone v Pollard* (1857) 24 Beav 283; *Marshal v Crutwell* (1875) LR 20 Eq 328; *Redington v Redington* (1794) 3 Ridg Parl Rep 106; *Shephard v Cartwright* [1955] AC 431.

[33] *Jones v Maynard* [1951] Ch 572.

[34] *Re Bishop* [1965] Ch 450.

[35] The creation of such an account would be a disposition of a testamentary nature not made in accordance with the Wills Act 1837 and ought therefore to be void; however a specific exception was created by Romer J in *Young v Sealey* [1949] Ch 278, approved in *Re Figgis* [1969] 1 Ch 123.

Failed purpose trusts

Possibly the most interesting manifestation of the resulting trust is that which arises in circumstances such as those of *Barclays Bank Ltd v Quistclose Investments Ltd*[36]. In such cases A pays money to B for the express purpose of allowing B to discharge a debt which he owes to C. Such an arrangement sounds like a purpose trust, which is, at English law, unenforceable[37]. However, the point which was taken in *Quistclose* and which has been repeated extra-judicially by Millett J is that where the transfer to B does not create an express trust in favour of C, it may well create a resulting trust in favour of A. Thus, where it becomes impossible to apply the property for the stated purpose (for example if C, being a company, had been struck off the Register of Companies and thus ceased to exist), A may assert a proprietary right to recover it. Analyses of *Quistclose* trusts are liable to omit to mention that they only arise in very unusual circumstances indeed—as a general rule, where B borrows money from A to apply for a particular purpose he will merely become A's debtor for the money advances, and A will have to exercise a very high degree of control indeed over the monies advanced before an express purpose trust will be held to have arisen, as the party seeking to assert the existence of such a trust will face the evidential burden of proving the three certainties (subject-matter, object and intention) necessary to create a trust.

Dispositions pursuant to illusory agreements

This class of agreements can best be illustrated by the 'swaps' cases. In *Hazell v London Borough of Hammersmith and Fulham*[38] it was held that local authorities did not have the power to enter into swap transactions as a means of raising revenues. This created considerable difficulties for the large numbers of banks who had already entered into such contracts with local authorities, and much litigation resulted as they sought to recover sums paid pursuant to these contracts. Now in such cases the facts appear very close to the ordinary situation of a voluntary transfer. Since the payment had been made pursuant to a contract which had never existed, then the position appeared to be on all fours with the classical resulting trust cases where a voluntary payment might be recovered from the payee.

However this analysis was considered in some depth by the House of Lords in *Westdeutche Landesbank Girozentrale v Islington LBC*[39]. The first thing which must be said about this case is that it is of dubious authority, since the points which were raised on appeal to the Lords were very narrow, and much of the general principle contained in the speeches of their Lordships are by no means essential components of the *ratio decidendi* of the case. Lord Browne-

---

[36] [1970] AC 567. For such trusts see also *Carreras Rothmans v Freeman Mathews Treasure Ltd* [1985] 1 All ER 155; *Re EVTR Ltd* [1987] BCLC 646; and Millett in (1985) LQR 101 at 269.
[37] *Morice v Bishop of Durham* (1804) 9 Ves 399 at 405; *Re Astor's Settlement Trusts* [1952] Ch 534.
[38] [1992] 2 AC 1.
[39] [1996] 2 WLR 802. On this decision see Birks [1996] *Restitution Law Review* 3; Cope (1996) 112 LQR 521; McCormack [1997] JBL 48.

Wilkinson considered the resulting trust claim in detail, and found that the underlying reasoning (set out above) was incorrect.

Lord Browne-Wilkinson started from the premise that a resulting trust is imposed by law in order to give effect to the parties' intentions. In the cases outlined above, the voluntary payment cases were all cases in which the trust was imposed where the surrounding facts indicated an intention not to make an absolute transfer. Now in the *Westdeutche* case there was no doubt over both parties' intentions as at the time of making the agreement. There was no intention on either part that the transfer of funds should be anything other than a complete and absolute transfer, and there was no evidence before the court at any time to suggest otherwise. In these circumstances, it was held, following an article by William Swadling[40], that since the test of intention to make a gift failed, then the presumption of resulting trust arose, but was defeated by proof of the making of the contract. The fact that the contract never took effect was not relevant to the parties' intention and therefore the existence or otherwise of the resulting trust.

The court noted, but disagreed with, restitution lawyers' views as expressed in an article by Peter Birks[41] to the effect that English law required the resulting trust to perform exactly this function in order to provide a restitutionary remedy in cases of 'subtractive unjust enrichment'. This argument necessarily implied that the trust is required to take effect at the date of the enrichment of the recipient of the property, and this was not a proposition which Lord Browne-Wilkinson was prepared to accept. He objected to the idea that a trust could take effect from any date earlier than the date upon which the putative trustee acquired knowledge (or notice) of the facts which gave rise to the trust. Where the recipient of property acquires notice of the relevant facts after he has received the property, then it would be practical to impose a trust obligation on him in respect of such property at that time, but such a trust would not be a resulting but a constructive trust. Lord Browne-Wilkinson said, perfectly correctly, that to the extent that the case of *Chase Manhattan v Is-raeli-British Bank*[42] was to be followed it was as an authority for the creation of a constructive trust in such circumstances, and to the extent that *Sinclair v Brougham*[43] is any authority for the proposition that a resulting trust would arise in such circumstances, to that extent the case was wrongly decided.

Since in the case of a contract which is void for mutual mistake it is necessarily true that neither party will be aware of the facts which render the contract void at the time of its making, it would seem to follow that a resulting trust will never be available in such a case. This conclusion seems valid. The idea that a property interest can be created with retrospective effect is a complex and difficult one, and at odds with the ordinary principles of property law. It is therefore necessary to look at why the availability of a constructive rather than a resulting trust will make a difference.

---

[40] 16 *Legal Studies* at 133.
[41] In Goldstein (ed), *Equity; Contemporary Legal Developments* (1992).
[42] [1981] Ch 105.
[43] [1914] AC 398.

Constructive trusts

In *Metall und Rohstoff AG v Donaldson Inc*[44] the court considered the flavours of constructive trust. In the United States there are now two distinct classes of constructive trusts: institutional constructive trusts, which are created automatically by operation of law upon the occurrence of specified events, and remedial constructive trusts, which are created by order of the court as a species of equitable relief[45]. These latter flourished briefly in England under the tutelage of Lord Denning[46], but a backlash set in after his retirement. The best explanation of this backlash is that '[f]or the hard-nosed property lawyer, the "finding" of a remedial constructive trust is an act of intellectual bankruptcy, amounting effectively to a judicial confession that no convincing reason can be found in law for giving judgement to a deserving plaintiff'[47], and by 1980 the remedial constructive trust could still be described as a 'novel concept in English law'[48]. The concept has been further criticised by Oakley[49], who has argued that it is important to maintain the principle that existing property rights must not be determined according to what is reasonable and fair or just in all the circumstances[50].

The primary difference between an institutional and a remedial constructive trust is that an institutional constructive trust arises immediately as a matter of law upon the occurrence of a particular set of events. The beneficiary therefore acquires an interest in the trust property at that time, and any subsequent interests will rank after him. Thus on the insolvency of the constructive trustee the beneficiary can call for his property to be returned to him in priority to the unsecured creditors and to any secured creditors whose security was created after the property was acquired. A remedial constructive trust, by contrast, arises as a result of the judgment which recognises it. A court creating such a trust may of course 'backdate' it, but it will do so only to the extent that such 'backdating' does not prejudice other acquired rights in the relevant property[51]. This in turn has the interesting side-effect that a remedial constructive trust is most unlikely to be of any great assistance against an insolvent trustee, the very circumstances in which a proprietary claim is most desirable, since to prejudice claims of secured creditors or indeed the general body of credi-

---

[44] [1990] 1 QB 391 at 478–80.
[45] See, for example, *Simonds v Simonds* (1978) 408 NYS2d 359 at 362 and J L Dewar, *The Development of the Remedial Constructive Trust* (1982) 60 CBR 265. On UK remedial constructive trusts see *Lonrho plc v Al Fayed (No 2)* [1992] 1 WLR 1 at 9; *Re Goldcorp ExchangeLtd* [1994] 2 All ER 806 at 822; and see Millett J in (1991) 107 LQR at 71.
[46] See for example *Cooke v Head* [1972] 1 WLR 518 and *Eves v Eves* [1975] 1 WLR 1338.
[47] Gray, *Elements of Land Law*, 2nd edn (Butterworths, 1993), p 454, fn 5. This work contains (at pp 450–9) an excellent analysis of the modern development of the remedial constructive trust in English law.
[48] *Re Sharpe (a Bankrupt)* [1980] 1 WLR 219 at 225.
[49] *Constructive Trusts*, 3rd edn (Sweet & Maxwell, 1997), pp 25–8.
[50] See *Pettitt v Pettitt* [1970] AC 777, per Reid LJ at 793, Morris LJ at 801–5, Hodson LJ at 809, Diplock LJ at 825, for a strong judicial reaffirmation of the inviolability of the principles of property law.
[51] Per Browne-Wilkinson LJ in *Westdeutche Landesbank Girozentrale v Islington LBC* [1996] 2 WLR 802 at 837; see also *Muschinski v Dodds* (1985) 160 CLR 583 at 615.

tors is not ordinarily considered equitable[52].

Remedial constructive trusts arising out of dishonesty are discussed in the section of this book on remedies. What follows here is a summary of the circumstances in which an ordinary institutional proprietary trust of property is created by law.

Institutional constructive trusts

Profits made by fiduciary
Where a fiduciary makes a profit resulting from his position as fiduciary, he receives such profit upon trust for the beneficiary. The leading case is *Boardman v Phipps*[53], in which the defendants were trustees of a family settlement which held a substantial minority interest in a company. They bought, with their own money, more shares in the company which, along with the trust shares, they then used to take over the company and restore its profitability. It was held that the profit which they made on their own holdings was held upon constructive trust for the trust beneficiaries. This form of trust may be said to have some of the characteristics of the remedial constructive trust in that it sometimes arises on a default. It is, however, properly regarded as institutional, since the trust arises automatically upon the occurrence of a particular set of facts, without the necessity for any deliberate or intentional wrongdoing by any person.

Sale under specifically enforceable contract
Where a contract is specifically performable the vendor holds the property as constructive trustee for the purchaser from the moment of entry into the contract[54], and if he sells the property to another, he holds the proceeds of sale upon constructive trust in the same way[55]. However, until the date specified in the contract for conveyance has been reached he preserves a very large degree of freedom in his dealings with the property[56], and it is only upon the conveyance date that he becomes a bare trustee without rights to the property[57]. The right is absolute, where a receiver of a vendor company is appointed after contract but before completion he must complete[58].

Conveyance by fraud
Where a person has defrauded another of property, he may hold the property as constructive trustee. This is a mechanism by which the absolute nature of a written conveyance may be overturned[59]. However, the constructive trust will only be imposed in some cases after detailed examination of the conduct of all parties[60].

---

[52] *Re Goldcorp Exchange Ltd* [1994] 2 All ER 806.
[53] [1967] 2 AC 46.
[54] *Oughtred v IRC* [1960] AC 206.
[55] *Lake v Bayliss* [1974] 1 WLR 1073.
[56] *Cuddon v Tite* (1858) 1 Giff 395.
[57] *Lloyds Bank v Carrick* [1996] 4 All ER 630.
[58] *Freevale Ltd v Metrostore (Holdings) Ltd* [1984] 1 All ER 495.
[59] *Rochefoucauld v Boustead* [1897] 1 Ch 196; *Bannister v Bannister* [1948] 2 All ER 133.
[60] *Lonrho v Al Fayed (No 2)* [1992] 1 WLR 1.

Murder

Where a person kills another[61], any benefit which the person may derive from the death is held on constructive trust for the estate of that person. The rule applies in the case of testamentary gifts, benefits acquired upon intestacy, and under insurance policies[62]. A joint tenant or co-owner who kills another co-owner holds any increment to his share of the jointly owned property upon trust for the estate of his victim[63]. Interestingly, in cases of manslaughter (but not murder) the court has jurisdiction under s 2(2) of the Forfeiture Act 1982 to relieve the killer of this consequence.

---

[61] All forms of murder and also some forms of manslaughter, since the test is the doing of an act intending harm (*Gray v Barr* [1971] 2 QB 554; *Re K (dec'd)* [1986] Ch 180; *Re H (dec'd)* [1990] 1 FLR 441).

[62] As a separate rule, a person who kills their partner is prevented thereby from claiming the partner's pension (*R v Chief National Insurance Commissioner, ex p Connor* [1981] 1 QB 758).

[63] *Re K (dec'd)* at first instance [1986] Fam 180.

Chapter 9

Proprietary Interests Arising From Estoppel

The operation of the equitable doctrine of estoppel cannot create title, but it can prevent a rightful owner asserting his title, or some part of his title, in circumstances in which it would be inequitable for him to be able to do so. Estoppel is a doctrine of the common law, but it has been developed by the courts of equity into a flexible instrument for doing justice in relation to property rights. Estoppel operates in respect of personal and real property alike. In the case of sales of goods the operation of the doctrine has been codified to some extent by s 21(1) of the Sale of Goods Act 1979 in relation to representations as to title made by a true owner, and by s 2 of the Factors Act 1889.

A definition of estoppel is as follows[1]:

[W]here a person has by words or conduct made to another a clear and unequivocal representation of fact, either with knowledge of its falsehood or with the intention that it should be acted upon, or has so conducted himself that another would, as a reasonable person, understand that a certain representation of fact was intended to be acted upon, and the other person has acted upon such representation and thereby altered his position to his prejudice, an estoppel arises against the party who made the representation, and he is not allowed to aver that the fact is other than he has represented it to be.

There is a dispute over whether estoppel is a rule of evidence[2] or a substantive rule of law[3]. This dispute is probably irrelevant for all practical purposes, although the idea of estoppel as a rule of evidence does at least explain the otherwise difficult rule that estoppel operates only as a defence and does not give an independent cause of action[4].

Common law estoppel

The origins of the doctrine of estoppel are to be found in the common law concepts of estoppel by record, estoppel by deed and estoppel in pais. Estoppel

---

[1] 16 Halsbury's para. 955, approved in *Re the Local Government Superannuation Acts 1937 and 1939, Algar v Middlesex County Council* [1945] 2 All ER 243 at 250, DC.

[2] *Low v Bouverie* [1891] 3 Ch 82 at 105; *Re Ottos Kopje Diamond Mines Ltd* [1893] 1 Ch 618 at 628; *Re Sugden's Trusts, Sugden v Walker* [1917] 1 Ch 510 and [1917] 2 Ch 92.

[3] *Canada and Dominion Sugar Co Ltd v Canadian National (West Indies) Steamships Ltd* [1947] AC 46 at 56; *Moorgate Mercantile v Twitchings* [1976] QB 225 at 241.

[4] *Low v Bouverie* [1891] 3 Ch 82.

by record is also known as estoppel *per rem judicatem*, since it operates to prevent a party to litigation denying in subsequent litigation the truth of a fact which has been determined by the tribunal[5]. Estoppel by deed operates in the same way to prevent a party to a deed denying the truth of any statement made by him in the deed in a dispute between the parties thereto[6]. It is probable that a statement made in a deed poll binds the person executing the deed against all the world.

Estoppel in pais is more complex. The original common law rule of estoppel in pais was that it prevented the defendant from denying the inferences which could be drawn from acts as public as the execution of deeds or the entry of judgements—for example livery, entry and acceptance of an estate[7]. However it also arises as between parties to transactions entered into otherwise than by deed where the entry into the transaction itself could be held to constitute a representation of a fact. It is for this reason that where a landlord accepts rent from a tenant who takes a leasehold estate, the landlord is estopped from denying the tenancy and the tenant is estopped from denying the landlord's estate[8]. For the same reason, where a person accepts property from another as bailee, the bailor is estopped from denying the bailment and the bailee from denying the bailor's title. A further manifestation is the common law doctrine of election (not to be confused with the equitable doctrine of election, a very different beast) which holds that a person may not at the same time maintain two inconsistent claims and, having knowingly abandoned one claim in order to proceed with the other, may not thereafter reverse his decision[9]. This is expressed in the maxim that a person may not at the same time approbate and reprobate[10]. The most common example is that a person who takes a benefit under a deed cannot thereafter dispute the terms of the deed[11].

Equitable estoppel

Equitable estoppel is not a separate doctrine of equity in its own right, but a development by the courts of equity of the common law rules of estoppel in pais[12]. It was the rules of estoppel in pais which the courts of equity developed

---

[5] Where the tribunal is not a court of record but a court or other body constituted by agreement of the parties, the estoppel still exists and is known as estoppel quasi by record.

[6] This is the original reason for recitals in deeds. The recitals, being statements made by both parties, might be denied by neither.

[7] Co. Litt 352A.

[8] Co Litt 352; *Phipps v Sculthorpe* (1817) 1 B & Ald 50; *Doe d Jackson v Wilkinson* (1824) 3 B & C 413.

[9] *United Australia Ltd v Barclays Bank Ltd* [1941] AC 1.

[10] See *Lissenden v CAV Bosch Ltd* [1940] AC 412. A person will not be regarded as having elected until such time as he has taken a benefit under or arising out of the course of conduct which he has first pursued and with which his subsequent conduct is incompatible (*Banque des Marchands de Moscou (Koupetschesky) v Kindersley* [1951] Ch 112), and in any event the court retains a jurisdiction to relieve the plaintiff of the result of an election made by mistake (*Kaprow & Co v Maclelland* [1948] 1 KB 618).

[11] Eg *Ashe v Hogan* [1920] 1 IR 159; *Tito v Waddell (No 2)* [1977] Ch 106.

[12] See *Citizens' Bank of Louisiana v First National Bank of New Orleans* (1873) LR 6 HL 352 at 360. In *Lovett v Lovett* [1898] 1 Ch 82 Romer J sought to distinguish them by confining the term 'estoppel at law' to mean estoppel by deed, which is incorrect. Estoppel in pais is a common law doctrine.

in order to produce the true equitable estoppels, the promissory and the proprietary estoppel.

Promissory estoppel

Promissory estoppel extends the ordinary common law doctrine of estoppel in that a common law estoppel may only be founded upon a statement of present fact. A promissory estoppel may, by contrast, be founded upon a statement of future intention—in effect, a promise. The promise must be clear and unequivocal[13], to have been intended to affect a pre-existing or future legal relationship[14], and intended to be acted on accordingly[15]. If the promise was not given for good consideration it can be withdrawn at any time. The action therefore only arises where the promissor cannot (or will not) restore the promisee to the position in which he would have been had he not relied upon the promise[16], and in this respect is very similar to the equitable doctrine of rescission. The doctrine is a relatively recent development, dating from either 1877[17] or 1947[18] according to taste. It takes effect purely to prevent a person relying upon their strict legal rights where it would be inequitable for them to do so.

Proprietary estoppel[19]

Proprietary estoppel is usually encountered in the context of real property. However there seems to be no doubt that the principal 'may extend to other forms of property'[20]. Proprietary estoppel is a much more interesting animal from the property lawyer's perspective, if only in that it (may) give rise to proprietary rights.

An equitable proprietary estoppel arises where a person who owns property has so conducted himself, either by encouragement or by representations, that the claimant believes that he has or will acquire some right or interest in the land and has so acted to his detriment on that basis[21]. It has three ingredients.

(1)   The person to whom the representations are made must have acted to his detriment in reliance thereon.

(2)   The acts must have been motivated by either an expectation or a belief that the representee either owned or would obtain an interest in property of some description.

---

[13] *Woodhouse A C Israel Cocoa Ltd SA v Nigerian Produce Marketing Co Ltd* [1972] AC 741.

[14] *Bank Negara Indonesia v Philip Hoalim* [1973] 2 MLJ 3, PC.

[15] *Kammin's Ballrooms Co Ltd v Zenith Investments (Torquay) Ltd* [1971] AC 850.

[16] *Ajayi v R T Briscoe (Nigeria) Ltd* [1964] 1 WLR 1326 at 1330, PC.

[17] *Hughes v Metropolitan Rly Co* (1877) 2 App Cas 439.

[18] *Central London Property Trust v High Trees House Ltd* [1947] KB 130.

[19] See generally Mark Pawlowski, *The Doctrine of Proprietary Estoppel* (1996); Gray, *Elements of Land Law*, 2nd edn (Butterworths, 1993), pp 356–68.

[20] Per Megaw LJ in *Western Fish Products Ltd v Penwith District Council* [1981] 2 All ER 204, CA; see also *Peruvian Guano Co Ltd v Dreyfus Bros & Co* [1892] AC 166 at 176; *Greenwood v Bennett* [1973] QB 195; and per Denning LJ in *Moorgate Mercantile v Twitchings* [1976] QB 225 at 242 The principle is espoused in s 6(1) of the Torts (Interference with Goods) Act 1977, which provides for statutory compensation for a mistaken improver of goods.

[21] Pawlowski, *The Doctrine of Proprietary Estoppel*, p 1.

(3) His belief must have been positively encouraged by the property owner or his predecessor in title.

Because the doctrine is an equitable doctrine, there must be no equitable bar to recovery (clean hands, laches etc).

A proprietary estoppel differs in a number of ways from the promissory estoppel discussed above[22]. First, it gives rise to a separately existing cause of action in its own right[23], and is not a mere defence. Secondly, it only arises in respect of a belief in a particular pattern of property ownership which is incorrect at law but which has been encouraged. It is submitted that there is a further requirement that a proprietary estoppel can only arise in respect of specified property[24]. The key to proprietary estoppel is that where the conditions for the estoppel arise, the court will prevent the person estopped from exercising his rights of ownership over the property in respect of which the estoppel arises. This raises a familiar issue. Where the court intervenes to deprive one person of some part of his rights over his property, and to vest those rights in another, the ordinary and conventional analysis should be that there is a transfer of a property right. As discussed below, the issue of the nature of duration and extent of this property right is complex and difficult, but that the effect of the doctrine of proprietary estoppel is to effect such a transfer seems to be clear.

Proprietary estoppel and constructive trust

The distinction between a right in property acquired by virtue of a proprietary estoppel and a right acquired by the operation of a constructive trust is that the estoppel arises on an inducement. The distinction is sometimes very marginal—*Gissing v Gissing*[25], for example, is a case in which the plaintiff's right of action arose from a breach by the defendant of an obligation to transfer the legal estate in property—in other words, the attempt to assert legal title in breach of equitable obligations.

It seems likely that an equitable estoppel would arise in most constructive trust cases. The importance of the doctrine is therefore that it is wider than the doctrine of constructive trusts. Because a constructive trust claim involves a claim for the transfer of equitable title to property, the claimant must show one of a recognised number of classes of detriment[26]. It seems that the equitable proprietary estoppel rests on 'wider equitable principle' than that which

---

[22] And at least one learned commentator suggests that promissary estoppel may not be a manifestation of estoppel at all, but a separate equitable doctrine (Snell, *Principles of Equity*, 29th edn, 573).

[23] *Dillwyn v Llewellyn* (1862) 4 De G F & J 517; *Inwards v Baker* [1965] 2 QB 29; *Moorgate Mercantile v Twitchings* [1976] QB 225; *Crabb v Arun DC* [1976] Ch 179; *Pascoe v Turner* [1979] 1 WLR 431, CA.

[24] *Layton v Martin* [1986] 2 FLR 227; *cf Baumgartner v Baumgartner* (1988) 62 ALJR 29. The apparent contradiction of this proposition by *Re Basham Dec'd* [1986] 1 WLR 1498 is due to a rather technical dispute over how clearly defined the relevant item of property requires to be before the estoppel will bite, and whether the property is present or future. This dispute does not affect the fundamental premise that a proprietary estoppel is, when made out, an interest in property.

[25] [1971] AC 886.

[26] *Lloyds Bank v Rosset* [1991] 1 AC 107.

underlies constructive trust liability[27], and that an equitable proprietary estoppel is available in cases which would not ordinarily satisfy the criteria for a full equitable constructive trust[28]. The person seeking to set up a proprietary estoppel is also assisted in that where the false promises can be shown, reliance is presumed unless the representor can prove otherwise[29].

Although a proprietary estoppel may be wider than a constructive trust claim, it is not necessarily weaker. A proprietary estoppel raises an equity which is satisfied according to all the circumstances, and an equity founded on proprietary estoppel may be satisfied by an absolute transfer of the whole of the interest in the disputed property[30]. It is true that the usual satisfaction of a claim based upon equitable proprietary estoppel is the grant of an irrevocable licence[31], but there does not appear to be any rule of law or practice that the fact that a claim is brought alleging equitable proprietary estoppel rather than constructive trust necessarily implies that the plaintiff will be awarded a lesser interest in the property concerned if he can prove his claim.

Creation of proprietary rights by operation of estoppel

The 'equity' which arises in a case of equitable proprietary estoppel is created as soon as the representor attempts to resile from his representation—in equitable terms, when the representor's conscience is affected[32]. The court's function is merely to recognise the equity and to 'satisfy' it by making the appropriate order dealing with the relevant property. It has been said that, either through the operation of the maxim that 'equity looks on as done that which ought to be done' or by the operation of some variant of the doctrine of relation back, this results in the estate which is awarded in satisfaction of the equity taking effect as from the date when the equity arose[33].

It is therefore clear that after judgment a property right may have been created. The main question, however, is whether the equity which exists prior to judgment constitutes in itself a property interest.

The position of such 'mere equities' in modern English law is complex. *National Provincial Bank v Ainsworth*[34] seems fairly clear authority that they are not property interests, but merely personal rights, but modern thought has been strongly influenced by the Australian decision in *Latec Investments Ltd*

---

[27] *Morris v Morris* [1982] 1 NSWLR 61 at 63.

[28] See in particular *Grant v Edwards* [1986] Ch 638, in which Browne-Wilkinson V-C described the grounds for an equitable proprietary estoppel very broadly as 'any act done to [the plaintiff's] detriment' (at 656–7). His conclusion that a constructive trust might be found in every case where the ground supported an equitable estoppel has been overruled by the House of Lords (*Lloyds Bank v Rosset* [1991] 1 AC 107) but it is submitted that his statement of the grounds which may found an equitable proprietary estoppel is still good law.

[29] *Coombes v Smith* [1986] 1 WLR 808.

[30] *Pascoe v Turner* [1979] 1 WLR 431 at 439.

[31] See eg *Bristol & West Building Society v Henning* [1985] 1 WLR 778.

[32] *Lim Teng Huan v Ang Swee Chuan* [1992] 1 WLR 113 at 117.

[33] Gray, *Elements of Land Law*, 2nd edn (Buttreworths, 1993), p 360, citing *Commonwealth v Verwayen* (1990) 170 CLR 394 at 437; *Voyce v Voyce* (1991) 62 P & CR 290 at 294.

[34] [1965] AC 1175.

v Hotel Terrigal Pty Ltd (1965) 113 CLR 265, which indicates clearly that they are property interests. The primary ground for this belief is that many equities are exercisable against successors in title[35]. The primary ground for rejecting it is that a mere equity will usually be displaced by a purchaser for value of an equitable interest[36].

The test of a property right is whether it is good against third parties. The equity created by the doctrine of equitable proprietary estoppel does not prevail against the class of purchasers for value without notice of an estate in the property[37], but then neither does a full equitable interest, which undoubtedly is an interest in property. The test of the proprietary nature of an equitable right is whether it binds a volunteer transferee. Equities of this form have been held to bind a transferee of the property[38], the trustee in bankruptcy of the property owner[39], an associated company[40] and a successor local authority[41], and the answer in this case is that such an interest clearly is a property interest.

The matter may further be tested by enquiring whether the right may be transferred. This is a harder question. In *Fryer v Brook*[42] Oliver LJ found that the equity which arose out of an equitable proprietary estoppel was similar to the personal right of occupancy created by a statutory tenancy, which was not transmissible to others. However in *E R Ives Investment Ltd v High*[43] Denning MR indicated that the right was transmissible to successors[44]. In his *Elements of Land Law*, Gray[45] suggests that the prevailing trend will be in favour of the recognition of such equities as being transferable, based upon the relevant Australian authorities, which are firmly in favour of the transmissibility of such equities[46]. It is submitted that this is the better view, if only because the denial of such transmissibility serves no good jurisprudential purpose, and denies the equity one attribute of a property right whilst leaving it with most of the others.

It therefore seems reasonable to conclude that the equity which arises out of an equitable proprietary estoppel is an independently existing equitable interest in property.

---

[35] The right to have a deed set aside on account of fraud (*Bowen v Evans* (1844) 1 Jo & Lat 178 at 263, 264) or undue influence (*Bainbrigge v Browne* (1881) 18 Ch D 188); the right to have a document rectified for mutual mistake (*Garrard v Frankel* (1862) 30 Beav 445); the right of a mortgagor to reopen a foreclosure (*Campbell v Holyland* (1877) 7 Ch D 166 at 172–5); and, possibly, the rights of a contractual licencee (*Westminster Bank Ltd v Lee* [1956] Ch 7 at 20, *sed quaere* given *Ashburn Anstalt v Arnold* [1989] Ch 1).

[36] *Phillips v Phillips* (1861) 4 De G F & J 208 at 218.

[37] It seems that constructive notice will suffice in this context (*The Duke of Beaufort v Patrick* (1853) 17 Beav 60 at 78; *Bristol & West Building Society v Henning* [1985] 1 WLR 778 at 781).

[38] *Voyce v Voyce* (1991) 62 P & CR 290; *Torrisi v Magame Pty Ltd* [1984] 1 NSWLR 14.

[39] In *Re Sharpe (A Bankrupt)* [1980] 1 WLR 219.

[40] *E & L Berg Homes Ltd v Grey* (1980) 253 EG 473.

[41] *Salvation Army Trustee Co Ltd v West Yorkshire MCC* (1981) 41 P & CR 179.

[42] (1984) LS Gaz R 2856, CA.

[43] [1967] 2 QB 379.

[44] At 395. Winn LJ declined to express a view on the point (at 403).

[45] At 364.

[46] *Hamilton v Geraghty* (1901) 1 SRNSW (Eq) 81; *Cameron v Murdoch* (1986) 63 ALR 575; *affmg* [1983] WAR 321.

Chapter 10

The Purchaser's Equitable Interest in Property

It is clear that there are some circumstances in which equity grants an interest to the purchaser in the property purchased as soon as the contract to sell is complete. This is frequently explained as arising out of some sort of deemed specific performance, the test for the existence of such a right being said to be whether a decree of specific performance would be available. However, this mode of expression is unhelpful. The availability of specific performance is constrained not by the power of the court but by its discretion. Specific performance is *available* in respect of every contract ever made, although the courts frequently exercise their discretion to refuse it. In circumstances where the dispute arises out of a contract for sale, it is unlikely that the criteria which are applied to determine the grant or refusal of specific performance will be identical to the criteria which will be applied to determine the presence or absence of an equitable interest in property.

It does not, however, follow that it is completely mistaken to proceed on the analogy of the discretion to award or refuse specific performance, since the test of the 'availability of specific performance' may be restated as follows. When A, who owns X, agrees to sell X to B, what is important is the parties' intention. If it is clear, either from the agreement itself or from the circumstances of the case, that what was intended was that that particular X was to be sold, it is appropriate that B should be treated as having an equitable interest in that X. However, the position is otherwise if it was in the parties' reasonable contemplation that A should be able to sell that X to a third party and replace it with some other X, which he has bought for the purpose. In other words if A intended, or in all the circumstances must necessarily have expected, that the X in his hands at the time of the making of the contract would be the X to be delivered to B, then B has an equitable interest in that X. A grant of an interest can be unilateral as long as it is enforceable, and B may therefore acquire an interest even though he does not know whether A possesses one X or several. However, if B knows that A owns only one X and is unlikely to find another, then the case that B acquires an equitable interest at the moment of contracting becomes extremely strong.

Another way of expressing this proposition is that property may only be described as subject to a binding contract for sale if it is identifiable as such. This is in fact no more than a manifestation of the sale of goods rule that property is only sold when it is appropriated to the contract. If I own £100 of

Government Treasury 8% stock, and I agree to sell you that amount of stock, then it is arguable that no act of appropriation is necessary, and an equitable interest in the stock will arise whether or not any act of appropriation has been performed. If, by contrast, I own £1,000,000 of the same stock and agree to sell you £100 of it, it is extremely difficult to argue for the existence of such an equitable interest.

Tangible and intangible property

The question of the existence of the purchaser's equitable interest in the property purchased is of no interest in the context of goods, since the issue is already perfectly treated in the sale of goods legislation. In the context of intangibles, however, where the sale of goods legislation does not apply, the point is suddenly of great interest. It has been suggested that the rule of equity as to when an equitable proprietary interest arises in the case of an intangible should be assessed in exactly the same way as the question of whether a legal proprietary interest would have arisen in the case of a sale of goods. This view is most clearly advanced in *Underhill & Hayton's Law Relating to Trusts and Trustees*[1], in which it is asserted that there is no basis in law for distinguishing between the rules of equity as between trusts of tangibles and trusts of intangibles. However, this view has been rejected, both by the Court of Appeal in *Hunter v Moss*[2] and at first instance in *Re Harvard Securities Ltd (In Liquidation), Holland v Newberry & another*[3]. In *Hunter v Moss* Dillon LJ had considered the decision in *Re London Wine Shippers*[4], in which it had been held that no equitable interest had arisen in the case of contracts for the sale of an unallocated quantity of wine. He held that the case was not authority for any proposition relating to the application of the rules of equity to a declaration of trust of a quantity of shares, as in the case before him. The facts of *Hunter v Moss* were that Moss, who was the owner of 950 shares in a private company, had agreed that he would hold 50 of the shares on trust for Hunter. It was held that although , if the case had involved goods, no property interest would have arisen, this was not relevant in determining the validity of the declaration of trust. The commentary on the case in *Underhill & Hayton* holds that it is wrongly decided. However, although the case was decided before the House of Lords' decision in *Re Goldcorp Exchange Ltd*[5], it does not seem that that decision has any bearing on this point.

In *Re Harvard* the issue arose whether a contract for the sale of shares gave rise to an equitable interest therein. Neuberger J found that, had the contract been for the sale of goods, no such interest would have arisen, following *Goldcorp*. However, he held that he was bound by the Court of Appeal deci-

---

[1] 15th edn (1995).
[2] [1994] 1 WLR 452.
[3] (1997) *The Times*, 18 July.
[4] [1986] PCC 121.
[5] [1995] 1 AC 74.

sion in *Hunter v Moss*, and, perhaps more importantly, that he was unable to distinguish that decision in the light of the subsequent decision in *Goldcorp*.

It seems to follow from these decisions that there is no force left in the old argument that such equitable rights only arise where equity would award specific performance.

In equity all legal obligations are specifically enforceable unless there is something repugnant to equity in their formation (eg an obligation procured by undue influence does not exist at equity at all, and is not specifically enforceable). All other legal obligations are in principle enforceable in equity. Equity does not choose to enforce a number of them on the grounds that there is no necessity for the specific relief which equity can provide (ie on the basis of the rule that damages are an adequate remedy), but this does not mean that equity will disregard them. As MacNaughten LJ said in *Tailby v The Official Receiver*:

> you have only to apply the principle that equity considers done that which ought to be done if that principle is applied under the circumstances of the case. The doctrines relating to specific performance do not ... afford a test or measure of the rights created.

This argument to the contrary is based on Atkin LJ's speech in *Re Wait*[6]. However, it has been convincingly criticised[7], and in *Re Bond Worth*[8] it was assumed that a contract for the sale of goods passed an equitable interest in those goods[9]. The point is still open for decision, but it should be borne in mind when considering equitable interests in personal property that although express trusts of personal property will operate in the same way, and give rise to the same remedies, as express trusts of land, issues of whether resulting or constructive trusts of personalty have arisen, or whether other equitable interests in personal property have arisen, may be answered more restrictively in the case of personal property than in the case of land.

---

[6] [1927] Ch 606; approved per Lord Brandon in *Leigh & Sillavan Ltd v Aliakmon Shipping, The Aliakmon* [1986] AC 785 at 812–3.
[7] See eg the decision of the Supreme Court of South Australia in *Graham v Freer* (1980) 35 SASR 424.
[8] [1980] Ch 228.
[9] *Contra*, there are indications in *Tailby v The Official Receiver* (1888) 13 App Cas 523 that even specific performance does not give rise to an equitable interest in goods.

Chapter 11

Mistake

The issues which arise in respect of transfers of title made under the influence of a mistake are some of the most complex of the issues in property law[1]. The area must be carefully distinguished from the ordinary area of mistake, in which a contract which parties have voluntarily entered into is sought to be set aside on the grounds of some misapprehension on the part of one or both parties. In property mistake cases the transaction commences with the transfer of property made other than pursuant to any obligation, and the issue is to determine what consequences flow from the transfer. The rationale for the separate treatments is that in contract the principle of finality operates to entrench every agreement, which will not be disturbed without good cause[2]. However in cases of mistaken payment there is no such principle in operation, and in such cases the law is that if a person pays money to another under a mistake of fact which causes him to make the payment he is *prima facie* entitled to recover it unless that other has a good defence. The result of a mistake which cannot be reversed is to constitute a gift of property.

Claims for restitution of money

The form of action for the return of money paid under a mistake is usually an action for money had and received, and there is little doubt that the action for the return of money paid by mistake is a restitutionary action which arises as a result of an unjust enrichment of the receiver at the expense of the transferor at the expense of the transferee[3]. However mere injustice does not of itself give rise to legal remedies.

The circumstances in which money paid by mistake may be recovered were set out in *Barclays Bank Ltd v WJ Simms, Son & Cooke (Southern) Ltd*[4] as that:

> ... if a person pays money to another under a mistake of fact which causes him to make the payment he is prima facie entitled to recover it as money paid under a

---

[1] See Goff & Jones, *The Law of Restitution*, 4th edn (Sweet & Maxwell, 1993), pp 107–228 for a very detailed treatment of this subject.
[2] Goff & Jones *above*, p 110; Palmer, *Mistake and Unjust Enrichment* (1962), pp 8, 25.
[3] *Kiriri Cotton Co v Dewani* [1960] AC 192; *Fibrosa Spolka Akcyjna v Fairbairn Lawson Combe Barbour* [1943] AC 32.
[4] [1980] QB 677.

mistake of fact. His claim may however fail if (a) the payer intends that the payee shall have the money at all events, whether the fact be true or false, or is deemed in law so to intend; or (b) the payment is made for good consideration, in particular if the money is paid to discharge, and does discharge, a debt owed to the payee ... or (c) the payee has changed his position in good faith, or is deemed in law to have done so.

Requirement for mistake to be mistake of fact

In order to be recoverable the payment must ordinarily have been made as a result of a mistake of fact or, where it has been made as a result of mistakes of both law and fact, the dominant mistake must be one of fact[5]. There has been substantial criticism of the rule that a payment may only be recovered where it is made under a mistake of fact and not of law[6] (the obvious mistake of law being that one is indebted in the first place[7]), and the Law Commission has recommended its abolition[8]. Mistakes which have been held to be mistakes of law include mistaken interpretations of a covenant to pay money as well as mistaken interpretations of Tax Acts[9]. However, in most cases payments are made because of a congeries of facts which give rise to the belief that there is an obligation to pay, and it is on those facts that the mistake will arise. Indeed in practice recovery on the grounds of mistake of law has only been denied to those who paid solely upon the strength of a representation to the effect that they were legally obliged to do so. It is therefore probably safe to say that the large majority of mistaken payments are made because of a mistake relating to the facts motivating the transfer rather than the law relating to it. In the context of banking note that payment on a forged cheque[10], payment contrary to a stop instruction[11] and payment to a person other than the named payee[12] are all payments made as a result of a mistake of fact and can therefore be recovered.

There is an important exception to the rule that mistake of law will not found an action for recovery of property, and that is where the mistake relates to property rights in the very property transferred. The authority for this is *Cooper v Phibbs*[13], in which a person agreed to take a lease of a fishery from

---

[5] *Trigge v Lavallee* (1863) 15 Moo PCC 270; *Home & Colonial Insurance Co Ltd v London Guarantee and Accident Co Ltd* (1928) 45 TLR 134.

[6] *Woolwich Building Society v Commissioners of Inland Revenue* [1993] AC 70. The High Court of Australia has permitted money to be recovered after a payment based upon a mistake of law (*David Securities Pty Ltd v Commonwealth Bank of Australia* (1990) 175 CLR 353); also the rule restricting recovery to mistakes of law is not a part of the law of Scotland (*Morgan Guaranty Trust Co of NY v Lothian Regional DC* [1995] SLT 299). There are some circumstances in which such a mistaken payment may be recovered at English law (see Goff & Jones at fn 1 *above*, passim).

[7] *Re Hatch* [1919] 1 Ch 351.

[8] *Mistakes of Law and Ultra Vires Public Authority Receipt and Payment*, Law Com No 227.

[9] *Whiteley Ltd v R* (1909) 26 TLR 19.

[10] *National Westminster Bank v Barclays Bank International Ltd* [1975] QB 654.

[11] *Barclays Bank Ltd v W J Simms, Son & Cooke (Southern) Ltd* [1980] QB 677.

[12] *Kleinwort Sons & Co v Dunlop Rubber Co* (1907) 97 LT 263.

[13] (1867) LR 2 HL 149.

another in circumstances where, unbeknownst to him, he already owned it. Lord Westbury held that rights of ownership are matters of fact rather than matters of law, and therefore a mistake of title was sufficient to ground a right to recover property.

The nature of the mistake required to found a restitutionary action for the recovery of money paid by mistake is probably different from the mistake required to avoid a contract[14]. Mistakes over creditworthiness and arithmetic have been sufficient to ground restitutionary actions[15], where such mistakes would not have been sufficient to avoid a contract.

The mistake must have been the sole or primary cause of the payment, and the mistake must be the payer's mistake. It is not necessary that the mistake be mutual—a payment is recoverable where the payee knows of the mistake and either deliberately conceals it from the payer or does not know of the payer's mistaken belief[16]. However, where the payee can show that the payer would not have appreciated the materiality of the fact, or would have paid in any event, then the payer will not recover[17].

Where one person pays out as agent for another, an agent's mistake is sufficient to invalidate the transaction[18]. There is some authority for the proposition that the mistake must be between the payer and the payee—thus, for example, where a bank pays money out under the misimpression that it has sufficient funds in its client account, it has been held that this mistake does not invalidate the transfer since it is not a mistake 'between the payer and the payee'. It is doubted whether this is still good law[19].

A person who pays out money whilst himself in possession of the information necessary to discover his mistake is undoubtedly negligent. However, he is not necessarily thereby debarred from recovering the payment. Neither is he estopped from denying the incorrectness of the payment[20].

It has been suggested that it is never possible to recover a mistaken payment made on a bill of exchange. This is too strong, but it is certainly true that there are authorities to the effect that a payment made by mistake in respect of a bill of exchange is harder to recover than a payment made on an ordinary mistake[21].

---

[14] *Chitty on Contracts*, 27th edn, para 29-019; *Midland Bank plc v Brown Shipley & Co* [1991] 2 All ER 690.

[15] *Kerrison v Glyn, Mills, Currie & Co* (1911) 81 LJKB 465; *Weld-Blundell v Synott* [1940] 2 KB 107.

[16] *Westminster Bank Ltd v Arlington Overseas Trading Co* [1952] 1 Lloyd's Rep 211.

[17] *Home & Colinial Insurance Co v Ltd v London Guarantee and Accident Co Ltd* (1928) 45 TLR 134.

[18] *Lloyds Bank Ltd v The Hon Cecily K Brooks* (1950) 6 Legal Decisions Affecting Bankers 161 at 164.

[19] *Paget's Law of Banking*, 11th edn, pp 360–1; *Barclays Bank Ltd v W J Simms, Son & Cooke (Southern) Ltd* [1980] QB 677.

[20] *Kelly v Solari* (1841) 9 M & W 54 at 59, approved by the House of Lords in *R E Jones v Waring & Gillow Ltd* [1926] AC 670.

[21] *Price v Neal* (1762) 3 Burr 1354 and *Smith v Mercer* (1815) 6 Taunt 76 are said to be authorities for the proposition that a payment negligently made may not be recovered. See *Cocks v Masterman* (1829) 9 B & C 902 for the propositon that a payment may not be recovered if the payee may have suffered detriment. Neither principle is unassailable.

Defences to claim for recovery based upon mistake

The primary defence which is available to a claim to recover money paid by mistake is a defence of change of position. Mere spending of money must be distinguished from change of position[22], and what must be shown is that the defendant has done some act which he would not otherwise have done in reliance upon the receipt. This defence was formerly regarded as a species of estoppel operating against the payer[23], but after the House of Lords' decision in *Lipkin Gorman v Karpnale*[24] it is better regarded as a separate defence[25]. In particular, in *RBC Dominion Securities Inc v Dawson* (1994) 111 DLR (4th) 230 the court indicated that it was prepared to anatomise the previous authorities where they led to the application of the principles of estoppel—which constitute a complete defence to the entire claim—in circumstance in which it appeared that the true defence of change of position would operate only *pro tanto*. In the light of the decision in *Boscawen v Bajwa*[26] decision it is hard to believe that English law will not also develop in this way.

A payment may also be upheld, even if mistaken, if it is given for good consideration, or as it is put in *Chitty*[27], 'Money paid in discharge of a genuine legal obligation cannot be recovered merely because the payer was induced to fulfil his legal obligation by a mistake of fact'.

Where money is transferred as a result of a mistake, the transferor enjoys no right of property in the money after the transfer, as the legal title passes upon the transfer, and a mistaken payment does not give rise to an equitable interest in the funds paid. To some extent this is a manifestation of the principle enunciated in *Re Bond Worth*[28] that one cannot grant away a legal estate whilst retaining an equitable estate. However, the argument was formerly employed that the transferee was, by the transfer, constituted a fiduciary, with the result that the funds could be traced into his hands. This view was based on the decision in *Chase Manhattan Bank NA v Israeli-British Bank (London) Ltd*[29], which has now been overturned by the House of Lords in *Westdeutsche Landesbank Girozentrale v Islington LBC*[30]. Lord Browne-Wilkinson pointed to the absurdity of a person's conscience being affected by a fact of which he was unaware, and clearly rejected the idea that a mere transferee might by virtue of the transfer become liable to repay. Note, however, that this finding would not necessarily have reversed the actual decision in *Chase Manhattan*. In that case, the bank made two identical payments in quick succession where

---

[22] *Larner v LCC* [1949] 2 KB 683.

[23] See eg *Lloyds Bank Ltd v The Hon Cecily K Brooks* (1950) 6 Legal Decisions Affecting Bankers 161.

[24] [1991] 2 AC 548.

[25] In *Boscawen v Bajwa* [1995] 4 All ER 796 it was said that the cases which constituted authority for an estoppel should be revised where basic principles appear to have been distorted in order to avoid injustice.

[26] [1995] 4 All ER 796.

[27] *Chitty on Contracts*, 27th edn (Sweet & Maxwell, 1994), para 29-022.

[28] [1980] Ch 228.

[29] [1981] Ch 105.

[30] [1996] 2 All ER 961.

only one was intended. It seems likely that the receipt of a second identical payment in such a case might have been sufficient to put the recipient on enquiry, and, if the facts warranted it, to constitute him a fiduciary. However, the idea that he is rendered a fiduciary by mere transfer was rightly rejected as unacceptable.

Claims for restitution of property other than money

Restitution of property delivered pursuant to a mistake of fact may be given in the same way as restitution for money paid[31]. The cases are usually framed as cases in rectification of deeds, in that a voluntary transfer of goods created as a result of a mistake takes effect as a bailment[32]. Where a person executes a deed disposing of property, the relief sought is often in the form of rectification. However where the deed itself effects the disposal, rectification of the deed has the necessary consequence of reversing the disposal and revesting the property in the donor, and in many respects this is a distinction without a difference. Where services are rendered pursuant to a mistake a claim for *quantum meruit* will arise[33], and where improvements to land or chattels are made as a result of a mistake an equitable proprietary estoppel will arise[34].

---

[31] *Gibbon v Mitchell* [1990] 1 WLR 1304; *Lady Hood of Avalon v MacKinnon* [1909] Ch 476; *Re Butlin's ST* [1976] 1 Ch 251.

[32] *Folkes v King* [1923] 1 KB 282; *Pearson v Rose & Young Ltd* [1951] 1 KB 275. It seems from these decisions that the effect of the mistake is to vitiate the transfer of title completely.

[33] *British Steel Corp v Cleveland Bridge & Engineering Co Ltd* [1984] 1 All ER 504.

[34] *See* p 92 *below*.

Section 4

Transfers of Title

Contents

Chapter 12

Proprietary Aspects of the Sale of Goods

The law of sale was radically simplified in the UK by the Sale of Goods Act 1893, now re-enacted with amendments as the Sale of Goods Act 1979, which provides a complete code governing all contracts for the sale of goods. There is authority for the proposition that the code is intended to be exclusive, and relevant common law rules are displaced by it[1]. However this propositon should be approached with caution. Section 62(2) of the Act provides that:

> The rules of the common law, including the law merchant, except in so far as they are inconsistent with the provisions of this Act, and in particular the rules relating to the law of principal and agent and the effect of fraud, misrepresentation, duress or coercion, mistake, or other invalidating cause, apply to contracts for the sale of goods.

In addition to this general provision there are specific provisions in individual sections of the Act that relevant sections are not intended to exclude the operation of common law doctrines[2]. In any event equitable obligations will arise in respect of any contract which may be required to be specifically performed.

The Hague Convention on the International Sales of Goods was introduced into English law by the Uniform Law on International Sales Act 1967, but applies only where it is selected by the parties. The Convention does not contain provisions relating to the passing of title to goods and deals only with the obligations of seller and buyer. Many of the countries which signed the Convention have denounced it in favour of the UNCITRAL Convention signed in Vienna in 1980. If the United Kingdom accedes to the Convention (which seems most unlikely, since it contains a sizeable admixture of civil law concepts) it will apply automatically to contracts of sale unless formally excluded. However Art 4(*b*) of the Vienna Convention specifically excludes matters relating to the passing of title to goods from its scope[3].

Scope of the Sale of Goods Act

The Act applies only to transactions which can properly be described as 'sales of goods'; in respect of all other transactions, the common law rules apply. It

---

[1] *Transport and General Credit Corp v Morgan* [1939] Ch 531.
[2] Eg s 20(3), which preserves the common law rules of bailment in respect of delivered goods; s 21(1), which preserves the common law power of sale.
[3] Although it does govern the passing of risk.

is therefore important to be able to distinguish to which transactions the Act applies.

The Act applies to contracts by which 'the seller transfers or agrees to transfer the property in goods to the buyer for a money consideration, called the price'[4]. Thus there are two criteria which must be satisfied. First, the transaction must be a 'sale', and secondly, the subject-matter of the transaction must be 'goods'.

Sale

The following transactions require special consideration, since although they have some of the characteristics of a sale they fall outside the annuity of the Sale of Goods Act.

(1) *Gifts[5], including promotional 'free offers'* In this context 'gift' includes anything transferred under a non-financial obligation; the provision of medicines by the National Health Service is outside the Act[6].

(2) *Exchange or barter transactions, in which goods are exchanged for other goods[7]* Part-exchange transactions are probably sales of goods for this purpose[8], but barter transactions are not.

(3) *Contracts for work and materials* A contract for service is clearly outside the Sale of Goods Act. However, where the contract involves the supply of a thing along with a service to be performed (for example the supply of building materials along with an obligation to build) for questions arising over whether the contract constitutes a contract of sale of goods, the test is that if the primary obligation under the contract is to exercise skill and labour, and any obligation to transfer title to the goods involved is ancillary to that main purpose, the contract is not a contract of sale of goods[9]. Such contracts are governed under implied terms by the Sale of Goods and Services Act 1982, but the rules relating to passing of title to the property encompassed in such transactions are those of the common law and not those of the Act.

(4) *Hire and hire-purchase* A contract of hire is outside the Sale of Goods Act, although it is caught by the Sale of Goods and Services Act 1982[10]. The hire-purchase contract was invented specifically to be outside the Sale of Goods Act, and in particular the provision that the buyer in possession can pass good title before he has paid the price[11] and the

[4] Sale of Goods Act 1979, s 2(1).
[5] *Chappell & Co v Nestlé Co Ltd* [1960] AC 87.
[6] *Pfizer Corp'n v Ministry of Health* [1965] AC 512.
[7] *Harrison v Luke* (1845) 14 M & W 139; *Simpson v Connolly* [1953] 1 WLR 911.
[8] Either because there are reciprocal sales with set-off of payment obligations (*Sheldon v Cox* (1824) 3 B & C 420), or because the buyer has the option of satisfying his payment obligation by delivering goods instead (*G J Dawson (Clapham) Ltd v H & G Dutfield* [1936] 2 All ER 232).
[9] *Robinson v Graves* [1935] 1 KB 579, in which a contract to paint and deliver a portrait was held not to be a contract for the sale of goods.
[10] Section 7.
[11] Although this provision was promptly recreated by Pt III of the Hire-Purchase Act 1964 in relation to motor vehicles (re-enacted by Consumer Credit Act 1974, Sched 4, para 22).

supplier's warranties as to quality[12]. Conditional sale agreements, whereby the purchaser pays the price by instalments but title remains vested in the seller until the last payment, are within the Act.

(5) *Mortgages* A mortgage of goods may be characterised as a sale with a provision for resale, but despite this the transfer which creates a mortgage is excluded from the Act by s 62(3). A pledge, by contrast, is not created by a contract of sale since the pledgor retains the general property in the goods.

Goods

Goods are defined as 'all personal chattels other than things in action and money[13] ... and in particular includes emblements[14], industrial growing crops, and things attached to or forming part of the land which are agreed to be severed before sale or under the contract of sale ... and includes an undivided share in goods'[15]. The term therefore excludes land, including leaseholds, but includes all chattels having physical existence[16]. Although choses in action are excluded, a part share in goods is goods for some purposes[17]. (The position for intangible things other than choses in action is unclear—there is some authority that the sale of computer software constitutes the sale of goods[18].

Passing of property under Sale of Goods Act

The key to understanding the proprietary elements of the Sale of Goods legislation is the idea of the passing of property. Before the property has passed, the buyer has nothing but a claim against the seller, either for the return of the price or, if the price has not been paid, for breach of the contract. After the property has passed the buyer has a property claim and is in effect secured. Thus prior to the property passing the buyer is bearing the risk of the seller's insolvency. If the property passes before the buyer has paid the price then the seller is bearing the risk of the buyer's insolvency until payment, but this tends to be a lesser risk since modern sales documentation traditionally embodies retention of title language to the effect that even if there is delivery before payment, title can remain vested in the seller until payment in full not only of the price of those goods, but also of the price of any other goods unpaid for[19].

---

[12] Reimposed as the Supply of Goods (Implied Terms) Act 1973.
[13] Although a coin bought as a curiosity is 'goods' for this purpose (*Moss v Hancock* [1899] 2 QB 111).
[14] It is a rule of law that where a tenant for life of an estate sows and cultivates crops on the estate, if the tenancy determines before those crops are harvested, the tenant's estate continues to own the crops. Such crops are known as emblements.
[15] Sale of Goods Act 1979, s 61(2).
[16] Including ships (*Behnke v Bede Shipping Co* [1927] 1 KB 649).
[17] Ie between part-owners (s 2(2); *Nicol v Hennessey* (1896) 1 Com Cas 410)
[18] *St Albans City and District Council v International Computers Ltd* [1995] FSR 686; and see *Toby Constructions Products Pty Ltd v Computa Bar (Sales) Pty Ltd* [1983] 2 NSWLR 48.
[19] *Aluminium Industrie Vaassen BV v Romalpa Aluminium Ltd* [1976] 1 WLR 676.

The primary rule on the passing of property is that 'property is transferred at such time as the parties intend it to pass'. Since the parties do not always specify exactly when property is to pass, s 18 then provides a series of 'rules' (in fact presumptions) which are to be applied to determine when the property did in fact pass; subject to s 17(2) which provides that for 'the purpose of ascertaining the intention of the parties regard shall be had to the terms of the contract, the conduct of the parties, and the circumstances of the case', these are as follows.

Rule 1   Unconditional sale of specific goods

Where the contract is for the sale of specific goods, property passes when the contract is made, whether payment and delivery are contemporaneous or subsequent. Since a contract is made where there is a *consensus ad idem*, and since subsequent documentation is ineffective to disturb existing property rights, it follows from this rule that where there is an unconditional agreement to sell goods and a document is subsequently signed retaining property in the goods to the seller until payment, that document is ineffective as property has already passed at the time of the contract[20].

Rule 2   Sale of goods requiring further work

Where there is a sale of goods in relation to which something further needs to be done for the purpose of putting them into a deliverable state, property passes when the further work is completed and the buyer has notice that it has been done

Rule 3   Sale of goods which seller is bound to weigh, test or measure

This does not apply where the seller has a mere right to weigh, measure etc, or is obliged to do so only to satisfy the buyer that the goods correspond with the delivery obligation[21], but only where the weighing or measuring is in some way essential to the delivery. This must be rare.

Rule 4   Sale or return

Where goods are sold on a sale or return basis, property passes to the buyer only when
- (a)   the buyer does an act accepting the property, such as reselling it or pledging it with a pawnbroker[22], or
- (b)   the buyer retains the goods past the return date or, if there is no return date, for longer than 'a reasonable time'.

---

[20] *Dennant v Skinner and Collom* [1948] 2 KB 164.
[21] *Nanka-Bruce v Commonwealth Trust Ltd* [1926] AC 77.
[22] *Kirkham v Attenborough* [1897] 1 QB 291.

Rule 5   Unascertained or future goods

Rule 5 is divided into sub-rules. Sub-rule (1) provides that where there is an enforceable agreement to sell (ie where the goods which are the subject of the transaction are not specific goods in the hands of the seller at the time of the contract), that property passes where goods which satisfy the relevant description are unconditionally appropriated to the contract 'either by the seller with the assent of the buyer, or by the buyer with the assent of the seller'. Assent may be either express or implied from conduct[23]. The question of whether an appropriation is unconditional is of some difficulty, since even where goods are separated out the seller may reserve the right to change goods between unfilled orders. Thus in practice it is very hard to show that a seller has unconditionally appropriated goods to a specific contract whilst they remain in his hands.

Sub-rule (2) provides that goods are appropriated for this purpose where they are delivered to a carrier or bailee for the buyer, or to the buyer himself. Note that where goods are delivered to a carrier unsegregated then property does not pass—thus if I have a lorry loaded with two tonnes of wheat with the intention of delivering two one-tonne loads to two different customers, property will not pass upon delivery to the carrier[24].

Sub-rule (3) is dealt with at p 110 below.

Unlike s 16, the s 18 rules can be bypassed by contrary arrangement. This point usually arises in the context of sales of unfinished goods, where the parties agree that property will pass whilst the goods are on the seller's premises and work is being done to them. In *Re Blyth Shipbuilding and Dry Docks Co*[25] it was held that such a clause was valid to pass property in a half-complete ship to the buyer[26]. However, such a clause will only be effective to transfer property in individual items when they have been affixed or in a reasonable sense made part of the thing which is eventually to be sold[27].

Transactions in mixed goods

It is clear that if I agree to sell you a single item which I currently own, then there is a valid sale of what are called in the Act 'specific goods'. If, prior to the conclusion of such a contract the goods are destroyed, then my liability under the contract ceases[28], and if, unbeknownst to me, the item had been destroyed prior to the conclusion of the contract, the contract is also void. Further, under the provisions of s 18, rule 1, *prima facie* property in the item passes to you upon the making of the contract.

---

[23] *Pignataro v Gilroy* [1919] 1 KB 459.
[24] *Healey v Howlett & Sons* [1917] 1 KB 337.
[25] [1926] Ch 494.
[26] However, clear words are required to get to such an arrangement, which will not be lightly implied (*Sir James Laing & Sons v Barclay Curle & Co* [1908] AC 35).
[27] *Seath & Co v Moore* (1887) 11 App Cas 305 at 318.
[28] Sale of Goods Act 1979, s 7.

What if I contract to sell you a single identifiable item which I do not yet own (known as 'future goods'[29])? Although such a contract might be characterised as a grant of an intangible right and therefore outside the Act, the correct answer is that the contract takes effect as an agreement to sell goods[30]. Agreements to sell are 'sales of goods' within the meaning of the Act, and the Act will therefore apply if the goods, when received, would constitute 'goods'. By s 18, rule 5(1), property in the item will pass to you as soon as I receive it.

Sale of goods forming part of a bulk

The position is harder when I contract to sell you goods which are at the time of the contract of sale mixed with other goods belonging to other people. As we have seen, where my goods are mixed with the goods of others, what I own is an interest in the mixture rather than the goods themselves. Thus, if I contract to sell the goods to you, I can contract in one of two ways: either to convey to you immediately my share of the total bulk, or to convey to you a fixed amount of goods to which I do not yet have title. The second is a sale of future goods[31], under the ordinary rules. The first is a sale of a share in a mixture. Both are simple concepts, but there is a difficulty in distinguishing between them—specifically, is a contract to sell 500 of the 1,000 tonnes which compose the cargo of the SS Peerless a contract for the sale of a half-share in the cargo or a contract for the sale of 500 tonnes of unspecified grain?

Section 16 of the Act prevents any property passing until such time as the relevant property is 'ascertained'—ie identified, extracted from the bulk and appropriated to the contract. This section cannot be excluded by contract, and it therefore follows that where I sell a bulk which I own to several buyers, those buyers will have to bear the risk of my insolvency until such time as the property is ascertained, and this will be true even if I have bound myself to deliver goods exclusively from that mixture and no other[32]. The operation of the new ss 20A and 20B as inserted by the Sale of Goods (Amendment) Act 1995 is to vary to some extent the rule embodied in s 16.

Section 20A provides that where there is a sale of a goods out of an identified bulk[33], property in an undivided share in the bulk is transferred to the buyer as soon as the buyer pays the price. It follows from this that it is up to the buyer to require that the property is separated out and attributed to the contract.

The difficulty which this creates is that which arises where dealings in shares of a bulk turn out to have been conducted upon the basis of a misunder-

[29] Section 61(1).
[30] Section 5(3).
[31] *Re Wait* [1927] 1 Ch 606.
[32] *H R & S Sainsbury Ltd v Street* [1972] 1 WLR 834.
[33] Defined as 'a mass or collection of goods of the same kind which is contained in a defined space or area; and is such that any goods in the bulk are interchangeable with any other goods therein of the same number or quality' (s 61(2), added by the Sale of Goods (Amendment) Act 1995).

standing over the bulk's volume. If I sell you my half-share in a bulk which I believe to be 100 tonnes of wheat, what happens where the bulk turns out to be only 97 tonnes? The difficulty here is that this fact will only come to light when the last appropriation is made; and consequently if the other co-owner has removed his 50 tonnes, leaving me with 47, I must recover my 1.5 tonnes from him. If there are several other co-owners this rapidly becomes difficult, and it ceases to be difficult and become impossible if goods have been added to the bulk subsequent to my acquisition of the share.

Section 20B provides for this possibility by providing that a person who acquires a share of a bulk in this way is deemed to consent to all transactions with or by other co-owners. Thus in the circumstances identified above, the last deliveree of goods (ie usually the person who finds out that the bulk is short) is prevented from bringing any action against any of the persons who received delivery against their shares. As a consolation prize, he acquires property in the remaining goods as soon as the penultimate withdrawal is complete (rule 5(3)). Where the co-owners discover that the bulk is short whilst there is still a number of joint interests in it, the amounts of the joint interests are reduced *pro tanto*[34].

Passing of risk

The Sale of Goods Act permits the transfer of risk separately from the transfer of property. In principle risk passes with property, such that the ordinary rules of property law apply[35]. However by agreement of the parties risk may pass at some time other than the time of passing of the property. What this means is that either the buyer or the seller can act as insurer of the goods for some part of the transaction whilst property vests in the other. Where the seller retains the risk after property has passed he is in effect guaranteeing to the buyer that the goods will not deteriorate in transit, and where the buyer accepts the risk before the property has passed, he is in effect acting as the seller's insurer of the goods.

The time at which risk passes is assessed in relation to the agreement between the parties[36], the parties' conduct and trade usage[37]. Risk may pass in unascertained goods, and this is very useful in transactions in undivided parts of a larger bulk[38]. The time of passing of risk is established by custom in respect of overseas sales. Where goods are sold on a c.i.f. basis the risk passes to the buyer on shipment, although he does not acquire property in the goods until payment, and likewise, in an f.o.b. contract the risk passes on shipment.

---

[34] Sale of Goods Act 1979, s 20A(4).
[35] Section 20(1).
[36] *Castle v Playford* (1872) LR 7 Ex 98.
[37] *Bevington v Dale* (1902) 7 Com Cas 112.
[38] *Sterns Ltd v Vickers Ltd* [1923] 1 KB 78.

Chapter 13

Retention of Title

The Sale of Goods Act 1979, s 19(1) provides that the seller may reserve the right of disposal of the goods until certain conditions are fulfilled, and in such a case, notwithstanding delivery of the goods to the buyer, the property in the goods does not pass to the buyer until the condition is satisfied. The condition referred to is almost invariably the payment of the price. Section 19(2) deems that there is such a reservation of title in a case where goods are shipped by the seller and the bill is made out to the seller rather than to the buyer.

The right described in s 19 is the basis for the standard retention of title clause, which provides that title to the goods delivered does not pass to the buyer until the buyer has paid the price to the seller. These clauses are known as 'Romalpa' clauses, after the decision in *Aluminium Industrie Vaassen BV v Romalpa Aluminium Ltd*[1] which established the effectiveness of such clauses. Where it is only equitable ownership which is retained, the effect of such a clause is to create a charge which will be void if not registered because, since it is not possible to grant away a legal interest whilst retaining an equitable interest, the operation of the clause must be to vest the complete title in the goods in the buyer subject to a grant back of an equitable interest to the seller[2]. However, an absolute retention of title does not suffer from this defect—since the buyer never acquires any property in the goods, he cannot be said to have granted a charge over them[3]. Likewise, the seller's right to recover the goods on the buyer's insolvency is a right to retake possession of his own goods, and not a right granted to him by the buyer[4].

Section 19 provides no limits to the conditions which may be specified. There is therefore no reason why title to an item should not be retained until the whole invoice upon which the item was supplied is paid[5], or indeed all indebtedness owing to the seller by the buyer is paid[6].

Where goods are supplied on Romalpa terms it seems that the buyer is the bailee of the seller in respect of the goods[7]. As with any other bailee, *prima facie* if he disposes of the goods of which he is a bailee he is liable to his

---

[1] [1976] 1 WLR 676.
[2] *Re Bond Worth* [1980] Ch 228, in which Slade J came as near as he decently could at first instance to holding that *Romalpa* had been wrongly decided by the Court of Appeal.
[3] *Clough Mill Ltd v Martin* [1985] 1 WLR 111.
[4] *McEntire v Crossley Bros* [1895] AC 457.
[5] *Re Peachdart Ltd* [1984] Ch 131.
[6] *Armour v Thyssen Edelstahlwerke AG* [1991] 2 AC 339. Their Lordships speculated on, but did not decide, the issues which would arise if the seller sought to repossess all the goods delivered to the buyer if the buyer had paid some but not all of the relevant outstanding invoices.

bailor in conversion, and this can be extremely difficult in the context of goods held as commercial stock. It is therefore conventional that a modern retention of title clause gives the buyer the right to deal with or to sell the goods[8].

Dealing with the goods

In *Borden (UK) Ltd v Scottish Timber Products Ltd*[9] it was held that where a buyer dealt with goods before he obtained title to them, the ordinary rule of wrongful mixing would apply. In that case the product supplied was resin which was applied in the manufacture of chipboard. This gave rise to a *confusio* followed by a *specificatio*, as a result of which the seller's title to the resin was completely extinguished[10]. In *Clough Mills v Martin* Goff LJ reasserted the rule of specification that 'the property in new goods will generally vest in [the maker], at least where the goods are not reducible to the original materials'[11]. In *Hendy Lennox (Industrial Engines) Ltd v Grahame Puttick Ltd*[12] an engine which had been incorporated into a larger machine, but which could be removed with two hours' work, was not sufficiently mixed to constitute a confusion and the title of the seller endured.

It is not uncommon to find retention of title clauses which seek to extend the seller's ownership into products made using the goods sold. However it seems clear that the only way in which such an interest could arise is by a grant by the buyer. The proprietary analysis of the *specificatio* involved in any substantial reworking of goods is that the seller's right is extinguished, and any right which the seller acquires in the new thing must be acquired by grant. Such a grant would require registration as a company charge, and would be invalid in the absence of registration[13]. However, where the process involved a simple mixing without further work, it seems very likely that the correct proprietary analysis of the mixing is a *confusio*, in which case it is highly arguable that the seller becomes a co-owner of the mixture by operation of law.

Where the subject-matter is building materials, note that the directional rule *quicquid plantatur solo, solo cedit*, which applies in the case of specificatio involving land, deprives the applier of title as soon as the fixture is complete.

---

[7] *Aluminium Industrie Vaassen BV v Romalpa Aluminium Ltd* [1976] 1 WLR 676. Dicta to the contrary in *Borden (UK) v Scottish Timber Products Ltd* [1981] Ch 25 and *E Pfeiffer Weinkellerei-Weineinkauf GmbH & Co v Arbuthnot Factors Ltd* [1988] 1 WLR 150 criticised in McCormack, *Reservation of Title*, 2nd edn, p 84.

[8] Although it is arguable that the effect of s 21(1) of the Act is sufficient to create an immunity from suit on conversion by the seller (McCormack *above*, p 205.

[9] [1981] Ch 2; see also *Highway Foods International (in administrative receivership)* [1995] BCLC 2095.

[10] Eg *Re Peachdart Ltd* [1984] Ch 131 (leather used to make handbags); *Modelboard Ltd v Outer Box Ltd* [1993] BCLC 623 (cardboard made into boxes); *Ian Chisholm Textiles v Griffiths* [1994] BCLC 96 (cloth made into garments).

[11] [1985] 1 WLR 111 at 119.

[12] [1984] 1 WLR 485.

[13] *Re Peachdart Ltd* [1984] Ch 131, although there are dicta to the contrary in *Clough Mills v Martin* [1985] 1 WLR 111 at 119, 124.

Dealing with proceeds of sale of goods

A disposal by a bailee of goods which he holds does not give the bailor any proprietary interest in the proceeds of sale[14]. The bailor will of course have a personal action in damages in conversion, but since he already has a money claim for the price, and cannot recover twice in respect of the same loss, this will be of no value whatsoever in an insolvency of the buyer. Determined attempts have therefore been made to extend the proprietary effect of the Romapla clause to the proceeds of sale of the goods. This is effected by erecting a fiduciary duty owed by the buyer to the seller in respect of the goods, or possibly a full-blown trust of the proceeds of sale—in both cases with the aim of enabling the seller to trace into the proceeds of sale.

This is a difficult exercise. Where a person receives money in respect of a transaction entered into on behalf of another, he is not bound to segregate that money, and is a mere debtor[15], unless he has assumed an express function as trustee. Such a function could be demonstrated if the requirement were to maintain such proceeds in a segregated account. However, the difficulty arises that the proceeds will be held as security for the repayment of the debt under an arrangement which appears to fall within both the facts of *Swiss Bank Corp'n v Lloyds Bank Ltd*[16], and the dictum of Slade LJ in *Re Bond Worth* to the effect that '... any contract which by way of security for the payment of a debt, confers an interest in property defeasible or destructible upon payment of such debt, or appropriates such property for the discharge of the debt, must necessarily be regarded as creating a mortgage or charge, as the case may be'[17]. If the agreement were to be held to create a charge, such charge would be void for want of registration.

Romalpa clauses against individuals

The foregoing discussion has been on the basis of the assumption that the buyer is a company. If the buyer is an individual there is, of course, no requirement to register any security created with the Registrar of Companies. However, there are other issues which arise. The most important is the Bills of Sale Acts[18]. A retention of title provision does not require registration as a security bill of sale[19], but it seems likely that any attempt to extend the effect of the clause beyond a mere retention of title would be ineffective since it would require registration[20].

[14] A bailor is not *per se* a fiduciary of his bailee (*Kirkham v Peel* (1880) 43 L.T. 171; *Re Coomber* [1911] 1 Ch 723).

[15] *Foley v Hill* (1848) 2 HLC 28, and see *Neste Oy v Lloyds Bank plc* [1983] 2 Lloyd's Rep 658.

[16] *See* p 236 *below*.

[17] [1980] Ch 228 at 248.

[18] *See* Chapter 25 *below*.

[19] *McEntire v Crossley Bros* [1895] AC 457.

[20] *Chitty on Contracts*, 27th edn (Sweet & Maxwell, 1994), para 41-142.

Chapter 14

Transfer of Title by Non-Owners

At common law, no-one can give better title to a thing than he has himself—a principle usually summarised as *nemo dat quod non habet.* Thus where X has defective title to a thing, any purported transfer to Y will vest in Y no more than the title which X had. The rule applies generally and not just in the context of the sale of goods; however, it is embodied in s 21(1) of the Sale of Goods Act 1979, which provides that 'where goods are sold by a person who is not the owner, and who does not sell them under authority or with the consent of the owner, the buyer acquires no better title to the goods than the seller had'. The owner may recover his goods, either by self-help or by means of an order for delivery up[1], or may sue in conversion, an action to which a complete ignorance of the existence of the owner's right provides no defence[2].

As a principle this is potentially productive of great injustice. It is not generally possible to investigate title to goods in the same way as it is possible to investigate title to land, and it is therefore necessary to protect merchants in their transactions. However, goods cannot simply be made negotiable, since the effect of this would be to enable owners to be deprived of their title capriciously; put another way, title which can be extinguished at will by a third hand is no title.

The tension between these different objectives—the protection of commerce and the protection of title—was well described by Denning LJ in *Bishopsgate Motor Finance v Transport Brakes Ltd*[3], where he said[4]:

> In the development of our law, two principles have striven for mastery. The first is for the protection of property: no-one can give a better title than he himself possesses. The second is for the protection of commercial transactions: the person who takes in good faith and for value without notice should get a good title. The first principle has held sway for a long time, but it has been modified by the common law itself and by statute so as to meet the needs of our own times ...

The initial response to the commercial uncertainty created by the rule of *nemo dat* was the doctrine of market overt, by which good title could be obtained in markets conducted in an open fashion[5]. The other exceptions have developed over the years as commercial practice has developed from formal local mar-

---

[1] Torts (Interference with Goods) Act 1977.
[2] *Hollins v Fowler* (1875) LR 7 HL 757.
[3] [1949] 1 KB 322.
[4] At 336–7.
[5] Coke, 2 Inst 713; Bl Comm ii.

kets to global exchange of commodities. The exception for market overt has now been abolished completely[6], but the other relevant exceptions are set out below.

Estoppel

The doctrine of estoppel is expressly introduced into the sale of goods by s 21(1) of the Sale of Goods Act 1979. The rule is that where the true owner allows another to sell the goods, he is thereafter estopped from asserting his title thereto. This is an estoppel by representation, the representation being spelled out of his act or his silence.

Issues of estoppel tend to revolve around their particular facts, and little of general value can be said about them. However, it may be mentioned that simply delivering possession of goods to another is not sufficient to constitute an estoppel[7]. Equally, the owner is not deemed to have been the author of any representation made by the seller unless he in some way authorised or consented to the seller making the representation[8]. The representation must be clear and unambiguous[9], and may be implied from conduct[10]. Although an estoppel may be grounded upon negligence[11], a breach of an existing duty of care is necessary, and mere carelessness, such as failing to report a theft[12], is insufficient. Taken together these criteria form a very high barrier, and except in cases of deliberate fraud 'there are very few reported cases in which a plea of estoppel has in fact succeeded[13]'.

Disposition by mercantile agent

Section 2(1) of the Factors Act 1889 provides that:

> Where a mercantile agent is, with the consent of the owner, in possession of goods or of the documents of title to goods[14], any sale, pledge, or other disposition of the goods, made by him when acting in the ordinary course of business of a mercantile agent, shall, subject to the provisions of this act, be as valid as if he were expressly authorised by the owner of the goods to make the same; provided that the person taking under the disposition acts in good faith, and has not at the time of the disposition notice that the person making the disposition has not authority to make the same.

---

[6] Sale of Goods (Amendment) Act 1995.
[7] *Central Newbury Car Auctions v Unity Finance Ltd* [1957] 1 QB 371.
[8] *Pickard v Sears* (1837) 6 Ad & El 469.
[9] *Moorgate Mercantile Co v Twitchings* [1977] AC 890.
[10] *Eastern Distributors Ltd v Goldring* [1957] 2 QB 600 at 614.
[11] *Johnson v Crédit Lyonnais Co* (1877) 3 CPD 32; *Moorgate Mercantile Co v Twitchings* [1977] AC 890.
[12] *Debs v Sibec Developments Ltd* [1990] RTR 91.
[13] *Chitty on Contracts*, 27th edn (Sweet & Maxwell, 1994), para 41-153.
[14] The term 'document of title' has an artificial meaning in this statute, considered above at p 47.

A mercantile agent is defined as one having, in the course of his business as such agent, authority either to sell goods, or to consign goods for the purpose of sale, or to buy goods, or to raise money on the security of goods[15]. The question of who is a 'mercantile agent' has varied with the courts' attitude to the protection of title, since a substantial weakening of that protection can be achieved by a minor expansion of the definition of a mercantile agent. There does not appear to be any specific set of categories of mercantile agents[16], and the issue of whether any given person is a mercantile agent in respect of a particular type of goods appears to be a question to be decided on its individual facts. Number of clients is not a factor[17], although the fact that the person lives by trading seems to be[18]. The element of agency, however, is important: a person who is known to buy and sell on his own account is not ordinarily treated as a mercantile agent[19], and neither is a person who deals for others only on very few occasions[20]. A person is only a mercantile agent in a particular type of business; he may very well be a mercantile agent for cars, but not for furniture[21].

By s 1(2) of the Factors Act 1889, a person is in possession of goods or documents of title to goods where the goods or documents are in his actual custody or they are held by any other person on his behalf. The goods must be in the possession of the mercantile agent with the owner's consent; the owner may have given the goods to the mercantile agent for some other reason or in some other capacity than as mercantile agent, in which case the agent is a mere bailee[22]. This point usually arises in the case of garages. Many garages sell cars as mercantile agents, but a person who gives his car to a garage purely for the purposes of repair is not giving it to the garage as mercantile agent, and the garage therefore cannot give good title to it under s 2(2). However, if the car is given to the garage in order to get a price for it and is subsequently wrongfully sold, the sale is a sale as mercantile agent[23]. If the mercantile agent obtains the property by deception it is still in his possession with the owner's consent[24], but the position is otherwise if he obtains it by force[25].

The burden of proof over whether the defendant was a purchaser in good faith without notice seems to rest on him[26].

By s 2(4) of the Act the owner's consent is presumed unless the contrary can be shown.

---

[15] Factors Act 1889, s 1(1).
[16] *Weiner v Harris* [1910] 1 KB 285.
[17] *Lowther v Harris* [1927] 1 KB 393.
[18] *Weiner v Harris* [1910] 1 KB 285.
[19] *Belvoir Finance Co Ltd v Harold G Cole & Co Ltd* [1969] 1 WLR 1877.
[20] *Heap v Motorists Advisory Agency Ltd* [1923] 1 KB 577.
[21] *Newtons of Wembly Ltd v Williams* [1965] 1 QB 560; *Lloyds & Scottish Finance Ltd v Williamson* [1965] 1 WLR 404.
[22] *Staffs Motor Guarantee v British Wagon Co* [1934] 2 KB 305; *Pearson v Rose & Young Ltd* [1951] 1 KB 275; *Astley Industrial Trust Ltd v Miller* [1968] 2 All ER 36.
[23] *Pearson v Rose & Young Ltd* [1951] 1 KB 275.
[24] *Whitehorn Bros v Davison* [1911] 1 KB 463; *Folkes v King* [1923] 1 KB 282; *Ingram v Little* [1961] 1 QB 31.
[25] *Debs v Sibec Developments Ltd* [1990] RTR 91 (vehicle obtained at gunpoint).
[26] *Heap v Motorists Advisory Agency Ltd* [1923] 1 KB 577.

Disposition by seller in possession

Section 24 of the Sale of Goods Act provides that:

> Where a person having sold goods continues or is in possession of the goods, or of the documents of title to the goods, the delivery or transfer by that person, or by a mercantile agent acting for him, of the goods or documents of title under any sale, pledge, or other disposition thereof, to any person receiving the same in good faith and without notice of the previous sale, has the same effect as if the person making the delivery or sale were expressly authorised by the owner of the goods to make the same.

This provision applies whenever a seller continues in possession of the property sold. In *Pacific Motor Auctions Pty Ltd v Motor Credits (Hire Finance) Ltd*[27] it was held that all that was necessary for the section to take effect was continuity of possession in the hands of the seller, and the fact that the seller may be holding the goods on specific terms (eg as bailee) prohibiting the disposition of the goods was immaterial. The section applies to any disposition, not just a sale, and therefore presumably embraces declarations of trust and, possibly, gifts[28].

Disposition by buyer in possession

Section 25 of the Sale of Goods Act provides that:

> Where a person having bought or agreed to buy goods obtains, with the consent of the seller, possession of the goods or the documents of title to the goods, the delivery or transfer by that person, or by a mercantile agent acting for him, of the goods or documents of title under any sale, pledge, or other disposition thereof, to any person receiving the same in good faith and without notice of any lien or other right of the original seller in respect of the goods, has the same effect as if the person making the delivery or transfer were a mercantile agent in possession of the goods or documents of title to the goods with the consent of the owner.

It seems from the decision in *Newtons of Wembly Ltd v Williams*[29] that the significance of the words 'bought or agreed to buy' is that where a person agrees to buy property in such a way that the seller is entitled to avoid the contract, the fact of the agreement plus the delivery to the buyer means that the buyer is *ipso facto* brought within the ambit of this section, and a subsequent avoidance of the contract by the original seller is ineffective to prevent the buyer giving good title under this section. Note also that 'agreed to buy' is interpreted as meaning 'under a binding obligation'. In a hire-purchase con-

---

[27] [1965] AC 867, PC.
[28] *Kitto v Bilbie Hobson & Co* (1895) 72 LT 266; *Worcester Works Finance Ltd v Cooden Engineering Co Ltd* [1972] 1 QB 210.
[29] [1965] 1 QB 560.

tract the purchaser is not under an obligation to buy but has an option to buy, and therefore cannot pass good title under this section of the Act[30]; this is also true where goods have been supplied on a sale or return basis[31].

It is not at all clear why a disposition under s 25 is said to be 'as if the person ... was a mercantile agent' instead of the formula 'as if he were expressly authorised by the owner of the goods to make the same', which is used in s 24 and in the Factors Act itself. It is suggested that this has the effect of importing into the operation of s 25 a requirement to the effect that a person seeking to defend a sale under s 25 must show that the sale was in the ordinary course of business[32].

Delivery, in the context of a sale by a buyer in possession, may be constituted by constructive delivery. Thus where the seller of goods agrees to hold the goods as bailee for the buyer, if the buyer subsequently sells the goods, the subsequent purchaser acquires good title under this section[33].

Sale under common law or statutory powers

The primary example of a sale under a common law power is the pledgee's right to sell goods deilvered to him by way of pledge. Although the pledgee does not have a complete property in the goods, when he disposes of them under his power of sale he gives complete title to the purchaser. The same is true of a sale by a mortgagee in possession.

The majority of sales under this head are sales under statutory powers. These include the powers given to sheriffs to levy execution by seizure and sale of property[34], of liquidators of companies[35] and trustees in bankruptcy of individuals[36] and under many other provisions. The Sale of Goods Act gives the unpaid seller after property has passed to the buyer a similar right by s 48.

A final point should be made about sheriffs and writs of execution. A High Court writ of execution binds the property to which it relates from the moment of its issue[37], and therefore in theory binds all subsequent acquirers of the property. If the possessor sells property subject to a writ of execution before possession is taken to a person in good faith without notice of the writ's existence, a statutory exemption is available to the disposition such that the buyer takes free of the writ[38].

---

[30] *Helby v Matthews* [1895] AC 471; see now the provisions of Pt III of the Hire-Purchase Act 1964 in relation to the sale of motor cars on hire-purchase. Such a sale confers good title.

[31] *Edwards v Vaughan* (1910) 26 TLR 545.

[32] *Newtons of Wembly Ltd v Williams* [1965] 1 QB 560 at 579.

[33] *Gamers Motor Centre (Newcastle) Pty Ltd v Natwest Wholesale Australia Pty Ltd* (1987) 63 CLR 236; followed in *Forsyth International (UK) Ltd v Silver Shipping Co Ltd* [1993] 2 Lloyd's Rep 268.

[34] Supreme Court Act 1981, s 138B.

[35] Insolvency Act 1986, ss 165–7.

[36] Insolvency Act 1986, s 134.

[37] Supreme Court Act 1981, s 138.

[38] Supreme Court Act 1981, s 138(2).

Sale or pledge under voidable title

A person has a voidable title to goods where the original owner has been induced to part with title in such a way as to give him a right in equity to have the contract set aside. The most common circumstances in which such a right arises are cases where the contract of sale was induced by a misrepresentation or was entered into on the basis of a mutual mistake. However, note that where the contract was based on a fraudulently induced mistake of identity, then the mistake may eliminate the contract's whole substructure to render it void. The rules relating to sale by a person holding under a voidable title have no application in the case of a void contract.

Where a person holds goods with voidable title, then a sale or pledge of the goods passes good absolute title to the purchaser and extinguishes the original owner's right to re-assert his title to the property. The original owner is left with his action against the contractual counterparty, but may not proceed against the goods themselves.

A voidable contract becomes void when the person entitled to avoid it communicates the avoidance to the other party. Avoidance is alternatively complete when the party entitled to avoid the contract has taken every step which he can to announce his avoidance to the other party[39]. However, although valid communication of avoidance prevents a disposition of the property from taking effect at common law, the effect of the *Newtons of Wembly Ltd v Williams* decision[40] that the person in possession after the title has been avoided can still make a valid disposition under the sale by buyer in possession rule laid down in s 25 of the Sale of Goods Act.

Section 23 governs the position where a person with a voidable title sells goods, but there is an equivalent right in respect of pledge at common law[41].

---

[39] Proof of actual communication is not necessary (*Universal Car Finance v Caldwell* [1965] 1 QB 525).

[40] [1965] 1 QB 560.

[41] *Babcock v Lawson* (1880) 5 QBD 284; *Whitehorn Bros v Davison* [1911] 1 KB 463; *Phillips v Brooks* [1919] 2 KB 243.

Chapter 15

Assignment, Novation and Acknowledgement

At the heart of the law relating to intangible property is the concept of assignment. Assignment is a term which is occasionally misused to cover transfers of chattels, but here it is employed only in its technical sense of a transfer of a right in action.

Choses in action as property

Before the idea of transferability is brought into play, the idea that a right in action is a species of property is not helpful, as a right in action is not a piece of property as between the parties thereto—if A has a contractual right to sue B, it is redundant to say that, as between A and B, A has property in his right to sue B. The term 'property' in this sense means no more than a right which can be asserted against third parties. In the case of a contractual right there is no third party against whom the right can be or needs to be asserted—A can sue B in contract because he has a contract with B, or in tort because B has caused him injury. C, who neither has a contract with B nor has been injured by B, is prevented from intervening by the general law. It is only where issues of transferability arise that the question of whether it is helpful to regard legal rights as property arises.

Roy Goode[1] has correctly identified the fact that an assignment, whether by transfer of a negotiable instrument or in any other way, is distinguished by the fact that it extinguishes the assignor's right at the same time as it creates the assignee's right. It would be perfectly possible—and indeed easier—to have the debtor grant new rights to the assignee, and in such a case the analogy with property law would be open to question. The fact that the assignor under a valid assignment may not of his own volition sue the debtor, despite the previously existing rights between them, confirms that intangible assets are indeed property rights, and that a transfer of a chose in action is a disposition of property rather than a rearrangement of personal claims.

The special position of bills of exchange is mentioned below[2]. A bill of exchange is a bundle of rights embodied in a single document, and the fact that by the custom of merchants the transfer of the document created a trans-

---

[1] Goode, *Commercial Law*, 2nd edn (Penguin, 1995), pp 53–4.
[2] *See* Chapter 18.

fer of the rights was the first true exception to the rule against assignments. It is clear, however, that such an assignment was a special case. A bill of exchange can only embody one specific type of intangible—a money debt. Since the transfer of an undisputed claim to pay a specified amount of money could not prejudice the debtor, who under the traditional bill of exchange structure was required to endorse the bill with a statement of his own liability on it (acceptance) before the action could be brought against him.

Origins of law of assignment

The law of assignment has developed as a series of exceptions to a prohibition on transfer of rights of action. The prohibition has now effectively disappeared, but its ghost still haunts the structure of the law. In principle there were good reasons why rights in action should not be transferable, these being primarily points relating to maintenance, champerty and the general undesirability of allowing one man to become engaged in another man's dispute, which was believed to be '... the occasion of multiplying of contentions and suits, of great oppression of the people ... and the subversion of the due and equal execution of justice'[3]. This principle is reflected in the only true common law exception to the rule against assignment: that rights could always be assigned to the Crown, which might have good reasons for pursuing an action which the injured party was unable or unwilling to pursue.

Prior to 1875, therefore, legal rights were not transferable at common law. The courts of equity took a different view. Buller J famously said of the common law prohibition on transfer of rights that 'courts of equity from the earliest times thought the doctrine too absurd for them to adopt'[4] and in equity rights were always assignable. This created a problem for the courts of equity. There was no difficulty allowing the assignment of things which fell within their exclusive jurisdiction (ie equitable things, such as an interest in a trust, a legacy[5], an interest in an unadministered estate[6], surplus proceeds of sale in the hands of a mortgagee[7] or a right to relief against forfeiture[8]) since such rights were enforced in the courts of equity in any event, which could admit as plaintiffs whoever they chose. However, in the case of the courts of law, since there was only one plaintiff in respect of a legal chose in action, the courts of equity proceeded by granting an assignee a mandatory injunction requiring the assignor to permit his name to be used in the exercise of the right at common law[9].

---

[3] *Lampet's Case* (1612) 10 Co Rep 46b at 48.
[4] *Master v Miller* (1791) 4 TR 320 at 340.
[5] *Seys v Price* (1740) 9 Mod 217.
[6] *Re Leighs WT* [1970] Ch 277.
[7] *Bucknell v Buknell* [1969] 1 WLR 1204.
[8] *Howard v Fanshawe* [1895] 2 Ch 581.
[9] *Row v Dawson* (1749) 1 Ves Sen 331; *Ryall v Rowles* (1750) 1 Ves Sen 348.

Statutory assignment under Law of Property Act 1925, s 136

A general right to assign was created in 1875 with the passing of the Judicature Act 1873. Section 25(6) of that Act provided that an assignment in writing in the form indicated by the section would be effective to transfer a right of action from one person to another. That subsection was re-enacted as s 136 of the Law of Property Act 1925, which provides that:

> Any absolute assignment by writing under the hand of the assignor[10] (not purporting to be by way of charge only) of any debt or other legal thing in action, of which express notice in writing has been given to the debtor, trustee or other person from whom the assignor would have been entitled to claim such debt or thing in action, is effectual in law (subject to equities having priority over the right of the assignee) to pass and transfer from the date of such notice—
> (a) the legal right to such debt or thing in action,
> (b) all legal and other remedies for the same, and
> (c) the power to give a good a discharge for the same without the concurrence of the assignor:
> Provided that, if the debtor, trustee or other person liable in respect of such debt or thing in action has notice—
> (a) that the assignment is disputed by the assignor or any person claiming under him; or
> (b) of any other opposing or conflicting claims to such debt or thing in action;
> he may, if he thinks fit, either call upon the persons making the claim thereto to interplead concerning the same, or pay the debt or other thing in action into court under the provisions of the Trustee Act 1925.

The introduction of a statutory mechanism for assignment was held not to affect the validity of equitable assignments[11], and consequently there are two independent forms of assignment available today—legal and equitable. Their continued coexistence creates some difficulties, but as a general rule, the fact that the rules of equity are always at least as permissive as those of the law means that assignments which fail to take effect as legal assignments pursuant to s 136 will usually take effect in any event as equitable assignments. However, it is worth analysing the structure of s 136 in order to see how it operates.

'Debt or other legal thing in action'

The courts have interpreted the section substantially since its enactment. In particular, the reference to 'legal thing', which would seem to restrict the section to legal things in action existing at common law only, has been held to

---

[10] It is suggested that the signature must be that of the assignor himself and not of his agent (*Wilson v Wallani* (1880) 5 Ex D 155). This is in line with the requirements generally attributed to ss 40 and 53 of the Law of Property Act 1925.
[11] *Brandt's Sons & Co v Dunlop Rubber Co* [1905] AC 454.

encompass equitable things, since otherwise the reference to trustees later on in the section is incomprehensible[12].

'Absolute and not by way of charge'

This is a strange provision. It is presumed that the mischief at which it was aimed was that where a person assigned a debt by way of charge, what they were in fact doing was undertaking to employ the proceeds of that debt as a fund out of which they agreed to pay a particular liability of their own[13]. This matter has nothing to do with the debtor, who must continue to pay the original creditor in any event, and it is submitted that these words were included in the section primarily to ensure that legal charges of debts were not required to be made in accordance with the section.

It is, of course, perfectly possible to create security over a receivable by means of a s 136 assignment simply by transferring the debt by way of mortgage (ie by an absolute transfer with a provision for retransfer upon repayment). This does not in any way prejudice the debtor's position, who will at all times know who to pay. The fact that such an assignment may be expressed on its face to be given as security for a loan does not exclude it from the section[14]. It seems that this principle may apply generally to all conditional assignments[15].

'in writing'

A statutory assignment must be in writing, but there is no prescribed form. There is authority that a written direction to the debtor to pay the assignee is insufficient to satisfy this requirement[16], but almost any written record between the assignor and the assignee will suffice. In addition, the assignment does not take effect until written notice is received by the debtor.

Equitable assignments do not in general require writing. However any transfer (including an assignment) of an equitable interest is required by s 53(1)(c) of the Law of Property Act 1925 to be in writing and signed by the person making it. Failing this the disposition is void.

Parties

Strictly speaking it is still the case that where a legal right in action is assigned by an equitable assignment the assignee as well as the assignor should be made a party to the action. However, it was held in *The Aiolos*[17] that where joinder of the assignor serves no good purpose it can be dispensed with. This

---

[12] *Torkington v Magee* [1902] 2 KB 427 and [1903] 1 KB 644; *Re Pain* [1919] 1 Ch 38.
[13] See per Atkin LJ in *National Provincial and Union Bank of England v Charnley* [1924] 1 KB 431 and per Buckley LJ in *Swiss Bank Corp'n v Lloyds Bank Ltd* [1982] AC 584 at 594–5.
[14] *Durham Bros v Robertson* [1898] 1 QB 765.
[15] *The Balder London* [1980] 2 Lloyd's Rep 489.
[16] *Curran v Newpark Cinemas Ltd* [1951] 1 All ER 295.
[17] [1983] 2 Lloyd's Rep 25.

follows from RSC Ord 15, r 6, which provides that non-joinder of a party is not fatal to any action, although the court may of its own motion require a party to be joined if non-joinder would prejudice the hearing.

Notice in writing

[It] is wrong to suppose that a separate document purposely prepared as a notice, and described as such, is necessary in order to satisfy the statute. The statute only requires that information relating to the assignment shall be conveyed to the debtor, and that it shall be conveyed in writing[18].

There is a great deal of authority on how sketchy, vague or incorrect the notice may be in order to qualify as such[19], but the general rule seems to be that any document which discloses the fact of the assignment constitutes good notice as from the date upon which it was actually received by the debtor[20].

Notice, once given, is irrevocable. 'After notice of an assignment of a chose in action the debtor cannot by payment or otherwise do anything to take away or diminish the rights of the assignee as they stood at the time of the notice'[21].

Assignments required to be in writing by the Law of Property Act 1925, s 53(1)(c)

Section 53(1)(c) of the Law of Property Act 1925 provides that a 'disposition of an equitable interest or trust subsisting at the time of the disposition must be in writing signed by the person disposing of the same, or by his agent thereunto lawfully authorised in writing or by will'.

This section is difficult to apply. It is by no means easy to ascertain what is meant by the term 'disposition of an equitable interest'. Equitable interests clearly include interests under trusts, but as mentioned above[22] there are certain equitable rights whose status as equitable interests is unclear.

The first point to note is that the section applies only to 'subsisting' equitable interests. Thus where a person declares a trust of property owned by him for the benefit of another, the declaration, although taking effect to transfer the equitable interest to the beneficiary, need not be in writing. Since equitable title to property does not arise unless the beneficial and legal interests are separated, a transfer of absolute ownership from one person to another is not treated as transferring legal and equitable title. Thus the section does not apply to absolute transfers.

The requirement of writing is absolute: the transfer must be in writing, rather than merely evidenced in writing, and therefore the number of occa-

[18] *Van Lynn Developments v Pelias Construction Co Ltd* [1969] 1 QB 607 at 615.
[19] The leading authorities are collected in *Chitty on Contracts*, 29th edn (Sweet & Maxwell) in the footnotes to paras 19-007 and 19-008.
[20] *Holt v Heatherfield Trust Ltd* [1942] 2 KB 1.
[21] *Bergmann v Macmillan* (1881) 17 Ch D 423.
[22] At pp 73–4.

sions in which the requirement can be satisfied by incidental correspondence is low. However, it is possible, and several writings may be pieced together to satisfy the requirement[23].

Beneficial interests under express trusts

Where a beneficiary directs a trustee to hold property upon trust for another, there is again a transfer of the beneficial ownership of the property from one person to another, although the transfer is not effected by a transaction between the two persons concerned. In such a case the trustee must give the instruction to the trustee in writing in order to satisfy the requirements of the section[24]. If the beneficiary declares himself a trustee of his beneficial interest for a third person then the declaration will not be a disposition but a new creation, and will not require writing[25].

Where a beneficiary directs a trustee to transfer trust property to another, the effect of that transfer is to vest the property in the other absolutely as if the transfer were absolute. In this case the equitable title is not transferred, but is extinguished by the transfer (since equitable title does not continue to exist where equitable and legal title to property are vested in the same person), and there is no requirement of writing[26].

Beneficial interests under constructive trusts

Where property is held by one person on constructive trust for another, s 53(1)(c) should have no application by reason of the terms of s 53(2), which provides that '[s 53] does not affect the creation or operation of resulting, implied or constructive trusts'. This point usually arises in the case of a specifically enforceable contract of sale of property, in which the seller becomes a constructive trustee for the buyer as soon as the sale agreement takes effect, and it is tolerably clear that s 53(2) exempts transfers of property under these circumstances from the requirement of writing[27]. There is authority that this may not be the case where stamp duty is chargeable[28].

Where there is an equitable assignment of future property, the conventional analysis is that as soon as that property passes into the assignor's hands the assignee acquires an equitable interest in it. However, prior to the assignor's acquiring the assigned property, it has been said that the assignee's interest is

---

[23] *Re Danish Bacon Co Staff Pension Fund Trusts* [1971] 1 WLR 248.
[24] *Grey v IRC* [1960] AC 1; *Re Tyler* [1967] 1 WLR 1269.
[25] However, if the terms of the two trusts are identical then the principle in *Grainge v Wilberforce* (1889) 5 TLR 436 may be applied. This is to the effect that where A holds as bare trustee for B, and B declares himself a bare trustee of his interest for C, then B will be ignored and A will be treated as holding directly for C. In this case the true effect of the transaction would be a transfer from B to C. The question of whether a court would be prepared in such a case to hold that s 53(1)(c) applies to substance rather than form has yet to be determined.
[26] *Vandervell v IRC* [1967] 2 AC 291.
[27] *DHN Food Distributors v Tower Hamlets LBC* [1976] 1 WLR 852; *Chinn v Collins* [1981] AC 533.
[28] *Oughtred v IRC* [1960] AC 206.

more than a mere contractual right against the assignor but has some property element[29]. However, this property element is insufficient to permit the interest to be characterised as an equitable interest, since it is very hard to see how an equitable interest in property may be created by a person other than the property's legal owner. To the extent that the assignee's rights arise upon acquisition of the assigned property by the assignor, such rights will arise under a contractual constructive trust similar to those considered above, and s 53(1)(*c*) will be disapplied by s 53(2). This may be tested as follows. In all cases in which specific performance of the contract to deliver the property would be ordered, the contractual constructive trust arises. In other cases, the obligation to deliver will be recognised in equity. However, where such recognition is not accompanied by a right to order specific performance, it is incorrect to describe the assignee's interest as a full equitable interest quasi-under a trust. The right is in fact to have the act treated as done as against third parties. This is a form of mere equity which, if transferable at all, is transferable without writing since it is wholly outside s 53(1)(*c*). It seems that the effect of such a transfer would be to render the transferee directly entitled as against the debtor, rather than giving the transferee a claim against the assignor's claim against the debtor[30].

Incomplete assignments

Issues may also arise where the assignment process involves a number of steps, which have been interrupted. A valid gift is unchallengeable, but equity does not perfect an imperfect gift. The test of when a gift has been perfected is to ascertain the time when the donor has done everything in his power to complete the gift. After that time, if the gift fails for want of the act of a third party, then the gift must be treated as having been completed, and equitable title to the relevant property vests in the donee. If, however, there were still steps which the donor could have taken but did not, then the donee has acquired no property right[31].

Perhaps paradoxically, it is not possible to assign a presently payable debt to take effect at a future time. Thus if I purport to assign to you on the first anniversary of this date a debt which is payable to me now, the effect of my agreement is not to make a present transfer to take effect at a future date, but to make a contract now which will take effect in a year's time. Thus, although I could have transferred the debt immediately without consideration, if I wish to transfer it at a future date I must make a binding contract to do so and give consideration[32]. In any other event my disposition is incomplete and unenforceable.

---

[29] *Re Lind* [1915] 2 Ch 345.
[30] *Berkley v Earl Poulett* (1977) 242 EG 39.
[31] *Re Rose* [1949] Ch 78; *Re Rose* [1952] Ch 499; *Letts v IRC* [1957] 1 WLR 201.
[32] *Re McArdle* [1951] Ch 669.

Assignment of part of debt

Part of a debt may not be assigned at law[33]. The reason for this is that the law does not permit multiplication of creditors, taking the view that to give the assignor the power to increase the number of plaintiffs and actions against a single debtor would be contrary to the principle that the assignor may not make the position of his assignee any worse by means of the assignment[34]. In equity no such objection arises, since equity reconstitutes a single action with a single plaintiff (ie the assignor) and part of a debt may be assigned in equity. Note, however, that where a debt is partially discharged, what remains is not a part of the original debt but a single action, albeit for a smaller amount, and such a single right of action may be assigned at law as well as in equity[35].

The 'no detriment' rule

An assignee cannot recover more from the debtor than the assignor could have recovered had there been no assignment[36]. This rule is part of a wider rule that the debtor must not suffer any detriment as a result of the assignment, since for him to do so would be inequitable.

What rights can be assigned

Since most rights which cannot be assigned at law can be assigned in equity, it is the restrictions which equity imposes upon assignability which are relevant, as it is only if a right is non-assignable in equity that it is genuinely non-assignable[37].

Rights which as created are non-assignable

The largest and most important class of rights which cannot be assigned are those which are created so. Where a contractual right is created, the nature of the right itself is determined by the terms of that contract. If one of the terms is that rights created under it shall not be transferable, then non-transferability is built into the very nature of the right, and any purported transfer of it is absolutely ineffective as against the debtor. This is true both where the contract contains an absolute prohibition, and where the contract provides that a given right is not to be assignable without the debtor's consent if an assignment is entered into without the relevant permission being granted[38].

---

[33] *Forster v Baker* [1910] 2 KB 636; *Re Steel Wing Co* [1921] 1 Ch 349.
[34] *Roxburghe v Cox* (1881) 17 Ch D 520 at 526.
[35] *Walter & Sullivan v Murphy & Sons Ltd* [1955] 2 QB 584.
[36] *Dawson v Great Northern & City Railway Co* [1905] 1 KB 260.
[37] *Tolhurst v Associated Portland Cement Manufacturers* [1902] 2 KB 660; *Torkington v Magee* [1902] 2 KB 427.
[38] *Linden Garden Trust v Lenesta Sludge Disposals Ltd* [1993] 3 All ER 417.

However, as between the parties to the assignment agreement the agreement itself remains valid. 'A prohibition on assignment normally only invalidates the assignment as against the other party to the contract so as to prevent a transfer of the chose in action: In the absence of the clearest words it cannot operate to invalidate the contract between the assignor and the assignee, and even then they may be ineffective on grounds of public policy'[39]. In other words, if you agree to transfer to me a right of action which is in fact non-transferable, you have made a valid contract to do the impossible, and I can sue you on it in the same way that I could if you had contracted that the sun will rise tomorrow in the north-west.

Where a contract provides that a right is not transferable, that is not necessarily the end of the story. Where the debtor has behaved in such a way as to give the impression that he consents to the transfer, he may well find that he is estopped from asserting the non-assignability clause in his defence[40].

Contingent future receivables

A future receivable (ie an obligation which is not yet due but will become so at a future time) can be transferred by entry into a binding agreement to transfer. If this is done, the agreement will effect an automatic conveyance when the receivable becomes due. Where, however, at the time the binding obligation is entered into it is not certain that the obligation will become due at all (ie the obligation is a contingent future receivable), problems will arise.

The difficulty with transferring a contingent future receivable by the contract and subsequent automatic conveyance method is that the process of serving notice becomes complex. It is not possible to perfect an assignment by serving notice upon the debtor in advance of the transfer[41]. Therefore in theory the earliest point at which notice may be given to the debtor is the date of the occurrence of the contingency. This has the important aspect that it is therefore not possible to prevent set-off accruing against the assignee in respect of actions arising against the assignor—the usual function of notice—until the occurrence of the relevant contingency[42]. Transfers of receivables are discussed below at pp 151–3.

Rights in tort

Non-contractual rights create particular problems. Assignments which savour of maintenance or champerty[43], or otherwise constitute assignments of a bare

---

[39] Per Browne-Wilkingon LJ in *Linden Garden Trust v Lenesta Sludge Disposals Ltd* [1993] 3 All ER 417 at 431.

[40] *Orion Finance Ltd v Crown Financial Management* [1994] 2 BCLC 607.

[41] *Somerset v Cox* (1865) Beav 634; *In re Dallas* [1904] 2 Ch 385.

[42] This proposition has been rejected by the Canadian Supreme Court in *Dommerich & Co v Canbadian Admiral Corp* [1962] OR 902, and has been criticised by Derham (*Set-off*, 2nd edn (OUP, 1996), pp 576–7).

[43] Maintenance and champerty were abolished both as torts and as crimes by the Criminal Law Act 1967. However Lord Roskill said in *Trendtex* at 702 that it 'seemed plain that Parliament intended to leave the law as to the effect of maintenance and champerty upon contracts unaffected by the abolition of them as crimes and torts'.

right to litigate, are invalid. The rule appears to be that an assignment of any right is enforceable as long as it is assigned for valid commercial reasons or as part of a larger transaction in which other property passes[44]. Thus, upon a sale of property it is perfectly proper to transfer all the rights which surround it, both contractual and otherwise[45].

Where the transfer is not made alongside a transfer of other property, but is made for good commercial reasons, the fact that enforcement of the right will necessarily result in litigation does not render that right a 'bare right to litigate', as a debtor cannot be allowed to render a debt untransferrable simply by disputing it. A transfer of a disputed debt is perfectly valid, even if the transfer is purely a transfer for the purpose of suing the debtor on the debt[46]. However, an assignment is invalidated if it is a transfer to 'a third party who has no genuine commercial interest in the claim'[47], and is taking the assignment primarily for the purpose of making a profit out of the litigation itself[48].

For this reason there are clearly some rights which cannot be assignable, since they are personal to the assignor. These include the right to sue for defamation, for trespass to the person or for assault. However, there would be no harm in an assignment of the proceeds of an action in respect of any of these torts, since the proceeds of an action, being a contingent future receivable, may be made the subject of a valid contract to assign which will take effect upon receipt by the assignor of the proceeds[49]. However, care needs to be taken by the assignee, in that he must not play any substantial part in the litigation.

Personal rights

Personal contracts are not assignable. This class is confined to rights where the personal nature of the service is implicit in the very nature of the service itself, and consequently there are very few rights which fall into it, since in the case of an obligation to pay money or to let out premises, it matters not to the debtor who his creditor may be. The issues which will be considered in this context are very few—for example, in *Fitzroy v Cave*[50] where the assignee's objective in procuring the assignment was to effect the debtor's bankruptcy, this was held to be insufficient to found an objection on this basis.

The components of this class are contracts whereby a personal service is performed: neither employer nor employee may assign the benefit of a contract of employment[51], and a publisher cannot assign the benefit of a contract

---

[44] *Trendtex Trading v Credit Suisse* [1982] AC 679.
[45] Eg *Dickinson v Burrell* (1866) LR 1 Eq 337; *GUS Property Management Ltd v Littlewoods Mail Order Stores Ltd* 1982 SLT 533.
[46] *County Hotel and Wine Co v London and North Western Railway* [1918] 2 KB 251; *Fitzroy v Cave* [1905] 2 KB 364.
[47] *Trendtex Trading v Credit Suisse* [1982] AC 679 at 704.
[48] *Advanced Technology Structures Ltd v Clay Valley Products* [1993] BCLC 723.
[49] *Glegg v Bromley* [1912] 3 KB 474.
[50] [1905] 2 KB 364.
[51] *O'Brien v Benson's Hoisiery (Holdings) Ltd* [1980] AC 562.

to write a book with a particular author[52]. Although they may be in a different category, motor insurance policies are also non-assignable on the basis that they are personal to the insured. However, in all these cases, although the right itself may not be assigned, the proceeds of the right may be.

Note that this rule is wider than a mere prevention of assignments. In the case of contracts the performance of which is personal, not only may the benefit of the contract not be assigned, but the contracting party may not delegate another person (either as agent or otherwise) to perform the contract. Thus, where a person hires a car for a given period, the car-hire company will have considered his record as a driver, and the hirer cannot give the car to another for the hire period[53]. However, where the contract involves the performance of work, the nature of the work is crucial in determining whether the contracting party must perform the work himself[54].

Rights whose nature would be changed by the assignment

An assignor cannot by an assignment materially increase the burden upon the debtor. This point has arisen in a number of cases where the assignment had the effect of altering the nature of the commitment envisaged at the time of the original contract. In *Tolhurst v Associated Portland Cement Manufacturers Ltd*[55], for example, the defendant contracted with a small company to supply them with as much chalk as they might require for making cement on a particular site. The small company assigned the contract to an enormous cement manufacturing concern, and the debtor sued to be released from the extra burden which was imposed on him. The court held that because the initial obligation had been expressed to be for a particular period and related to a particular site, there was no substantial change. By contrast, in *Kemp v Baerselman*[56] a similar contract to supply a cake manufacturer with all the eggs which he might require was struck down on the basis that there was no evident limitation on the demands which the assignee might place upon the debtor equivalent to the limitation implied by the size of the site in the *Portland Cement* case.

Assignment and set-off

As a general rule, the debtor may set off against the assignor all rights of action which have accrued to him against the assignor in respect of the debt up to the moment of receipt of notice of the assignment. Thereafter he may only set off against the assignee claims which he has against the assignee. In *Business Computers Ltd v Anglo-African Leasing Ltd*[57] the rule was stated to be that:

---

[52] *Stevens v Benning* (1855) De G M & G 223.
[53] *Robinson & Sharpe v Drummond* (1831) 2 B & Ad 303.
[54] *British Wagon Co and Parkgate Wagon Co v Lea* (1880) 5 QBD 149.
[55] [1902] 2 KB 660.
[56] [1906] 2 KB 604.
[57] [1977] 1 WLR 578.

A debt which accrues due before notice of an assignment is received, whether or not it is payable before that date, or a debt which arises out of the same contract which gives rise to the assigned debt, or is closely connected with that contract, may be set off against the assignee. A debt which is neither accrued nor connected may not be set off even though it arises from a contract made before the assignment.

The logic of this is clear. Prior to the assignment, the debtor has a net exposure to the assignor which may arise in a number of different ways. If he were to be prevented from raising those set-offs his net exposure would be very different. Thus, the rule that the debtor may treat his net exposure to the assignor as at the date of the assignment as his net exposure to the assignee thereafter is another manifestation of the rule that the assignor may not in any way damage the debtor's position by the assignment[58]. This rule operates in effect as a denial of set-off for claims accruing after notice of the assignment has been received, and a grant of set-off in the period between the written assignment and the giving of notice. Note also that if the assignment is regarded as inchoate until the grant of notice to the debtor, some of the more complex theoretical problems which arise out of this structure can be elided.

An equitable set-off may be available to the debtor in a claim arising after the receipt of notice. This occurs where, as for any other equitable set-off, the title to sue itself is impeached such that it would be inequitable to allow the claim to be separated from the counterclaim by assigning it. Thus in *Government of Newfoundland v Newfoundland Railway Co*[59], a construction company assigned a claim to payment for a construction project to a third party and gave notice of the assignment. It was held that the claim against the company for failing to complete the project could be asserted against the assignee in equity[60].

Novation and transfer of obligations

Assignment is a means of transferring the benefit of a contract. Where it is desired to transfer the burden of an obligation the obligee's consent must be obtained, and the transfer must be accomplished by means of a novation. It follows that it is not possible by assigning a contractual benefit to transfer any contractual burden. In *Pan Ocean Shipping Ltd v Creditcorp*[61] this point arose in connection with an assignment of the benefit of hire payments under a charterparty. The charterers paid the hire in advance to the assignee. When the owner failed to make the ship available to the charterer, the charterer sued the assignee in restitution for the return of part of the hire payment. It was held by

---

[58] This is limited in one respect. Where the debtor has a set-off against the assignor for an amount greater than the debt (ie after the set-off the debtor is in fact a creditor of the assignor) the debtor may only plead his set-off in extinction of the debt when sued by the assignee, and may not counterclaim for the balance (*Young v Kitchin* (1878) 3 Ex D 127).
[59] (1888) 13 App Cas 199.
[60] See also *Lawrence v Hayes* [1927] 2 KB 111.
[61] [1994] 1 All ER 470.

the House of Lords that there was no liability on the assignee arising out of the assignment, and the charterers should pursue their action under the charterparty against the owner[62].

This principle was considered by Megarry V-C in *Tito v Waddell (No 2)*[63], where he distinguished two circumstances in which an assignee might acquire a burden pursuant to the assignment. One is in the case of a conditional benefit, where the right to the benefit assigned is subject to the doing of an act such that the doing of such act is an integral part of the right assigned. The second is the 'pure principle of benefit and burden'. This is a rule that in some cases an independent benefit and burden arising under the same instrument should be transferred together. In the light of the observations of Lord Templeman in *Rhone v Stephens*[64] in the House of Lords it is debatable to what extent the 'pure principle' continues to exist. However, it is clear that there are some circumstances in which a burden may travel under an assignment.

Alternatively, the ordinary way in which an obligation can be transferred is by novation. Where a right has been created by a contract, an identical right can necessarily be created in favour of another person by another contract. If the second contract is coupled with a third contract between the original parties extinguishing the prior liabilities, then a transaction which is apparently identical to a transfer of property will have been accomplished by the extinguishing of one item of property in exchange for the creation of another between different parties. This is a novation. The important part of a novation is that it involves at least two contracts and usually three, for if A, who is owed money by B, agrees to novate the debt to C, he is unlikely to be doing so other than pursuant to a contract with C. These contracts are referred to as follows:

(1)   The contract which releases B's liability to A is 'the first contract'.

(2)   The contract which creates B's liability to C is 'the second contract'.

(3)   The agreement between A and C, if there is one, is 'the third contract'.

All these contracts must satisfy the formal tests for validity—in particular there must be consideration moving from each promisee, and there must be consent of all parties.

Consideration is a difficult issue in the context of novation. In respect of the first contract, consideration must move from B, and can be inferred from B's entry into the second contract. In respect of the second contract, however, consideration must move from C. Where C enters into the third contract which, being a commercial contract, is valid on other grounds, then the three contracts may become self-supporting. However, where there is no third contract (ie a situation where C, if he had been a transferee, would have been a volunteer) there is a danger that the second contract will simply constitute an un-

---

[62] The rule against set-off of freight payments does not apply to hire payments under a charter, so that if the assignor had (prior to the assignment) sued for the hire the charterer would have had a valid set-off, and the same would have been true had the assignee sued for the hire prior to its payment. However, this point was specifically considered by the Lords to be irrelevant to the fundamental principle that an assignment transfers rights only and not liabilities.

[63] [1977] Ch 106.

[64] [1994] 2 AC 310 at 322.

supported promise to pay which, not being under seal, is unenforceable. In such a case, the question is whether the failure of the second contract necessarily invalidates the first contract. If the consideration for entry into the first contract was entry into the second, then the first contract also fails and the *status quo ante* is restored. However, if the debtor gives additional consideration under the first contract then he may have a claim to be released from his debt under the first contract whilst declining to accept any liability under the unenforceable second contract[65].

A further difficulty is that novation is not usually used to transfer rights, but to transfer obligations. Thus, the position above may be restated from a starting point where at the outset A owes money to B. In this context, the first contract releases A's liability to B, and the second contract constitutes the creation of C's liability to B. In this case, the first contract releasing the debt from A to B requires consideration to move from A (which it may well have done, moving from A to C under the third contract) and the second contract, creating the liability from C to B, requires consideration to move from B.

In the context of transactions of the more common second type, where what is sought is to achieve the equivalent of a transfer of an obligation, issues of consent arise. There can be no contract without knowledge, since the incurring of contractual obligations requires an intention to be bound. This point usually arises in the context of mergers and other substitutions where one person takes up or carries on a business formerly conducted by another. In such cases there is an issue of whether B, the customer, voluntarily entered into the novation[66].

It is also highly likely that this is the way in which payment for purchases by means of a credit card operates. The point here is that the discharge of a debt by means of the presentation of a negotiable instrument operates only as a conditional payment, such that if the negotiable instrument is for any reason dishonoured then the supplier may proceed against the customer under the underlying contract of sale[67]. The rule in relation to payments by credit cards is different; where a credit card is presented in settlement of a debt it seems that there is a novation of the obligation to pay from the purchaser to the credit card company. As Browne-Wilkinson V-C said in the Court of Appeal in *Re Charge Card Services Ltd*[68], 'the [supplier is] accepting the [credit card] company's obligation to pay instead of cash from a purchaser of whose address he was totally unaware'[69]. His Lordship described the structure as a

---

[65] These issues are considered in *Olsson v Dyson* (1969) 120 CLR 365 at 390; see also *Tatlock v Harris* (1789) 3 TR 174; *Cuxon v Chadley* (1824) 3 B & C 591; *Whjarton v Walker* (1825) 4 B & C 163.

[66] *Chitty on Contracts*, 27th edn (Sweet & Maxwell, 1994), para 19-050.

[67] *W J Allen & Co Ltd v El Nasr Export & Import Co Ltd* [1972] 2 QB 189; *E D & F Man Ltd v Nigerian Sweets & Confectionery Co Ltd* [1977] 2 Lloyd's Rep 50 (payments by letters of credit); and see *Sayer v Wagstaff* (1844) 14 LJ Ch 116; *In Re London, Birmingham and South Staffordshire Banking Co Ltd* (1865) 34 Beav 332; *In re Romer & Haslam* [1893] 2 QB 286; *Allen v Royal Bank of Canada* (1925) 95 LJPC 17; *Bolt and Nut Co (Tipton) Ltd v Rowlands Nicholls & Co Ltd* [1964] 2 QB 10 (payments by cheque and other negotiable instruments).

[68] At 513.

[69] [1989] Ch 497.

'quasi-novation', but it is hard to see anything 'quasi' about it. However, it should be emphasised that what was novated was the obligation to pay, not the contract as a whole.

Acknowledgement

There is a line of authorities to the effect that where a person who holds a fund for another is directed by that other to make a payment out of the fund to a third party, and communicates his agreement to do so to the third party, the third party acquires a right of action against the person holding the money. This is known as 'acknowledgement'. It bears more relation to an attornment than to an assignment, but since there cannot be a bailment of money *qua* currency[70] it is clearly not an attornment. The doctrine of acknowledgement resurfaced in *Shamia v Joory*[71] in which it was incorrectly applied to a mere debt rather than a fund of money. The decision in *Shamia v Joory* has been strongly criticised[72] and it is questionable whether the doctrine of acknowledgement continues to exist.

---

[70] *See* pp 144 *below*.

[71] [1958] 1 QB 448.

[72] Goff & Jones, *The Law of Restitution*, 4th edn (Sweet & Maxwell, 1993), pp 573–5; *Chitty on Contracts*, 27th edn, para 19-051.

Particular Types of Property

Contents

Chapter 16

The Law of Money

The greater part of the world's wealth is held in the form of money. Money is in some respects property, but in others it is a thing *sui generis*. The English law of money has been both blessed and cursed by the presence of a colossus in the form of Dr F A Mann—blessed in that the first edition of his *The Law of Money* was itself both the first and the last word upon the subject; cursed for the same reason in that in the light of Mann's enormous erudition and scholarship the field has remained largely empty of other scholars, conscious perhaps that there is little to do other than to add footnotes to his existing work. This author is no exception, and it is freely acknowledged that the bulk of the content of this chapter is a restatement of the work and analysis of Dr Mann. However, the task is ventured and, it is submitted, is of value as a first step in the task of integrating to some extent the law of money into the English law of personal property, a task which, as recent decisions of the English courts have shown, remains at least incomplete, and in some areas unstarted.

Nature and boundaries of the concept of money

Far from there being a single concept of 'money', there is a central concept of currency in the form of coins, and a penumbra of other classes of property which do duty in various degrees as substitutes for negotiable currency. In the nearest class we find bank notes and negotiable instruments. Next are bank deposits, building society deposits and letters of credit. In the next circle again are to be found debt securities. It is clear that the purchase of an interest-bearing debt security from its initial issuer is economically identical to the advancing of a loan of money to that person for a period[1]. We should therefore acknowledge debt securities as forming a part of the universe of 'money'. The next circle again is the concept of the equity security, equivalent to the advance of a sum of money to an enterprise upon terms that the repayment will be in the form of a share in the enterprise's profits. However, at this stage we can draw a fairly clear line between money and property. The purchase of debt security from a company is a purely financial transaction in the sense that money is paid for money. The purchase of an equity security, however, is

---

[1] It is incorrect to say that the fact that a bondholder has rights against the issuing company differentiates him from a lender, since the rights of the bond holder are analogous to the rights created by the restrictive covenant and event of default provisions under ordinary loan documentation.

a purchase not of money but of rights against the company, and it is clear that an equity share is not 'a sum of money settled upon terms'[2]. The purchase of a newly created equity share is in fact a purchase of rights from the existing shareholders rather than from the issuing company, albeit that the right purchased may be newly created rather than pre-existing[3] equity securities are therefore true property rather than money.

Money in law

As a result of the existence of the penumbra of concepts identified above, the vast majority of what we mean when we say 'money' is not, in law, money. Money in law means notes and coins. 'Bank money', that is money owed to a person by a bank, may in many circumstances be treated as being as good as money, and indeed in many circumstances has completely replaced notes and coins as the means of settling transactions. 'Money is not the same as credit, nor is the law of money identical with the law of credit, nor does the fact that "bank money" largely functions as money prove that in law it necessarily and invariably is money.'[4]

Money initially meant coinage, and was defined by reference to its physical attributes such as weight and fineness[5], and even with modern coins it is still the case that gold coins of less than a specified weight or fineness are not legal tender[6]. This led in the early days of paper currency to the view that bank notes were not 'money', and although this view was overcome relatively easily[7], ghosts of the idea that something without an inherent value was not really 'money' endured as late as the early nineteenth century[8]. However, it is now accepted that in order to function as money a token need not have any inherent value at all. Thus 'in law the quality of money is to be attributed to all chattels which, issued by the authority of the law and denominated with reference to a unit of account, are meant to serve as universal means of exchange in the state of issue'[9].

In order to understand the nature of money it is necessary to begin with a hierarchy.

The *concept of money* is an intangible. There is no such thing as a 'pound'; the unit of currency is not a thing in itself but is the measure of all things. It is created by an exercise of the sovereign will and exists by continuing exercise of that will.

Coins are the only component of the monetary system which have an intrinsic value—intrinsic in the sense that they are not claims upon some other

[2] See Gower, *Principles of Modern Company Law*, 6th edn (Sweet & Maxwell, 1997), Ch 13.
[3] Although since the new shareholders acting together will have the same rights in total as the old shareholders acting together, it may be fallacious to distinguish between the creation of new rights and the sub-division of existing rights.
[4] F A Mann, *The Law of Money*, 5th edn (OUP, 1992), p 6; and see *Re Diplock* [1948] Ch 465 at 519.
[5] *Case de Mixt Moneys* (1604–5) Dav Ir 18.
[6] Coinage Act 1971, s 2(1).
[7] *Wright v Reed* (1790) 3 TR 554.
[8] *R v Hill* (1811) Russ & Ry 191 (bank notes held not to be 'money').
[9] Mann, *op cit*, p 8.

person. A coin has its value because statute says that a piece of metal with that composition, of that design, and manufactured in that way, has that value. Title to coins is transferred by delivery of physical possession of the coins.

Bank notes are claims on the Bank of England for their face value embodied in a piece of paper, title to which is transferable by delivery. They are in principle no different from any other note, but have by statute the characteristic of being legal tender—ie that when they have been offered in settlement of a debt, the creditor cannot demand an alternative form of payment.

Bills, notes and cheques are claims on a person[10] which are embodied in a piece of paper (called an instrument). Title to the claim embodied in the instrument is transferred by delivery of the instrument if

    (a) the instrument satisfies one of the various criteria set out in the Bills of Exchange Act 1882, or

    (b) the instrument is negotiable by custom of merchants.

Debts are claims on any person which are not embodied in any physical object. They are transferable by assignment, and are subject to the doctrine of set-off.

Legal essentials of money

One of the core characteristics of money is that it must be denominated—gold is an excellent store of value, but gold is not and cannot be currency until it has been struck into unitary measures. It follows that 'a chattel cannot in law be regarded as money if it represents anything else than the mere embodiment of a unit of account, its fraction or multiple'[11].

'Only those chattels are money to which such character has been attributed by law, ie by or with the authority of the state'[12]. This is the sovereign theory of money. It holds that one of the essential aspects of statehood is the power to regulate financial transaction within the state, and that it therefore follows that only the state can designate what chattels may be used as currency. Mann argued that the sovereign theory meant that the European Monetary Union necessarily involved a fusion of the sovereignties of the individual European states[13]. It is submitted that this is not completely accurate. As in the case of monetary zones, there is no reason why a state should not, in the exercise of its state powers, designate that the currency of another state should be legal tender within its own territory. Neither is there any reason why a state should not designate some other circulating medium of another state as currency within its own territory. Thus if state A has two common means of settlement, glass beads and pearls, and it has designated glass beads as its currency, there is no reason why the neighbouring state B should not designate A standard pearls as its own currency[14]. This is true whether or not state A exists as a sovereign entity. Thus the fact that the European Union is not a state, and the ECU is

---

[10] Including the Bank of England.
[11] Mann, p 24.
[12] Mann, p 14.
[13] Mann, p 16, fn 69.
[14] Mann disagrees, holding that a currency is only a currency where it embodies a 'distinct unit of account' unique to the state concerned. But this cannot be right, since it undermines the absolute authority of the state over its currency which is the basis of the sovereign theory.

therefore not a unit of currency in its own right, does not (and indeed could not) prevent the UK Government through its own sovereign act constituting the ECU legal tender in the United Kingdom.

Title to currency

The law relating to title to currency has been developed through the use of remedies relating to goods in the context of physical money. The mediæval action for the recovery of money was the action in debt. This action was subject to procedural difficulties, and from 1500 onwards, attempts were made to synthesize an action for the recovery of money from the action on the case in conversion. The first of these is *Miller v Dymock*[15], in which a plaintiff sought to recover from his agent the price of his property which the agent had sold by suing the agent alleging conversion of the money received as the price. Although the plaintiff succeeded in *Miller v Dymock* this approach was flawed in that the money received by an agent was not the property of the principal upon receipt, and thus conversion could not lie[16]. The courts went on to develop the action in action for 'money had and received to the use of the plaintiff' to deal with this circumstance[17].

The case had still to be resolved on the position of a 'bailment of money'—that is, the circumstance where A has obtained possession of money from B otherwise than for value and refused to return it. In *Halliday v Higges*, decided in 1600[18], it was held that the action in conversion was inapplicable to money in a two-party situation. The facts did not in fact give rise to a two-party situation, but the action was phrased as an action in conversion *sur trover*, and was therefore decided on the basis of the legal fiction that the plaintiff had lost the chattel (in this case the money) and that the defendant had found it. The court held that by asserting the fiction of loss the plaintiff deprived himself of the only way of showing that the money in the hands of the plaintiff was indeed his money, since money might not be followed by any 'earmark'.

The logic of the decision seems to be that the only way that I can prove that money in your hands is my money is to prove on the facts that that money is the very money which was given by me into your immediate possession. To show that money which was once mine is currently in your hands is insufficient, for transfer for value passes good title. In other words, assume that I mark a note with a secret, indelible mark. Assume that that note is stolen from me and subsequently found in your hands. Is the note mine? On the evidence it is impossible to say. If you took the note from me and held it then it is mine. But if you took the note from me, spent it at a corner shop, and subsequently

---

[15] (1530) KB 27/1077, m 72A.
[16] *Orwell v Mortoft* (1505) CP 40/972, m 123.
[17] Eg *Beckingham and Lambert v Vaughan* (1616) Moore KB 854. The action for money had and received is an offshoot of the action *in indebitatus assumpsit* the essence of which is that where a person receives the money of another other than in settlement of an obligation to himself, he is deemed to have made a promise to repay it immediately upon the receipt, the promise being actionable as an action in debt.
[18] (1600) Cro Eliz 638.

received it back in change, the note is yours, since the transaction for value restores the title of the holder for the time being (the shopkeeper), who can subsequently give good title back to you. For the plaintiff to prove his case he must prove that the note has *never* passed into currency—that is, that it left him otherwise than for value, and that value has never been given for it.

The decision in *Halliday v Higges* was recorded in the rolls as being to the effect that 'this action lies not for money found, unless it be in a bag or chest'. In 1627 in *Kynaston v Moore*[19] this was criticised. The proposition that money was presumed to have passed into currency unless the contrary could be proved was affirmed. However, the jury having found on the facts that the identity of the money was proved, the appeal appears to have been based upon the proposition that *Halliday v Higges* established a rule of law that such identity might never be proved. This proposition was rejected.

This rejection was clearly correct, since if absolute title to money were to move with mere possession, then a thief might acquire good title to stolen money immediately upon the theft.

It is unfortunate that the decision in *Kynaston v Moore* is frequently reported as having been to the effect that the action might lie for money 'out of a bag, as well as in', since this summary, although picturesque, is unhelpful. What the case decided is that the plaintiff may as a matter of law prove on the facts that the money which is in the hands of the defendant is the very same money which the defendant took from him other than for value, and that it has not subsequently passed out of and returned to the defendant's hands. In order to prove this, it would be virtually essential to prove that the money concerned was 'in a bag' or maintained some other identifiable physical distinction. However such proof can be given[20], the proof itself was a matter of fact for the jury.

It is strongly presumed that title to money passes with its possession unless it can be proved that the transfer of possession was in fact wrongful (ie theftous). A thief acquires no title to money simply by acquiring possession of it, and is liable in conversion if he is found in possession of a stolen note[21]. However, the thief can give good title by transferring the money for value. In the context of instruments, this is called negotiating the instrument. In the context of notes and coins, it is called 'passing into currency'. The concepts are different names for the same thing, since the idea of negotiability of notes was developed to mimic the concept of 'passing into currency'.

Title to any note or coin is irretrievably lost when the note or coin 'passes into currency'[22]. The meaning of the phrase 'pass into currency' was considered by the Court of Appeal in *Re Diplock*[23], in which it was said that 'where moneys are handed by way of a transfer to a person who takes for value without notice, the claim of the owner of the money is extinguished'. This rule

---

[19] (1627) Cro Car 89, 1 14.

[20] *Miller v Race* (1758) 1 Burr 452 at 457–8, per Mansfield LC.

[21] *Thomas v Whip* (1714) Buller NP 130a.

[22] *Solomons v Bank of England* (1791) 13 East 135; *King v Milson* (1809) 2 Camp 5; and see F A Mann, *The Legal Aspect of Money*, 5th edn (OUP, 1992), pp 7–13.

[23] [1948] Ch 465 at 539.

seems to apply even where the basis of the transfer has been vitiated. For example, if I give a builder a marked £50 note in exchange for his agreement to complete a piece of work for me, I cannot recover back the note upon his breach of the agreement unless I can show total failure of consideration, in which case the position is as if no value had been given[24].

These principles state a code. Title to individual notes and coins exists in the same way as title to any other thing, but it passes according to special rules of its own, and those rules are exhaustive. Money is not an asset like any other, but has a unique status as a medium of exchange and a store of value[25], and for this reason the ordinary rules of property are modified in the case of money. The primary modification is that title to notes and coins is presumed to be vested in the possessor for the time being. The underlying logic of this rule is a matter of public policy. As Best CJ said in *Wookey v Pole*[26]: 'The true reason of this rule is that by the use of money the interchange of all other property is most readily accomplished. To fit it for its purpose, the stamp denotes its value, and possession alone must decide to whom it belongs'. Put another way, if the merchant had to investigate the title of his customer to the notes and coins which he tendered in payment, commerce would cease.

Foreign money as money

There is substantial authority at English law that foreign money is to be treated as a commodity[27]. However, there are also numerous cases in which it is treated as money[28], and the House of Lords' decision in *Miliangos v George Frank (Textiles) Ltd*[29] has now put it beyond doubt that in some contexts at least foreign money should be treated as money.

This conflict of approaches led to the establishment of the orthodoxy that an amount payable as a sum of foreign money might be treated either as an obligation to pay money or as an obligation to deliver a commodity, depending on the nature of the transaction. However, this approach has never been entirely satisfactory. In the case of the foreign exchange markets in particular, the question of whether contracts for the sale and purchase of foreign currency are contracts for the purchase of commodities or contracts for the mutual payments of sums of money is a matter of some importance. Mann took the view that such contracts constituted contracts for the purchase and sale of commodities[30], and that presumably a contract for the exchange of French francs for US dollars made in London constitutes a contract for the exchange

---

[24] *Fibrosa Solka Akcyjna v Fairbairn Lawson Combe Barbour Ltd* [1943] AC 32.
[25] See Mann.
[26] (1820) 4 B & Ald 1 at 7.
[27] *Marrache v Ashton* [1943] AC 311; *In Re British American Continental Bank Ltd, Credit General Liegois' Claim* [1922] 2 Ch 589 at 595; *Rhokana Corp Ltd v Inland Revenue Commissioners* [1938] AC 380; *Landes Bros v Simpson* (1934) TC 62; *Imperial Tobacco v Kelly* [1943] 2 All ER 119; and see *Vishipco Line v Chase Manhattan Bank*, 754 F 2d. 452 (1985).
[28] *McKinlay v H T Jenkins & Sons* (1926) 10 TC 372; *Davies v The Shell Company of China* (1951) 32 TC 133.
[29] [1976] AC 443.
[30] Mann, pp 197–8.

of commodities, as in such a contract neither sum is more entitled than the other to be treated as the price rather than the subject-matter of the contract. In particular, the fact that without an express agreement there is no set-off of an obligation to deliver goods against an obligation to pay money[31], but only between obligations to pay money, created difficulties.

However, Mann's view has now been rejected by the Court of Appeal in *Camdex International Ltd v Bank of Zambia*[32]. In this case the issue arose whether, where a sum of foreign currency (Zambian Kwacha) payable under a foreign exchange contract was not paid, the default gave rise to an action in debt for recovery of a sum of money, or an action in damages for breach of a contractual obligation to deliver a commodity.

At first instance Morison J, relying on *In Re British American Continental Bank Ltd, Lisser & Rosenkranz' Claim*[33] and following Mann, held that the contract was one to deliver a commodity, and that the remedy was therefore in damages. The Court of Appeal disagreed. Simon Brown LJ held that[34]:

> Of course, if one is concerned with rare coins or the manufacture of bank notes or something of that kind money may indeed be a commodity rather than a medium of exchange. But where, as is the usual case, the obligation in question is simply the payment of a stipulated sum in a stipulated currency, then, whether that obligation arises from a loan, a sale, or any other contract or set of circumstances, it is an obligation properly described as one of debt.

Phillips LJ considered in some detail the authorities which had been relied upon at first instance, and concluded that they could not stand alongside the House of Lords' decision in *Miliangos v George Frank (Textiles) Ltd*[35]. *A propos* foreign exchange transactions he said:

> I recognise that an exchange transaction is *sui generis*, but its true nature is the incurring of mutual money obligations, not the barter of commodities. If one party performs and the other does not, the latter will be and remain indebted to the former, in the sum of currency that he has failed to provide, unless, of course, the former accepts that the failure to perform as a repudiation, and claims restitution of his own payment. In either case the primary relief will be a claim in or in the nature of debt, although an additional claim for damages may lie—see *President of India v Lips Corporation*[36]. Where one party to a foreign exchange transaction performs his obligation and the other does not, I see no reason why the obligation of the latter should not be subject to attachment as a debt ...

In *Banco de Portugal v Waterlow & Sons Ltd*[37], Messrs Waterlows had printed a series of notes for the Portugese Government. Rogues convinced them to manufacture and deliver a quantity of these notes approximately equal to the quantity legitimately printed, and these notes were delivered to the rogues.

---

[31] *Green v Farmer* (1768) 4 Burr 2214.
[32] [1997] 6 Bank LR 43.
[33] [1923] Ch 726.
[34] At 51–2.
[35] [1976] AC 443.
[36] [1988] AC 395.
[37] [1932] AC 452.

Because the second series of notes was printed on the same paper and with the same plates as the original series, the two were indistinguishable. The Bank of Portugal, when it discovered the fraud, withdrew the whole issue of notes from circulation but announced its intention to replace all the notes with genuine notes of a different series, thereby (in effect) accepting the forged notes into circulation. When the Bank sued the printers the issue arose whether the loss to the Bank of Portugal was to be estimated at the face value of the fraudulent notes, or was merely the cost of reprinting a new series of notes to replace the existing series—in other words, had the Bank lost anything by accepting the forged notes into circulation. The Court of Appeal and the House of Lords both accepted that it had suffered a loss equal to the liability which it had been forced to assume. Thus, it is accepted that foreign money is to be treated in the English courts as bearing its face value.

The incidents of foreign money are to be determined according to English law. Although a simplifying assumption may be made that foreign money is subject to the same rules as English money, this assumption is akin to the simplifying assumption that all foreign legal systems are identical to the English system—it will give way immediately in the face of any challenge. Thus, in *Picker v London & County Banking Co* the question of whether German legal tender was negotiable in England was held to be a question of fact required to be proved by evidence rather than a question of law[38].

Coins

Gold coins in England are legal tender by virtue of s 2(1) of the Coinage Act 1971, and cupro-nickel coins are legal tender by virtue of s 2(2) thereof. However there are quantitative limits imposed by the Act: coins of more than 10 pence are only legal tender up to £10 value, coins of between 2 and 10 pence up to £5 and bronze coins up to 20 pence—hence the rule that 'not all money is legal tender, but all legal tender is money'[39].

Money is, by definition, a medium of, and not an object of, exchange. It follows from this that where money is dealt with other than as a medium of exchange it is not 'money'[40]. Thus the sale of coins as curiosities or as collectors items is a sale of goods and not an exchange of money[41]. There is an unfortunate decision of the European Court of Justice[42] to the effect that coins should always be treated as money and not as goods where they are current legal tender in their state of origin, but this decision has been subjected to

---

[38] Its kissing cousin, *Williams v Colonial Bank* (1888) 38 Ch D 388, [1890] 15 AC 267 developed the disconcerting point that since the finding of a court as to a matter of fact does not create a precedent, the question of whether a particular German note was negotiable in England would have to be proved afresh in every case relating to the notes.

[39] Mann, p 192.

[40] *Moss v Hancock* [1899] 2 QB 111.

[41] See the US cases *Gay's Gold* (1879) 13 Wall 358; *Peabody v Speyers* (1874) 56 NY 230; *Fowler v New York Gold Exchange Bank* (1867) 67 NY 138; and the New Zealand case *Morris v Ritchie* (1934) NZLR 196.

[42] *R v Thompson* [1980] QB 229.

convincing criticism[43], has been disregarded by the Court of Appeal[44] and may be taken to have been wrongly decided. The true test is whether, in the context of the transaction concerned, the coins were used by way of trade or by way of payment.

Title to money is transferable by delivery. This is presented as an exception to the principle *nemo dat quod non habet*, but the rule is most easily explained as being a manifestation of the fact that currency is negotiable. Where it has passed in good faith for value without notice it cannot be recovered even if it can be identified,

> 'for if his guineas or shilling had some private marks on them by which he could prove that they had been his, he could not get them back from a bona-fide holder. The true reason of this principle is that by the use of money the interchange of all other properties is most readily accomplished. To fit it for its purpose the stamp denotes its value and possession alone must decide to whom it belongs.[45]

Thus the transferee of money gets good title even though the transferor has none.

These principles mean that, except in rare circumstances[46], one cannot have a bailment of notes or coins[47]. Where one person hands money to the other it is presumed that the idea is that the other will return an equivalent amount of currency, not the identical notes and coins delivered, and their relationship is therefore one of debtor and creditor rather than bailor and bailee.

Bank notes

A bank note embodies a chose in action against the bank issuing it. Although this theory may be redundant in the case of English currency, it survives in s 1(3) of the Currency and Bank Notes Act 1954 which provides that a bank note shall be 'payable' at the head office of the Bank of England.

Bank notes are legal tender for any amount in England by virtue of s 1(2) of the Currency and Bank Notes Act 1954. It seems that the sovereign right to designate instruments as currency is unlimited—at the beginning of the First World War postal orders were made legal tender in the United Kingdom by s 1(6) of the Currency and Bank Notes Act 1914.

Since a bank note is a promissory note under the Bills of Exchange Act 1882[48], the holder of a bank note is entitled to avail himself of the presumptions set out in ss 30 and 90 of that Act to the effect that good faith and value are presumed in favour of a holder.

---

[43] Mann, p 27.

[44] *Allgemeine Gold- und Silberscheideanstalt v Commissioners of Customs & Excise* [1980] QB 390.

[45] *Wookey v Pole* (1820) 4 B & Ald 1,7 per Best J.

[46] Ie where a specific, tangible sum is accepted by a person on an express or implied mandate to return the identical money at some futute time or to apply it, without alteration or substitution, in its exact original form as delivered by the bailor (*R v Mason* (1890) 16 VLR 327).

[47] *R v Hassall* (1861) Le & Ca 58 at 62; see generally *Palmer on Bailment*, pp 178–82.

[48] Although the Act applies only 'with the necessary modifications' (s 89).

Chapter 17

The Law of Debts

As noted above, the vast majority of the 'money' in circulation in the economy at any given time is not in the form of notes and coins but in the form of credit and debit balances existing between persons—primarily, but not exclusively, banks. The common denominator of all such claims is that they are debt claims.

Not all claims for money are necessarily properly regarded as items of property. Money claims may be divided into claims based on an action in debt, that is, an action for a sum certain in money which it is alleged is due, and claims based on an action in damages, which is an action for compensation for the failure of a person to perform an obligation, whether positive or negative. The distinction is that an action in debt is an action for the enforcement of a promise to pay money, whereas an action in damages arises out of the breach of an obligation for which the plaintiff seeks compensation. A debt is an item of property which can be transferred without restriction[1], whereas a right to sue for damages may be transferred only in certain circumstances[2]. The law has developed a number of ways in which rights of action in debt can be transferred from one person to another in settlement of obligations, and these are dealt with herein under the headings of assignment and negotiable instruments.

The most important thing about a debt claim is that because it is a claim for a certain amount, it is not susceptible to being reduced by the ordinary principles of the calculation of damages. There is no defence of remoteness or mitigation to a claim in debt. The failure to pay a debt on time may give rise to a separate claim for damages, but this is distinct from and different to the claim itself[3]. Equally there is no need to prove loss suffered by the plaintiff; all that must be proved is the agreement to pay upon condition, performance by the plaintiff of the condition, and demand by the plaintiff of the defendant for payment. Strictly speaking a demand is not necessary, since a defendant is obliged to pay money when due[4]. However, if demand is not made the action could be met by a defence of tender which, when coupled with a payment into court of the amount tendered, has the result that the plaintiff is denied interest on the amount due and is obliged to pay the costs of the action[5]. Thus in

---

[1] *Comfort v Betts* [1891] 1 QB 737; *Fitzroy v Cave* [1905] 2 KB 364; *County Hotel and Wine Co Ltd v London and North Western Railway* [1918] 2 KB 251 at 258–62.

[2] See *Trendtex Trading Corp v Credit Suisse* [1982] AC 679.

[3] *Trans Trust SPRL v Danubian Trading Co Ltd* [1952] 2 QB 297.

[4] *M S Fashions Ltd v Bank of Credit and Commerce International SA* [1993] Ch 425 at 436 (per Hoffman LJ) and at 447 (per Dillon LJ).

[5] *Chitty on Contracts*, 27th edn (Sweet & Maxwell, 1994), pp 1067 and 1072, fn 94.

practice demand is an essential ingredient of the action. Note that a defendant may not refuse tender of legal currency in order to keep the debt alive, since the rule above as to interest and costs applies as from the date of tender, not from the date of payment in the action.

Types of debts

Debts can be classified into debts which are immediately due and payable, debts which become payable at a specified future time, and debts which will become payable upon the occurrence of a contingency (contingent future receivables). Even though equity does not enforce a contract to pay money[6] it seems that rights in equity are not rights in damages only and there can be such a thing as an equitable debt. However at common law a debt which is not currently due and payable is not an item of property. Consequently debts which are immediately due and payable may be either legal or equitable choses but debts which are payable either in future or upon a contingency are equitable only.

Debts immediately due and payable

Debts which are immediately due and payable can be assigned either in equity or under the statute without difficulty.

Debts due but not yet payable

Debts which will become payable at a specified future time are existing property in equity although not at common law. Thus a transfer of an existing debt which will certainly become payable upon the elapsing of a period of time is an equitable chose which is transferable under the statute or in equity.

Contingent future receivables

A future debt which is payable upon a contingency is not an existing item of property. Since it does not exist it may not be transferred. There are many contingent rights which fall clearly into this category—for example the right to inherit under the will of a person who is still alive[7], or the right to monies payable under a contract which has not yet been made[8]. However, there are significantly more complex examples than these. There is authority that the right to receive money under a contract is an existing rather than a future chose in action, even though the money will only become payable if the contract is performed[9]. There is Australian authority that interest payable under a contract of loan is not assignable if the loan is repayable, as the repayment

---

[6] *South African Territories Ltd v Wallington* [1898] AC 309, except where to fail to do so would produce inequity—*Beswick v Beswick* [1968] AC 58.
[7] *Meek v Kettlewell* (1843) 1 Ph 342.
[8] *E Pfeiffer Weinkellerei-Weineinkauf GmbH & Co v Arbuthnot Factors Ltd* [1988] 1 WLR 150.
[9] *Hughes v Pump House Hotel Co Ltd* [1902] 2 KB 190.

would eliminate the receivable[10]. The test seems to operate by application of the maxim *omnia praesumuntur rite esse acta*, that where an amount will certainly become payable if the parties to the contract perform the contract then the amount is an existing future debt, whereas if either party can create a situation in which the debt is not payable without breaching the contract, then the receivable is a contingent receivable which is not assignable. An interesting case is *Glegg v Bromley*[11], in which an assignment was made of the proceeds of an action for defamation. It was held that this was a contingent receivable since the outcome of the action was uncertain.

Where a right is a contingent receivable, although it cannot be assigned in law or in equity, if the parties make a binding agreement to transfer it, it comes into the hands of the person contracting to transfer it there will be an automatic transfer by operations of law at that moment. In the case of physical goods this was decided in *Holroyd v Marshall*[12], and this principle was extended to choses in action in *Tailby v The Official Receiver*[13]. However, it is very important to remember that the effect of these decisions is not to render future contingent receivables transferable, but to impose upon the parties to the contract a binding obligation to transfer such that as soon as the contingency occurs and the absolute right to payment vests in the assignor, that right is immediately by operation of law transferred to the assignee without the necessity (or possibility) for any further act by the assignor.

The distinction which in practice requires to be drawn is therefore between existing future receivables, which may be assigned, and contingent future receivables, for which a valid obligation to assign effects an automatic assignment at a later date. The obligation to transfer may be created either by deed or by contract; mere agreement is not enough. This means that all the ingredients of a contract must be present—including consideration. This is awkward. An assignment of an existing piece of property does not require consideration, since a person may make a valid gift of any form of property, whether it be a chose in action or in possession[14]. However, a contract to assign a future contingent receivable, if made without consideration, is wholly unenforceable. There are some dicta to the effect that all equitable assignments require consideration[15] apparently based on the application of the maxim that equity will not assist a volunteer. Yet this is incorrect—a completed voluntary disposition is perfectly effective in equity and does not offend against the maxim. The rule is that 'if under the authority of an ineffective assignment the property is actually transferred to the assignee, the assignor cannot make the assignee refund it; for he has received it under a valid unrevoked authority, and it matters not that he could not have compelled the transfer'[16]. It is for this reason also that the debtor cannot refuse to pay the assignee of a contingent future receivable

---

[10] *Norman v Federal Commissioner of Taxation* (1963) 109 CLR 9.
[11] [1912] 3 KB 474.
[12] (1862) 10 HLC 191.
[13] (1888) 13 App Cas 523.
[14] *Chitty on Contracts*, 27th edn (Sweet & Maxwell, 1994),, para 19-018.
[15] See eg *Glegg v Bromley* [1912] 3 KB 474 at 491.
[16] *Snell's Equity* (P V Baker, ed), 29th edn, p 83.

on the grounds that the assignment was not made for good consideration[17].

It is an obscure point, but one which must be made, that the structure of contract to assign followed by automatic assignment is not quite the end of the story. The reason for this is that because equity looks on as done that which ought to be done, the effect of the contract is not merely to create personal rights against the assignor, but to create a sort of inchoate right in the future property. This is a property right rather than a mere obligation. This follows from the decision in *Re Lind*[18], in which it was held that where a person had assigned a contingent future receivable to another, gone bankrupt and been discharged before the contingency occurred, upon the occurrence of the contingency the assignee was entitled to the assigned property. Since the effect of personal bankruptcy was then and is now the discharge of the bankrupt from contractual obligations incurred prior to the bankruptcy, it is clear that if the obligation under the assignment had been a mere contractual obligation the assignees' claims would have been defeated.

Multiple debts and set-off

Where parties have multiple dealings with each other, or where they engage in any transaction more complicated than a single payment in return for a single chattel or service, the point may be raised whether the party concerned has the benefit of one debt or several. This point can be elided, as there is a tendency to consider many contractual relationships as giving rise to a single net balance. However, the importance of the point cannot be over-estimated. If my bank account is £1,000 overdrawn whilst my savings account has £1,000 in it, the question whether I can pay my rent depends entirely on whether what exist are separate rights or a single right. The reason why the point occasionally presents difficulty is that there is a tendency to consider it in response to the question 'when can rights be combined?', to which the answer tends to be that, since the net balance due is the same in any event, it does not much matter. The correct way to ask the question is 'when can countervailing separate rights be considered as separate entities rather than netted off?' The response to the latter question signifies a great deal about the commercial flexibility of the system of which it is asked.

The reason for this is explained on policy grounds by Philip Wood[19]. Set-off between solvent parties has the effect of enabling a debtor to avoid paying his creditor by asserting a counterclaim for some other debt, and produces a position in which the debtor's payment to his creditor can be put off until after litigation. Where no set-off is available, the effect is otherwise, and the creditor can effectively insist upon a 'pay now/litigate later' position. Consequently commercial efficacy is promoted by keeping solvent set-off within the narrowest possible bounds. The principle for insolvent set-off is exactly the re-

---

[17] *Walker v Bradford Old Bank* (1884) 12 QBD 511.
[18] [1915] 2 Ch 345; and see also *Joseph v Lyons* (1884) 15 QBD 280.
[19] P Wood, *The Law and Practice of International Finance; Title Finance, Derivatives, Securitisations, Set-off and Netting* (Sweet & Maxwell, 1995), pp 71–5.

verse; the set-off operates to benefit the commercial creditor, since in respect of the amount owed by him to the debtor he is in effect paid at 100p in the pound by the cancellation of the debt due from him, and only the balance will have to be proved as a debt.

Since English law is particularly receptive to the needs of commerce, this dynamic has driven the development of the English rules of set-off. In insolvency, set-off is as wide as possible; between solvent creditors it is closely confined.

Solvent set-off

The rules of solvent set-off in England have been described as lacking logic and sense[20]. The reason for this is that they have developed piecemeal over a prolonged period, for most of which the idea of set-off of mutual debts was regarded with suspicion, if not outright hostility.

The origins of solvent set-off at English law are to be found in the Statutes of Set-Off 1729 and 1735. Prior to these enactments there was no general right of set-off at common law. There was, however, a right to set off in equity[21] if there had been a specific agreement to set off[22] through the mechanism of an injunction restraining proceeding in the common law courts with the relevant counterclaim. Although the courts have been fused by the Judicature Acts these two strands of authority at English law have continued their separate existence. In order to know the precise identity of one's property it is therefore necessary to look at set-off both in equity and at common law.

Statutory set-off at common law

As a matter of property law, common law set-off does not affect the nature of the property owned but merely places a procedural barrier in the way of its employment. Two separate and distinct debts remain in existence until such time as they are fused in a judgement for a single amount[23]. Common law set-off is therefore a procedural defence rather than a doctrine of property law. It follows from this that in principle a person who owns a debt may, at common law, transfer the debt freely whether or not it is subject to a set-off, and the debtor who has a set-off against A will simply lose the benefit of his set-off if the debt is transferred at law to B.

Statutory set-off is only available in cases where the debt sought to be set off is due and payable at the time of the action[24]. The most important element

---

[20] *Axel Johnson Petroleum AB v MG Mineral Group AG* [1992] 1 WLR 270 at 274.

[21] *Arnold v Richardson* (1699) 1 Eq Ca Abr 8.

[22] *Jeffs v Wood* (1723) 2 P Wms 128.

[23] Per Hoffman LJ in *Stein v Blake* [1995] 2 All ER 961 at 964; see also R Derham, *Set-Off*, 2nd edn (OUP, 1996), pp 20–7; P Wood, *English and International Set-Off* (Sweet & Maxwell, 1989), pp 43–4; McCracken, *The Bankers' Remedy of Set-Off* (Butterworths, 1993), pp 53, 128–30.

[24] *Pilgrim v Kinder* (1744) 7 Mod 462; *Evans v Prosser* (1789) 3 TR 186; *Maw v Ulyatt* (1861) 31 LJ Ch 33.

of this rule is that the debt must be due. Contingent debts[25], or debts which are not yet due[26], may not be set off.

The old rule was that in order to be available for set-off a debt must have fallen due and payable prior to the date of commencement of the action[27]. It has been suggested that this rule is still law[28], but the better view seems to be that a set-off is available whether the debt concerned arises before or after the date of commencement of the action[29] as long as it has fallen due by the date of judgment. Statutory set-off is only available where both claims are 'in respect of liquidated debts, or money demands which can be readily ascertained'[30]. This means that the claim which it is sought to set off must be a money claim. This head encompasses both claims for specific debts and claims for amounts which are to be struck by reference to a formula[31] (although not claims whose amount is to be determined by expert arbitration[32]). It also encompasses claims for liquidated damages[33], although not claims for general damages[34].

In this context, an interesting question arises over liabilities which are certain in amount but uncertain in liability—that is, guarantees and indemnities which have not been called upon or otherwise become due. In principle a guarantee, which is an undertaking to procure that another performs his obligation[35], should not be capable of being set off against a money claim, since the claim on the guarantor would be a claim in damages for breach of his contract rather than an action for debt. However, this interpretation is probably over-technical, and it does not seem likely that the guarantor's liability under a guarantee would be barred from being set off at modern English law[36]. The position for indemnities is much clearer, as an indemnity is indisputably an independent obligation to pay money, and a claim under an indemnity is only disallowed in the context of a set-off if the indemnity were against an amount of unliquidated damages[37]. However, note in this context that policies of indemnity insurance (that is, most insurances) have traditionally been classified as indemnities against unliquidated damages, and there is therefore no set-off in respect of the proceeds of a policy of insurance[38].

For the purposes of common law set-off, all debts howsoever arising may be set off between two parties as long as those parties are the legal owners of

---

[25] *Fromont v Coupland* (1824) 2 Bing 170; *Leman v Gordon* (1838) 8 Car & P 392.
[26] *Pilgrim v Kinder* (1744) 7 Mod 462; *Smith, Fleming & Co's Case* (1866) LR 1 Ch App 538.
[27] *Richards v James* (1848) 2 Ex 471.
[28] Per Donaldson MR in *Edmunds v Lloyds Italico SpA* [1986] 1 WLR 492; per Hoffman LJ in *Stein v Blake* [1995] 2 All ER 961 at 694.
[29] R Derham, *Set-Off*, 2nd edn (OUP, 1996), p 12.
[30] Per Cockburn CJ in *Stooke v Taylor* (1880) 5 QBD 569 at 575.
[31] *Axel Johnson Petroleum AB v MG Mineral Group* [1992] 1 WLR 270.
[32] *B Hargreaves v Action 2000 Ltd* [1993] BCLC 1111.
[33] *President of India v Lips Maritime Corp* [1988] 1 AC 395.
[34] *Seeger v Duthrie* (1860) 8 CB(NS) 45.
[35] *Moschi v Lep Air Services Ltd* [1973] AC 331.
[36] *The Raven* [1980] 2 Lloyd's Rep 266.
[37] *Cooper v Robinson* (1818) 2 Chit 161; *Hardcastle v Netherwood* (1821) 5 B & Ald 93.
[38] *Grant v Royal Exchange Assurance Co* (1815) 5 M & S 439; *Castelli v Boddington* (1852) 1 El & Bl 66; *Luckie v Bushby* (1853).

the relevant debts. It has been noted that set-off is not permitted between two legal owners of debts in circumstances where one of the owners holds the debt as trustee or as equitable assignee for another person. However, Derham has explained that this results not from a confusion of the rules of law and equity, but from a manifestation of the rule that equity will restrain an unconscionable action in law[39], and it would clearly be unconscionable to allow a defendant to take advantage of a set-off against a debt which he holds for a third person. A set-off between the legal owner of a debt and an equitable owner of a debt is therefore always equitable.

Set-off in equity

As a matter of property law an equitable set-off changes the nature of a debt owned. The owner of a debt subject to an equitable set-off is in a position not dissimilar to that of a person who has received property pursuant to a revocable contract. The decision whether to enforce the set-off is in the hands of the debtor, and the owner of the debt can only wait to see whether he will enforce his right.

The primary distinction in equity is that in some circumstances equity does not permit a debtor to transfer the ownership of his debt to a third person where the result is to deprive the creditor of a defence of set-off. Assume that B owes A £10. Assume that, at some later time (*t*), A incurs a debt to B of £5. Now if A transfers title to his debt to C before *t*, C acquires a complete right against B for £10. However, if A transfers title to his debt to C after *t*, then all that C acquires is a right against B for £5, as equity does not permit C to enforce his debt against B without giving credit for B's set-off against A. Note that even after the date of the assignment equities may continue to accrue against C. In the example above, assume that after *t* A incurs a further debt to B of £3. Unless B has been given notice of the assignment he can also assert this claim in reduction of his initial indebtedness, such that the value of the claim in C's hands suddenly shrinks to £2. Thus, in equity the property in his hands has changed its nature (or at least its value). Therefore in equity the accrual of a right of set-off against a particular debt changes the nature of the debt itself as from the time of accrual of the set-off.

The legal structure of this analysis is that C will sue, citing A's title and in A's name. B will therefore assert his set-off as against A. The law entitles him to do this in all circumstances, but equity prevents him doing so after he has received notice of the assignment[40].

This outcome appears repugnant to ordinary equitable principles, since even if C is a purchaser for value without notice of the debt he will still not take free of the existing set-off. This is because the 'policy' of equity in such circumstances is that A must not in any way be allowed to prejudice B's position by means of a transaction which B cannot prevent[41].

---

[39] Derham, *Set-Off*, 2nd edn (OUP, 1996), pp 328–9.
[40] Ibid, p 570.
[41] *See* p 130 *above*, the 'no detriment' rule.

The rules for set-off in equity are multi-faceted.

(1) Equity enforces any agreement to grant set-off, and 'the least evidence of an agreement of set-off will do'[42].

(2) Equity acts in parallel with statutory set-off in cases where one of the debts is held under a trust or by virtue of an equitable assignment such that it is the beneficial owner rather than the legal owner who is entitled to the set-off[43]. This has the effect of equity creating the mutuality which is absent at law. In such a case, the equitable set-off fails if there is evidence of circumstances which would render the set-off unjust.

(3) Equity acts in parallel with the statute in circumstances in which one or both of the debts which it is sought to set off exist only in equity. This has the effect of equity giving effect to an obligation which is invisible to the common law. Again, the equitable set-off fails if there is evidence of circumstances which would render the set-off unjust.

(4) Equity creates a separate right of set-off where it is just to do so. This independent equitable set-off is first seen in the speech of Lord Cottenham in *Rawson v Samuel*[44], in which he expressed the general principle that equity would allow any two claims to be set off one against the other in circumstances in which the defendant could argue that the plaintiff's title to his demand is impeached. This loosely translates into a requirement that the cross-claim must call in question, impugn, disparage or impede the plaintiff's title to his claim[45], or as in a recent English statement, that it must 'go to the very root of the plaintiff's claim'[46]. The test of impeachment is a difficult one to apply. The examples given by Lord Cottenham were a claim in damages for negligence to be set off against a solicitor's action for payment of his bill[47], and a tenant's action against his landlord for damage to the tenement set off against the landlord's action for rent[48]. In *Rawson v Samuel* itself, however, the plaintiff sought damages for breach of contract, and sought to have an account of profits taken so that the amount found to be due could be set off, and Lord Cottenham found that the issues were 'totally distinct', the fact that the two arose from the same subject-matter being insufficient to ground an equitable set-off.

Because of the difficulty of the 'impeachment' test, the test for the availability of equitable set-off has tended to metamorphose over the years into a test that the relevant claims should be closely connected and should arise out of the same transaction. This tendency was noted by the House of Lords in *Bank of Boston Connecticut v European Grain and Shipping Ltd*[49], in which Lord Brandon said that an equitable set-off should be available if there is a cross-

---

[42] Per Sir Joseph Jeckell in *Jeffs v Wood* (1723) 2 P Wms 128.
[43] Spry, *Equitable Remedies*, 172–3 and the authorities cited thereto.
[44] (1841) Cr & Ph 161.
[45] Per Tadgell J in *MEK Nominees Pty. Ltd v Billboard Entertainments Pty Ltd* (1993) V Conv R 54-486.
[46] *British Anzani (Felixstowe) Ltd v International Marine Management (UK) Ltd* [1980] QB 637.
[47] *Piggott v Williams* (1821) 6 Madd 95.
[48] *Beasley v Darcy* (1800) 2 Sch & Lef 403n.
[49] [1989] 1 AC 1056.

claim 'flowing out and inseparably connected with the dealings and transactions which also give rise to the claim'[50]. This has been criticised by Derham[51] as being unduly mechanistic, and likely to permit equitable set-off in all cases where the actions arise out of the same transaction, regardless of whether there is any justice in the set-off being obtained. However, it does not seem that the decision has overruled the numerous authorities to the effect that an equitable set-off should be permitted if the set-off would create an injustice in all the circumstances of the case[52].

In theory mutuality is not a requirement of an equitable set-off, which may be granted in any circumstances in which the relevant debts are closely connected and the justice of the case requires it. Consequently there are some circumstances in which set-off is available in equity but not in law such as in cases where a joint-debtor can set off against his creditor's claim a debt owed by the creditor to him singly[53]. However, in most cases there is no great or apparent justice in allowing claims between different persons to be set off.

Abatement

The common law remedy of abatement has been largely subsumed in the development of the law of set-off. Abatement was (and is) a specific common law defence by which a purchaser of goods could show that the goods were worth less than the purchase price by reason of defects manifest in them upon delivery[54]. This action still exists and is currently embodied in s 53(1)(*a*) of the Sale of Goods Act 1989, which provides that a damages claim may be set up in diminution or extinction of the price. However, it seems that abatement is only available in the context of transactions for the sale of goods. It seems that the defence is substantive[55], and it would seem to follow that where a vendor delivers defective goods subject to abatement, what he owns is not an action for the full price subject to a defence, but an action for the net price after abatement.

Insolvent set-off

Insolvent set-off is a matter for insolvency text books and is not dealt with here. However, note that upon the onset of insolvency of a debtor, all outstanding transactions between that person and any other person are automatically consolidated by statute into a single amount[56] due from the insolvent person, and the creditor is entitled to prove for that amount in the liquidation or, if the amount is negative, to contribute that amount to the insolvent's assets.

---

[50] At 1102–3.
[51] R Derham, *Set-Off*, 2nd edn (OUP, 1996), p 52.
[52] Collected in R Derham, *Set-Off, above*, p 66.
[53] *Ex p Hanson* (1811) 18 Ves Jun 232.
[54] *Mondel v Steele* (1841) 8 M & W 858.
[55] Per Diplock LJ in *Gilbert-Ash (Northern) Ltd v Modern Engineering (Bristol) Ltd* [1974] AC 689; *Aectra Refining and Manufacturing Inc Exmar NV* [1994] 1 WLR 1634.
[56] Insolvency Rules 1986, r 4.90; *Stein v Blake* [1995] 2 All ER 961.

Chapter 18

Negotiable Instruments[1]

The law of negotiable instruments is somewhat arcane, but is essential to the understanding of the law of personal property. The negotiable interest stands Janus-faced between the worlds of tangible and intangible property; being both a chose in action and a physical thing. This practical solution to the employment of debts in commerce may well be one of the most important economic innovations in commercial history. The bill of exchange today in its traditional form rarely serves the purpose of modern commerce—indeed the elimination of the paper which is the essence of the bill is one of the primary goals of modern business management. However, by examining what was achieved in the past we equip ourselves with the armoury of concepts which may be applied to solve the challenges of the present.

Development of the concept of negotiability

The conventional explanation of the development of the law of negotiable instruments is that it is based on seventeenth- and eighteenth-century endeavours by merchants to evade the operation of the common law principle that choses in action were not assignable[2]. Recent work has cast doubt upon this venerable thesis[3], and it is necessary to examine briefly the history of the development of the law of transferability and negotiability in order to understand the modern position.

Transferability

The original trade bill was an instruction to a mercantile factor based in another place to disburse funds. The mercantile factor indicated, by signing the bill as acceptor, that he had in his hands funds belonging to the drawer which he was prepared to pay to the drawee. From that moment on the factor undoubtedly treated the money as already gone. Thus in the proto-transaction there appears to be no infringement of the prohibition on assignment. The factor does not merely receive notice of the assignment, as would a modern debtor, but by his acceptance he actively participates in the transaction. If necessary it would be possible to spell a new contract with valid considera-

---

[1] Statutory citations in the footnotes to this chapter are to the Bills of Exchange Act 1882 unless otherwise stated.

[2] See eg Holden, *History of Negotiable Instruments* (University of London, 1955).

tion passing between the acceptor and the payee of the bill.

The point in relation to assignment arises from the fact that the payee of the bill might thereafter transfer it by endorsement. Since the endorsement was perceived as a transfer of the right against the acceptor, it seems that here was a flagrant breach of the rule against assignment. However, that is not how the courts of the time characterised the transaction. In their view 'the indorsement is quasi a new bill, and a warranty by the indorser that the bill shall be paid; and the party may bring his action against any of the indorsers, if the bill be not paid by the acceptor'[4]. In other words, since the payee of an existing bill could perfectly validly have drawn a new bill in favour of a third party, presented the new bill to the drawee for acceptance and then delivered it, what he was doing by endorsing the bill was short-cutting this process by warranting that it might validly be done[5]. The action clearly created some category problems; a variant of assumpsit was pressed into use, and the action *onorabilis assumpsit* was being brought on bills as an action 'derived from the custom of merchants' early in the seventeenth century[6]. However, it seems clear that the custom which was relied upon in these cases was a voluntary assumption of liability by the endorsee and the acceptor rather than a claim by merchants to be exempt from the ordinary law of the land as regards assignment.

It is for this reason that Holt CJ was in 1702[7] so astonished by the suggestion that the rule relating to the transferability of bills of exchange should be extended to promissory notes—or, as he perceived the issue, whether the special action based on the custom of merchants should be extended to every written acknowlegement of a debt. His concerns were overridden by statute 3 & 4 Anne, c 9, which enacted that

> all notes in writing ... made and signed by any person or persons ... whereby such person or persons ... promise to pay to any other person or persons ... or their order, or unto bearer, any sum of money mentioned in such note shall be assignable or endorseable over, in the same manner as inland bills of exchange ... according to the custom of merchants; and that the person or persons to whom such money is or shall be by such note made payable, shall and may maintain an action for the same, in the same manner as he, she or they might do upon any inland bill of exchange, made or drawn according to the custom of merchants.

It is only fair to Lord Holt to point out that after the enactment of this statute the courts spent the next 50 years struggling to distinguish between promissory notes and mere memoranda of debts[8].

---

[3] J S Rogers, *The Early History of the Law of Bills & Notes* (Cambridge University Press, 1995), on whose work much of what follows is based.

[4] Per Holt CJ, *Anon* (1673) Holt 15.

[5] This construction seems to explain the reported cases in which endorsement is treated as perfectly normal (eg *Dashwood v Lee* (1667), 2 Keb 303; *Tercese v Geray* (1677) Finch 301; *Death v Serwonters* (1685) 1 Lutw 885), although these are reported in courts which at the time eschewed assignment.

[6] *Oaste v Taylor* (1612) Cro Jac 306; *Woodford v Wyatt* (1626) HLS MS 106.

[7] *Clerke v Martin* (1702) 2 Ld Raym 757; *Buller v Cripps* (1703) 6 Mod 29.

[8] See eg *Garnet v Clarke* (1709) 11 Mod 226; *Roberts v Peake* (1757) 1 Burr 323; and see the cases collected in Rogers (*see* fn 2 *above*), p 185.

Negotiability

The essence of negotiability is that a person who takes a bill *bona fide* for value without notice of any defect is not affected by any defect in title to the bill of the transferee or any equity arising between the drawee and any other holder, including the transferee—in other words, that he gets better title to the bill than the transferor. The rules on the rights of *bona fide* holders are as old as the rules relating to transferability; in 1698 Holt CJ ruled that no action in trover would lie against a person who had given valuable consideration for a bank bill, even though the bill was identifiable as a bill that the plaintiff had lost[9].

Negotiability was not a new concept. The aim was to give to bills and notes the characteristics which were already possessed by circulating coins—that is, the characteristics of currency. This was clearly spelt out in the judgment of Lord Mansfield in *Miller v Race*[10], where he said that 'bank notes ... are not goods, nor securities, nor documents for debts, nor are so esteemed: but are treated as money, as cash, in the ordinary course of and transaction of business by the general consent of mankind; which gives to them the credit and currency of money, to all intents and purposes'[11]. He also went on to disapprove the part of the judgment of Holt CJ in *Ford v Hopkins*[12] in which he had given the impression that bank notes were to be treated like ordinary goods. Although *Miller v Race* itself related to bank notes, it was made clear that the doctrine extended to bankers' drafts[13] and to inland bills[14] immediately thereafter. In the latter case Lord Mansfield drew a clear distinction between the position of a holder for value of a bill and an assignee of a debt. He said[15]:

> the holder of a bill of exchange, or promissory note, is not to be considered in the light of an assignee of the payee. An assignee must take the thing assigned, subject to all the equity to which the original party was subject. If this rule applied to bills and promissory notes, it would stop their currency. The law is settled, that a holder coming fairly by a bill or note, has nothing to do with the transaction between the original parties.

The Bills of Exchange Act

The law of bills of exchange was codified in 1882 by the Bills of Exchange Act. This Act was intended to codify the existing law, so that pre-1882 deci-

---

[9] *Anon* (1698) 1 Ld Raym 725.
[10] (1758) 1 Burr 452.
[11] At 457.
[12] (1700) Holt 119.
[13] *Grant v Vaughan* (1764) 3 Burr 1516.
[14] *Peacock v Rhodes* (1781) 2 Doug KB 633.
[15] With respect to this last point, Rogers at p 192 notes the relative scarcity of cases seeking to raise equities against holders of bills arising out of the original transaction, and points out that as a general rule such equities would only have amounted to defences after the nineteenth-century revolution in the law of set-off. Thus we have an example of a solution developed in the seventeenth century to a problem which arose in the nineteenth.

sions retain their authority where they do not conflict with the Act. The Act itself is a masterpiece of concision and good drafting, and has been described as 'the best drafted Act of Parliament ever passed'[16], a title for which it vies with its brother codifying acts of the 1890s; the Partnership Act 1890 (Pollock) and the Sale of Goods Act 1893 (also drafted by Chalmers).

The essence of a bill of exchange is that it is created by a separate contract all of its own. Where a bill is employed, for example, in settlement of an obligation to pay for goods acquired by a contract of sale, a new contract is created in relation to the bill which is independent of and separate from the existing contract of sale. Thus if the bill is not honoured, the seller has two actions—one under the contract of sale, and a second for breach of the contract which created the bill. Defences under the contract of sale—breach of warranty of quality and the like—are not available in respect of the action on the contract creating the bill.

Because the bill is created by a separate contract, all of the ordinary requirements of contract—agreement between the parties, intention to create legal relations, capacity to contract and consideration—must all be present. Thus an infant[17] or lunatic[18] who does not have contractual capacity cannot draw a valid bill, and a bill is unenforceable against a corporation which enters into it *ultra vires*. The contract creating the bill can be entered into by one person as agent for another, as with contracts generally. However, a person who endorses a bill as agent for another is personally liable on it unless he indicates that he is signing as agent and names his principal on the bill[19].

The requirement for consideration would be troublesome in this context were it not for s 27(1)(*b*) of the Act, which provides that: 'Valuable consideration for a bill may be constituted by ... an antecedent debt or liability'. This in effect reverses the common law rule on the invalidity of past consideration, and has the effect that any bill which is drawn in order to satisfy an existing obligation is validly constituted. This has the interesting side-effect that a bill which is drawn for purely voluntary purposes (as for a gift) is not enforceable by the payee[20]. However, this rule if strictly enforced would have the irritating side-effect that the endorsee of a bill would have to enquire into the circumstances in which the bill was originally drawn—a difficult process. The rule is therefore modified such that where consideration is given for a bill which was originally voluntary, it is thereafter enforceable in the hands of later holders as against those holders who acquired the bill after value had been given. The Act further raises a presumption that all bills have been given for value, and it is the defendant's task to prove otherwise[21].

---

[16] Per McKinnon LJ in *Bank Polski v Mulder* [1942] 1 KB 497 at 500.
[17] *Re Soltykoff* [1891] 1 QB 413 at 415 (presumably aliter if the bill is drawn for 'necessaries' after the Minors Contracts Act 1987).
[18] *Re Walker* [1905] 1 Ch 160 at 178.
[19] Bills of Exchange Act 1882, ss 26(1) and 31(5); *Elliott v Bax-Ironside* [1925] 2 KB 301.
[20] *Oliver v Davis* [1949] 2 KB 727.
[21] Section 30(1) provides that 'every party whose signature appears on a bill is prima facie deemed to have become party thereto for value'.

Formal requirements for bill of exchange

The form of a bill is defined in s 3(1) of the Act. It must be

> ... an unconditional order in writing addressed by one person to another, signed by the person giving it, requiring the person to whom it is addressed to pay on demand or at a fixed or determinable future time a sum certain in money to or to the order of a specified person, or to bearer.

Section 3(2) provides that:

> An instrument which does not comply with these conditions, or which orders any act to be done in addition to the payment of money, is not a bill of exchange.

The consequence of not being a bill of exchange is, in effect, unenforceability. A document which fails to satisfy the definition of a bill of exchange is neither negotiable nor transferable, and is nothing more than a piece of documentary evidence of the intentions of some of the parties thereto. It is therefore important to consider in some detail the issue of what is, and what is not, a bill of exchange.

'an unconditional order'

This precludes politeness—'please let bearer have £7 and place it to my account and you will oblige your humble servant' is not a valid bill[22], although 'Mr Nelson will much oblige Mr Webb by paying to J Ruff 20 guineas on his account' is[23]. Any condition invalidates the bill, as does any instruction to do any act other than pay money. However, by virtue of the specific exceptions contained in s 3(3) of the Act, a reference to the transaction which gives rise to the bill or a specific fund out of which the bill is to be paid does not render the bill conditional. Thus a bill in the form 'pay £100 to Y and debit my account number XXX' is not conditional and is valid.

'in writing'

Writing includes any form of physical record, including non-permanent physical records such as pencil[24]. There is no authority directly on the point, but it seems clear that a bill of exchange cannot be created entirely through electronic means, although a print-out of an electronic instruction could constitute a bill. There is no authority on whether a bill may be in any language other than English, and there seems no reason why a foreign bill, at least, should not be in the language of the drawee. There is, however, authority that the wording of any endorsement should be in the language in which the bill is expressed, otherwise the bill is irregular on its face[25].

---

[22] *Little v Slackford* (1828) Moore & M 171.
[23] *Ruff v Webb* (1794) 1 Esp 130.
[24] *Geary v Physic* (1826) LJKB Hil T 147 at 149.
[25] *Arab Bank v Ross* [1952] 2 QB 216 at 228 per Denning LJ.

'signed by the person giving it'

The signature probably must be manual. In most other cases, including for the purposes of endorsement of the bill once created[26] and generally for the purposes of the statute of frauds, the signature may be by typing, printing or by a rubber stamp. For the purpose of the creation of the bill actual writing may still be necessary[27]. The signature may be that of some other person acting with authority[28].

'requiring the person to whom it is addressed'

A bill must be addressed either to a named person or to a person whose identity may be ascertained with reasonable certainty[29]. It may be drawn on two drawees so as to make them jointly liable on the bill[30], but a bill addressed to two persons in succession or to either of two persons at the election of the holder is not a bill[31]. In other words, a bill drawn on 'X and Y' is valid, but a bill drawn on 'X or Y' is not.

'on demand or at a fixed or determinable future time'

By default, all bills are payable immediately on demand unless a future time is specified for their payment[32]. A bill may be made payable at a time calculated in any way that may seem fit to the drawer—a bill expressed to be payable 30 days after the drawer's death is a valid bill. However, bills couched in such terms must be predicated upon an event the occurrence of which is certain, otherwise they are void as conditional—the otherwise useful formula 'X days after delivery of the cargo ex SS Y' is ineffective for this reason whether or not the SS Y actually arrives[33].

The primary function of dating a bill of exchange is to provide a base for the computation of the payment date for a time bill. There is therefore no requirement that the bill be dated the date upon which it was drawn, and a bill expressed to be payable 30 days after a date regardless of when it is dated 30 days prior to the date of drawing functions as a good sight bill. A time bill must be presented for payment on the specified day (or, if that day is not a business day, the next business day).

'a sum certain in money'

This need not mean a single payment—an instruction to pay in a specified

---

[26] *Bird & Co (London) Ltd v Thomas Cook & Son Ltd and Thomas Cook and Son (Bankers) Ltd* [1937] 2 All ER 227.
[27] Chalmers, *Bills of Exchange*, p 285.
[28] Section 91(1).
[29] Section 6(1).
[30] Section 6(2).
[31] Section 6(2).
[32] Section 10.
[33] *Palmer v Pratt* (1824) 2 Bing 185. See also *Korea Exchange Bank v Debenhams (Central Buying) Ltd* [1979] 1 Lloyd's Rep 548, in which it was held that a bill endorsed 'pay 90 days after acceptance' was invalid since the bill might never be accepted.

number of instalments of a determinable amount is valid, although an instruction to pay periodic amounts until the occurrence of a specified event is not[34].
A bill may provide for the payment of interest over the period to presentation
as long as the rate and means of calculation are stated sufficiently for it to be
possible to calculate the exact sum due[35]. Where the amount involved is set
out in both words and numbers it not infrequently happens that the two differ.
In this case the drawee is entitled to rely on the words[36], although he may if he
wishes reject the document as uncertain.

'to or to the order of a specified person or to bearer'

A bill may be made payable to 'bearer'. It then becomes a bearer instrument
payable to the person who has physical possession of it. Note that the requirement is that the word 'bearer' itself must appear— other commonly used syno-
nyms (such as 'cash') invalidate the bill[37]. If a particular payee is named then
it is presumed to be payable either to that person or to any person to whom he
may endorse it (his 'order'), unless it contains words explicitly limiting its
transferability[38]. A bill made out to a particular named person or to bearer is
treated as a bearer bill. A bill may be made payable to the drawer or to the
drawee—common examples are cheques made out to the account-holder when
drawing cash, or to the account-holding bank when, eg, buying foreign currency.

A person may be specified in a number of ways other than by his name. A
bill may be validly drawn in favour of an office holder for the time being (eg
the treasurer of the X Cricket Club) or presumably by citing some other distinguishing feature, such as perhaps a National Insurance number. A bill drawn
in favour of two or more persons jointly is a good bill as long as the persons
are sufficiently identifiable. Where a bill is made payable to a wholly fictitious person, it is treated as being payable to bearer; ie if I persuade you to
draw a bill addressed to me whilst I am masquerading as 'Mr Brown', if it can
be proved that there is no such person as Mr Brown, the bill is treated as
payable to bearer[39]. Note that this is true even if you do indeed know a Mr
Brown but believe that I am he[40].

A bill which does not exactly correspond with the above requirements may
be rectified by a court if the court is satisfied that the defect in the bill appears
by inadvertence[41]. However, since a bill is not invalidated by the absence of a
date, mention of value given, or place payable[42] there are relatively few defects which can require remedy. The most important—failure to complete payee

[34] *Worley v Harrison* (1835) 111 ER 568.
[35] Section 9(3).
[36] Section 9(2).
[37] *Cole v Milsome* [1951] 1 All ER 311.
[38] Section 8(4).
[39] Section 7(3).
[40] *Bank of England v Vagliano Bros* [1891] AC 107.
[41] *Druiff v Parker* (1868) 18 LT 46.
[42] Section 3(4).

or amount—may be rectified by any holder in due course, to whom the transfer operates as a grant of authority to complete the bill as he thinks fit[43].

Promissory notes

Promissory notes, as we have seen above, have been considered to be negotiable instruments for some considerable time. The law relating to bills applies to promissory notes as it applies to bills with necessary modifications.

A promissory note is[44]:

> an unconditional promise in writing made by one person to another signed by the maker, engaging to pay, on demand or at a fixed or determinable future time, a sum certain in money, to or to the order of a specified person or to bearer.

There are some features of this definition which require explanation.

'promise'

A promise must be distinguished from a mere written acknowledgement of debt[45]. The words 'John Mason, 14 February 1836 borrowed of M A M his sister the sum of £14 in cash a loan, in promise of payment which I am truly thankful for' is a promise[46], whereas 'Borrowed this day of J H the sum of £100 for one or two months' is a mere memorandum[47]. A promise to pay on or before a given date has been held to be invalid as a promissory note because of the contingent element of the date of payment, and although this seems very dubious as logic, in law the point must be treated as settled[48].

'made by one person'

A promissory note may be made by one person. Persons joining together to sign a promissory note may bind themselves by it either jointly or jointly and severally[49]. However, a note which purports to create several liability of the makers for determinate shares in the debt[50], or to render the makers liable in succession[51], is not a promissory note.

'a specified person or to bearer'

Section 5(2) of the Act provides that where a person draws a bill on himself, or on a fictitious person, or on a person who has no capacity to contract, the

---

[43] Section 20(1), and see *Haseldine v Winstanley* [1936] 1 All ER 137.
[44] Section 83(1).
[45] *Gould v Coombes* (1845) 135 ER 653; *Akbar Khan v Attar Singh* [1936] 2 All ER 545.
[46] As well as being dreadful English—*Ellis v Mason* (1839) 8 LJQB 196.
[47] *Hyne v Dewdney* (1852) 21 LJQB 278.
[48] *Williamson v Rider* [1962] 2 All ER 268; followed in *Claydon v Bradley* [1987] 1 All ER 522.
[49] Section 85(1).
[50] *Gardener v Walsh* (1855) 24 LJQB 285.
[51] *Ferris v Bond* (1821) 106 ER 1085.

holder may treat it as either a bill or a note at his option. This is important, not because the legal liabilities are different (they are not), but because in some circumstances a bill which is invalid as a bill of exchange is valid as a promissory note[52].

Liability on promissory note

By s 89(2) the maker of a promissory note is treated as the acceptor of a bill and the first endorser with the drawer of an accepted bill payable to the drawer's order. However, no liability is incurred by any endorser of a bill until it is presented to the maker for payment[53].

Promissory notes and the Consumer Credit Act 1974

One of the great advantages of the regime relating to promissory notes which should be mentioned here: unlike bills of exchange, they may (and usually do) contain security provisions[54]—provisions which would not be permitted to be included in an ordinary bill as being provisions requiring something to be done other than a payment of money[55]. Note that in almost all cases of promissory notes given by individuals such security provisions require registration under the Bills of Sale Acts. The advantage of dividing the two is that where a security bill is invalidated by the Bills of Sale Acts it is invalidated *in toto*, such that the obligation to pay is extinguished along with the security[56]. However, where the promise is embodied in a separate document, the promissory note will survive the avoidance of the bill of sale[57].

It was common practice prior to the passing of the Consumer Credit Act 1974 for finance companies to require hire-purchase customers to execute promissory notes for the amount due under the agreement in addition to the agreement itself. The hire-purchase company would then negotiate the bills to a finance company. This had the unpleasant side-effect that if the customer wished for any reason to return the goods under the hire-purchase agreement he was still fully liable on the note[58].

The Consumer Credit Act 1974, which applies to all consumer credit agreements for less than £15,000, prohibits the lender from accepting any negotiable instrument in discharge of any sum payable under a regulated agreement[59]. Bank notes are (obviously) excepted, as are cheques provided that the cheque is not negotiated[60]. Any breach of this section renders the regulated agreement unenforceable without a court order[61]. The bill itself, however, remains en-

---

[52] Admittedly fairly rare: see *Mason v Lack* (1929) 45 TLR 363.
[53] Section 87(2).
[54] Section 83(3) of the 1882 Act.
[55] Section 3(1) invalidates a bill of exchange in this form.
[56] *See* p 264 *below*, and see *Davies v Rees* (1886) 17 QBD 408.
[57] *Monetary Advance Co v Carter* (1888) 20 QBD 785.
[58] *Acceptance Co Ltd v Cutner* (1964) 108 SJ 298.
[59] Consumer Credit Act 1974, s 123.
[60] Section 123(2).
[61] Section 124.

forceable subject to conditions. In particular, any person who takes a bill created in breach of this provision with notice of the fact that it was created in breach of the Consumer Credit Act is debarred from becoming a holder in due course[62], although a person who takes such a note in good faith without notice of the defect is a holder in due course and may enforce it[63]. In such a case the consumer has a right of indemnity against the person who initially required the note[64].

Promisory notes have the same characteristics as bills of exchange (with some minor exceptions listed in s 89 of the 1882 Act), and hereafter the term bills is used to include notes unless otherwise specified.

Delivery

There is one further requirement which a bill or note must satisfy before it can be accepted under the 1882 Act, and that is that it must have been 'delivered'[65]. The delivery may be actual or constructive (ie it need not involve any physical movement of the relevant piece of paper)[66], and the delivery need not be successful; an act proving the holder's intention to deliver is sufficient, and actual receipt by the deliveree is not necessary[67].

The object of the requirement for delivery seems to be that the drawer of a bill should have a *locus poenitentiae* after he has drawn up the bill and had it accepted—for example, in *Bromage v Lloyd*[68], where the drawer of a bill died before the bill was delivered, it was held to be invalid for want of delivery.

In order to ensure that there is no requirement to investigate the prehistory of a given bill in order to ensure delivery, delivery is conclusively presumed in favour of a holder in due course[69].

Negotiation and transfer

Bearer and order bills

A bill made payable to bearer is transferable by mere delivery. The transferor of such a bill need do nothing more than deliver it, and the title to the claim embodied in the bill is complete in the recipient at the time of receipt. The transferor need not sign the bill, nor do any other act than deliver it—he is a 'transferor by delivery'[70].

---

[62] Section 125(1).
[63] Section 125(4).
[64] Section 125(3).
[65] Section 21(1) of the 1882 Act.
[66] *Kleinwort v Comptoir D'Escompte* [1894] 2 QB 157.
[67] This normally happens where a person posts a bill which is subsequently intercepted. The act of posting is good delivery (*Kleinwort v Comptoir D'Escompte*, above). However, if the use of the post was expressly excluded by the parties then the sender can be required to send a second bill (*Pennington v Crossley* (1897) 13 TLR 513).
[68] (1847) 1 Ex 32.
[69] Section 21(2).
[70] Section 58(1).

A bill made out to X 'or order', however, can only be transferred by X's endorsing his order on the bill itself. X's order can either be an endorsement in blank (ie a bare signature) in which case the bill is thereafter in effect a bearer bill, or a 'special endorsement', in which X endorses the bill to Y by name. In such a case Y must in turn endorse the bill if he wishes to transfer the bill to Z. Where X endorses a bill he may make it subject to a variety of restrictions, such as making it non-negotiable[71], non-transferable[72] or by prescribing any restrictions upon subsequent transactions in the bill which could have been imposed by the original drawer[73]. These restrictions are enforceable.

Classes of holder

The Act recognises three types of holder of a bill:
  (a) the mere holder, defined by s 2 of the Act as the payee, endorsee or bearer of a bill who is in actual possession of it;
  (b) a holder for value, ie a holder of a bill for which value has been given, whether or not by him;
  (c) a holder for value without notice, ie a holder for value who has taken without notice of any defect in title of the person who negotiated it to him. Such a holder for value without notice is entitled by s 29(1) a 'holder in due course'.

The mainspring of the bills of exchange legislation is the idea of the holder in due course. A holder in due course:
  (i)   can enforce a bill free from any defect of title of the prior parties and without regard to any personal defences any prior party may have[74];
  (ii) can enforce payment against all parties liable on the bill;
  (iii) can give good title to a bill to a transferee, even though his own title is not good[75];
  (iv) is not affected by a previous dishonour[76];
  (v)   may sue any endorser for the value represented by the bill[77].

Other advantages which accrue to the holder in due course are that valid delivery[78] and due execution[79] are presumed in his favour.

The holder in due course is a close cousin of the idea 'purchaser for value of the legal estate without notice', against whom no prior right prevails. In both cases, a successful claim to such status is 'an absolute, unqualified, unanswerable defence against the claims of any prior equity'[80]. However, whereas in equity a person claiming the status of the purchaser for value without no-

---

[71] Section 35(1).
[72] Section 8(1).
[73] Section 35(1).
[74] Section 38(2).
[75] Section 38(3).
[76] Section 36(5).
[77] Section 56.
[78] Section 21(2).
[79] Section 20(2).
[80] *Pilcher v Rawlins* (1872) Ch App 259 at 269 per James LJ.

tice must prove that he is such[81], in the law of bills every holder is presumed to be a holder in due course unless the contrary is proved[82].

By s 29(1) of the Act a holder in due course is defined as a holder

who has taken a bill complete and regular on the face of it, under the following conditions; namely,

(a) That he became the holder of it before it was overdue, and without notice that it had been dishonoured, if such was the fact previously:

(b) That he took the bill in good faith and for value, and that at the time the bill was negotiated to him he had no notice of any defect in the title of the person who negotiated it.

Again, it is necessary to examine this provision in detail.

'holder'

A holder for the purposes of the Act is either an endorsee or the bearer. A payee is not a holder in due course for reasons explained below.

'complete and regular on the face of it'

This means free from apparent defects (ie a break in the chain of endorsements). Denning LJ said in *Arab Bank v Ross*[83] that the test of 'regularity on its face' is whether the bill would ordinarily be questioned if it were circulating amongst city bankers—in other words, the test is as to what would give rise to question in ordinary market practice. The usual irregularity on the face of a bill is an endorsement where the name endorsed differs from that of the named payee. It is impossible to become a holder in due course of a bill marked 'not transferable' or 'not negotiable', since such words render the bill not regular on the face of it—ie expressly negative its being used in transactions of the form ordinarily effected by bills of exchange.

'without notice of dishonour'

Notice in this case clearly means actual notice and not constructive notice, as constructive notice is not ordinarily to be imputed to commercial transactions[84].

'in good faith'

Section 90 of the Act provides that a thing is done 'in good faith' if it is done honestly, whether or not it is done negligently. It is tentatively submitted that the test of the status of holder 'in good faith' for the purpose of the Act may now be indistinguishable from the test of 'dishonesty' applied by the Privy

---

[81] *Re Nisbet & Potts' Contract* [1906] 1 Ch 386 at 402.

[82] Section 30(2).

[83] [1952] 2 QB 216 at 227.

[84] Per Lindley LJ in *Manchester Trust v Furness* [1895] 2 QB 539.

Council in *Royal Brunei Airlines Sdn Bhd v Tan*[85] in determining liability as a constructive trustee.

'for value'

By s 2 'value' means valuable consideration. This means that a donee of a bill cannot sue on it. However, where the donee of a bill negotiates it for value, the person who gives value becomes a holder in due course.

'negotiated to him'

By s 31 a bill is 'negotiated' when it is transferred from one person to another. In *R E Jones v Waring and Gillow*[86] it was held that the initial delivery of a bill to its payee is not a 'negotiation', and therefore the initial payee of a bill (or its first bearer if it is made out to bearer) is not a holder in due course. This means that where A defrauds B into making out a bill payable to C, C cannot claim payment under the bill. However, if C were to negotiate the bill to D for value, D could claim payment under the bill since, as holder in due course, he would take free from any counterclaim that B may have.

Liability of drawer on the bill

The drawer of bill undertakes by drawing it that it will be paid, and he is liable on the bill if it is not[87], in addition to any liability which he may have purported to satisfy by the delivery of the bill, which remains intact (although in most cases the agreement between the parties that the underlying liability is satisfied by delivery of the bill constitutes an agreement that extinguishes the underlying liability). Where the drawee has negotiated the bill for value, the person to whom he has negotiated the bill may sue the drawer on the bill in any event. The Act permits the drawer to restrict his liability by endorsing the bill with such a restriction—for example, a bill can be created without recourse to the drawer[88].

Liability of acceptor on the bill

A drawee is only liable on a bill where he has accepted it, and his liability therefore arises *qua* acceptor rather than *qua* drawee. Some bills may be valid bills even though they have not been accepted, in the sense that they transfer a contingent claim against the drawee in any event[89]. However, the holder of a bill which has not been endorsed by the drawee as acceptor has a mere spes

---

[85] [1995] 2 AC 378.
[86] [1926] AC 670.
[87] Section 55(1)(*a*).
[88] Section 16.
[89] Section 39 sets out the circumstances in which a bill must be presented for acceptance.

that the bill will be paid, and if it is not his only remedy is against his transferee and any other endorser.

The drawee may accept the bill either absolutely or with a qualified acceptance. The acceptance may be qualified as to amount, time of payment, conditional upon the occurrence of a specified event or in a number of other ways. A holder of a bill who, upon presenting it to the drawee for acceptance, receives a qualified acceptance, is entitled to treat the bill as dishonoured.

An acceptor is prevented from raising defences based on the capacity or authority of the drawer[90]. He is only liable for his original acceptance, and where a bill is tampered with after acceptance but prior to presentation for payment, the transferee, even if he is a holder in due course, can only claim up to the original acceptance[91].

The acceptor is excused if the bill is not presented for payment promptly at a reasonable hour on a business day at the place specified for payment or at the places specified in s 45 of the Act. 'Promptly' in the case of a time bill means on the very day specified for payment[92], but for bills payable on demand the issue of when they should be presented is an issue for the court, which will take into account the nature of the bill, any applicable usage of the relevant trade and any other relevant facts[93]. However, the harshness of this rule is more apparent than real. The endorser of a bill is liable to his endorsee for the whole of the contract limitation period, and an endorsee who fails to obtain payment of a bill by presenting it after the due date can claim from his endorser, who in turn can claim back up the chain of endorsements to the drawer and the acceptor in any event. For this reason, many acceptors do not assert their strict legal right to refuse to pay bills presented shortly after their due date. As mentioned above, time bills must be presented 'within reasonable time'. In this context, the most important fact is the rule of practice among clearing banks that they will not pay cheques presented more than six months after their due date.

Liability of endorser on the bill

An endorser becomes liable on a bill merely by signing it. Any signature which appears on a bill other than as drawer or acceptor is taken to be that of an endorser, and renders the signatory liable as such[94].

The point here is that any person who endorses a bill becomes liable on it as (in effect) a guarantor of the bill's validity. A holder of a bill who is not paid when he presents it for payment may sue any endorser of the bill on the basis that each endorser has, by signing it, independently guaranteed its value[95].

---

[90] Section 54(2)(*a*).
[91] *Scholfield v Londesborough* [1896] AC 514 (bill accepted for £500 altered after acceptance to £3,500, negotiated and then presented. Held that acceptor liable only for £500).
[92] Section 45(1), except in the circumstances specified in ss 39(4) and 52(2) of the Act.
[93] Section 45(2).
[94] Section 56.
[95] Section 55(2)(*b*).

A transferor by delivery is not liable on a bill merely by virtue of having transferred it—if X has a bill made out to bearer which he hands to Y for value, Y cannot sue X if the bill is dishonoured upon presentment for payment. The result of this is that Y usually requires X to endorse the bill as a condition of his accepting it in payment of whatever liability it discharges. A person who endorses a bearer bill becomes liable on it in the same way as the endorser of an order bill is liable by s 56 of the Act which provides that any person who signs a bill 'otherwise than as drawer or acceptor ... thereby incurs the liabilities of an indorser'.

This rule has created a business whereby persons of good financial standing, for a fee, allow others to draw on them in order to raise money. Such bills are called accommodation bills, and are economically identical to credit being given by the payee to the drawer guaranteed by the drawee. The accommodation bill has the characteristic that it remains alive after it has been paid by the accommodating party until the accommodating party is paid by the drawer[96]. A virtually identical transaction is achieved where the person who wishes to provide financial assistance simply endorses his name on the bill.

Note that this creates some difficulty in the United Kingdom by reason of the continental European practice of signing bills *par aval*. A signature *par aval* is intended to (and, in Europe does) have the effect of guaranteeing the liabilities of one particular signatory. In other words, where X, holding the bill, wishes to negotiate it to Y, Y may require X to have Z sign *par aval* for X. In continental practice, this means that Z assumes a contingent liability for X's debt. X remains liable as endorser to subsequent holders of the bill, but such subsequent holders may only claim against Z if X has been claimed against. The operation of s 56 eliminates the possibility of the endorsement *par aval* on an English bill, and a person who endorses *par aval* becomes directly liable as an endorser to every subsequent holder[97].

Liability of transferor by delivery on a bearer bill

As mentioned above, where a bill is endorsed to bearer (or is created to order but subsequently generally endorsed), a person who subsequently acquires possession of it may negotiate it by mere delivery without endorsing it. By s 58 such a transferor is not liable on the bill, and cannot be sued by subsequent holders. However a transferor by delivery can be sued by the person to whom he negotiates the bill as he is deemed to have warranted that the bill is good for payment[98], and if the bill is dishonoured this warranty is breached. In this way a chain of liabilities may develop upon transfers of a bearer bill. However, whereas any holder of an order bill may sue any endorser, the holder of a bearer bill may only sue his immediate transferee, who may sue his own transferee in turn.

---

[96] Section 59(3).
[97] *Grunzweig und Hartmann Montage GmbH v Rahim Mottaghi Irvani* [1989] 1 Lloyd's Rep 14.
[98] Section 58(3).

Forged endorsements

A forged endorsement has, by s 24 of the Act, the effect that the forged signature is wholly void, and no person may rely on it in order to establish their claim. This rule has a number of interesting results. Where the drawer's signature is forged the bill is, of course, not a bill at all[99]. Where the acceptor's signature is forged there has been no valid acceptance and the bill may be presented for acceptance in the normal way. However, where an endorser's signature is forged, the forgery in effect breaks the chain of endorsement. Thus, where A endorses to B, B endorses to C and C endorses to D, each of A, B, C and D may recover against the drawer. However if Z steals the bill from A and negotiates it to B by forging A's endorsement, B, C and D (if they are holders in due course) may sue each other but may not sue A or the drawer because the forged endorsement breaks the chain of liability. The bill must be returned to A, whose rightful property it remains, D will successfully sue C and C will successfully sue B, who will bear the loss unless he can find and sue the forger.

Note that this rule only applies where the forged endorsement is a necessary part of the transaction. In the case of a bearer bill, a forged endorsement is of no consequence since the bill is validly transferred by mere delivery without reference to the endorsement.

Finally, note that by the terms of s 24 a forgery is treated as genuine where an estoppel arises against the person concerned. Thus in *Greenwood v Martins Bank*[100], a man who knew that his wife was forging his signature in order to draw money out of his account was held to be estopped from denying the veracity of the signatures in an action brought against the bank for paying the cheques.

Where a bill is altered as to its amount, tenor or any other term after it has been drawn and accepted, this does not count as a forgery. In such a case, the rules provided in s 64 of the Act govern. Clearly the amendment does not affect the drawer's or the acceptor's liability. If the alteration is apparent, then all the endorsees subsequent to the alteration may recover from each other the face amount, but none of them may recover anything from the original drawer or acceptor. If the alteration is not apparent, then any holder may recover the initial amount from the drawer or acceptor.

Autonomy of the bill

A bill of exchange is created by a separate and independent contract. This has the disadvantage that the bill's validity may be challenged where all of the ingredients of an ordinary contract are not present (see above), but the advantage that the bill remains fully enforceable regardless of the enforceability or

---

[99] A bill is a document 'signed by the person giving it' (s 3) or 'signed by the maker' in the case of a promissory note.
[100] [1933] AC 51.

otherwise of the original contract. This is clearly seen in cases such as *Glasscock v Balls*[101] in which a person gave a negotiable instrument for a debt along with a mortgage. The creditor transferred the mortgage to one person and the note to another. The defendant was not allowed to raise a defence to the action on the instrument that he could not be liable both on the instrument and on the mortgage, on the basis that to allow such a defence would be to infringe the autonomy of the instrument. This rule applies even to counterclaims, and in *Brown Shipley v Alicia Hosiery*[102] Denning LJ said: 'judgement upon the bill of exchange should be given as for cash, and it is not to be held up by virtue of some counterclaim which the defendant may assert, even, as in this case, a counterclaim relating to the specific subject-matter of the contract'[103]. This rule takes effect to exclude even the ordinary rules of court, and RSC Ord 18, r 17, which ordinarily allows counterclaims to be set off against the plaintiff's claim, is disapplied in the case of actions brought upon bills of exchange[104].

It may be noticed that this conclusion does not automatically follow from the fact of the separateness of the two contracts, since equitable set-off is available where cross-claims arise out of separate but connected contracts. The unavailability of equitable set-off in this case is in fact based upon policy grounds, and in particular the preservation of the commercial efficacy of bills[105]. It seems, however, that the unavailability of equitable set-off is only a bar to the drawer and the acceptor. A holder of an instrument may set off the debt owed on the instrument against a claim for damages by a third party who is liable on the instrument[106].

In the context of common law set-off, it has been said that a liquidated cross-demand cannot be set off in law against a liability under the bill[107], and there is some authority for this proposition[108]. However, the better view seems to be that set-off at law is always available in respect of liquidated amounts presently due, whether on a bill or otherwise, since common law set-off is a creature of statute, and the statute makes no express exception for negotiable instruments from its general scope[109].

It will therefore be seen that the only defences which are likely to assist the drawer are those to the effect that the bill has not satisfied the requirements of

---

[101] (1889) 24 QBD 13.
[102] [1966] 1 Lloyd's Rep 668.
[103] At 669.
[104] *Lamont v Hyland* [1950] 1 KB 585. For a full citation of the authorities for this proposition see R Derham, *Set-Off*, 2nd edn (OUP, 1996), pp 98–9, fn 618–22.
[105] *Nova (Jersey) Knit Ltd v Kammgarn Spinnerei GmbH* [1977] 1 WLR 713. However, see *Barclays Bank Ltd v Aschaffenburger Zellstoffwerke AG* [1963] 1 Lloyd's Rep 387, in which a stay of execution was granted in an action on a bill pending arbitration of a counterclaim. The decision was disapproved by the Court of Appeal in *Cebora SNC v SIP (Industrial Products) Ltd* [1976] 1 Lloyd's Rep 271.
[106] *Williams v Davies* (1829) 2 Sim 461.
[107] Wood, *English and International Set-Off* (Sweet & Maxwell, 1989), pp 700–1.
[108] *Cebora SNC v SIP (Industrial Products) Ltd* [1976] 1 Lloyd's Rep 271, followed in *Power Curber International Ltd v National Bank of Kuwait* [1981] 1 WLR 1233.
[109] Derham, *Set-Off*, 2nd edn (OUP, 1996), pp 106–10; *Hong Kong & Shanghai Banking Corp v Kloeckner & Co AG* [1990] 2 QB 514.

the Act (ie is not in proper form) or that the contract by which it was created was for some reason void. In general, this means a claim that consideration has totally failed[110]. Claims of this form are usually made where the bill is drawn in payment under a contract the performance of which constitutes the consideration for the giving of the bill in the first place. Thus if I agree to pay you £10 for the use of your garden for a garden party and it is agreed between us that the agreement will be cancellable if it rains, where I give you a bill for the money in advance, upon the rain falling your right to collect the bill will fall away, since there is no consideration to support the action[111]. However, once the bill has been negotiated, the holder may sue on it whether or not the consideration for the initial transaction pursuant to which the bill was created was void[112], and it seems that this is true whether or not the holder knew of the invalidity of the consideration on the underlying contract[113].

As in many other fields, the doctrine of estoppel may be brought into play to defeat claims under a bill. Thus where a person has by his words or conduct led another to rely to his detriment on an actual or apparent undertaking not to do something, he is not thereafter allowed to do it. The ordinary case of estoppel arises where a person leads another to believe, by words or by conduct, that he will not enforce his strict legal rights and, where such a person has acted to his detriment in reliance upon such a representation, equity restrains the enforcement of the strict legal rights except in so far as such enforcement is consistent with the representation. In the context of bills this usually arises in the case of agreements to defer payment, but can arise in circumstances where a person prepares a defective bill for another to sign[114].

Discharge of the bill

A bill is discharged by payment, by express waiver[115], by cancellation[116], by alteration without the consent of all parties[117] or in circumstances where the acceptor is the holder at the maturity date[118]. Payment in due course is the usual way in which a bill becomes discharged. Payment in due course is defined as payment made by or on behalf of the drawee or acceptor in good faith at or after maturity to the holder without notice that his title is defective[119]. Where an endorser pays on the bill it is not discharged. The same is true when the drawer pays, for he can recover from the acceptor[120].

---

[110] It is unusual for a person to seek to set up his own incapacity, and defences based on fraud, duress and undue influence only arise in fairly specialised circumstances.

[111] *Elliott v Crutchley* [1906] AC 7.

[112] *Banco Di Roma v Orru* [1973] 2 Lloyd's Rep 505.

[113] *Fitch v Jones* (1855) 24 LJQB (Trin T) 295; *Lilley v Rankin* (1886) 56 LJQB 248; although *contra Lloyd v Davis* (1824) 3 LJ (OS) KB (Mich T) 3.

[114] *Durham Fancy Goods Ltd v Michael Jackson (Fancy Goods) Ltd* [1968] 2 QB 839.

[115] Section 62.

[116] Section 63.

[117] Section 64.

[118] Section 61.

[119] Section 59(1).

[120] Except in the case of an accommodation bill (s 59(3)).

Dishonour

The concept of dishonour is unique to bills of exchange. Upon dishonour, it suddenly becomes of the greatest importance for the holder to give notice to all other parties of the dishonour. The reason for the great haste is that, as Byles puts it[121]:

> The law presumes that, if the drawer has not had due notice, he is injured because otherwise he might have immediately withdrawn his effects from the hands of the drawee and that, if the endorser has not had timely notice, the remedy against the parties liable to him is rendered more precarious. The consequence, therefore, of neglect of notice is that, that the party to whom it should have been given is discharged from all liability, whether on the bill or on the consideration for which the bill was paid. It has long been settled that the want of notice is a complete defence, and that evidence tending to show that the defendant was not prejudiced by the neglect is inadmissible ...

This rule is construed very strictly. In *Yeoman Credit Ltd v Gregory*[122] the lapse of two days before notice was given was sufficient to discharge the liability of an endorser of the bill. As a general rule, the notice must be dispatched no later than the day after dishonour[123].

A bill may be dishonoured in two ways. Where a bill is circulating in drawn-up form without having been accepted, if when it is presented to the drawee for acceptance the drawee refuses to accept it the bill is dishonoured. In such a case the holder may sue on the bill immediately without representing it for payment. The second is upon non-payment of the bill itself. Note that upon a partial payment the holder may elect to treat the bill as dishonoured as to the unpaid part only. Note also that where the bill is paid by cheque the actual transaction is a substitution of one bill for another which has the effect of discharging the first bill. The notice of dishonour must be given according to the detailed rules set out in s 49 of the Act.

Protest

Where a foreign bill (ie a bill drawn on a person outside the British Isles or upon a person not resident therein) is dishonoured, either by non-acceptance or by non-payment, it must be 'protested'. This means that it must be taken to a notary public who in effect notarises the fact that the bill has not been paid. Again, Byles explains that[124]:

> By the law of many foreign countries a protest is essential in the case of dishonour of any bill or note, whether inland or foreign, and it is for the sake of uniformity in

---

[121] *Byles on Bills of Exchange,* 26th edn (Sweet & Maxwell, 1988), pp 177–8.
[122] [1963] 1 All ER 245.
[123] Section 49(12).
[124] *Byles on Bills of Exchange* (*see* fn 122 *above*), pp 186–7.

international transactions that by English law, as in that of the United States, foreign bills must be protested. Besides, a protest affords satisfactory evidence of dishonour to the drawer, who, from his residence abroad, might experience difficulty in making proper inquiries on the subject.

The basis of the process is that 'a notary public by the law of nations has credit everywhere'[125]. The mechanism of protest may be abridged by a shorter process, called noting, which in effect operates as a preliminary which allows the bill to be formally protested at an unspecified later date. A version of the protest mechanism can be used in respect of inland bills in order to enable acceptance and payment 'for honour'[126] or 'for better security'[127].

---

[125] *Hutcheon v Mannington* (1802) 6 Ves 823.
[126] Sections 65 and 67.
[127] Section 51(5).

Chapter 19

Cheques

General

A cheque is a bill of exchange drawn on a banker payable on demand[1]. Two elements of this definition require comment:

'drawn on a banker'

In the context of the Bills of Exchange Act and the Cheques Acts, 'banker' does not have its ordinary statutory meaning of an institution licensed to accept deposits under the Banking Act 1987[2], but is defined as 'a body of persons whether incorporated or not who carry on the business of banking'[3]. This may be because, even though the Banking Act 1987 provides that only institutions authorised thereunder may describe themselves as banks[4], s 69(4) preserves the right of persons not authorised under the Act to take advantage of any other enactment which applies to a person by virtue of his being a bank or banker. The question of who qualifies as a 'banker' for the purposes of the Act is important, primarily because the Cheques Act 1957 is construed as one with the Bills of Exchange Act[5], and the protections it provides to 'bankers' are therefore available to anyone who falls within the definition contained in the Act.

It seems most likely that the test to be applied of whether a person is a 'banker' within the meaning of the Act (and therefore of whether a document is a cheque) is the common law test as identified in *United Dominions Trust Ltd v Kirkwood*[6]. In that case the issue arose whether UDT was a 'bank' within the meaning of the Moneylenders Acts 1900 and 1927 and therefore exempt from the documentation requirements of those Acts. This was a matter of great importance to a number of institutions, since compliance with the Moneylenders Acts was in effect incompatible with conducting the business of a finance house in the 1960s. The decision in *Kirkwood* was so unsatisfactory in terms of enabling an institution to identify whether it was a bank or not that

---

[1] Section 73 of the Bills of Exchange Act 1882.
[2] Eg Bankers Books Evidence Act 1879, s 9, which also includes building societies, the National Savings Bank and the Post Office within the definition.
[3] Section 2.
[4] Banking Act 1987, s 67.
[5] Cheques Act 1957, s 6(1).
[6] [1966] 2 QB 431. The relevant authorities prior to the decision are listed in *Paget's Law of Banking*, 11th edn (1996) 104, fn 7.

the following year the Companies Act 1967 introduced a mechanism whereby the Board of Trade could issue a conclusive certificate to the effect that a given institution was a bank[7]. That system has now gone, being replaced in its function by the licensing provisions of the Consumer Credit Act 1974, but the legal uncertainty of the common law meaning of 'bank' remains.

In *Kirkwood*[8], the Court of Appeal by a two to one majority held that there were three characteristics of a 'bank' at common law, ie

(a) the conduct of current accounts,

(b) the payment of cheques, and

(c) the collection of cheques for customers,

such that any institution which had these characteristics was necessarily a bank. However, they further held (by the same majority) that the absence of any of these three characteristics did not necessarily render an institution not a bank, and that where the institution could be shown to enjoy the reputation of a 'bank' then it could be considered as such even though it did not have any of these characteristics[9]. Lending alone did not constitute the lender a bank[10].

However Scarman LJ, who dissented, held that the definition to be applied was that set out in *Bank of Chettinad Ltd of Colombo v IT Comrs, Colombo*[11] that a banker is one who carries on as his principal business the accepting of deposits of money on current account or otherwise, subject to withdrawal by cheque, draft or order, and he declined to accept that mere reputation was sufficient to constitute a person a 'banker'.

It has been suggested that only institutions which are authorised under the Banking Act 1987 to accept deposits can qualify as banks under the three criteria laid down by the majority in *Kirkwood*, on the basis that a current account could not be conducted without 'accepting deposits'[12]. This is incorrect. The statement is true in the ordinary meaning of the words, but the statutory definition of the term carves out a number of transactions. Most importantly, reg 15 of the Banking Act 1987 (Exempt Transactions) Regulations 1997 (SI No 817) permits any person authorised under the Financial Services Act 1987 to accept deposits in the course of the business for which he is authorised under that Act. Consequently, it seems clear that there are potentially a number of persons who, although not authorised institutions under the Banking Act 1987, may potentially qualify as bankers for the purposes of the Bills of Exchange Act.

'payable on demand'

A post-dated cheque is not a cheque within the meaning of the Act, but an ordinary time bill. Because a cheque is payable on demand it must be presented for payment within a reasonable time of its being drawn[13]. However it

---

[7] Companies Act 1967, s 123.

[8] *See* fn 6 *above*.

[9] per Denning MR and Diplock LJ.

[10] Followed in *Hafton Properties v McHugh* (1988) 59 TC 420.

[11] [1948] AC 378.

[12] Paget, *Law of Banking*, 11th edn (1996) 104.

[13] Section 45(2).

need not be presented for acceptance prior to payment[14].

However, note that the fact that a bill is not a 'cheque' within the meaning of the Act (either by virtue of being post-dated or by virtue of its being made out to 'cash') does not necessarily deprive the collecting banker of the protections of the Cheques Act with respect to it[15].

Crossing and marking[16]

The Act provides a special regime for cheques relating to what are known as 'crossings'. A crossing is an endorsement on a cheque, usually in the form of lines drawn across it, which has the effect of preventing the acceptor from obtaining a good discharge if he pays the bill to any person other than a bank claiming to collect on the part of the holder. This, in effect, requires the accepting bank to make payment only to another bank[17]. Crossings come in two flavours: general (ie the cheque can be paid to any bank), and special (ie the cheque may only be paid to a named bank). If the payee of a specially crossed sheque does not have an account at the named bank he must open one in order to collect on the cheque himself.

A crossing merely limits the identity of the person to whom payment of the cheque gives good discharge. A marking restricts the transferability of the cheque itself[18]. A cheque marked 'not negotiable' may be freely transferred, but the person to whom such a cheque is transferred does not become a holder in due course. This means that

(a) he takes the cheque subject to any defences which may have arisen pursuant to the contract on the cheque (ie where the consideration for a cheque marked 'not negotiable' has wholly failed, the cheque is not enforceable by a subsequent holder without notice of the failure), and

(b) he gets no better title than the transferor (ie if a thief transfers for value a cheque marked 'not negotiable', the transferee gets no title to the cheque[19]).

A bill, whether or not a cheque, marked 'not transferable' is not transferable. It creates rights between the drawer, the drawee bank and the payee, but between no other persons, and its transfer is a nullity as far as the creation of new rights on the bill is concerned[20]. The same result can be achieved on a cheque by the application of the marking 'account payee' or 'a/c payee'[21].

Since this last marking, accompanied by a crossing, is printed as a matter of course on the cheques issued by all the major banks, the jurisprudence of

[14] Section 39(3).
[15] *Orbit Mining & Trading v Westminster Bank Ltd* [1963] 1 QB 794.
[16] Sections 76–82.
[17] The term having in this context its common law meaning.
[18] It is probable that only cheques can be marked 'not negotiable' (*Paget's Law of Banking*, 11th edn (1996), p 251; *Byles on Bills of Exchange*, 26th edn (Sweet & Maxwell, 1988), pp 85–6, *per contra Hibernian Bank v Gysin & Hanson* [1939] 1 KB 483.
[19] *Wilson & Meeson v Pickering* [1946] KB 422.
[20] Section 8(1).
[21] Cheques Act 1992, adding s 81A to the Bills of Exchange Act 1882.

crossing and marking of cheques is of limited importance. Although the drawer of a cheque may delete the printed crossing prior to drawing the cheque, many banks will decline to pay on such cheques without adequate safeguards.

Banks' liabilities in respect of processing cheques

'To require a thorough enquiry into the history of each cheque would render banking business impracticable'[22]. In the interests of the efficiency of the banking system the Cheques Act 1957 amends the ordinary law of duties and obligations on bills in order to reduce the liabilities of banks dealing with cheques in respect of such dealings.

Liabilities of the paying banker

As a general rule, banks pay cheques which are presented to them for the purpose. Consequently the liabilities of the paying bank will arise out of payment by the bank of invalid cheques rather than non-payment of valid ones. The bank's duty to pay cheques is founded on the contract of banker and customer, by which the bank undertakes to pay cheques drawn by the customer where there are funds available to do so. Non-payment may also constitute defamation[23].

In addition to its duty to obey its mandate, a bank also owes a duty to safeguard its customer's assets. As far as a paying bank is concerned, its relationship with its customer is governed by the duties which would arise as between principal and agent[24]. Thus the bank owes to its customer a duty to take care in making payments on his behalf[25]. This duty arises both in tort and under the contract between banker and customer[26]. It is therefore in principle the responsibility of a paying banker, when a cheque drawn by or on behalf of his customer is presented to him for payment, to satisfy himself that the cheque is validly and properly drawn and that he is authorised and entitled to pay it. The enquiry by which standard of care which is expected of a paying banker in this regard is to be determined was explained by Parker LJ in the Court of Appeal in *Lipkin Gorman v Karpnale* as that[27]:

> The question must be whether if a reasonable and honest banker knew of the relevant facts he would have considered that there was a serious or real possibility, albeit not amounting to a probability that his customer might be being defrauded ... If it is established then in my view a reasonable banker would be in breach of duty if he continued to pay cheques without enquiry. He could not simply sit back and ignore the situation.

---

[22] Per Scrutton LJ, *Lloyds Bank v Chartered Bank of India* [1929] 1 KB 40 at 59.
[23] A presumption of damage arises in every case of non-payment (*Kpoharor v Woolwich Building Society* (1995) *The Times*, 8 December).
[24] *Westminster Bank Ltd v Hilton* (1926) 135 TLR 124 at 126.
[25] *Royal Products Ltd v Midland Bank Ltd* [1981] 2 Lloyd's Rep 194.
[26] *Barclays Bank v Quincecare Ltd* [1992] 4 All ER 363; *Lipkin Gorman v Karpnale* [1989] 1 WLR 1340, CA.
[27] [1992] 4 All ER 409 at 441.

This must be understood in the context of the decision in *London Joint Stock Bank Ltd v Macmillan*[28] to the effect that the customer may not put upon the banker, and the banker need not accept, any risk or liability not contemplated in or ordinarily arising out of the ordinary routine of business.

The customer is not necessarily obliged to reimburse the bank in respect of all payments made by the bank on his account. The terms of the mandate given by the customer to his bank will determine under what circumstances the bank may or may not pay cheques drawn on the account[29]. A common example is a company mandate which requires two signatures for payment. A cheque drawn on the account but signed by only one signatory is outside the mandate, and the bank must seek to recover otherwise than under the agreement. The same is true of payments made on forged cheques. If banks pay out on cheques which are not the customers, they are acting outside their mandate and cannot plead his authority in justification of their debit to his account. That is a risk of the service which it is their business to offer.

Common law defences of the paying banker

The paying bank may defend its debiting of the account of the customer in one of four ways.

Estoppel

An estoppel will arise against the customer in circumstances where he has either drawn a cheque in a way which facilitates a fraud or forgery (eg by leaving a space after the amount which can subsequently be filled up with a larger amount[30]) or where the customer knows that the cheque has been fraudulently produced or amended and did not disclose this fact to the bank[31]. It seems that these categories are now exhaustive and will not be extended[32].

Ratification

This arises where the customer has adopted the defective cheque as his own, as, for example, in *London Intercontinental Trust Ltd v Barclays Bank Ltd*[33], where a company resolved to take no action over cheques which had been paid by the company's bank on the signature of a single director where two signatures were required by the mandate.

Equitable defence of discharge

The equitable defence of discharge of the plaintiff's debt arises where the effect of the payment is to confer a benefit on the account-holder. In *Liggett v*

---

[28] [1918] AC 777.
[29] Per Scarman J in *Tai Hing Cotton Mill v Liu Chong Hing Bank Ltd* [1986] AC 80.
[30] *London Joint Stock Bank v Macmillan and Arthur* [1918] AC 777.
[31] *Greenwood v Martins Bank* [1933] AC 51.
[32] *Tai Hing Cotton Mill v Liu Chong Hing Bank Ltd* [1986] AC 80.
[33] [1980] 1 Lloyd's Rep 241.

Barclays Bank Ltd[34] the bank (again) paid cheques required by the mandate to be signed by two directors which had in fact been signed only by one. The cheques were paid to creditors of the company in discharge of the company's debts. It was held that the bank was subrogated to the rights of the creditor thus discharged, and could therefore debit the company's account in respect of the claim which it had acquired by the subrogation. The difficulty was of course to distinguish the case from that of a payment by a mere volunteer which, it is trite law, does not discharge the debt of another. If A owes B £5 and C pays B £5, in the absence of a direct connection between the two C's payment does not extinguish A's debt. In the instant case it was held that the fact of the signatory's directorship created an implied authorisation to discharge the company's debts, and that the act of inducing the bank to discharge the debt was pursuant to this implied authority and established the necessary connection[35].

Payment in due course

Section 59 of the Bills of Exchange Act provides that the bank upon which a cheque is drawn is discharged by payment in due course to the holder for the time being unless the bank has notice that the holder's title to the bill is defective. Where a cheque is treated as discharged the bank has performed its obligations under the bill in accordance with the contract, and is entitled to reimbursement in accordance with that contract. However, note that this may still leave the bank liable to the customer for breach of the mandate if it has paid a cheque which is incorrectly signed or subject to a stop order. The definition of the concept of discharge by payment also leaves a number of circumstances in which the bank, having made payment, is not discharged and remains liable to another person (eg where payment is made to a person claiming under a forged endorsement (ie a person with no title at all) or where the document is not a 'cheque' at all (ie where it is post-dated)).

Statutory defences of the paying banker

Payment is important partly because it is the usual way in which cheques are dealt with, but also because the various statutory protections which are available to a paying banker take effect to deem him discharged by payment despite the existence of facts which render his payment otherwise than good discharge. These are as follows.

Section 60 of the Bills of Exchange Act 1882 protects the banker who pays out on a bill in good faith and in the ordinary course of business[36] in circumstances where one of the endorsements on the bill is forged or made without

---

[34] [1928] 1 KB 48.
[35] *Re Cleadon Trust* [1939] Ch 286; *Barclays Bank v Simms* [1980] 1 QB 677; and see *AEG (UK) v Lewis* (1992) *The Times*, 29 December.
[36] This seems to be a different and lower standard than negligence, in that a bank may act in the ordinary course of business whilst at the same time acting negligently (*Carpenters Co v British Mutual Banking Co Ltd*).

authority. The bank is treated as if it had discharged the bill, and is therefore relieved from liability on the bill and entitled to seek reimbursement from its customer. Section 60 applies only to bills which are payable to order. As a result of the 1992 Cheques Act modern cheques are not usually payable 'to order', and the section probably does not apply in these cases.

Section 19 of the Stamp Act 1853 was the statutory predecessor of s 60 above. It has been held to have been deliberately left unrepealed by the Bills of Exchange Act on the basis that it applies not only to bills but also to drafts or orders drawn upon the bank[37]. Section 19 has the same effect as s 60 in respect of these documents save that there is no requirement of dealing in the ordinary course of business for the protection to arise.

Section 1 of the Cheques Act 1957 supplements the foregoing provisions. It applies to banks acting 'in good faith and the ordinary course of business', and it may therefore be available in circumstances in which s 80 is not available. The protection is in two parts. Section 1(1) provides that where a banker pays a cheque he does not incur any liability by reason of any endorsement appearing thereon being irregular, or being absent altogether, and is discharged by payment. Section 1(2) provides that where a banker pays 'a document issued by a customer of his which, though not a bill of exchange, is intended to enable a person to obtain payment from him of the sum mentioned in the document' (ie post-dated cheques, cheques made out to 'cash' and other documents which, by reason of formal irregularities, are not properly bills of exchange) or a draft payable by him he does not incur any liability by reason of the absence or irregularity of any endorsement and is also discharged. The protection afforded in the absence of an endorsement means that the paying bank may, in effect, assume an endorsement from the payee to the person presenting the cheque for payment.

Section 80 of the Bills of Exchange Act 1882 relates to payments made contrary to their crossing or marking. The section has the effect that where, in good faith and without negligence, a banker pays a cheque in accordance with its crossing, the banker is to be treated 'as if the cheque has been paid to the true owner thereof' (ie the bank is treated as if it had discharged the cheque). It is therefore relieved from further liability on the bill and entitled to claim reimbursement from the customer. The purpose of this section requires a little explanation. A cheque which has been crossed may only be presented to the paying banker for collection by another banker. When a banker presents the cheque for collection, he will not disclose to the paying bank the identity of his customer. Consequently, as far as the paying bank is concerned he has discharged his duty if, the cheque being crossed generally, he pays the cheque to a bank or, the cheque being crossed specially to X & Co, he pays the cheque to X & Co. He need not concern himself with how the cheque came into the hands of the relevant bank—it is the responsibility of the bank presenting the cheque for collection to establish whether its customer has a right to the cheque, and the paying bank has no liability for the act of the collecting bank.

This reasoning explains the provisions of s 81A(2) of the Bills of Exchange

[37] *Jones v Gordon* (1877) 2 App Cas 616.

Act, which in effect allow the paying bank to disregard the a/c payee marking which renders the cheque non-transferable. If this were not the case the paying bank might be put upon enquiry to determine whether the payee of the cheque had an account with the bank presenting the cheque for payment—an unreasonable requirement.

The requirement for establishing the protection of s 80 is that the paying bank shall have acted 'without negligence'. As mentioned above, this is a higher standard than 'in the ordinary course of business', so the protection of s 80 may not be available in situations in which the protections of s 60 and s 1 of the Cheques Act 1957 are available.

Liabilities to third parties of the paying banker

Where a paying banker has paid a cheque, he is usually safe against claims by the account holder. However, the position must also be considered from the perspective of the rightful owner of the instrument where the payment has been made to a different person.

Conversion

The paying bank owes no duty in negligence to the payee of a cheque[38]. However, he may be sued in conversion[39]. Where the drawee has delivered the cheque to the payee, from whom it is stolen, if the thief presents the cheque and it is paid, the payment does not discharge the bank, which remains liable to the true owner. There has therefore been no interference with the title of the holder, and therefore no conversion. The same applies if the cheque is fraudulently endorsed[40]. The action against the bank will therefore be in respect of a breach of the terms of the crossing. Where a cheque is paid contrary to the terms of its crossing, the payment still discharges the liability under s 59 of the Act and therefore appears to be a conversion of the cheque as against the true owner. However, it has been held that in reality there is no such conversion. In *Charles v Blackwell*[41] the point arose, and the Court of Appeal held that, because the cheque had been paid within the terms of s 19 of the Stamp Act (now s 60 of the Act) it had therefore been discharged. The court went on to hold that because the payment had discharged the instrument, the plaintiffs no longer had any property in it. Cockburn CJ observed that when a cheque was paid, the customer ceased to be entitled to it, and the paying banker was himself the person immediately entitled to possession thereafter[42].

This argument that payment of the cheque destroys the owners' immediate right to possession thereof is an interesting one, in that the very act of conversion destroys the possessory base needed to bring the action. This argument

---

[38] *National Westminster Bank v Barclays Bank International Ltd* [1975] QB 654.
[39] *Smith v Union Bank of London* (1875) LR 10 QB 291.
[40] *Lacave v Credit Lyonnais* [1897] 1 QB 148.
[41] (1877) 2 CPD 151.
[42] (1877) 2 CPD 151 at 162–3.

seems to be challengeable in principle on the basis that the wrongdoer should not be able to set up his own wrong as a defence to liability, but it does not seem to have been so challenged.

In modern practice the action will be brought upon a non-transferable cheque which has been paid to a person other than the named payee rather than on a bill which has been transferred by a false endorsement. In such a case protection is provided by s 80 rather than s 60 of the Act (as was relied upon in *Charles v Blackwell*), which has the effect that the bank is deemed to have made the payment 'to the true owner of the cheque' rather than 'to the holder thereof in good faith and without notice' as is the effect of ss 59–60. Since the true owner is the only person entitled to bring an action in conversion, the effect of this provision is, on the reasoning of *Charles v Blackwell*, to extinguish the liability in conversion. Note, however, that s 80 only provides its protection in the event that the banker acts 'in good faith and without negligence'. If the banker does not act in this way then the action in conversion is effective.

Constructive trust

The paying bank may also be liable in constructive trust based upon knowing assistance in the disposition of trust assets[43]. Such liability on the part of a paying bank was found in both *Selangor United Rubber Estates v Cradock (No 3)*[44] and *Karak Rubber Co Ltd v Burdon (No 2)*[45]. In the case of the bank's customer there is nothing to be gained by adding a constructive trust claim to an ordinary contractual claim for breach of the bank's duty of care in respect of the customer's assets[46]. However such an action will be the only remedy available to the beneficiaries of the assets in respect of which the account holder may have been a trustee. In reality, this point tends to arise primarily in the case of actions brought by companies in respect of unauthorised payments out of a company bank account made by directors.

Liability in knowing assistance requires proof of actual dishonesty. This was finally determined by the Privy Council in *Royal Brunei Airlines Sdn Bhd v Tan*[47], which swept away the scale of degrees of constructive knowlege[48] and replaced the test for liability in constructive trust with a single test of 'dishonesty'. The problem for banks in the past had been that too significant a degree of ignorance on their part of their own activities had been liable to be construed by the courts as constructive notice. It is a great deal harder to prove dishonesty on the part of a bank than it is to prove incompetence or ignorance, and it is suggested that in the aftermath of *Tan* this head of liability will disappear.

---

[43] Note that a paying bank is not liable in knowing receipt.
[44] [1968] 1 WLR 1555.
[45] [1972] 1 WLR 602.
[46] *Lipkin Gorman v Karpnale* [1989] 1 WLR 1340, CA.
[47] [1995] 2 AC 378.
[48] Set out in *Baden Delvaux v Société Generale pour Favoriser le Dévéloppement du Commerce et de l'Industrie en France SA* [1983] BCLC 325 at 404.

The collecting banker

A collecting bank acts as agent for its customer in presenting bills for payment, and as such owes and is owed all the normal duties associated with an agency. In particular, where the bank employs an agent to collect cheques, the bank is liable for the acts of its sub-agents[49]. The primary role of the collecting bank is to present a cheque for acceptance, although pursuant to the Deregulation (Bills of Exchange) Order 1996 this may now be accomplished electronically at a single address rather than by physical presentment of the individual cheque at the branch upon which it was drawn, as was previously the custom. Where a cheque is dishonoured, the usual custom is to return it to the person presenting it with instructions to 'refer to drawer'. In order to preserve the drawer's liability on the cheque it is necessary for that person to protest the dishonour to the drawer within a very short space of time (usually one day)[50].

The means by which the collecting bank acquires the cheque is of interest. As a general rule the cheque is simply presented to him for use in the collection process—in which case he is simply its bailee, although he has a banker's lien against it in respect of debts due to him from the customer[51]. However, in some circumstances the cheque may be negotiated to him so that he becomes a holder in due course. In such a case he is entitled not only to collect the cheque but also to sue the drawer directly on the bill, and is not liable to the true owner in conversion. In the ordinary course of events the paying bank rarely gives value for a cheque, and value is not given where the bank merely credits the account of the customer before collecting the cheque[52]. By s 27(3) of the Act the holder of a bill is deemed to have given value if he has a lien over the bill up to the amount secured by the lien, and this is frequently the case in respect of bank's collecting cheques for customers who are overdrawn[53]. In such a case the bank is both holder and agent for collection, and there is no repugnance between these two statuses[54].

By s 2 of the Cheques Act 1957 a bank which has a lien upon a cheque delivered to it for collection has the same rights as if the cheque had been endorsed to it in blank. The value of this section is, however, almost completely destroyed by the ordinary bank practice of delivering unpaid cheques back to the customer concerned. Such a redelivery, it has been held, destroys the bank's lien, and a subsequent re-redelivery to the bank for the purposes of suing the drawer will not revive it[55].

---

[49] *Mackersey v Ramsays, Bonars & Co* (1843) 9 Cl & Fin 818; *Prince v Oriental Bank Corp'n* (1873) 3 App Cas 325.
[50] *Lombard Banking Ltd v Central Garage & Engineering Co* [1963] 1 QB 220.
[51] *Giles v Perkins* (1807) 9 East 12; *Brandao v Barnett* (1846) 12 Cl & Fin 787, HL; *Re Firth, ex p Schofield* (1879) 12 Ch D 337.
[52] *A L Underwood v Barclays Bank Ltd* [1924] 1 KB 775.
[53] If the overdraft is less than the value of the cheque the bank may sue as holder for value up to the amount of the overdraft and as mere holder for the balance (*Barclays Bank v Aschaffenburger Zellstoffwerke AG* [1967] 1 Lloyd's Rep 387).
[54] *Barclays Bank Ltd v Astley Industrial Trust Ltd*.
[55] *Westminster Bank Ltd v Zang* [1966] AC 182.

Liabilities of collecting bank

The potential liabilities of the collecting bank are fourfold.

Conversion

Although conversion only lies for interference with an immediate right to possession of property, and does not normally allow for recovery of value lost, by a legal fiction the physical embodiment of a negotiable instrument is deemed to bear the face value of the instrument[56], and where the instrument is not negotiable, it seems that a person who succeeds in obtaining value for it is estopped from denying that it bears the value which he obtained[57].

Where the collecting bank obtains value for the bill in circumstances where title to it is vested in some other person, the act of the collecting bank in collecting the bill constitutes a conversion of the bill[58]. This occurs where the bill has been stolen, transferred via a forged endorsement, or bears a crossing which renders it non-negotiable and is being collected for someone other than the named payee. Given the universality of the a/c payee crossing after the 1992 Cheques Act, the last will invariably be the case whenever any bank collects a cheque for the benefit of any person other than the named payee.

The basis of an action in conversion is a right to immediate possession. In the context of cheques, this can create problems. For example, where A opens an account with bank X & Co in the name of B in order to pay into it cheques stolen on their way to B, X & Co commits no conversion against B by collecting the cheques, since B has no immediate right to possession[59]. The position is otherwise where the cheques have reached B but then been stolen from him, for the theft does not destroy his immediate right to possession. Likewise, it is probable that where someone steals my cheque-book and forges my signature on one of my cheques, I have no action in conversion against the collecting bank. The cheque-book remained at all times the property of the bank itself, and the forged signature, being a complete nullity, does not create in me any right to possession of the cheque[60]. Further, where I receive a bill under a voidable contract, if the contract is avoided whilst the bill is in my hands the right to immediate possession of the drawer immediately revives, and a bank which collects it is liable to the drawer in conversion for interference with that right. However, where the contract is merely voidable, no such action arises[61].

Where an agent misappropriates a cheque due to his principal, the right to sue remains vested in his principal. Thus in *Great Western Railway Co v London & County Banking Co Ltd*[62], the GWR made out a cheque for a rates bill

---

[56] *Morrison v London, County & Westminster Bank Ltd* [1914] 3 KB 356.

[57] *Bavins Junior and Sims v London and South Western Bank* [1900] 1 QB 270, CA.

[58] *Morison v London, County & Westminster Bank Ltd* [1914] 3 KB 356; *Lloyds Bank Ltd v Chartered Bank of India, Australia and China* [1929] 1 KB 40.

[59] *Robinson v Midland Bank Ltd* (1925) 41 TLR 402.

[60] *Arrow Transfer Co Ltd v Royal Bank of Canada, Bank of Montreal and Canadian Imperial Bank of Commerce* [1972] 4 WLR 70, *affmg* [1971] 3 WLR 241.

[61] *Midland Bank Ltd v Brown, Shipley & Co* [1991] 1 Lloyd's Rep 576.

[62] [1901] AC 414.

to the rates collector, one Huggins, personally, so that the cheque was to 'Huggins or Order'. Huggins paid it into his personal account. It was held that his principals could sue on the conversion of the cheque even though it was made out to Huggins personally, since it had been given to him for their benefit. Note, however, that in *Australia and New Zealand Bank v Ateliers de Constructions Electriques de Charleroi*[63], the opposite conclusion was reached where it was proved that the principal had permitted the agent to pay cheques into his own account in this way.

Where a bank is liable in conversion, it may probably debit the customer's account with any damages awarded against it[64]. However doubt has been cast on this proposition on the basis that the indemnity would be in respect of the bank's own negligence[65] (if the bank had not been negligent it would have been entitled to the protection of s 4 of the Cheques Act 1957—see below).

Money had and received

This lies wherever one person has received money for the benefit of another. As discussed below[66], wherever conversion lies the plaintiff can elect to waive the tort and sue in money had and received to his use. The structure of the liability is that the law implies a debt, which is sued for[67].

An action for money had and received lies against the successor holder to the use of the plaintiff. However, such an action will not be against an agent where the agent has paid over the amount to his principal in such a way as to give him a defence of change of position[68]. It seems that the bank will only be said to have irretrievably altered its position if, subsequent to the customer having been credited with the proceeds of the money, the account has been closed, reduced to a nominal amount, or there is some other reason why the bank cannot debit the account with the outstanding amount. If the account is in credit to the amount of the claim then there is no alteration of position[69], and therefore no defence.

Constructive trust

Constructive trust liability is incurred by a collecting bank as soon as it receives the funds. It is important in the context of the liability of the receiving bank to distinguish between liability incurred by a knowing recipient of trust funds and liability incurred as a knowing assistant in the disposal of trust

---

[63] [1967] 1 AC 86, PC.

[64] *Sheffield Corp v Barclay* [1905] AC 392; *Stanley Yeung Kai Yung v Hong Kong and Shanghai Banking Corp* [1981] AC 787.

[65] *Redmond v Allied Irish Banks plc* [1987] 2 FTLR 264.

[66] *See* pp 322–5 *below*.

[67] *Fibrosa Spolka Akcyjna v Fairbairn Lawson Combe Barbour Ltd* [1943] AC 32 at 62.

[68] Dicta of Millett LJ to the contrary in *Agip (Africa) v Jackson* [1990] 1 Ch 265 are misconceived, based as they are on the premise that the result in *Banque Belge pour L'Etranger v Hambrouck* [1920] 1 KB 321, which arose as the result of an accident of pleading, was based on legal principle—see Birks [1989] LMCLQ 296.

[69] *Bavins Junior and Sims v London and South Western Bank* [1900] 1 QB 270, CA.

funds[70]. It is clear from the decision in *Royal Brunei Airlines Sdn Bhd v Tan*[71] that liability for knowing assistance requires proof of dishonesty. However, liability in knowing receipt has always been said to require a lower level of knowledge of the relevant breach of trust than liability in knowing assistance[72], and it seems probable that this has survived the decision in *Tan*. Consequently, the mental state required to show liability in respect of knowing receipt of trust property is less than dishonesty, and it seems that the pre-*Tan* authorities to the effect that constructive knowledge not involving fraud or dishonesty but founded simply upon a failure to make enquiries is still good law[73]. Banks and other financial businesses are now under a positive duty to make enquiries about their customers, and in particular whether their customers are acting for the benefit of other persons[74]. This clearly increases the number of facts in respect of which they will be deemed to have knowledge, since constructive knowledge is imposed in relation to all facts which the person concerned would have learned had he made the inquiries which he should reasonably have made[75].

Where a collecting bank is liable in constructive trust, its liability is as knowing recipient rather than as knowing assistant. A collecting bank receives the money which it collects directly for its own benefit. Although it acts as agent for the collection, when it receives the money it receives it absolutely for its own benefit, and where it employs that money in transactions the customer on whose behalf it has collected the money has no right to the profit made on such transactions[76]. Consequently the collecting bank can be made liable as a constructive trustee on proof of mere constructive knowledge as opposed to dishonesty.

A collecting bank does not have a defence to a claim in constructive trust that it is a purchaser for value without notice of the proceeds of the cheque, partly because by definition it does have notice, but in any event because it is not a 'purchaser'. It has been argued that the provision of ordinary banking services pursuant to the contract of banker and customer constitutes giving value for the deposit[77], but the better view is that this is not the case and the bank, as a mere transferee, is a volunteer as against an equitable owner of the money received[78].

---

[70] These liabilities were first distinguished in *Barnes v Addy* (1874) 9 Ch App 244.

[71] [1995] 2 AC 378.

[72] See eg *Eagle Trust v SBC Securities* [1993] 1 WLR 484.

[73] *Belmont Finance Corp'n v Williams Furniture (No 2)* [1980] 1 All ER 393, CA; *International Sales & Agencies v Marcus* [1982] 3 All ER 551. There is an argument that liability for receipt of trust property is strict, but this has been doubted in the House of Lords (*Westdeutsche Landesbank Girozentrale v Islington LBC* [1996] AC 669 at p 707, per Browne-Wilkinson LJ).

[74] Money Laundering Regulations 1993, reg 9.

[75] *Cowan de Groot Properties v Eagle Trust plc* [1992] 4 All ER 700. No account is taken of the fact that if the enquiry had been made the answer would certainly have been false (*Agip (Africa) v Jackson* [1990] 1 Ch 265).

[76] See S J Gleeson, 'The Involuntary Launderer' in Birks (ed) *Laundering and Tracing* 1995 at pp 126–7; [1996] JBL 165 (M Bryan).

[77] Per Bingham J in *Neste Oy v Lloyds Bank plc* [1983] 2 Lloyd's Rep 658 at 667.

[78] Per Templeman LJ in *Lipkin Gorman v Karpnale Ltd* [1991] 2 AC 548 at 563 and see per Wilberforce LJ in *Barclays Bank Ltd v Quistclose Investments* [1970] AC 567; *Paget's Law of Banking*, 11th edn (1996) p 434.

Negligence

It appears that a bank does not owe a duty of care in negligence to the true owner of a cheque which it collects[79].

Statutory protection of the collecting banker

Section 4 of the Cheques Act 1957[80] protects a banker who, in good faith and without negligence, receives payment for a customer of an instrument in circumstances where the customer has no title to the instrument. This is explicitly stated to include circumstances in which the cheque concerned is crossed 'a/c payee' and is therefore non-transferrable pursuant to the Cheques Act 1992. The section provides that in such a case the banker does not incur any liability to the true owner by reason only of having obtained payment thereof. The section applies to a wide variety of instruments besides cheques. Section 4(3) further provides that a banker is not to be taken to have been negligent merely because the instrument is missing an endorsement.

The dynamic of the section is that, as Lord Wright explained in *Lloyds Bank v E B Savory & Co*[81], since the liability of the collecting bank in conversion and/or money had and received is effectively irresistible in such circumstances, the effect of the section is to limit the liability of the bank to circumstances in which it has acted negligently, and since the onus is on the banker to prove that the defence applies, he must prove absence of negligence rather than the plaintiff proving negligence in the traditional fashion.

Requirement of good faith

The bank must prove that it acted in 'good faith' throughout the transaction, not simply that it entered into it in good faith[82]. Good faith is partially defined in the Bills of Exchange Act itself, which provides in s 90 that a thing is deemed to be done in good faith where it is in fact done honestly, whether it is done negligently or not. The leading English common law authority on the meaning of the term good faith is 'without bad faith'[83], and it is suggested that the term 'honestly' as used in the Act should be construed as meaning 'not dishonestly'. 'Dishonesty' is defined in the context of criminal proceedings as meaning '[Acting] in a way which [the defendant] knows ordinary people would consider dishonest, even if he asserts, or genuinely believes that he is

---

[79] *Paget's Law of Banking*, 11th edn, p 434 citing *Groves-Raffin Construction Ltd v Canadian Imperial Bank of Commerce* [1976] 2 WLR 673.

[80] Introduced as s 12 of the Crossed Cheques Act 1876, this provision became s 82 of the Bills of Exchange Act 1882 before being re-enacted with amendments as s 4 of the Cheques Act 1957.

[81] [1933] AC 201 at 229.

[82] *Marfani & Co Ltd v Midland Bank Ltd* [1968] 2 All ER 573.

[83] Per Kekewitch J in *Mogridge v Clapp* [1892] 3 Ch 382. This is arguably the least helpful judicial definition in the law reports.

[84] Per Lane LJ in *R v Ghosh* [1982] QB 1053. His Lordship went on to cite the example of Robin Hood and his merry men as an example of dishonesty under this test.

morally justified in acting as he did'[84]. This is supported by the words of Lord Blackburn in *Jones v Gordon*[85] that

> If the facts and the circumstances are such that the jury ... came to the conclusion that he was not honestly blundering and careless, but that he must have had a suspicion that there was something wrong, and that he refrained from asking questions because he thought in his own secret mind—I suspect there is something wrong, and if I ask questions and make further enquiry, it will no longer be my suspecting it, but my knowing it, and I shall not be able to recover—I think that is dishonesty[86].

It is further submitted that this is the same 'dishonesty' that is the required component of liability in knowing assistance in *Royal Brunei Airlines Sdn Bhd v Tan*[87].

Without negligence

'Negligence' in this context is strictly speaking a misnomer, since negligence proper involves the breach of a duty of care, and it is clear that no duty of care is owed by the collecting bank to the true owner. What is actually involved is a statutory duty to take care. However, the only way in which the statutory duty differs from the common law duty is that the burden of proof is positively on the banker to prove it rather than on the plaintiff to disprove it[88]. The level of care which the statute requires is generally accepted to be the level of care which is the ordinary practice of bankers[89]. There are a number of discrepant authorities which set out various descriptions of this standard[90]. The following or otherwise of the bank's internal guidelines is not decisive for this purpose. As Donaldson J said in *Lumsden & Co v London Trustee Savings Bank Ltd*[91]:

> I fully accept that the defendant's own instructions [to its managers as to the proceedures to be followed on the opening of an account] are not conclusive of the standard to be applied. They may set too high or too low a standard. They do, however, provide some evidence of what can reasonably be expected, and [the bank] can hardly complain if I treat them as correct.

The primary defaults which have led to the establishment of negligence in previous cases have been failure to make proper enquiries on the opening of

---

[85] 2 App Cas 616.
[86] Followed and applied in the context of the Act in *Tatam v Hasler*, 23 QBD 345.
[87] [1995] 2 AC 378.
[88] *Bissell & Co v Fox Bros & Co* (1884) 51 LT 663.
[89] *Taxation Comrs v English, Scottish and Australian Bank* [1920] AC 683.
[90] '[T]he same care as a reasonable businessman would bring to bear on similar business of his own' (*Lloyds Bank v Chartered Bank of India, Australia and China* [1929] 1 KB 40); a requirement that the cashiers of the bank concerned exhibit the degree of intelligence and knowlege ordinarily required of them (*Ross v London, County, Westminster and Parr's Bank Ltd* [1919] 1 KB 678); the practice of reasonable men in carrying on the business of bankers (*Lloyds Bank Ltd v E B Savory & Co* [1933] AC 201); a banker must exercise reasonable care in all the circumstances of the case (*Marfani & Co Ltd v Midland Bank Ltd* [1968] 2 All ER 573).
[91] [1971] 1 Lloyd's Rep 114.

an account[92] and failure to make special enquiries where the balance in an account suddenly changes dramatically[93]. In addition to these, payment into an account other than the account of the named payee has been held to put a bank on enquiry[94].

Regardless of what the position may have been before the 1992 Act, it seems clear that the collection of a cheque for any person other than the named payee constitutes a *prima facie* case of negligence[95]. The current custom of bankers is that cheques drawn on all UK clearing banks are crossed pursuant to the Act and are therefore no longer transferable. Thus where A presents for collection a cheque drawn on an English clearing bank payable to B, if the bank collects the cheque it is outside the s 4 protection and liable in conversion to B. This applies where B is a company of which A is a director or officer[96], a partnership in which A is a partner[97] or the title of an office which A holds[98].

The use of a London clearing bank (the receiving bank) by a non-clearing bank (the transmitting bank) to collect cheques is normal banking practice, and where a transmitting bank uses a receiving bank in order to collect a cheque, the transmitting bank retains the s 4 protection[99].

Note that s 4 only applies to 'cheques' properly so-called. Where a document has been forged, and in particular where the drawee's signature has been forged, the whole document is a nullity, and if the bank collects it it is outside the s 4 protection[100]. The rule in respect of cheques which have been 'raised'[101] is as above—where the raising has been facilitated by the drawing of the cheque, the customer is prevented from denying that the alteration is valid; where the raising is 'apparent', the drawer is discharged altogether and a bank which collects the cheque is liable in money had and received; where the raising is not apparent, the cheque is recoverable for the initial amount and the collecting bank is (probably) entitled to the s 4 protection on the basis that the altered cheque is covered by the definitions in s 42(*a*) and (*b*) of the Cheques Act 1957.

Contributory negligence

Negligence on the drawer's part has always been a defence for the benefit of

---

[92] *Turner v London and Provincial Bank Ltd* (1903) 2 Legal Decisions Affecting Bankers 33.
[93] *Slingsby v District Bank Ltd* [1932] 1 KB 544, *sed contra Morison v London County and Westminster Bank Ltd* [1914] 3 KB 356.
[94] *Thackwell v Barclays Bank plc* [1986] 1 All ER 676.
[95] The learned editors of *Paget's Law of Banking* were of the view that this was the case prior to the 1992 Act (see the current (11th) edn, p 454).
[96] *United Australia Ltd v Barclays Bank Ltd* [1941] AC 1 at 21–34.
[97] *Re Riches and Marshall's Trust Deed, ex p Darlington District Joint Stock Banking Co* (1865) 4 De G J & Sm 581; *Bevan v National Bank Ltd* (1906) 23 TLR 65.
[98] *Ross v London, County, Westminster and Parr's Bank Ltd* [1919] 1 KB 678.
[99] *Akrokerri (Atlantic) Mines Ltd v Economic Bank* [1904] 2 KB 465.
[100] *Kulatilleke v Bank of Ceylon* (1957) 59 Ceylon NLR 188.
[101] A cheque is 'raised' where a person adds words and numbers to it after it has been drawn to make it appear that the cheque is for a larger amount than that for which it was originally drawn.

the paying banker[102]. In *Lumsden & Co v London Trustee Savings Bank*[103] a clerk in a firm of stockbrokers altered his employer's cheques after they had been validly issued and paid them into his own account. The firm successfully sued the bank in conversion as the bank was held to have been negligent and therefore outside the s 4 protection. The bank then argued that, even though it had been negligent, the plaintiffs' conduct in the way they dealt with their cheques once drawn gave rise to a defence of contributory negligence. Donaldson J decided that a defence of contributory negligence was available to the bank, assessed at 10 per cent. In 1977 the effect of this decision was reversed by statute by s 11 of the Torts (Interference With Goods) Act 1977, which provided that contributory negligence was not available as a defence in proceedings founded on conversion or trespass to goods, but in 1979 the *status quo ante* was restored by s 47 of the Banking Act 1979, which provided that contributory negligence was available in respect of actions on cheques. This is the only section of the 1979 Act which is still in force.

---

[102] *London Joint Stock Bank v Macmillan & Arthur* [1918] AC 777.
[103] [1971] 1 Lloyd's Rep 114.

Chapter 20

Securities

The root of the special nature of the securities transaction at English law is the peculiar nature of a security. There is no definition of the term. The Stock Transfer Act 1963, s 4 attempts the task:

> shares, stock, debentures, debenture stock, loan stock, bonds, units of a collective investment scheme ... and other securities of any description.[1]

Despite this lack of a workable definition there are some generalisations about securities which may safely be ventured. The most important is that a security is not a single piece of property, but a bundle of rights against the issuer thereof[2]. This bundle of rights may for convenience be dealt with together as a single piece of property, and is conventionally measured by a sum of money, but is not in any respect a sum of money settled on terms[3]. It follows from this that the value of a security lies in the value of the rights which it embodies against its issuer. Since these rights are financial rights, their value is in turn a function of the issuer's financial condition.

Securities may be issued by corporations or individuals, but in practice are issued only by corporations. A security issued by an individual would ordinarily be characterised as a promissory note subject to conditions[4], and additionally or alternatively, if conditions on security were involved, as a bill of sale[5].

It is now nearly a century since the first parliamentary intervention in the area of securities liability, and nearly a decade since the statutory rights of action for securities transactions were systematised in the Financial Services Act 1986. It may therefore occasion some surprise that the fundamental principles of UK securities law remain so unclear[6].

---

[1] The slightly desperate note struck by the last few words of this definition is echoed in the US Securities Act 1933, the definition in s 2(1) of which provides a longer list of examples but concludes '... or, in general, any interest or instrument commonly known as "a security"'.

[2] For a more detailed analysis of the nature of a share, see Gower, *Principles of Modern Company Law*, 6th edn (Sweet & Maxwell, 1997), Ch 13.

[3] *Borlands Trustees v Steel Brothers & Co Ltd* [1901] 1 Ch 279, per Farwell J.

[4] *See* pp 166–8 *below.*

[5] Such conditions render the document outside the terms of the definition of 'promissory note' in the Bills of Exchange Act 1882, and therefore non-transferrable except by assignment.

[6] See *R v Panel on Take-Overs and Mergers, ex p Datafin plc* [1987] QB 815 for this view. Even in the US, the primary civil liability provision of the post-crash securities legislation of the 1930s, s 11 of the Securities Act 1933, was not tested before the Supreme Court until 1968.

Legal nature of securities

As mentioned above, a security is a bundle of rights against its issuer. In this respect it is identical to a promissory note, which embodies in itself a congeries of rights. Ordinarily legal rights must be transferred by assignment, either legal or equitable as the case may be. However, statute provides for certain clumps of rights to be 'glued together' into a single right called a security, providing also a formal method of transfer for the new items of property so created. Thus the transfer of the security becomes a streamlined process. These are statutory securities.

A non-statutory security is a bundle of rights which is not stuck together by the statutory 'glue'. Non-statutory securities must be transferred by means of an assignment according to the relevant applicable law. The private market has developed systems which mimic the statutory regime for transfer in respect of a non-statutory security, and it is not usually a matter of great concern to the security holder whether he is required to transfer it through the statutory mechanism or by non-statutory means.

The two classes of securities

Whereas a statutory security may take one of a small number of forms, a non-statutory security may take any form. This means that a non-statutory security may be created which takes a form identical to that of a statutory security, and this is sometimes done. Preference shares and eurobonds are an example.

The distinctions between statutory and non-statutory securities arise primarily on regulatory and fiscal grounds. An interesting example is the minor industry which has grown up around the process of creating a form of non-statutory instrument which resembles an ordinary share sufficiently for banking regulators to treat it as a share for the purposes of calculating the bank's available risk capital. Accounting, tax and insolvency are other areas in which the distinction between the security's statutory or non-statutory nature is of importance.

Shares

The classic statutory security is the share. Interestingly, the share was in origin a non-statutory security which became embodied in a statutory form. The deed of settlement company, the predecessor of the modern limited company, was established through a deed which settled the relevant property upon trustees and provided for the rights of the contributors by allocating them into aliquot shares which were freely transferrable[7]. The regulation of these companies, and their eventual development into the modern incorporated com-

---

[7] A B Dubois, 'The English Business Company after the Bubble Act, 1720–1800 (NY 1938)' in Gower, *Company Law*, 5th edn, p 30.

pany, owes much to a desire on the part of government to protect the owners of such shares, and it is to this impulse that the very high level of regulation of the rights and liabilities of shareholders as against the issuer of the shares may be associated.

It is interesting to note that at one stage in the development of English company law the introduction of a system of limited parterships on the model of the European *société en commandite* was considered as a possible alternative to the development of share-issuing companies[8]. A limited partnership provides an equivalent structure to a share-issuing company—it is also a bundle of rights 'glued' together, although it is glued into a status which can be assumed and discarded rather than into an item of property which can be bought and sold. In the United States today limited partnerships are bought and sold as investments.

A share has been defined as:

> the interest of a shareholder in the company measured by a sum of money, for the purpose of liability in the first place, and of interest in the second, but also consisting of a series of mutual covenants entered into by all the shareholders inter se ... The contract contained in the articles of association is one of the original incidents of the share. A share is not a sum of money ... but is an interest measured by a sum of money of a more or less amount.[9]

The primary characteristics of a share are as follows:

(1) The company which issues shares is required to keep a register of its members. The shareholders for the time being are those who are registered in the register of members, and a transaction intended to transfer title to a share is wholly ineffective to transfer any legal property interest in the share until such time as the register of shareholders has been amended accordingly. Companies may retain the right to elect not to register transfers at their discretion—in such a case a company can prevent a person obtaining any right of legal (although not equitable) property in the share.

(2) On the insolvency of a company, the shareholders ordinarily rank after all other creditors. After other creditors have been paid they are entitled to have any surplus divided between them; before other creditors have been paid they are entitled to nothing at all. The shareholders may as between themselves regulate which of them will be paid out in what order; such agreements often lead to the creation of different classes of shares, including preference shares (see below).

(3) Payments by the company to its shareholders are limited by reference to the company's profits. A company may pay interest out of any cash which it may have to hand, and likewise may pay any claim arising out of a non-statutory security. However, it may only pay dividends to

---

[8] See the report of Bellendedker to the Board of Trade 1837; Gower, *Company Law*, 5th edn, pp 41–3.
[9] Per Farwell J in *Borland's Trustee v Steel* [1901] 1 Ch 279 at 288, approved by the House of Lords in *IRC v Crossman* [1937] AC 26.

shareholders in accordance with the statutory formula.

(4) A company may not retire or redeem its shares without the court's permission (in large quantities) or the sanction of the shareholders (in small ones).

(5) A shareholder has the right to be consulted on the company's management and administration to the extent provided for in the company's articles of association. These must require the holding of a general meeting at least once a year[10].

A company is conventionally required by its articles to provide members with certificates for the number of shares which they are registered as holding. A share certificate is an ornamental document of no value—it simply acts as a representation by the company concerned, made under the company's seal, as to the state of its register. In some circumstances a form of estoppel may operate against the company to the extent that it may be estopped from denying the truth of a statement made in a share certificate, but certificates are irrelevant to the transmission of a property interest in the share except to the extent that the production of a certificate may be a condition precedent to the registration of a transfer.

The division of a company's share capital into different classes of shares is not a statutory phenomenon; shares with different rights may occupy the same statutory category (eg 'A' and 'B' shares which differ only in their voting rights are both 'ordinary' shares for statutory purposes). However, the common law has developed subdivisions of the unitary class of shares which the Companies Act 1985 provides for, and the division of share capital into classes, and the ascription of the term 'preference' to those classes which are in some way different from other classes, is a common law mechanism. The primary characteristics (there are others) of preference shares are as follows:

(1) All shares have the same rights in respect of
   (a) dividends,
   (b) return of capital, and
   (c) attendance and voting at company meetings
   as any other shares unless the contrary otherwise appears from the company's articles of association.

(2) Any right conferred on a particular share in a particular respect is assumed to be exhaustive. Thus where the holders of a class of shares are entitled to a return of capital in advance of other classes, they are not entitled to share in any surplus[11]; where holders of a class are entitled to a specified dividend paid in advance of the other dividends, they receive no more than their preferred amount[12].

(3) If a preference dividend is provided for, it is presumed to be cumulative[13].

---

[10] CA 1985, s 366.
[11] *Scottish Insurance v Wilsons & Clyde Coal Co* [1949] AC 462.
[12] *Will v United Lankat Plantations Co* [1914] AC 11.
[13] *Webb v Earle* (1875) LR 20 Eq 556.

Transfer of shares

The mechanisms which are used for the transfer of shares vary according to whether the shares have been issued in registered or bearer form.

Registered shares

A shareholder's rights are conferred upon him as a 'member' of the company. A person becomes a member by satisfying two conditions. One is that a share or shares in the company are transferred to him (a pure property transaction). The second is that he is entered into the register of members as a member. The register is *prima facie* evidence of the true state of the membership[14]. The right to register is the directors' right, and they cannot be compelled to register a transferee as a member if they are acting bona fide within the company's articles for proper purposes[15]. The directors may have a power to refuse to register the person as a member. The property which the transferor of shares seeks to transfer is the rights against the company which are acquired by virtue of the status of member. The key to membership is title to the shares, in that only a person who has such title may become a member. However where a purported transfer of the property in the shares has been met with a refusal to register the transfer, the transfer is said to have failed and the shares themselves are said to remain vested in the transferor. This is not wholly logical, since the position where A is a shareholder but B has the rights which accrue to the holder of the shares is by no means intolerable (it simply produces a discrepancy). However for reasons of practicality, upon a failure by the directors to register it is said that the property transfer has wholly failed and legal title to the shares remains with the transferor.

The property transfer must be performed by the completion of a 'proper instrument of transfer'[16]. Such an instrument may be in any form prescribed by the articles or in the forms prescribed by the Stock Transfer Act 1963. The instrument does not need to be executed by the acquirer of the shares, although the form provided by the 1963 Act requires the transferee's name and address to be included by the disponor of the shares which must, once completed, be sent to the company for registration.

Sections 182 and 183 of the Companies Act 1985 provide that a company must keep a register of members and provide for the mechanisms of transfer. As mentioned above it is conventionally said legal title to shares follows registration as a member. However, strictly speaking this is incorrect, since where a person is registered without having complied with any necessary requirements for membership (eg as contained in the articles) then it seems that that person is not a member, and the court (and the company) have the power to rectify the register of shareholders in favour of the true member[17].

---

[14] CA 1985, s 361.
[15] *Re Smith & Fawcett Ltd* [1942] Ch 304.
[16] CA 1985, s 183(1).
[17] *POW Services Ltd v Clare* [1995] 2 BCLC 435.

Where a company refuses to register an otherwise proper transfer, the transfer's effect is to constitute the transferor a trustee of the shares for the transferee[18]. But if the shares are not sufficiently specified specific performance will not be ordered until specific shares are allocated to the contract[19].

Securities of companies which are listed on the London Stock Exchange are usually transferrable by means of the CREST[20] system. CREST is implemented in the United Kindom by the Uncertificated Securities Regulations 1995[21], which apply to both shares and registered debentures. The object of the system is to replace the physical share transfer forms prescribed by the Stock Transfer Act 1963 with an electronic messaging system which automatically updates the share register of the company concerned and maintains share accounts for buyers and sellers. Cash settlement of transactions is also effected through the system through the membership of banks. CREST is a mechanism for the transfer of securities, and its use in respect of shares is only appropriate in the case of shares in UK-registered companies.

Bearer shares

Bearer shares, rare in the United Kingdom, pass by delivery by statute. Section 188 of the Companies Act 1985 provides that a company may issue a bearer warrant in respect of a particular amount of securities. The effect of the warrant is that the bearer is entitled to the shares specified therein. It is possible that such documents are negotiable[22], but they are clearly transferrable. The company enters on its register the fact that a given parcel of shares is represented by such warrants, and the holder, although entitled to a share, is not a member of the company, although he may present his warrant to the company and obtain registration as a member. Whilst the shares are in bearer form the rights of the shareholder against the company are therefore to some extent in abeyance.

Statutory debentures

Preference shares usually pay a fixed dividend, expressed as a percentage of a nominal value. In this they precisely resemble debentures, which are simply fixed interest securities. A statutory debenture is a debenture which is governed by Pt VIII of Companies Act 1985. A company elects to have a particular issue of debentures exist as statutory debentures by maintaining a register of them in accordance with s 182 of the 1985 Act. If it does so, no transfer of the debenture is lawful unless made on the statutory form provided by the Stock Transfer Act 1982.

---

[18] *Re National Bank of Wales, Taylor, Phillips and Rickards' Case* [1897] 1 Ch 298.
[19] *Duncuft v Albrecht.*
[20] There is an unverifiable legend that the Bank of England director responsible for naming the system selected the name because he liked it and because it would be many years before anyone worked out that it was not in fact an acronym for anything.
[21] Made pursuant to s 207 of the Companies Act 1989.
[22] *Webb, Hale & Co v Alexandria Water Co* (1905) 21 TLR 572.

There are some curious provisions relation to the difference between shares and debentures—for example a share may (but a registered debenture may not) be made the subject of a bearer warrant issued by the company itself[23], and a debenture issued by the company may be repurchased by the company and then re-issued[24], although a share cannot. However the primary difference is that whereas the company must have a share register[25], it may or may not keep a register of holders of debentures as it wishes, although if it does so it must comply with the statutory requirements relating thereto. Therefore the term 'debentures' includes both statutory and non-statutory securities.

Transfer of statutory debentures

The rules relating to shares apply equally to registered (ie statutory) debentures. However, the complex provisions relating to membership and the transfer of title to shares are not applicable. There is no absolute requirement to maintain a register, although it is only where securities are registered that it is possible to employ the statutory stock transfer form to transfer title thereto. It is only if the company wishes to issue debentures in uncertificated form within CREST that it is required to maintain a register. A holder of a statutory debenture may transfer it by execution of an appropriate stock transfer form, and the company has no statutory power, by refusing registration, to interfere with the passing of property in the security[26], which will therefore take effect upon delivery of the form to the company.

Note that in the context of securities 'registered' means registered in a register maintained by or on behalf of the company. All Eurobonds are registered in the sense that their ownership is recorded within Euroclear or CEDEL. However, these are not registers maintained 'by or on behalf of' the issuing companies, and these securities are therefore properly classed as unregistered debentures.

Non-statutory debentures

A non-statutory security is simply a security which does not fall within one of the Companies Act 1985 categories. Non-statutory securities are protean. They also form the bulk of the securities currently traded world-wide. Following the categorisation of the attributes of shares given above, the primary attributes of a non-statutory security are:

(1) Title to the securities can be transferred by assignment or (sometimes) by delivery, in the case of bonds. The company, unless it has placed any specific restrictions on transfer in the securities themselves, can-

---

[23] CA 1985, s 188.
[24] CA 1985, s 194.
[25] CA 1985, s 352.
[26] Although such a power may well be contained in the instruments constituting the debenture, which will take effect as between the debenture holder and the company in the same way as the terms of the articles of association in respect of a share.

not affect the passing of legal title thereto.

(2) On an insolvency, the holders of non-statutory securities rank *pari passu* with other unsecured creditors (unless the securities are subject to some further agreement over their being either deferred or secured).

(3) A payment to a holder of a non-statutory security is in the nature of a contractual payment, usually by way of the discharge of a claim in debt. Such payments are characterised as payments of interest.

(4) A company may redeem its non-statutory securities (and its statutory debentures) as it wishes.

Transfer

An unregistered debenture is, in principle, a contractual claim against the company embodied in a document. As such, it is transferrable by assignment, and the ordinary rule of assignment should apply that the transfer is completed in equity upon the parties thereto entering into a binding contract to transfer it, and the legal title to the claim will be vested in the transferee upon completion of an absolute written assignment and the giving of written notice to the company[27].

The holy grail of transfer of non-statutory securities has been to achieve negotiability. Statutory securities are in effect negotiable, in that registration as the owner of a share constitutes a vesting of absolute legal title, and a transferee bona fide without notice of any equitable defect in title is therefore as fully protected as a holder in due course of a negotiable instrument. Non-statutory securities, however, have the disadvantage that at heart they are merely choses in action against the issuing company, and, like any other chose in action, they are in principle transferrable only subject to equities.

The parties to an instrument cannot render it transferrable, much less negotiable, simply by agreement[28]. Such an agreement would be an agreement between two parties to benefit a third and which is unenforceable by that third party[29]. There is, however, a class of written instruments at English law whose physical transfer has the effect of an assignment of a claim; these are known as negotiable instruments. It is accepted that a document is treated as negotiable at English law if it is rendered negotiable either (a) by statute, or (b) by 'mercantile custom'.

In the case of instruments (that is, undertakings to pay money) statutory negotiability may only be obtained within the statutory definition of a bill of exchange or a promissory note pursuant to the Bills of Exchange Act 1882. A bond is certainly not a bill of exchange under the Act. Neither is it usually a promissory note, since the terms and conditions usually contain provisions which exclude it from the category of an 'unconditional promise to pay' as required by s 83[30]. It will be negotiable therefore only if it is negotiable by

---

[27] *See* pp 125–7 *below.*
[28] *Bechuanaland Exploration Co v London Trading Bank Ltd* [1898] 2 QB 658.
[29] *Tweddle v Atkinson* (1861) 1 B & S 393; *Beswick v Beswick* [1968] AC 58—the third party is prevented from suing absolutely by the rule of privity of contract.
[30] An analysis of some of the more common discrepancies may be found in Tennekoon, *The Law and Regulation of International Finance* (Butterworths, 1991), p 164.

custom of merchants.

The classical form of the company bond was a document executed under the seal of the company undertaking to pay a sum of money at particular intervals. The document was executed as a deed poll. Such bonds were replaced in the mid-nineteenth century by debentures, which usually contained security provisions as well as a promise to repay.

The nineteenth-century company debenture was in form a promise under the company seal to pay the bearer a certain sum of money, along with interest at a stated rate for a particular period. There seems to have been considerable doubt over whether such an instrument, when issued by a company, counted as a negotiable promissory note under the statute of 1704 3 & 4 Anne, c 9[31]. However, by the middle of the nineteenth century it had become accepted that bearer bonds issued by foreign companies and governments were treated in the city as negotiable[32], and in 1873 the first bearer bond issued by an English company came before the court in *Crouch v Crédit Foncier of England*[33]. The bond was in the form of a promise under seal to pay the bearer the face amount, and was unsecured. The court held that the bond was a valid obligation of the issuer but was not negotiable by custom of merchants, since the court clearly took the view that the 'ancient law merchant' was a good source of customary law, whereas recent practice was not.

The decision in *Crédit Foncier* was distinguished out of existence in the 50 years which followed, first in *Goodwin v Robarts*[34], then in *Rumball v Metropolitan Bank*[35] and then in *Bechuanaland Exploration Co v London Trading Bank*[36], which indicated with increasing strength that a bond issued by a company (whether English or foreign) promising to pay money to bearer was negotiable by the custom of merchants. Finally, in 1902, Bingham J suggested that it was so well known that bearer bonds were negotiable that a judge should be prepared to take judicial notice of the fact without requiring it to be proved to him[37].

There is a separate head of negotiability by estoppel which also appears for consideration. A person who issues notes described as negotiable bearer notes is estopped from denying in a suit brought by the buyer that they are negotiable, and therefore from setting up any defence which it may have against a previous holder[38].

Negotiability requires paper. This is simply because the delivery of a piece of paper operates as a kind of 'constructive assignment' of the right of action

---

[31] The predecessor of s 83 of the Bills of Exchange Act 1882, passed to reverse the decision of Holt CJ in *Buller v Crips* (1703) 6 Mod 29; *see* p 160 *below*.

[32] *Georgier v Mieville* (1824) 3 B & C 45 (Prussian bearer bonds); *A-G v Bouwens* (1838) 4 M & W 171 (Russian, Spanish and Dutch bearer bonds).

[33] (1873) LR 8 QB.

[34] (1875) LR 10 Ex 76 and (1876) 1 App Cas 476.

[35] (1877) 2 QBD 194. This case related to scrip certificates issued by an English company, and produced *Webb Hale and Co v Alexandria Water Co* (1905) 93 LT 339, which stands as English authority for the proposition that a bearer share warrant is also a negotiable instrument.

[36] [1898] 2 QB 658.

[37] *Edelstein v Schuler & Co* [1902] 2 KB 144.

[38] *Re General Estates Co* (1868) LR 3 Ch 758; *Re Imperial Land Co of Marseilles* (1870) LR 10 Eq 478.

concerned. Dematerialised securities, therefore, are not strictly speaking negotiable, since if what is required is a transfer of the right of action without physical interference the legal mechanism of assignment is already available, and the purpose and logic of negotiability falls away[39]. However, this is not to say that the concept is lost. It is undoubtedly still the case that an issuer who represents that what he has issued is functionally identical to a bearer bond will still be estopped from denying the fact. However, holders will take subject to any defects in the title of their transferors.

Eurobonds

The legal nature of a Eurobond requires one further word of explanation. A Eurobond has a distinct series of features which arise from its documentation. The most important of these is that most bonds which are settled through the Euroclear[40] and CEDEL[41] clearing systems (ie virtually all Eurobonds) exist in the form of a global note. This is a single debenture executed by the issuing company, and constitutes an obligation by the issuing company to issue definitive notes upon request. The global note provides that it is in respect of an amount of £100m in denominations of £10,000 and £100,000, or some similar figure. Transactions in the bonds and settlement of the amounts due proceed on the basis that imaginary pieces of paper in these denominations are circulating within the clearing systems to the total amount of the global note.

The global note is delivered to a 'common custodian', who holds the security for the benefit of Euroclear and CEDEL. These are the two major clearing systems, with which all bond traders have accounts. The clearing systems operate on a pooled basis. Euroclear is governed by Belgian Royal Decree No 62 of 10 November 1967, which provides that the account holders in the system are (in English terms) tenants in common of the securities held by Euroclear. A similar result is obtained by the Luxembourg legislation which applies to CEDEL. The account holder within Euroclear and/or CEDEL is more often than not a custodian or account operator. Thus in order to obtain definitive securities the buyer must ask his account operator to ask the clearing system to ask the common custodian to ask the issuer to issue the securities.

With any actual securities four removes away from the user of the system it is perhaps unsurprising that the idea of owning a property interest in securities is leaching out of the system. It is, however, being replaced by direct actionability under the most important component of the Eurobond documentation structure, the deed of covenant. Along with the other documentation signed by the issuer, a deed poll in the form of a deed of covenant is entered into undertaking to deal with the holders from time to time of the securities as registered in the books of Euroclear and CEDEL *as if they were* the holders of

---

[39] This argument is developed in greater length in Benjamin, *The Law of Global Custody* (Butterworths, 1996), pp 16–18.
[40] Euroclear Clearance System Société Cooperative, a subsidiary of Morgan Guaranty Trust Company of New York.
[41] CEDEL Bank SA, a co-operative of euromarket banks.

real securities. This is the key document in a Eurobond structure. It operates as an actionable undertaking in favour of third parties. Because it is in favour of the account holders for the time being, issues as to the validity of transfers of securities are left out of account. If a holder has obtained a transfer of securities into his account by fraud, this is nothing to the effect of the covenant, which is in favour of the account holder *simpliciter*. Transferors and transferees may solve their differences between themselves without concerning subsequent purchasers, and thus the essence of negotiability is achieved. It is interesting that this is the result of an abandonment of the concept of property in favour of an abstract acceptance of liability. However, this is only rational in the case of a piece of property which carries with it the right to sue as an unsecured creditor, and may be taken to be another manifestation of the slight eccentricity of the law relating to securities.

Transfers of securities

Securities transactions can be categorised into primary issuance and secondary trading.

(1) Primary issuance is the issue of new securities. When an issuer is issuing securities for the first time it is customary (and usually compulsory) for substantial written disclosure to be made to potential offerees of the securities as to the issuer's financial condition in addition to information about the rights attaching to the shares. This disclosure is required to be contained in the prospectus, and those responsible for the prospectus's preparation have a statutory liability for the truth of its contents. Any statement made in the course of an initial offer, whether in the prospectus or outside it, is actionable at common law by an initial placee of the securities offered.

(2) Secondary trading is the process of purchase and sale of securities between investors. In the secondary market it is uncommon for representations concerning the issuer's status to be made by the buyer to the seller since neither party necessarily has better information than the other. Where such representations are made then the ordinary remedies of deceit, misrepresentation and negligent misstatement are available. The greatest area of difficulty in respect of secondary transactions is that relating to secondary purchases of securities made in reliance upon statements contained in a prospectus. In this situation the common law remedies are generally not available, and the secondary purchaser must rely on the statutory liability of those responsible for the prospectus.

The division of this information in this way enables the distinctions between the forms of offer to be more clearly perceived:

(1) Information about the security itself and the rights attaching thereto is given in respect of every transaction. These rights are almost never spelt out in full. It is probable that there is an implied term in most securities transactions to the effect that 'this security has the rights

which normally accompany ownership of a security of this class'.

(2) Information about the issuing company's ability to meet its obligations to the security is usually given where the security is being offered for the first time. The form in which this information is given varies according to the classification of the offer.

(3) Market information is almost never given by any party to the transaction to any other. Where it is, it is usually actionable (in misrepresentation if incorrect, as insider dealing if correct).

Statutory liability in primary transactions

At English law a primary securities transaction is called an 'offer', and this term is used here. The statutory securities actions arise only where there has been an offer accompanied by a statutory prospectus, and arise only in respect of the contents of that prospectus. Thus the most important criterion in identifying the extent of this liability is to determine which transactions require a prospectus and which do not.

English law categorises offers of securities into offers to the public and offers which are the private concern of those involved. An offer which is made 'to the public' must be accompanied by a prospectus containing specified information about both the issuer and the securities issued.

The question of when an offer is an offer to the public is a difficult one. It is perfectly clear that where a small company with a few employees wishes to make one of its employees a shareholder it should not be obliged to go to the expense of producing a full prospectus. However, the cases under the Companies Acts drew the boundaries of the term 'the public' very narrowly, and there was authority that an offer to a single person might constitute an offer 'to the public'[42].

The matter is now dealt with by the express provision of 'safe harbours'. Parliament has provided a list of 25 separate safe harbours, such that an offer falling within one or more of these is deemed not to be an offer 'to the public'[43]. Different parts of an issue may be sheltered in different harbours; thus an issue to securities professionals may be offered to up to 50 persons in addition to those professionals. It may be technically possible for an offer to fall outside all of these safe harbours and still to pass the common law test of an offer not 'to the public', although a factual example is hard to imagine.

The prospectus

The Companies Act 1844[44] first introduced a requirement that an offer of shares

---

[42] *Lynde v Nash* [1928] 2 KB 93.

[43] Public Offers of Securities Regulations 1995 (SI No 1537). The primary safe harbours are those relating to offers to those who are engaged in the securities business, offers to those sufficiently expert to understand the risks involved, offers in connection with the arrangement of underwriting, offers of Euro-securities and offers to groups of less than 50 people.

[44] 7 & 8 Vict, c 110. The Act was passed in response to a report of a Select Committee on Joint Stock Companies.

for subscription be accompanied by a disclosure document requiring registration, the document being described as a prospectus. The force of this requirement was somewhat muted by the lack of specification of what the document should contain. The Companies Act 1867 introduced some content requirements, but it was not until the 1900 Act that the modern concept of a detailed list of the information required was adopted.

The Financial Services Act 1986, whilst retaining the division of public and private offers, subdivided the category of public offers into offers of listed and unlisted securities[45]. Where there is an offer of unlisted securities, the prospectus must be produced in accordance with the requirements of Schedule 1 to the Public Offers of Securities Regulations 1995 (the POS Regulations). Where the shares are to be listed on the London Stock Exchange, the prospectus is required to comply with the Stock Exchange listing rules.

For private offers (ie offers other than to the public), there is no requirement to employ any offer document at all. However, if such a document is used it must either conform with the requirements of the Financial Services Act (Investment Advertisements) (Exemptions) (No 2) Order 1995 (a further attenuated set of prospectus requirements), or be restricted in its circulation, or be approved by a person who is authorised to do investment business under the Financial Services Act 1986. The authorised person concerned is required by its rule book to show that before approving the document it took steps to ensure that it was fair and not misleading[46].

Finally, note that the requirement to produce a prospectus is not limited to offers of new shares. The POS Regulations, reg 13(1)(e) makes clear that the requirement is equally present in the case of a holder of securities who wishes to make an offer to the public for the first time of those particular securities. The statutory regime bites on offers of securities, not issuance of securities.

Offers of listed securities

The key provision for offers to the public of listed securities is s 150 of the Financial Services Act 1986, which provides that:

> the person or persons responsible for any listing particulars ... should be liable to pay compensation to any person who has acquired any of the securities in question, and suffered loss in respect of them as a result of any untrue or misleading statement in the particulars or the omission from them of any matter required to be included [therein].

This formulation is very wide, and clearly gives a right of action to both primary and secondary purchasers. An example illustrates the extent of the s 150 liability. A company with shares already trading in the market makes an offer of new shares accompanied by listing particulars. Those listing particulars

---

[45] Strictly speaking it subdivided all offers, public and private, since it is in theory possible to have a private offer of listed securities. However this eventuality is not frequently encountered. 'Listed' in this context means full-market listed—shares listed on the Alternative Investment Market are not 'listed' for this purpose.
[46] Eg SFA, rule 5-9.

contain a misstatement which causes the shares' value to fall. A person unconnected with the company takes the opportunity to buy existing shares from
shareholders who wish to sell because of the information in the prospectus.
The inaccuracy of the information is then revealed, whereupon the shares
climb to their previous level. The company is liable to the shareholders who
were induced to sell their shares by the misstatement. The fact that those shareholders have no connection with the issue to which the listing particulars relate, and that the benefit of the misstatement was collected by the unconnected
buyer, does nothing to eliminate the liability of the person responsible for the
misstatement in the prospectus, whose obligation is to make full restitution to
the losing shareholders.

This liability is subject to a 'due diligence' defence provided by s 151,
which saves any person who:

> at the time when the particulars were submitted to the competent authority, rea-
> sonably believed, having made such enquiries as were reasonable, that the state-
> ment was true and not misleading or that the matter whose omission caused the
> loss was properly omitted.

The liability which this section creates is upon the 'persons responsible' for
the listing particulars. The list of 'persons responsible' is given in s 152 of the
Act. It includes:

- the issuer
- the issuer's directors[47]
- any person who has agreed to become a director
- any person who explicitly accepts responsibility for any part of the particulars in respect of that part
- any person who has authorised any part of the particulars in respect of
  that part.

The last category is indeterminate, and it is fair to say that no one knows
what the word 'authorise' means in the context of this part of this section. It
clearly means something different from an explicit acceptance of responsibility, since this is a separate area of viability. The concepts are difficult to distinguish—it is difficult to see how one might authorise a document without
accepting responsibility for it, and vice versa—but together clearly catch the
'promoter' of the company[48]. In particular, a person who allows his name to
appear prominently on the cover of the prospectus or to be the person arrang-
ing or making the offer of securities is clearly 'authorising' any prospectus
distributed in the course of such an offer, and this is true regardless of any
formal acceptance or rejection of liability in the prospectus itself.

---

[47] The personal liability of directors and potential directors does not apply in the case of offers of
Eurobonds (s 152(6)).

[48] The predecessor of this provision, s 43 of the Companies Act 1948, expressly provided that
liability should rest upon 'every person being a promoter of the company', promoter being
defined in turn (in s 43(5)(*a*) of that Act) as a person who '... was a party to the preparation of
the prospectus, or of the portion thereof containing the untrue statement, but does not include
any person by reason of his acting in a professional capacity for persons engaged in procuring
the formation of the company'.

This conclusion is supported by s 152(1), which provides that nothing in s 152 shall be construed as making a person responsible for any particulars by reason of giving advice as to their contents in a professional capacity. The only head of liability under which a person might be caught in this way is authorisation of the prospectus. It follows from this exclusion that the statute contemplates liability attaching to a person whose name appears nowhere in the listing particulars, but whose advice is contained therein. It must follow that a formal statement of authorisation is not a pre-requisite of liability.

Offers of unlisted securities

Where an offer is made to the public of shares which are neither listed nor the subject of an application for listing on the London Stock Exchange the offer is regulated, as to both documentary content and issuer liability, by the POS Regulations, which replace Pt V of the Financial Services Act which, having been enacted, was never brought into force.

The English legislation is drawn up so that liability for offers of unlisted securities should follow as closely as possible liability for offers of listed securities. Therefore the provisions of the POS Regulations replicate wherever possible the provisions of Pt IV of the Financial Services Act. The section of the POS Regulations which mirrors s 150 is reg 14, which reads:

> the person or persons responsible for a prospectus or supplementary prospectus should be liable to pay compensation to any person who has acquired the securities *to which the prospectus relates* and suffered loss in respect of them as a result of any untrue or misleading statement in the prospectus of the omission from it of any matter required to be included [therein]. (Italics supplied.)

It would ordinarily be expected that the liability created by this section would be commensurate with the liability created by s 150, such that it too would create a right of action available to both primary and secondary purchasers of securities. However, there is some doubt that this is indeed the case. The words in italics represent a difference of drafting between s 150 and reg 14, and the effect of this difference has recently been considered by Lightman J in *Possfund Custodian Trustee Ltd and another v Diamond and another*[49]. His comments on the point and upon the correct interpretation of the difference in drafting between the two sections, although obiter, are the first time that this point has been the subject of judicial utterance, and his words are therefore important.

Section 150 confers a statutory action upon any person who acquires 'the securities in question'. Regulation 14, by contrast, confers an action upon any person who acquires 'the securities to which the prospectus relates'. It was argued that a prospectus is produced for a particular transaction—that is, the offer itself. 'The shares to which the prospectus relates' must therefore mean the shares which the prospectus is used to offer at the moment of offer. The present tense is significant because from the perspective of a secondary pur-

---

[49] [1996] 2 All ER 774.

chaser the shares are shares to which the prospectus *related*, not shares to which the prospectus *relates*. For this reason, His Lordship indicated that in his view reg 14 would not be effective to confer a statutory action upon a secondary purchaser. It is submitted that this somewhat surprising conclusion is wrong for the following reasons:

(1) The major difference between the POS Regulations and Pt IV is that Pt IV does not contemplate offers by persons other than the issuer of the securities concerned, whereas the Regulations do[50]. The formulation used in Pt IV, 'the securities in question', would be inapplicable to the regime governing offers to the public by persons other than the issuer of the securities, since in the case of an offer by a non-issuer the paragraph would be ambiguous as between the securities offered and the securities currently in issue. Thus the narrower term 'securities to which the prospectus relates' is used for this reason. There is no internal or external indication that this minor change in phraseology was intended to make a substantial difference to the scope of the liability created by the Regulations.

(2) There is express reference within the Regulations themselves to liability arising after the moment of issue of the prospectus. Regulation 15(1)(*d*) provides that it is a defence for a person liable under reg 14 to show that 'the securities were acquired after such a lapse of time that he ought in the circumstances reasonably to be excused'. The only possible interpretation of this defence is that liability may arise in respect of a purchase of securities made after the date of issuance of the prospectus. It is hard to see how this is capable of being reconciled with the idea that the prospectus has only a single instant of legal efficacy, at the moment of its publication. It would also seem to follow that if Parliament has created a defence to a statutory liability, it would need remarkably clear wording to indicate that it did not intend to create the liability. Such clarity is not easily discernable in an inference drawn from a change of tense[51].

Statements made outside the prospectus

The position on statutory liability for statements made in the course of an offer outside the prospectus is extremely difficult. For offers of unlisted securities there is no such liability. However, for offers of listed securities s 154 of the Financial Services Act provides that there are penalties for any such statement made without the approval of the Stock Exchange. One of these penalties is the provision that 'an authorised person who contravenes this section shall be treated as having contravened rules made under the conduct of busi-

---

[50] Compare, for example, s 152 of the Financial Services Act 1986 with reg 13 of the POS Regulations.

[51] It may be noted that the symmetrical provision in respect of listed securities, s 151(1)(*d*) of the Financial Services Act 1986, restricts this defence 'until after the commencement of dealings in the securities following their admission to the official list'. This seems to be the clearest possible indication that the defence arises only in respect of secondary market purchases.

ness rule-making powers conferred by the Act on the SIB'[52]. The reason that this obscurely worded provision might create a civil right to damages requires a word of explanation.

Section 62 of the Financial Services Act provides that substantially any breach of the Act or any rule made by a regulator pursuant to the Act shall be actionable in damages at the suit of a person suffering injury thereby. As enacted this was a radical provision, and the Government did not maintain the nerve required to carry it through. Section 62 was therefore emasculated by s 62A (inserted by the Companies Act 1989). However, s 62A did not abolish the s 62 right, but merely confined it to private investors. It therefore seems clear that where s 154 is breached, then a private investor has a right of action in damages against the person responsible for the breach in any event.

Since nothing is ever simple in financial services law, regulations were then made disapplying s 62A in some circumstances[53]. One of these circumstances is where the breach complained of is a breach of rules other than the conduct of business rules. The meaning of this rule is highly obscure, but one possible interpretation is that it permits actions under s 62 to be brought by non-private investors where the breach complained of is a 'deemed' breach (such as that created by s 154) rather than an actual breach[54].

Common law liabilities in securities transactions

Whereas statutory liabilities arise only in respect of specific classes of transactions, the common law actions are available to any securities transaction, primary or secondary and regardless of classification.

Deceit

An action in the tort of deceit may be brought by any person to whom a deceitful representation has been made[55], and may be in respect of any of the classes of information given above. A representation may be made to one person, or to a class of persons, or to the public at large, and in each case the test is one of whether the representation is made 'with a view to its being acted on' by a person who does do so and suffers loss[56]. This is true whether or not the person concerned has any relationship, contractual or otherwise, with the deceiver[57].

---

[52] Section 154(2).

[53] The Financial Services Act 1986 (Restriction of Right of Action) Regulations 1991 (SI No 489).

[54] Anyone who is by now thoroughly confused is recommended to Lomnicka & Powell, *Encyclopædia of Financial Services Law* (Sweet & Maxwell, looseleaf), para 4-353 where this topic is discussed more fully.

[55] Except in the case of fraudulent representations as to the credit of a person, which are actionable only if in writing and signed, by virtue of s 6 of the Statute of Frauds Amendment Act 1828, also known as Lord Tenterden's Act).

[56] *Commercial Banking Co of Sydney v R H Brown & Co* [1972] 2 Lloyd's Rep 360, H Ct of Aust. See also *Richardson v Silvester* (1873) LR 9 QB 34, where liability arose by reason of a misleading advertisement in a newspaper.

[57] *Pasley v Freeman* (1789) 3 TR 51.

However, there is an important modification of the general principles of the tort of deceit in securities cases. This is the rule to the effect that a purchaser in a secondary transaction who purchases securities in reliance upon a prospectus published by the issuer cannot sue. The leading case is *Peek v Gurney*[58], in which it was held that a prospectus is a representation made only to the initial subscribers, and that a person who is deceived into a secondary purchase by the prospectus is not a person to whom the representation is made. Consequently, in the case of this particular deceit a secondary purchaser has no action.

This rule seems to be strictly confined to statements made in the prospectus, and it probably does not prevent a secondary purchaser taking action in respect of statements made by the issuer to prospective purchasers of the shares outside the prospectus. It further seems to be the case that where a statement made outside the prospectus is rendered deceitful by being read together with the prospectus then the action in deceit will still lie. In *Andrews v Mockford*[59] it was held that a secondary purchaser could sue where the purchaser had been deceived by the whole course of conduct of the company, and for this purpose the contents of the prospectus were taken into account as one part of the larger deceit. In that case a telegram subsequently released by the company was read together with the prospectus, and the whole was taken to constitute a deceit upon the secondary purchasers of the shares in the market.

The action in deceit lies only where the statement concerned was made fraudulently. The test of what is meant by 'fraudulently' underwent a sea-change upon the decision in *Derry v Peek*[60]. Prior to that decision the courts had been very flexible in their use of the term 'deceit', and in many cases representations were held to be deceitful which in our terms would be classified as merely negligent[61]. In *Derry v Peek* it was held that 'fraud' embraces only two circumstances: where there is a deliberate intention to decieve, and where the person making the statement is utterly careless whether it be true or false.

This requirement makes deceit a difficult cause of action. What must be proved is in effect the criminal *mens rea* of intention or recklessness, and although the standard is the civil standard of proof[62], the rule that fraud 'must be distinctly alleged and as distinctly proved'[63] in reality places a higher burden of proof, even in the civil courts, upon a plaintiff who pleads fraud than upon one who pleads negligence[64].

---

[58] (1873) LR 6 HL 377.
[59] [1896] 1 QB 372.
[60] (1889) 14 App Cas 337.
[61] See *Snell's Equity* (P V Baker, ed), 29th edn, 548–9 for an explanation of the extraordinary width of the term 'fraud' as used in the Courts of Equity. It is this very wide reading which underlies the view that 'all Lincoln's Inn considered [*Derry v Peek*] to be wrongly decided'.
[62] Despite the fact that what is alleged is usually tantamount to a commission of a criminal offence (*Hornal v Neuberger Products Ltd* [1957] 1 QB 247).
[63] Per Theisger LJ in *Davy v Garrett* [1877] 7 Ch D 473.
[64] Per Denning LJ in *Bater v Bater* [1951] P 35 at 37.

Misrepresentation

The question of the existence or otherwise of a misrepresentation is one of pure fact. If what was said was not true, then there is a misrepresentation. However, the consequences of making a misrepresentation have long been dependent upon the state of mind of their maker. Misrepresentations are categorised on this basis into fraudulent and innocent misrepresentations. Any misrepresentation entitles the misrepresentee to rescind his contract, but only where there has been fraudulent misrepresentations does he also have a right to sue for money damages.

The shortcoming of this rule was illustrated in *Derry v Peek*. As with almost all securities actions rescission of the contract of allotment of shares was barred, since the company had gone into insolvent liquidation and third party rights had intervened. The plaintiffs' position was therefore that if they had no claim in fraudulent misrepresentation then they had no remedy. Because the court found no positive intention to deceive, there was no claim in fraudulent misrepresentation. No action in negligence was considered possible—when *Derry v Peek* was decided *Hedley Byrne v Heller*[65] was 75 years in the future, and the law was universally believed to be that 'in the absence of contract, an action for negligence cannot be maintained where there is no fraud'[66]. Thus although those who prepared the prospectus were clearly grossly negligent, those who had been injured by their negligence were left without a remedy against them.

In respect of primary issues made by prospectus this situation was corrected by the Directors Liability Act 1890, passed in response to *Derry v Peek*, which aimed to reverse the decision and render directors liable for negligently prepared prospectuses. This Act was the progenitor of the modern statutory prospectus actions. However, this act did not benefit secondary purchasers, or indeed those who purchased shares in response to misstatements made outside the prospectus.

After 1964, as a result of the decision in *Hedley Byrne v Heller* both of these could sue in the tort of negligent misstatement. However, the position of those who purchased shares in reliance upon misrepresentations by the immediate vendor has improved by the enactment of the Misrepresentation Act 1967 which provided as between contracting parties an effective reversal of part of the *Derry v Peek* decision.

The scheme of the Misrepresentation Act is to deem all misrepresentations to be fraudulent. This is known as the 'fiction of fraud'[67]. The Act goes on to provide that this deeming provision may be defeated by the defendant's proving 'that he had reasonable ground to believe and did believe *up to the time the contract was made* that the facts represented were true'[68]. Section 2(2) of

---

[65] [1964] AC 465.

[66] *Le Lievre v Gould* per Lord Esher MR [1893] 1 QB 491 at 498, explaining the law as he believed it to have been restated by the House of Lords in *Derry v Peek* (1889) 14 App Cas 337.

[67] Atiyah and Treitel (1967) 30 MLR 396 at 373.

[68] Section 2(1) (italics supplied). Note that this 'due diligence' defence is only a defence against an award of damages under the Act, and not against rescission of the underlying contract.

the Act provides that rescission is not available as of right in the case of innocent misrepresentation, and that the court has a power to award damages instead of rescission in these circumstances.

In retrospect it seems probable that the Act's objective was no more than to make a remedy in damages available to misrepresentees. Unfortunately the Act's draftsman had not anticipated the decision in *Doyle v Olby (Ironmongers) Ltd*[69]. Denning LJ's judgment therein established that damages for fraud should be calculated on a very different basis from those used in cases of ordinary negligence. This point is discussed further below, but at this stage it must be noted that the Act's effect was not simply to create a remedy in damages, but to select as between two modes of calculation of damages.

Negligence

Since *Hedley Byrne & Co v Heller & Partners*[70], the branch of the tort of negligence known as the tort of negligent misstatement is available to the disappointed shareowner. An action in negligent misstatement may be brought by any person owed a duty of care by the representor. The action is therefore wider in its scope than the action in misrepresentation, and in the absence of deceit it is the only way in which a purchaser of securities in a secondary transaction has a cause of action against anyone other than the immediate vendor[71]. As noted below the rules for the calculation of quantum of damages in negligence are less favourable to the plaintiff than those in misrepresentation, deceit or the statutory action. Thus the action in negligence is of interest primarily to secondary purchasers who do not have recourse to these actions.

The ordinary rule of liability in negligent misrepresentation is also varied in respect of securities transactions. In *Al-Nakib Investments (Jersey) Ltd v Longcroft*[72] the court explicitly adopted the decision in *Peek v Gurney*[73] to be a decision of general principle, and held that where a negligent misstatement is made in a prospectus, the relevant duty of care is owed only to the initial placees. Secondary purchasers, no matter how reasonable it may have been for them to act in reliance upon the statement made, are owed no duty and have therefore no action.

It is easy to see why *Al-Nakib* is an unpopular decision[74], not least because the 'principle' which it purports to extract from the decision in *Peek v Gurney* was expressly overturned by statute in 1986[75]. However, its effect whilst it stands is to carry into the sphere of negligence the same rigid rule, arrived at without reference to market practice, which renders the common law remedies unsatisfactory in securities matters.

---

[69] [1969] 2 QB 158.
[70] [1964] AC 465.
[71] Traditionally the auditors of the company concerned.
[72] [1990] 1 WLR 1390.
[73] At 1396.
[74] Gower (*Company Law*, 5th edn (Sweet & Maxwell), p 498) observes that the decision should be reversed by statute as otherwise 'its contagion may spread'.
[75] Financial Services Act, s 150. *See below* for a discussion of whether the principle has been completely repealed, or whether it still applies in respect of unlisted securities.

The measure of securities liability

The existence of a liability is the beginning rather than the end of the analysis. Part of the nature of a security is that it has no intrinsic value, and its worth may fluctuate wildly by reference to factors wholly outside the contemplation of all concerned in the original transaction.

Deceit and misrepresentation

These two heads are taken together since the decision in *Royscot Trust Ltd v Rogerson*[76], in which it was held that the 'fiction of fraud' drafting in the Misrepresentation Act meant that the damages which the Act prescribes are to be calculated by reference to the measure in deceit rather than the ordinary tortious measure.

The question of the measure of damages for a deceit inducing a securities transaction has recently been considered in the House of Lords in *Smith New Court Securities Ltd v Scrimgeour Vickers (Asset Management) Ltd*[77]. In that case the defendants had deceitfully sold to the plaintiffs 28 million shares in Ferranti. The shares were sold at 82.25p, at a time when their market value was 78p. However, due to an undiscovered fraud the shares' value plumeted, and the investor subsequently sold the shares for an average price of 44p. At first instance the plaintiffs were awarded the amount of their loss—82p less 44p. But on appeal it was held that the measure of damages was the difference between what had been paid and the market price at the moment of the purchase.

In reaching this decision the court was applying some established rules for the calculation of damages in securities actions. These rules may be summarised as follows:

(1) Where the shares are valueless, the measure is the amount paid[78]. Where the shares have a true value, the measure is the difference between the amount paid and the true value[79].

(2) The price at which the shares stand in the market is not to be taken as the true value, but merely as evidence which may be taken into account in calculating the true value[80]. The reason for this rule is that the market price may itself be infected by the misrepresentation made, and the true value is therefore taken to be the price at which the shares would stand in the market if all the facts were known.

(3) The date of valuation of the shares is the date of allotment (or, in the case of a secondary transaction, the date of transfer). There is a presumption that the allotment takes place on the day after posting of the

---

[76] [1991] 2 QB 297.
[77] [1996] 4 All ER 769. The report of the Court of Appeal hearing is to be found at [1994] 1 WLR 1271.
[78] *Twycross v Grant* (1877) 2 CPD 469, CA.
[79] *Peek v Derry* (1887) 37 Ch D 541, CA; *Glasier v Rolls* (1889) 42 Ch D 436; *Cackett v Keswick* [1902] 2 Ch 456.
[80] *Twycross v Grant* (1877) 2 CPD 469 at 489–90.

notice of allotment[81]. This rule has some interesting consequences. One is that a misrepresentation in the prospectus which is cured after the date of allotment is dealt with as if it had never been cured. Thus, in *McConnel v Wright*[82], the prospectus represented that the issuer had acquired valuable property. In fact the company was, at the date of allotment, in the process of acquiring the property, and did not complete the acquisition until after the date of allotment. It was held that the deceit was actionable *per se* unless it could be proved that at the date of the prospectus the acquisition of the property was virtually certain. By contrast, in *Waddell v Blockey*[83] a very substantial deterioration in the value of the shares purchased after the transfer date was held to be wholly immaterial to the quantum of damage for the initial misrepresentation. This rule is, however, subject to the general principle that subsequent developments, although not capable of affecting the valuation directly, constitute good evidence of the true value of the shares at the time of the allotment. In *Derry v Peek* Cotton LJ observed that even the subsequent winding-up of the company and the amount returned to the shareholders may be taken into account for this purpose.

(4) Damages should not be reduced to take into account the fact that the plaintiff might have sold at a profit before the discovery of the fraud. As Cotton LJ said in *Peek v Derry* 'it cannot be unreasonable of a purchaser not to sell'[84].

(5) Consequential losses (such as interest costs in respect of borrowings to finance the purchase) are in principle not recoverable.

When *Smith New Court* came before the House of Lords, their Lordships delivered a strong restatement of the rule in *Doyle v Olby (Ironmongers) Ltd*[85] that the liability of a defendant in deceit should be quantified primarily by the identification of all the injury suffered by the defendant as a result of his entry into the transaction, without reduction for remoteness. The authorities cited above upon which the Court of Appeal relied should not be applied in cases of deceit since, although they were reached in cases pleaded in deceit, they were all decided pre-*Doyle v Olby*, and to the extent that they were incompatible with the principles laid down in *Doyle v Olby* they were no longer law. Indeed Lord Steyn criticised the idea that shares should be treated differently from any other class of property for this purpose.

Negligence

There is an important distinction between the quantum of damages which may be awarded for negligent misstatement and the quantum which will be

---

[81] *Stevens v Hoare* (1904) 20 TLR 407.

[82] [1903] 1 Ch 546, CA.

[83] (1879) 4 QBD 678, CA.

[84] (1887) 37 Ch D 541 at 593; see also *Twycross v Grant* (1877) 2 CPD 469 at 490 per Coleridge CJ: 'the plaintiff was not bound to sell, and after he discovered the fraud, he could not sell'.

[85] [1969] 2 QB 158.

awarded for fraudulent misrepresentation. Both start from the same basis—
that the measure of damages is the 'reliance loss': that is, the amount necessary to put him back into the position in which he was before the tort was
committed. However:

(1) In negligent misstatement, the measure of loss is the loss which flows
     from the statement; in deceit the measure of loss is the loss which
     flows from the transaction[86].

(2) The amount of this loss is reduced in negligent misstatement by any
     loss as was not a reasonably foreseeable consequence of the misstate-
     ment. No such restriction is applied in the case of deceit.

The rule in respect of actions in deceit, misrepresentation and breach of
the s 150 and reg 14 obligations is that they are calculated on the basis of the
measure of damages in the tort of deceit. This includes all losses, no matter
how unforeseeable, as long as they are not too remote[87]. Thus in many cases
the amount of the potential liability in negligence will be less than the amount
of the liability in any of the other actions.

Statutory liability

Prima facie the liability which is created by s 150 is a liability for breach of
statutory duty. In principle an action under a statute is not an action for damages, but the precise nature of a statutory claim varies from statute to statute.
In the case of this particular claim (or its predecessor under the 1928 Companies Act) the matter was decided by Lord Atkin in *Clark v Urquhart*[88] as that
the measure of damages for the statutory prospectus action 'is precisely the
same as in an action of deceit'. This conclusion is reinforced by the fact that
the statutory drafting of s 150 is identical in form to that of the Misrepresentation Act, although there is no express 'fiction of fraud' language. The conclusion is also appealing in that the two symmetrical actions for primary and
secondary transactions should give rise to the same measure of damages.

Financial Services Act 1986, s 47

Section 47 is a criminal provision importing criminal sanctions. The market
has completely discounted the possibility of an action for breach of statutory
duty by a private individual for a breach of s 47. It is unquestionably unwise
to have done so. The US equivalent of s 47 is Rule 10b-5 of the SEC, a regulation couched in similar terms to s 47, and the action for breach of the duty
imposed by Rule 10b-5 is now the primary securities action in the United
States. Although there is a strong trend in the English courts against the creation of actions for breach of statutory duty[89], the rule is that where a provision

---

[86] *Banque Bruxelles Lambert SA v Eagle Star Insurance Co Ltd* [1996] 3 WLR 87.
[87] *Royscot Trust v Rogerson* [1991] 3 WLR 57.
[88] [1930] AC 28.
[89] *M v Newham LBC* [1994] 2 WLR, and see *Clerk & Lindsell on Torts*, 17th edn (1995) para 11-
19.

of a statute imposes a duty sanctioned only by criminal prosecution, a civil action for breach of such statutory duty may be derived where the obligation is created for the express benefit of a class of individuals, or where a duty is created for the benefit of the public as a whole and an individual suffers special damage through a breach of that duty[90]. It is submitted that a person who suffers damage through a breach of s 47 is potentially within either category but particularly the first in that the whole object of the Financial Services legislation is to protect a particular class of individuals—that is, investors[91].

---

[90] *Lonrho Ltd v Shell Petroleum Co Ltd (No 2)* [1982] AC 173.
[91] The analogy may be far-fetched, but an equivalent right was held to exist in *London Passenger Transport Board v Upson* [1949] AC 155 for users of a zebra-crossing.

Section 6

Security Interests in Property

Contents

Chapter 21

Elements of Security

Possessory and title security

The primary distinction in the field of security law is between possessory security (pledges) and title security (charges). Loosely, a possessory security is one which is created by the grantor parting with his right to possession of an asset (but retaining title to it), and is generally created by physical delivery of the security asset. Under a possessory security the person delivering possession of the asset is entitled to its return upon payment of the secured debt. A title security is created by the grantor parting with his ownership of the asset (usually retaining possession) by conveyance of title to it. Under a title security the grantor is entitled to a reconveyance of title to the asset upon discharge of the secured debt, possessory securities are referred to as pledges, and title securities are charges. It follows from this classification that tangible assets may be either pledged or charged, whereas intangible assets cannot be pledged but can only be charged. Pledges may be protected either by physical delivery or by registration (or by both); charges may only be protected by registration.

Publicity

A security is an absolute transfer of an interest in property coupled with an enforceable right vested in the transferor to compel retransfer upon the satisfaction by the transferor of a condition. It is therefore created using the normal means of transfer—anything which can be sold or given away may be made the subject of a security arrangement. However, at the heart of almost all systems of security law is a prohibition on the creation of secret security. The reasons for this prohibition are twofold:

(1) To show other creditors that assets of the debtor are not his own. The aim here is that those considering dealing with a particular person should be able to form a true estimate of his assets, and where that person appears to own assets which he has in fact granted to another, his potential creditors are thereby misled. This is known as the doctrine of false wealth or reputed ownership, and is a bankruptcy doctrine.

(2) To protect existing and potential pledgees and chargees. If it can be made clear that particular assets are subject to a security, third parties,

such as buyers and mortgagees, are protected from double dealing by the owner.

These rules operate in effect as a prohibition on all security arrangements, howsoever created, which do not satisfy a requirement of publicity.

Where possession of an asset is transferred, the transfer of possession itself may be regarded as sufficient to publicise the security. However, where title alone is transferred the necessary publicity can only be created by registration. Thus prior to the development of concepts of registration the effect of the requirement of publicity was in many legal systems completely to extinguish the ability to create security by transfer of title alone. But modern civil law-based systems have managed to overcome this problem and to create valid title security—for example, the modern German system still has a prohibition on the creation of non-possessory security, but title security is created by an absolute grant of both title and possession to the grantee followed by a grant of an immediate right to possession back to the grantor.

Tangible assets

During the earliest period of the commercial system the only way of creating publicity was by physical transfer. This avoids false wealth and protects priorities—the pledgor no longer physically has the asset.

The requirement for physical possession is not always physically possible: I can have physical possession of a coin, or ten coins, but a million coins present a problem. Consequently, in addition to a transfer of physical possession, a transfer of control and dominion over the goods may suffice. In such a case actual delivery can be replaced by the 'key of the door' principle, as where the pledgee takes the key to a locked room which contains the pledged goods.

Separate again is the idea of constructive delivery. Here, a third person (the bailee of the goods) has physical possession of the goods throughout. Constructive delivery happens where the true owner of the goods instructs the bailee to hold the goods to the order of another. When the bailee acknowledges the instructions and agrees to hold the goods for the benefit of that other person, the other person is said to have acquired constructive possession of the goods. In almost all legal systems constructive possession is equal in all respects to true possession.

Constructive possession must be carefully distinguished from actual possession by means of control. For example, if a warehouseman has a warehouse in which there is a locked room with a single key, if the owner of the goods in the room transfers the key to another with the intention to transfer possession of the contents of the room, then what happens is a transfer of actual possession by a transfer of the means of control. Where, however, the room is unlocked and is controlled by the warehouseman, an instruction to the warehouseman by the owner to hold the contents of the room to the order of another effects, when that instruction is acknowledged, a transfer of constructive possession.

Intangible assets

As mentioned above, possession of an intangible cannot be transferred. In principle this does not create a problem since intangibles, being imperceptible to potential creditors, do not give rise to 'false wealth'. However, the fact that the person taking security cannot take physical delivery of an intangible asset imperils his position. In the case of debts, the most common intangibles dealt with in this way, 'possession and control' is transferred by the transferee giving a compulsory notice to the debtor so that in effect the transferee has full control, dominion and possession of it. This is why in many countries this notice is compulsory in order to perfect the security: if the transferor or transferee does not give notice to the debtor, then the security has not been properly publicised for the purposes of insolvency and therefore fails on the *transferor's* insolvency.

This compulsory notice rule must be distinguished from situations where the notice is permissive or optional. Thus in most English-based countries, the failure to serve notice does not invalidate the security on the assignor's insolvency but has various advantages, eg to protect priorities, to secure payment to the assignee and to obtain certain, less essential procedural advantages.

The fact that the giving of a compulsory notice is wholly inefficient to achieve the purpose of publicity (in that creditors cannot see the receivable in any event, let alone know whether notice has been given) has led to the progressive removal of the rule in a number of countries which still have it but progress on this is slow. The presence of the compulsory notice rule also led to the development of techniques of avoiding it in trade transactions, eg negotiable instruments and bills of lading.

Often the compulsory notice requirement is not necessary if the debtor consents to the assignment or acknowledges the assignment—but usually this acknowledgement must be in writing.

Public registration

Delivery of possession is a logical requirement for possessory security. It is neither rational nor desirable in the case of security created by a grant of title to property as opposed to security created by a grant of possession of property; indeed, it would abolish the distinction between title and possessory security to require that title security should be publicised by delivery of possession. Thus in order to publicise title security many countries have installed a public registration or filing system whereby the secured creditor must publicise the security in an official register which can be inspected by third parties. The main objective of these registration systems is to notify unsecured creditors of the presence of security for insolvency purposes by reason of the doctrine of false wealth or reputed ownership. Some registration systems go further by also endeavouring to deal with priorities as between buyers, second chargees and others. Article 9 of the American Uniform Commercial Code and Pt XII of the Companies Act 1985 both do this to some extent. The English-based corporate charge registration systems are directed against insolvency false wealth and are only incidentally priority systems.

Some registration systems register the creation of possessory security. This may seem paradoxical, since where a possessory security is created the transfer of possession involved would seem sufficient to satisfy the requirement for publicity. However, the logic of registration is that not all possessory securities transfer possession. This is because many civil systems follow the Roman classification of securities, and divide them not into two (title and possessory) but into three—title, possessory and hypothecs. A hypothec is loosely a security in which the grantor grants neither title nor possession but the right to immediate possession, such right being suspended whilst repayments continue. Such a right is not self-publicising in the way that most possessory security is self-publicising, and may therefore require registration.

The doctrine of specificity

The doctrine of specificity holds that in order to transfer or to create security over an asset it is necessary to specify the asset with particularity. The purpose of the doctrine is mainly to avoid fraud and also to meet the apparently commonsense approach that one cannot transfer anything without identifying what it is. Even in England a grant of property under which the property granted is unidentifiable is ineffective[1].

Security agreements may take two forms. The security may be granted over a single specified asset or over a class of assets. Where security is granted over a class of assets, jurisdictions differ over how precisely the class needs to be specified in order for the security to take effect. Thus, whereas in the United Kingdom a grant of security over all the grantor's assets, present and future, is a valid security, in some civil law jurisdictions it is necessary to specify the individual assets concerned with some particularity in order for the security to take effect.

There are many degrees of specificity. At the most liberal extreme, in the English-based jurisdictions, the doctrine has virtually disappeared and it is possible to create security over a generic class of asset (eg all goods present and future): it is sufficient if one can tell at the time whether the asset is or is not a member of the class. At the most restrictive extreme are requirements for detailed particularisation (eg the bags of grain on board the ship m.v. 'Argos' numbered 1–52 and marked as the property of Grain Company Ltd).

The classification of securities—common law and Roman law

At Roman law securities were divided into *fiducia*, *pignus* and *hypotheca*. The schema of the distinction is that in *fiducia* security was created by trans-

---

[1] *Mogg v Baker* (1838) 3 M & W 195 at 196–8, per Parke B.

fer of title; in *pignus* security was created by transfer of possession; and in *hypotheca* neither title not possession was transferred, but the hypothecator assumed an enforceable obligation to deliver the property to the beneficiary of the hypothec which was unenforceable against successors in title to the property subject to the hypothec. This structure sounds similar to the common law division between mortgage, pledge and charge. Interestingly, it was not. No English lawyer could possibly say of the distinction between pledge and charge, as Marcian said of the distinction between *pignus* and *hypotheca*, that it was nothing except the sound of the words[2], and if this were true no Roman lawyer should have been able to go on to say, as Ulpian did, that the theoretical distinction was that one involved the delivery of possession[3]. In order to understand this it is necessary to say a little about Roman concepts of possession.

All legal systems protect possession—English law through the action in the tort of conversion, Roman law through the possessory interdicts[4]. However, there is a distinction between physical possession and the 'possession' which is protected at law. English law protects almost every possession with a very few exceptions; indeed the only significant exception is the 'custodianship' exception where property is in the physical possession of an employee in the course of his employment is treated as being possessed by the employer and not the employee. Roman law approached the matter very differently. Actual physical possession—*naturalis possessio*—was of little interest. What was important was juristic or legal possession—*possessio civilis*, or simply *possessio*. *Possessio* was only enjoyed by those who had the *animus domini*, or intention to possess as owner[5]. Thus in cases of consensual bailment—deposit, loan, hire, mandate and so forth—the bailee, since he did not have the *animus domini*, did not have juristic possession and therefore the benefit of the possessory interdicts.

The reason for this is that 'a possessor is always thought of [in Roman law] as a potential defendant in a real action, and therefore one who is and will remain owner, unless the plaintiff can oust him by proof of his title'[6]. Roman possession was something to be defended, and it would have been wholly unreasonable to throw the burden of defending the bailor's right to possession upon the bailee. Further, all possession *animus domini* ripened into ownership through usucapion in a very short space of time, and it would be inappropriate to allow this in the case of bailees.

Thus where a Roman lawyer spoke of possession what he meant was not *possessio naturalis* but something which is almost identical to what we mean when we speak of ownership of a chattel. The principle was that no one who

---

[2] Dig 20. 1.5, 1.
[3] Dig 13. 7. 9. 2.
[4] Buckland & McNair observe that the possessory interdicts 'are the remote ancestors of our possessory assizes which, however, they do not much resemble' (*Roman Law and Common Law*, 2nd edn (Cambridge University Press, 1952), p 421.
[5] This is Savigny's theory, based upon Paulus. *Contra* Ihering, who took the view that the location of juristic possession was determined entirely by operation of law.
[6] Buckland & McNair *above*, p 74.

had acquired *possessio naturalis* of a thing by virtue of a contract recognising the ownership of another could be treated as having juristic possession. This created difficulties in the context of the contract of pledge, the whole point of which was that at the time of the contract it was not at all clear in whom the property was eventually to vest. The pledgee was eventually treated as entitled to possession, and had the *actio Serviana*[7] to recover the property from a third hand. However, given Roman notions of juristic possession as being predicated upon *animus domini*, once it had been agreed between the parties that the pledgee was to have dominium over the property, its *possessio naturalis* became a matter of no interest, and it might as well be left with the pledgor, who might use it, as with the pledgee, who might only store it.

Thus the idea of the non-possessory pledge, which is a contradiction in terms in English law, became a common place of Roman law.

The *hypotheca* was a real security created by mere agreement. It developed in the context of land, where delivery was impossible, and in the case of farm implements and livestock, for which delivery would have extinguished the hypothecator's ability to work his land and thereby accumulate the money to repay the debt. However, given the close similarity between Roman concepts of possession and of ownership it is not surprising that the distinction between the *hypotheca* and the *pignus* diminished, and the action which the beneficiary of the hypothec has for the recovery of his property—the *actio hypothecaria*—has the same base, in the *actio Serviana*, as the action which the beneficiary of the *pignus* has for the recovery of his property. In both cases the action could be brought against third parties into whose hands the property had come.

The security created by *mancipatio* (or in *jure cessio*) *cum fiducia*, by contrast, seems to have been a close replica of the modern mortgage. Yet by the time of the publication of the *Digest* it had almost completely disappeared from view along with the formal methods of conveyance, and we have been able to reconstruct its incidents only through careful detective work.

---

[7] In its form of the *actio pigneraticia in rem.*

Chapter 22

Mortgages and Charges

A security interest is 'an aggregation or bundle of proprietory rights though not necessarily of ownership rights'[1]. Securities created by the transfer of possession are treated in Chapter 24, 'Pledge'. This chapter deals with securities created by the transfer of rights of ownership. However, the point which does require to be explored is the rationale for the maintenance of a distinction between the two classes of title security: mortgage and charge.

Legal mortgage

A mortgage is created by an absolute transfer of title of the mortgaged property by the mortgagor to the mortgagee 'as a security for the payment of a debt or the discharge of some other obligation for which it is given'[2]. Any property which is capable of transfer can be mortgaged. Where the transfer concerned is a legal transfer, the result is a legal mortgage. Where only an equitable interest is transferred the result is an equitable mortgage.

The mortgagor constitutes the mortgage by making an absolute transfer of title to the property, and immediately acquires a bundle of rights known as the equity of redemption. This equity is 'an equitable right inherent in the [property]'[3], and is treated as being equal to any other interest: indeed in *Fawcett v Lowther*[4] a right of redemption of land passed by gavelkind on the mortgagor's death.

The intervention of equity in the common law mortgage was on the basis of the jurisdiction to relieve from forfeiture, to the extent that equity would rewrite the express terms for redemption in the legal transfer with an absolute right for the mortgagor to have his property back upon discharge of the debt. This has resulted in two substantial interventions of equity into any transfer or property:

Recharacterisation
An equity of redemption may be found in any transaction where property is transferred with a provision for retransfer upon condition, regardless of whether the parties express themselves to be creating a mortgage, or indeed intended

---

[1] Sykes and Walker, *The Law of Securities*, 5th edn (Law Book Company, 1993), p 10.
[2] *Santley v Wilde* [1899] 2 Ch 474 per Lindley MR.
[3] *Pawlett v A-G* (1667) Hard 465 at 469 per Hale CB, and see *Re Wells* [1933] Ch 29 at 52.
[4] (1751) 2 Ves Sen 300.

to do so. Equity looks to the substance of the transaction and not merely the form[5]. This can create particular problems in the context of repurchase, or 'repo', transactions where an asset is sold at one price and at the same time an agreement is made that it will be repurchased at another, since such transactions are functionally identical to secured loans, with the difference between the purchase and the resale price being the cost of borrowing. The courts will look at all the circumstances of the individual case in order to determine whether a particular transaction is to be treated as a mortgage, but the primary test is the parties' intention[6]. The importance of the different treatment is that in the case of a purchase with an agreement to repurchase, the vendor has no property interest in the property. However, in the case of a mortgage the mortgagee retains his property right in the property throughout, and is entitled to have it reconveyed to him upon discharge of the outstanding debt. It is frequently suggested that most of the repo agreements in use in the capital markets are potentially recharacterisable as mortgages of securities, but this remains to be tested.

Clogs upon equity of redemption
Equity restrains any onerous condition which is imposed upon the redemption of the mortgage. Any term which has the effect of absolutely barring the mortgagor's right to redeem is invalid in equity[7], as is any term which would result in the mortgaged property reverting to the mortgagor subject to encumbrances[8]. There was at the turn of the twentieth century a tendency to construe any provision in a mortgage requiring anything other than the repayment of capital and interest as a 'clog', but modern courts accept that the financial markets may create new forms of security[9]. The modern rule is that[10]

> there is now no rule in equity which precludes a mortgagee, whether the mortgage be made upon the occasion of a loan or otherwise, from stipulating for any collateral advantage, provided such advantage is not either (1) unfair and unconscionable, or (2) in the nature of a penalty clogging the equity of redemption, or (3) inconsistent with or repugnant to the contractual and equitable right to redeem.

Examples of permissible and valid conditions are common; the most usual is a requirement in a mortgage of a public house to a brewery that the mortgagor will sell only the beer of that brewery for the duration of the mortgage[11]. However, a provision that the mortgagor should continue to buy beer exclusively

---

[5] *Re Watson, ex p Official Receiver in Bankruptcy* (1890) 25 QBD 27; *Re Lovegrove* [1935] Ch 464; *Grangeside Properties v Collingwood's Securities Ltd* [1964] 1 WLR 140.
[6] *Manchester, Sheffield and Lincs Rly v North Central Wagon Co* (1888) 13 App Cas 554.
[7] *Howard v Harris* (1683) 1 Vern 190.
[8] *Kreglinger v New Patagonia Meat and Cold Storage Co Ltd* [1914] AC 25.
[9] For example mortgages whose repayments are linked to indices or to foreign currency movements have been approved for this purpose; see *Nationwide BS v Registry of Friendly Societies* [1983] 1 WLR 1226 (index-linked); *Multiservice Bookbinding v Marden* [1979] Ch 84 (currency-linked).
[10] *Kreglinger v New Patagonia Meat and Cold Storage Co Ltd* [1914] AC 25 at 61, per Parker LJ.
[11] *Biggs v Hoddinott* [1898] 2 Ch 307.

from the brewery after the repayment of the mortgage is contrary to the rule against clogs upon the equity of redemption, since the property which is received back is subject to an incumbrance[12]. Yet the jurisdiction to relieve on the grounds of unconscionability is still exercised[13]. A provision which takes effect to postpone redemption is not *per se* a clog, and in *Knightsbridge Estates Trust Ltd v Byrne*[14] a provision which rendered the mortgage irredeemable for 40 years was held to be valid[15]. However a provision which renders the right to redeem illusory—for example where a mortgage of a lease is expressed to be irredeemable for a period equal to the duration of the lease—will be struck down[16]. Note that a mortgage made by a company may be rendered irredeemable by statute[17].

Chattel mortgages

The position of the mortgagor of a chattel in the course of a chattel mortgage depends on the construction of the instrument. Two constructions are possible: one is that the chattel has been delivered to the mortgagee and redelivered to the mortgagor to hold as bailee; the other is that the chattel remains in the mortgagor's possession subject to a power vested in the mortgagee to take immediate possession[18]. The difference is that in the second case the mortgagor cannot take possession except in accordance with the terms of the grant and, in the absence of a breach of the terms of the agreement giving rise to an immediate right to possession, he cannot sue either third parties nor the mortgagor in detinue or conversion.

It appears that a mortgagee of a chattel has an implied power of sale at law[19], although the instrument creating the security usually creates an express power. It also appears that the doctrine of consolidation does not apply to successive mortgages of a chattel[20].

This full equitable interest is extinguished by foreclosure, and the enduring right of the mortgagor to reopen the foreclosure is a mere equity[21].

Remedies of the legal mortgagee

The mortgagee usually has five remedies: an action on the covenant for payment; sale; foreclosure; taking possession; and appointing a receiver. It seems

[12] *Noakes & Co v Rice* [1902] AC 24.
[13] *Cityland and Property (Holdings) Ltd v Dabrah* [1968] Ch 166.
[14] [1939] Ch 441.
[15] This was based in part on the fact that the lender was prohibited from calling in the loan for the same period—if this had not been the case the decision might have been different (*Morgan v Jeffreys* [1910] 1 Ch 620).
[16] *Fairclough v Swan Brewery Co Ltd* [1912] AC 565.
[17] Companies Act 1985, s 193.
[18] *Gale v Burnell* (1845) 7 QB 850; *Fenn v Bittleston* (1851) 7 Ex 152; *Moore v Shelley* (1883) 8 App Cas 285, PC.
[19] *Re Morritt* (1886) 18 QBD 222 at 233, deplored in Sykes & Walker, *The Law of Securities*, 5th edn (Law Book Company, 1993), p 609.
[20] *Chesworth v Hunt* (1880) 5 CPD 266, deplored in Sykes & Walker, above, at p 610.
[21] Megarry & Wade, *The Law of Property*, 5th edn (Stevens, 1984), p 146.

probable that a mortgagee owes a duty to exercise these remedies in good faith and not to achieve any collateral aim of his own[22].

Action on covenant

This is always available. In any agreement to grant security in relation to a debt there is a deemed covenant to repay[23]. Note that this obligation does not pass with the property, and where a person transfers an equity of redemption, the transferee does not thereby become liable upon the covenant[24].

Sale

The mortgagee's power of sale is created either by the terms of the mortgage document or, where the mortgage is made under seal, by operation of statute[25]. The statutory power may not be exercised until after

(a) the secured amount has become due and notice has been served upon the mortgagor to repay[26],

(b) the payment is more than two months overdue, or

(c) there has been a breach of some other term of the mortgage[27].

A sale by or on behalf of a mortgagee confers good title upon the purchaser regardless of the title of the mortgagor and the mortgagee[28]. The mortgagee is a constructive trustee of the proceeds of sale over and above the amount needed to discharge the secured debt[29]. The mortgagee may not purchase the mortgage security[30], and if he does so the purported disposition is ignored and the mortgagee is treated as continuing in possession. However, if after such a purported sale the mortgagee purports to sell the property on to a third party, the sale to the third party is treated as a valid exercise of the mortgagee's power of sale, subject, of course, to the fact that any proceeds of sale over the mortgage debt are held upon constructive trust for the mortgagor[31].

Foreclosure

Foreclosure is accomplished by the extinction of the equity of redemption, thereby rendering the mortgagee's title absolute. *Snell's Equity* describes the process as 'asking the court to set limits to its own indulgence, and to decree that a mortgagor who is already too late to redeem at law shall be deprived even of his equitable right'[32]. Foreclosure can thus only be accomplished by means of an application to the court[33], and by making all subsequent

---

[22] *Downsview Nominees Ltd v First City Corporation Ltd* [1993] AC 295.

[23] *Meynell v Howard* (1696) Prec Ch 61; *King v King* (1735) 3 P Wms 358; *Sutton v Sutton* (1882) 22 Ch D 511, CA.

[24] *Re Errington* [1894] 1 QB 11.

[25] Law of Property Act 1925, s 101.

[26] *Barker v Illingworth* [1908] 2 Ch 20.

[27] Law of Property Act 1925, s 103.

[28] Law of Property Act 1925, s 104(2).

[29] See below.

[30] *Henderson v Astwood* [1894] AC 150.

[31] *Henderson v Astwood* [1894] AC 150.

[32] 29th edn, p 418.

[33] *Ness v O'Neil* [1916] 1 KB 706 at 709.

incumbrancers party to the proceedings[34]. Foreclosure is difficult to obtain, and even after a foreclosure order has been obtained there is an equity in the mortgagor to have the foreclosure re-opened if he can show good enough cause[35]. The Law Commission has recommended that foreclosure be abolished[36].

Taking possession

A mortgagee is *prima facie* entitled to possession of the mortgaged property, and may retain possession until the security is redeemed[37]. As a general rule this does not happen, not least because if the mortgagee had wanted a possessory security he would have taken a pledge. However, if a mortgagee does obtain possession of the mortgaged property he must account strictly to the mortgagor for its revenues on a 'wilful default' basis, ie he must account not only for amounts received but also for amounts which he should have received but did not because of his own default.

Appointment of receiver

A receiver is an agent of the mortgagor, appointed by the mortgagee, responsible for recovering any income of the property and exercising any powers which may have been granted to him. A typical mortgage document provides in great detail for the powers and authority of a receiver, but if these provisions are not set out in the mortgage document then, if the mortgage is made by deed, the Law of Property Act 1925 provides for the appointment of a receiver with statutory powers. A receiver can only be appointed over the charged property, although, where the security is a floating charge over 'substantially the whole of a company's property', an 'administrative receiver' having the powers of an administrator may be appointed[38].

Equitable mortgage

An equitable mortgage of personalty is identical to a legal mortgage of personalty, save for the fact that it is constituted not by a transfer of title to the charged asset but by entry by the chargeor into a binding agreement to transfer which is treated in equity as having been performed. In *Holroyd v Marshall*[39] the concept of the equitable mortgage was said to rest on the availability of specific performance of the contract to transfer; this is true to the extent that an equitable mortgage cannot arise in a case where equity has no jurisdiction to award specific performance. However, the guidelines on the exercise of the jurisdiction are to be disregarded for this purpose. Thus the fact that the asset is of no intrinsic value does not prevent an equitable charge from being cre-

---

[34] *Gee v Liddell* [1913] 2 Ch 62.
[35] *Campbell v Holyland* (1877) 7 Ch D 166.
[36] *Transfer of Land—Land Mortgages*, Law Com No 204.
[37] *Four-maids Ltd v Dudley Marshall (Properties) Ltd* [1957] Ch 317.
[38] Insolvency Act 1986, s 28.
[39] (1862) 10 HLC 191.

ated over it even though a court would not ordinarily exercise its discretion to award specific performance in such a case.

In the case of a mortgage of an existing chattel owned by the chargeor there is no substantial distinction between a legal and an equitable mortgage. In the case of chattels not yet owned by the mortgagor, a legal mortgage can only be created in two cases:

(1) A charge of potential property takes effect at law. Potential property is the fruit of property currently owned by the mortgagor (eg crops). A mortgage of crops to be grown on a certain piece of land by the land-owner takes effect to vest legal title to the crops in the chargee as soon as they are severed from the realty[40].

(2) A mortgage of future property takes effect to vest legal title to the property when it has passed into the ownership of the mortgagor and the mortgagor has done an act with the consent of the mortgagee appropriating the property to the mortgage—the doctrine of *novus actus*. The *novus actus* must be an act over and above the ordinary collection of the goods into the mortgagor's possession[41]. The *novus actus* must also be sufficient to enable it to be ascertained which property is appropriated to the mortgage—a manifestation of the doctrine of specificity.

In all other cases, a mortgage of future chattels can only be created in equity. In equity, future property is automatically vested in the mortgagee as soon as it is acquired by the mortgagor without the necessity for any *novus actus*[42] as long as the property is sufficiently identified in the mortgage document[43]. Thus an equitable mortgage of all after-acquired property would in principle be effective. This rule is subject to the rule set out below on floating charges.

Note that there is no chattel equivalent to the equitable mortgage of land by deposit of deeds. A security characterised by a transfer of actual possession or constructive possession by delivery of a document of title to goods is characterised as a pledge[44] and does not ordinarily give the holder any proprietory right in the chattel.

Where property is equitable property (for example an interest in a trust of personal property, or a second mortgage of a chattel), it can only be mortgaged by way of an equitable mortgage.

Remedies of equitable mortgagee

An equitable mortgage of personalty probably does give the mortgagee a right to possession[45]. The rule that an equitable mortgagee of land does not acquire

---

[40] *Grantham v Hawley* (1615) Hob 132; *Petch v Tutin* (1846) 15 M & W 110; Benjamin, *Sale of Goods*, 4th edn, para 5-095; see also *Re New Bullas Trading* [1994] 1 BCLC 485.

[41] *Lunn v Thornton* (1845) 1 CB 379; *sed quaere* given *Reeves v Barlow* (1884) 12 QBD 436.

[42] *Holroyd v Marshall* (1862) 10 HLC 191.

[43] *Tailby v Official Receiver* (1888) 13 App Cas 523; *Re Wait* [1927] 1 Ch 606; and see *King v Greig* [1931] VLR 413 and *ex p Dalgety Farmers Ltd* [1987] 2 Qd R 481.

[44] *Sewell v Burdick* (1884) 10 App Cas 74 at 95–7.

[45] Sykes & Walker, *The Law of Securities*, 5th edn (Law Book Company, 1993), p 616.

a right to possession is based on the fact that an equitable mortgagee could not bring an action for ejectment[46], and an action for ejectment was never available in respect of chattels. It seems that aside from statute and any provisions of any relevant statute, the only powers which the mortgagee of a chattel has are to foreclose and to apply to the court for the appointment of a receiver.

Charges

Legal charges

A legal charge over personal property is an impossibility. A legal charge is a creature of statute, and the provisions of Pt III of the Law of Property Act 1925, which create the legal charge, apply only to securities over land.

Equitable charges

An equitable charge arises where the debtor intends to give limited rights to an asset less than full ownership. Since the legal ownership of a chattel is indivisible, all such securities must necessarily be created in equity. Thus any enforceable agreement the effect of which is to grant a person rights over assets which remain in the grantor's possession, and to which title remains vested in the grantor, constitutes an equitable charge[47].

The charge in its original form was a species of equitable relief. The examples given in *Snell's Equity*[48] are in fact illustrative of the two different types of transaction which together contributed to the formation of the general law relating to charges.

(1) *The charge by devise* This may well be the oldest of the components, and arises where land is devised (usually by will) by A to B on the condition that B pay £x to C. Such a transaction clearly fell outside the ordinary rules of mortgage as the document simply could not be construed as a conveyance to anyone except B. Further, equity could not simply order the creation of a legal mortgage as the consciences of the parties concerned were clearly not bound to do anything of the kind, and a personal remedy against the devisee, although available, was clearly inadaequate as the chargee's interest was in the specific property charged rather than a general right of action against all the devisee's property.

(2) *The charge by covenant* In this case a chargeor covenanted that repayment of a loan should be 'out of' or 'secured by' a particular fund. This was an easier case, in that the covenant was clearly a promise to do something and the enforcement of promises is second nature to a court of conscience. However this form of creation ran into the prob-

---

[46] *Fisher & Lightwood's Law of Mortgages*, 8th edn, p 332; Sykes & Walker, *above*, pp 161–4.
[47] See eg *ex p North Western Bank; Re Slee* (1827) LR 15 Eq 69; *Brown v Bateman* (1867) LR 2 CP 272.
[48] 29th edn (1990) at p 443.

lems of construction so common in the nineteenth century. A covenant to pay money out of the income arising out of a particular asset clearly charged that asset with the repayment. However a covenant to pay money without designation of the asset charged was merely a covenant to charge and without more did not create a charge[49]. This created problems where the charge was of as much property as was necessary to secure a specified amount[50], as such a charge did not take effect as a charge on all of the existing property but only on such property as should be attached to the charge by a subsequent instrument. In both of these cases it is clear that what was created was a power *simpliciter*. However, this power rapidly came to be recognised as creating an equitable interest in that property over which the power might be exercised. Where a contracting party is given a contractual recourse to some specific asset of the other contracting party, equity enforces the right over the specific asset rather than leaving the parties to their action in damages, and in *Palmer v Carey*[51] it was said that '[it is a] familiar doctrine of equity that a contract for valuable consideration to transfer or charge a subject matter passes a beneficial interest by way of property in that subject matter ...'.

In *Swiss Bank Corp'n v Lloyds Bank Ltd*[52] the House of Lords considered the issue of how much and to what extent it was necessary for a particular fund to be appropriated to pay a particular debt before a charge was created. Approving the dictum cited above from *Palmer v Carey*[53], Lord Wilberforce went on to consider whether the relevant clause was a mere restrictive covenant. If it was, he said, such a covenant could not of itself create any interest in property. In the Court of Appeal Buckley LJ said that Browne-Wilkinson V-C had in the court below addressed only the question of equitable charge as mortgage[54], and proceeded to consider the question of whether the document might have created an equitable charge which did not create an interest. He held that it did not, but his reasons for holding such were that:

> ... whether a particular transaction gives rise to an equitable charge of this nature must depend on the intention of the parties ascertained from what they have done in the then existing circumstances. The intention may be expressed or it may be inferred. If the debtor undertakes to segregate a particular fund or asset and to pay the debt out of that fund or asset, the inference may be drawn, in the absence of any contra indication, that the parties' intention is that the creditor should have such a proprietary interest in the segregated fund or asset as will enable him to realise it out of the amount owed to him by the debtor: compare *Nanwa Gold Mines Ltd*[55] and contrast *Moseley v Cressey's Co*[56] where there was no obligation

---

[49] *Ravenshaw v Hollier* (1834) 7 Sim 3, upheld (1835) 4 LJ Ch 119, followed in *Montagu v Earl of Sandwich* (1886) 32 Ch D 525.
[50] *Freemould v Dedine* 1 P Wms 429 applied in *Countess of Markington v Keane* 2 De G & J 297.
[51] [1926] AC 703.
[52] [1979] Ch 548 at 595 and [1982] AC 584 at 613.
[53] [1926] AC 703, 706–7.
[54] At p 595.
[55] [1955] 1 WLR 1080.
[56] (1865) LR 1 EQ 405.

to segregate the deposits. But notwithstanding that the matter depends upon the intention of the parties, if upon the true construction of the relevant documents in the light of any admissible evidence as to surrounding circumstances the parties have entered into a transaction the legal effect of which is to give rise to an equitable charge in favour of one of them over the property of the other, the fact that they may not have realised this consequence will not mean that there is no charge. They must be presumed to intend the consequence of their acts.

Thus, in any circumstances where on the construction of the charge documents there is some segregation of assets and an intention to pay the debt out of those assets, an equitable charge is created. The question which then arises is whether both of these indicia are required to create an equitable charge. The decision in the House of Lords that an undertaking not to pay out of any other assets is insufficient despite the segregation suggests that both are required, and this finding is consistent with the authority of *Moseley v Cressey's Co* as cited by Buckley LJ, where the intention to repay out of a particular fund was explicit on the face of the agreement, but the assets concerned were paid into a general pool[57].

Does an equitable charge create equitable interest in charged property?

This importance of this question lies in the field of priorities. If charged personal property is sold to a bona fide purchaser without notice the chargee cannot recover the proceeds of sale from the chargeor. The doctrine of overreaching does not apply, since it arises only in relation to land[58], and the chargee cannot trace the proceeds into the hands of the chargeor since the chargeor is not a fiduciary of the chargee with respect to the charged property[59]. The reason for this is that the two parties to the charge will clearly wish to negotiate the payment of the secured debt and the release of the charge, and to place the parties in a fiduciary relationship would obstruct the negotiating power of the chargeor. This conclusion is supported by the words of Slade J in *Re Bond Worth Ltd*[60] that

> where an alleged trustee has the right to mix tangible assets or moneys with his own other assets or moneys and to deal with them as he pleases, this is incompatible with the existence of a presently subsisting fiduciary relationship in regard to such particular assets or moneys.

Thus the chargee's only proprietory remedy in the event of a wrongful disposal by the chargeor is against the charged property itself. If the property has been disposed of to a purchaser for value without notice of the legal estate, then the chargee's equitable interest in the property is extinguished. However, if the purchaser took with notice of the existence of the charge, then the question of whether the chargeor can assert a claim against the charged asset de-

---

[57] The question of an equitable charge was not raised in this case.
[58] Law of Property Act 1925, s 2(1).
[59] *Re Oliver* (1890) 62 LT 533.
[60] [1980] Ch 228 at 261.

pends on the answer to the question whether the charge constitutes a property interest, which can affect subsequent holders, or a mere covenant to apply the property in a particular way, which cannot bind a subsequent holder[61].

In this context it is important to distinguish the equitable charge from the equitable mortgage created by entry into an enforceable agreement to assign property. An equitable mortgage is constituted by a transfer of equitable ownership, but 'A charge ... does not pass either an absolute or a special property in the subject of the security.'[62] In *National Provincial & Union Bank of England v Charnley*[63] Lord Atkin made it clear that in his view for an equitable charge other than by way of equitable mortgage the chargee gets ' no legal right of property, either absolute or special, or any legal right to possession, but only gets a right to have the security made available by an order of the court'. These dicta would indicate that a charge does not constitute an equitable right in property.

However, it is submitted that the true analysis of an equitable charge properly so-called is that it does create an interest in property. There are three strands of authority which may be invoked in defence of this proposition. The first of these is the testamentary cases. Where there is a gift of the income from a fund indefinitely, that gift is automatically enlarged at law into a gift of the fund itself absolutely[64]. Where the gift is of a wasting asset—such as the profits of a leasehold—the interest passed is not only the rents themselves but the absolute right to the land itself when it reverts[65].

The second strand is that not all the cases which assert that an equitable charge does create an interest in property are in fact based on a confusion between equitable charge and equitable mortgage by enforceable agreement to transfer. In *Reeve v Whitmore*[66] an equitable charge was considered as against a mere power to seize goods, and was distinguished on the basis that the equitable charge created a property interest in the goods. Day J said in *Burlinson v Hall*[67]: 'A charge differs from an assignment. A charge on a debt confers rights on the person to whom the charge is given to have it enforced by assignment'. In *Rodick v Gandell*[68] Lord Truro said that an agreement to pay a debt out of a specific fund 'will create a valid equitable charge on such fund, in other words will operate as an equitable assignment of the debts or funds to which the order refers'. These words of Lord Truro were cited in *Palmer v Carey*[69]; there the court went on to hold that:

> An agreement for valuable consideration that a fund shall be applied in a particular way may found an application to restrain its application in another way. But if

---

[61] *See* pp 20–4 *below.*
[62] *Fisher & Lightwood's Law of Mortgage,* 10th edn, p 22.
[63] [1924] 1 KB 431.
[64] *Jennings v Bailey* 17 Bea 118; see also *Jarman on Wills,* 8th edn, p 1172 and the cases cited in note (t) thereat.
[65] *Watkins v Weston* 32 Bea 238; *Jarman,* p 1281.
[66] (1863) 33 LJ Ch 63 at 66.
[67] (1884) 12 QBD 347 at 350.
[68] (1851) 1 De G M & G 763 at 777–8.
[69] [1926] AC 703 at 706.

there is nothing more, such a stipulation will not amount to an equitable assignment. It is necessary to find further that an obligation has been imposed in favour of the creditor to pay the debt out of the fund. This is but an instance of a familiar doctrine of equity, that a contract for valuable consideration to transfer or charge a subject matter passes a beneficial interest by way of property in that subject matter if the contract is one of which the court will decree specific performance.

In *Phillips v Phillips*[70] a charge of £20 annually on land was held to be an equitable interest in the land.

The third strand of authority is to be found in the decision in *Harrison v Southcote*[71]. That case concerned an equitable lien which arose upon the sale by a Roman Catholic in England of land. Under the statute 11 & 12 Will III a Roman Catholic was prohibted from having any property interest in any land in England, but not from exercising other legal rights. Lord Hardwicke LC considered the position where a Roman Catholic vendor was not paid in full on the sale of land. He accepted that ordinarily a lien on the land would arise for the unpaid vendor's benefit, but held that where the vendor was barred by statute from holding any interest in land, then the lien did not operate as a matter of law[72]. Now it is clear that a vendor's lien for the purchase price may be said to stand proxy for an equitable charge, and it is also clear that this was not a case in which the charge could be classified as an enforceable agreement to create a mortgage. The conclusion may therefore be derived that where a charge on property is taken by one who is not capable of holding an interest in that property then the charge itself will fail. This must suggest that a charge creates a property interest in the charged property[73].

It follows from all of this that a purchaser of a chattel with notice of the fact that it was, at the time of disposal, charged with the payment of a debt, takes the asset subject to that charge. This conclusion is supported by implication by the decision in *Re Charge Card Services*[74], in which it was held that 'the availability of equitable remedies has the effect of giving the chargee a proprietary interest ... in the property charged'[75], and further support is to be found in the House of Lords' decision in *Morris v Rayners Enterprises Inc*[76].

Remedies of the equitable chargee

The equitable chargee's primary remedy is an application to the court that the property be applied in accordance with the charge. If the property charged is a fund of money the application is for payment of that sum to the chargee; if the property charged constitutes assets of any other kind the application is that the assets be sold and the proceeds applied in extinction of the debt. A chargee cannot foreclose, as there is no equity of redemption to extinguish.

---

[70] (1861) 4 De G F & J 208.
[71] (1751) 2 Ves 389 at 393.
[72] See also *Mackreth v Symmons* (1808) 15 Ves Jr 329 at 337.
[73] This conclusion is also reached by Sykes & Walker, *The Law of Securities*, 5th edn, p 616, and Gough, *Company Charges*, 2nd edn (Butterworths, 1996), p 19.
[74] [1987] Ch 150.
[75] At 176D.
[76] 30 October 1997.

The floating charge[77]

An equitable charge cannot take effect unless the chargee acquires enforceable rights against the property. If the chargee does not acquire such rights, then the charge is ineffective. In the context of individuals this dichotomy is absolute: if the chargee can deal with the charged property of his own motion, there is no charge but merely a contractual right against the grantor. In the case of companies, however, there is a half-way house between chargeor control and chargee control—this being the floating charge.

A floating charge is one which exists in the abstract over either a designated class of a company's assets or the whole of a company's assets, present and future. The holder of a floating charge has no equitable interest in any of the assets subject to the floating charge, which may therefore be dealt with freely by the company. However, upon the occurrence of a designated event (usually insolvency) the charge 'crystallises' and becomes fixed; the chargee acquires an equitable interest in every asset in the company's hands at the time of crystallisation, and assets acquired by the company post-crystallisation are free of the charge.

A floating charge takes effect as from the date of its creation, and the date of crystallisation is unimportant. As against other charges, a subsequently created floating charge cannot rank anywhere but after a prior floating charge[78], although a subsequently created floating charge over a sub-class of the assets comprised in the prior charge may, by agreement, take priority over the prior charge[79]. However, a subsequently created fixed charge takes priority over a floating charge, since the equitable interest in the charged property arises immediately upon creation of the fixed charge, whereas the equitable interest of the floating charge-holder is only created upon crystallisation[80]. Finally, the Insolvency Act 1986 postpones any charge which 'as created was a floating charge'[81] to the outstanding preferential debts of the relevant company[82].

The question of whether any particular charging document creates a fixed or a floating charge is determined according to the terms of the charge document, without reference to its self-designation[83]. If the charge has the characteristics that it attaches to all assets, both present and future, including those which would ordinarily be expected to be bought and sold in the ordinary course of the company's business, in such a fashion that the company is free to deal with those assets in the course of its business without recourse to the chargee, then the charge is taken to be a floating charge[84].

---

[77] An excellent review of the law of floating charges is to be found in *Gower's Principles of Modern Company Law*, 6th edn (Sweet & Maxwell, 1997), pp 362–89.

[78] *Re Benjamin Cope & Co* [1914] 1 Ch 800.

[79] *Re Automatic Bottle Makers Ltd* [1926] Ch 412, CA.

[80] *Wheatley v Silkstone & Haigh Moor Coal Co* (1885) 29 Ch D.

[81] Insolvency Act 1986, s 251.

[82] Insolvency Act 1986, s 175.

[83] *Re Armagh Shoes Ltd* [1984] BCLC 405, ChD (NI).

[84] *Re Yorkshire Woolcombers Association Ltd; sub nom Illingworth v Holdsworth* [1903] 2 Ch 284, CA; [1904] AC 355, HL.

Charges and charge-backs

One of the most common forms of charge is the charge which is taken by a bank over a cash deposit made with it in order to secure lending by it to the depositor. These 'charge-back' arrangements are popular, not least with banks who take the view that a deposit of cash is the best form of security imaginable, and wish themselves to hold any security deposits made by their customer. The question of whether a bank in this situation can take a charge over such a deposit—in other words, whether it can have a property interest in a debt owed by itself—has resulted in some of the most interesting debate in relation to the nature of the equitable charge as a security.

In *Re Charge Card Services*[85], Millett J addressed the problem of a charge to a bank of a deposit by its customer, and found that such a charge was impossible in law. The impact of this judgment was immediate in that the registrar promptly refused to accept for registration bank charges over deposits (although solicitors continued to submit them for registration in order to obtain the protection of the *Slavenberg* case[86]), and it has been commercial orthodoxy since that date that any rights over a debt owed by the lender to the borrower must be created by contract rather than by the creation of a security interest in the debt. *National Westminster Bank v Halesowen Presswork & Assemblies*[87] was relied upon by analogy to the effect that if a bank could not have a lien upon its own indebtedness to a customer it could therefore not have a charge on such indebtedness. However, it has been pointed out in the House of Lords by Lord Hoffman (in *Morris v Rayners Enterprises*) that these statements are in fact no more than objections to the fact that a legal lien such as the bankers' lien cannot arise over an intangible asset such as a bank debt.

The reason which is usually given as to why a bank should not take a charge over a deposit which it holds is that since no one may be both plaintiff and defendant in an action, and a debt is a chose in action, and since the action is extinguished as a matter of law, then the debt (which is, after all, only the fruit of the action) is also extinguished. This appears similar to the doctrine of merger. However, the equitable doctrine of merger does not operate automatically. There is no reason at all why a man should not be, for example, his own landlord as long as he manifests a clear wish to maintain the estates. He cannot create himself his own landlord, but the acquisition of a lease by a landlord, for example, is perfectly capable of continuing the separate existence of the lease[88]. What is important is the acquirer's intention[89]. This doctrine applies with equal force to charges. Where someone entitled to property subsequently becomes entitled to a charge upon it the charge endures where there is an expression of intention that the charge shall not merge[90]; this should be

---

[85] [1987] Ch 150.

[86] See Lingard Bank Security Documentation 18.2.

[87] [1972] AC 785.

[88] See eg *Brandon v Brandon* (1861) 31 LJ Ch 47 at 49.

[89] *Forbes v Moffatt* (1811) 18 Ves 384; *Symons v Southern Rly Co* [1935] 153 LT 98; and see *Golden Lion Hotel (Hunstanton) Ltd v Carter* [1965] 1 WLR 1189.

[90] *Watts v Symes* (1851) 1 De GM & G 240; *Adams v Angell* (1877) 5 Ch D 634, CA.

sufficient to keep it alive[91].

There are two authorities which appear to be contrary to the conclusion reached in *Charge Card*. In *Webb v Smith*[92] an auctioneer's lien on the proceeds of an auction was upheld. Since those proceeds included the debt due to him as auctioneer for his services it is clear that in that case at least the debt remained in the debtor's hands without being extinguished. In *Ex p Mackay*[93] a debtor gave his creditor a charge on monies accruing to the creditor but due to him. Thus the creditor clearly had a charge over his own debt, and it was argued by counsel for the debtor that this charge was a nullity as no man can have a charge on a debt due from himself. Their Lordships rejected this contention and held that there was a valid charge.

In *Welsh Development Agency v Export Finance Co*[94] at first instance Browne-Wilkinson V-C said that he had considerable doubts about the decision in *Re Charge Card Services* but would follow it 'in the interests of preserving consistency'. However, when the case came to the Court of Appeal ([1992] BCLC 148) Dillon LJ said that:

> I have very considerable difficulty with the view expressed by Millett J ... I see no basis for this conclusion in the judgement of Millett J himself. I see no reason why the transaction which took place in *Ex p Mackay*[95] and was upheld by this court ... should not be valid in law. The same applies to the auctioneer's lien on his client's moneys in his hands which was upheld by this court in *Webb v Smith*[96]. However I do not see that this arises in the present case.

In *Re Bank of Credit and Commerce International SA (No 8)*[97] at first instance Rattee J, following the dicta of Dillon LJ cited above, held that a particular document did have the effect of giving a bank a security interest in a debt due from it. The Court of Appeal[98] reversed this finding, holding that[99]:

> The difficulty that needs to be faced is that the debtor cannot be made to own the debt which he owes and which he is incapable of assigning. This is not merely a matter of semantics. The distinction between property and obligation lies at the heart of our jurispridence.

However the fact that such arrangements are ineffective to create charges does not leave them ineffective to secure the bank lender. In the conclusion to this part of his judgment in *Re Charge Card Services* Millett J said that[100]:

---

[91] Halsbury's Laws of England, Vol 16, para 884.
[92] (1885) 30 Ch D 192.
[93] (1873) LR 8 Ch App 643 (more fully reported in 42 LJ (NS) Bankruptcy 68).
[94] [1991] BCLC 936 at 953.
[95] (1873) LR 8 Ch App 643.
[96] (1885) 30 Ch D 192.
[97] [1994] 3 All ER 565.
[98] [1996] 2 All ER 121.
[99] At 131.
[100] Now s 323 of the Insolvency Act 1986 with respect to individuals and r 4.90 of the Insolvency Rules with respect to companies.

It does not, of course, follow that an attempt to create an express mortgage or charge of a debt in favour of the debtor would be ineffective to create a security. Equity looks to the substance, not the form, and while in my judgement this would not create a mortgage or charge, it would no doubt give a right of set-off which would be effective against the creditor's liquidator or trustee in bankruptcy, provided it did not purport to go beyond the what is permitted by s 31 of the Bankruptcy Act 1914.

As Oditah points out it is commonplace for insurance companies to take charges over policies of assurance issued by themselves. However the reason that they do so is illustrated by *Sovereign Life Assurance Co v Dodd*[101]. In that case a borrowing from a customer of the insurance company secured against the proceeds of policies with the company held by him was held to give rise to a valid set-off on the basis of s 38 of the Bankruptcy Act 1883, the precursor of s 323 of the Insolvency Act 1986. The validity of the charge does not seem to have been argued but its existence provided the source of the mutuality found. This appears to bear out Millett J's observations. Interestingly the validity of such a set-off was confirmed in *Re Bank of Credit and Commerce International (No 8)* by Rose J, who said that[102]:

> If the reasoning in *Re Charge Card Services Ltd* led to the conclusion that chargebacks were invalid or ineffective to give security in the event of the chargeor's insolvency, then the reasoning would be suspect, and if it could not be faulted we would be prepared to sacrifice doctrinal purity on the altar of commercial necessity. But we are satisfied that neither conclusion would be justified.

The position of a bank's charge over a deposit held with itself is now put beyond doubt by the House of Lords' decision in *Morris v Rayners Enterprises Inc*[103]. Lord Hoffman, giving a speech with which the other four law lords agreed, said that

> The depositor's right to claim payment of his deposit is a chose in action which the law has always recognised as property. There is no dispute that a charge over such a chose in action can validly be granted to a third party. In which respects would the fact that the beneficiary of the charge was the debtor himself be inconsistent with the transaction having some or all of the various features which I have enumerated? The method by which the property would be realised would differ slightly: instead of the beneficiary of the charge having to claim payment from the debtor, the realisation would take the form of a book entry. In no other respect, as it seems to me, would the transaction have any consequences different from those which would attach to a charge given to a third party. It would be a proprietary interest in the sense that, subject to questions of registration and purchaser for value without notice, it would be binding upon assignees and a liquidator or trustee in bankruptcy. The depositor would retain an equity of redemption and all the rights which that implies. There would be no merger of interests because the depositor would

---

[101] [1892] 1 QB 405.
[102] At 134.
[103] Speeches 30 October 1997. The case had not yet been reported at the time of going to press.

retain title to the deposit subject only to the bank's charge. The creation of the charge would be consensual and not require any formal assignment or vesting of title in the bank. If all these features can exist despite the fact that the beneficiary of the charge is the debtor, I cannot see why it cannot properly be said that the debtor has a proprietary interest by way of charge over the debt.

The policy grounds given by Lord Hoffman for his decision are interesting. One is the (entirely reasonable) point that 'in cases where there is no threat to the consistency of the law or to public policy ... the courts should be very slow to declare a practice of the commercial community to be conceptually impossible'. The second is the more interesting point about the availability or otherwise of set-off in the absence of such charges. As Scott V-C pointed out in *Re Bank of Credit and Commerce International SA (No 10)*[104], there is a substantial difference between the common law and civil law traditions in terms of their attitude to set-off. To adopt Philip Wood's categorisations[105], the common law jurisdictions are highly creditor-friendly, confining set-off within the narrowest bounds between solvent parties (thus restricting the availability of defences to creditor claims) and expanding it to its greatest limit on insolvency (thus ensuring that creditors are only exposed to the extent of their net claim—in effect allowing full recovery of amounts due from the insolvent debtor to the creditor). The civil law traditions are more debtor-friendly, widening solvent set-off to provide debtors with defences to claims, and narrowing it on insolvency to enable the greatest possible degree of recovery of assets for the debtor. The result of this asymmetry is that insolvent set-off is frequently unavailable in continental European countries in circumstances in which it would be available in England. The rationale for the development of the charge over bank deposits by creditor banks in the civil law systems was precisely the need to address the unsatisfactory nature of civil law insolvency set-off.

For English domestic business this is not a significant problem. Judges in earlier hearings had drawn attention to the fact that the 'charge card' problem was, in the UK, a non-issue, since everything that the charge was required to do was accomplished at English law by the rules of insolvent set-off. However, cross-border cases such as *BCCI* illustrate the difficulties which arise as a result of reliance upon set-off rather than a charge in a multi-jurisdictional setting. There the principal law of the liquidation was a civil law system, Luxembourg, but recoveries fell to be made in England as an auxiliary jurisdiction. In *Re Bank of Credit and Commerce International SA (No 10)*[106] the English system of set-off was held to prevail in respect of English recoveries since rule 4.90 of the Insolvency Rules (which requires insolvent set-off), being a rule of public policy, was applied even though the English proceed-

---

[104] [1997] 2 WLR 172.
[105] *Law & Practice of International Finance; Principles of International Insolvency* (Sweet & Maxwell, 1995), pp 2–7.
[106] Ibid.

ings were of an entirely auxiliary nature[107]. The English court nonetheless accepted that the Luxembourg courts would have applied their own variant of the set-off rule as a mandatory rule of Luxembourg law had the opportunity arisen to do so, and that such a conflict of rules of public policy was not resolvable. The English court therefore ordered that the English recoveries be applied according to the principles of English law.

Because the validity of a charge is determined by the proper law of the asset over which it is granted, the existence of the charge card problem meant that charges over debts governed by English law were theoretically invalid, regardless of the governing law of the security agreement creating the charge. Thus balances held with English banks were subjected to an arbitrary and irrational disadvantage, and banks lending under English law in international and cross-border transactions, or engaging in domestic transactions with overseas parties, were deprived of an important security technique. Consequently the banking community in England will breathe a large collective sigh of relief that it is now permitted to have recourse to the charge over deposits.

---

[107] Applying *British Eagle International Airlines v Compagnie Nationale Air France* [1975] 1 WLR 758; *Stein v Blake* [1996] AC 243.

Chapter 23

Lien

The law of lien requires a separate chapter for itself. A lien is loosely defined as a right of one person against property, title to which is vested in another, which does not constitute a legal or equitable interest in that property. A lien can exist both at law or in equity.

The common law lien

At common law a lien is a possessory right to property—a right to retain the property of another until the possessor's claim against that other is satisfied[1]. The nature of the legal lien can therefore be described simply as a pledge arising by operation of law rather than by agreement of parties[2] (although there are differences). Liens arise by custom or by express agreement.

A common law lien is a bare right of retention, and confers no right to sell the property, although an unsatisfied holder of a common law lien may apply to the court for an order for sale[3]. A common law lien may be either particular (in relation to obligations arising in connection with the particular goods for which the lien exists) or general (relating to all obligations owed by the property owner to the possessor). As a general rule liens are particular—for example, where goods are delivered to a tradesman to work on[4], or where property is left in the custody of innkeepers[5], packers[6] or carriers[7], the lien which arises will be a particular lien. General liens arise by trade custom, and have been held to arise in favour of solicitors[8], stockbrokers[9], factors[10] and bankers[11], although not in the case of warehousemen[12] and possibly not in the case of accountants[13].

---

[1] *Hammonds v Barclay* (1802) 2 East 227.
[2] *Brandao v Barnett* (1846) 12 Cl & Fin 787 at 806.
[3] *Larner v Fawcett* [1950] 2 All ER 727.
[4] *Keene v Thomas* [1905] 1 KB 136.
[5] *Robins v Gray* [1895] 2 QB 501.
[6] *Re Witt* (1876) 2 Ch D 489.
[7] *Skinner v Upshaw* (1702) 2 Ld Raym 752.
[8] *Barratt v Gough-Thomas* [1951] Ch 242.
[9] *Re London and Globe Finance Corp* [1902] 2 Ch 416.
[10] *Kruger v Wilcox* (1755) Amb 252.
[11] *Brandao v Barnett* (1846) 12 Cl & Fin 787.
[12] *K Chellaram & Sons (London) Ltd v Butlers Warehousing and Distribution Ltd* [1978] 2 Lloyd's Rep 412.
[13] *Woodworth v Conroy* [1976] QB 884.

Particular liens

A legal lien arises where goods have been lawfully delivered to a person[14] upon terms which impose upon that person an obligation to improve those goods. A mere finder who takes care of goods does not thereby acquire a lien upon them[15]. Mere supervision does not ordinarily give rise to a lien, and it is for this reason that a farmer tending stock acquires no lien[16]. The mere prevention of deterioration constitutes maintenance only, and does not give rise to a lien[17], but the prevention of deterioration must be distinguished from repair (or, in the case of animals, cure of illness), which does[18]. This principle has two significant exceptions: carriers, who are entitled to a lien by virtue of their common law obligation to accept all goods for carriage[19], and innkeepers, who are entitled to a lien upon the property of their customers left within the inn by virtue of their common law obligation to receive and afford proper entertainment to everyone who offers himself as a guest and safely and securely to keep the goods brought by the guest[20]. The case of custodians is problematic. In general a custodian does not acquire a lien upon the goods which he guards, as he is a mere maintainer[21], but there are some categories of custodian who have been held to be entitled to a lien by custom of their particular trades[22].

The delivery must be legal—in other words, it must be by the person who has title to the goods or by his agent. Thus where a car is given to a repairer by a hire-purchaser after the termination of the hire-purchase agreement had resulted in the hire-purchaser losing his right to possession, the repairer did not acquire a lien on the car for the value of his repairs[23]. Neither is there a lien for incomplete work[24] unless the reason that the work is incomplete is the interference of the owner[25].

By s 41 of the Sale of Goods Act 1979 a common law lien arises in favour of the seller of goods whilst he remains in possession of them. This is important, since the seller will ordinarily retain possession until such time as he has parted with the bill of lading which, in a modern documentary credit transaction, is against payment.

General liens

The test for the existence of a general lien is that the usage in a particular trade

[14] *Tappenden v Artus* [1964] 2 QB 185.
[15] *Nicholson v Chapman* (1793) 2 Hy Bl 254.
[16] *Re Southern Livestock Producers Ltd* [1964] 1 WLR 24.
[17] *Hatton v Car Maintenance Co Ltd* [1915] 1 Ch 621.
[18] *Albermarle Supply Co v Hind & Co* [1928] 1 KB 307.
[19] See Halsbury's Laws of England, 4th edn Carriers, paras 323 *et seq.*
[20] See Halsbury's Laws of England, 4th edn Inns, paras 1245–55.
[21] See eg *Chitty on Contracts*, 27th edn (Sweet & Maxwell, 1994), para 32-037.
[22] Notably *WharfingersBock v Gorrissen* (1860) 2 De GF & J 434 and arguably railway companies—*Singer Manufacturing Co v London and South Western Railway Co* [1894] 1 QB 833.
[23] *Bowmaker Ltd v Wycombe Motors Ltd* [1946] KB 505.
[24] *Pinnock v Harrison* (1838) 3 M & W 532.
[25] *Lilley v Barnsley* (1844) 1 Car & Kir 344.

in a particular locality must be certain and reasonable and so universally acquiesced in that everyone in the trade knew of, or on inquiry could have ascertained, its existence[26]. This is a very high standard, and outside certain very well-defined instances general liens arise otherwise than by usage. In particular, they are usually created:

(1) *By contract*   A general lien created by contract is indistinguishable from an agreement for a pledge[27]—especially since a lien cannot be created by mere agreement (any more than a pledge can be created by mere agreement) and specific appropriation of the property is required[28]. A contractual lien supersedes any customary lien which might arise between the parties to the contract[29].

(2) *By statute*   Many general liens arise by statute; for example, by s 7(1) of the Factors Act 1889, where an owner has given goods to another to be consigned, or has shipped the goods in another's name (as in an extended f.o.b. contract), the carrier has a lien upon the goods for advances made as if the shipper were the true owner. The Solicitors Act 1974, s 73 provides solicitors with a particularly wide general lien, covering all property recovered and preserved in the course of any suit in which the solicitor is instructed.

(3) *By notice*   Where a body of persons (eg a body of tradesmen) gives notice that it will do work only on terms that they have a general lien upon goods delivered to them for the purpose, this will take effect to create a general lien if the customer concerned had actual notice of the agreement[30].

A legal lien is more precarious than a pledge, in that where the lienee voluntarily parts with possession of the goods the lien is destroyed[31] unless the delivery is to the owner under an agreement that the lien will continue[32], or is to a bailee of the lienee[33]. Note that a right to possession of goods is lost if they are affixed to real property[34]. The destruction of the lien is a matter of substantive law, and the court has no power to declare it subsisting[35]. Where the lienee parts with the goods by mistake the lien is extinguished for good[36], but where the lienee is deceived into parting with possession of the goods, the lien revives if the lienee obtains possession of the goods again[37].

---

[26] 28 Halsbury (4th edn) para 528; *Plaice v Allcock* (1866) 4 F & F 1074.

[27] *Gladstone v Birley* (1817) 2 Mer 401.

[28] *Jones v Starkey* (1852) 16 Jur 510.

[29] *Inman v Clare* (1858) John 769.

[30] *Kirkman v Shawcross* (1794) 6 Term Rep 14; *Jowitt & Sons Union Cold Storage Co* [1913] KB 1.

[31] *Sweet v Pym* (1800) 1 East 4.

[32] *Albermarle Supply Co v Ltd v Hind & Co* [1928] 1 KB 307.

[33] *Levy v Barnard* (1818) 8 Taunt 149.

[34] This means that a building contractor who continues to build with goods subject to a lien loses his lien as the building progresses.

[35] *The Gaupen* [1925] WN 138

[36] *Dicas v Stockley* (1836) 7 C & P 587; *Bligh v Davies* (1860) 28 Beav 211.

[37] *Mason v Morley (No 1)* (1865) 11 Jur NS 459; *Earl of Bristol v Wilsmore* (1823) 1 B & C 514; *Hawse v Crowe* (1826) Ry & M 414.

Enforcement of legal liens

At common law a lien is not a positive right but a defence to a claim by the person entitled to the goods for their delivery[38]. Thus, strictly speaking, a legal lien is not enforced at all. However, once a lien has been exercised the person in possession of the goods is no longer entitled to claim his costs of storage or care of the goods from the true owner[39], and the person asserting the lien will want to release himself from the burden of their care. This involves an application to the court to order a sale of the goods[40], or to apply the income generated by the property in reduction of the debt[41]. This is not always necessary, since in certain circumstances there may be a customary right of sale which will be given effect by the courts[42]. Alternatively a lien may attract a statutory power of sale, and this is the case in respect of innkeepers[43], carriers[44], vendors of chattels[45] and any bailee of uncollected goods.[46]

A legal lien is not transferable. Even if the property is transferred along with an assignment of the benefit of the debt due, since the lien is destroyed when the property passes out of the lienee's hands for any reason[47].

Equitable liens

An equitable lien is the right in equity to a charge on property. The right arises in respect of all property[48], but is superseded where particular statutes provide for alternative lien arrangements. The foundation of the equitable lien is the idea that where a person has obtained property (or an improvement to property) which was obtained pursuant to a contract or similar obligation to pay money, equity imposes on the property a charge for the obligation whilst it remains undischarged. The element of legal obligation is key here. A man does not acquire a lien on the property of another by voluntarily spending money on it.

> The general principle is, beyond all question, that work and labour done or money expended by one man to preserve or benefit the property of another do not according to English law create any lien upon the property saved or benefited nor, even if standing alone, create any obligation to repay the expenditure. Liabilities are not

---

[38] For this reason a legal lien does not become statute-barred (*Higgins v Scott* (1831) 2 B & Ad 413).
[39] *Somes v British Empire Shipping Co* (1860) 8 HL Cas 338.
[40] RSC Ord 29, r 4.
[41] RSC Ord 29, r 8.
[42] Eg in the tea trade, *Re Tate, ex p Moffat* (1841) 2 Mont D & De G 170.
[43] Innkeepers Act 1878, s 1.
[44] Railway Clauses Consolidation Act 1845, s 97; Transport Act 1962, Sched 2, Pt IV.
[45] Sale of Goods Act 1979, s 39(1)(c).
[46] Torts (Interference with Goods) Act 1977, s 12.
[47] *Wilkins v Carmichael* (1779) 1 Doug KB; *Daubigny v Duval* (1794) 5 Term Rep 604 at 606; *Donald v Suckling* (1866) LR 1 QB 585.
[48] *In re Stucley* [1906] 1 Ch 67, approved in *Transport & General Credit Corp v Morgan* [1939] Ch 531.

to be forced upon people behind their backs any more than you can confer a benefit on a man against his will.[49]

Aside from express contracts, equity will find an obligation sufficient to support the creation of a lien in the case of trustees[50], of mortgagees and of persons who by performing the work will be subrogated to enforcement against the property[51]. The expenditure of money upon the property of another is also sometimes sufficient to establish a proprietary estoppel[52]. An equitable lien may also arise out of the relationship between persons, as for example the partners' lien upon partnership property after dissolution[53] or the lien created by a company's articles of association[54].

The primary distinction between an equitable lien and a common law lien is that the equitable lien can be asserted against property in the hands of another. Minor distinctions are that an equitable lien may be defeated by the Limitation Acts, and that the equitable lien carries with it an implied power of sale.

The most important manifestation of the equitable lien is the vendor's lien upon property for payment of the price. If title to property passes prior to possession, the vendor has a legal lien on it for the price. However, a transfer of possession to the purchaser destroys the legal lien, and the vendor has only the equitable lien.

Where a specifically enforceable contract for sale is made, the vendor, although he retains legal ownership of the property, becomes in equity a constructive trustee of the property for the benefit of the purchaser, and is accountable to the purchaser for any damage done during this period[55].

There is a symmetrical purchaser's lien where a purchaser has paid part of the price to the purchaser[56] in advance[57]. This lien takes effect upon a repudiation by the vendor[58] or upon the exercise by the purchaser of a right not to proceed with the transaction in accordance with the contract[59], but is extinguished by a repudiation of the contract by the purchaser himself[60]. At the same time as this trust arises, the vendor also acquires a lien as against the trust property for the purchase price[61]. The lien is not excluded by the fact that the instrument of transfer contains a receipt for the full purchase price, but

---

[49] *Falcke v Scottish Imperial Insurance Co* (1886) 34 Ch D 234 at 238, per Bowen LJ.

[50] A trustee is entitled to a lien upon trust property in respect of all of his costs. This rule is now statutory (Trustee Act 1925, s 30(2)) but previously existed as a rule of common law (*Re Beddoe* [1893] 1 Ch 547).

[51] *Re Leslie* (1883) 23 Ch D 552.

[52] *See* pp 92–5 *above*.

[53] *Aberdaire and Plymouth Co v Hankey* (1887) 3 TLR 493.

[54] Eg Companies Act 1985, Table A, paras 8–12.

[55] *Lysaght v Edwards* (1876) 2 Ch D 499; *Rayner v Preston* (1881) 18 Ch D 1.

[56] Not to a stakeholder (*Combe v Swaythling* [1947] Ch 625).

[57] *Burgess v Wheate;* (1759) 1 Eden 177, and see the authorities collected in 28 Halsbury (4th edn) para 560, fn 4.

[58] *Lee-Parker v Izzet* [1971] 1 WLR 1688.

[59] *Whitbread & Co Ltd v Watt* [1901] 1 Ch 911 at 915; [1902] 1 Ch 835.

[60] *Dinn v Grant* (1852) 5 De G & Sm 451; *Ridout v Fowler* [1904] 2 Ch 93.

[61] *Re Birmingham* [1959] Ch 523.

endures until the purchaser has paid the price and in addition discharged any other obligations under the contract of sale (eg an obligation to collect back rental or hire payments owing and to account to the vendor for those accruing prior to completion[62]).

An equitable lien does not arise in the context of a sale of ordinary commercial goods, since it is displaced by the lien created by s 41 of the Sale of Goods Act 1949[63]. However, this was explained in *Transport & General Credit Corp v Morgan*[64] as being due to the fact that the Sale of Goods Act should be treated as a complete code in relation to such sales without intermixture of the earlier doctrines of common law. It must be assumed that this is confined to the ambit of the sale of goods legislation (sale and purchase of tangible property) since there is authority that an equitable lien may arise in relation to intangible property such as debts[65] and shares[66].

The operation of the equitable doctrine of subrogation renders equitable liens to some extent transferable. Where a person makes a payment which is secured by the lien, as, for example, where a person makes part of a payment of a purchase price for an asset over which a vendor's equitable lien exists, that person is subrogated to the rights of the lienee as against the original purchaser[67].

An equitable lien may be created *inter partes* by enforceable agreement. If the agreement is an express written agreement it is registrable, if created by an individual, under the Bills of Sale Acts and, if created by a company, under the Companies Act 1985. If it is created by enforceable agreement other than in writing it will be avoided as against an individual by the Bills of Sale Acts, but will still require registration under the Companies Act if created by a company. There is authority that liens arising by operation of law do not require to be registered under the Companies Acts[68].

Extinction of equitable lien

An equitable lien can be excluded either by express or implied agreement[69] or by conduct. The latter occurs when the vendor agrees to accept some form of conditional payment (eg a cheque). If the cheque is not met, the lien does not revive[70]. Equally the vendor loses his lien if he takes any security for the purchase money[71]. In other respects it acts as any other equitable interest—it is defeated by laches and by the intervention of a purchaser for value of the legal estate without notice of the lien, but otherwise ranks in priority against other

---

[62] *Uziell-Hamilton v Keen* (1971) 22 P & CR 655.
[63] *Transport & General Credit Corp v Morgan* [1939] Ch 531.
[64] Fn 63 *above*.
[65] *Re Crossman, Salaman v Crossman* [1939] 2 All ER 530.
[66] *Re Nanwa Gold Mines Ltd, Ballantyne v Nanwa Gold Mines Ltd* [1955] 1 WLR 1080.
[67] *Boodle Hatfield & Co v British Films Ltd* [1986] PCC 176.
[68] *London & Cheshire Insurance Co v Laplagrene Property Co Ltd* [1971] Ch 499. This issue is discussed in greater detail in McCormack, *Registration of Company Charges*, pp 16–22.
[69] *Dixon v Gayfere* (1857) 1 De G & J 655.
[70] *Parrott v Sweetland* (1835) 3 My & K 655; *Buckland v Pocknell* (1843) 13 Sim 406.
[71] *Mackreth v Symmons* (1808) 15 Ves 329.

interests according to the time of its creation. By definition any purchaser of property (other than in a transaction for the sale of goods) who knows that his vendor has not yet paid for the property will take subject to the unpaid original vendor's lien.

Enforcement of equitable lien

An equitable lien is enforced by a writ issued in the Chancery Division, endorsed with a claim by the plaintiff for a declaration that he is entitled to a lien. Such a declaration has the effect of entitling the plaintiff to all the rights and remedies which he would be entitled to had he had a properly enforceable and valid charge on the property[72].

---

[72] *Rose v Watson* (1864) 10 HLC 672; *Re Stucley* [1906] 1 Ch 67.

Chapter 24

Pledge

A pledge is a security which is created by a physical transfer of possession of goods. It is a bailment of goods whereby the law implies a number of special terms into the contract creating the bailment. The special contract is brought into being where the bailor delivers goods to the bailee in consideration of a loan of money[1] upon terms that the bailee may retain possession of the goods until such time as the debt is repaid. Thus far it is indistinguishable from a legal lien. However, the distinction lies in the fact that the law implies into the contract of bailment a term that the pledgee may sell the property and apply the proceeds in extinction of the debt[2].

It is important to distinguish the true contract of pledge from a legal or contractual lien. A contractual lien is 'a mere personal and passive right to retain possession of chattels until certain monies due to the person exercising the lien are paid'[3].

Because there is no transfer of title to the pledgee he may not foreclose, and is therefore in the position of a chargee in that he may not have the security property for himself[4]. In addition, a pledgee may not sub-pledge the pledged goods without breach of the contract. However, the benefit of a lien may be transferred[5]

A pledge is constituted by the physical or constructive delivery of the goods concerned. The delivery need not be simultaneous with the making of the contract, but must be within a reasonable time[6]. The handing over of a key constitutes good physical delivery of goods which are accessed by the key[7] as long as the effective transfer is of control over the goods. The endorsement of a bill of lading constitutes good physical delivery of the cargo to which the bill relates, as by virtue of the Carriage of Goods by Sea Act 1992[8] a bill of lading constitutes a document of title whose delivery conveys possession of the goods to which it relates[9]. There are a few other documents which are

---

[1] The loan may be past or future (*Blundell-Leigh v Attenborough* [1921] 3 KB 235).
[2] *Re Hardwick, ex p Hubbard* (1886) 17 QBD 690; *Re Morritt ex p Official Receiver* (1887) 41 Ch D 222.
[3] *Crossley Vaines' Personal Property* (Palmer, ed), 5th edn (Butterworths, 1973), p 459.
[4] *Carter v Wake* (1877) 4 Ch D 605; *Fraser v Byas* (1895) 11 TLR 481.
[5] *Donald v Suckling* (1866) LR 1 QB 585.
[6] *Hilton v Tucker* (1888) 39 Ch D 669.
[7] *Wrightson v McArthur and Hitchisons (1919) Ltd* [1921] 2 KB 807.
[8] And formerly s 1 of the Bills of Lading Act 1885.
[9] *Glyn, Mills, Currie & Co v East and West India Dock Co* (1880) 6 QBD 475.

rendered documents of title by statute[10] whose delivery constitutes constructive delivery of the goods to which they relate, but in most cases delivery of
documents relating to goods constitutes nothing more than delivery of the
ipsa corpora of those documents[11]. In such a case, or in other cases where
goods are in the possession of a third party bailee, possession can only be
delivered by an attornment by the carrier, warehouseman or whoever has actual possession of the goods.

The implied power to sell the pledged goods and give good title thereto is
the primary distinguishing characteristic of the pledge. This right of sale is
implied at common law, and is therefore subject to the usual restraints; a pledgee
can almost certainly not sell the pledge to himself[12]. He may elect to retain the
pledge and sue for the debt[13], but if he elects to sell the pledge before the debt
has fallen due he is not liable for even nominal damages unless the debt is
paid[14].

Because a pledge is a possessory security there can be no pledge of intangibles. Thus a pledge of shares by delivery of the share certificates is invalid,
since shares in a company, being intangible, cannot be possessed[15]. However,
in the case of bearer bonds (or, presumably, bearer shares), delivery of the
paper in which the right has become embodied may be a valid pledge[16].

A pledgee has no ownership interest in the goods pledged[17]. A pledgeor
has no immediate right to possession of the goods pledged: indeed, until tender of the amount owed (or breach of the contract of pledge[18]) he has no
possessory right at all. However, he retains full and unrestricted title to the
goods, and may dispose of the title to them despite the pledge. The transferee
of the pledgeor's title stands in all respects in relation to the pledgee as if he
were the pledgeor, and is absolutely entitled to delivery of the goods upon
satisfaction of the condition of the pledge or to damages against the pledgee
for conversion if he fails to deliver up the goods pledged[19].

The pledgee's right to possesion of the pledge is no better than that of the
pledgeor. Thus, if the pledgeor were holding the goods despite an immediate
right to possession of a third party, the pledgee would commit a conversion
against that third party by accepting the goods as a pledge. However, where
the pledgeor is a mercantile agent the Factors Act 1889 protects the position
of any pledgee of goods held by him in such a fashion, so that the true owner
would have to pay the amount secured by the pledge in order to be entitled to

---

[10] Ie dock warrants complying with the conditions set out in the Port of London Act 1968, s
146(4), the Mersey Docks Consolidation Act 1858, s 200, the Trafford Park Act 1904, ss 33 and
34, and the Liverpool Mineral and Metal Storage Co Ltd (Delivery Warrants) Act 1921, ss 3
and 4.
[11] *Official Assignee of Madras v Mercantile Bank of India Ltd* [1935] AC 53.
[12] *Crossley Vaines' Personal Property* (Palmer, ed), 5th edn (Butterworths, 1973), p 461.
[13] *South Sea Co v Duncomb* (1731) 2 Stra 919; *Jones v Marshall* (1889) 24 QBD 699.
[14] *Halliday v Holgate* (1868) LR 3 Ex 299.
[15] *Harrold v Plenty* [1901] 2 Ch 314.
[16] *Carter v Wake* (1877) 4 Ch D 605.
[17] *The Odessa, the Woolston* [1916] 1 AC 145.
[18] *Cooke v Haddon* (1862) 3 F & F 229.
[19] *Franklin v Neate* (1844) 13 M & W 481.

delivery of the pledge. The point here is that the rule *nemo dat quod non habet* applies as much to the right to possession as it does to title, and is subject to the same broad exceptions in the case of pledge as it is in the case of sale.

A pledgee is in many ways treated as the person entitled to the goods for the duration of the pledge. He is entitled to the possessory remedies against any third party interfering with the goods (ie trespass and conversion), and is entitled to use the goods in whatever way is neither detrimental to the goods nor contrary to the contract of bailment[20]. He may also sub-pledge the pledged goods as he wishes unless there is an express term of the pledge agreement preventing this[21]. A pledgee's creditor may seize the pledged goods in execution of a judgment against him, although a pledgeor's creditor may not[22].

The interaction of the Bills of Sale legislation and the contract of pledge is a matter of some difficulty. In theory a pledge is constituted by mere delivery and there is therefore no requirement for any document to be prepared. However, it is usual for a written agreement to be entered into setting out the terms of the pledge. Where property is actually delivered in accordance with such an agreement, the agreement is *prima facie* not a bill of sale[23]. This is also true where there is constructive delivery by a transfer of the means of control, although the point is harder in such a case[24]. In any event, the important point is that the delivery must be valid; in *Dublin City Distillery v Doherty*[25] it was held that an attempt to deliver possession by the delivery of a 'delivery warrant' which was not a bill of lading or a statutory document of title was completely ineffective to transfer possession.

Requirement for physical delivery

In many continental legal systems it is possible to have a constructive delivery of property by mere agreement. The way in which this works is that a person agrees to transfer property to another, and the other immediately bails it back to him. This is in effect a method of creating a proprietary security by writing alone, and flourishes in those jurisdictions in which restrictions upon 'false wealth' render it difficult or impossible to create securities by transfer of title alone.

In the United Kingdom it has never been possible to do this. An agreement which purports to transfer possession so as to create a possessory security is known in civil law countries as a *hypothecation*. Hypothecation in this sense is not permitted at English law[26]. This may seem paradoxical, in that it ap-

---

[20] *Coggs v Bernard* (1703) 2 Ld Raym 909, per Holt CJ.
[21] *Donald v Suckling* (1866) LR 1 QB 585.
[22] *Re Rollason, Rollason v Rollason, Halse's Claim* (1887) 34 Ch D 495; *Rogers v Kennay* (1846) 9 QB 592.
[23] *Re Hardwick, ex p Hubbard; Johnson v Diprose* [1893] 1 QB 513; *Ramsay v Margrett* [1894] 2 QB 18.
[24] *Wrightson v McArthur and Hitchisons (1919) Ltd* [1921] 2 KB 807.
[25] [1914] AC 823.
[26] *Howes v Ball* (1827) 7 B & C 481; *Donald v Suckling* (1866) LR 1 QB 585; *Sewell v Burdick* (1884) 10 App Cas 74.

pears to be an anomalous exception to the rule that in equity a thing is treated as having been done if an enforceable contract exists by which it could have been compelled to be done[27]. Why, it may be asked, should a contract to transfer title create a valid equitable title in the transferee, whereas a contract to deliver possesion does not create 'equitable possession' in the transferee?

The reason is that there is no such thing as equitable possession[28]: the concept is redundant. In a case where an action is brought for the enforcement of a contract to deliver possession, a court may award damages at common law for non-delivery. This satisfies the requirements of the underlying transaction in every case bar one, that being an agreement for a pledge. What is being aimed at in the case of a requirement to deliver property under an agreement to deliver it, however, is the completion of a legal security—in other words, the order for delivery of possession which would be sought from the court would be a mere component of the completion of the common law security. This is a very long way around a short point and the courts of equity, which do nothing in vain, deal with this situation not by ordering delivery of possession, but by awarding an equitable security—an equitable lien[29], or in some cases an equitable charge[30] —over the goods. Equity does not need to concern itself with possession, as by dealing with possession it would be constituting a legal security composed of an incompatible jumble of equitable and legal elements. It is easier and better, surely, to look to the parties' intention, see that what has been achieved is an enforceable contract to create a security, and therefore in response to create a remedial security in the goods concerned[31].

Redelivery

A pledge is constituted by the delivery of possession of the pledged item. It therefore follows that a pledge is destroyed by redelivery of possession to the pledgeor[32]. This is not, in fact, an absolute rule—at common law redelivery is permitted where it is for a limited purpose on the clear understanding that the pledge is not to be affected thereby and that the pledgeor's temporary possession is held on the pledgee's behalf[33]. It is therefore possible to continue a pledge after delivery of possession to the pledgeor, as where a bank delivers the bill of lading to its customer as buyer of the goods so that the buyer can

---

[27] *Snell's Equity* (P V Baker, ed), 29th edn, p 40.
[28] Goode, *Commercial Law*, 2nd edn (Penguin, 1995), p 677.
[29] *Brown v Bateman* (1867) LR 2 CP 272; *Re Slee, ex p North Western Bank* (1872) LR 15 Eq 69.
[30] *Re Hamilton, Young & Co, ex p Carter* [1905] 2 KB 772; *Official Assignee of Madras v Mercantile Bank of India Ltd* [1935] AC 53.
[31] See Palmer, *Bailment*, 2nd edn (Sweet & Maxwell, 1991), pp 1398–1400 in which these issues are addressed in more detail. Palmer cites the speech of Templeman LJ in *Maynegrain Pty Ltd v Compafina Bank* (1984) 58 ALJR 389 as indicating that the Privy Council was prepared to admit the possibility of an equitable pledge, but he concludes that this is not a tenable view.
[32] *Reeves v Capper* (1838) 5 Bing NC 136 at 140–1; *Dundas Hamilton v Western Bank* (1857) 28 LTR 376.
[33] *North Western Bank Ltd v John Poynter, Son & Macdonalds* [1895] AC 56.

collect them from their port of arrival and resell them in order to pay back the bank. This is done under a trust receipt which in English law has been treated as preserving the pledge even though the bank loses actual possession[34]. The practical advantages of the scheme are very great[35].

Pawnbroking

The most common form of pledge was until relatively recently the pawn. The pawnbrokers' shop has largely disappeared from modern high streets, although in recent times the concept appeared to be undergoing something of a revival.

The Pawnbrokers Acts 1872–1960 were replaced by the Consumer Credit Act 1974. The 1974 Act's operative provisions apply only to transactions of less than £15,000, so that transactions in excess of this amount are now unregulated by any statute[36]. In order to engage in the business of pawnbroking a person must be licensed under the 1974 Act, but there is no separate category of licences for pawnbrokers. Pawns entered into outside the course of business[37], in respect of documents of title[38] and of bearer bonds[39] are also excluded from the Act. The Act requires that the pawnee must provide the pawnor with a pawn-receipt and must enter into a written agreement with him setting out the terms of the pawn and the associated borrowing. Both the format and the content of the agreement and the terms of the pawn-receipt are governed by express provisions made under the Act[40]. The Act also provides for a form of written declaration to be delivered in lieu of the pawn-receipt in cases where the pawnor has lost the receipt[41]. The failure to deliver the pawned item against tender of the outstanding debt is rendered a criminal offence[42], and the burden of proof to show that the failure to return the property was reasonable is on the pawnee[43]. Where the pawnee sells the property, if the amount received is more than the debt he is obliged to pay the surplus over to the pawnor[44] and he is required to show that he did so. Goode[45] says that although in such a case the pawnor has no right to interest either at common law or under s 35A of the Supreme Court Act 1981, the fiduciary relationship

---

[34] *Re David Allester* [1922] 2 Ch 211.
[35] *Lloyds Bank v Bank of America NT & SA* [1938] 2 KB 147 at 166, per MacKinninon LJ.
[36] Save that the 1974 Act gives a court a residual power to reopen any credit transaction which it considers to be extortionate (s 137(1)). In *Castle Phillips & Co Ltd v Wilkinson* [1992] CCLR 83, for example, a mortgage of land at a rate of 48 per cent per annum was struck down on this basis.
[37] Section 114(3)(*b*).
[38] Section 114(3)(*a*).
[39] Section 114(3)(*a*).
[40] Consumer Credit (Agreements) Regulations 1983 and Consumer Credit (Pawn-Receipts) Regulations 1983 respectively.
[41] Section 118.
[42] Section 119.
[43] Section 171(6).
[44] Section 121(3).
[45] *Consumer Credit Legislation*, Vol 1, para 2106, fn 1.

between the pawnee and the pawnor entitles the pawnor to interest in equity[46]. The rule that equitable interest cannot be claimed in respect of a common law action[47] is not breached, since the action is equitable for breach of the fiduciary duty rather than on the statute or the common law liability *qua* bailee.

Where the amount which is realised on disposal is less than the amount due the pawnee may sue for the total debt, giving credit for the sale proceeds of the pawned item less reasonable expenses of sale. However, the burden is upon him to show that he took reasonable care to ensure that the true market value was obtained for the pawn[48], and that the expenses of sale were not unreasonably high[49]. If he cannot prove either of these elements, the amount due from the pawnor is recalculated as if the true market value had been obtained or as if the expenses of sale had been reasonable.

---

[46] The principles upon which equitable interest is calculated may be found in *Snell's Equity*, pp 288–9; see also *Wallersteiner v Moir (No 2)* [1975] QB 373 at 397; *Guardian Ocean Cargoes Ltd v Banco di Brasil (No 3)* [1992] 2 Lloyd's Rep 193; *Matthew v T M Sutton Ltd* [1994] 1 WLR 1455.

[47] *Westdeutche Landesbank Girozentrale v Islington LBC* [1996] AC 669.

[48] Section 121(6).

[49] Section 121(7).

Chapter 25

Security Interests Created by Individuals—The Bills of Sale Acts

The core of the law of security is a repugnance to the appearance of 'false wealth'—the idea that a man may appear to the world to be solvent and credit-worthy whereas in fact he has title to none of the assets which he appears to own. The conventional response to false wealth is a requirement for publicity, such that a creditor may discover whether his debtor truly owns the assets which he appears to own, coupled with legislation which strikes down secret transfers by way of security. Such features may be found in very many legal systems[1].

The key to the system is the striking-down legislation. In England this was for many years the Fraudulent Conveyances Act 1587, 27 Eliz I c.4 (which became s 172 of the Law of Property Act 1925 before being repealed by the Insolvency Acts 1981–6), which struck down 'fraudulent conveyances' (ie such secret conveyances and mortgages as were in fraud of creditors). It was presumed that any transaction whereby the grantor retained possession of the assets concerned was fraudulent unless the contrary was proved[2]. This arrangement seems to have ensured that most securities were enforceable only after a good deal of dispute over whether they were fraudulent[3]. To complicate matters further, the doctrine of 'reputed ownership' might in any event take effect to vest title to property in the hands of a bankrupt in his trustee in bankruptcy for distribution regardless of the true position[4].

This system began to be amended by the Bills of Sale Act 1854. The policy of the Bills of Sale legislation was to enable unchallengeable security to be granted over assets other than land by ensuring that such securities were in written form and were registered in a public register. The legislation did not automatically avoid all securities not effected in the statutory form; it merely provided that any document effecting such a disposition was to be in a certain form and to be registered. Thus it was (and remains) perfectly possible to create security orally without coming into contact in any way with the Bills of

---

[1] See P Wood, *The Law and Practice of International Finance, Comparative Law of Security and Guarantees* (Sweet & Maxwell, 1995).

[2] *Twyne's Case* (1602), 3 Co Rep 80.

[3] See eg per Lord Blackburn in *Cookson v Swire* (1884) 9 App Cas 653 at 664, and see Muir, *Hunter on Personal Insolvency* at para 3-465.

[4] The doctrine of 'reputed ownership' was last seen in s 38 of the Bankruptcy Act 1914 (repealed by the Insolvency Act 1986). It provided that upon the bankruptcy of an individual, goods which were not his own but which were in his possession in the course of his trade or business, by the true owner's consent and permission, vested in his trustee in bankruptcy for distribution amongst his creditors.

Sale legislation[5], in the same way in which it is possible to transfer property orally without coming into contact with the Stamp Duty legislation. However, the reliability of oral contracts is such that the draftsmen of the statute correctly reasoned that by catching grants of security embodied in documents they would catch effectively all grants. Note that the parole rule of evidence is to the effect that verbal evidence of a written agreement is not admissible: thus, where the document is inadmissible, oral testimony of the transaction which it records is also inadmissible, and the transaction may therefore not be proved at all[6].

In order to understand the operation of the Bills of Sale Acts it is necessary to understand the distinction which the Acts make between security bills, given by way of security for an advance of money, and absolute bills, given in order to transfer title to property. The 1878 Act applies to absolute bills only, the 1882 Act to security bills.

The importance of this distinction is that the 1878 Act takes effect to avoid any disposition of property by an absolute bill only upon insolvency (and against execution creditors seeking to enforce against the relevant asset prior to insolvency). An absolute bill is and remains enforceable between the parties thereto whilst the parties remain solvent, whether or not it is registered in accordance with the Act. The effect of the 1882 Act, however, is to render an unregistered security bill void as against everyone, including the parties thereto. This is similar to the effect of the Consumer Credit Act 1974, and for much the same reason. Part of the mischief which the 1882 Act was aimed at was oppressive requests for security made by moneylenders, and the object of the Act was at least in part to protect borrowers from such pressure.

It is interesting to note that the passing of the first Bills of Sale Act in 1854 was contemporaneous with the abolition of all other statutory regulation of lending practices.

> Apart from the Bills of Sale Acts and pawnbroking legislation, the lenders of money enjoyed an unparalleled era of freedom and prosperity between 1854 and [the enactment of the Moneylenders Act 1900]. Trickery and extortion were rampant and borrowers suffered misery and hardship through ruthless enforcement of security. The Report of the House of Commons Select Committee on Money-Lending, published in 1898, showed that one lender had admitted charging on occasion interest rates as high as 3,000%, while another confessed that to avoid the notoriety likely to result from his activities he had traded under no less than 34 different aliases.[7]

This was the environment in which the Bills of Sale legislation developed.

Absolute bills and the 1878 Act

The 1878 Act was aimed at the contrived sale by a businessman of all his

---

[5] Litt S 365; *Reeves v Capper* (1838) 5 Bing NC 136; *Flory v Denny* (1852) 7 Exch 581; *Newlove v Shrewsbury* (1888) 21 QBD 41.
[6] *Newlove v Shrewsbury* (1888) 21 QBD 41.
[7] Goode, *Consumer Credit Law* (Sweet & Maxwell, looseleaf), para 4.

assets to a friendly party who could be relied upon to hold them for him during any unforeseen period of insolvency. The law saw no reason why the friendly party should not be entitled to enforce the transaction whilst the transferor remained solvent, but declined to allow the transaction to remain enforceable upon insolvency unless it was publicly registered and therefore publicly known.

The underlying mechanism of both Acts is that any relevant transaction which is recorded in writing is void unless the writing is in the prescribed form and registered[8]. The shape of the avoidance, however, differs between the Acts. Security bills which do not satisfy the 1882 Act's requirements are void absolutely, including as between the grantor and the grantee of the security. This is a measure for the relief of debtors, and may be referred to the market conditions alluded to above. An absolute bill, however, is void except as between the parties thereto. In other words, upon the grantor's insolvency, the grantee may not employ the bill to vindicate the assets concerned as against the grantor's trustee in bankruptcy's estate. However, if the grantee decides that he wishes to claim the assets, the grantor cannot set up the Act to challenge the validity of his own gift. There is a certain 'serves you right' element to this principle of selective validity, but it has its counterpart in the modern law of company charges, which are valid between the parties thereto whether registered or otherwise[9].

The application of the Acts

The courts have held that the Bills of Sale Acts do not apply to companies on the basis that the Companies Acts provide for a distinct and separate registration regime[10]. The issue of whether they apply to other corporations appears to be still open. However, in practice the Acts are treated as applying only to natural persons. Neither do the Acts catch supplies of goods or services on credit[11] or reservation of title clauses[12].

As mentioned above, the Acts catch documents, not transactions, and under the Acts the nature of the documents caught has been widely defined. Thus, not only is a document setting out the terms of the transaction caught, but so is any document transferring title, recording the terms of the agreement or acting as any record of the transaction[13]. A receipt may therefore be caught by the Acts[14].

---

[8] This approach was adopted into the Consumer Credit Act 1974, although that Act permits the enforcement of an agreement which, although otherwise valid, does not comply with the 1974 Act requirement, with the sanction of a court order (s 65(1)).
[9] Companies Act 1985, s 395. Note that a document in the form of a security bill of sale created by a company is not void as between grantor and grantee.
[10] *Re Standard Manufacturing Co* [1891] 1 Ch 627.
[11] *Beete v Bidgood* (1827) 7 B & C 453; *Olds Discount Co v Cohen* [1938] 3 All ER 281n.
[12] *McEntire v Crossley Bros Ltd* [1895] AC 457.
[13] The authorities are collected in *Crossley Vaines' Personal Property* (Palmer, ed), 5th edn (Butterworths, 1973), p 452, n (k).
[14] *Youngs v Youngs* [1940] 1 KB 760.

Nature of bill of sale

The definition of the term 'bill of sale' in the 1878 Act includes any of the following:

(a) documents given to pass the legal property in goods retained by the grantor (ie bills of sale proper);
(b) assignments;
(c) transfers;
(d) declarations of trust without transfer;
(e) inventories of goods with receipts attached thereto;
(f) receipts for purchase moneys of goods;
(g) any other assurance of personal chattels;
(h) powers of attorney, authorities or licences to possession of personal chattels as security for any debt;
(i) any agreement, whether or not intended to be followed by the execution of any other instrument, by which a right in equity to any personal chattel, or to any charge or security thereon, is conferred,
(j) every attornment, instrument or agreement whereby a power of distress is given by way of security for a debt or advance and rent is reserved as a mode of providing interest or otherwise for the purpose of such security only.

'Personal chattel' as used in the Act has a special meaning. The term is defined to exclude shares, government securities and choses in action. This exclusion is very important in the context of the modern law of security, and in particular in modern banking practice, in which banks frequently accept security of this kind from individual customers without compliance with the Bills of Sale Acts.

The difficulty with the legislation was that transfers of title without possession were and are an everyday part of international commerce. Consequently, a series of exceptions from the Act were provided for goods in foreign parts or at sea, including goods represented by bills of lading. By the Bills of Sale Act 1891 a further exception was provided for imported goods at any time prior to their delivery to a warehouseman or the eventual buyer or to their reshipment. Another case in which the 1878 Act created difficulties was that of farmers seeking to finance their activities by granting security over their livestock. This was dealt with by exempting such securities from the operation of the Acts completely by the Agricultural Credits Act 1928, which enables individual farmers (uniquely) to grant floating security over their herds. Other, less important exclusions from the 1878 Act include general assignments for the benefit of creditors[15], marriage settlements and transfers of ships.

Goods

One of the issues which is regularly encountered in security law is what is known as the 'doctrine of specificity'[16]. This is a rule that a grant of security

---

[15] Loosely, the pre-1986 equivalent of an individual voluntary arrangement.

over an asset or assets is only valid if it identifies the asset with sufficient particularity. The rule varies in its strength from jurisdiction to jurisdiction, and in modern English law it is particularly weak in that company charges may be valid even though they give only the vaguest indication of the assets concerned. In bills of sale, however, the doctrine continues in full force. The statutory requirement that the schedule to the bill must specifically describe the chattel secured is strictly enforced, and where the description is insufficiently specific the bill is void against third parties. Thus a bill given by a tradesman in respect of his stock in trade was held to be void because it referred only to items 'at 47, Mortimer Street'[17]. Equally a bill given in respect of 'Stock; 2 horses, 4 cows', was void for want of specificity[18]. However, perhaps strangely, items can be specified by reference to a document not itself registered—a bill relating to items 'as per catalogue' was valid even though the catalogue was a separate document outside the bill of sale[19].

Where a bill refers to goods of which the grantor was not the 'true owner' at the time of the bill's execution, it is void in respect of those goods as against third parties[20]. Thus where a person executes a bill of sale for goods which he holds subject either to a hire purchase contract[21] or to a prior absolute bill[22], the bill is void except as against the grantor. Therefore, if the grantor subsequently acquires legal ownership of the thing the grantee of the bill may recover it from him. But if the grantee acquires the goods after the grantor's insolvency he cannot retain possession as against the trustee in bankruptcy of the grantor[23].

Avoidance of absolute bills

Absolute bills are avoided by s 8 of the 1878 Act, which provides that bills which do not comply with the formalities '... shall be deemed fraudulent and void so far as regards ... chattels comprised in such bill which, at or after the time of filing of the petition for bankruptcy, or of the execution of [an assignment for the benefit of creditors], or of executing process [of any court ordering the seising of chattels] ... and [were, seven days after the making of the bill,] in the possession or apparent possession of the person making such bill of sale'.

Thus an absolute bill of sale is valid in respect of property which was, either in the week after making the bill or at the time of filing the petition, not in the possession or apparent possession of the grantor of the bill. 'Apparent

---

[16] See Wood *above*.
[17] *Witt v Banner* (1887) 20 QBD 114.
[18] *Davies v Jenkins* [1900] 1 QB 133.
[19] *Davidson v Carlton Bank Ltd* [1893] 1 QB 82.
[20] 1882 Act, s 5.
[21] *Lewis v Thomas* [1919] 1 KB 319.
[22] *Tuck v Southern Counties Deposit Bank* (1889) 42 Ch D 471. If the goods are subject to a prior security bill then the second bill operates as a form of 'second mortgage' of the equity of redemption under the first bill (*Thomas v Searles* [1891] 2 QB 408).
[23] *Newlove v Shrewsbury* (1888) 21 QBD 41.

possession' is partially defined in the statute as meaning on land occupied by the person or otherwise enjoyed by him[24], but its true meaning has been said to be '"apparently in possession" as distinguished from "actually in possession" such that goods may be in the true and actual possession of one, and in the apparent possession of another'[25]. This extended concept of possession survives the abolition of the concept of 'reputed ownership'. However, because s 283 of the 1986 Insolvency Act defines the bankrupt's estate as extending only to property beneficially owned by the bankrupt, this section has no effect on property which is, at the time of the grantor's bankruptcy, in the possession of the bankrupt but is beneficially owned by someone other than the grantee.

Avoidance of security bills

A security bill must be in the form specified in Sched 1 to the 1882 Act, which sets out the individual assets over which the security is created, the amount advanced, the terms of repayment and the interest rate. Curiously, any bill of sale is also void which is given in respect of an advance of less than £30[26].

Because Sched 1 requires that the form of the bill contains the interest provisions along with a promise to repay, it is unusual to include these items in a second separate agreement. This means that, because the Act renders the whole bill void if it is in any way defective on its face, as a general rule the covenant to repay and the obligation to pay interest at the contract rate is also void. However, the courts will permit the lender to recover the sum advanced together with interest at 5 per cent[27].

Yet there are some minor defects which, although they avoid the security element of the bill, do not affect the covenants as to repayment and interest. These are a failure to (a) have the bill properly attested, (b) register, or (c) set out the consideration[28].

Registration

The Bills of Sale Acts' registration requirements are to be found in s 11 of the 1882 Act and in the Bills of Sale (Local Registration) Rules 1960. These require that every bill of sale must be registered within seven days of its execution, either with the Registrar of the Bills of Sale at the Central Office of the Supreme Court or with the local County Court Registrar. The registration must be renewed every five years. There is no necessity for transfers of the benefit of the bill to be registered[29]. Priorities amongst bills are determined in accordance with their date of registration.

---

[24] Bills of Sale Act 1878, s 4.
[25] Per Williams J in *Robinson v Tucker* (1883) Cab & El 173 at 178.
[26] 1882 Act, s 12.
[27] *Davies v Rees* (1886) 17 QBD 408.
[28] 1822 Act, s 8.
[29] *Re Parker, ex p Turquand* (1885) 14 QBD 636; *Marshall & Snelgrove v Gower* [1923] 1 KB 356.

A bill must be endorsed with a memorandum of satisfaction when it is discharged. By an interesting echo of post-O'Brien legal practice, an absolute bill is required to be attested by a solicitor who must state on the face of the document that he has explained its effect to the grantor[30]. Security bills, however, need only be attested by a credible witness.

Enforcement of security bill

The grantee of a security bill of sale may only enforce his rights against the goods in the following circumstances[31]:

(a) default by the grantor under the terms of the bill (this may include failure to pay principal or interest, and failure to perform any covenant specified in the agreement—eg a covenant to insure);

(b) the grantor's bankruptcy;

(c) distraint upon the goods for rent[32], rates or taxes[33];

(d) if the grantor fraudulently removes, or suffers the goods to be removed from the specified premises;

(e) if the grantor refuses to provide the grantee with up-to-date receipts for rent, rates and taxes;

(f) if execution has been levied against any goods of the grantor.

The procedure for seizure is that the grantee must give notice to the grantor of the seizure but may not remove the goods from the grantor's premises for a period of five days, during which time the grantor has a *locus poenitentiae* to repair whatever default gave rise to the right to seize[34].

---

[30] 1878 Act, s 10.

[31] 1882 Act, s 7.

[32] Section 4 of the Law of Distress Amendment Act 1908 provides that a bill of sale is no defence to distraint by a landlord for rent.

[33] Section 14 of the 1882 Act provides that a bill of sale is no defence to distraint for rates and taxes.

[34] 1882 Act, ss 13 and 7.

Chapter 26

Security Interests Created by Companies and Registration of Charges[1]

Security interests in the property of English companies must be registered with the Registrar of Companies in a public register by Pt XII of the Companies Act 1985. Initially companies were required to maintain a private register of securities granted over their property[2], and this register was to be open to the public for inspection. However, it was held that failure to maintain such a register was a mere misfeasance by the directors, and did not invalidate the relevant security[3]. Consequently these registers became largely redundant, and by s 14 of the Companies Act 1900 companies were required to file particulars of charges created with the Registrar of Companies. Failure to register such a charge invalidated it.

Principles of registration

The object of the public registration requirements was and is to ensure publicity and to avoid problems of 'false wealth'[4]—in other words, to give creditors notice of the amount of unencumbered assets owned by the company.

Registration has a Janus-faced aspect. For the secured lender it is highly desirable. Registration gives notice to all the world of the security's existence, and therefore renders it impossible for any person to acquire a subsequent charge over the asset without acquiring constructive notice of the prior charge[5]. However, the better view appears to be that the registration of the charge does not affect trade purchasers, since a trade purchaser is not expected to investigate the register of charges of the company concerned before dealing with it[6].

---

[1] The Companies Act regime applies to charges and mortgages alike. However, the Act uses the term 'charge' throughout to apply to both forms of security, and that usage is followed for this chapter.

[2] Companies Act 1862, s 43.

[3] *Re General South America Co* (1876) 2 Ch D 337; *Wright v Horton* (1887) 12 App Cas 371.

[4] See per Cozens-Hardy MR in *Re Yolland, Husson & Birkett Ltd* [1908] 1 Ch 152, and the Report of the Diamond Committee (February 1989) which reviewed the basis of the charge registration system.

[5] See eg per Lord Watson in *Salomon v Salomon & Co Ltd* [1897] AC 22 at 40. Registration of a charge on land has this effect by statute by the Law of Property Act 1925, s 198(1). Gough takes the view that the 'constructive notice' analysis is unhelpful, in that the problem should be perceived as a priority problem and dealt with by a statutory rule of priorities (*Company Charges*, 2nd edn, p 832).

[6] McCormack, *The Registration of Company Charges*, pp 141–4.

For the borrower, however, registration has no advantages, but has a substantial disadvantage in that it makes the company's borrowings a matter of public record. Companies are instinctively averse to disclosing their security arrangements, since this may damage their credit and thereby increase their cost of borrowing. As a general rule, therefore, tension exists between the borrower's desire to avoid registration and the lender's desire to register.

The Companies Acts

The Companies Act 1989 embodied a series of registration provisions which were intended to replace the existing Pt XII of the Companies Act 1985. These provisions are unsatisfactory in a number of respects and are unlikely ever to be brought into force[7], and this chapter therefore discusses only the provisions of the existing Pt XII.

By Pt XII the major headings under which securities require registration are:

(1) A charge created or evidenced by an instrument which, if executed by an individual, would require registration as a *bill of sale*[8]. This head includes all non-possessory securities in goods. Registration is not usually required under this head for

   (a) a possessory pledge of goods,

   (b) a charge on goods which is not in writing (because the Bills of Sale legislation bites on documents, not transactions),

   (c) a charge over identified goods to be imported in certain very restricted cases,

   (d) charges on goods situated outside England and Wales, and

   (e) a charge on a chose in action, such as a contract right.

(2) A charge on the company's *book debts*. This probably means commercial or business receivables and has been defined as 'debts arising in a business in which it is the proper and usual course to keep books and which ought to be entered in the books'[9]. The test to be applied is whether as a matter of ordinary accounting practice the debt would be recorded in the company's books[10] under the heading of 'debtors'.

(3) Charges to secure any *issue of debentures*.

(4) *Floating charges* created by a company (including partial floating charges).

In addition to these there is a series of minor headings, which includes charges on the uncalled share capital of a company and a charge on calls made but not paid. Special mention is made of three classes of assets for which a separate

---

[7] See McCormack, *The Registration of Company Charges*.

[8] *See* p 262 *above* for a definition of what this involves—in effect any grant of an interest in property without transfer of possession of that property.

[9] *Official Receiver v Tailby* (1888) 13 App Cas 523, HL, *affmg* (1886) 18 QBD 25 at 29.

[10] *Paul & Frank Ltd v Discount Bank (Overseas) Ltd* [1967] Ch 348; *Re Brightlife Ltd* [1987] Ch 200 at 209.

registration is required in a designated register—land[11], ships[12] and aircraft[13]. These provisions are included to make clear that double registration is required: that is to say, a company creating a charge over an asset of any of these types is required to register the charge at Companies House in addition to registering it with the relevant specialist registry. Finally, two classes of intangible assets are brought within the registration provisions—goodwill and intellectual property[14].

Charges which do not require registration

Because the Act is structured as a list of types of charge which require registration, any charge which does not appear on the list is effective without registration. The Companies Registry should reject registration filings over assets which do not fall within the classes of charges which require registration. This means that the lender has no means of giving the world notice of his security, and remains vulnerable to double-dealing by the grantor of the security by the creation of a second charge. From the lender's perspective, the fact that a charge cannot be registered makes it less valuable as a security because of the increased risk of double-dealing. Conversely, from a borrower's perspective, the fact that a charge over a given item of property need not be registered renders it more attractive as a potential security.

The most important—and certainly the most commonly encountered—of the items which are not included in the registration requirements of Pt XII are shares, debentures and other securities. This is sometimes aggressively employed by borrowers who grant security over assets by transferring them to a subsidiary company and granting security over the shares in the subsidiary. Conversely, the security can be made registrable by taking a charge over the shares themselves and the dividends paid thereon; the latter constitute future book debts of the company, and therefore the charge requires registration.

An insurance policy is not a book debt, since the amount which may be received under it is not a book debt, being payable only upon a contingency. Consequently, a charge over an insurance policy's proceeds cannot be registered[15]. The position for a true life assurance policy (ie one where the contingency—death—is certain, and only the amount receivable is variable) is very unclear, but it seems that a charge over an interest in such a policy is not registrable.

A bank account is not a book debt, and therefore a charge over an account

---

[11] The Land Registry is established by the Land Registration Act 1925.

[12] The Merchant Shipping Act 1894, as amended by the Merchant Shipping (Registration) Act 1993, provides that legal mortgages of ships must be registered at the central register of British ships to be maintained by the Registrar General of Shipping and Seamen.

[13] The Civil Aviation Act 1982, s 86 creates a separate register of aircraft mortgages to be maintained by the Civil Aviation Authority.

[14] Most charges over intellectual property now additionally require to be registered under the Copyright, Designs and Patents Act 1988, but for most of the life of the existing company registration system such property, and interests therein, was unregistered.

[15] *Paul & Frank Ltd v Discount Bank (Overseas) Ltd* [1967] Ch 348.

balance is not registrable[16]. To some extent this makes perfect sense—the amount of the credit or debit balance in a bank account is usually kept secret in any event, and the lack of publicity for such a security is no detriment to creditors.

A pledge does not require to be registered because it is not within any of the headings above. However, the logic which excluded pledges from the registration provisions of the Bills of Sale legislation is equally applicable to the Companies Acts; the transfer of possession concerned is itself sufficient to publicise the transaction[17]. Although it is clear beyond doubt that a pledge created by actual delivery of possession is exempt from the registration provisions[18], some doubt has been expressed over whether a pledge created by constructive delivery by attornment is also outside the provisions[19].

Liens created by operation of law do not require registration, but a lien created by contract between parties is registrable as a charge. Thus, for example, a lien on sub-freights created by a company under a time charter in the owner's favour is a charge on a book debt and registrable as such[20].

Effect of non-registration

Registration is usually on a form setting out prescribed particulars of the security and attaching the document (if any) creating the charge. A failure to register a charge within 21 days of its creation is a misfeasance by the company and by its directors, and both they and the company are liable to a daily fine for every day after the permitted period on which the charge remains unregistered[21].

This is, however, incidental to the main sanction for non-registration, which is that the charge is void as against the liquidator or administrator or any secured[22] creditor of the company[23] if it is not registered within 21 days of the date of its creation. Note that the charge remains valid as against the company, which cannot escape from its liabilities thereunder by reference to non-registration for as long as it remains solvent[24]. This point is of importance in cases where charges have remained unregistered through mischaracterisation. For example, it is common practice in trade finance transactions to rely on 'letters of hypothecation' of particular cargoes to pay particular borrowings, usually supported by deposit of a bill of lading or of warrants of some form.

---

[16] Per Hoffman J in *Re Brightlife Ltd* [1987] Ch 200 at 209. However, he did explain in *Re Permanent Houses (Holdings) Ltd* [1988] BCLC 563 that it did not follow from *Re Brightlife* that a bank balance could never be a book debt, merely that this was not the usual state of things.

[17] For an explanation of the nature of a pledge see *Re Morritt, ex p Official Receiver* (1887) 41 Ch D 222.

[18] *Wrightson v McArthur and Hitchisons (1919) Ltd* [1921] 2 KB 807.

[19] Per Parker LJ in *Re Hardwick, ex p Hubbard* (1886) 17 QBD 690 at 854.

[20] *Re Welsh Irish Ferries Ltd* [1985] 3 WLR 610.

[21] Companies Act 1985, s 399(2).

[22] *Re Telomatic Ltd* [1994] 1 BCLC 90 at 95.

[23] Section 395.

[24] *Re Ehrmann Bros Ltd* [1906] 2 Ch 697; *Re Monolithic Building Co* [1915] 2 Ch 643.

Where what is deposited is not a bill of lading (or some other negotiable document of title to goods) the agreement takes effect as an equitable charge of the cargo which is ordinarily void for non-registration, since it is not usual to register charges created under letters of hypothecation. In such a case, if the lender can seize the cargo prior to the onset of the borrower's insolvency he may perfect his claim under the letter of hypothecation and obtain a valid pledge, which is enforceable against the liquidator[25].

However, as a general rule, where the company is solvent the value of the charge is negligible, and it is only upon insolvency that the charge has any value to the chargee. Thus an unregistered charge is in practice nearly valueless.

Where A creates a charge in favour of B, any interested person (in practice B) has 21 days in which to register it. If the charge is not registered within this period, it ceases to be effective upon insolvency. Registration after the lapse of the 21-day period is ineffective unless a successful application is made to the court for an order extending the period[26]. Such an order is not made post-liquidation[27] except in extraordinary circumstances, but in *Re R M Arnold & Co Ltd*[28] late registration was permitted post-insolvency in order to give effect to a pre-existing agreement between secured creditors of the distribution of assets upon insolvency in circumstances where all the secured creditors agreed to the registration and there was evidence that the unsecured creditors' positions would not be affected.

Registration does not affect priorities. Thus where two charges are created consecutively, the fact that the second is registered before the first does not affect its ranking as long as both are registered within the 21-day period. This creates a period of vulnerability for anyone taking a charge over the property of a company, since a prior charge created less than 21 days previously, although unregistered at the time of taking the charge, has priority over it if registered thereafter.

Where neither of two charges are registered the position is more complex. Neither is effective against a liquidator, administrator or creditor of the company, but otherwise the ordinary principles of equitable priorities apply such that if the second chargee is a purchaser for value without notice, he acquires good title to the property and takes priority over the prior chargee[29]. If such a person does have notice of the first charge's existence, his interest, being later in time, should rank in equity after the existing security[30]. However, it is quite possible that if the principles developed in *Re Monolithic Building Co*[31] in the context of the registration of land charges are applied in the context of company charges, a person who creates a second charge with knowledge of the

---

[25] *Mercantile Bank of India v Central Bank of India, Australia and China* [1937] 1 All ER 231.
[26] Companies Act 1989, s 404(2).
[27] *Re S Abrahams & Sons* [1902] 1 Ch 695.
[28] [1984] BCLC 535.
[29] *Watson v Duff Morgan & Vermont (Holdings) Ltd* [1974] 1 WLR 450.
[30] Since legal estates cannot be created in personal property, such charges are almost always equitable.
[31] [1915] 1 Ch 643.

existence of that prior charge acquires priority both against a liquidator, administrator or secured creditor *and* against the prior chargee, since the gravamen of that case seems to be that where a statutory mechanism is provided for notice by registration, notice by knowledge may be disregarded. The rule is that except in a case of fraud, a subsequent chargee who takes with actual notice of a prior unregistered charge is absolutely entitled to the charged assets[32]. This rule is a curious exception to the ordinary rule of notice, and has been strongly criticised[33].

Effect of defective registration

Defective registration arises where the particulars which are submitted to the Registrar are incorrect. The Registrar's certificate is conclusive evidence of the registration of a charge[34], and one of the effects of this 'conclusive evidence' rule is that even where the details of the charge given to the Registrar are incorrect, the charge is still taken to be properly registered. This applies in the case of serious inaccuracies, including cases where the charged property is incorrectly identified[35], where the amount secured is incorrectly stated[36], and where the date of creation of the charge is given incorrectly[37]. It is presumably the case that if a set of charge particulars differed so substantially from the actual charge created so as to be unrecognisable as such then there might be an argument to the effect that the certificate was invalidly granted as being *ultra vires* the Registrar, but it is hard to imagine a set of circumstances in which this could be the case.

In this context, note that registration has no effect upon the charge registered. Where a charge is defective, registration cannot cure any defect in the charge itself[38].

---

[32] *Re Monolithic Building Co* [1915] 1 Ch 643, approved by the House of Lords in *Midland Bank Trust Co v Green* [1981] AC 513. Both cases relate to the rules concerning the registration of charges over land, but it seems that the principles to be applied are identical.

[33] See eg Gray, *Elements of Land Law*, 2nd edn (Butterworths, 1993), p 131: 'It may well be that, in the eyes of the law, it is not fraud to take advantage of the folly of another, but it remains an uncomfortable fact of life that most fraud consists in doing precisely that'. The Law Commission has indicated its disapproval of the decision (*Property law: Third Report on Land Registration* (Law Com No 158, 31 March 1987, para 4.15).

[34] Section 401(3).

[35] *National Provincial and Union Bank v Charnley* [1924] 1 KB 431.

[36] *Re Mechanisations (Eaglescliffe) Ltd* [1966] Ch 20.

[37] *Re Eric Holmes (Property) Ltd* [1965] Ch 1052.

[38] Gower, *Principles of Company Law*, 6th edn (Sweet & Maxwell, 1997), p 381.

Chapter 27

Priorities

Issues of property law frequently resolve themselves in practice into questions as to which of a number of competing interests should take priority in an asset. Such issues frequently can be resolved by examining the constitution of each property interest individually, since it is less common that one would imagine for competing interests in property to have all been validly created. However, where this is the case the rules of priority must be applied.

Competing legal interests

Double-dealing

The most common manifestation of competing legal title to property arises where a vendor sells goods twice over to different parties. This is known as 'double-dealing', and the issue which arises is which of the two purchasers gets the goods. Where the transaction is a sale of goods and the seller remains in possession of the goods after the first sale, the point is dealt with by s 24 of the Sale of Goods Act 1979, which provides that a seller in possession of goods after sale who resells them to a second purchaser can give good title to the goods. If the seller is not in possession, or the transaction is outside the ambit of the Sale of Goods Act and the Factors Acts, then the rule *nemo dat quod non habet* applies and the second purchaser receives nothing[1]. In the context of double-dealing in property other than goods, in most cases conflicts over legal title are dealt with according to the ordinary rules governing successive assignments[2].

Consecutive pledges

Consecutive pledges by actual delivery are in theory impossible, since after the first pledge the pledgee has no possession to transfer and a redelivery of the property to the pledgor by the first pledgee will destroy the pledge. However, consecutive pledge problems can arise where pledges are created by actual or constructive attornment[3] by a bailee.

---

[1] Unless one of the other obstacles to the rule (ie an estoppel against the first purchaser) applies: *see* Chapter 14 *above*.

[2] *See* pp 282–3 *below* and Chapter 15 *above*.

[3] A constructive attornment occurs where a document of title to goods is delivered.

There is a statutory element to consecutive pledges of goods which must be considered. Sections 2, 8 and 9 of the Factors Act 1889 provide that in the case of a pledge of goods by (a) a mercantile agent who is in possession of the goods with the owner's consent, (b) a seller who has retained possession of the goods, and (3) a buyer who has obtained possession of but not title to those goods, the pledge is valid. Neither the second nor the third of these applies in the case of consecutive pledges, for the good reason that these sections regulate priorities as between a first sale and a subsequent sale or pledge. Only the first can apply in the case of consecutive pledges. The reason why it applies at all is to be found in *Lloyds Bank v Bank of America*[4], where it was said that, even though the pledgor retains ownership of the pledged goods, the effect of a pledge is to constitute the *pledgee* the 'owner' as the term is used in the Factors Acts. Thus , if the pledgeor is otherwise a 'mercantile agent', if he acquires possession of the pledged goods with the pledgee's consent (usually under a trust receipt structure) so as to be able to repledge them, then he is in possession 'with the consent of the owner' (ie the first pledgee) and the second disposition is given priority by the operation of the Act.

The position at common law outside the special Factors Acts' mechanism is different. It is submitted that the rule of *nemo dat quod non habet* applies to possession as well as to title, so that the second pledge is completely ineffective, the possessor having, by the first pledge, divested himself of all that he had; he has nothing with which to create the second pledge[5]. The first pledgee therefore has priority. This is a similar position to repledging, where a person who has himself only a special property in goods as bailee pledges those goods to a pledgee representing as he does so that the goods are his own[6]. In the majority of such cases the true owner may recover the goods directly from the pledgee without discharging the secured debt[7]. However, the second pledgee may be able to argue that the first pledgee, by delivering the documents to the pledgeor, is estopped from denying the pledgeor's power to pledge.

The most important issue for common law priorities is therefore whether the pledge is indeed made by a person to whom the goods have been delivered in his capacity as a mercantile agent. A mercantile agent for this purpose is defined as a person who has 'in the customary course of his business as such agent authority either to sell goods, or to consign goods for the purposes of sale, or to buy goods, or to raise money on the security of goods'. The question of whether a particular individual is a mercantile agent is therefore a question of fact. Note that delivery to a person who does business as a mercantile agent is not sufficient; the delivery must be to that person *in his capacity as* mercantile agent. Thus, delivery to a warehouseman who also conducts

---

[4] [1938] 2 KB 147.

[5] *Meyerstein v Barber* (1866) LR 3 CP 38 and 661, in which the consecutive pledges were accomplished by delivery of different copies of the same bill of lading.

[6] Such a representation is implied in every pledge (*Cheesman v Exall* (1851) 6 Ex 341; *Singer Manufacturing Co v Clark* (1879) 5 Ex D 37 at 42.

[7] *Singer Manufacturing Co v Clark* (1879) 5 Ex 37 (pledges by thieves); *Helby v Matthews* [1895] AC 471 (pledges by hirers of goods— *sed quarere* given *Belsize Motor Supply Co v Cox* [1914] 1 KB 244); *Hoare v Parker* (1788) 2 TR 376 (pledges by a tenant for life); *Attenborough & Son v Solomon* [1913] AC 76 (pledges by trustees).

business as such an agent does not constitute such a person a mercantile agent in possession with the owner's consent[8]. It appears that the same is true of a custodian whose role is simply to take care of documents of title.

Note also that there is a quasi-security interest which inheres for the benefit of a seller of goods known as the right of stoppage *in transitu*. This is an overriding right of an unpaid seller to require the carrier of goods to hold them to the order of the seller for as long as the goods are in the carrier's possession. This right is defeated by a pledge of the bill of lading by the purchaser[9], although the pledgee must pay over to the seller any surplus of the sale proceeds of the goods pledged[10]. Such a right is also defeated by a pledge of such a document by a buyer in possession[11].

Competing equitable interests

The equitable rules relating to priorities amongst competing interests may be shortly stated:

    (1) A disposition of a legal interest in property to a purchaser for value of the legal estate without notice of a prior equitable interest extinguishes that interest and leaves the purchaser with good absolute legal title[12].

    (2) Successive dispositions of legal interests in property other than to a purchaser for value without notice take effect in equity in order of creation, the rule being *qui prior est tempore, potior est jure*[13].

    (3) Successive dispositions of an equitable interest in property take effect in the order in which notice of the dealings was given to the owner of the legal interest in the property. This is the rule in *Dearle v Hall*[14].

The logic of there being different rules of priority for dispositions of equitable and legal property is, to say the least, obscure. *Snell's Equity* observes that 'the principle has been lost sight of, and at the present day the [rule in *Dearle v Hall*] will not be extended'[15]. Thus, it may be assumed that the rule *qui prior est tempore, potior est jure* applies in all cases except those to which the rule in *Dearle v Hall* is to be applied.

Purchaser for value without notice

The status of purchaser for value without notice of the legal estate is an important feature of property law in the context of equitable interests in property. An equitable interest prevails against a donee of trust property[16], but is ineffective against a purchaser for value without notice. Such a purchaser not

---

[8] *Cole v North Western Bank* (1875) LR 10 CP 354.
[9] *Re Westzinthus* (1833) 5 B & Ad 817.
[10] *Spalding v Ruding* (1846) 15 LJ Ch 374; *Kemp v Falk* (1882) 7 App Cas 573.
[11] Factors Act 1889, s 10; Sale of Goods Act 1979, s 47(2).
[12] *Wilkes v Spooner* [1911] 2 KB 473.
[13] *Barclays Bank v Bird* [1954] Ch 274 at 280.
[14] (1823–28) 3 Russ 1.
[15] 29th edn, p 66.
[16] *Re Diplock* [1948]Ch 465 at 544–5.

only acquires absolute equitable title but can pass it on, and a person who purchases property from such a purchaser acquires absolute title even if he himself had notice of the pre-existing equity[17]. In other words, where property passes to a purchaser for value without notice any existing equities are extinguished. The status of purchaser for value of the legal estate without notice is a claim to privilege, and the person claiming it must prove his claim[18].

'purchaser'

The term 'purchaser' in law means one who acquires property as the result of an another's act, and it is used in contradistinction to persons who acquire property by inheritance or escheat[19]. Thus a person who acquires property by a voluntary transfer is nonetheless a purchaser[20]. The term extends to the acquirer of any property interest, and therefore includes a mortgagee or lessee[21].

'for value'

'Value' includes all consideration, both in money or in money's worth[22]. By a vagary of equity marriage constitutes good consideration for this purpose[23], although cohabitation does not[24]. It may be noted that neither the provision of love and affection[25] nor the relief of tedium[26] constitutes consideration, so that the emotional and social side of such relationships must be disregarded. The doing of an act can constitute good consideration, and this is true if the act constitutes a detriment to the actor, whether or not it also confers a benefit upon the other party[27]. This leads to the interesting argument that all transfers of property between a cohabiting couple are potentially transfers for value, although transfers between a married couple may not be, by reason of the rule that performance of an existing obligation does not constitute consideration for a different transaction[28].

'of the legal estate'

The basis of the doctrine is that where equities are equal, equity follows the law. As between two persons who are both in equity entitled to the property, the rule is that the legal estate is determinative[29]. Thus the true inwardness of

---

[17] *Wilkes v Spooner* [1911] 2 KB 473.
[18] *Re Nisbet & Potts' Contract* [1906] 1 Ch 386.
[19] *Powell v Cleland* [1948] 1 KB 262.
[20] A person who acquires title through extinctive possession by expiry of the limitation period is not a purchaser for this purpose.
[21] *Kingsnorth Finance Co v Tizard* [1986] 1 WLR 783.
[22] *Thorndike v Hunt* (1859) 3 De G F & J 563.
[23] *De Mestre v West* [1891] AC 264; *A-G v Jacobs-Smith* [1895] 2 QB 341.
[24] *Banque Belge pour L'Etranger v Hambrouck* [1921] 1 KB 321.
[25] *Bret v J S* (1600) Cr Eliz 755; *Tweddle v Atkinson* (1861) 1 B & S 393.
[26] *White v Bluett* (1853) 23 LJ Ex 36.
[27] *Chitty on Contracts*, 27th edn (Sweet & Maxwell, 1994), paras 3-004 to 3-008.
[28] *Stilk v Myrick* (1809) 2 Camp 317, although *quaere* given the potential application of the maxim that equity treats as done that which ought to be done, so that the doing of an act pursuant to an existing obligation may not be recognised in equity at all. Query further the availability of specific performance.
[29] *Pilcher v Rawlins* (1872) 7 Ch App 259.

the rule is that where a person with a legal and equitable interest confronts another with a mere equitable interest, the equities cancel out and the holdership of the legal title is decisive.

A purchaser of an equitable estate takes free of mere equities (such as a right to have a conveyance rectified)[30].

Where the competition is between two owners of the equitable estate, the position is otherwise, as where equitable interests compete the rule is that the first in time prevails[31]. Since these issues tend to arise where A, who is under an existing obligation to transfer property to X, wrongfully transfers it to Y, the question of whether X or Y is entitled to the property in equity depends on whether Y is a transferee of the legal estate or an equitable interest.

The test which is applied is not simply whether the purchaser has the legal estate, but whether he has the better right to the legal estate[32]. Where a purchaser of property has it conveyed to a trustee to hold on his behalf, he takes an equitable interest in the property. However, because he has a better right to call for the legal estate than the person having the prior equitable interest, his right to the property prevails. This rule operates only where there is a change of trustee, and it has no application where the legal estate in the property remains vested in a single trustee throughout[33]. The position where a sale is effected by the vendor declaring himself a trustee for the purchaser's benefit is more complex still, in that the issue may be determined by the date of the declaration of trust[34].

This is of great importance in the context of transactions in securities held by custodians. Where A acts as custodian for X, A is a trustee for X[35]. Assume that A holds shares for X which, unbeknownst to both A and X, are subject to an equitable interest in favour of a third party. X agrees to sell the shares to Y, who in turn has a custodian B. Neither Y nor B has any notice of the prior equitable interest in the shares. The share transfer from custodian A to custodian B renders Y safe, since he has the better right to call for delivery of the shares from custodian Y. But if, as is not unlikely, both X and Y have the same custodian, the transaction is settled by book entry in the books of that custodian. Thus Y, even though he is without notice, takes the securities subject to the prior equitable interest.

A potential purchaser in such circumstances cannot necessarily protect himself even by insisting on a separate custodian. Where securities are held in an electronic clearing system—the US Depositary Trust Corporation (DTC) clearing system, for example—they are registered in the name of the DTC nominee company, CEDE & Co. Any transfer of shares within the DTC therefore

---

[30] *Phillips v Phillips* (1861) 4 De G F & J 208 at 218; *National Provincial Bank v Ainsworth* [1965] AC 1175.

[31] *Qui potior est in tempore, potior est in jure*; *Barclays Bank Ltd v Bird* [1954] Ch 274 at 280.

[32] *Wilkes v Bodington* (1707) 2 Vern 599; *Taylor v London and County Banking Co* [1901] 2 Ch 231.

[33] *Assaf v Fuwa* [1955] AC 215; *McCarthy & Stone Ltd v Julian S Hodge & Co Ltd* [1971] 1 WLR 1547.

[34] *McCarthy & Stone Ltd v Julian S Hodge & Co Ltd*, above.

[35] Benjamin, *The Law Of Global Custody* (Butterworths, 1996), pp 1–11.

involves no transfer of the legal ownership. Where intermediate custodians are involved, the position is that X, the investor, employs A as his custodian. A operates an account with the DTC which records A's beneficial ownership of the total amount of the relevant security held by CEDE & Co. Thus, the asset which A holds on trust for X is (at English law) an equitable interest in a trust of which CEDE & Co is the trustee. If X sells the asset to Y, then the mechanics of the transfer are that A, the custodian for X, transfers to B, the custodian for Y, an equitable interest in the trust property of which CEDE & Co is the trustee[36]. Whether this constitutes Y as the person entitled to the better right to the legal estate is very unclear. It is submitted that this is not the case, since the existence of a hierarchy of trustees should not be allowed to obscure the fundamental point that there is no transfer of the legal estate, and it is only a transfer of the legal estate which should, as a special case, be allowed to interfere with the ordinary equitable rule that interests rank in order of creation. This rule has been described as lying at the heart of equity[37], and it would be paradoxical if an equitable transfer of equitable property were to interfere with the equitable rule of priorities absent some change of legal title. Yet it follows from this that the position of a purchaser of securities held in a clearing system seems to be necessarily more vulnerable than that of an equivalent purchaser of identical securities held outside such a system, since upon a purchase for value without notice the first does not, but the second does, take free from prior equitable interests. The counter-argument to this conclusion was described by Millett LJ in *Macmillan Inc v Bishopsgate Investment Trust*[38] as resting upon

the correctness or otherwise of dicta in *Assaf v Fuwa*[39], described in Meagher, Gummow and Lehane, *Equity Doctrines and Remedies*, 3rd Ed. (1992) as 'an impermissible extension' of *Wilkes v Bodington*[40], itself described as 'an impermissible extension of the doctrine of *tabula in naufragio*.'

Milett LJ did not find it necessary to decide the point, but his expression of it creates little confidence that an argument based on it would be successful in any future case.

Where the very transaction by which the legal estate is transferred to the purchaser is itself a breach of trust the doctrine does not apply[41], and 'if the legal estate is subject to a prior equity inconsistent with the purchaser's title, it will necessarily be a breach of trust to convey it to him, whether or not the facts are known to the person conveying it'[42]. This can be illustrated by refer-

---

[36] We shall disregard for this purpose the alternative *R v Preddy* analysis that A's interest in the trust is extinguished and B's is simultaneously and equally created, although this would be the case if, for example, what was happening was the equivalent to the revocation and re-exercise in favour of a different beneficiary of a revocable power of appointment.
[37] Per Browne-Wilkinson LJ in *Barclays Bank v O'Brien* [1994] 1 AC 180.
[38] *(No 3)* [1995] 1 WLR 978 at 1002.
[39] [1955] AC 215.
[40] (1707) 2 Vern 599.
[41] *Harpham v Shacklock* (1881) 19 Ch D 207.
[42] Megarry & Wade, *The Law of Real Property*, 5th edn (Stevens, 1984), p 147.

ence to the Credit Suisse transaction in *Macmillan*. Credit Suisse perfected its equitable security by having the trustee (CEDE & Co) transfer the shares to it. Since CEDE & Co had no notice of the prior equity, the transfer was effective to constitute Credit Suisse purchaser for value without notice of the legal estate. However, if CEDE & Co had been trustee for the true beneficiaries directly, then the transfer would have been in breach of trust and Credit Suisse would not have become purchasers for value without notice of the legal estate. Thus in most cases which relate to securities, where a person is given an equitable mortgage by delivery of a share certificate and share transfer form, or is otherwise given the means whereby he can procure his registration as owner of the shares, he may thereafter vest legal title in himself without recourse to the legal owner and therefore without any breach of trust.

If a purchaser for value without notice acquires an equitable estate by his purchase, he acquires an interest which ranks after the prior existing equitable interest. However, if he subsequently acquires the legal interest, then he becomes a purchaser for value without notice of the legal estate, and his interest is promoted over that of the prior encumbrancer[43].

'without notice'

The doctrine of notice is one of the more complex elements of the doctrines of equity. In its pure form (ie as applied to real property) the rule is that where an equitable interest exists in property, a purchaser is taken to have notice of that equitable interest unless he can show that 'he took reasonable care and made enquiries, and that, having taken that care and made inquiry, he received no notice of the trust which affected the property'[44]. The point here is that persons have notice not only of what they did know but of what they would have known had they made the enquiries which should have been made.

This rule is relaxed in the case of personal property. The reason is that, as Lindley LJ said in *Manchester Trust v Furness*[45],

> as regards the extension of the equitable doctrines of constructive notice to commercial transactions, the courts have always set faces resolutely against it. The equitable doctrines of constructive notice are common enough in dealing with land and estates, with which the court is familiar; but there have been repeated protests against the introduction into commercial transactions of anything like an extension of those doctrines, and the protest is founded in perfect good sense. In dealing with estates in land title is everything, and it can be leisurely investigated; in commercial transactions possession is everything, and there is not time to investigate title; and if we were to extend the doctrine of constructive notice to commercial transactions we should be doing infinite mischief and paralysing the trade of the country.

In *Cowan de Groot v Eagle Trust*, Vinelott J observed that this was particu-

---

[43] It has been contended that this rule was abolished by s 94(3) of the Law of Property Act, which abolishes 'tacking'. However, it was held in *McCarthy & Stone Ltd v Julian S Hodge & Co Ltd* [1971] 1 WLR 1547 that this section has no effect upon the operation of the doctrine of purchaser for value of the legal estate.
[44] *Re Morgan* (1881) 18 Ch D 93 at 102 per Fry J.
[45] [1895] 2 QB 539 at 545.

larly the case in respect of payments of money.

The purchaser of personalty has notice of interests of which he has actual knowledge[46], and of facts which he would have discovered had he made investigations in respect of a transaction which was probably improper[47]. Another way to express this principle is that 'the court will impute knowledge on the basis of what a reasonable person would have learnt, to a person who is guilty of commercially unacceptable conduct in the particular context involved'[48]. However, particularly in commercial cases, the courts will be very slow to apply the doctrine of constructive notice.

Knowledge and notice must be distinguished, as 'knowledge' is not a synonym for 'notice'[49].

A man may have actual notice of a fact and yet not know it. He may have been supplied with a document and so have actual notice of its content, but he may not in fact have read it; or he may have read it some time ago and have forgotten its content[50].

In such cases the notice acquired is actual, not constructive. Actual notice is derived from assuming knowledge of all the facts which the defendant would have had he grasped all the information within his actual possession. Constructive knowledge is the knowledge which he would have acquired had he made the enquiries which should have been made.

The time of the notice is important. Clearly, where the purchaser receives notice of the equitable interest after he has completed the transaction by acquisition of the legal estate he is unaffected by it. Equally, where he receives notice before he enters into an enforceable agreement to do the transaction he is bound by it. Difficult questions arise, however, where notice is received between these two points.

The general rule is that[51]:

A purchaser without notice who at the time of purchase fails to obtain either a legal estate or the better right to one will nevertheless prevail over a prior equity if, without being party of the breach of trust, he subsequently gets in a legal estate, even if he then has notice of the equity.

Since notice received prior to the transfer of the legal estate in almost all cases constitutes notice that the transferor is in breach of trust in effecting the transfer, the transferee's participation in the breach of trust as a result of this notice is sufficient to ensure that he cannot rely on the doctrine. Thus in the case of most forms of real property the question of notice is determined by reference

---

[46] *Nelson v Larholt* [1948] 1 KB.

[47] *Macmillan Inc v Bishopsgate Investment Trust plc (No 3)* [1995] 1 WLR 978.

[48] Per Knox LJ in *Cowan de Groot Properties Ltd v Eagle Trust plc* [1992] 4 All ER 700.

[49] *Re Montagu's Settlement Trusts Duke of Manchester v National Westminster Bank Ltd* (1985) [1992] 4 All ER 308.

[50] Per Vinelott J in *Eagle Trust plc v SBC Securities Ltd* [1992] 4 All ER 488 at 497–8.

[51] *Snell's Equity* (P V Baker, ed), 29th edn, p 50.

to the point of transfer of the legal estate.

In the case of shares, however, what is important is notice received as at the date of entry into the transaction, not at the date of acquiring the legal estate by registration on the register of shareholders. This is true for absolute transfers as well as mortgages[52]. A person who has the ability to obtain the legal estate through his own act (ie if he has and can deliver a share certificate plus a signed share transfer form) necessarily acquires the legal estate without breach of trust[53]. It therefore follows that for most transactions in securities the time of notice is the time of the transaction, and subsequent notice is ineffective. It is, though, questionable whether the doctrine will be applied outside the field of securities law[54].

The question of notice has difficult ramifications in the context of companies. Where one person in a company knew one thing and someone else knew another, it is tempting to allege a corporate consciousness which is simultaneously aware of everything of which the corporation is aware and, possibly more importantly, is put on notice to inquire into by discrepancies between the knowledge of the two persons. It seems that this approach does not meet with judicial favour. Notice and knowledge are concepts which are proper to persons, not organisations. A corporation is not put on notice by conflicting stories told to different employees unless it is reasonable for those two employees to have compared notes. Attention may be paid to the systems which a reasonable corporation in that line of business is expected to have in place for the dissemination of information concerning customers between employees, and if such systems are not in place the corporation may in some circumstances find itself fixed with constructive notice of facts of which no individual employee had constructive notice. However, in the case of both employees and the corporation as a whole, commercial companies are entitled to be treated with great circumspection in the assessment of what they ought to have done. 'The practice of merchants ... is not based upon the supposition of possible frauds. The object of mercantile usages is to prevent the risk of insolvency, not of fraud ... credit, not distrust, is the basis of commercial dealings ...'[55].

Qui prior est tempore, potior est jure

This rule has its origin in Roman law[56]. In the absence of a purchaser for value without notice of the legal estate, property rights rank in order of creation. In law this rule was absolute, and where there were successive creations of legal mortgages by demise (possible prior to the 1925 legislation) the second mortgage was automatically postponed to the first on this basis[57].

---

[52] *Bailey v Barnes* [1894] 1 Ch 25 at 37; *Powell v London & Provincial Bank Ltd* [1893] 2 Ch 555.
[53] *Dodds v Hills* (1865) 2 Hem & M 424.
[54] Per Millett LJ in *Macmillan Inc v Bishopsgate Investment Trust plc* [1971] 1 WLR 978 at 1004.
[55] Per Bowen LJ in *Sanders Bros v Maclean & Co* (1883) 11 QBD 327 at 343.
[56] Cod 8 17 (18) 2.
[57] *Mason v Rhodes* (1885) 53 LT 322.

The rationale of this rule for equitable interests is a variation of the principle that *nemo dat quod non habet.* 'Every conveyance of an equitable interest is an innocent conveyance, that is to say, the grant of a person entitled merely in equity passes only that which he is justly entitled to and no more.'[58]

The rule of priority in time does not take effect in the case of what are called 'mere equities'. An equitable interest in property is a right existing in equity which has some of the indicia of a property interest, notably transferability and assignability. A right existing in equity which does not have these indicia is a mere equity[59]. Mere equities come in two flavours; personal equities, that is, rights which are personal to the plaintiff and are therefore not transferable[60], and proprietary equities, that is, rights to have completed transactions adjusted (such as rights to have a conveyance rectified or to have a transaction set aside for mistake or misrepresentation). In relation to priorities it was held in the Australian case of *Latec Investments Ltd v Hotel Terrigal Pty Ltd (in liquidation)*[61] that the words of Lord Westbury cited above applied only to equitable interests. Thus where a person has an equitable interest in property subject to a mere equity, a transfer can be made of the whole equitable interest, and the mere equity, being a personal right against the owner of the equitable interest, is in effect extinguished. It therefore follows that a subsequent transfer of an equitable interest has priority over a prior equity unless the transferee takes with notice of the equity[62].

Consecutive equitable assignments: the rule in *Dearle v Hall*

The rule in *Dearle v Hall*[63] applies to all equitable interests in personal property. By s 137(1) of the Law of Property Act 1925 it is extended to equitable interests in real property. It does not apply to dealings in shares[64].

The rule is that as between competing assignments of the same claim (ie in the standard case of double-dealing where a person purports to transfer the same claim to two different persons), the person who has priority is the person whose claim is first notified to the debtor, unless he knew of the other assignment when he gave notice[65]. Although the rule is an equitable one it applies to legal assignments, and where there is a prior equitable assignment

---

[58] *Phillips v Phillips* (1861) 4 De G F & J 208 at 215, per Westbury LC.

[59] *National Provincial Bank v Ainsworth* [1965] AC 1175; *Latec Investments Ltd v Hotel Terrigal Pty Ltd (in liquidation)* (1965) 113 CLR 265.

[60] The 'deserted wife's equity', the primary example of a personal equity, has now been extinguished by the House of Lords (*National Provincial Bank v Ainsworth* [1965] AC 1175). Gray in 'Property in Thin Air' [1991] CLJ 252 has criticised the circularity involved in determining the proprietary nature of the right by asking whether it has the characteristics of property.

[61] (1965) 113 CLR 265.

[62] *Stump v Gaby* (1852) 2 De G M & G 623, which is authority for the proposition that a right to have a conveyance set aside, a mere equity, constitutes the owner of that right the owner in equity of the property itself, and is transferrable as property; this was distinguished as applying only to transferability and not to priority.

[63] *Société Générale de Paris v Walker* (1885) 11 App Cas 20.

[64] (1823–28) 3 Russ 1.

[65] In the event of a simultaneous notice, the assignments take effect in order of creation (*Calisher v Forbes* (1871) 7 Ch App 109; *Johnstone v Cox* (1880) 16 Ch D 571; (1881) 19 Ch D 17).

followed by a subsequent legal assignment, the point is tested by reference to the rule[66]. Strictly speaking this is an anomaly, since the transferee of a legal interest in the debt ought to take priority over a transferee of a mere equitable interest, which is in theory all that the equitable assignment can confer[67].

There is much confusion about the logical basis of the rule in *Dearle v Hall*, but it is submitted that the confusion arises in good part from a failure to consider the logic of the case itself. Vice-Chancellor Plumer clearly explained that the rule's logic was that an assignee who had not given notice to the debtor was in the position of a purchaser of goods who had not yet taken possession of them. A purchaser of goods who leaves the seller in possession runs the risk that the seller will dispose of those goods again[68], and can only protect himself by taking possession of the goods themselves. It was held that in the same way an assignee can only protect himself by giving notice. Thus the true reason for the rule may be said to be that no assignment, whether legal or equitable, is complete until notice of the assignment is given to the debtor. There is no scope for assignments to rank in priority in order of their date of creation, since they are completely created not on the date when the agreement between assignor and assignee is made, but on the date when they are perfected by notice to the debtor.

Note also that in any dealing with an equitable interest, not only must the transfer of the equitable interest be in writing, but so must the notice to the trustee[69].

In the case of successive assignments, the position in respect of rights which accrue due against the intermediate holder of the debt is complex. Where A assigns to B, and B assigns to C, what is the position of the debtor in respect of counterclaims which accrued whilst the debt was in B's hands? When C gives notice he should in principle be affected by all set-offs which accrued prior to his doing so[70]. However, there is authority for the alternative view that a debtor may only raise against an assignee claims which have accrued against that particular assignee[71]. To complicate matters further, the rule may be different depending on whether the assignment concerned is legal or equitable, since in the case of a legal assignment the rule is that 'the debt is transferred to the assignee and becomes as though it had been his from the beginning; it is no longer to be the debt of the assignor at all, who cannot sue for it, the right to sue being taken from him'[72]. If this is true it seems to follow that where the chain of assignments is by legal assignment the debtor can apply all available

---

[66] *E Pfeiffer Weinkellerei-Weineinkauf GmbH & Co v Arbuthnot Factors Ltd* [1988] 1 WLR 150.
[67] It is possible that a legal assignee who actually acquired the proceeds of the debt might be able to claim to be a transferee for value without notice of the proceeds, and therefore to take free from the prior equitable interest. This was conceded in *Compaq Computers v Abercorn Group* [1991] BCC 484 at 500. However, in the light of the decision in *Re New Bullas Trading* [1994] 1 BCLC 485 it seems very doubtful that this concession was properly made.
[68] The rule now embodied in s 24 of the Sale of Goods Act 1979.
[69] Law of Property Act 1925, s 137(3).
[70] Treitel, *The Law of Contract*, 8th edn, p 594; R Derham, *Set-Off*, 2nd edn (OUP, 1996), pp 590–2.
[71] *The Raven* [1980] 2 Lloyd's Rep 266 at 273.
[72] *Read v Brown* (1888) 22 QBD 128 at 132, per Lord Esher MR.

set-offs against the current assignee, whereas if the assignment is equitable the debtor cannot plead any set-offs other than those which in equity may be raised against any claim on that particular debt and such other set-offs as may have arisen against the original debtor.

Competing legal and equitable interests in property

Some charges over goods do not require registration[73], and it is therefore possible that goods which have been pledged through a document evidencing possession (such as a bill of lading) may have been charged prior to the pledge being created. The importance of registration in this context is that registration constitutes notice to all the world. After a charge has been registered it is impossible for any person to acquire an equitable interest prior to the charge, since he is affixed with notice of the charge. If, however, the charge is not a registrable charge the position is difficult.

Pledge followed by charge

Where goods are pledged and then charged, the charge is good as a charge of the 'general property' which a bailor retains after he has transferred the 'special property' to his bailee. This is in effect a security created over the difference between the goods' value and the amount secured by the pledge equivalent to the 'equity of redemption'. Where it is purported to create a charge over the goods themselves, the question arises whether the recipient of this charge can claim to be a purchaser for value without notice of the legal estate, and therefore absolutely entitled as against the pledgee.

The issue here is whether the legal possessor should be affected by the subsequent equitable charge, and the answer is the same as it would be for any other competing prior legal and subsequent equitable transfers. The ordinary rule is that the principal of *nemo dat quod non habet* applies, and the beneficiary of the subsequent equitable interest has no claim against the goods charged or transferred. However, there are two circumstances in which the true legal owner of the goods may find his interest in the goods postponed to that of the equitable transferee. These are set out in *Northern Counties Fire Insurance v Whipp*[74], and are where either the owner of the legal estate has been party to some fraud by which the equity is created[75], or the legal owner has given another a power to deal with the property and that person deals in excess of his authority. It seems that the requirement of fault on the part of the legal estate owner is one of either fault or 'gross' negligence[76], and that in the case of ordinary negligence the legal estate owner retains his priority.

---

[73] Bills of Sale Act 1890; Companies Act 1985, s 396.
[74] (1884) 26 Ch D 482.
[75] The term 'fraud' is here clearly used in the equitable rather than in the common-law sense.
[76] Sykes & Walker, *The Law of Securities*, 5th edn (Law Book Company, 1993), pp 400–2.

Charge followed by pledge

Where goods are charged to a person and then pledged to another, two issues arise: whether the pledge's validity is affected, and whether the position is different if the pledge holder has notice of the prior charge.

A charge, whether legal or equitable, does not interfere with the chargeor's right to possession, and it is out of the right to possession that a pledge is created. Thus it seems that a person can create a valid charge and a valid pledge of the same goods. This may be demonstrated by reference to the rules of common law liens: if my car is subject to a chattel mortgage, and I give it to a garage to repair, then the garage acquires a legal lien upon it. It is clearly not the case that the mortgagee is entitled to recover the car from the garage without paying for the work done. What the pledgeor may be doing by the pledge is breaching either an express or an implied term of the charge agreement that he will not do anything which would have the effect of diminishing the chargee's rights under the charge.

A pledgee does not acquire either a legal or an equitable estate in the goods pledged[77]. In *Whitehorn Bros v Davison*[78] a pledgeor of goods who had, at the time of the pledge, good title to them subject to an equity[79] was held to be able to give a good pledge. The court seems to have assumed that the pledgee was entitled to maintain his pledge unless the rightful owner could show that he took with notice of the pledgeor's defective title. It does not follow from this that the court must have treated the pledgee as one who had acquired a legal estate, since the acquirer of an equitable interest also takes free from a 'mere equity'[80].

---

[77] Since legal estates cannot be created in personalty what the pledgee acquires is no more than a 'special property'.
[78] [1911] 1 KB 463.
[79] The goods had been acquired by fraud, and the true owner was entitled to avoid the transfer.
[80] *Phillips v Phillips* (1861) 4 De G F & J 208 at 215–6, and see *Cave v Cave* (1880) 15 Ch D 639; *Westminster Bank Ltd v Lee* [1956] Ch 7; *National Provincial Bank v Ainsworth* [1965] AC 1175 at 1238; *Allied Irish Banks Ltd v Glynn* [1973] IR 188.

Chapter 28

The Protection of Title to Goods

At English law the remedies available to an owner of goods arise out of his right to possession rather than his right of ownership.

The fundamental distinction between personal property and land is that personal property may only be possessed, whereas the landowner does not possess his land but is seised of it. The mediæval doctrine of seisin is of largely historical value, but the fundamental principle of personal property law is the idea of possession. 'Seisin is possession' as Pollock and Maitland bluntly asserted[1], and it is to the development of the protection of seisin that we must look for principles governing the protection of possession.

Protection of interests in land

The feudal system is best seen as one of taxation, having the characteristic of deeming relationships into a fiscally convenient pattern. Thus feudal ownership of land was divided into two aspects: tenure (roughly, what taxes were owed), and estate (roughly, for how long the person concerned might have the tenure, and to whom that tenure should pass upon the determination of his occupation thereof). It is sometimes forgotten that revenues from feudal status were derived in the form of feudal incidents and dues, and the reason for ancient rules such as those surrounding the passing of seisin have eminently practical roots; for example, the rule that property should never be without seisin and that the person in possession should be deemed to be seised derives from the need of those who came seeking feudal incidents to be able to exact them from the person in actual occupation of the land, unless he could point them to another.

Thus for the feudal lawyer the division of property was between that which did, and that which did not, attract feudal incidents. However, as is common the system deemed into place by the revenue-raising authorities did not correspond with the situation as it actually existed. Where a person wished to go into actual occupation of land he could not rationally demand enfeoffment on every occasion, and thus the extra-feudal device of the lease developed. Again, the surprise sometimes expressed that the lease of land was never recognised within the system may miss the point that had it so been another extra-sys-

---

[1] *The History of English Law* (S F C Milsom, ed), 2nd edn (Cambridge University Press, 1968), vol II, p 29.

tematic device would immediately have been invented to fill the gap. The lease, being a right relating to land but outside the existing system, became a thing *sui generis*. The category of chattel real was invented especially for it, since it was not a 'real' interest in land but a mere chattel. It is notable that leaseholders' claims to a property interest in land manifest themselves only after the demise of the feudal incident as the primary tool of royal revenue-raising.

The writ of right and the battle

The great writ of right, the 'most solemn action in real property law'[2], purported to determine the best right to seisin. The action was therefore hedged about with every imaginable precaution against injustice, since the effect of a decision was to deprive a man forever of what he claimed to be his property. Amongst these precautions were the doctrine of *essoins* and the danger of trial by battle.

The jurisprudence of essoins was an offshoot of the rule that very man must present his own case[3]. The inconvenience of a procedure which the defendant might at any time bring to a halt for a year and a day by taking to his bed[4] is clear. In any event, the ordinary mode of trial for the writ of right was the battle. By the Assize of Windsor in 1179 Henry II had introduced for every defendant to the great writ of right to elect the grand assize, a process whereby a jury of 12 knights was charged to say whose right to the land was the better[5]. However, this election involved the possibility of a number of issues being raised beyond the specific issue of title, and in any event involved the removal of the case into the King's court. The ever-present risk that a hard-pressed defendant might exercise his right to battle did much to eliminate the writ of right as a remedy[6].

Novel disseisin

The writ of right was displaced briefly by the writ of entry. The writ of entry challenged the right of the current occupier to the land by means of asserting

---

[2] Plucknett, *Concise History of the Common Law*, 5th edn (Little, Brown & Co), p 358.

[3] This was a universal rule (Fitzherbert's *La Graunde Abridgment* (1577 edn) 25; *Blackstone Commentaries on the Laws of England III*, 25). Blackstone notes that the power to appoint an attorney was a royal prerogative which was not available unless specially granted, and that 'an idiot cannot appear to this day by attorney, but in person, for he hath not discretion to appoint a proper substitute'.

[4] See *Bracton*, fo 256b for a description of this process. A deputation of four knights was dispatched from the court, and appears to have tested the defendant's degree of indisposition by examining his state of undress. The less clothing, the more acceptable the *essoin*.

[5] J H Round, 31 *English Historical Review* 268.

[6] Trial by battle was in fact abolished in 1819 by the statute 59 Geo III, c 46 after an attempt to assert the right in *Ashford v Thornton* (1818) 1 B & Ald 405. The last recorded judicial battle in the law reports may be found in *Claxton v Lilborn* (1638) Cro Car 522. For expressions of judicial regret at its abolition see per Harman J in *Serville v Constance* [1954] 1 WLR 487, 491.

a defect in the grant under which he had initially entered it. It was not a proprietary action but employed pleadings and procedures copied from the writ of right. It was displaced in turn by the *novel disseisin*[7].

The petty assizes—*novel disseisin, mort d'ancestor, darrein presentment* and *utrumque*—were all in theory possessory remedies whose object was to determine a particular set of facts. Since they did not decide absolute title but only relative right they were not subject to the procedural complications which had strangled the writ of right, and there was no danger of the appeal to trial by battle. The issue which was to be put to the jury was simply the question of whether the plaintiff had been 'disseised of his free tenement' and, if so, whether the disseisin had been unjustified.

The novel disseisin became the action of choice for the wronged of England. However, having commenced as a tribunal for determining better right, it became a forum for hearing questions of absolute right. Initially an ejector would become seised of land if the true owner did not attempt to recover it within five days, and this represented the time limit for the action. However a combination of judicial unwillingness to deny the novel disseisin to persons who had not acted immediately and an administrative concern to enhance the novel disseisin led to a gradual removal of the limits of novelty. Thus the focus of the action changed from determining recent possession to determining original possession, and thus on to determining absolute title. By 1400 novel disseisin was the almost exclusive vehicle for determining questions of right to land[8].

The owners of intangible property rights were also eager to make use of this new remedy; hence incorporeal hereditaments were held to be capable of being the subject of seisin. Where a tenant has refused to perform a service which the lord says is due, the lord has against his tenant the action *de consuetudinibus et servitiis*, an action virtually identical to and following the same rules as the writ of right. As mentioned above, this was a disastrously inefficient remedy. However, by pleading that he is seised of the services of his tenant he can bring the assize of novel disseisin[9]. The boundaries of what things could be incorporeal hereditaments are to be sought in some fairly dry distinctions between periodic payments. On the above argument, novel disseisin clearly lay for a rent service—ie a rent due as a result of the tenure of the land. Equally, where a payment is charged on a piece of land there is seisin; which arises both where the beneficiary can (rent charge) and cannot (rent seck) distrain on the land for the money. Finally there is the annual payment out of rent received known as a chamber rent (because it issues out of

---

[7] However by the fourteenth century the novel disseisin was being used to try matters of entry (J H Baker, *Introduction to English Legal History*, 3rd edn (Butterworths, 1990), p 270).

[8] It is this expansion which led to the increase in the ambit of the term *seisin* which has rendered the term incomprehensible to modern lawyers.

[9] Strictly speaking, withholding services would not be a disseisin. However, if the lord distrains for the services and the tenant resists the distraint then an actionable disseisin arises. Equally, rendering such services to any other person would constitute a disseisin of the lord (*Bracton*, f 169, 203; *Note Book*, pl 1239; *Britton*, vol I, 281, 290; Pollock & Maitland (*see* fn 1 *above*), vol II, p 126.

the chamber of the lord concerned[10]). The beneficiary of such a charge cannot, it is decided, have the novel disseisin: there is no land which the jurors can view and no free tenement from which the service springs[11].

Yet the novel disseisin itself had, having acquired the function of a hearing as to absolute right, accumulated many of the excrescences which had rendered the writ of right obsolete. Those who wished to determine matters of fact were therefore set upon their wits to discover a new means of doing so.

Trespass

The answer was found in the writ of trespass. This writ had the advantage of being a mechanism for putting a simple question of fact before a jury, and, being a flexible instrument[12], it could be adapted to the task without undue strain. However the right which it asserted was personal and not proprietary, and this meant that the only award which the successful plaintiff could hope for was money damages. An order requiring the defendant to give up possession of the disputed property was not available, and since the major objective of parties litigating over land is to have, if not title, then at least possession of the land, the action did not at first seem suitable.

Action in ejectment

The particular variant of the writ of trespass which applied to possession of land, the writ of ejectment, was at this point being developed by a group of landholders to whom the writs of right had never been available. These were those who possessed their land by virtue of a lease rather than a feudal grant.

In 1290 the statute Quia Emptores abolished subinfeudation. This meant that any attempt to alienate land for a term within the feudal system would automatically be executed by the statute into a permanent alienation without right of recovery. The lease therefore became the only practical method of getting someone else to farm one's own land other than as a paid labourer. By 1360[13] the action of ejectment[14] had been developed and was available to protect the termor's rights. Since the action of ejectment was not a real action, the only remedy was damages[15]. It was not until 1500 that it was decided that the

---

[10] The correct modern term would be personal annuity. The reason for granting these may be gleaned from Rot Cart p 14, where King John grants an annuity of 40 marks 'to be received from our chamber until we assign them in some certain and competent place'.

[11] *Bracton*, f 180, 203 b.

[12] If writs *in consimili causu* are included in the classification, then the writ of trespass and its progeny may be said to be the origin of all modern procedure.

[13] 100 Selden Society lxxiii.

[14] Strictly the action *de ejectione firmae*. This is not to be confused with the action *quare ejecit infra terminum*, a one-off writ invented by William Raleigh in the 1230s which could be had by a leaseholder against another claiming as grantee of his lessor, and was therefore of use only where a lessor made two incompatible leases of the same property.

[15] In 1382 Belknap CJ ruled that this was the case (Pas 6 Ric II; Fitzherbert's *Abridgment., Ejectione firme*, pl 2; [1976] *Cambridge Law Journal* 325 n 40.

termor might recover his term in ejectment[16]. It has been suggested that this was the result of a confusion with the rights created by the writ *quare ejecit infra terminum*[17], and it seems undoubted that the decision to give the termor a proprietary remedy was in effect the creation of a new legal rule (or, more strictly, exception). However, the result of this creation was that the action in ejectment, as well as being quicker and more effective than the equivalent real actions, now offered in effect an equivalent remedy. By 1570 freeholders had joyfully abandoned the real actions and were using the action in ejectment to decide matters of title[18]. Perhaps more importantly, a remedy based upon trespass had acquired a proprietary function.

Because ejectment was in its origins a remedy developed by the lease-holder, it was unnecessary to prove seisin (as a leaseholder was not seised of the land in any event). What had to be proved was simple possession, and possession is a great deal easier to prove than seisin. Thus seisin's importance declined with the actions based on it, and simple (or the better right to) possession became the root of actions for recovery of land.

This remained the case from the sixteenth century to the nineteenth. The real actions did continue a ghostly existence, and it was felt necessary to provide by statute in 1833 that ejectment was to be the only action brought for real property[19]. Ejectment was finally abolished in 1852[20].

Modern actions

The modern remedy for recovery of land is still based on a claim of the better right to possession. As Professor Baker has said[21]:

> The present action to recover possession of land is nevertheless the direct successor of ejectment and the rules about proof of title are, with statutory alterations, those developed in that action rather than in the old real actions.

For this purpose it is possession that forms the basis of title, and in particular possession of land is taken to be *prima facie* evidence of seisin in fee simple[22].

---

[16] *Gernes v Smyth* (1500) CP 40/948.
[17] Milsom, 74 LQR 200–1; YB Mich 33 Hen VI, Jo 42, Pl 19. A proprietary remedy was always available in *quare ejecit* since the very point at issue was the validity of competing grants.
[18] The process involved a fictional action between John Doe and Richard Roe being commenced by the actual plaintiff, the court allowing the actual defendant to intervene only on the grounds that he accepted the fictional action. The improbability of this structure is itself graphic witness to the unsatisfactory nature of the freehold actions of the time.
[19] Real Property Limitation Act 1833, 3 & 4 Will IV, c 27.
[20] Common Law Procedure Act 1852, 15 & 16 Vict, c 76.
[21] Baker, *Introduction to English Legal History*, 3rd edn (Butterworths, 1990), p 343.
[22] *Peaceable D Uncle v Watson* (1811) 4 Taunt 16 at 17; *Jayne v Price* (1814) 5 Taunt 326; *Re Atkinson & Horsell's Contract* [1912] 2 Ch 1 at 9; Lightwood, *Possession of Land*, pp 114-121; (1940) 56 LQR 376, A D Hargreaves.

Protection of rights to personal property

Title to chattels is and has always been indivisible[23]. Thus the law of title to chattels must remain simple and apparently archaic compared with the law of title to land. As Pollock puts it[24]:

> On the land dominium rises above dominium; a long series of lords who are tenants and of tenants who are lords ... [this] compatibility of diverse seisins permits the rapid development of a land law which will give both letter and hirer, feoffor and feoffee, rights of a very real and intense kind in the land, each protected by its own appropriate action, at a time when the backward and meager law of personal property can hardly sanction two rights in one thing, and will not be dissatisfied with itself if it achieves the punishment of thieves and the restitution of stolen goods to those from whose seisin they have been taken.

Professor Baker has taken this to its logical conclusion, and argues that[25]

> there was no such thing as *dominium*, absolute abstract ownership or right [in chattels]. The most a person out of possession could claim was a better right to possession than the person in possession.

It is a truism that early English law was procedural in structure, with the availability of a remedy dependent on there being a writ, and thus a procedure, to establish it. The lack of any equivalent of the writ of right for chattels is therefore a contributor to the theory that English law does not admit the absolute ownership of chattels, since title was the one thing which might not be determined, there being no writ available with which to make such determination.

This apparently absurd rule is in fact perfectly sensible. The logic which produced the desuetude of the writ of right applies to any hearing which purports to define title for all time against all the world—that notionally all relevant persons and all relevant material should be considered, a requirement impossible of fulfilment. Thus the only question which can be decided as between two parties is of better right between them, not best right as between all men. This in turn explains the bar on pleading the *jus tertium*, that the right of a third party may not be considered in proceedings between two others, since such consideration amounts to trying his title *in absentia*. Thus what appears to be a pettifogging mediæval inefficiency may be seen in practice to be an expression of a fundamental and true principle of substantive law.

It may be objected that this 'fundamental principle' is nothing of the kind since at Roman law questions of title were frequently tried. Two points may be made in response to this. One is that the Roman system is almost unique in this, the classical Greek systems having been as averse to the trial of matters of title as our own[26]. The second is a matter of practicality. As Buckland and

---

[23] Pollock & Maitland, vol II, p 181.
[24] Ibid, p 183.
[25] Baker (*see* fn 21 *above*), p 439.
[26] Mitteis, *Reichsrecht und Volksrecht*, p 70.

McNair point out[27], before the statute 32 Hen VIII, c 2 there was almost no such concept in English law as limitation, and roots of title were required to be deduced from unrecorded antiquity. This statute and others allow limitation but grudgingly and from only slightly less remote antiquity. Thus the prospect of proving absolute title is remote, and proof of better right is all that can in practice be encompassed. At pre-*Digest* Roman law, by contrast, the period of 'adverse possession' required for *usucapio* is two years for immovables and one year for movables. Since the title acquired by *usucapio* is no mere extinctive prescription but absolute title, the proof of title becomes a matter of the greatest ease[28]. It may be most accurate to say that in fact the Roman system determined title rather than possession because the rule of *usucapio* meant that in practice possession was title.

Possession and title

We must now come to the question of what is the relationship between possession and title? '[P]ossession is equivalent to title against a mere wrongdoer, and this is a substantive rule of law not affected by forms of action.'[29] This is clearly true—there is authority in the actions of ejectment that prior possession will defeat subsequent possession, even where the latter has been under colour of title[30], and that possessory title may be settled such that the beneficiary obtains better right than a subsequent possessor[31], but it does not help us with the relationship between the two ideas. For an explanation we are thrown back more than a century to an argument which is as true today as on the day when it was published[32]:

[P]ossession confers more than a personal right to be protected against wrongdoers; it offers a qualified right to possess, a right in the nature of property which is valid against every one who cannot show a prior and better right. Having reached this point the law cannot stop at protecting and assisting the possessor himself. It must protect those who stand in his place by succession or purchase; the general reasons of policy are at least as strong in their favour as in his, their case at least is meritorious. And the merits of a purchaser for value, who perhaps has no means of knowing the imperfections of his vendor's title, are clearly greater than those of the vendor himself. The qualified right of property which arises from possession must therefore be a transmissible right, and whatever acts and events are capable of operating to confirm the first possessor in his tenure must be capable of the same operation for the benefit of those who claim through him by such a course of transfer as would be appropriate and adequate, if true ownership were present in the first

[27] *Roman Law and Common Law*, 2nd edn (Cambridge University Press, 1952), p 69.
[28] Justinian lengthened the periods to three years for movables and ten or 20 years for immovables; these periods have endured into the European legal systems based on Roman law.
[29] Pollock & Wright, *Possession in the Common Law* (Clarendon, 1888), p 91, and see *Jeffries v Great Western Railway Co* (1856) 5 El & Bl 802, at 805. Interestingly, this rule is embodied in the form of the Roman *actio publiciana* (Inst 4. 6 4, D 21.3.3).
[30] *Doe D Smith v Webber* (1834) 1 A & E 119.
[31] *Asher v Whitlock* (1865) LR 1 QB 1.
[32] Pollock & Wright (*see* fn 29 *above*), p 93.

instance, to pass the estate or interest which is claimed. Hence the rule that possession as a root of title is not only an actual but also a necessary part of our system.

Once possession is admitted as a root of title it becomes the only possible root of title for chattels which preserve a separate identity[33]. Statute may, and frequently does, replace prior possession by some other characteristic, whether registration, purchase, or delivery of an instrument in particular circumstances. However in almost every such case the statute operates to deem the possessor for the time being the absolute owner, and cases where statute removes title from an actual possessor are few. Thus the effect is no more than to truncate the time period required to show title to zero, such that the rule becomes one that he who has possession at this time also has title.

There is never any suggestion that there should be a general recognition of multiple property interests in chattels at law. Such a development is unnecessary, given that from the earliest times it has been possible to settle a chattel in succession by settlement of the use of it[34]. Whereas a chattel might not be settled on a limited number of persons, its use might be settled in this way, and thus was developed the ability to settle chattels in tail. Given that land, where settled, was almost invariably settled in tail, the ability to settle chattels which in practice were a necessary part of the working of the land in the same way must have been exceptionally valuable[35]. Thus, since chattels could be settled without division of title, then title could remain unitary.

Actions for recovery of chattels

Actions for recovery of stolen goods are probably a universal feature of early legal systems and, in particular, in the Anglo-Saxon system, 'If only cattle lifting could be suppressed, the legislators will have done all or almost all that they can hope to do for the protection of the owner of movables.'[36]

The earliest restitutionary action in English law was therefore the criminal appeal of larceny. This highly unsatisfactory remedy carried a double jeopardy, one being the danger of trial by battle and the other being the possibility of losing the goods to the Crown if the appeal failed[37]. The remedy for these defects, as for almost all mediæval formal defects, was the development of an appropriate remedy in trespass. Initially the only writ of trespass which was available was the writ of trespass *vi et armis*, that is with force of arms. This worked perfectly for cases of theft but less well in cases of bailment, since a bailor could hardly claim that his bailee had deprived him with force of arms

---

[33] Mixtures are dealt with below.

[34] Such a use was not executed by the Statute of Uses (*Mayntell's Case* (a 1553) cit In Bl Ms Harley 1691, fo 91v).

[35] The parallel with the development of the idea of seisin of the benefit of a service is almost exact.

[36] Pollock & Maitland, *History of English Law*, p 157.

[37] The author of *Britton*, vol I, 123 advises his readers against the appeal of larceny to recovery goods.

of the goods which he had himself voluntarily delivered to him[38]. By 1360[39] the writ of trespass based on the special case was available, and in the special case the plaintiff need not have pleaded force of arms, although he might (and did) plead almost any other form of wrongdoing.

This procedure developed into the writ of trespass *de bonis asportatis*. However, the logic of this writ was semi-criminal: its penalty was that the defendant should be imprisoned until he paid his fine and damages. There are no grounds for bringing such an action against one who has not trespassed upon the plaintiff's land, but has merely acquired the plaintiff's property from the trespasser. Pollock and Maitland suggest that this reasoning was imported into the action of trespass *de bonis asportatis* by analogy from its close relative, the action in trespass *de clauso fracto,* and this seems highly likely. However, in the case of trespass *de clauso fracto*, the reason that it could not be brought against the disseisor of a previous disseisor was that there was a proper remedy available for the purpose, and trespass should not be brought in such a case. In the case of goods there was no such remedy. Thus an asymmetry was built into the very foundation of the law: that whereas a man might recover land from a third hand, he might not recover goods. It is this structure which seems to have confused early lawyers into ascribing property in stolen goods to a thief, since as the thief might in effect give good title, then he must by implication be taken to have acquired good title himself[40].

Detinue

Thus the primary remedy for the recovery of goods in the hands of another was the writ of *præcipe*, which doubled as a claim for the recovery of goods (known after its formula as detinue) and the payment of money[41]. This writ developed into two separate writs, one each for the recovery of money and of goods. The action for the repayment of money developed separately, and indeed still stands today as the action in debt. The action in detinue for the recovery of goods had a less happy history.

Detinue for goods, in its original formulation, required the proof of all the matters which would ordinarily be expected to be proved in the context of a debt—that there was entitlement to possession of the goods, that they were in the defendant's possession, and that the defendant had refused to return them.

---

[38] Although it seems that this plea was sometimes made in the hope that the defendant would not take the point (*Knoston v Bassyngburn* (1329) SS 97 at 363, Eyre of Northamptonshire).

[39] Baker, *Introduction to English Legal History*, 3rd edn (Butterworths, 1990), p 446.

[40] There is also a mysterious civil action *de re adirata* about which opinions are divided The options are a petition in eyre, or a petition at gaol delivery, or an action in trespass. *Britton* (vol I, 57, 68), seems to treat it as trespass, but it is not clear why if this were the case it would have been so separate and so little-used.

[41] The form of the writ, *præcipe D quod reddat P catalla quae injuste detinet* , and its defence, the plea of *non detinet*, were not only applicable to both goods and money but were in fact formally identical—indeed the formal entry on the Roll for an attempt to recover goods was a 'plea of debt' *(?)* (Milsom 77 LQR 273, and see 105 SS 86 (Baker, *Introduction to English Legal History*, p 442).

This action placed a heavy burden on the plaintiff. Attempts to evade this requirement by employing the action of assumpsit failed when the action itself became caught up in the Tudor development of the doctrine of consideration, restricting its use to cases of bailment for reward.

Detinue sur trover

The problems of proof which the action in detinue presented were overcome by an elaborate fiction of finding, or trover, and the action on the fiction was known as the detinue sur trover. The fiction was that the chattel concerned had been lost, the defendant had found it and refused to return it. This dispensed with the troublesome requirement for proof of initial title, and the defendant might defend himself only by demonstrating that he had acquired the chattel legitimately. Thus the litigation's effect was to place the burden of proof on the defendant to show that the chattel concerned was his.

The writ of detinue sur trover, however, was at heart a writ of præcipe. Writs of præcipe were unfortunate for a number of reasons; they lay only for complete non-performance and were defeated by imperfect performance, they did not lie where the defendant could prove the destruction of the thing sought, and above all the defendant retained the right to take the general issue and offer wager of law.

It seems that from its inception the writ of detinue had the aspect that the defendant might keep the chattel by paying its value. This again may be to do with the origin of the writ of detinue as a writ of debt for the recovery of money, but in any event the form of the writ required that the value of the chattel detained be specified, and the defendant might therefore retain the chattel by paying this amount. Further, if the plaintiff obtained judgment, the judgment would be enforced not by taking and returning to him the chattel, but by taking and selling the defendant's goods until the plaintiff might be paid the amount specified. Thus, although the action was in form a real action which purported to determine title, it became in effect personal action against the defendant sounding only in damages. Bracton says of this development[42]:

> It would seem at first sight that the action in which a movable is demanded should be as well *in rem* as *in personam* since a specific thing is demanded and the possessor is bound to restore that thing, but in truth it is merely *in personam*, for he from whom the thing is demanded is not absolutely bound to restore it, but is bound alternatively to restore it or its price; and this, whether the thing be forthcoming or no.

Although this may seem to us to be a substantial defect in the law of property, it does not seem to have caused any remark or comment for many centuries after it became settled law. Pollock and Maitland have suggested that this is owing to 'the pecuniary nature of chattels', and would have been a natural

---

[42] *Bracton*, f. 102 b.

rule in an early age in which the concepts of chattels and money were interchangeable. What is asserted is a concept of fungibility: that all chattels are fungible *inter se* such that an action for one chattel can be satisfied in full by the delivery of any other chattel of the same value. As to whether this is a true account of the concepts underlying the development of the doctrine we can only speculate, but at this stage it is necessary to note that the idea that the only action available for the recovery of a chattel is an action for damages is almost as old as our legal system.

Conversion

The action in conversion was in origin an action of trespass on the case. It was developed to deal with the difficult case of the bailee who damaged the goods entrusted to him and then returned them, and who was therefore invulnerable to the detinue sur trover[43]. By the sixteenth century conversion was established as a distinct tort, parallel with but different from detinue, and the action was swiftly developed against persons other than bailees. The common denominator was the allegation of deliberate damage or withholding. The mechanism of the 'fiction of finding' was imported into the action in conversion by analogy, and by 1531 we find a fully formed declaration of conversion sur trover[44] in the King's Bench, and the Court of Common Pleas approved the form of declaration in 1555[45]. At this point a spat similar to that over the use of the action of assumpsit for debt broke out between the Common Pleas and the King's Bench. The Common Pleas seems to have held a candle for the wager of law (or at least to have held that it was unfair to deny the defendant the benefit of electing wager of law), and argued that to permit the action in conversion to be used in cases sounding in detinue was to deprive the defendant of a legitimate juridicial advantage[46]. In the King's Bench, however, the rule that neither the allegation of finding nor the allegation of conversion were traversible meant that the action in conversion lay for a refusal to deliver *simpliciter*, and had become an exact mimic of the action in detinue save for the non-availability of wager of law[47]. The matter was finally decided in favour of the King's Bench in 1596[48].

The procedure adopted by the King's Bench, however, led to the conclusion that every detention was a conversion. Although conversion initially lay only for deliberate damage or withholding, the forms of procedure which the King's bench had adopted meant that an innocent possessor might be held to have converted the goods of another, and the King's Bench was forced to concede that where goods had, for example, been pawned, then no conversion

---

[43] *Rilston v Holbeck* (1472) CP 40/844M, 322; *Calwodelegh v John* (1479) YB Hil 18 Edw IV, Jo 23 pl 5.

[44] *Wysse v Andrewe* (1531) 94 SS 252.

[45] *Lord Mounteagle v Countess of Worcester* (155) BL MS Horley 1691, Jo 94.

[46] *Anon* (1582).

[47] *Anon* (1579) Li MS Misc 488 p 64.

[48] *Eason v Newman* (1596) HLS MS 110 Jo 218v.

arose[49]. Yet the rigid exclusion of considerations of innocence or culpability necessary to establish the action had left it with all the characteristics of a real action bar one. It lay for the recovery of goods, it was unaffected by right save right to the goods, and it could be brought by one with imperfect title (eg a finder) against a subsequent taker[50]. The one characteristic which it lacked might well be said to be the *sine qua non* of a real action—it did not necessarily recover the goods for which it lay.

The last stage in the action of conversion's development was that since it lay for any denial of title, any dealing by any person was potentially a conversion. The action therefore lay not only against a person found in possession of the goods, but also against any person through whose hands the goods had passed, since by dealing with the goods that person had interfered with the owner's title[51]. It was at this stage that Lord Mansfield felt able to say that 'trover [ie conversion] is merely a substitute for the old action of detinue ... [it] is not now an action *ex maleficio* though it is so in form, but it is founded on property'[52].

The abolition of wager of law by the Uniformity of Process Act 1832 gave rise to an Indian summer for some of the old forms of action which had been abandoned because of the danger thereof. Chief among these was the action in detinue itself, which took its place in the sun as an action parallel to but distinct from conversion. The coexistence of an identical real action and tortious action caused little difficulty since in reality what was revived was the name without the substance[53]. The two actions coexisted through the interesting asymmetry that since detinue was nominally a real action it led to a claim for the asset's value at the date of judgment, whereas conversion, being an action for damages for a wrong done, valued the wrong at the date of its commission.

Title to goods—possession and bailment

The problems of the leaseholder of land were echoed by the problems of the bailee of goods. The primary problems which arose were those created where one person delivers voluntarily[54] his goods to another and then at some later time required them to be returned. This issue arises in the Year Books of Henry VII's reign[55], where there appears for the first time the idea that where goods are transferred to another by way of bailment the transferee (the bailee) acquires a 'special property' in the goods, whilst the transferor (the bailor) retains the 'general property'.

---

[49] *Isaack v Clarke* (1615) 2 Bulst 306.
[50] *Armory v Delamirie* (1722) 1 Stra 505; followed in *Parker v British Airways Board* [1982] 1 All ER 834.
[51] *Hartop v Hoare* (1743) 2 Stra 1187; *Cooper v Chitty* (1756) 1 Burr 20.
[52] *Hambly v Trott* (1776) 1 Cowp 371 at 374.
[53] Indeed in *Bryant v Herbert* (1878) 3 CPD 389, detinue was held to be a tort.
[54] I ignore, for the moment, the debate as to the possibility of involuntary bailment.
[55] Y B Hill 21 Hen VII, fo 15, pl 23.

Remedies against bailees

The problem which existed in the case of bailment of goods was that there was no scope for the action in detinue sur trover between the bailor and the bailee, since the allegation of loss was logically incompatible with a claim of bailment. The action therefore took on a separate life of its own as the action of detinue sur bailment.

It is important to notice at this stage that the action of detinue sur bailment lay solely against the bailee himself[56]. The bailor was thus prevented from bringing any action to recover his goods from any person to whom the bailee wrongfully gave them. Where goods were stolen from the bailee, he alone might bring an action to recover them.

The difficulty of recovering damages from a person who had damaged goods bailed to him was initially tackled by means of the action in assumpsit. The form of the action in trespass was originally that the bailee had breached a duty to look after the goods or to use them in a particular way[57]. A count of assumpsit was added, but it is believed that this originally recorded the assuming of possession by the bailee of the goods rather than the assuming of a separate obligation to take care[58]. Thus the assumpsit was initially no more than an allegation of the fact of the bailment, and this is the explanation for the rule that the count of assumpsit could not be traversed, since it was implicit in the very nature of bailment[59]. Unfortunately, this innovation was made at a time when the action in assumpsit itself was undergoing a rapid change. Initially developed to provide a remedy in cases of breach of agreement, it was caught up in the development of the Tudor doctrine of consideration, and the King's Bench held in 1539[60], and again in 1563[61], that assumpsit was not actionable without consideration. The immediate result was the division of remedies as between the bailee for reward and the gratuitous bailee, leaving the bailee for reward strictly liable in assumpsit for any defect in the goods bailed as well as for their theft or loss, whilst the voluntary bailee was liable only for deliberate damage.

This unsatisfactory situation was to some extent resolved in *Coggs v Barnard*[62], in which a voluntary bailee accidentally damaged goods in his possession. The immediate decision was that assumpsit did lie against a voluntary bailee since the bailee, by 'actual entry upon the thing, and taking the trust upon himself', had rendered himself liable. Holt CJ, relying on *Bracton*, proceeded to analyse the relation of bailor and bailee in terms of Roman law. Holt's own comment that he had 'stirred up many new points which wiser

---

[56] And, eventually, his executors.
[57] See, for example, the *Humber Ferry Case, Bukton v Tounesende* (1348) Li MS Hale 116, 82 ss 66.
[58] Baker, *Introduction to English Legal History*, p 446.
[59] *Bourgchier v Cheseman* (1504) Mitch 20 Hen VII, Jo 4 pl 13; 94 SS 249; *Rycroft v Gamme* (1523) Spelman Rep (93 SS) 3; *Warton v Ashpole* (1524) Spelman Rep (93 SS) 4.
[60] *Marler v Wilmer* (1539) KB 27/1111, m 64.
[61] *Isack v Barbour* (1563); see M S Arnold (ed), *The Laws and Customs of England* (1981) 353, n 61.
[62] (1703) 2 Ld Raym 909.

heads in time may settle' is an understatement. In fact he had planted the seed of the idea that bailment is a peculiarly Roman concept, alien to the common law and capable of being treated only *sui generis*. The fruits of this idea are still visible in modern English law, and the result is that the doctrines of property in personalty have been divorced from their natural habitat. By 1600 the action in conversion was permitted to be brought against a bailee, and from that point the law of personal property began to coalesce around the action in conversion as its core remedy.

The defendant's option to purchase

Under the action in conversion, and its successors under the Torts (Interference with Goods) Act 1977, the defendant may keep the property by paying damages. There is a savour of injustice about the idea that a man can gain an interest in goods simply by misappropriating them. This regret is normally expressed as that English law has no remedy corresponding to the Roman action of *vindicatio*.

The first thing which must be said about this observation is that it is (probably) nonsense. We do not know as much as we would like about Roman procedure, but certainly the example given by Gaius of the formula to be used to commence an *actio vindicatio rei* is as follows[63]:

> Be Titius judge: if it appears that the Cornelian estate, now in question, belongs to Aulus Agerius by Quiritary title, and the said land shall not to your satisfaction be restored to Aulus Agerius, at what sum soever the amount shall be assessed, in so much money, judge, condemn Numerius Negidius to Aulus Agerius: if it does not appear, absolve.

This is the form of an action for damages with an option of specific performance. The defendant had, in effect, an absolute right to pay the damages and keep the property[64], and in this respect the Roman action of *vindicatio* was very little different from our own chattel torts.

At first glance this seems monstrously unjust. If a thing is mine, and I retain title to it, then I should be entitled to have it. The idea that a person who furtively removes my property from my possession can subsequently in effect compel me to sell him that property is at first glance inimical to some of the most fundamental concepts of justice. It may well be true that 'a very true and intense ownership of goods can be pretty well protected by actions in which nothing but money can with any certainty be obtained'[65], but an application of Occam's Razor suggests that if property is protected by awarding damages rather than by ordering redelivery of the property then there is some other fact

---

[63] G 4. 41, 51. Although the formula gives the judge the power to assess the value of the compensation to be set at any value he likes, it was the practice to require the plaintiff to swear the value of the thing in advance (Dig 12.3.1).
[64] Dig 6.1.46.
[65] Pollock & Maitland, vol II, pp 181–2.

to be taken into account.

The explanation for this mode of procedure is that, with a few exceptions, property is misappropriated in order to be used. The circumstances in which A's property, having made its way into B's hands, is to be found any time after that in unaltered form without depreciation of value, are interestingly rare. Leaving tracing considerations aside, if you steal my bricks and use them to build your house it gives rise to a substantial injustice if I can demand the return of those very bricks. What I want, and am entitled to, is the value of those bricks, or possibly sufficient money to replace them. Note also that where property does not appreciate it tends to depreciate. If you take my car when it is worth £15,000, and you are apprehended a year later, at that time it might be worth only £12,000. If I have a right to reclaim the car you should have a converse right to require me to accept the car in settlement of my claim. It is only if I have a right to damages that it is just that you be required both to return the car and to pay me the £3,000 difference. This argument does not work in all cases—if you steal the Mona Lisa it should be theoretically possible to assess the value of your wrongdoing, but it is a great deal easier in practice to award the return of goods than to assess the measure of damages—but it works in most.

Chapter 29

Remedies at Common Law

The remedies available at English law for interference with goods are collectively christened the remedies for 'wrongful interference' by the Torts (Interference with Goods) Act 1977. Sadly the Act provided only a name and not a systematisation, and consequently the individual torts continue in existence although the procedures for their enforcement are affected by the Act.

Trespass to goods

Trespass has been defined as 'committing without lawful justification any act of direct physical interference with goods in the possession of another person'[1]. This may not be perfect: although in practice the essence of trespass is physical contact, it can in (rare) cases be committed without such contact. Exposing undeveloped film to the light would be a trespass even though there is no physical contact with the film.

As well as being the oldest, trespass is also the most catholic of the chattel torts, since it is available in almost all circumstances. This is because buried deep in its historical sub-structure is a fiction of violence (*vi et armis*) constituting a breach of the King's peace, and it was this fiction which made trespass actionable in the first place. When the writ of trespass developed to cover wrongdoings whose facts could not conceivably be stretched to accommodate the fiction of violence, there developed a number of special writs (writs of trespass on the special case). The action in conversion was one such. Actions in case had a number of procedural advantages, one of which was the fact that the defendant might not 'wage his law' by swearing to his innocence, and was required to prove his case before a jury. However, the absence of the count of *vi et armis* mean that some extra fact required to be proved to show that what had been done was wrong, and for this reason actions which are descended from actions in case require both the fact of damage and the intention to damage to be proved before they can be successful, whereas actions in the form of the old writ of trespass are actionable *per se* without proof of either actual[2] or the intention to damage.

---

[1] Salward & Heuston, *The Law of Torts*, 21st edn (Sweet & Maxwell, 1996), p 94.
[2] This correspondence between the requirement for proof of damage and descent from the action in case is not universal—eg libel is actionable without proof of damage, although the action in defamation is descended from the action in case—but will do for practical purposes.

This lack of a requirement for damage means that it is a trespass to do a number of things which, although undoubtedly offensive, result in no quantifiable financial harm. The action in trespass has been successfully used to obtain satisfaction from defendants who have breached requirements of confidentiality (eg showing a private letter to a third party[3]) or who have withheld the plaintiff's own property from him for periods too short to result in actual damage[4]. The lack of a requirement of an intention to damage is a feature of all actions in trespass[5].

The measure of damages in trespass is sometimes problematic. In the case of the goods' complete destruction, the measure is the chattel's full value[6], but there is some authority that this should also be awarded if it is removed and subsequently returned[7]; doubt has been cast on whether this authority would be followed[8]. It has also been suggested that where a person severs something from land (thereby committing a trespass to both land and goods) the measure of damages is determined by the loss to the land[9].

This is subject to two caveats. The first is that where no actual damage can be shown to have befallen the plaintiff his position, even after he has succeeded in his action, is precarious. He is entitled to his costs, but the monetary award (if any) which he obtains is entirely at the court's discretion, and the court is not known for its generosity. The second is that in cases of mutual trespass the writ avails no one. In the case of a motor accident, for example, it is virtually certain that all the participants are victims of a trespass, whether to their property or their persons or both. In practice the actions in trespass cancel out and the issue falls to be decided entirely as a matter of negligence, which involves analysis of both damage and fault.

Trespass to goods is committed by an interference with possession. A man can therefore commit a trespass to his own goods if they are lawfully in the possession of a third person[10]. However, it follows that a bailee can never commit trespass to goods, since by definition the goods are already in his possession. Equally a man who removes goods from the possession of another who is wrongfully in possession of them is liable in trespass, even if he removes the goods to return them to their rightful owner[11]. The policy objective of these rules is clearly to promote quiet possession.

---

[3] *Thurston v Charles* (1905) 21 TLR 659.

[4] *White v Brown* (1983) CLY 972.

[5] Even this requirement is now largely historic. In *National Coal Board v Evans* [1951] 2 KB 861, CA it was held that it was a good defence to an action in trespass to show that the trespasser was entirely without fault.

[6] *The Mediana* [1900] AC 113.

[7] *Rundle v Little* (1844) 6 QB 174.

[8] *MacGregor on Damages*, 11th edn, p 954.

[9] *MacGregor on Damages* at p 959, citing *Moore v Drinkwater* (1858) 1 FtF 134. In conversion only the goods' value may be claimed (*Clarke v Halford* (1848) 2 C&K 540).

[10] *Keenan Bros v CIE* (1962) 97 ITLR 54.

[11] Torts (Interference With Goods) Act 1977, s 8. In such a case the possessor is necessarily also a trespasser, but in this case there is no cancellation of liabilities, since they are not mutual.

Self-help and right to repossess

In some respects the most important thing about trespass to goods is that it gives rise to the right to self-help. The English law of trespass has always permitted the wronged possessor to recover his goods, and although there are volumes of judicial dicta disapproving recourse to self-help[12] the remedy continues in rude health.

The primary difficulty in helping oneself in this context is the general rule that a victim of a trespass may only recover his property by using 'reasonable' force[13]. The courts do not view the use of any force leniently, and the question of what is reasonable is a difficult point at the best of times. To compound the difficulty, the goods concerned are unlikely to be on the rightful owner's land, and therefore a trespass to the land of another is necessary to recover them in all circumstances where they are not to be found on the public highway[14]. It seems clear that some element of trespass is permitted in the recovery of goods[15], although this is viewed more leniently when it is to recover goods which have been forcibly removed from the owner's own land[16].

Conversion

Conversion may be defined as 'an act, or a complex series of acts, of wilful interference without lawful justification, with any chattel in a manner inconsistent with the right of another, whereby that other is deprived of the use and possession of it'[17].

Unlike trespass, conversion cannot occur without intention: there is in theory no such thing as a completely accidental conversion. However, intention is readily implied from the doing of an act which necessarily challenges the existing owner's right, even though the person doing the act may have no knowledge of the owner's identity nor any intention deliberately to challenge such ownership[18]. It is for this reason that a person who deals with an object which he genuinely believes to have been abandoned thereby commits a conversion[19]. This is most commonly encountered where a person finds goods in circumstances in which they are clearly someone else's property (eg a gold bracelet found in an airport departure lounge, as in *Parker v British Airways Board*[20]), in which case he is committing a conversion against the true owner.

An interference with another's possession of goods without any intention to interfere in any way with the title of the person entitled thereto is not a

---

[12] See eg *Billson v Residential Apartments Ltd* [1992] 1 AC 494 at 524–5 and 536.
[13] *Blades v Higgs* (1861) 10 CBNS 713.
[14] Eg vehicles subject to a broken hire contract.
[15] *Anthony v Haney* (1832) 8 Bing 186.
[16] *Patrick v Colerick* (1838) 3 M & W 483.
[17] *Lewis Trusts v Bambers Stores* [1983] FSR 453 at 459.
[18] *Moorgate Mercantile Finance Co v Fitch* [1962] 1 QB 701.
[19] Although the conversion itself will not occur unless (a) at the time he found the item it could not possibly have been abandoned, or (b) the rightful owner demands it back.
[20] [1982] QB 1004.

conversion[21] (it is a trespass). For example,the removal of unsafe items from an air traveller's luggage by airline security staff is not a conversion by the security staff, as they have no intention to interfere with the title of the person concerned to the goods[22], but they do commit a trespass.

Liability in conversion is strict. The owner of goods is entitled to possession of them at all times, and where a person deprives him of that possession, that person must compensate him for all the damage flowing from his interference. Mistake is no defence, and an honest delivery of goods to a person believed to be the owner is actionable in conversion by the true owner[23]. Equally, no reduction in liability is permitted owing to the true owner's contributory negligence[24], and neither is there any reduction in damages as a result of the remoteness of the likelihood of the damage to the goods at the time of the conversion[25]. In the case of a temporary taking in which restoration of the goods taken has become impossible through the act of a third party or through accident, the taker has no defence that he is only partly to blame for the failure to restore the goods, but is under a strict liability either to return the goods themselves or to reimburse the owner for their whole value[26]. The proper defendant in an action in conversion is the person responsible for the interference, and even if that person acted solely as the servant or minister of another he is not thereby excused from liability[27].

This situation must be clearly distinguished from the case where a person who is lawfully in possession of another's goods is unable to deliver them to the rightful owner upon demand because they have been destroyed or stolen by a third hand. This is not a conversion[28], and the possessor's liability to the rightful owner arises either in negligence or under the terms of the contract pursuant to which he held the goods.

It is possible to interfere with another's title to goods without interfering with the goods themselves. For example, where a person holds the registration document of a car belonging to another, by failing to return it upon demand he thereby interferes with the owner's ability to demonstrate his title to the car. Thus, in addition to converting the document itself, he also commits a conversion in respect of the car[29], even though he may never have come into contact with it, and the same is true of any act done by a possessor which evidences absolute denial and repudiation of the plaintiff's title[30]. However, enabling another to deal with an asset belonging to a third party is not a con-

---

[21] *Wilson v New Brighton Panel Beaters Ltd* [1989] 1 NZLR 74 at 77.

[22] *Fouldes v Willoughby* (1841) 8 M & W 540, followed in *Leitch & Co v Leydon* [1931] AC 90 and *Bearman v ARTS Ltd* [1948] 2 All ER 89, 92.

[23] *Consolidated Co v Curtis* [1892] 1 QB 495.

[24] Torts (Interference With Goods) Act 1977, s 11(1).

[25] *Wilson v New Brighton Panel Beaters Ltd* [1989] 1 NZLR 74.

[26] *Wellington City v Singh* [1971] NZLR 1025 at 1027.

[27] *International Factors Ltd v Rodriguez* [1979] QB 351.

[28] *Barclays Mercantile Business Finance v Sibec Developments Ltd* [1992] 1 WLR 1253. If the defendant destroyed or wilfully abandoned the goods, he converted them at the moment of doing so, but even in this case his refusal to redeliver is not in itself actionable.

[29] *Bryanston Leasings v Principality Finance* [1977] RTR 45.

[30] *Douglas Valley Finance Co Ltd v Hughes (Hirers) Ltd* [1969] 1 QB 738.

version against that party[31], although it may well be actionable in negligence.

The clearest possible case of conversion is destruction. Where a person destroys another's goods he is immediately liable in conversion; this is the case regardless of whether the destruction is by consumption, by direct action or by inaction[32]. This is also true where a person in possession of goods allows those goods to be mixed in such a way that the title of the goods' true owner is extinguished[33]. It seems that where the effect of a mixture is to render the owner the co-owner of part of a bulk rather than the absolute owner of specific property there is no conversion, as the owner's title, although modified, is neither extinguished nor materially affected in value[34]. This appears to follow from the authorities to the effect that damaging goods is no conversion, but a mere trespass[35].

Demand

If no demand has been made, no conversion is committed where the possessor of goods to which he has no title continues in possession without doing any act otherwise incompatible with the true owner's title. This is very common, and arises where a bailee holds over at the end of the term of his bailment[36], usually whilst awaiting instructions for the goods' disposition.

The essence of conversion is a withholding. Where a person has removed goods from the other's possession, the withholding occurs at that moment, and the owner may proceed without formally demanding the goods' return[37]. In cases where the defendant has come into possession of the goods by legal means, the conversion is proved by failure to redeliver them on demand[38]. There are clear rules for what is necessary in order to constitute a 'demand for this purpose'. Perhaps most importantly, the demand must have been conveyed to the defendant: it is a valid defence to an action in conversion that a proper demand, although dispatched by the plaintiff, was never received[39]. Other relevant rules are that the demand must specify the goods demanded (a general demand for 'everything that you have which is mine' is invalid[40]) and the demand must be unconditional[41]. If the response to the demand is anything other than the goods' immediate redelivery a conversion is thereby committed; an equivocal response which professes willingness to return the goods but cites reasons why this should not or cannot be done immediately is equiva-

---

[31] *Ashby v Tolhurst* [1937] 2 KB 242.
[32] *Hollins v Fowler* (1875) LR 7 HL 757.
[33] *Northern Ireland Master Butchers' Wholesale Supply Ass'n v Belfast Corp* [1965] NI 30.
[34] Although such a mixing would be a trespass to the goods.
[35] *Simmons v Lillystone* (1853) 8 Ex 431.
[36] *Mitchell v Ealing LBC* [1979] QB 1. The bailee is almost certainly guilty of a breach of the contract of his bailment.
[37] *Cuff v Broadlands Finance Ltd* [1987] NZLR 343.
[38] *Capital Finance Co v Bray* [1964] 1 WLR 323.
[39] *King v Walsh* [1932] IR 178.
[40] *Abington v Lipscomb* (1841) 1 QB 776.
[41] *Rushworth v Taylor* (1842) 3 QB 699.

lent for this purpose to a refusal, and is therefore actionable[42].

Note that the demand and refusal to deliver is not an ingredient of the action in conversion, but simply a convenient procedure for proving the conversion. This may be proved by other facts not involving the making of a demand (eg where the defendant has destroyed the plaintiff's goods and this can be proved there is no need to prove a demand for their return[43]).

Wrongful disposition and wrongful delivery

In many cases a person who holds goods for another's benefit has at law the power to dispose of them in such a way as to pass title to them to the disponee. In this case possession is irrelevant; the wrong is done to the owner's title. For example, the vendor of goods who remains in possession of them after title has passed to the initial purchaser may enter into a second sale of the same goods to a second purchaser; that second sale deprives the first purchaser of his title and confers good title to the goods on the second purchaser[44]. Even though the goods may remain at all times in the vendor's lawful possession, at the moment of disposition to the second purchaser the vendor commits a conversion against the first, and is liable accordingly[45]. However, the purported sale must be effective to transfer title before the liability in conversion arises. A purported sale outside any of the exceptions to the rule of *nemo dat* unaccompanied by delivery of possession is at law a complete nullity, and for this reason does not constitute a conversion[46]. This rule is not absolute, and there are a number of circumstances in which there is an implied permission to alienate (eg where goods are delivered to a repairer, he acquires a repairer's lien on the goods for the cost of the repair without incurring liability in conversion, although the creation of such a lien constitutes a partial interference with the absolute title of the goods' owner).

Where a purported but ineffective sale is accompanied by a transfer of possession, or where possession is transferred without authority, a conversion is committed through the goods' wrongful delivery. In this case the conversion is complete upon delivery. The conversion is committed whether or not the person in possession of the goods knows that the person to whom he is delivering them is entitled to them; where A, holding goods for B, is defrauded into delivering them to C, then he is liable to B for their value regardless of whether he has received any value from C[47].

Where a person who is delivering goods commits a conversion, what is the recipient's position? The answer is that he commits a conversion by mere receipt, whether he takes delivery under a purported sale[48] or as pledgee or

---

[42] *Howard E Perry v British Railways Board* [1980] 1 WLR 1375.
[43] *Cuff v Broadlands Finance Ltd* [1987] NZLR 343.
[44] Sale of Goods Act 1979, ss 22 and 24.
[45] *Worcester Works Finance v Cooden Engineering Co Ltd* [1972] 1 QB 210.
[46] *Consolidated Co v Curtis* [1892] 1 QB 495.
[47] *Hollins v Fowler* (1875) LR 7 HL 757.
[48] *M'Combie v Davies* (1805) 6 East 538.

bailee[49]. In such a context innocence is no defence to the action in conversion[50]. However, note that it is a defence to an action in conversion that a person receiving goods in such circumstances has returned them to the person from whom he received them before he had any notice of the fact that there were other claims either to possession or to ownership of such goods. In the light of what has gone before this is an anomalous defence, but it operates on the logic that the deposit and return in no way affect the position of the goods' true owner, since he is in the same position after the return as he was before the delivery[51]. This is also true if the goods, instead of being returned to the person who initially provided them, are delivered to the order of that person[52] on the basis that, again, nothing has happened to affect the rightful owner's title or claim to possession which would not have happened without his intervention. There is authority to the effect that this is true even where the person concerned knows that the transaction will pass title to a new owner[53]. However, all this is true only as long as the person in actual possession of the goods remains ignorant that there is any question over the title or right to possession of the goods' depositor. As soon as he has notice of such doubt, then he is liable for conversion upon delivery[54].

Cheques and negotiable instruments

If I steal a cheque made out by A to B and present it to my bank, the legal analysis of my bank's position is that it takes the piece of paper upon which the order to pay is written and presents it to A's bank for payment. The piece of paper has no value, and is used merely as a token to instruct various banks to adjust their accounts in a specified way. Strictly speaking no property has passed[55] from or to anyone other than the relevant piece of paper, and although the transaction's effect is to diminish the debt owed from A's bank to A, and to increase by an equivalent amount the amount owed by my bank to me, it is very hard to see a conversion of any valuable asset.

It is therefore troublesome that the traditional remedy for a stolen cheque is an action in conversion. This is accomplished by a legal fiction to the effect that the cheque's value is of its face amount, and that when I appropriate the cheque made out by A to B, then I am appropriating a valuable asset of the value of the cheque[56].

---

[49] Torts (Interference With Goods) Act 1977, s 11(2), reversing the previous common law position.

[50] *Hilbery v Hatton* (1864) 2 H & C 822.

[51] *Hollins v Fowler* (1875) LR 7 HL 757.

[52] *Barker v Furlong* [1891] 2 Ch 172.

[53] *National Mercantile Bank v Rymill* (1881) 4 LT 767, doubted in *Willis v British Car Auctions* [1978] 1 WLR 438, but approved in *Barker v Furlong* [1891] 2 Ch 172.

[54] *Winter v Bancks* (1901) 84 LT 504.

[55] *R v Preddy* [1996] AC 815.

[56] *Morison v London County & Westminster Bank* [1914] 3 KB 356; *Lloyds Bank v Chartered Bank of India, Australia and China* [1929] 1 KB 40.

Right to sue in conversion

The proper plaintiff in an action in conversion is the rightful possessor at the time of the conversion[57], quite regardless of whether or not he is the owner[58]. The importance of this rule is that a person who holds goods for another can sue anyone who interferes with those goods in his own name without joining the true owner as a party[59]. Thus where a person's goods are in the hands of a bailee at will, subject to an arrangement that the bailor may repossess the goods at any time, then upon a conversion both the bailee at will and the rightful owner may sue[60], jointly or separately, although the measure of damages between them cannot be more than the goods' value.

An old chestnut in the law of conversion is the position between co-owners. Where one co-owner of a chattel appropriates it entirely to his own use, the old rule was that the other(s) could sue in conversion only where the other's act amounted to a claim to exclusive possession. If the co-owner's act was merely to employ the chattel for its ordinary purpose then no conversion was committed, even if the use diminished the chattel's value. This rule has been preserved by s 10(1)(*a*) of the Torts (Interference with Goods) Act 1977, which helpfully provides that any attempt by one co-owner to sell the relevant chattel may constitute a conversion if done without the consent of the other(s).

Where the true owner is out of and has no immediate right to possession, he cannot bring an action for conversion[61]. Where the offence complained of is one against the true owner's title, it is the true owner alone who may sue[62]— but again only if he has an immediate right to possession. Equitable ownership alone does not give the right to sue in conversion[63]. Immediate in this context means unqualified. A person who has bought goods which are being held by the seller to his order does not have an immediate right to possession, since the seller has a lien for the price. It is submitted that the fact of the existence of any lien for any amount has the same effect, such that no owner of property subject to any possessory lien may sue in conversion[64].

A person who has no right in the goods but merely a contractual right to have goods delivered cannot sue in conversion. However, this is subject to the important exception that a bailee who does an act which is 'wholly repugnant to' the bailor's title thereby determines the bailment and causes the rightful owner's claim to possession to revive[65]. Thus where a person who has goods in his possession *qua* bailee sells them, the act of sale causes the finance company's title to revive and it can thereafter sue the auction house which

---

[57] *Winkworth v Christie Manson & Woods Ltd* [1980] Ch 496.
[58] *Lipkin Gorman v Karpnale Ltd* [1991] 2 AC 548.
[59] *Burton v Hughes* (1824) 2 Bing 173.
[60] *USA v Dollfus Mieg et Cie* [1952] AC 582.
[61] *Lord v Price* (1874) LR 9 Ex 54.
[62] *International Factors v Rodrigues* [1979] QB 351.
[63] Per Lord Brandon in *Leigh & Sillavan Ltd v Aliakmon Shipping Co, The Aliakmon* [1986] AC 785 at 809.
[64] *Lord v Price* (1874) LR 9 Ex 54.
[65] *North General Wagon & Finance Co Ltd v Graham* [1950] 2 KB 7; *Union Finance v British Car Auctions Ltd* [1978] 2 All ER 385.

sells the goods and any person who acquires them[66]. But note that an act which is sufficient to cause the true owner's right to possession to revive may itself be less than sufficient to constitute a conversion[67].

This rule produces at fairly regular intervals the circumstance in which the converter's defence is that he acted on the instructions or with the authority of the goods' rightful owner, who was himself entitled to immediate possession. Prior to the passing of the 1977 Act this was not a good defence to an action. The rule of *jus tertii* applied such that where there had been interference with actual possession, the measure of damages should be assessed as if the possessor were absolutely entitled to the goods, without regard to the question of whether the plaintiff in the action had any title to them. It was only where an owner sued relying on an immediate right to possession that the defendant might put the title of the goods' owner in issue.

The rule of *jus tertii* was abolished by s 8(1) of the Act. The importance of the abolition lies largely in the field of damages. The problem was that if a person in actual possession sued a converter he might recover the full value of the goods converted[68]. The true owner might then separately sue, citing an immediate right to possession, and, in theory, recover the chattel's value over again[69]. The Act permits the defendant to join all parties with an interest in the goods in the action, and thereby ensures that the value of the award of damages is divided amongst all of the parties thereto in proportion to their right.

The right to possession can be based on the flimsiest of grounds. In *Armory v Delamirie*[70] a chimney sweep boy had found a gem and took it to a jeweller for valuation. The jeweller refused to return the gem to the boy, who successfully sued in conversion, the court treating the boy as entitled to possession. However, the rules of possession[71] are applied by the court in order to determine whether the plaintiff ever had possession at all. In *Parker v British Airways Board*[72] it was held that the British Airways Board could not bring an action in conversion against a person who found a gold bracelet in a departure lounge. The facts of the case were that the finder handed the bracelet to a British Airways employee, requesting that it be returned to him if the true owner were not found. The true owner was not found, the Board refused to return the bracelet, and was successfully sued in conversion.

A right to possession may also be vested in the owner of the land upon which the property is at the moment of the conversion. Chattels attached to or

---

[66] *North General Wagon & Finance Co Ltd v Graham* [1950] 2 KB 7.

[67] Palmer, *Bailment*, 2nd edn (Sweet & Maxwell, 1991), p 211, and see the authorities collected in notes 88–94 therein.

[68] *The Winkfield* [1902] P 42.

[69] Because payment of the full price of the goods to the possessor does not extinguish the true owner's title (*Attenborough v London & St Katherines Dock Co* (1878) 3 CPD 450). Note however that if the order of the actions is reversed, payment of the full value to the owner entitled to immediate possession would extinguishes the possessor's right (Holdsworth, *History of English Law*, vol II, pp 461–2; *Eastern Construction Co v National Trust Co* [1914] AC 197; *Morrison Steamship Co v Greystoke Castle (Cargo Owners)* [1947] AC 265).

[70] (1722) 1 Stra 505.

[71] *See* Chapter 3 *above*.

[72] [1982] QB 1004.

lying under land are in the landowner's possession[73] (ie the freeholder or lease-holder, but probably not a licensee).

The Limitation Act 1980 has the effect of extinguishing a true owner's title to a chattel where steps have not been taken to recover it six years after the date of its conversion[74]. This rule does not apply where the original conversion was by way of theft, as a person encountering his stolen property may in principle recover it at any time. However, the Act does provide that where a thief has sold stolen property which is subsequently disposed of to a purchaser in good faith, the time period begins from the date of the disposition.

Proprietary effects of conversion as a remedy

Conversion is not ordinarily characterised as a proprietary remedy, in that it is a tortious action for damages. However, it has certain proprietary characteristics. In practice the remedy in conversion does prevail in this way. The reason is that if you have my goods wrongfully, and become insolvent, I can sue your trustee in bankruptcy, or liquidator, personally in conversion if he does not return my goods to me. Since he will be able to claim any damages which I recover out of your general assets in priority to all other creditors, this means that the proprietary right is as fully protected as it would be if the action were a proprietry action. The point is that for practical purposes the question of whether a right can be classified as proprietary can be shortly stated as whether, in the defendant's insolvency, the plaintiff's right would prevail over the other creditors' interest.

Detinue and damages

Section 1(1) of the Torts (Interference with Goods) Act famously provides that 'Detinue is abolished'. This clause has given rise to some difficulty.

> The precise meaning of this terse enactment is unclear. The Writ of Detinue had been abolished long before. The fact of detinue cannot be abolished, because people will continue wrongfully to detain other people's goods. The legal consequences of detaining (as opposed to converting) goods may certainly be abolished, but Parliament went to some trouble to preserve them.[75]

It is this last point which is important. What is meant by 'the legal consequences of detinue' is the mechanics of calculation of damages.

As mentioned above, the old writ of detinue was in effect superseded by the writ of conversion, since the defendant could avoid the action in detinue by waging his law. The abolition of this possibility in 1833 brought a revival

---

[73] *London Corp v Appleyard* [1963] 1 WLR 982.

[74] Limitation Act 1980, s 3(2). Note that it is the original conversion which is important; subsequent conversions do not commence limitation periods of their own, but all subsequent conversions cease to be actionable six years after the date of the initial conversion (per s 3(1)).

[75] J H Baker, *Introduction to English Legal History*, 3rd edn (Butterworths, 1990), p 452.

of the old action, primarily because of its rule of calculation of damages. In an action in detinue the amount of money which might be awarded in damages upon its being made out was the goods' value at the moment when the true owner was deprived of them. The reasons for this are clear from the origins of the writ of detinue: the writ was developed as the chattel equivalent of an action in debt[76], and in debt liability is assessed at the date upon which the obligation falls due without reference to any subsequent fluctuation in value of the amount owed. Hence the rule that one should sue on conversion in a rising and detinue in a falling market[77].

Measure of damages[78]

The question of whether damages for the unitary tort of interference with goods should be calculated on the conversion or the detinue measure was not solved by the abolition of detinue as a separate tort. Instead, s 3 of the Act provides for three different potential awards in favour of a successful plaintiff:

    (a)   the chattel's value (assessed at such time as the court may feel to be desirable[79]) plus damages for its detention;

    (b)   return of the chattel plus damages for its detention; and

    (c)   either payment or return of the chattel (at the defendant's option) plus damages for its detention.

Note that this structure has the effect of removing from the plaintiff's hands the choice as to the time of assessment of the value of the plaintiff's loss and placing it in the hands of the court.

The principles which are applied in calculating the asset's value are as follows:

    (1)   The property's value should in principle be assessed at the time of the tort[80]. If the property depreciates, then the loss falls on the converter, who must pay the price at the time of the conversion without receiving any benefit from the depreciation[81]. If the property appreciates, the plaintiff is entitled to recover the appreciation as special damages[82], unless the appreciation either is due to the defendant's act, in which case the plaintiff has no right to it[83], or was foreseeable by the plaintiff, in which case he should have mitigated his loss by making an equivalent purchase[84].

---

[76] The original form of the writ was *injuste debet et detinet* (Milsom 77 LQR at 243).

[77] *Rosenthal v Alderton & Sons Ltd* [1946] 1 KB 374.

[78] See Tettenborn, 'Damages in Conversion' [1993] CLJ 128; Hudson, 'Money Claims for the Misuse of Chattels' in *Interests in Goods* (Mckendrick & Palmer, eds) (Lloyds of London Press, 1993), p 548.

[79] *IBL Ltd v Coussens* [1991] 2 All ER 133 at 140.

[80] *Caxton Publishing Co v Sutherland Publishing Co* [1939] AC 178; *Brandeis Goldschmidt v Western Transport Ltd* [1981] QB 864; *BBMM Finance (Hong Kong) Ltd v Eda Holdings Ltd* [1990] 1 WLR 409.

[81] *Solloway v McLaughlin* [1938] AC 247.

[82] *Aitken v Gardiner and Watson* (1956) 4 DLR (2nd) 119.

[83] Torts (Interference with Goods) Act 1977, s 6(1).

[84] *Sachs v Miklos* [1948] 2 KB 23.

(2) 'The plaintiff may recover, in addition to the value of the property or his interest in it, any additional damage which he may have sustained by reason of the conversion which is not too remote.'[85] Where the converter returns the goods, this counts in reducing his liability[86], as does any payment made by him in respect of the goods[87]. However, a mere payment by him not specifically related to the goods and accepted by the plaintiff with knowledge of the conversion does not reduce such liability[88].

(3) Where a person converts goods in a bailee's possession, as between those two the fact that the bailee might have been called upon to give up the property at a moment's notice is nothing to the purpose in the award's calculation. This translates in practice into a rule that a person in actual possession may sue for the goods' full value. However, an owner with an immediate right to possession may sue only for the value of his interest—in other words, if he could only obtain immediate possession by payment of a sum of money (or refunding a sum of money), then the award of damages in his favour against a converter is the value of his interest. In an action between an owner and a person who has acquired possession of the goods as part of a security arrangement, the owner will not be successful in his action unless he has made tender of the debt secured by the pledge[89], and in the case of an action by a hirer under a hire-purchase agreement against the debtor under the agreement, the hirer can sue only for the balance due under the agreement and not for the goods' full value[90].

(4) Where the possessor is a bailee, the amount of damages should be the value of the property as a whole and not the amount which the bailee would be liable to pay to the true owner if he had destroyed the property himself[91]. However, where the amount received by the bailee exceeds the amount of his liability, he holds the balance for the benefit of the true owners, who can proceed against him in an action for money had and received to recover it[92]. There is a specific exception to this rule for finance companies whose rights to immediate possession have arisen as a result of a disposition of the property subject to the hire agreement by the hirer. In such cases, where the property has been disposed of for a price in excess of the amount due under the finance agreement, the award of damages to the finance company is limited to the amount outstanding under the agreement.

(5) Any difficulties of valuation or identification are resolved against the interest of the defendant who, by failing to produce the chattel, is taken

---

[85] Salward & Heuston (*see* fn 1 *above*), pp 115–16; *Hillesden Securities Ltd v Ryjack Ltd* [1983] 1 WLR 959.
[86] *USA v Dollfus Mieg* [1952] AC 582.
[87] *Liggett (Liverpool) v Barclays Bank* [1928] 1 KB 48.
[88] *Lloyds Bank v Chartered Bank of India, Australia and China* [1929] 1 KB 40.
[89] *Donald v Suckling* (1866) LR 1 QB 585.
[90] *Wickham Holdings v Brooke House Motors* [1967] 1 WLR 295.
[91] *The Winkfield* [1902] P 42.
[92] *A Tomlinson (Hauliers) Ltd v Hepburn* [1966] AC 451.

to have caused the difficulty, as *omnia præsumuntur contra spoliatorem*[93].

An order under the Act has the effect of an offer made by the defendant to the plaintiff to purchase the asset at the price stated. The plaintiff need not accept this offer but may (if he wishes) seize the chattel. If he does so, the order lapses[94]. The court will not order the plaintiff to accept money damages instead of his chattel; that is an election for the plaintiff. It will, however, occasionally and 'where the justice of the case requires it', oblige him to accept redelivery of the chattel instead of allowing him to sue for damages[95].

Replevin

The right to replevy goods is the right of an owner of goods, which are wrongfully in another's possession, to recover the goods from a third hand who has levied distress or any other form of authorised taking on the goods of that other[96]. Replevin is not available where the goods are lawfully in the possession of the person suffering distraint, but only where that person has come into possession of the goods by trespass against goods which were, at the time of the trespass, in the plaintiff's possession. In other words, where the owner had voluntarily bailed the goods, and the defendant had merely failed to return them, then no action for replevin is available.

The point of replevin is that the owner is entitled to his goods back immediately pending investigation of his title. It is therefore in the nature of an interlocutory remedy, as it does not determine right or title but merely preserves a status quo pending determination of right and title. However, the eventual proceedings are also in the form of an action in replevin in which, if the owner is successful, he may keep his property and claim damages from the defendant for any loss which he may have incurred as a result of the wrongful seizure[97].

The action in replevin has for almost all purposes been superseded by the provisions of s 4 of the 1977 Act, which create a procedure for interim custody by a third party pending trial.

Rescous and pound-breach

These two obscure torts have a happy and lively continuing existence in the field of insolvency practice. Rescous is the tort of taking back distrained goods before they reach the 'pound', or place in which they are to be kept, and pound-breach is, as it sounds, the tort of taking back goods after they have been placed in the pound. In both cases, the point is that after goods have been

---

[93] *Armory v Delamirie* (1721) 1 Stra 505.
[94] *Ellis v John Stenning & Son* [1932] 2 Ch 81.
[95] *USA v Dollfus Mieg* [1952] AC 582.
[96] Although replevin is usually encountered in the case of goods distrained upon, it is available for any form of authorised taking (*Shannon v Shannon* (1804) 1 Sch & Lef 324).
[97] *Smith v Enright* (1893) 69 LT 724.

distrained upon they are in *custodia legis*, and it is a particularly serious legal wrong to remove them. The reason that the distrainor chooses to proceed in the torts of rescous and pound-breach rather than in the tort of conversion is that liability for both torts is strict—ignorance that the goods have been distrained upon is no defence—and, more importantly, that they give rise to a liability for triple damages[98].

The reason that these two are important is that the modern bailiff does not in fact haul goods off to an identifiable and designated pound, but takes a 'walking possession' order which allows the goods' possessor to retain them after having signed a written acknowledgement to the effect that they have been distrained upon. This leaves the possessor liable in pound-breach if he moves any chattel for any reason after having signed such an order. More controversially, a third party who moves any such goods is equally liable, even though he may have had no way of knowing that the goods had been distrained upon[99]. It is probably for this reason that the Law Commission has recommended the abolition of these torts[100].

Injury to reversionary interest[101]

As mentioned above, both conversion and trespass are remedies which are only available either to possessors or to persons with an immediate right to possession. Where the true owner is out of possession and has no immediate right to it, he cannot bring an action for conversion[102] or for trespass. Under the old law such a person could bring a special action on the case for damage to his reversionary interest[103], and this action (presumably) continues to exist, although there is doubt over whether it is within the umbrella category of the tort of wrongful interference with goods under the Act[104]. Such persons cannot recover the goods themselves, since they do not have any immediate right to the goods and to make such an award in their favour would be to dispossess a prior claimant with a better right. However, the claim for money damages should proceed in the normal way[105]. It would seem that the effect of the Sale of Goods (Amendment) Act 1995 means that a purchaser of an unseparated part of a larger bulk can now bring this action against a purchaser of a part of the bulk which has been wrongfully sold.

---

[98] Distress for Rent Act 1689, s 3.

[99] *Lavell & Co v O'Leary* [1993] 2 KB 200, although it is accepted that a third party is not so liable in the case of walking possession if he does not know that the goods are impounded (*Abingdon RDC v O'Gorman* [1968] 2 QB 811).

[100] Law Com No 194 (1991).

[101] This topic is fully dealt with in Tettenborn, 'Reversionary Damages to Chattels' [1994] CLJ 326.

[102] *Lord v Price* (1874) LR 9 Ex 54.

[103] *Gordon v Harper* (1796) 7 TR 9; Clerk & Lindsell, p 108.

[104] Clerk & Lindsell, *Torts*, 17th edn, para 13-167.

[105] See *Tancred v Allgood* (1859) 4 H & N 438; Palmer, *Bailment*, p 259; *Candlewood Navigation Corp v Mitsui OSK Lines, The Mineral Transporter* [1986] AC 1; see also *The Jag Shakti* [1986] AC 337.

Negligence

Where a person damages my goods, he is almost certainly acting in a way which could be characterised as negligent. Consequently, if a duty of care can be established he is liable to me in negligence as well as in conversion. The action in negligence for damage to goods has, however, been incorporated by the 1977 Act into the general tort of interference with goods[106], and there should therefore be no procedural advantages to proceeding in negligence rather than conversion.

The action in negligence is, like the action in conversion, limited in its availability to persons having an immediate right to possession of the goods[107]. The theoretical base for this restriction is that negligence is only actionable where a person has suffered damage to his physical property. Where the defendant does not have an immediate right to possession, his loss by virtue of the negligence is only 'economic' loss, which is not recoverable in negligence[108]. The underlying rationale for this bar is a rule of foreseeability, and it seems that the underlying principle of English law is that there is an irrebuttable presumption of law that economic loss is not foreseeable[109].

Money

Conversion does not lie for money[110]. This is because it is the rule of law that there is no property in currency[111], and a person who deprives another of currency does not therefore interfere with their property right in it. For the same reason, the transfer of notes and coins to any person does not create a bailment[112], as it follows that the return of the specific notes and coins concerned is not intended by either party[113] and cannot be compelled by law. What is important is the value, not the physical existence, of the money. The rule is best treated as one of law. A person seeking to recover stolen or otherwise misappropriated money must therefore seek to reclaim its value, and not the money itself. This is achieved by means of the action for money had and received. This remedy is discussed in Chapter 30.

---

[106] Clerk & Lindsell, *Torts*, 17th edn, para 13-163.

[107] *Leigh & Sillivan Ltd v Aliakmon Shipping Co, The Aliakmon* [1986] AC 785; *Candlewood Navigation Co v Ltd v Mitsui OSK Lines Ltd, The Mineral Transporter* [1986] AC 1.

[108] *Spartan Steel & Alloys Ltd v Martin & Co (Contractors)* [1973] QB 27.

[109] See Clerk & Lindsell, *Torts*, 17th edn, para 7-57; but see *Caltex Oil (Australia) Pty v The Dredge 'Willemstad'* (1976) 136 CLR 529 and *Morrison SS Co v Greystoke Castle* [1947] AC 265 for possible exceptions in the context of damage to goods.

[110] *Orton v Butler* (1822) 5 B & Ald 652 (an action in detinue, but the same principles are applicable). In *Lipkin Gorman v Karpnale* [1991] 2 AC 548 Nicholls LJ suggested that conversion was available for currency, but in the House of Lords Goff LJ corrected this view (at 570).

[111] Per Templeman LJ in *Lipkin Gorman v Karpnale* [1991] 2 AC 548 at 563.

[112] Pollock & Wright, *Possession in the Common Law* (Clarendon, 1888), p 161.

[113] Although conversion will lie if the relevant notes and coins are earmarked or segregated (*Halliday v Higges* (1600) Cro Eliz. 638). Thus a customer who, distrusting his bank, placed his money in a locked safe deposit box at the bank rather than in a bank account, could bring an action in conversion if the bank appropriated the money.

Chapter 30

Restitution

There is much debate on and some dispute over the correct employment of the term 'restitution'. In principle, a restitutionary claim arises as a result of an 'unjust enrichment'; that is in circumstances where a person has been enriched at another's expense and it is unjust to allow him to retain that benefit. Yet it has recently been suggested that 'unjust enrichment' is the name of a cause of action (or a number of different causes of action sharing the same primary characteristics), and restitution is properly the name of the remedies which arise out of that cause of action[1]. This is the usage adopted in several leading works[2], and it is adopted here. First the origin of the restitutionary remedies is explained, and then some of those remedies are considered in the context of property law.

Contract, tort and the *tertium quid*

There is a continuing illusion in the common law context that all that is not contract is tort and vice versa[3]. This idea has respectable roots in Roman law: Justinian had divided obligations into a fourfold paradigm—obligations which arose *ex contractu* (from contract), *ex delicto* (loosely, from tort[4]), *quasi ex contractu* and *quasi ex delicto*[5]. It is possible that this categorisation is derived from Gaius[6], although Gaius had in fact said that obligations were threefold, arising from delict, contract or other operation of law[7]. This threefold categorisation has been described as having 'practical utility, if no scientific value'[8]. Justinian's fourfold categorisation, by contrast, had immense scientific value but no practical utility, in that it compelled the recharacterisation of Gaius' 'other causes' into artificial classes of quasi-delict or quasi-contract.

---

[1] This contention renders the leading textbooks on the subject misnamed, since they tend to concern unjust enrichment rather than restitutionary remedies.

[2] Particularly *Chitty on Contracts*, 27th edn (Sweet & Maxwell, 1994).

[3] See eg Viscount Haldane's speech in *Sinclair v Brougham* [1914] AC 398 at 415.

[4] The identity of tort and delict is by no means complete (eg a delictual action was primarily brought to impose a penalty, whereas a tortious action at common law is brought to recover compensation) but the two are close enough to be assimilated for this purpose. See Buckland & McNair, *Roman Law and Common Law*, 2nd edn (Cambridge University Press, 1952), p 338–51 for a comparison.

[5] Institutes 3.13.2.

[6] In the *Digest* it is attributed to the *Aurea* (Dig 44.7.5).

[7] Dig 44.7.1.pr.

[8] R W Lee, *Elements of Roman Law*, 4th edn (Sweet & Maxwell, 1956), p 284.

The development of a law of unjust enrichment is an attempt to escape from the results of this mischaracterisation by admitting the existence of obligations which do not owe their origin to either contractual or tortious duties. Yet the idea that obligations not tortious were contractual proved so appealing, and the concept of the actionable obligation arising neither in contract nor in tort was so revolutionary that the development of non-contractual non-tortious obligations was embodied in a structure entitled 'quasi-contract'.

The true origins of the restitutionary remedies are older than those of the action in contract, and it is only by reason of the fact that the action on a contract swallowed up, in procedural terms, the independent actions arising out of obligations incurred otherwise than by contract that the illusion that restitution is a form of quasi-contract has arisen. One way to express this conclusion is to say that in the nineteenth century, lawyers facing a non-contractual action (debt) clad in the form of a contractual action (assumpsit) made the mistake of disregarding the legal form of the action and paying too much attention to its procedural garments, reasoning that any action which involved an assumpsit must be an action in contract, or at least quasi in contract[9]. To understand how this mistake was made it is necessary to explain the origins of the action in *indebitatus assumpsit*.

Origins of the idea of quasi-contract

English law never knew a writ in respect of contract *per se*. The usual contractual remedies in the thirteenth century were the præcipe writs on a covenant and in debt. A præcipe writ asserted a right and demanded performance. 'Covenant', at that time, was not restricted to documents under seal, and might embrace virtually any obligation. However, by 1321 the royal courts, at least, had decided that they would hear no action in covenant unless the promise sued upon was in writing and sealed[10]. In all other cases, the only action available was the action in debt.

An action in debt might have been brought upon proof of an agreement accompanied by a *quid pro quo*, and therefore did not require a deed. There was no requirement that the sum need be due under a contract, and the action lay equally for the recovery of rent, a loan, the price of goods sold where consideration had wholly failed, or penalties due under a statute. Some of these functions were also or additionally performed by the writ of account[11]. However, the only defence to an action in debt was the general issue, a plea of *nil debet*.

The fact that the action in covenant was restricted to actions upon a deed

---

[9] This error was also responsible for the mischaracterisation of bailment. Bailment, being neither contractual nor tortious, might have been explained by the theory of quasi-contract, and the fact that it was not is the origin of the concept that all bailments were ultimately contractual.

[10] See D Ibbetson, 4 JLH 71.

[11] Created by the Statute of Marlborough 1276, c 23; see Jackson, *History of Quasi-Contract*, pp 8–17 and 32–4.

led to the development of assumpsit to cover other obligations. Assumpsit was not a præcipe writ asserting a right and demanding performance, but an *ostensurus quare* writ of trespass, asserting a default and requiring an explanation. Thus in order to have an assumpsit, a duty needed to be shown. The earliest writs in assumpsit originally lay in any case where a person, having agreed to do an act, failed to do it properly[12] (eg a veterinary surgeon who, having undertaken to cure a horse, killed it[13]). The basis of the action was the obligation, but the obligation in this case was an implied obligation—a person who had commenced to do something assumed an obligation to do it properly—and it applied in all cases regardless of whether the obligation was undertaken for reward or otherwise. This reasoning had one very significant drawback: that the action could only lie where something had been done wrong (ie misfeasance), and not where it had never been done at all (nonfeasance).

Assignment was developed to cover nonfeasance by recourse to the concept of *quid pro quo*, such that a failure to do a thing once having been paid to do it was characterised as misfeasance rather than a nonfeasance[14]. The concept of *quid pro quo* then became entangled with the cannon law concept of *causa* (the idea that a man should only be bound by those of his agreements which he had made for good *causa*[15]), and by 1565[16] the concept of consideration was established at English law as necessary for an assumpsit. From shortly thereafter 'the English law of contract might truly be said to be consensual; despite its trespassory guise, liability was based upon reciprocal agreement'[17].

The action in debt lasted longer and ranged wider than covenant before it, too, was swallowed up in assumpsit. The reason for its longevity was that it was an effective and popular action; the reason for its demise was that it was a writ of the court of the Common Pleas. The Common Pleas, as has been seen, held a candle for a long time for the wager of law as the defendant's right[18], and this was a great inconvenience for those who wished to collect their debts using the action.

Assumpsit was extended to embrace the recovery of debts through the development of the separate action of *indebitatus assumpsit.* This action was developed, like the action in *detinue sur trover,* by the employment of legal fictions. The fiction involved in the *indebitatus assumpsit* was that the defendant owed a fictional debt to the plaintiff. In extinction of this debt, the

---

[12] See in particular the Humber Ferry case, *Bukton v Tounesende* (1348) 22 Lib Ass pl 41.
[13] *Waldon v Mareschal* (1369) YB Mich 43 Edw III, fo 33 pl 38.
[14] *Orwell v Mortoft* (1505) CP 40/972, m 123.
[15] It is the concept of *causa* which gives rise to the maxim that *ex nudo pacto non oritur actio* (*C St German, Doctor & Student* (1531) 91 SS 228–33.
[16] *Sharington v Strotton* (1565) Plowd 298.
[17] J H Baker, *An Introduction to English Legal History*, 3rd edn (Butterworths, 1990), p 388.
[18] Wager of law involved the defendant in swearing to his innocence along with eleven oath-helpers—a system which probably originally functioned in local courts as a form of jury trial; if the defendant could convince eleven men of his innocence he probably was. But in latter days, a defendant who was happy to perjure himself might find a crowd of oath-helpers around the courts prepared to swear to anything for a fee. Wager of law was sometimes known as the 'lesser law', in the context of being inferior to the ordeal (abolished in 1215 by the Lateran Council in the ecclesiastical courts) and the trial by battle (abolished in 1818 by 59 Geo III, c 46.

defendant was deemed to have undertaken to pay the sum to him. If the promise were broken then an action in case might be brought[19]. The advantages to the plaintiff of electing this step have been canvassed before: the cheapness of the bill procedure, the simplicity of pleading and, above all, the avoidance of wager of law. The Common Pleas resisted this innovation, and in a rerun of the earlier dispute regarding bailment[20], the recently formed Court of Exchequer chamber decided in *Slade's Case*[21] that assumpsit, and the fictional debt which lay at its heart, was a valid procedure. This established the *indebitatus assumpsit* in cases of contract, and over the ensuing period the assumpsit expanded its scope further, so that it gradually came to embrace non-contractual liabilities[22]. In time it also embraced improper application of legal process[23], waiver of tort[24], and duress of goods[25].

The fictional debt which lay at the heart of the *indebitatus assumpsit* was a device capable of overcoming the rules on consideration which had been developed for the ordinary assumpsit. Eventually seven distinct *indebitatus* counts appeared, known as the common counts, which embraced goods sold and delivered, or bargained and sold, for work done, money lent, money laid out to the plaintiff's use at his request, money due upon an account stated and, most importantly, money had and received to the plaintiff's use. The limits of the *indebitatus assumpsit* were set by Holt CJ in a series of celebrated cases in the late seventeenth century[26], but it still remained a powerful action capable of remedying most legal wrongs. The fictional promise which lay at the root of the *indebitatus* count endured as a necessary component of the action until the abolition of the forms of action. Indeed the Common Law Procedure Act of 1852 provided that 'the statement of promises which need not be proved, as promises in *indebitatus* counts, need not be pleaded'[27].

The apotheosis of the *indebitatus assumpsit* was *Moses v Macferlan*[28] in which Lord Mansfield, relying on Roman law sources, laid down the broad proposition that[29]

> if the defendant be under an obligation from the ties of natural justice, to refund; the law implies a debt, and gives this action, founded in the equity[30] of the plain-

[19] [1954] CLJ 105 SFC Milsom.
[20] *Eason v Newman* (1596) Cro Eliz 495.
[21] (1602) 4 Co Rep 92a.
[22] *Lady Cavendish v Middleton* (1628) Cro Car 141.
[23] *Newdigate v Davey* (1693) 1 L Raym 742.
[24] *Lamine v Dorrell* (1701) 2 Ld Raym 1216.
[25] *Astley v Reynolds* (1731) 2 Str 915.
[26] *Shuttleworth v Garnett* Comb 151; *Hussey v Fiddall* 12 Mod 324, pl 558.
[27] Section 49; see also *Fibrosa Spolka Akcyjna v Fairbairn Lawson Combe Barbour Ltd* [1943] AC 32 at 63–4, per Lord Wright.
[28] (1760) 2 Burr 1005.
[29] 1008.
[30] 'Equity' is used here to mean 'natural justice' with a civil lawyer's disregard for the fact that it is a term of art at English law. For a general consideration of Roman law influences on Mansfield's reasoning see 'English and Roman learning in Moses v Macferlan' by Prof P H Birks in [1984] CLP 1.

tiff's case, as it were upon a contract (*quasi ex contractu*, as the roman law expresses it).

Under the tutelage of Lord Mansfield the count for money had and received became one of the most widely used actions of the nineteenth century as a flexible action which might be employed in new circumstances based upon general principles. These general principles were analysed in the late nineteenth century[31], and became in the United States the foundation of the doctrines of restitution, and the relief of unjust enrichment. In England, however, it was only with the House of Lords' decision in *Fibrosa Spolka Akcyjna v Fairbairn Lawson Combe Barbour Ltd*[32] when restitution returned to the mainstream of English legal thought.

It is perfectly clear that the development of the action for money had and received is an example of the procedural tail wagging the substantive dog. The fact that the action is based on that of assumpsit does not make it a contractual action, and if the older actions of debt and account had survived it would have been perfectly clear that the potential liability to repay benefits acquired unjustly would have had a separate and continuing identity clearly distinct from the action on contract. However, the fact that the action in assumpsit replaced the action in debt before it gave birth to the *indebitatus* counts has created the legal illusion that an action which is fundamentally a debt action has something in common with an action in contract—which it does not. It is for this reason that Goff and Jones say that 'In our view, the concept of implied contract is ... a meaningless, irrelevant and misleading anachronism'[33]. Some authority is cited in support of the proposition, much of it obiter[34]. But the question remains whether the words of Lord Templeman in *Guinness plc v Saunders*[35], supporting as they do the restrictive interpretation of the law of *quantum meruit* that there can be no such award in circumstances where a contract in the same terms could not have been made, constitute authority for a continued adherence by English law to the principles of 'strict' quasi-contract.

Restitutionary remedies

The thrust of the modern development of the law of unjust enrichment has been in the spheres of constructive trusts, tracing and mistake, which are dealt with elsewhere in this volume. However, there are a number of remedies which fall clearly into the restitutionary camp if only because the development of a coherent law of restitution has enabled them to be perceived within the overall structure of law rather than marginalised as 'sports'. The common denominator of these remedies is that they arise from a factual set of circumstances

---

[31] In particular in the US; see J B Ames (1888) 2 HLR 66 and W A Keener, *The Law of Quasi-Contracts* (1893).
[32] [1943] AC 32.
[33] Goff & Jones, *Introduction to the Law of Restitution*, p 10.
[34] Ibid, p 10, fn 51–60.
[35] [1990] 2 AC 663 at 689.

which give rise to a claim in unjust enrichment, and they result in a transfer of property rights. The greatest of these, mistake, is discussed at Chapter 10. In this chapter there are reviewed three of the lesser brethren of restitution: the actions for property based on waiver of tort; for money had and received; and that based on total failure of consideration.

Waiver of tort

A restitution analysis of personal property law must begin with the doctrine of waiver of tort. Although anathema to many restitution lawyers as being illustrative of what they perceive as the quasi-contract fallacy, waiver of tort is a useful starting point for the examination of restitutionary remedies for interference with goods.

The doctrine of waiver of tort resembles nothing so much as an exercise of the principle of ratification[36]. The idea is that where someone has appropriated your goods and put them to productive use, rather than suing in conversion for the goods' value at the time of the appropriation, you may elect to 'waive the tort' and assert that all that has been done with the goods has been done for your benefit. Therefore you may claim the proceeds of such activity by asserting a proprietary right and, if the goods have been sold on, proceeding by means of an action for money had and received.

It seems clear that the restitutionary remedy which is available through waiver of tort is additional, and not alternative, to the action in conversion. This follows from the House of Lords' decision in *United Australia Ltd v Barclays Bank Ltd*[37], in which a cheque made out to United Australia was appropriated by one of its employees who fraudulently endorsed it over to a company called MFG. Barclays, who were bankers to MFG, collected the cheque. As a matter of ordinary banking law the remedy available to United Australia was an action against Barclays for conversion of the cheque, an item in which it had an immediate right to possession. However, United Australia's first step was to commence an action for money had and received against MFG. When it subsequently commenced an action in conversion against Barclays, Barclays' defence was that by commencing the action for money had and received against MFG, United Australia had irreversibly waived the tort of conversion, and that it could not simultaneously assert and waive the tort in simultaneous proceedings. The House of Lords explained that this was incorrect, since there were in fact two distinct remedies for interference with goods, these being compensatory damages under the chattel torts on the one hand and restitutionary damages on the other. As Birks explains: 'on these facts, the tort was just as much the cause of action whether the damages sought were restitutionary or compensatory. In short, the one wrong gave rise to both remedial possibilities'[38].

---

[36] Although the two are distinct (*Verschures Creameries Ltd v Hull & Netherlands Steamship Co* [1921] 2 KB 608).
[37] [1941] AC 1.
[38] Goff & Jones (*see* fn 33 *above*), p 316.

The point of the restitutionary action is to obtain greater damages. The basis of the restitutionary calculus is to be found in the decision of Denning LJ in *Strand Electric v Brisford Entertainments*[39]. The facts were that a theatre hired lighting from a commercial hirer and declined to return it for 43 weeks after its return had been properly requested. The lighting was returned in (it seems) no worse condition than it was when it was hired out. The action was brought in the form of an action in detinue[40]. Of primary interest is Denning LJ's reasoning in calculating the quantum of damages. He based his approach on a general principle that where a wrongdoer makes use of goods for his own purposes, he must pay a reasonable hire. The argument is based on the premise that if the defendant had agreed with the plaintiff that he should keep the goods for the duration of the detainer, then the plaintiff would have been entitled to rent at a market rate, and the defendant should not be allowed to get away with paying a lesser sum by reason of his own wrongdoing[41]. It is unclear whether this principle is of general application or applies only in cases where the plaintiff is a commercial hirer of equipment of the type detained; however, Birks at least takes it to be of general application.

There is substantial debate, summarised and analysed by Ewan McKendrick[42], on the *ratio decidendi* in *Strand Electric*. The detailed analysis may be left to the curious reader, but it is necessary to summarise the various conclusions in order to shape the answer to the question of who may sue (and on what grounds) for a restitutionary remedy in cases of interference with goods.

(1) It is suggested that the decision in *Strand* simply enunciates a rule of calculation of damages in the tort of detinue in a particular set of circumstances, and is not in fact a restitution decision at all[43]. Although this is the most natural interpretation, it is also the least helpful, since there is no combination of existing principles of assessment of damages which can give rise to the quantum of damages set in *Strand*[44].

(2) It is suggested that although the cause of action in *Strand* was the tort of detinue, the relief granted was as a result of the fact that the plaintiffs' claim was not a tortious but a dependent restitutionary claim. The division of restitutionary claims into dependent and independent claims is a construct of Professor Birks[45], and is not universally ac-

---

[39] [1952] 2 QB 246.
[40] Although the decision has been applied in cases of conversion (*Hillesden Securities Ltd v Ryjack Ltd* [1983] 2 All ER 184) and trespass to goods (*Penarth Dock Engineering Co Ltd v Pounds* [1963] 1 Lloyd's Rep 359).
[41] The defendants had claimed in the proceedings that the plaintiffs would not in fact have been able to let out the equipment continuously for such a long period, and this had been accepted. Consequently the result of the decision seems to be that the *plaintiffs* were unjustly enriched.
[42] 'Restitution and the Misuse of Chattels' in *Interests in Goods* (Mckendrick & Palmer, eds) (Lloyds of London Press, 1993), p 599.
[43] Sharpe & Wadams, 'Damages for Lost Opportunity to Bargain' (1982) 2 OJLS 290.
[44] The only way in which the measure arrived at can be achieved using ordinary principles is to postulate an entirely fictitious contract of hire at a fictitious price, and then require payment of the hire due under this contract. Such an approach to the assessment of damages would be unique in English law.
[45] Goff & Jones, *Introduction to the Law of Restitution*, pp 39–40.

cepted[46]. Independent claims arise directly from unjust enrichment; dependent claims arise as a result of a specific wrong done by the defendant to the plaintiff. Birks analyses the distinction as between circumstances in which restitution provides a remedy in cases where the cause of action is unjust enrichment, and cases where restitution provides a remedy for a wrong which is already characterised as such by the system[47]. Here, identification of the wrong (the tort of conversion) gives rise to a restitutionary remedy in damages calculated according to the principles in *Strand* as an alternative to damages calculated according to the ordinary principles of conversion. The primary objection to this argument is that, if the waiver of tort analysis is sufficiently accurate to accommodate the dependent restitutionary claim analysis, then the decision in *Chesworth v Farrar*[48] becomes incomprehensible. In that case actions for money had and received and in conversion were pleaded arising out of the same facts. The court held that the latter was time barred, the former not, because actions in restitution and quasi-contract were of different natures and were governed by different parts of the Limitation Act. Limitation applies to causes of action, not remedies, and if a dependent restitutionary claim were merely a restitutionary remedy arising from a tortious right then there would be no such difference.

(3) It is further suggested that the cause of action in *Strand* was an 'ordinary' independent restitutionary claim. This is the only kind of restitutionary claim which Beatson[49] recognises, and is based on satisfaction of the four criteria for a claim in unjust enrichment. These are that:

(a)   the defendant was enriched[50];

(b)   the enrichment must have been at the plaintiff's expense;

(c)   there must be an element of injustice in the enrichment; and

(d)   there are no bars to restitution.

There is no difficulty in showing these incidents on the facts of *Strand*,

---

[46] See Goff & Jones, *The Law of Restitution*, 4th edn (Sweet & Maxwell, 1993), pp 56–9; Beatson, 'The Nature of Waiver of Tort' in *The Use and Abuse of Unjust Enrichment*, pp 242–3.

[47] Birks' approach is more attractive in that it is clearly based, consciously or not, upon an Occamist principle that *entia non est multiplicanda praeter necessitatem*—in other words, there is no point in creating a new cause of action in unjust enrichment where there is a perfectly good existing cause of action in tort. Beatson's view, on the other hand, seems to be a simplification which does not in fact simplify, since it requires a complex reinterpretation of existing decisions.

[48] [1967] 1 QB 407.

[49] Beatson, 'The Nature of Waiver of Tort' in *The Use and Abuse of Unjust Enrichment*, pp 242–3.

[50] This is more difficult than it sounds. It is accepted that not all cases of enrichment are actionable (eg where a defendant is enriched without his knowledge or consent there is no restitutionary action against him) and the consensus view is that in order for there to be actionable enrichment, the enrichment must be either knowingly and freely accepted by the defendant, or must be 'incontrovertible' (ie must constitute the saving of an inevitable expense, or must confer on the defendant a realisable benefit).

and this analysis appears to be the most satisfactory solution to the problem posed by the decision.

This last point, however, leads on to another. The waiver of tort analysis provides relatively simple answers to the question 'who can sue?', to which the answer is the proper plaintiff in an action in tort where the tort alleged is one of those which can be waived. There is relatively clear authority for which torts can and cannot be waived: assault, battery, malicious prosecution, negligence and defamation are all examples of torts which cannot be waived since they do not ordinarily enrich the tortfeasor, and if they do it is in such an indirect way that an action for restitution would be virtually impossible to maintain. Conversion and deceit, by contrast, are the prime examples of torts which may be waived. This gives rise to a relatively simple classification in which restitution becomes little more than a method of calculation of damages.

However, if the fully-fledged independent cause of action in unjust enrichment is to be deployed in this cause, then the number of circumstances in which property rights may be protected has expanded substantially. Restitutionary remedies, on this analysis, are available wherever the four criteria set out above are satisfied regardless of whether the act complained of constitutes a tort.

The non-tortious grounds for unjust enrichment giving rise to a restitutionary remedy may be grouped as follows: crime, breach of fiduciary duty, breach of confidence, breach of contract, and a residual category loosely entitled 'benefits acquired by reprehensible means'[51]. Work in all these areas is continuing.

Action for money had and received

This action proceeds by the identification of a specific payment rather than an assessment of value. The historical reason for this is that the action against a person who has received value due to the plaintiff is one of account, in which an assessment is made of a number of transactions in order to come up with a net balance. The action for money had and received identifies a particular sum which, *being the plaintiff's property*, has been paid to the defendant but which is unconscionable for the defendant to retain.

The action for money had and received is therefore available in any circumstances in which A receives money in circumstances which he should not keep it for himself. Thus the action lies against a person who has either

(a) wrongfully received the money as a gift or for no consideration[52],
(b) received the money in exchange for consideration which the law will not accept as valuable[53],
(c) otherwise received the money knowing that it did in fact belong to some other person than the person giving it, or
(d) possibly, received the money as the proceeds of an oppressive transaction[54].

---

[51] See Goff & Jones, *The Law of Restitution*, Chs 32–7, of which these are the headings.
[52] There is a difference (*Lipkin Gorman v Karpnale* [1991] 2 AC 548).
[53] Sexual favours (*Banque Belge pour l'Etranger v Hambrouck* [1920] 1 KB 321), or participation in an illegal lottery (*Clarke v Shee & Johnston* (1774) 1 Cowp 197; Lofft 756).

The action for money had and received was favoured in the eighteenth century as a means of doing a 'large and liberal' justice in the King's Bench. The *locus classicus* of the action is to be found in Lord Mansfield's speech in *Moses v Macferlan*[55]:

> [the action for money had and received] lies for money paid by mistake; or upon a consideration which happens to fail; or for money got through imposition (express or implied); or extortion; or oppression; or an undue advantage taken of the plaintiff's situation, contrary to the laws made for the protection of persons under those circumstances. In one word, the gist of this kind of action is that the defendant, upon the circumstances of the case, is obliged by the ties of natural justice and equity to refund the money.

Lord Mansfield explained further in *Clarke v Shee & Johnston*[56]:

> [The action for money had and received] is a liberal action in the nature of a bill in equity; and if, under the circumstances of the case, it appears that the defendant cannot in conscience retain what is the subject matter of it, the plaintiff may well support this action ... Where money or notes are paid bona fide, and upon a valuable consideration, they never shall be brought back by the true owner; but where they come mala fide into a person's hands they are in the nature of specific property; and if their identity can be traced and ascertained, the party has a right to recover ... Here the plaintiff sues for his identified property, which has come to the hands of the defendant iniquitously and illegally, in breach of the Act of Parliament[57], therefore they have no right to retain it; and consequently the plaintiff is well entitled to recover.

So, it is clear that the point of the action is that the plaintiff can only maintain his action if he can show that the money which the defendant received was his property at the time when the defendant received it. The action for money had and received is an action which is available in any case where one person has received money which was at the time of receipt the property of another. It has a proprietary base, in that in order to succeed it is necessary to show that the money received by the defendant is the same money as that which is due to the plaintiff. This is most easily accomplished in the case of a single payment, as where money due to B is paid to A, and in the classical action for money had and received a principal sues his agent for the sale proceeds of the principal's goods.

However, the action also has an application where a third party takes money belonging to A and gives it to B. Here, there are two payments: the payment

---

[54] This is speculative, but *Moses v Macferlan* (1760) 2 Burr 1005 and *Browning v Morris* (1778) 2 Cowp 790 are both authority for the proposition that the action for money had and received provides a common law remedy for money obtained through an unconscionable transaction; a modern precedent is to be found in *Kiriri Cotton v Dewani* [1960] AC 192, PC, per Denning LJ. See also *Bainbrigge v Browne* (1881) 18 Ch D 188.

[55] (1760) 2 Burr 1005, 1012.

[56] (1774) 1 Cowp 197 at 199–201.

[57] The Lottery Act 1772.

from A to the third party, and the payment from the third party to B. Now in such a case the action can only succeed where the third party can be (as it were) cancelled out of the equation such that the transfer can be treated as a transfer from A to B. It is this case in which we are interested, since it forms the basis for what is known as the common law tracing action.

The important question is whether the intervener has acquired title himself to the money. Now the rule of law is that money is presumed to be owned by the possessor for the time being, but this is a mere presumption and a thief does not acquire absolute and indisputable title to money simply by appropriating it. What is in fact happening is that money ceases to be the property of its true owner and becomes the property of its possessor when it 'passes into currency'[58]. The meaning of this phrase was explained in *Re Diplock*[59] as that 'where money is handed by way of transfer to a person who takes for value without notice, the claim of the owner of the money is extinguished just as all other equitable estates are extinguished by a purchaser for value without notice'[60]. Although this looks very similar to the equitable rule it is in fact a distinct and separate rule of common law. Professor Birks has commented on a puzzling legal illusion which has appeared in the context of some of the analysis of the action of money had and received[61]. Despite the references cited above to 'equity', the action for money had and received is without question a purely common law action. The defence of bona fide purchaser for value is one only to an action in equity, and the common law admits no such defence. However, the frequent references to 'good faith' above give the impression that the defence of purchaser for value without notice is being successfully deployed against a common law action. In fact, however, the analysis is simply that money can be followed only where it was not 'passed into currency', a process which happens where it is given in good faith for value.

Total failure of consideration

Where money has been paid under a transaction which, subsequently to the money being paid, becomes ineffective, the payer may recover his money. The logic of this action is quasi in debt rather than quasi in contract, since the amount which may be recovered is that paid without regard to considerations of remoteness or foreseeability. The action may be brought in any case where the contract has been discharged, whether for frustration or by a deliberate or accidental breach by the other party of a condition of the contract entitling the other party to treat the contract as discharged. The discharge of the contract is an essential part of this action: any act appearing to affirm the contract is fatal to an action in this form[62].

---

[58] *Solomons v Bank of England* (1791) 13 East 135; *King v Milsom* (1809) 2 Camp 5; and see generally F A Mann, *The Legal Aspect of Money*, 5th edn (OUP, 1992), pp 7–13.

[59] [1948] Ch 465 at 539.

[60] See also *Miller v Race* (1758) 1 Burr 452.

[61] 'Misdirected Funds, Restitution from the Recipient' [1989] LMCLQ 296.

[62] *Dies v British and International Mining and Finance Corp Ltd* [1939] 1 KB 724; *Kwei Tek Chao v British Traders and Shippers Ltd* [1954] 2 QB 459.

The failure of consideration must be total[63], and any contractual benefit accruing to the plaintiff[64] is sufficient to bar such a claim, and restricts the plaintiff to his claim in damages[65]. This does not mean that the innocent party must have received no benefit under the contract, but that he must have received no part of the benefit for which he contracted. Incidental collateral benefits are ignored. Thus, where a person sells to another an item of property to which he has no title in circumstances in which none of the exceptions to the maxim *nemo dat quod non habet* apply, the true owner may recover the property from the purchaser. The purchaser can then bring an action against the vendor to recover the purchase price, as the consideration for which he bargained—title to the item—has wholly failed. The fact that he may have had use of the object for a period does not diminish this[66].

Where the contract is divisible, a divided part of a larger contract may be said to have wholly failed, even though the overall contract proceeds[67].

Note also that by s 6(3) of the Torts (Interference with Goods) Act 1977, where a person is sold goods in such circumstances and improves them before selling them to another, the improver is entitled to an allowance for his work in an action by the purchaser based on total failure of consideration.

---

[63] Where there is a partial failure of consideration, the Law Reform (Frustrated Contracts) Act 1943 provides that restitution may still be available subject to a claim for set-off for expenses (*BP Exploration Co (Libya) Ltd v Hunt (No 2)* [1979] 1 WLR 783).

[64] *Whincup v Hughes* (1871) LR 6 CP 78.

[65] Eg the rather unfortunate Australian case, *Baltic SS Co v Dillon* (1993) 67 AJLR 228, in which the plaintiff's complaint was that the cruise ship upon which he was taking his holiday sank on the tenth day of a 14-day cruise. It was held that there was no total failure of consideration, as some of the contractual benefit had been enjoyed.

[66] *Rowland v Divall* [1923] 2 KB 500; *Johnson v Johnson* (1802) 3 B & P 162.

[67] *Deveaux v Conolly* (1849) 8 CB 640; *Ebrahim Dawood Ltd v Heath Ltd* [1961] 2 Lloyd's Rep 512.

Chapter 31

Constructive Trusts

We have already examined the institutional constructive trust (the constructive trust implied by law in circumstances where equity deems a full equitable interest to have arisen by reason of the parties' conduct). This chapter considers the remedial constructive trust.

Constructive trusteeship and remedial vesting of property

The idea that where property is vested in A a court can make an order to the effect that it is now vested in B suggests a power to disturb title at random which is inimical to ordinary commercial relations. The key to the idea of remedial constructive trust liability is that it arises on the wrongful acquisition of property. Thus where a fiduciary makes use of that status to obtain a benefit for himself, that benefit comes into his hands impressed with a constructive trust in favour of the person to whom he owes a fiduciary obligation.

There are two reasons for wanting to assert a proprietary rather than a personal claim. One is that the property concerned has increased in value. The other is that the person concerned is insolvent, and judgement on a personal claim would rank as an unsecured creditor. Strictly speaking money cannot increase in value, although close money substitutes (eg zero-coupon bonds) can. Thus the use of a claim of constructive trusteeship to recover money in the hands of a fiduciary is usually only relevant where the fiduciary is insolvent.

Basis of remedial constructive trusteeship

As mentioned above[1] there are certain circumstances in which a constructive trust arises by operation of law upon the occurrence of a certain set of facts. Such constructive trusts are known as institutional constructive trusts. These must be distinguished from remedial constructive trusts. The remedial constructive trust in this sense must not be confused with the 'constructive trust of a new model' as popularised by Denning MR. The 'new model' constructive trust constituted an attempt to upset property rights in favour of abstract principles of justice, and as such failed as the general interest of mankind in relative certainty of title prevailed, as it is bound to do, over judge-made law

---

[1] At p 87.

which tends towards the conclusion that all cases must be litigated before certainty can be achieved. The remedial constructive trust, as the term is used herein, refers to the constructive trust which is imposed by a court as a result of positive wrongdoing.

Wrongdoing by fiduciary

It is clear beyond doubt that where a trustee misapplies trust property any resulting gain is held by him on constructive trust for the trust's beneficiaries[2], and this is an institutional rather than a remedial constructive trust.

Wrongdoing by non-fiduciary

There are two cases in which a non-fiduciary may render himself liable as a fiduciary: he may incur both a personal obligation to repay and/or find a proprietary right created in an asset owned by him. These are cases where the non-fiduciary either assists the fiduciary in the disposition of assets in breach of his fiduciary obligation, or receives such assets for himself knowing them to have been transferred to him in breach of a fiduciary obligation.

These categories are known respectively as 'knowing assistance' and 'knowing receipt'. The terms are derived from Lord Selborne's speech in *Barnes v Addy*[3], and despite continued terminological onslaught these phrases have remained current, perhaps because they are almost perfectly descriptive.

There is no difference between the two personal liabilities. A person who knowingly[4] misappropriates trust assets himself is under no heavier personal liability than a person who knowingly assists him to do so. The old rule that an accessory could not be liable, even if he was dishonest, if his principal was not dishonest has now been swept away by the Privy Council in *Royal Brunei Airlines Sdn Bhd v Tan*[5], which has replaced the different tests with a single test of dishonesty. A person who dishonestly deals with trust property, either by receiving it or by assisting in its disposition, is personally liable in equity to the rightful owner thereof.

The dishonesty which is required in order to impose equitable liability is different from the test which is applied by the criminal law. Criminal dishonesty, the primary ingredient of common law theft, was described in primarily objective terms by Lane CJ in *R v Ghosh*[6]:

> In determining whether the prosecution has proved that the defendant was acting dishonestly, a jury must first of all decide whether according to the ordinary stand-

---

[2] *Boardman v Phipps* [1967] 2 AC 46, and *see* p 76 *above*.
[3] (1874) 9 Ch App 244.
[4] The point should be made here that, in addition to the usual issues of what level of suspicion indicates knowlege of a beneficial interest, an issue also arises of when information about a claimed beneficial interest becomes knowlege that it is valid (see *Carl Zeiss Stiftung v Herbert Smith & Co (No 2)* [1969] 2 Ch 276).
[5] [1995] 2 AC 378.
[6] [1982] QB 1053 at 1064.

ards of reasonable and honest people what was done was dishonest. If it was not dishonest by those standards, then that is the end of the matter and the prosecution fails.

If it was dishonest by those standards, then the jury must consider whether the defendant himself must have realised that what he was doing was by those standards dishonest. In most cases, where the actions are obviously dishonest by ordinary standards, there will be no doubt about it. It will be obvious that the defendant himself knew that he was acting dishonestly. It is dishonest for a defendant to act in a way which he knows ordinary people to consider to be dishonest, even if he asserts or genuinely believes that he is morally justified in acting as he did. For example, Robin Hood or those ardent anti-vivisectionists who remove animals from vivisection laboratories are acting dishonestly, even though they may consider themselves to be morally justified in doing what they do, because they know that ordinary people would consider these actions to be dishonest.

There is authority that the criminal and civil tests for dishonesty are identical[7]. However, in *Royal Brunei Airlines* Nicholls LJ rejected this proposition, and emphasised that the test to be applied for equitable liability was a purely objective one[8]:

The standard of what constitutes honest conduct is not subjective. Honesty is not an optional scale, with higher or lower values according to the moral standards of each individual. If a person knowingly appropriates another's property, he will not escape a finding of dishonesty simply because he sees nothing wrong with such behaviour.

The incorporation of the concept of 'constructive dishonesty', analogous to constructive knowledge, may provide some interesting lines of argument for the future, but is no more than an employment of a principle that everything is to be presumed against the defaulter in equity.

The test of dishonesty has replaced an earlier 'five-point scale' constructed in *Baden Delvaux*[9], which purported to analyse scientifically how much notice of a fact constituted constructive knowledge of it. Its demise is unmourned, although post-*Baden Delvaux* experience suggests that what has changed is the content of counsels' closing speeches rather than what it is sought to be proved in evidence.

The dishonest accessory is personally liable to the property's rightful owner. However, the recipient of trust property is, in addition to his personal liability, required to hand back trust property in his hands to the rightful owner along with any profits made from its use. The question of how much can be recovered is considered in Chapter 31 in the context of tracing, but there are a few points which require to be made here.

The first is in the context of the non-dishonest recipient. A person who receives property without knowing that it has been given to him in breach of

---

[7] Per Kerr LJ in *Att-Gen's Reference (No 2 of 1982)* [1984] QB 624.

[8] [1995] 2 AC 378 at 389.

[9] *Baden Delvaux and Lecuit v Société Générale pour Favouriser le Developpement du Commerce et de l'Industrie en France SA* [1983] BCLC 325.

trust is not only liable to return the property if he still has it, but incurs a personal liability in the amount of the property received which is not extinguished by a transfer on unless that transfer on is in the context of an act amounting to a change of position. It has been suggested that such a transferee is not to be treated as a constructive trustee for all purposes, and in particular he is not liable to repay with interest[10]. It is therefore still important in some cases to determine whether the recipient took the property with knowledge of the trust's existence. There is some authority that actual knowledge is necessary for this liability to arise[11], but the better view is that constructive knowledge suffices[12]. This apparently harsh result has been defended on the basis that restitutionary liability is receipt based, not fault based. It also seems that 'notice' in the context of a volunteer has a different meaning from 'notice' in the context of purchaser. Very little is required to affix a volunteer with notice, but in the context of a purchaser for value it seems that little short of actual knowledge renders him a constructive trustee of the property concerned[13].

In the context of recipient liability, there is a defence of ministerial receipt where a person receives property purely as a minister of another. The distinction here is benefit; where a person has received property purely for the benefit of another then he is not liable if that property turns out to be trust property. The defence was successful in *Agip (Africa) Ltd v Jackson*[14] in respect of persons who had simply acted as conduits for money. But note that if such dealing is dishonest then the defence of ministerial receipt does not avail against a claim based upon knowing assistance. A bank, when it receives money from a depositor, receives it as principal and not as minister, and thus there is no defence of ministerial receipt available[15].

Note that where there is a claim for knowing receipt there is often a common law claim for money had and received.

Equitable personal liability

In addition to the constructive trustee's obligation to transfer the property subject to the trust to its beneficial owner, a constructive trustee is under a separate personal liability to make up any loss to the beneficiary which results

[10] Goff & Jones, *The Law of Restitution*, 5th edn (Sweet & Maxwell, 1993), p 672.

[11] *Re Montagu's ST* [1987] Ch 264; *Westdeutche Landesbank Girozentrale v Islington LBC* [1996] AC 669; *Powell v Thompson* [1991] 1 NZLR 597; *Royal Brunei Airlines Sdn Bhd v Tan* [1995] 2 AC 378.

[12] *Belmont Finance Corp v Williams Furniture Ltd (No 2)* [1980] 1 All ER 393; *Eagle Trust v SBC Securities Ltd* [1993] 1 WLR 484; *El Ajou v Dollar Land Holdings plc* [1993] 3 All ER 717.

[13] *Polly Peck Int'l plc v Nadir (No 2)* [1992] 4 All ER 769; *Eagle Trust v SBC Securities Ltd* [1993] 1 WLR 484; *Cowan de Groot Properties Ltd v Eagle Trust plc* [1992] 4 All ER 700; *El Ajou v Dollar Land Holdings plc* [1993] 3 All ER 717 (at first instance).

[14] [1990] Ch 265.

[15] [1996] JBL 165 (M Bryan); Hanbury & Martin, *Modern Equity*, 15th edn (Sweet & Maxwell, 1997), p 302.

from his act. Equitable personal liability is imposed on any person who is in breach of an equitable obligation. The liability is compensatory, the rule being that the fiduciary must make good any detriment to the beneficiaries caused by his act. The liability is assessed on a restitutionary basis, and the ordinary principles of remoteness and foreseeability are not used. This in theory places upon the fiduciary an absolute and unlimited obligation to make good any detriment to the beneficiary, no matter how remote or peripherally related to the fiduciary's default. However, some limits have been placed on the obligation in *Target Holdings Ltd v Redferns (a firm)*[16], in which a trivial breach of an obligation by a trustee occurred in a transaction in which the beneficiary lost £1m. Lord Browne-Wilkinson said that the equitable personal liability was not in fact infinite, but was restricted to those losses which could be seen with hindsight to have resulted from the breach of duty[17]. This has been formulated as a rule that 'Equity does not require a [fiduciary] to compensate for a loss which would have occurred had there been no breach of trust'[18].

Note that these principles only apply where the breach is one of fiduciary duty rather than of a duty owed by a fiduciary. The breach must be one of a duty of a type which is characteristic of the fiduciary relationship. Where the breach is of an ordinary duty the ordinary common law rule applies[19]. A fiduciary is a fiduciary in respect of a particular duty, and not at large. My solicitor is my fiduciary as regards my legal affairs, and owes me a fiduciary duty to conduct them in my best interests. However, if I give him my watch to look after he is not my fiduciary *qua* solicitor, since safekeeping of valuables is no part of a solicitor's duty. As La Forest J said in *Lac Minerals Ltd v International Corona Ltd*: 'not every legal claim arising out of a relationship with fiduciary incidents will give rise to a claim for breach of fiduciary duty'[20].

Equitable personal liability is not confined to defaulting trustees. In *Re Diplock*[21] it was held that where an innocent volunteer receives trust property, in addition to the beneficiaries' proprietary interest in the property received, the beneficiaries also have a personal claim against the innocent volunteers. This draconian finding amounts to a rule that where any person receives money which is rightfully the property of another, he is in equity bound to pay to that other the relevant amount regardless of whether he still owns it. This rule thus recreates the common law rule in relation to the action for money had and received to the effect that the action accrues and is completed at the time of receipt. Thus if A wrongfully gives £1,000 of trust property to B, who gives it in turn to C, then both B and C are liable to the beneficiary in the sum of £1,000, although the beneficiary is not permitted to recover more than £1,000 in total from the two together. There are, however, a number of important

[16] [1996] 1 AC 421.
[17] Contrast *Bristol & West BS v May May & Merrimans* [1996] 2 All ER 801, in which the loss suffered was caused (in part) by the breach of trust, in which the defendants were held to be liable in full for the loss.
[18] Hanbury & Martin (*see* fn 15 *above*), p 636.
[19] *Bristol & West Building Society v Mothew* [1996] 4 All ER 698.
[20] (1989) 61 DLR (4th) at 28.
[21] [1948] Ch 465.

restrictions on this right. First, it lies for the principal sum alone, without interest and credit for any accrual through its investment. Secondly, the claim against the volunteer and subsequent transferees is for such amount as may not be recovered from the trustee, who is primarily liable. Thirdly, there is some authority that the doctrine applies only to the administration of estates and does not arise in the context of *inter vivos* settlements[22].

The severity of this rule is much mitigated by the subsequent recognition of the defence of change of position, which applies both to the proprietary claim for return of the property and to the personal claim.

---

[22] Per Lord Simonds in *Ministry of Health v Simpson* [1951] AC 251 at 265–6, although there are dicta to the contrary in *Butler v Broadhead* [1975] Ch 97 and *Re J Leslie Engineers Co Ltd* [1976] 1 WLR 292.

Chapter 32

Following and Tracing at Law and in Equity

The law of following and tracing is one of the more complex areas of English law. The distinction between the two concepts may be easily expressed—following is an assertion of an existing proprietary right against an asset, whereas tracing is the name of the legal process by which one asset is deemed to be another.

Following

Following is the process whereby title to an asset is vindicated. If you steal my bicycle, it remains mine. If you give it away, it remains mine. If you sell it to a purchaser for value without notice, it remains mine. If he in turn sells it on, it remains mine. No matter how many hands it passes through, it is still mine unless at some stage it is disposed of in such a fashion as to pass good title to the recipient. In the case of goods this is very difficult: now that the sale in market overt has been abolished, none of the remaining exceptions to the rule of *nemo dat quod non habet* are of much practical assistance to the thief. In the case of money and negotiable instruments, by contrast, it is very easy: as soon as the instrument is passed to another for value without notice my title to it is extinguished.

Following operates in equity as well as in law. If I have an equitable interest in property which is held by a trustee, in principle if the trustee transfers the property to another I can assert my equitable interest against that other. In practice the trustee can extinguish my right with ease by making a disposition to a purchaser for value without notice of my interest, but in principle the rule is the same for equitable as for legal interests—ownership endures until it is extinguished, and whilst it endures the relevant property can be claimed from whatever hand it has come to.

Tracing begins where following ends. Where a thing in which I have a property right has been dealt with so that my property right in it is extinguished, the rules of tracing sometimes allow me to assert a property right against other property which is in some way connected with the original property. Given that both following and tracing are proprietary remedies for wrongs, the wrongs concerned can be grouped as follows: following is the remedy for wrongful transfers which do not pass title; tracing is the remedy for wrongful transfers which do pass title.

Tracing

English law has two distinct systems of tracing—tracing at law and tracing in equity. This distinction is frequently criticised, and has been regularly declared redundant, impractical and characterised as being based on arbitrary rules. There is some force in many of these criticisms. But common law and equitable tracing are different tools designed for different tasks, and in order to understand the law of tracing as it currently exists in England it is important to keep the distinction in mind.

Tracing is a legal calculus by which a wrong is related to a remedy. Thus a prerequisite of tracing is a wrong and, since tracing is a proprietary remedy, the relevant wrong must be one relating to property (eg defamation does not initiate an application of the doctrine of tracing)[1]. Proprietary wrongs may themselves be divided into those which do, and those which do not, involve the passing of title. These categories may very loosely be rendered as 'theft' and 'fraud'. In this chapter neither term is used in any technical sense, but the two together express the division. Where a person obtains property of mine from me without my consent or approval he may be said to have stolen it. Where a person procures a transfer by me of my property to him in a wrongful way, he may be said to have been fraudulent. These two categories between them embrace the universe of wrongful transfers.

Common law tracing and wrongs which do not pass title

The primary remedy in the case of theft is the retaking of possession of the property. In terms of property law, theft is a nullity: my property after being stolen is as much my property as it was before it was stolen, and if I can locate it I can reclaim it. A difficulty arises, though, where the thief has disposed of the property in such a fashion as to give the disponee good title to it. In the case of goods, and now that the market overt doctrine has been abolished, this is exceedingly difficult—a thief cannot be a mercantile agent (since he does not receive the property as agent); neither is he a buyer or seller in possession, and nor can he by his conduct raise an estoppel against the true owner. However, it almost inevitably occurs in two important cases: mixing, and negotiable instruments and money. In both cases it is important to determine what the remedy should be against the thief, since it cannot be allowed that by effecting a successful disposition of the stolen property for value he can thereby render himself absolute owner of the value received, for this would enable him to improve his position as against the true owner of the original property.

Equitable and legal tracing are different tools which perform different tasks. Legal tracing, like legal following, is a tool for the recovery of stolen property, which endures for as long as the property can be identified and gives out

---

[1] This appears logically necessary, but in fact is not. An early example of personal wrongs giving rise to proprietary remedies was the rule of deodand, by which an item which caused a person's death was forfeited by its owner and vested in the dead man's estate. Deodand was abolished in 1846 shortly after executors began to seek to apply it to railway accidents (Holdsworth, *History of English Law*, vol II, p 47).

when it cannot. This reflects the primacy of sanctity of title in the common law. At common law following is the strong claim, and tracing an incident. The common law knows no defence of purchaser for value without notice. At common law the rule is *nemo dat quod non habet* and an item which has been stolen remains the property of its owner until it is destroyed. Thus the primary remedy at common law is following. It is only if the item followed has evaporated that it is necessary to have recourse to the doctrines of tracing.

Common law tracing will be found, upon inspection, to apply only in such cases. Where a person, having no title to property at all, manages to deal with it in such a way as to create a new title in a third party, then common law tracing will take effect to create for the benefit of the original owner of the property an ownership right in the exchange product. This anomalous exception to the ordinary common law rules of title is a product of the strong policy approach that every nerve should be strained to prevent a thief benefiting from his theft. The category is, of course, slightly wider than pure theft, since theft is not the only way in which a person may come to occupy a position in which he can exchange the property of another for his own benefit, and this is why I have used the slightly cumbrous heading of 'wrongs which do not pass title'. However any situation which triggers common law tracing will be found, on analysis, to be based upon the operation of a transfer of property under an exception to the rule of *nemo dat quod non habet*.

Equity and wrongs which pass title

In general, equity is the sole recourse for wrongs which pass title. Primarily within such recourse is the declaration of constructive trust, although equitable tracing may also be pressed into action where assets acquired as trust assets or in breach of fiduciary duty have subsequently been misapplied. The main issue here is why equitable tracing should only be applied in the context of wrongs which arise in breach of a fiduciary duty. This requirement of equity has been much criticised, and yet it is defensible upon its own terms.

It is a truism of English law that there can be no equitable tracing against a thief. Equitable tracing begins with a valid transfer of title to property which it is sought to reverse or to amend. This transfer can be one either from the beneficiary to a third party, or to a third party of property which should have been transferred to the beneficiary. The distinction from legal tracing is that legal tracing is triggered automatically by the breach of the *nemo dat* principle, regardless of the wrongfulness or otherwise of the act[2]. Equitable tracing is triggered by a wrongful act. The court of equity does not—and should not—have an absolute discretion to reverse any property transaction which it considers unconscionable, but has a strictly defined discretion in respect of those wrongs which are classified as 'breach of fiduciary duty'. This is in fact a necessary provision, since the uncertainty which would be introduced into commercial life if a court of equity could reverse all transfers of property of

---

[2] *F C Jones & Sons v Jones* [1996] 3 WLR 703.

which it disapproved would be substantial. Legal tracing is part of the common law's armoury of weapons against theft, whereas equitable tracing is part of equity's armoury of weapons against fraud.

This dichotomy breaks down where money is concerned. The concepts of currency and negotiability import the doctrines, if not the language, of the purchaser for value without notice into the common law. Thus the victim of a financial theft finds himself at common law in the position of the equitable plaintiff, in that his right to follow has been extinguished. Unless he has access to the equitable right to trace, common law tracing is unlikely to provide a satisfactory remedy. This position illustrates something which has been a theme throughout this book: that the old law of goods is incapable of accommodating the new world of finance. Professor Birks[3] has argued for a fusion of the rules of equitable and legal tracing, but this would be to ignore the different roles which the two doctrines play in the context of their two systems. Paul Matthews[4] demonstrates the chaos which can be wrought applying some of the more complex modern ideas of tracing to a bicycle rather than to a sum of money—a conclusion which supports the idea that there is nothing wrong with legal or equitable tracing, but merely with our law of money and monetary obligations. A unified law of tracing implies a unified law of title, and the ideas of separate legal and equitable title are not yet so archaic that they may cheerfully be discarded. The minimum necessary change is the recognition of the distinctly different nature of money claims from ordinary common law claims, and the acceptance of some of the concepts involved in equitable tracing to be applied in the context of money claims. Even this change may be softened to a simple acceptance that equitable tracing should be available in all cases involving financial misappropriation, whether legal or equitable. However, these are matters far beyond the scope of this work.

Common law tracing

The mechanism whereby the true owner of stolen property may recover substitute property from the thief is known as legal tracing. It was explained by Lord Ellenborough in *Taylor v Plumer*[5]:

> It makes no difference in reason or law into what other form, different from the original, the change may have been made, whether it be into that of promissory notes for the security of the money which was produced by the sale of the goods of the principal, as in *Scott v Surman*[6], or into other merchandise, as in *Whitcomb v Jacob*[7], for the product of or substitute for the original thing still follows the nature of the thing itself, as long as it can be ascertained to be such, and the right only ceases where the means of ascertainment fail ...

---

[3] *Making Commercial Law* (OUP, 1997).
[4] 'The Legal and Moral Limits of Common Law Tracing' in *Laundering and Tracing*, P Birks (ed) (OUP, 1995, pp 23–72).
[5] (1815) 3 M & S 562.
[6] (1742) Willes 400.
[7] (1710) Salk 160.

The most evident application of this principle is in cash transactions. Where a person steals money and pays it into a bank account, he is effecting an exchange whereby he gives up title to one asset (the money) in exchange for receiving a new asset (the debt due from the bank). Yet because he had no title to the money he can acquire no better title to the exchange asset.

The facts of *Taylor v Plumer* were that a thief had stolen money and expended some of it on the purchase of securities. The thief was apprehended and made bankrupt, and litigation ensued between the money's rightful owner and the thief's trustee in bankruptcy over the purchase's property law consequences. The trustee in bankruptcy argued that the rightful owner had no property right in the securities, but merely a personal right to be repaid an amount of money equivalent to the amount stolen. It was held that, since the securities were identifiably the product of the stolen money, they could be recovered by the true owner.

Taylor v Plumer was relied on in *Banque Belge pour L'Etranger v Hambrouck*[8], in which money belonging to the Banque Belge was stolen by Hambrouck, credited to his account at Bank Y, withdrawn by him in cash and paid to his mistress, who deposited it in Bank Z. Upon discovering the theft, the question arose over who was the owner of the money remaining in the account at Bank Z. The case proceeded on the basis that the accounts at Bank Y and Bank Z had not contained at any material time any money other than that originally drawn by Hambrouck from Banque Belge, that there had therefore been no mixing, and that the mistress was not a transferee for value[9].

The Court of Appeal held that since there had been no mixing of money, the amount remaining could be said to be Banque Belge's money at common law. This decision is at first glance surprising. Scrutton LJ said in his judgment: 'payment into Hambrouck's bank, and his drawing out other money in satisfaction, had changed its identity'[10], and went on to hold that the only claim which the Banque Belge had to the money was in equity. However, both Bankes and Atkin LLJ held that the money was Banque Belge's property at law, Atkin LJ explaining that 'the product of, or substitute for, the original thing ... follows the nature of the thing itself'.

Scrutton LJ's speech makes it clear that the decision in *Banque Belge*, like that in *Taylor v Plumer*, can be entirely explained by reference to the ordinary rules of equity. However, Atkin J's judgment clearly follows Lord Ellenborough's lead in suggesting that legal title to property can, after being extinguished in one asset, be reincarnated in another. This point has recently been considered in *Lipkin Gorman v Karpnale*[11], in which Lord Goff suggested that in fact legal title does not inhere automatically in a substitute asset at the moment of acquisition, but can be created subsequently to the acquisition by an election by the original asset's owner 'to assert his title to the product in place of the original authority'.

---

[8] [1921] 1 KB 321.
[9] A concession undoubtedly resented and controverted by mistresses worldwide.
[10] At pp 329–30.
[11] [1991] 2 AC 548.

The existence of common law tracing has been roundly and regularly attacked. Based as it is in a strong public policy bias to provide a remedy for owners against thieves, it sometimes sits ill with the certainties of conveyancing. The validity of the *Taylor v Plumer* decision has been impugned[12], and it has been said with some confidence that at English law 'there are not and never were any common law rights in respect of substitute assets'[13]. Yet the idea was recently supported by the Court of Appeal in *F C Jones & Sons v Jones*[14], in which the court considered the academic authorities mustered against the idea of common law tracing but concluded that, even though *Taylor* may be impugned in that direction, *Banque Belge* and *Lipkin Gorman* were now clear authority for the doctrine's existence. It is clear from the judge's reasoning that he was prepared to approach the issue on the basis that *communis error fecit ius*, but nonetheless unless the House of Lords is prepared to reconsider and reverse its own decision in *Lipkin Gorman*, it seems that the existence of common law tracing has now been convincingly established.

Jones v Jones is an interesting case, not least because it is one of the very few common law tracing cases not concerned with ordinary theft. *Taylor* itself was a clear case of theft; *Banque Belge* involved theft via stolen bank drafts; and *Lipkin Gorman* involved a partner stealing from a partnership[15]. In *Jones* the initial transfer was made by a bankrupt after the commission of an act of bankruptcy, an act which under the then prevailing bankruptcy legislation was incapable of passing any interest at all to the transferee, and placed her, in effect, in the position of a thief. It is notable that absent this provision, common law tracing would not have been available—indeed Millet J went out of his way to distinguish the transfer from one under a voidable or a void title, thereby suggesting that in neither of these cases would legal tracing have been available[16], and this seems to support the conclusion that common tracing is only available in cases of theft, whether actual or constructive.

Mixtures

A thief can affect title to stolen property other than money by mixing it. Where stolen property is mixed with the thief's own property, the punitive rule is applied that the whole of the mixture belongs to the innocent party[17]. Thus if a thief steals my sack of grain and mixes it with his, the combined bulk belongs to me. However, because of the different rule which applies to mixtures

---

[12] Lionel Smith, 'Equity in the court of King's Bench' [1995] LMCLQ 240.

[13] Birks, 'Overview' in *Laundering and Tracing*, P Birks (ed) (1995, Oxford University Press), p 298. In the same work Paul Mathews in 'Limits of Common Law Tracing' investigates the idea that such a concept may exist for goods exchanged for other goods, and has concluded that there is no such right at law.

[14] [1996] 4 All ER 721.

[15] This sounds impossible, since the partner is in effect stealing from himself. However the rule is that where he obtains partnership funds in breach of his authority, those funds vest in him absolutely and cease to be the partnership's property (see *Union Bank of Australia Ltd v McClintock* [1922] 1 AC 240 and *Commercial Banking Co of Sydney Ltd v Mann* [1961] AC 1.

[16] [1996] 4 All ER 721 at 726.

[17] *The Ypattiana* [1987] 3 All ER 839.

of *specie,* if a thief steals my £10 note, places it in his wallet next to his own £10 note such that the two are indistinguishable, and is apprehended immediately thereafter, my claim is only to one £10 note, since mixtures of money create a *commixtio* rather than a *confusio*[18].

Yet these facts could only be proved in a very exceptional situation. The facts of any given theft of money are such that the best that can be proved is that the defendant, having stolen £100, was subsequently found in possession of £100. In such a case there is no room for the application of the ordinary rules of legal tracing, since it is impossible to demonstrate a 'trail of exchanges'. It is in this sense that the words of Lord Ellenborough should be understood when he said that[19]

> the means of ascertainment fail ... when the subject is turned into money, and mixed and confounded in a general mass of the same description. The difficulty which arises in such a case is a difficulty of fact, and not of law, and the dictum that money has no ear-mark must be understood in the same way; i.e. as predicated only of an undivided and undistinguishable mass of current money. But money in a bag or otherwise kept apart from other money, guineas, or other coin marked (if the fact were so) for the purpose of being distinguished, are so far ear-marked as to fall within the rule on this subject ...

The most commonly encountered example of mixing is that of money, and the most usual transfer of physical money is payment into a bank account. Where this happens, the result is that title to the notes and coins is transferred absolutely to the bank, which in exchange creates a chose in action against it. The terms of this chose in action are determined by the terms of the contract between banker and customer and any specific agreement made at the time of the deposit[20]. The same is true where money is transferred from one bank account to another[21].

Where a person pays money which he owns into an account which contains other money of his own, then there is a mixing, which in this case is neither a *commixtio* nor a *confusio* but a *specificatio*. The account balance cannot be re-divided back into its component parts since it is now a new thing. Now in such a case the proprietary base which underlies common law tracing is destroyed. The rule on tortious mixings (*The Ypattiana*—if it applies at all) does not apply to *specificatio*, but only to *confusio*. Thus there is no basis in common law upon which the victim of the theft can point to the newly created

---

[18] *See* pp 61–2 *above*.

[19] *Taylor* is criticised on the ground that Lord Ellenborough was in fact giving a decision about equitable tracing, and not tracing in common law (see L Smith, 'Equity in the Court of King's Bench' [1995] LMCLQ 240.). However, in *F C Jones & Sons v Jones* [1996] 3 WLR 703, Millett LJ said that even if true this did not mean that the common law could not recognise claims to substitute assets—perhaps a humpty-dumpty attitude to precedent.

[20] Eg money paid into a high-interest account which prohibits withdrawal for a period.

[21] *R v Preddy* [1996] AC 815 which, pointing out as it did something which civil lawyers had known for years, caught criminal lawyers completely by surprise and necessitated an immediate amendment to the Theft Act 1968 to prevent the immediate acquittal of half of the fraudsters then in custody.

asset and say 'that is mine'.

This point may be most easily explained by considering the different possible analyses of the mixtures available to a thief. In the case of stolen specie the rule of *commixtio* solves all possible problems bar one: where the thief has mixed specie stolen from two or more persons and then spent some, but not all, of it. In this case it seems clear that the ordinary rule of wrongful mixing applies, and a joint tenancy is created. However, where a thief steals specie from a person and pays it into a bank account, if the bank account already contains his own money then he has effected a *specificatio*. If the account contains nothing at all then the account balance is a simple exchange product, which becomes the property of the money's owner[22]. If the account balance contains money which is already the property of another on this basis, then it would seem that a joint tenancy is created since the ordinary rules of wrongful mixing apply to bank account balances. It is only physical specie which is subject to the special rule of *commixtio*. Thus the only situation in which any objection may be raised to the rules of law is where the thief mixes the stolen money with his own in such a way as to extinguish the previous owners' right to it.

The conventional explanation for the reason that equity can trace into a mixed fund is that equity can impose a charge upon the mixed fund in the plaintiff's favour[23]. It may be objected to this that at law the same result could be obtained by creating a joint tenancy in the specified asset. The problem seems to be that a *specificatio* does not and cannot give rise to a joint tenancy in the new thing created, since it is the very essence of *specificatio* that title to the new thing is vested solely in the specificator.

An interesting issue relating to mixtures arises in the context of inter-bank payments. In *Agip (Africa) v Jackson*[24] the question arose whether for payments of unmixed funds through the clearing system the fact of the mixture within the clearing system brought into effect the supposed rule that at common law one cannot trace through a mixture. A relatively simple series of transactions, involving multiple bank transfers in different jurisdictions, had been entered into in order to launder stolen money. The thief had his bank in Tunis instruct a London bank to pay money to the defendants. The Tunis bank subsequently instructed a New York bank to reimburse the London bank. The payments were in dollars, and settlement between the New York and London banks was therefore through the New York interbank clearing system, in which banks settled the net balances of their total transactions for a business day. Two barriers to common law tracing were identified on these facts. First, the payment out to the defendants made prior to the reimbursement of the bank making the payment seems to have been overcome, since the requirement for exchange cannot really be contemporaneous. Secondly, though, the net settlement system in use in the New York interbank clearing rendered tracing impossible, since the mixing of moneys involved created exactly the difficulty

---

[22] *Banque Belge pour L'Etranger v Hanbrouk* [1921] 1 KB 321.
[23] *Re Diplock* [1948] Ch 465.
[24] [1991] Ch 547.

identified by Lord Ellenborough in *Taylor v Plumer*. It was held that there could be no tracing through this clearing system.

This decision has been criticised as craven, but has been at least approved, if not specifically followed[25]. It is submitted that it is incorrect in law. Where a payment is made by A to B by an interbank payment, the correct analysis of the position is that a debt owed by A's bank to A disappears, and a debt owed by B's bank to B is created. The way in which the banks concerned choose to settle the transaction between themselves is of not the slightest relevance to anyone, and especially not the account holders. The point may be tested in this way. If instructions of such a kind are given, the relevant accounts credited and debited, and immediately thereafter the US clearing system were to stop, the failure or otherwise of the clearing system would have no substantial effect on the position as between each bank and its customer. A would have transferred value to B, quite regardless of the interbank settlement system. On the exchange product analysis deployed in *Jones*, the asset in B's hands is the direct exchange product of the asset formerly in A's hands, and in this respect *Jones* may be taken to have overruled *Agip (Africa)*.

It can be seen, then, that tracing at law is confined to dealings with things. In the language of Smith[26] common law tracing is not in fact an exercise in tracing but in following, with the exchange product hypothesis engrafted onto it as a quasi-criminal provision. It therefore runs foul of the problem that the law recognises no estates in personalty, and, perhaps more importantly, recognises no such doctrine as the remedial joint tenancy. The law is concerned only with title, which means with whole assets. This conservatism on the part of the common law is frequently deprecated by those whose commitment to absolute justice outweighs their commitment to certainty of title. This dispute rages on in the field of real property, where the relative ease of investigation of title validates the former position. In the field of personal property, where 'possession is everything and there is no time to investigate title'[27], the overwhelming requirement for certainty of title to goods and to intangibles seems to set the opponents of the existing methodology of legal tracing a challenge to which they have not yet begun to respond.

Equitable tracing

Equitable tracing supplements common law tracing in two important respects. One is the mixture of money in a bank account described above as a *specificatio*, where the common law leaves the money's original owner without a remedy. The other, and far more important, is where wrongs have the effect of vesting the plaintiff's property in the wrongdoer or in a person who stands in the wrongdoer's shoes[28].

---

[25] *Nimmo v Westpac Banking Corp* [1993] 3 NZLR 218; *Bank Tejarat v Hong Kong and Shanghai Banking Corp (CI) Ltd* [1995] 1 Lloyd's Rep 239.

[26] *The Law of Tracing* (1997).

[27] Per Lindley LJ in *Manchester Trust v Furness* [1985] 2 QB 539 at 545.

[28] Ie a donee or any other person other than a purchaser for value without notice.

Requirement for fiduciary obligation

Equitable tracing is a proprietary calculus which gives rise to a declaration that property previously vested in one person is now vested in another. It disturbs title, upsets transactions and creates litigation. In the interests of promoting certainty of title, the Courts of Equity were not prepared to make equitable tracing available for all cases of wrongdoing, but confined themselves to cases in which there was an equitable wrong which required an equitable remedy. An equitable wrong may be characterised as a wrong done in breach of a duty recognised by equity (a fiduciary duty). The nature and incidents of a fiduciary duty are considered above at pp 74–8, but what is important at this stage is that a fiduciary relationship can almost be characterised as a relationship by which one person is given the power to effect common law title to the assets of another, either by having such title vested in him, as a trustee; or by being given power to acquire or dispose of them, as an agent or company director; or in a number of other ways. As noted above, a breach of fiduciary duty must be distinguished from one of a duty by a fiduciary, and it is only the former which gives rise to the right to trace. The equitable right to trace is therefore confined within the narrowest possible compass compatible with the general principle that if a man having a power to deal with the another's assets, and under a duty to deal with those assets for that other's benefit, deals with them otherwise, then he is liable for any loss which his breach of duty causes. Again, the fact that any disposition of such property is likely to divest the principal of even his equitable interest in it has the wholly virtuous side-effect that it is only the wrongdoer's assets which are subject to the proprietary right, and that that right can therefore be expanded beyond its normal compass without fear of interference with trade. The requirement for a fiduciary relationship before an equitable right to trace arises may in this way be seen as inherent in the concept of equitable tracing.

Equity and mixing

Where a person has mixed property wrongfully obtained with his own, the equitable owner has a charge over the mixed fund. For this purpose the equitable owner is referred to as a 'beneficiary', although the availability of equitable tracing is not confined to beneficiaries under formal trusts, and the wrongful mixer as a trustee. The rule of *specificatio* is reversed, such that the beneficiary is entitled 'to every portion of the blended property which the trustee cannot prove to be his own'[29]. If the mixed property has been invested the beneficiary is entitled to the whole of the profit which has accrued where the mixed fund has been used to enter into a transaction which the trustee could not have entered into on his own account[30], although where the outcome is merely that the trustee has purchased more of a particular investment than

---

[29] *Lewin on Trusts*, 16th edn, p 223, approved in *Re Tilley's Will Trust* [1967] Ch 1179 at 1182.
[30] *Paul A Davies (Australia) Pty Ltd v Davies* [1983] 1 NSWLR 440.

he otherwise would, the profits are shared rateably[31]. Thus, where a trustee has mixed a beneficiary's £100,000 with his own £100,000 to buy a £200,000 house, any capital gain on the house belongs exclusively to the beneficiary. However, where he has used the money to buy £200,000 of ICI shares, the capital gain on the shares is apportioned rateably.

There are limits to the doctrines of tracing into mixtures. It was pointed out in *Space Investments Ltd v Canadian Imperial Bank of Commerce Trust Co (Bahamas) Ltd*[32] that in pure theory, where a trustee has mixed trust property with his own, then the proper object of the tracing claim is the whole of the trustee's assets. However, in *Re Goldcorp Exchange Ltd*[33] this was disapproved as being contrary to both the general principles of distribution of assets upon insolvency[34] and the specific rules of tracing, which relate to mixed funds rather than to mixed assets generally. It seems therefore that the proprietary remedy against the trustee is limited to the particular asset with which the trust asset is mixed. In *Goldcorp* the point at issue was that the property which it was sought to trace had not been mixed with any particular assets of the company but had been swallowed up in the company's general funds. It was held that this was sufficient to extinguish any proprietary claim. The point was further considered in *Bishopsgate Investment Management Ltd v Homan*[35], in which the issue was money transferred to the trustee which had been employed to reduce the overdraft on a bank account rather than mixed with a specific fund, and again it was held that in the absence of a specific mixed fund there was no scope for the doctrine of equitable tracing to apply.

The true usefulness of the equitable doctrine of tracing is most clearly seen in the context of the problem which is created at common law by the payment of funds into a bank account. Here, equity imposes a charge over the resulting debt due from the bank to the trustee in the beneficiary's favour[36]. However, the amount of the charge is reckoned according to a precise calculus developed by equity. The basis for this is to be found in *Re Hallett's Estate*[37], in which it was said that whenever an act can be done rightfully 'a man is not allowed to say, against the person entitled to the property or the right, that he has done it wrongfully'[38]. In other words, the trustee cannot claim any money out of the fund if in order to do so he would have to say that he had misapplied

---

[31] *Australian Postal Corp'n v Lutak* (1991) 21 NSWLR 584. In *Re Tilley's Will Trusts, above*, the beneficiaries were held to have no interest at all in the profits made, since the trust moneys were negligible relative to the amount of capital employed by the trustee. This is an exceptional case, and the decision is not free from doubt.

[32] [1986] 1 WLR 1072. The case also appears to disregard the ordinary law relating to the nature of a bank deposit. It may be that special considerations arise in the (very unusual) case in which a bank is itself a trustee, but where (as is usual) the bank exercises its trustee function through a special trust company there is no more reason for disregarding the corporate veil between bank and trust company than there would be in any other case.

[33] [1995] 1 AC 74.

[34] If the trustee is not insolvent he is good for the personal claim and the proprietary issue does not arise.

[35] [1995] Ch 211.

[36] *Re Diplock* [1948] Ch 465.

[37] (1880) 13 Ch D 696.

[38] At 727.

trust moneys in making any payment which was not in accordance with his trust. Thus, where the trustee has drawn £100 out of the account to spend on himself, he may not deny that the money taken out was part of that money which he himself contributed. Equity thus goes through the books related to the fund, matching contributions and withdrawals, and applies each withdrawal against a relevant contribution until the contribution of one party is exhausted. Only then does it treat any withdrawal as being wrongful[39]. So, where a trustee has mixed £10,000 of his own with £10,000 belonging to a beneficiary and spent £12,000 of it in such a fashion that there is no property attributable to it, the balance is taken to be the beneficiary's property since the trustee is taken to have spent £10,000 of his own before touching the trust monies. But note that if some of the money had been spent on the purchase of valuable property, the property would have constituted trust property in the trustee's hands and would have been subject to the beneficiary's claims in priority to his own[40]. The same is true if the money is transferred into another account belonging to the trustee—the contents of that account thereby becomes part of the fund over which the beneficiary's charge may be asserted[41]. Professor Martin[42] suggests that such property remains part of a single trust fund, such that where a third beneficiary's money is subsequently mixed with the fund, that third beneficiary is entitled to a charge over the property purchased. This is close to the idea of 'backward tracing', which occurs where the trustee uses trust funds to discharge a debt incurred in the acquisition of property. Backward tracing has been condemned as contrary to the ordinary rules of tracing, but appears to be consistent with the objectives of the tracing rules and has received some judicial[43] and academic[44] support.

Backward tracing is closely related to the acquisition of a property interest by subrogation. Where A uses trust money to discharge his mortgage, the beneficiaries are subrogated to the lender's rights in respect of the property charged[45]. However, a person may only be subrogated to an existing right: if a trustee purchases a car on the strength of an unsecured personal loan and subsequently discharges the loan out of the trust fund, it is probable that the beneficiary acquires no interest in the car[46].

Because equity examines the source of any particular balance on any bank account, the equitable claim is liable to a defence that the trust money has

---

[39] The rule in *Re Hallett* seems to be discretionary, and both the US (*Cunningham v Brown*, 265 US 1 44 Sup Ct 424) and the English (*Re Eastern Capital Futures Ltd* [1989] BCLC 371) courts have refused to research individual account transactions where the volume of bookkeeping involved is very large.

[40] *Re Oatway* [1903] 2 Ch 356.

[41] *El Ajou v Dollar Land Holdings plc* [1993] 3 All ER 717.

[42] Hanbury & Martin, *Modern Equity* , 15th edn (Sweet & Maxwell, 1997), p 671.

[43] Per Dillon LJ in *Bishopsgate Investment Management Ltd v Homan* [1995] Ch 211.

[44] Prof D Hayton, 'Equity's Identification Rules' in *Laundering and Tracing*, P Birks (ed) (1995), p 18.

[45] *Boscawen v Bajwa* [1996] 1 WLR 328, in effect overturning dicta to the contrary in *Re Diplock* [1948] Ch 465.

[46] Although on the basis of the decision in *Napier and Ettrick (Lord) v Kershaw* [1993] AC 713 the beneficiary may have a lien upon it. It is not, however, clear whether this case is authority for any general proposition of law or is confined to insurance claims.

been completely or partially dissipated. If trust monies are mixed in an account whose balance falls to zero, it must follow that the trust monies have been spent, and any subsequent amounts credited to that account are not subject to any charge in the beneficiaries' favour. This argument applies to any other intermediate balance, such that if £10,000 of trust monies are paid into a mixed account which is subsequently depleted to a balance of £100, the beneficiaries' proprietary claim is limited to £100 regardless of the ultimate account balance[47].

Where there has been a mixing of the property of two trusts by the trustee, in principle the structure which is applied is that of co-ownership; thus, where trust assets have been mixed the beneficiaries are entitled to the mixture in proportion to their contributions[48]. However, in the case of mixing money in a bank account the rule in *Clayton's Case*[49] is applied. This rule is to the effect that as between innocents, where the only consideration is of where the inevitable loss will fall, contributions and withdrawals are dealt with on a first in, first out basis. Thus where £100 of beneficiary A's money is paid into an empty bank account, and subsequently £100 of beneficiary B's money is paid in, if the trustee withdraws £80 and spends it before going bankrupt the remaining £120 is held to belong as to £20 to A and £100 to B. There is no particular justice to this rule, but merely an acknowledgement that where equities are equal a mechanical formula must suffice. Note that the operation of this rule is displaced by evidence of a contrary intention on the part of any person. Thus if A and B in the above example had consented to the mixing on the basis that their money would be pooled, then they share equally in the resulting balance[50].

Equitable defence of change of position

The purchaser for value without notice of trust property is impervious to a claim for its return, since he is equity's darling. However, the innocent volunteer takes the property subject to any existing interest in it. Clearly, if he takes the money, pays it into a bank account and thinks no more about it then he should be required in equity to return it to its rightful owner, and this is indeed the case. But this is rarely the act of a donee of even a small sum of money. In such a case the courts recognise a defence of 'change of position' to the claim for return of the trust property where after receipt of the benefit circumstances have so changed that it would be inequitable to require its return[51]. The bare bones of the defence of change of position are still being fleshed out by the courts, but the following propositions appear from the existing decided cases.

(1) The defence is not available to someone who had actual or constructive notice of the interest's existence[52].

---

[47] *Roscoe v Winder* [1915] 1 Ch 62.

[48] *Re Diplock* [1948] Ch 465.

[49] (1817) 1 Mer 575; confirmed in *Barlow Clowes International Ltd v Vaughan* [1992] 4 All ER 22.

[50] *Barlow Clowes International Ltd v Vaughan*, above.

[51] *Lipkin Gorman v Karpnale Ltd* [1991] 2 AC 548.

[52] *South Tyneside MBC v Svenska International plc* [1995] 1 All ER 545.

(2) The defence operates as a defence to a personal as well as to a proprietary claim[53].

(3) The defence does not operate where the act relied upon is the payment of a debt which would have fallen to be paid in any event[54].

(4) The defence does not operate in favour of a person who has performed a service for the trustee in reliance upon the trustee's power to pay him where that person should have had notice of the potential equitable claim[55].

(5) The defence does not operate in favour of a person who has changed his position in reliance upon the promise of payment, but does operate in favour of a person who has actually received property, even though it may not be that property which he applies[56].

One of the more interesting phenomena which arise through the form of the action for money had and received is that when an identifiable sum of money belonging to A passes intact through B's hands and into C's hands, neither giving value in good faith, both B and C are liable to A as having received the money to his use[57]. This is because the action is complete at the moment of receipt. This position is identical to the difficulties which are created by the personal and proprietary actions in equity which the defence of change of position defeats. It seems that the defence is available in common law action as well as an equitable claim.

---

[53] *Lipkin Gorman v Karpnale Ltd* [1991] 2 AC 548.
[54] (1995) 54 CLJ 377 at 426 (A Oakley).
[55] *Gray v Richards Butler (a firm)* (1996) *The Times*, 23 July.
[56] *South Tyneside MBC v Svenska International plc* [1995] 1 All ER 545.
[57] See Millet LJ, 'Recovering the Proceeds of Fraud' (1991) 107 LQR 71 at 77.

Chapter 33

Specific Performance, Equitable Damages and Declaration

Specific performance and injunction are the primary remedies in equity. Whereas the common law can only award damages, equity, which acts upon the conscience, can require or prohibit a thing to be done. The prohibition, which arises through injunction, does not have a property element[1]. However, the order to do a thing can extend to an order to transfer property, and such an order is therefore capable of taking effect as a proprietary remedy.

Jurisdiction to award specific performance

Specific performance is not available as of right, but the court has a discretion to award it. However, the court cannot confer jurisdiction upon itself, and the first question which must be answered is of the scope of the jurisdiction to award specific performance. The primary rule seems to be that it is only contractual obligations relating to property which are specifically enforced, and contracts for services are outside the jurisdiction such that the court cannot grant specific performance of a contract for service even if it considers that the facts constitute a proper case for doing so[2]. Even this proposition has been doubted judicially[3], and it is in fact difficult to see in the cases any limitation on the court's jurisdiction to award specific performance. We may therefore say that any contractual or fiduciary obligation is potentially specifically performable.

Considerations employed in exercise of discretion to award specific performance

The nature of an order for specific performance is that it is 'an order of the court compelling the defendant personally to do what he has promised to do'[4].

---

[1] A mandatory injunction is only issued where the order is to undo a thing which has already been done. All orders to do a thing *de novo* are orders of specific performance.
[2] *Scandinavian Trading Tanker Co AB v Flota Petrolera Ecuatoriana* [1983] 2 AC 694.
[3] Per Megarry J in *C H Giles & Co Ltd v Morris* [1972] 1 WLR 307 at 318.
[4] Hayton & Marshall, *Commentary and Cases upon the Law of Trusts and Equitable Remedies*, 10th edn, p 949.

It is the mechanism by which equity can enforce the maxim that 'equity looks on as done that which ought to be done'—a maxim that would be without logic or sense unless there were a means of compelling individuals to perform their obligations. In equity a man who elects to break an obligation suffers progressively more severe sanctions (theoretically ending with sequestration of assets and indefinite imprisonment) until the obligation is performed. The formal structure of the rule is that equity compels the performance of all obligations but the court will exercise its discretion against awarding the remedy in a series of classes of cases, the largest of which classes being those in which 'damages are an adequate remedy'. However, before discussing the application of this rule it is necessary to explain its logic in more detail.

At common law a person may elect without penalty to break his contract and pay damages. As Oliver Wendell Holmes pointed out[5], breach of contract is not an unlawful act, since the contractual obligation itself is either to do an act or to pay a sum of money equal to the amount which the plaintiff has lost (or, in some circumstances, failed to gain[6]) by the failure to perform. The defendant may elect which to do, and legal sanctions only follow upon his failure to do either.

This view has been denied in theory but accepted in practice by English lawyers[7]. Offensive as the idea of a right to break a contract may be, the fact remains that there is no jurisprudential basis for the absolute enforcement of all obligations[8]. A person who, having entered into an obligation, wishes to be released from it should be entitled to do so by the payment of appropriate compensation. If the law does not permit this, the only practical effect is to increase the amount of money which the other contracting party can demand to secure the release, a system which would provide unjustified windfall gains on a random basis.

There are contracts for which this argument fails: where it is clear that it was not the parties' common intention to allow one of them to have an option to pay damages. An interesting example is provided by *City of New Orleans v Fireman's Charitable Association*[9], in which the City of New Orleans paid the Association a fixed fee for the provision of fire-fighting services, and the Association contracted to maintain a force of 124 men plus necessary equipment for the purpose. The Association maintained its force at a lower level than it had agreed, and as a result saved a substantial amount of money. The City sued the Association, claiming damages for breach of contract. But the City over-catered in its specifications for the fire-fighting resource it required in that the maintenance of the force at a lower level than that agreed resulted in all the relevant fires being put out in an acceptable time. Thus, since there was no loss, the City was entitled to no damages.

As a matter of the calculus of damages this is perfectly acceptable, but as a matter of principle it is not. To interpret the contract between the City and the

---

[5] *The Common Law* (1881).
[6] *Hadley v Baxendale* (1854) 9 Ex 341.
[7] Atiyah, *An Introduction to the Law of Contract*, 5th edn (OUP), pp 418–19.
[8] Millet LJ in *Restitution Law Review* (1993) 7.
[9] (1819) 9 So 486.

Association as a contract to the effect that the Association might either fight fires or pay damages is absurd, and clearly contrary to the parties' intention: the Association contracted as a fire brigade, not an insurance company.

This point illustrates the rationale for the division of contracts into those which can, and those which cannot, be interpreted as contracts giving rise to an option of whether to perform or pay. Because this distinction does not (possibly cannot) exist at law, it must be made in equity, where it is usually expressed as a distinction between obligations for a breach of which 'damages are an adequate remedy' and obligations which were assumed with the single intention of performance. It is wrong to say that contracts for which damages are an adequate remedy do not exist in equity—equity is cognisant of all obligations. However, the task performed by equity is to require that a person perform his obligation, and it is for a court of conscience to determine exactly what was the nature of the obligation which he took on—either to 'do or pay', or to 'do in any event'. In the case of the latter, equity compels performance. It may be said that in the same way as the doctrine of resulting trust is equity's rule of recognition of valid gifts, the rules relating to specific performance are equity's rules of recognition of obligations which are intended to be genuinely enforceable.

Enforceable obligations

Equity treats as enforceable both legal and equitable obligations; thus obligations arising under a contract and out of a trust are equally enforceable in equity. There is one important exception to this rule: equity does not recognise obligations created at common law under seal without consideration. At common law I can, by execution of a deed poll, bind myself to pay £100 to the first person I meet tomorrow morning, and the first person I meet tomorrow morning, provided he can prove that he is indeed such, has a common law action against me for the money. However, if I execute a deed poll undertaking to give the first person I meet tomorrow morning a single unique chattel, that person may have damages in law but may not have specific performance in equity. The reason is that 'equity will not assist a volunteer', and a person who has been given the benefit of a legal obligation is in equity as much a volunteer as if he had been made any other promise—without consideration he cannot enforce it[10]. It has been said of this line of authority that it 'makes false assumptions, contains various inaccuracies and, if correct, would have extraordinary results'[11].

Adequacy of damages

Adequacy in this context is a complicated concept. There can clearly never be specific performance of an obligation where the contract creating it contains a provision for a liquidated sum to be paid upon non-feasance, for such a provision is the clearest possible indicator that the obligation was not intended to

---

[10] *Re Pryce* [1917] 1 Ch 234; *Cannon v Hartley* [1949] Ch 213.
[11] Meagher, Gummow and Lehane, *Equity, Doctrines and Remedies*, 3rd edn, pp 54–5.

be absolutely performable[12]. Conversely specific performance is available in circumstances where the loss is very difficult to quantify, since this is a clear indication that the parties did not intend to allow performance by payment of damages[13]. The rule is directional in terms of enforcement of obligations. If, upon breach of contract by one party, the other elects to treat the contract as repudiated and to sue in damages, this is the clearest possible evidence that damages are an adequate remedy and specific performance is not thereafter ordered[14]. If, however, the plaintiff elects to sue for specific performance, the issue of adequacy of damages is at large, and the court may award either damages or specific performance as it sees fit. Equally, after a court has awarded specific performance, the plaintiff may subsequently elect to request damages, which should be awarded as a matter of course[15], either at common law or in equity under Lord Cairns' Act[16].

The test of adequacy of damages is objective, not subjective. The parties to a contract at the time of its making contemplate performance, not breach, and it can probably never be said that at the time of making the contract either party had applied their mind to the issue of whether damages would be an adequate remedy for non-performance. Frequently they do, in which case a provision for the payment of liquidated damages is usually inserted in the contract. However, because of the rule that an unreasonably high level of liquidated damages constitutes a penalty, there is no clear way for the parties to embody in their agreement an opinion that the ordinary contractual damages payable upon a breach would be inadequate.

These principles may be systematised into a series of presumptions arising out of different factual situations, which may be grouped together as follows.

Contracts relating to land

A contract for the sale of land is presumed by law to be one which contemplates only actual performance and not payment of damages. The reason is that[17]

> the damages for [failure to perform] would be negligible and, as in most cases of breach of contract for the sale of land at a market price by refusal to convey it, would constitute a wholly inadequate and unjust remedy for the breach. That is why the normal remedy is by a decree for specific performance by the vendor of his primary obligation to convey ...

This is true whether the contract concerned is for the sale of land, or for the grant of a lease, or the grant of an option to purchase[18].

This is merely a presumption, and there is no rule that specific performance is always available for transactions in land. In a proper case the contract is held to be one in which performance may be by payment of damages. How-

[12] *Legh v Lillie* (1860) 6 H & N 165.
[13] *Co-operative Insurance Society Ltd v Argyll Stores (Holdings) Ltd* [1996] Ch 286.
[14] *Meng Leong Development Pte Ltd v Jip Hong Trading Co Pte Ltd* [1985] AC 511, PC.
[15] *Johnson v Agnew* [1980] AC 367.
[16] *Biggin v Minton* [1977] 1 WLR 701.
[17] *Sudbrook Trading Estate Ltd v Eggleton* [1983] 1 AC 444.
[18] *Pritchard v Briggs* [1980] Ch 338.

ever, the presumption of performance in the case of land is so strong that it is only in a very special case that damages are awarded in lieu of an obligation to convey.

Where the transaction is for a grant of a mere permission to enter upon land, it might be thought that since no right in the land is conferred by such a permission[19], no order for specific performance could lie[20]. This has been held to be incorrect in *Verrall v Gt Yarmouth BC*[21], which concerned an organisation whose views were so unpopular that it was unable to hire premises for a public meeting other than those to which the licence in question related. It was held that this was clearly a contract which required actual performance. This is authority for the important proposition that specific performance is granted in the case of non-proprietary obligations.

Since a conveyance of land requires writing signed by the owner, it may be wondered how this signature is to be obtained in the face of a steadfast refusal. The traditional remedy of imprisonment until compliance having proved old-fashioned and unsatisfactory, the modern approach is to order an officer of the court to execute the relevant papers on the owner's behalf, by a kind of statutory power of attorney[22].

Contracts relating to personal property
It is presumed that commercial goods and stocks and shares are fungible in nature. Thus upon the failure of a supplier to deliver a thing, the disappointed purchaser is fully compensated by an award of sufficient money to purchase a replacement. This is true of contracts for the sale of goods[23] and for the purchase and sale of listed shares or stock[24].

Where the relevant goods are not fungible, specific performance will be ordered for personal property in the same way as for land. Thus in *Fells v Reed*[25] an order was made for the tobacco box which was of great symbolic significance to a club, although another could clearly have been procured[26]. The rule also applies where the contract to deliver chattels is closely connected with another contract which requires specific performance; for example, in *Record v Bell*[27] an order for specific performance was made for the sale of the contents as well as for the house. It also applies where the asset concerned is of particular value to the plaintiff[28], or where the property concerned

---

[19] *Ashburn Anstalt v Arnold* [1989] Ch 1, CA.
[20] *Booker v Palmer* [1942] 2 All ER 674.
[21] [1981] QB 202.
[22] Supreme Court Act 1981, s 39; Trustee Act 1925, ss 44 and 50; Administration of Estates Act 1925, s 43.
[23] *Dominion Coal Co v Dominion Iron & Steel Co Ltd* [1909] AC 293.
[24] *Cuddee v Rutter* (1720) 1 P Wms 570.
[25] (1796) 3 Ves 70.
[26] See also *Pusey v Pusey* (1684) 1 Vern 273, a fascinating case involving a horn supposedly given to the Pusey family by King Canute.
[27] [1991] 1 WLR 853.
[28] *CN Marine Inc v Stena Line A/B* (1982) *The Times*, 12 June (specific performance granted in respect of a ship); but see *Société des Industries Metallurgiques SA v The Bronx Engineering Co Ltd* [1975] 1 Lloyd's Rep 465 (specific performance refused in respect of a large and complex industrial machine which would take nine months to replace).

is, although fungible in theory, in practice completely unavailable from any-where else[29].

The jurisdiction for goods should be wider than that for intangible personal property in that s 52 of the Sale of Goods Act 1979 contains a statutory provision enabling the court to make an order for specific performance of a contract of sale of specific goods. However, the section has been interpreted as being no more than a statutory expression of the ordinary equitable rule of specific performance, and the ordinary rules relating to the grant of specific performance have been applied to it[30].

Contracts to advance money

The rule for contracts for lending or payment of money is complex. In the case of an obligation to pay money it seems necessarily true that specific performance can never be given[31], since damages would almost always equal the amount due. However, where the plaintiff is a borrower who has no other source of funding, and the defendant is a lender who has agreed to advance funds for a specified term at a specified rate of interest, it is difficult to see in theory why specific performance should not be granted, although in practice it is not[32]. Yet there are some circumstances where specific performance of a contract to pay money is granted.

Payments on contingencies:

(1) *Where A contracts to pay an annuity to B* If A simply breached the agreement, B's damages must be based on an actuarial valuation of his life expectancy[33], thereby throwing back upon B the very risk which he had disposed of to A. Thus damages are inadequate, and an order for specific performance of the obligation to make periodic payments will be made.

(2) *Contract to pay money out of particular fund* This sort of contract creates an equitable charge over the fund of property. Damages are inappropriate since the transaction is a grant of a contingent interest in property and there is no mechanism for measuring the contingency. As a general rule, at the time of agreeing to give such a charge there is no intention on the part of either party that the charge will ever be enforced—once the debt secured by the charge is repaid the interest lapses. The one thing that no one intends is that the chargee will receive a fixed amount, over and above the debt due, representing the percentage chance of its non-repayment. Thus, as in the previous case, specific performance will be made available.

Multi-party arrangements:

(1) *Where A and B contract that A shall pay money to C* If B sues A for non-payment, his award of damages will be notional, since he has suf-

---

[29] *Sky Petroleum v VIP Petroleum Ltd* [1974] 1 WLR 576.
[30] *Cohen v Roche* [1927] 1 KB 169.
[31] *South African Territories v Wallington* [1898] AC 309.
[32] *Locobail International Finance Ltd v Agroexport* [1986] 1 WLR 657.
[33] *Adderley v Dixon* (1824) 1 Sim & St 607.

fered no loss, whilst C is precluded from suing by the rule of privity. Thus damages are an inadequate remedy, and B may have an order for specific performance against A[34].

(2) *Where A contracts to indemnify B against a liability, upon the liability arising A is ordered to pay the debt directly* This arises where the obligation on the indemnifier is to hold B harmless (ie to ensure that he is never out-of-pocket) as opposed to an obligation to reimburse him at a later time once he has discharged his obligation[35].

(3) *Contract with a company to subscribe for debentures* This right is created by s 195 of the Companies Act 1985, and is anomalous, the logic presumably being that the failure to subscribe for the debentures injures those who have subscribed, and, since they cannot sue directly (and would receive no money if they did), the company can sue in their place to compel subscription.

Obligations to do an act

An obligation to transfer property may be relatively easily enforced. However, an obligation to do an act may be enforceable only with difficulty, and in such a case the court will not order specific performance unless it is confident that its decree will be enforceable. The only acts which it is relatively certain will be ordered to be done are those which are intermediate stages in the delivery of title, since they involve the exercise of a legal power, and the court can always vest such a power in a different person by its own order[36]. But where the act is not a legal act, the issue is whether the court can sensibly order it to be performed. In *Posner v Scott-Lewis*[37] an obligation to perform specific duties (through the employment of a porter) was held to be specifically performable, because the tasks concerned were sufficiently specified that it was possible to say with certainty whether they had been done properly.

A subdivision of the 'obligation to do an act' cases arises out of the fact that there are some acts which simply cannot be ordered. A person may be compelled by a court order to attend a concert, but he cannot be compelled to enjoy it. Thus, in cases where the act involves the actor's co-operation, specific performance is not ordered. The reasons were explained by Sir Robert Megarry in *C H Giles & Co Ltd v Morris*[38].

If a singer contracts to sing, there could no doubt be proceedings to for committal if, ordered to sing, the singer remained obstinately dumb. But if instead the singer

---

[34] *Beswick v Beswick* [1968] AC 58; *Gurtner v Circuit* [1968] 2 QB 587; cf *Coulls v Bagot's Executor and Trustee Co Ltd* (1967) 40 ALJR.

[35] *McIntosh v Dalwood (No 4)* (1930) 30 SRNSW 415.

[36] Strictly speaking the power to require executory contracts to be executed is specific performance proper, and the idea of requiring the performance of obligations under executed contracts a modern heresy; see Meagher, Gummow and Lehne, *Equity, Doctrines and Remedies*, 2nd edn, p 472.

[37] [1987] Ch 25. The case is also interesting for its use of the technique of 'distinguishing' a previous judgment in relation to *Ryan v Mutual Tontine Westminster Chambers Association* [1893] 1 Ch 116, in which exactly the opposite conclusion had been reached on nearly identical facts.

[38] [1972] 1 WLR 307 at 318.

sang flat, or sharp, or too loudly, or too quietly, or resorted to a dozen of the manifestations of temperament traditionally associated with some singers, the threat of committal would reveal itself as a most unsatisfactory weapon, for who could say whether the imperfections of performance were natural or self-induced? To make an order with such possibilities of evasion would be vain, and so the order will not be made ...

Such cases provide an interesting reversal of the approach outlined above, since there is clearly no expectation that damages are an even remotely adequate remedy. They represent, rather, a failing of the possibilities of legal enforcement, and damages are awarded not because they are adequate but because they are the only option.

Insolvency considerations

If an order for specific performance is available for the transfer of a property interest, the effect is to vest an interest in the defendant's property in the plaintiff. Where the defendant is in the process of becoming insolvent, the availability of specific performance is most important to the plaintiff if he has paid the purchase price, and in some cases even if he has not. If specific performance is available, he will receive the benefit which he bargained for upon payment of the price. If it is not, his obligation to pay the price may remain enforceable by the insolvent person, although he is entitled not to the property, but to a dividend in the insolvency. The grant of an order for specific performance in such circumstances clearly prejudices the rights of the other creditors, but the insolvency alone is not a bar to the grant of specific performance[39].

Mutuality

There is an old rule that specific performance is not available where there is no mutuality between the parties—in other words, where the contract is not of a form in which specific performance would be ordered against one party, it will not be ordered against the other either. The rule was formerly applied on an abstract basis, so that the test was applied as at the date of making contract, and if any obligation of either side was incapable of specific performance then the whole contract was incapable of specific performance on either side.

The modern rule of mutuality is confined to circumstances where the unperformed part of the contract is incapable of specific performance. The rule is that 'the court will not compel a defendant to perform his obligations specifically if it cannot at the same time ensure that any *unperformed* obligations of the plaintiff will be specifically performed'[40]. Thus, where a person makes a bargain that he will perform a service in exchange for the transfer of an interest in property, if he does not perform the service then the contract

---

[39] *Freevale Ltd v Metrostore (Holdings) Ltd* [1984] Ch 199; *Amec Properties Ltd v Planning Research & Systems plc* [1992] 1 EGLR 70.
[40] *Price v Strange* [1978] Ch 337 at 367.

cannot be specifically enforced by either party, since there is no mutuality. However, if he does perform the service the other party cannot refuse to transfer the property on the basis that he could not have compelled performance of the service, since the test is applied only to unperformed obligations and not to the totality of the contractual obligation.

General equitable defences

An order for specific performance may be resisted by an assertion of the usual equitable defences, such as that the plaintiff is partly to blame for the breach or has otherwise acted in such a fashion as to debar himself from equitable relief (the doctrine that 'he who comes to equity must come with clean hands'). In practice this means that he has either performed his own obligations, or is ready to perform them[41]. The plaintiff must sue within a reasonable time, otherwise he will find his action defeated by the doctrine of laches (based on the maxim that 'equity aids the diligent and not the tardy'). In the context of equitable remedies 'a reasonable time' is assessed with reference to the circumstances of the transaction, and in an ordinary commercial matter a lapse of more than a few months may be sufficient to prevent the plaintiff proceeding with his action[42]. The courts also look sympathetically on the position of a defendant upon whom the enforcement of his obligation would create intense hardship[43].

The point must be emphasised that an equitable defence operates only in equity. There is a series of old decisions, proceeding largely from Jessel MR's enthusiasm for the fusion of law and equity in the immediate aftermath thereof[44], which indicates that post-fusion equitable defences took effect in law as well as in equity. The leading case in this direction is *Dean v Prince*[45], but to the extent that this case is authority for any such proposition it must be taken to have been wrongly decided[46].

Damages in equity

Under the Chancery Amendment Act 1858, known as Lord Cairn's Act[47], the courts of equity were empowered to award damages either in addition to or in substitution for an order of specific performance. The jurisdiction to award damages is closely allied to the doctrines of specific performance; in particular, damages may be available in equity where they would not be available at law[48]. However, the power to award damages only arises for obligations of

---

[41] *National and Provincial Building Society v British Waterways Board* [1992] EGCS 149.

[42] *Huxham v Llewellyn* (1873) 21 WR 570. A delay which is not the fault of either party may still operate as a bar (*Patel v Ali* [1984] Ch 283).

[43] *Patel v Ali*, above.

[44] See O'Keefe, 'Sir George Jessel and the Union of Judicature' (1982) 26 Am J Legal Hist 227.

[45] [1954] Ch 409.

[46] *Legal and General Life of Australia v A Hudson Pty Ltd* (1985) 1 NSWLR 314.

[47] Now s 50 of the Supreme Court Act 1981.

[48] *Johnson v Agnew* [1980] AC 367.

which specific performance would be decreed in equity. Thus equitable damages are not available in any case in which a court of equity would not be prepared to award specific performance[49]. This extends to contracts for the sale of fungible goods or listed securities and to at least some contracts for personal services[50].

Although there is some authority to the contrary[51], it is now clear that damages under Lord Cairn's Act are calculated in the same way and on the same basis as damages at law[52]. The only exception seems to be where damages would not be available at law at all, or would be nominal, a Court of Equity may assess the injury to the plaintiff by refusing a discretionary order and make an award of damages to reflect that injury[53].

Declaration

An action for a declaration is an action requesting the court to declare a specific legal proposition to be the case, and it is of interest here primarily because a vindication of title can be effected by an application to the court for a declaration that the plaintiff is absolutely entitled to a particular piece of property. It is thus potentially an instrument to enable the courts to vest absolute title, a possibility which has been lacking in English law since the desuetude of the great writ of right.

The action for a declaration is an anomalous component of English law, having been introduced in the recent past from a civil jurisdiction. For many years the declaration was espoused by the Scottish courts, rejected by the English judiciary and admired by the English business community. It was introduced in England by the Court of Chancery Act 1850[54], and it is interesting to note that when this chancery innovation was introduced into the common law courts by the Supreme Court of Judicature Act 1873 there was no common law precedent at all for such a proceeding. Conceptually the action for a declaration was a matter of documentary construction, and its early usage was primarily to determine the true construction of wills[55]. However, it soon became clear that any document which purported to confer rights might be treated as being the subject of a declaration, and eventually the action for a declaration was made available to cover the interpretation of statutes[56].

The unique nature of the declaration is that it is a decision good against all the world. Thus one of the fundamental principles of the action for a declara-

---

[49] *Lavery v Pursell* (1888) 39 Ch D 508.
[50] *C H Giles & Co Ltd v Morris* [1972] 1 WLR 307, although the House of Lords has indicated that there may be no jurisdiction for any contract of services (*Scandinavian Trading Tanker Co A/B v Flota Petrolera Ecuatoriana* [1983] 2 AC 694).
[51] *Wroth v Tyler* [1974] Ch 30; *Oakacre v Claire Cleaners (Holdings) Ltd* [1982] Ch 197.
[52] *Johnson v Agnew* [1980] AC 367.
[53] *Wrotham Park Estates Ltd v Parkside Homes Ltd* [1974] 1 WLR 798; *Jaggard v Sawyer* [1995] 1 WLR 269.
[54] Also known as the Special Case Act or Sir George Turner's Act.
[55] See *Re Medland, Eland v Medland* (1889) 41 Ch D 476 at 492, CA, per Fry J.
[56] By the Rules of the Supreme Court 1883, Ord 54A, r 4.

tion is that the person bringing it must be able to secure a proper contradictor, that is someone presently existing who has a true interest to oppose the declaration sought[57]. The opponent can raise any objection to the declaration and, as with variation of trust applications, the court will protect the interests of parties not before it. If these conditions are complied with, the court makes a declaration of absolute title to property[58].

---

[57] *Russian Commercial and Industrial Bank v British Bank for Foreign Trade* [1921] 2 AC 438 at 448; approved in *Vine v National Dock Labour Board* [1957] AC 488 at 500.
[58] *Bridges v Mees* [1957] Ch 475.

Appendices

Contents

Appendix 1

Negotiable Instruments

Bills of Exchange Act 1882

PART I PRELIMINARY

1 Short title
This Act may be cited as the Bills of Exchange Act 1882

2 Interpretation of terms
In this Act, unless the context otherwise requires,—
'Acceptance' means an acceptance completed by delivery or notification.
'Action' includes counter claim and set off.
'Banker' includes a body of persons whether incorporated or not who carry on the business of banking.
'Bankrupt' includes any person whose estate is vested in a trustee or assignee under the law for the time being in force relating to bankruptcy.
'Bearer' means the person in possession of a bill or note which is payable to bearer.
'Bill' means bill of exchange, and 'note' means promissory note.
'Delivery' means transfer of possession, actual or constructive, from one person to another.
'Holder' means the payee or indorsee of a bill or note who is in possession of it, or the bearer thereof.
'Indorsement' means an indorsement completed by delivery.
'Issue' means the first delivery of a bill or note, complete in form to a person who takes it as a holder.
'Person' includes a body of persons whether incorporated or not.
'Value' means valuable consideration.
'Written' includes printed, and 'writing' includes print.

PART II BILLS OF EXCHANGE

Form and Interpretation

3 Bill of exchange defined
(1) A bill of exchange is an unconditional order in writing, addressed by one person to another, signed by the person giving it, requiring the person to whom it is addressed to pay on demand or at a fixed or determinable future time a sum certain in money to or to the order of a specified person, or to bearer.
(2) An instrument which does not comply with these conditions, or which orders any act to be done in addition to the payment of money, is not a bill of exchange.
(3) An order to pay out of a particular fund is not unconditional within the meaning of this section; but an unqualified order to pay, coupled with (a) an indication of a particular fund out of which the drawee is to re-imburse himself or a particular account to be debited with the amount, or (b) a statement of the transaction which gives rise to the bill is unconditional.
(4) A bill is not invalid by reason—
(a) That it is not dated;
(b) That it does not specify the value given, or that any value has been given therefor;

(c)   That it does not specify the place where it is drawn or the place where it is payable.

4   Inland and foreign bills

(1)   An inland bill is a bill which is or on the face of it purports to be (a) both drawn and payable within the British Islands, or (b) drawn within the British Islands upon some person resident therein. Any other bill is a foreign bill.

For the purposes of this Act 'British Islands' mean any part of the United Kingdom or Great Britain and Ireland, the islands of Man, Guernsey, Jersey, Alderney, and Sark, and the islands adjacent to any of them being part of the dominions of Her Majesty.

(2)   Unless the contrary appear on the face of the bill the holder may treat it as an inland bill.

5   Effect where different parties to bill are the same person

(1)   A bill may be drawn payable to, or to the order of, the drawer; or it may be drawn payable to, or to the order of, the drawee.

(2)   Where in a bill drawer and drawee are the same person, or where the drawee is a fictitious person or a person not having capacity to contract, the holder may treat the instrument, at his option, either as a bill of exchange or as a promissory note.

6   Address to drawee

(1)   The drawee must be named or otherwise indicated in a bill with reasonable certainty.

(2)   A bill may be addressed to two or more drawees whether they are partners or not, but an order addressed to two drawees in the alternative or to two or more drawees in succession is not a bill of exchange.

7   Certainty required as to payee

(1)   Where a bill is not payable to bearer, the payee must be named or otherwise indicated therein with reasonable certainty.

(2)   A bill may be made payable to two or more payees jointly, or it may be made payable in the alternative to one of two, or one or some of several payees. A bill may also be made payable to the holder of an office for the time being.

(3)   Where the payee is a fictitious or non-existing person the bill may be treated as payable to bearer.

8   What bills are negotiable

(1)   When a bill contains words prohibiting transfer, or indicating an intention that it should not be transferable, it is valid as between the parties thereto, but is not negotiable.

(2)   A negotiable bill may be payable either to order or to bearer.

(3)   A bill is payable to bearer which is expressed to be so payable, or on which the only or last indorsement is an indorsement in blank.

(4)   A bill is payable to order which is expressed to be so payable, or which is expressed to be payable to a particular person, and does not contain words prohibiting transfer or indicating an intention that it should not be transferable.

(5)   Where a bill, either originally or by indorsement, is expressed to be payable to the order of a specified person, and not to him or his order, it is nevertheless payable to him or his order at his option.

9   Sum payable

(1)   The sum payable by a bill is a sum certain within the meaning of this Act, although it was required to be paid—

(a)   With interest.

(b)   By stated instalments.

(c)   By stated instalments, with a provision that upon default in payment of any instalment the whole shall become due.

   (d)   According to an indicated rate of exchange or according to a rate of exchange to be ascertained as directed by the bill.
   (2)   Where the sum payable is expressed in words and also in figures, and there is a discrepancy between the two, the sum denoted by the words is the amount payable.
   (3)   Where a bill is expressed to be payable with interest, unless the instrument otherwise provides, interest runs from the date of the bill, and if the bill is undated from the issue thereof.

10   Bill payable on demand
   (1)   A bill is payable on demand—
   (a)   Which is expressed to be payable on demand, or at sight, or on presentation; or
   (b)   In which no time for payment was expressed.
   (2)   Where a bill is accepted or indorsed when it is overdue, it shall, as regards the acceptor who so accepts, or any indorser who so indorses it, be deemed a bill payable on demand.

11   Bill payable at a future time
A bill is payable at a determinable future time within the meaning of this Act which is expressed to be payable—
   (1)   At a fixed period after date or sight.
   (2)   On or at a fixed period after the occurrence of a specified event which is certain to happen though the time of happening may be uncertain.
   An instrument expressed to be payable on a contingency is not a bill, and the happening of the event does not cure the defect.

12   Omission of date in bill payable after date
Where a bill expressed to be payable at a fixed period after date is issued undated, or where the acceptance of a bill payable at a fixed period after sight is undated, any holder may insert therein the true date of issue or acceptance, and the bill shall be payable accordingly.
   Provided that (1) where the holder in good faith and by mistake inserts a wrong date, and (2) in every case where a wrong date is inserted, if the bill subsequently comes into the hands of a holder in due course the bill shall not be avoided thereby, but shall operate and be payable as if the date so inserted had been the true date.

13   Ante-dating and post-dating
   (1)   Where a bill or an acceptance or any indorsement on a bill is dated, the date shall, unless the contrary be proved, be deemed to be the true date of the drawing, acceptance, or indorsement, as the case may be.
   (2)   A bill is not invalid by reason only that it is ante-dated or post-dated, or that it bears date on a Sunday.

14   Computation of time of payment
Where a bill is not payable on demand the day on which it falls due is determined as follows:
   (1)   The bill is due and payable in all cases on the last day of the time of payment as fixed by the bill or, if that is a non-business day, on the succeeding business day.
   (2)   Where a bill is payable at a fixed period after date, after sight, or after the happening of a specified event, the time of payment is determined by excluding the day from which the time is to begin to run and by including the day of payment.
   (3)   Where a bill is payable at a fixed period after sight, the time begins to run from the date of the acceptance if the bill be accepted, and from the date of noting or protest if the bill be noted or protested for non-acceptance, or for non-delivery.
   (4)   The term 'month' in a bill means calendar month.

15 Case of need

The drawer of a bill and any indorser may insert therein the name of a person to whom the holder may resort in case of need, that is to say, in case the bill is dishonoured by non-acceptance or non-payment. Such person is called the referee in case of need. It is in the opinion of the holder to resort to the referee in case of need or not as he may think fit.

16 Optional stipulations by drawer or indorser

The drawer of a bill and any indorser, may insert therein an express stipulation—
    (1)   Negativing or limiting his own liability to the holder.
    (2)   Waiving as regards himself some or all of the holder's duties.

17 Definition and requisites of acceptance

    (1)   The acceptance of a bill is the signification by the drawee of his assent to the order of the drawer.
    (2)   An acceptance is invalid unless it complies with the following conditions, namely:
        (a)   It must be written on the bill and be signed by the drawee. The mere signature of the drawee without additional words is sufficient.
        (b)   It must not express that the drawee will perform his promise by any other means than the payment of money.

18 Time for acceptance

A bill may be accepted—
    (1)   Before it has been signed by the drawer, or while otherwise incomplete:
    (2)   When it is overdue, or after it has been dishonoured by a previous refusal to accept, or by non-payment:
    (3)   When a bill payable after sight is dishonoured by non-acceptance, and the drawee subsequently accepts it, the holder, in the absence of any different agreement, is entitled to have the bill accepted as of the date of first presentment to the drawee for acceptance.

19 General and qualified acceptances

    (1)   An acceptance is either (a) general or (b) qualified.
    (2)   A general acceptance assents without qualification to the order of the drawer. A qualified acceptance in expressed terms varies the effect of the bill as drawn.
    In particular an acceptance is qualified which is—
        (a)   conditional, that is to say, which makes payment by the acceptor dependent on the fulfilment of a condition therein stated:
        (b)   partial, that is to say, an acceptance to pay part only of the amount for which the bill is drawn:
        (c)   local, that is to say, an acceptance to pay only at a particular specified place:
        An acceptance to pay at a particular place is a general acceptance, unless it expressly states that the bill is to be paid there only and not elsewhere:
        (d)   qualified as to time:
        (e)   the acceptance of some one or more of the drawees, but not of all.

20 Inchoate instruments

    (1)   Where a simple signature on a blank . . . paper is delivered by the signer in order that it may be converted into a bill, it operates as a prima facie authority to fill it up as a complete bill for any amount . . . , using the signature for that of the drawer, or the acceptor, or an indorser; and, in like manner, when a bill is wanting in any material particular, the person in possession of it has a prima facie authority to fill up the omission in any way he thinks fit.
    (2)   In order that any such instrument when completed may be enforceable against

any person who became a party thereto prior to its completion, it must be filled up within a reasonable time, and strictly in accordance with the authority given. Reasonable time for this purpose is a question of fact.

Provided that if any such instrument after completion is negotiated to a holder in due course it shall be valid and effectual for all purposes in his hands, and he may enforce it as if it had been filled up within a reasonable time and strictly in accordance with the authority given.

21 Delivery

(1)   Every contract on a bill, whether it be the drawer's, the acceptor's, or an indorser's, is incomplete and revocable, until delivery of the instrument in order to give effect thereto.

Provided that where an acceptance is written on a bill, and the drawee gives notice to or according to the directions of the person entitled to the bill that he has accepted it, the acceptance then becomes complete and irrevocable.

(2)   As between immediate parties, and as regards a remote party other than a holder in due course, the delivery—

(a)   in order to be effectual must be made either by or under the authority of the party drawing, accepting, or indorsing, as the case may be:

(b)   may be shown to have been conditional or for a special purpose only, and not for the purpose of transferring the property in the bill.

But if the bill be in the hands of a holder in due course a valid delivery of the bill by all parties prior to him so as to make them liable to him is conclusively presumed.

(3)   Where a bill is no longer in the possession of a party who has signed it as drawer, acceptor, or indorser, a valid and unconditional delivery by him is presumed until the contrary is proved.

Capacity and Authority of Parties

22 Capacity of parties

(1)   Capacity to incur liability as a party to a bill is co-extensive with capacity to contract.

Provided that nothing in this section shall enable a corporation to make itself liable as drawer, acceptor, or indorser of a bill unless it is competent to it so to do under the law for the time being in force relating to corporations.

(2)   Where a bill is drawn or indorsed by an infant, minor, or corporation having no capacity or power to incur liability on a bill, the drawing or indorsement entitles the holder to receive payment of the bill, and to enforce it against any other party thereto.

23 Signature essential to liability

No person is liable as drawer, indorser, or acceptor of a bill who has not signed it as such: Provided that

(1)   Where a person signs a bill in a trade or assumed name, he is liable thereon as if he had signed it in his own name:

(2)   The signature of the name of a firm is equivalent to the signature by the person so signing of the names of all persons liable as partners in that firm.

24 Forged or unauthorised signature

Subject to the provisions of this Act, where a signature on a bill is forged or placed thereon without the authority of the person whose signature it purports to be, the forged or unauthorised signature is wholly inoperative, and no right to retain the bill or to give a discharge therefor or to enforce payment thereof against any party thereto can be acquired through or under that signature, unless the party against whom it is sought to retain or enforce payment of the bill is precluded from setting up the forgery or want of authority.

Provided that nothing in this section shall affect the ratification of an unauthorised signature not amounting to a forgery.

25 Procuration signatures

A signature by procuration operates as notice that the agent has but a limited authority to sign, and the principal is only bound by such signature if the agent in so signing was acting within the actual limits of his authority.

26 Person signing as agent or in representative capacity

(1) Where a person signs a bill as drawer, indorser, or acceptor, and adds words to his signature, indicating that he signs for or on behalf of a principal, or in a representative character, he is not personally liable thereon; but the mere addition to his signature of words describing him as an agent, or as filling a representative character, does not exempt him from personal liability.

(2) In determining whether a signature on a bill is that of the principal or that of the agent by whose hand it is written, the construction most favourable to the validity of the instrument shall be adopted.

The Consideration for a Bill

27 Value and holder for value

(1) Valuable consideration for a bill may be constituted by—

    (a) Any consideration sufficient to support a simple contract;

    (b) An antecedent debt or liability. Such a debt or liability is deemed valuable consideration whether the bill is payable on demand or at a future time.

(2) Where value has at any time been given for a bill the holder is deemed to be a holder for value as regards the acceptor and all parties to the bill who became parties prior to such time.

(3) Where the holder of a bill has a lien on it arising either from contract or by implication of law, he is deemed to be a holder for value to the extent of the sum for which he has a lien.

28 Accommodation bill or party

(1) An accommodation party to a bill is a person who has signed a bill as drawer, acceptor, or indorser, without receiving value therefor, and for the purpose of lending his name to some other person.

(2) An accommodation party is liable on the bill to a holder for value; and it is immaterial whether, when such holder took the bill, he knew such party to be an accommodation party or not.

29 Holder in due course

(1) A holder in due course is a holder who has taken a bill, complete and regular on the face of it, under the following conditions; namely,

    (a) That he became the holder of it before it was overdue, and without notice that it had been previously dishonoured, if such was the fact:

    (b) That he took the bill in good faith and for value, and that at the time the bill was negotiated to him he had no notice of any defect in the title of the person who negotiated it.

(2) In particular the title of a person who negotiates a bill is defective within the meaning of this Act when he obtained the bill, or the acceptance thereof, by fraud, duress, or force and fear, or other unlawful means, or an illegal consideration, or when he negotiates it in breach of faith, or under such circumstances as amount to a fraud.

(3) A holder (whether for value or not), who derives his title to a bill through a holder in due course, and who is not himself a party to any fraud or illegality affecting it, has all the rights of that holder in due course as regards the acceptor and all parties to the bill prior to that holder.

30   Presumption of value and good faith
(1)   Every party whose signature appears on a bill is prima facie deemed to have become a party thereto for value.
(2)   Every holder of a bill is prima facie deemed to be a holder in due course; but if in an action on a bill it is admitted or proved that the acceptance, issue, or subsequent negotiation of the bill is affected with fraud, duress, or force and fear, or illegality, the burden of proof is shifted, unless and until the holder proves that, subsequent to the alleged fraud or illegality, value has in good faith been given for the bill.

Negotiation of Bills

31   Negotiation of bill
(1)   A bill is negotiated when it is transferred from one person to another in such a manner as to constitute the transferee the holder of the bill.
(2)   A bill payable to bearer is negotiated by delivery.
(3)   A bill payable to order is negotiated by the indorsement of the holder completed by delivery.
(4)   Where the holder of a bill payable to his order transfers it for value without indorsing it, the transfer gives the transferee such title as the transferor had in the bill and the transferee in addition acquires the right to have the indorsement of the transferor.
(5)   Where any person is under obligation to indorse a bill in a representative capacity, he may indorse the bill in such terms as to negative personal liability.

32   Requisites of a valid indorsement
An indorsement in order to operate as a negotiation must comply with the following conditions, namely,—
(1)   It must be written on the bill itself and be signed by the indorser. The simple signature of the indorser on the bill, without additional words is sufficient.
An indorsement written on an allonge, or on a 'copy' of a bill issued or negotiated in a country where 'copies' are recognised, is deemed to be written on the bill itself.
(2)   It must be an indorsement of the entire bill. A partial indorsement, that is to say, an indorsement which purports to transfer to the indorsee a part only of the amount payable, or which purports to transfer the bill to two or more indorsees severally, does not operate as a negotiation of the bill.
(3)   Where a bill is payable to the order of two or more payees or indorsees who are not partners all must indorse, unless the one indorsing has authority to indorse for the others.
(4)   Where, in a bill payable to order, the payee or indorsee is wrongly designated, or his name is mis-spelt, he may indorse the bill as therein described, adding, if he think fit, his proper signature.
(5)   Where there are two or more indorsements on a bill, each indorsement is deemed to have been made in the order in which it appears on the bill, until the contrary is proved.
(6)   An indorsement may be made in blank or special. It may also contain terms making it restrictive.

33   Conditional indorsement
Where a bill purports to be indorsed conditionally the condition may be disregarded by the payer, and payment to the indorsee is valid whether the condition has been fulfilled or not.

34   Indorsement in blank and special indorsement
(1)   An indorsement in blank specifies no indorsee, and a bill so indorsed becomes payable to bearer.
(2)   A special indorsement specifies the person to whom, or to whose order, the bill is to be payable.

(3)   The provisions of this Act relating to a payee apply with the necessary modifications to an indorsee under a special indorsement.

(4)   When a bill has been indorsed in blank, any holder may convert the blank indorsement into a special indorsement by writing above the indorser's signature a direction to pay the bill to or to the order of himself or some other person.

35   Restrictive indorsement

(1)   An indorsement is restrictive which prohibits the further negotiation of the bill or which expresses that it is a mere authority to deal with the bill as thereby directed and not a transfer of the ownership thereof, as, for example, if a bill be indorsed 'Pay D. only,' or 'Pay D. for the account of X.,' or 'Pay D. or order for collection.'

(2)   A restrictive indorsement gives the indorsee the right to receive payment of the bill and to sue any party thereto that his indorser could have sued, but gives him no power to transfer his rights as indorsee unless it expressly authorises him to do so.

(3)   Where a restrictive indorsement authorises further transfer, all subsequent indorsees take the bill with the same rights and subject to the same liabilities as the first indorsee under the restrictive indorsement.

36   Negotiation of overdue or dishonoured bill

(1)   Where a bill is negotiable in its origin it continues to be negotiable until it has been (a) restrictively indorsed or (b) discharged by payment or otherwise.

(2)   Where an overdue bill is negotiated, it can only be negotiated subject to any defect or title affecting it at its maturity, and thenceforward no person who takes it can acquire or give a better title than that which the person from whom he took it had.

(3)   A bill payable on demand is deemed to be overdue within the meaning and for the purpose of this section, when it appears on the face of it to have been in circulation for an unreasonable length of time. What is an unreasonable length of time for this purpose is a question of fact.

(4)   Except where an indorsement bears date after the maturity of the bill, every negotiation is prima facie deemed to have been effected before the bill was overdue.

(5)   Where a bill which is not overdue has been dishonoured any person who takes it with notice of the dishonour takes it subject to any defect of title attaching thereto at the time of dishonour, but nothing in this sub-section shall affect the rights of a holder in due course.

37   Negotiation of bill to party already liable thereon

Where a bill is negotiated back to the drawer, or to a prior indorser or to the acceptor, such party may, subject to the provisions of this Act, re-issue and further negotiate the bill, but he is not entitled to enforce payment of the bill against any intervening party to whom he was previously liable.

38   Rights of the holder

The rights and powers of the holder of a bill are as follows:

(1)   He may sue on the bill in his own name:

(2)   Where he is a holder in due course, he holds the bill free from any defect of title of prior parties, as well as from mere personal defences available to prior parties among themselves, and may enforce payment against all parties liable on the bill:

(3)   Where his title is defective (a) if he negotiates the bill to a holder in due course, that holder obtains a good and complete title to the bill, and (b) if he obtains payment of the bill the person who pays him in due course gets a valid discharge for the bill.

General Duties of the Holder

39   When presentment for acceptance is necessary

(1)   Where a bill is payable after sight, presentment for acceptance is necessary in

order to fix the maturity of the instrument.

(2)   Where a bill expressly stipulates that it shall be presented for acceptance, or there a bill is drawn payable elsewhere than at the residence or place of business of the drawee, it must be presented for acceptance before it can be presented for payment.

(3)   In no other case is presentment for acceptance necessary in order to render liable any party to the bill.

(4)   Where the holder of a bill, drawn payable elsewhere than at the place of business or residence of the drawee, has not time, with the exercise of reasonable diligence, to present the bill for acceptance before presenting it for payment on the day that it falls due, the delay caused by presenting the bill for acceptance before presenting it for payment is excused, and does not discharge the drawer and indorsers.

40   Time for presenting bill payable after sight

(1)   Subject to the provisions of this Act, when a bill payable after sight is negotiated, the holder must either present it for acceptance or negotiate it within a reasonable time.

(2)   If he do not do so, the drawer and all indorsers prior to that holder are discharged.

(3)   In determining what is a reasonable time within the meaning of this section, regard shall be had to the nature of the bill, the usage of trade with respect to similar bills, and the facts of the particular case.

41   Rules as to presentment for acceptance, and excuses for non-presentment

(1)   A bill is duly presented for acceptance which is presented in accordance with the following rules:

(a)   The presentment must be made by or on behalf of the holder to the drawee or to some person authorised to accept or refuse acceptance on his behalf at a reasonable hour on a business day and before the bill is overdue:

(b)   Where a bill is addressed to two or more drawees, who are not partners, presentment must be made to them all, unless one has authority to accept for all, then presentment may be made to him only:

(c)   Where the drawee is dead presentment may be made to his personal representative:

(d)   Where the drawee is bankrupt, presentment may be made to him or to his trustee:

(e)   Where authorised by agreement or usage, a presentment through the post office is sufficient.

(2)   Presentment in accordance with these rules is excused, and a bill may be treated as dishonoured by non-acceptance—

(a)   Where the drawee is dead or bankrupt, or is a fictitious person or a person not having capacity to contract by bill:

(b)   Where, after the exercise of reasonable diligence, such presentment cannot be effected:

(c)   Where, although the presentment has been irregular, acceptance has been refused on some other ground.

(3)   The fact that the holder has reason to believe that the bill, on presentment, will be dishonoured does not excuse presentment.

42   Non-acceptance

When a bill is duly presented for acceptance and is not accepted within the customary time, the person presenting it must treat it as dishonoured by non-acceptance. If he do not, the holder shall lose his right of recourse against the drawer and indorsers.

43   Dishonoured by non-acceptance and its consequences

(1)   A bill is dishonoured by non-acceptance—

(a)   when it is duly presented for acceptance, and such an acceptance as is prescribed by this Act is refused or cannot be obtained; or

(b)   when presentment for acceptance is excused and the bill is not accepted.

(2)   Subject to the provisions of this Act when a bill is dishonoured by non-acceptance, an immediate right of recourse against the drawer and indorser accrues to the holder, and no presentment for payment is necessary.

44   Duties as to qualified acceptances

(1)   The holder of a bill may refuse to take a qualified acceptance, and if he does not obtain an unqualified acceptance may treat the bill as dishonoured by non-acceptance.

(2)   Where a qualified acceptance is taken, and the drawer or an indorser has not expressly or impliedly authorised the holder to take a qualified acceptance, or does not subsequently assent thereto, such drawer or indorser is discharged from his liability on the bill.

The provisions of this subsection do not apply to a partial acceptance, whereof due notice has been given. Where a foreign bill has been accepted as to part, it must be protested as to the balance.

(3)   When the drawer or indorser of a bill receives notice of a qualified acceptance, and does not within a reasonable time express his dissent to the holder he shall be deemed to have assented thereto.

45   Rules as to presentment for payment

Subject to the provisions of this Act a bill must be duly presented for payment. If it be not so presented the drawer and indorsers shall be discharged.

A bill is duly presented for payment which is presented in accordance with the following rules:—

(1)   Where the bill is not payable on demand, presentment must be made on the day it falls due.

(2)   Where the bill is payable on demand, then, subject to the provisions of this Act, presentment must be made within a reasonable time after its issue in order to render the drawer liable, and within a reasonable time after its indorsement, in order to render the indorser liable.

In determining what is a reasonable time, regard shall be had to the nature of the bill, the usage of trade with regard to similar bills, and the facts of the particular case.

(3)   Presentment must be made by the holder or by some person authorised to receive payment on his behalf at a reasonable hour on a business day, at the proper place as herein-after defined, either to the person designated by the bill as payer, or to some person authorised to pay or refuse payment on his behalf if with the exercise of reasonable diligence such person can there be found.

(4)   A bill is presented at the proper place:—

(a)   Where a place of payment is specified in the bill and the bill is there presented.

(b)   Where no place of payment is specified, but the address of the drawee or acceptor is given in the bill, and the bill is there presented.

(c)   Where no place of payment is specified and no address given, and the bill is presented at the drawee's or acceptor's place of business if known, and if not, at his ordinary residence if known.

(d)   In any other case if presented to the drawee or acceptor wherever he can be found, or if presented at his last known place of business or residence.

(5)   Where a bill is presented at the proper place, and after the exercise of reasonable diligence no person authorised to pay or refuse payment can be found there, no further presentment to the drawee or acceptor is required.

(6)   Where a bill is drawn upon, or accepted by two or more persons who are not partners, and no place of payment is specified, presentment must be made to them all.

(7)   Where the drawee or acceptor of a bill is dead, and no place of payment is specified, presentment must be made to a personal representative, if such there be, and with the exercise of reasonable diligence he can be found.

(8)   Where authorised by agreement or usage a presentment through the post office is sufficient.

46   Excuses for delay or non-presentment for payment

(1)   Delay in making presentment for payment is excused when the delay is caused by circumstances beyond the control of the holder, and not imputable to his default, misconduct, or negligence. When the cause of delay ceases to operate presentment must be made with reasonable diligence.

(2)   Presentment for payment is dispensed with,—

   (a)   Where, after the exercise of reasonable diligence presentment, as required by this Act, cannot be effected.

   The fact that the holder has reason to believe that the bill will, on presentment, be dishonoured, does not dispense with the necessity for presentment.

   (b)   Where the drawee is a fictitious person.

   (c)   As regards the drawer where the drawee or acceptor is not bound as between himself and the drawer, to accept or pay the bill, and the drawer has no reason to believe that the bill would be paid if presented.

   (d)   As regards an indorser, where the bill was accepted or made for the accommodation of that indorser, and he has no reason to expect that the bill would be paid if presented.

   (e)   By waiver of presentment, express or implied.

47   Dishonour by non-payment

(1)   A bill is dishonoured by non-payment (a) when it is duly presented for payment and payment is refused or cannot be obtained, or (b) when presentment is excused and the bill is overdue and unpaid.

(2)   Subject to the provisions of this Act, when a bill is dishonoured by non-payment, an immediate right of recourse against the drawer and indorsers accrues to the holder.

48   Notice of dishonour and effect of non-notice

Subject to the provisions of this Act, when a bill has been dishonoured by non-acceptance or by non-payment, notice of dishonour must be given to the drawer and each indorser, and any drawer or indorser to whom such notice is not given is discharged: Provided that—

(1)   Where a bill is dishonoured by non-acceptance, and notice of dishonour is not given, the rights of a holder in due course, subsequent to the omission, shall not be prejudiced by the omission.

(2)   where a bill is dishonoured by non-acceptance, and due notice of dishonour is given, it shall not be necessary to give notice of a subsequent dishonour by non-payment unless the bill shall in the meantime have been accepted.

49   Rules as to notice of dishonour

Notice of dishonour in order to be valid and effectual must be given in accordance with the following rules:—

(1)   The notice must be given by or on behalf of the holder, or by or on behalf of an indorser who, at the time of giving it, is himself liable on the bill.

(2)   Notice of dishonour may be given by an agent either in his own name or in the name of any party entitled to give notice whether that party be his principal or not.

(3)   Where the notice is given by or on behalf of the holder, it enures for the benefit of all subsequent holders and all prior indorsers who have a right of recourse against the party to whom it is given.

(4)   Where notice is given by or on behalf of an indorser entitled to give notice as

herein-before provided, it enures for the benefit of the holder and all indorsers subsequent to the party to whom notice is given.

(5)   The notice may be given in writing or by personal communication, and may be given in any terms which sufficiently identify the bill, and intimate that the bill has been dishonoured by non-acceptance or non-payment.

(6)   The return of a dishonoured bill to the drawer or an indorser is, in point of form, deemed a sufficient notice of dishonour.

(7)   A written notice need not be signed, and an insufficient written notice may be supplemented and validated by verbal communication. A misdescription of the bill shall not vitiate the notice unless the party to whom the notice is given is in fact misled thereby.

(8)   Where notice of dishonour is required to be given to any person, it may be given either to the party himself, or to his agent in that behalf.

(9)   Where the drawer or indorser is dead, and the party giving notice knows it, the notice must be given to a personal representative if such there be, and with the exercise of reasonable diligence he can be found.

(10)   Where the drawer or indorser is bankrupt, notice may be given either to the party himself or to the trustee.

(11)   Where there are two or more drawers or indorsers who are not partners, notice must be given to each of them, unless one of them has authority to receive such notice for the others.

(12)   The notice may be given as soon as the bill is dishonoured and must be given within a reasonable time thereafter.

In the absence of special circumstances notice is not deemed to have been given within a reasonable time, unless—

(a)   where the person giving and the person to receive notice reside in the same place, the notice is given or sent off in time to reach the latter on the day after the dishonour of the bill.

(b)   where the person giving and the person to receive notice reside in different places, the notice is sent off on the day after the dishonour of the bill, if there be a post at a convenient hour on that day, and if there be no post on that day then by the next post thereafter.

(13)   Where a bill when dishonoured is in the hands of an agent, he may either himself give notice to the parties liable on the bill, or he may give notice to his principal. If he give notice to his principal, he must do so within the same time as if he were the holder, and the principal upon receipt of such notice has himself the same time for giving notice as if the agent had been an independent holder.

(14)   Where a party to a bill receives due notice of dishonour, he has after the receipt of such notice the same period of time for giving notice to antecedent parties that the holder has after the dishonour.

(15)   Where notice of dishonour is duly addressed and posted, the sender is deemed to have given due notice of dishonour, notwithstanding any miscarriage by the post office.

50   Excuses for non-notice and delay

(1)   Delay in giving notice of dishonour is excused where the delay is caused by circumstance beyond the control of the party giving notice, and not imputable to his default, misconduct, or negligence. When the cause of delay ceases to operate the notice must be given with reasonable diligence.

(2)   Notice of dishonour is dispensed with–

(a)   When, after the exercise of reasonable diligence, notice as required by this Act cannot be given to or does not reach the drawer or indorser sought to be charged:

(b)   By waiver express or implied. Notice of dishonour may be waived before the time of giving notice has arrived, or after the omission to give due notice:

(c)   As regards the drawer in the following cases, namely, (1) where drawer and drawee are the same person, (2) where the drawee is a fictitious person or a person not having capacity to contract, (3) where the drawer is the person to whom the bill is presented for payment, (4) where the drawee or acceptor is as between himself and the drawer under no obligation to accept or pay the bill, (5) where the drawer has contermanded payment:

(d)   As regards the indorser in the following cases, namely, (1) where the drawee is a fictitious person or a person not having capacity to contract, and the indorser was aware of the fact at the time he indorsed the bill, (2) where the indorser is the person to whom the bill is presented for payment, (3) where the bill was accepted or made for his accommodation.

51   Noting or protest of bill

(1)   Where an inland bill has been dishonoured it may, if the holder think fit, be noted for non-acceptance or non-payment, as the case may be; but it shall not be necessary to note or protest any such bill in order to preserve the recourse against the drawer or indorser.

(2)   Where a foreign bill, appearing on the face of it to be such, has been dishonoured by non-acceptance it must be duly protested for non-acceptance, and where such a bill, which has not been previously dishonoured by non-acceptance, is dishonoured by non-payment it must be duly protested for non-payment. If it be not so protested the drawer and indorsers are discharged. Where a bill does not appear on the face of it to be a foreign bill, protest thereof in the case of dishonour is unnecessary.

(3)   A bill which has been protested for non-acceptance may be subsequently protested for non-payment.

(4)   Subject to the provisions of this Act, when a bill is noted or protested, it may be noted on the day of its dishonour and must be noted not later than the next succeeding business day. When a bill has been duly noted, the protest may be subsequently extended as of the date of the noting.

(5)   Where the acceptor of a bill becomes bankrupt or insolvent or suspends payment before it matures, the holder may cause the bill to be protested for better security against the drawer and indorsers.

(6)   A bill must be protested at the place where it is dishonoured: Provided that—

(a)   When a bill is presented through the post office, and returned by post dishonoured, it may be protested at the place to which it is returned and on the day of its return if received during business hours, and if not received during business hours then not later than the next business day:

(b)   When a bill drawn payable at the place of business or residence of some person other than the drawee has been dishonoured by non-acceptance, it must be protested for non-payment at the place where it is expressed to be payable, and no further presentment for payment to, or demand on, the drawee is necessary.

(7)   A protest must contain a copy of the bill, and must be signed by the notary making it, and must specify—

(a)   The person at whose request the bill is protested:

(b)   The place and date of protest, the cause or reason for protesting the bill, the demand made, and the answer given, if any, or the fact that the drawee or acceptor could not be found.

(8)   Where a bill is lost or destroyed, or is wrongly detained from the person entitled to hold it, protest may be made on a copy or written particulars thereof.

(9)   Protest is dispensed with by any circumstance which would dispense with notice of dishonour. Delay in noting or protesting is excused when the delay is caused by circumstances beyond the control of the holder, and not imputable to his default,

misconduct, or negligence. When the cause of delay ceases to operate the bill must be noted or protested with reasonable diligence.

52 Duties of holder as regards drawee or acceptor

(1) When a bill is accepted generally presentment for payment is not necessary in order to render the acceptor liable.

(2) When by the terms of a qualified acceptance presentment for payment is required, the acceptor, in the absence of an express stipulation to that effect, is not discharged by the omission to present the bill for payment on the day that it matures.

(3) In order to render the acceptor of a bill liable it is not necessary to protest it, or that notice of dishonour should be given to him.

(4) Where the holder of a bill presents it for payment, he shall exhibit the bill to the person from whom he demands payment, and when a bill is paid the holder shall forthwith deliver it up to the party paying it.

Liabilities of Parties

53 Funds in hands of drawee

A bill, of itself, does not operate as an assignment of funds in the hands of the drawee available for the payment thereof, and the drawee of a bill who does not accept as required by this Act is not liable on the instrument. This subsection shall not extend to Scotland.

54 Liability of acceptor

The acceptor of a bill, by accepting it—

(1) Engages that he will pay it according to the tenor of his acceptance:

(2) Is precluded from denying to a holder in due course:

(a) The existence of the drawer, the genuineness of his signature, and his capacity and authority to draw the bill;

(b) In the case of a bill payable to drawer's order, the then capacity of the drawer to indorse, but not the genuineness or validity of his indorsement;

(c) In the case of a bill payable to the order of a third person, the existence of the payee and his then capacity to indorse, but not the genuineness or validity of his indorsement.

55 Liability of drawer or indorser

(1) The drawer of a bill by drawing it—

(a) Engages that on due presentment it shall be accepted and paid according to its tenor, and that if it be dishonoured he will compensate the holder or any indorser who is compelled to pay it, provided that the requisite proceedings on dishonour be duly taken;

(b) Is precluded from denying to a holder in due course the existence of the payee and his then capacity to indorse.

(2) The indorser of a bill by indorsing it—

(a) Engages that on due presentment it shall be accepted and paid according to its tenor, and that if it be dishonoured he will compensate the holder or a subsequent indorser who is compelled to pay it, provided that the requisite proceedings on dishonour be duly taken;

(b) Is precluded from denying to a holder in due course the genuineness and regularity in all respects of the drawer's signature and all previous indorsements;

(c) Is precluded from denying to his immediate or a subsequent indorsee that the bill was at the time of his indorsement a valid and subsisting bill, and that he had then a good title thereto.

56 Stranger signing bill liable as indorser

Where a person signs a bill otherwise than as drawer or acceptor, he thereby incurs the liabilities of an indorser to a holder in due course.

57 Measure of damages against parties to dishonoured bill

Where a bill is dishonoured, the measure of damages, which shall be deemed to be liquidated damages, shall be as follows:

(1)   The holder may recover from any party liable on the bill, and the drawer who has been compelled to pay the bill may recover from the acceptor, and an indorser who has been compelled to pay the bill may recover from the acceptor or from the drawer, or from a prior indorser—

(a)   The amount of the bill:

(b)   Interest thereon from the time of presentment for payment if the bill is payable on demand, and from the maturity of the bill in any other case:

(c)   The expenses of noting, or, when protest is necessary, and the protest has been extended, the expenses of protest. ...

(3)   Where by this Act interest may be recovered as damages, such interest may, if justice require it, be withheld wholly or in part, and where a bill is expressed to be payable with interest at a given rate, interest as damages may or may not be given at the same rate as interest proper.

58 Transferor by delivery and transferee

(1)   Where the holder of a bill payable to bearer negotiates it by delivery without indorsing it he is called a 'transferor by delivery'.

(2)   A transferor by delivery is not liable on the instrument.

(3)   A transferor by delivery who negotiates a bill thereby warrants to his immediate transferee being a holder for value that the bill is what it purports to be, that he has a right to transfer it, and that at the time of transfer he is not aware of any fact which renders it valueless.

Discharge of Bill

59 Payment in due course

(1)   A bill is discharged by payment in due course by or on behalf of the drawee or acceptor.

'Payment in due course' means payment made at or after maturity of the bill to the holder thereof in good faith and without notice that his title to the bill is defective.

(2)   Subject to the provisions herein-after contained, when a bill is paid by the drawer or an indorser it is not discharged; but

(a)   Where a bill payable to, or to the order of, a third party is paid by the drawer, the drawer may enforce payment thereof against the acceptor, but may not re-issue the bill.

(b)   Where a bill is paid by an indorser, or where a bill payable to drawer's order is paid by the drawer, the party paying it is remitted to his former rights as regards the acceptor or antecedent parties, and he may, if he thinks fit, strike out his own subsequent indorsements, and again negotiate the bill.

(3)   Where an accommodation bill is paid in due course by the party accommodated the bill is discharged.

60 Banker paying demand draft whereon indorsement is forged

When a bill payable to order on demand is drawn on a banker, and the banker on whom it is drawn pays the bill in good faith and in the ordinary course of business, it is not incumbent on the banker to show that the indorsement of the payee or any subsequent indorsement was made by or under the authority of the person whose indorsement it purports to be, and the banker is deemed to have paid the bill in due course, although such indorsement has been forged or made without authority.

61 Acceptor the holder at maturity

When the acceptor of a bill is or becomes the holder of it at or after its maturity, in his own right, the bill is discharged.

62 Express waiver

(1)   When the holder of a bill at or after its maturity absolutely and uncondition-ally renounces his rights against the acceptor the bill is discharged.

The renunciation must be in writing, unless the bill is delivered up to the acceptor.

(2)   The liabilities of any party to a bill may in like manner be renounced by the holder before, at, or after its maturity; but nothing in this section shall affect the rights of a holder in due course without notice of the renunciation.

63 Cancellation

(1)   Where a bill is intentionally cancelled by the holder or his agent, and the cancellation is apparent thereon, the bill is discharged.

(2)   In like manner any party liable on a bill may be discharged by the intentional cancellation of his signature by the holder or his agent. In such case any indorser who would have had a right of recourse against the party whose signature is cancelled is also discharged.

(3)   A cancellation made unintentionally, or under a mistake, or without the au-thority of the holder is inoperative; but where a bill or any signature thereon appears to have been cancelled the burden of proof lies on the party who allege that the can-cellation was made unintentionally, or under a mistake, or without authority.

64 Alteration of bill

(1)   Where a bill or acceptance is materially altered without the assent of all par-ties liable on the bill, the bill is avoided except as against a party who has himself made, authorised, or assented to the alteration, and subsequent indorsers.

Provided that,

> Where a bill has been materially altered, but the alteration is not apparent, and the bill is in the hands of a holder in due course, such holder may avail himself of the bill as if it had not been altered, and may enforce payment of it according to its original tenour.

(2)   In particular the following alterations are material, namely, any alteration of the date, the sum payable, the time of payment, the place of payment, and, where a bill has been accepted generally, the addition of a place of payment without the accep-tor's assent.

Acceptance and Payment for Honour

65 Acceptance for honour suprà protest

(1)   Where a bill of exchange has been protested for dishonour by non-accept-ance, or protest for better security, and is not overdue, any person, not being a party already liable thereon, may, with the consent of the holder, intervene and accept the bill *suprà protest*, for the honour of any party liable thereon, or for the honour of the person for whose account the bill is drawn.

(2)   A bill may be accepted for honour for part only of the sum for which it is drawn.

(3)   An acceptance for honour *suprà protest* in order to be valid must—

(a)   be written on the bill, and indicate that it is an acceptance for honour:

(b)   be signed by the acceptor for honour.

(4)   Where an acceptance for honour does not expressly state for whose honour it is made, it is deemed to be an acceptance for the honour of the drawer.

(5)   Where a bill payable after sight is accepted for honour, its maturity is calcu-lated from the date of the noting for non-acceptance, and not from the date of the acceptance for honour.

66 Liability of acceptor for honour

(1)   The acceptor for honour of a bill by accepting it engages that he will, on due

presentment, pay the bill according to the tenor of his acceptance, if it is not paid by the drawee, provided it has been duly presented for payment, and protested for non-payment, and that he receives notice of these facts.

(2)   The acceptor for honour is liable to the holder and to all parties to the bill subsequent to the party for whose honour he has accepted.

67   Presentment to acceptor for honour

(1)   Where a dishonoured bill has been accepted for honour *suprà protest*, or contains a reference in case of need, it must be protested for non-payment before it is presented for payment to the acceptor for honour, or referee in case of need.

(2)   Where the address of the acceptor for honour is in the same place where the bill is protested for non-payment, the bill must be presented to him not later than the day following its maturity; and where the address of the acceptor for honour is in some place other than the place where it was protested for non-payment, the bill must be forwarded not later than the day following its maturity for presentment to him.

(3)   Delay in presentment or non-presentment is excused by any circumstance which would excuse delay in presentment for payment or non-presentment for payment.

(4)   When a bill of exchange is dishonoured by the acceptor for honour it must be protested for non-payment by him.

68   Payment for honour suprà protest

(1)   Where a bill has been protested for non-payment, any person may intervene and pay it *suprà protest* for the honour of any party liable thereon, or for the honour of the person for whose account the bill is drawn.

(2)   Where two or more persons offer to pay a bill for the honour of different parties, the person whose payment will discharge most parties to the bill shall have the preference.

(3)   Payment for honour *suprà protest*, in order to operate as such and not as a mere voluntary payment, must be attested by a notarial act of honour which may be appended to the protest or form an extension of it.

(4)   The notarial act of honour must be founded on a declaration made by the payer for honour, or his agent in that behalf, declaring his intention to pay the bill for honour, and for whose honour he pays.

(5)   Where a bill has been paid for honour, all parties subsequent to the party whose honour it is paid are discharged, but the payer for honour is subrogated for, and succeeds to both the rights and duties of, the holder as regards the party for whose honour he pays, and all parties liable to that party.

(6)   The payer for honour on paying to the holder the amount of the bill and the notarial expenses incidental to its dishonour is entitled to receive both the bill itself and the protest. If the holder do not on demand deliver them up he shall be liable to the payer for honour in damages.

(7)   Where the holder of a bill refuses to receive payment *suprà protest* he shall lose his right of recourse against any party who would have been discharged by such payment.

Lost Instruments

69   Holder's right to duplicate of lost bill

Where a bill has been lost before it is overdue the person who was the holder of it may apply to the drawer to give him another bill of the same tenor, giving security to the drawer if required to indemnify him against all persons whatever in case the bill alleged to have been lost shall be found again.

If the drawer on request as aforesaid refuses to give such duplicate bill he may be compelled to do so.

70 Action on lost bill

In any action or proceeding upon a bill, the court or a judge may order that the loss of the instrument shall not be set up, provided an indemnity be given to the satisfaction of the court or judge against the claims of any other person upon the instrument in question.

Bill in a Set

71 Rules as to sets

(1) Where a bill is drawn in a set, each part of the set being numbered, and containing a reference to the other parts the whole of the parts constitute one bill.

(2) Where the holder of a set indorses two or more parts to different persons, he is liable on every such part, and every indorser subsequent to him is liable on the part he has himself indorsed as if the said parts were separate bills.

(3) Where two or more parts of a set are negotiated to different holders in due course, the holder whose title first accrues is as between such holders deemed the true owner of the bill; but nothing in this sub-section shall affect the rights of a person who in due course accepts or pays the part first presented to him.

(4) The acceptance may be written on any part, and it must be written on one part only.

If the drawee accepts more than one part, and such accepted parts get into the hands of different holders in due course, he is liable on every such part as if it were a separate bill.

(5) When the acceptor of a bill drawn in a set pays it without requiring the part bearing his acceptance to be delivered up to him, and that part at maturity is outstanding in the hands of a holder in due course, he is liable to the holder thereof.

(6) Subject to the preceding rules, where any one part of a bill drawn in a set is discharged by payment or otherwise, the whole bill is discharged.

Conflict of Laws

72 Rules where laws conflict

Where a bill drawn in one country is negotiated, accepted, or payable in another, the rights, duties, and liabilities of the parties thereto are determined as follows:

(1) The validity of a bill as regards requisites in form is determined by the law of the place of issue, and the validity as regards requisites in form of the supervening contracts, such as acceptance, or indorsement, or acceptance *suprà protest*, is determined by the law of the place where such contract was made.

Provided that—

(a) Where a bill is issued out of the United Kingdom it is not invalid by reason only that it is not stamped in accordance with the law of the place of issue:

(b) Where a bill, issued out of the United Kingdom, conforms, as regards requisites in form, to the law of the United Kingdom, it may, for the purpose of enforcing payment thereof, be treated as valid as between all persons who negotiate, hold, or become parties to it in the United Kingdom.

(2) Subject to the provisions of this Act, the interpretation of the drawing, indorsement, acceptance, or acceptance *suprà protest* of a bill, is determined by the law of the place where such contract is made.

Provided that where an inland bill is indorsed in a foreign country, the indorsement shall as regards the payer be interpreted according to the law of the United Kingdom.

(3) The duties of the holder with respect to presentment for acceptance or payment and the necessity for or sufficiency of protest or notice of dishonour, or otherwise, are determined by the law of the place where the act is done or the bill is dishonoured. ...

(5) Where a bill is drawn in one country and is payable in another, the due date

thereof is determined according to the law of the place where it is payable.

PART III   CHEQUES ON A BANKER

73   Cheque defined
A cheque is a bill of exchange drawn on a banker payable on demand.
Except as otherwise provided in this Part, the provisions of this Act applicable to a bill of exchange payable on demand apply to a cheque.

74   Presentment of cheque for payment
Subject to the provisions of this Act—
(1)   Where a cheque is not presented for payment within a reasonable time of its issue, and the drawer or the person on whose account it is drawn had the right at the time of such presentment as between him and the banker to have the cheque paid and suffers actual damage through the delay, he is discharged to the extent of such damage, that is to say, to the extent to which such drawer or person is a creditor of such banker to a larger amount than he would have been had such cheque been paid.
(2)   In determining what is a reasonable time regard shall be had to the nature of the instrument, the usage of trade and of bankers, and the facts of the particular case.
(3)   The holder of such cheque as to which such drawer or person is discharged shall be a creditor, in lieu of such drawer or person, of such banker to the extent of such discharge, and entitled to recover the amount from him.

75   Revocation of banker's authority
The duty and authority of a banker to pay a cheque drawn on him by his customer are determined by—
(1)   Countermand of payment:
(2)   Notice of the customer's death.

Crossed cheques

76   General and special crossings defined
(1)   Where a cheque bears across its face an addition of—
(a)   The words 'and company' or any abbreviation thereof between two parallel transverse lines, either with or without the words 'not negotiable'; or
(b)   Two parallel transverse lines simply, either with or without the words 'not negotiable';
that addition constitutes a crossing, and the cheque is crossed generally.
(2)   Where a cheque bears across its face an addition of the name of a banker, either with or without the words 'not negotiable', that addition constituted a crossing, and the cheque is crossed specially and to that banker.

77   Crossing by drawer or after issue
(1)   A cheque may be crossed generally or specially by the drawer.
(2)   Where a cheque is uncrossed, the holder may cross it generally or specially.
(3)   Where a cheque is crossed generally the holder may cross it specially.
(4)   Where a cheque is crossed generally or specially, the holder may add the words 'not negotiable'.
(5)   Where a cheque is crossed specially, the banker to whom it is crossed may again cross it specially to another banker for collection.
(6)   Where an uncrossed cheque, or a cheque crossed generally, is sent to a banker for collection, he may cross it specially to himself.

78   Crossing a material part of cheque
A crossing authorised by this Act is a material part of the cheque; it shall not be lawful for any person to obliterate or, except as authorised by this Act, to add to or alter the crossing.

79 Duties of banker as to crossed cheques

(1) Where a cheque is crossed specially to more than one banker except when crossed to an agent for collection being a banker, the banker on whom it is drawn shall refuse payment thereof.

(2) Where the banker on whom a cheque is drawn which is so crossed nevertheless pays the same, or pays a cheque crossed generally otherwise than to a banker, or if crossed specially otherwise than to the banker to whom it is crossed, or his agent for collection being a banker, he is liable to the true owner of the cheque for any loss he may sustain owing to the cheque having been so paid.

Provided that where a cheque is presented for payment which dies not at the time of presentment appear to be crossed, or to have had a crossing which has been obliterated, or to have been added to or altered otherwise than as authorised by this Act, the banker paying the cheque in good faith and without negligence shall not be responsible or incur any liability, nor shall the payment be questioned by reason of the cheque having been crossed, or of the crossing having been obliterated or having been added to or altered otherwise than as authorised by this Act, and of payment having been made otherwise than to a banker or to the banker to whom the cheque is or was crossed, or to his agent for collection being a banker, as the case may be.

80 Protection to banker and drawer where cheque is crossed

Where the banker, on whom a crossed cheque (including a cheque which under section 81A below or otherwise is not transferable) is drawn, in good faith and without negligence pays it, if crossed generally, to a banker, and if crossed specially, to the banker to whom it is crossed, or his agent for collection being a banker, the banker paying the cheque, and, if the cheque has come into the hands of the payee, the drawer, shall respectively be entitled to the same rights and be placed in the same position as if payment of the cheque had been made to the true owner thereof.

81 Effect of crossing on holder

Where a person takes a crossed cheque which bears on it the words 'not negotiable', he shall not have and shall not be capable of giving a better title to the cheque than that which the person from whom he took it had.

81A Non-transferable cheques

(1) Where a cheque is crossed and bears across its face the words 'account payee' or 'a/c payee' either with or without the word 'only', the cheque shall not be transferable but shall only be valid as between the parties thereto.

(2) A banker is not to be treated for the purposes of section 80 above as having been negligent by reason only of his failure to concern himself with any purported indorsement of a cheque which under subsection (1) above or otherwise is not transferable. ...

PART IV PROMISSORY NOTES

83 Promissory note defined

(1) A promissory note is an unconditional promise in writing made by one person to another signed by the maker, engaging to pay, on demand or at a fixed or determinable future time, a sum certain in money, to, or to the order of, a specified person or to bearer.

(2) An instrument in the form of a note payable to maker's order is not a note within the meaning of this section unless and until it is indorsed by the maker.

(3) A note is not invalid by reason only that it contains also a pledge of collateral security with authority to sell or dispose thereof.

(4) A note which is, or on the face of it purports to be, both made and payable within the British Isles is an inland note. Any other note is a foreign note.

84   Delivery necessary

A promissory note is inchoate and incomplete until delivery thereof to the payee or bearer.

85   Joint and several notes

(1)   A promissory note may be made by two or more makers, and they may be liable thereon jointly, or jointly and severally according to its tenour.

(2)   Where a note runs 'I promise to pay' and is signed by two or more persons it is deemed to be their joint and several note.

86   Note payable on demand

(1)   Where a note payable on demand has been indorsed, it must be presented for payment within a reasonable time of the indorsement. If it be not so presented the indorser is discharged.

(2)   In determining what is reasonable time, regard shall be had to the nature of the instrument, the usage of trades and the facts of the particular case.

(3)   Where a note payable on demand is negotiated, it is not deemed to be over-due, for the purpose of affecting the holder with defects of title of which he had no notice, by reason that it appears that a reasonable time for presenting it for payment has elapsed since its issue.

87   Presentment of note for payment

(1)   Where a promissory note is in the body of it made payable at a particular place, it must be presented for payment at that place in order to render the maker liable. In any other case, presentment for payment is necessary in order to render the maker liable.

(2)   Presentment for payment is necessary in order to render the indorser of a note liable.

(3)   Where a note is in the body of it made payable at a particular place, present-ment at that place is necessary in order to render an indorser liable; but when a place of payment is indicated by way of memorandum only, presentment at that place is sufficient to render the indorser liable, but a presentment to the maker elsewhere, if sufficient in other respects, shall also suffice.

88   Liability of maker

The maker of a promissory note by making it—

(1)   Engages that he will pay it according to its tenour;

(2)   Is precluded from denying to a holder in due course the existence of the payee and his then capacity to indorse.

89   Application of Part II to notes

(1)   Subject to the provisions in this part, and except as by this section provided, the provisions of this Act relating to bills of exchange apply, with the necessary modi-fications to promissory notes.

(2)   In applying those provisions the maker of a note shall be deemed to corre-spond with the acceptor of a bill, and the first indorser of a note shall be deemed to correspond with the drawer of an accepted bill payable to drawer's order.

(3)   The following provisions as to bills do not apply to notes; namely, provisions relating to—

(a)   Presentment for acceptance;

(b)   Acceptance;

(c)   Acceptance *suprà protest*;

(d)   Bills in a set.

(4)   Where a foreign note is dishonoured, protest thereof is unnecessary.

PART V   SUPPLEMENTARY

90   Good faith
A thing is deemed to be done in good faith, within the meaning of this Act, where it is in fact done honestly, whether it is done negligently or not.

91   Signature
(1)   Where, by this Act, any instrument or writing is required to be signed by any person it is not necessary that he should sing it with his own hand, but it is sufficient if his signature is written thereon by some other person by or under his authority.

(2)   In the case of a corporation, where, by this Act, any instrument or writing is required to be signed, it is sufficient if the instrument or writing be sealed with the corporate seal.

But nothing in this section shall be construed as requiring the bill or note of a corporation to be under seal.

92   Computation of time
Where, by this Act, the time limited for doing any act or thing is less than three days, in reckoning time, non-business days are excluded.

'Non-business days' for the purposes of this Act mean—
   (a)   Saturday, Sunday, Good Friday, Christmas Day:
   (b)   A bank holiday under the Banking and Financial Dealings Act 1971:
   (c)   A day appointed by Royal proclamation as a public fast or thanksgiving day.
   (d)   a day declared by an order under section 2 of the Banking and Financial Dealings Act 1971 to be a non-business day.
Any other day is a business day.

93   When noting equivalent to protest
For the purposes of this Act, where a bill or note is required to be protested within a specified time or before some further proceeding is taken, it is sufficient that the bill has been noted for protest before the expiration of the specified time or the taking of the proceeding; and the formal protest may be extended at any time thereafter as of the date of the noting.

94   Protest when notary not accessible
Where a dishonoured bill or note is authorised or required to be protested, and the services of a notary cannot be obtained at the place where the bill is dishonoured, any householder or substantial resident of the place may, in the presence of two witnessed, give a certificate, signed by them, attesting the dishonour of the bill, and the certificate shall in all respects operate as if it were a formal protest of the bill.

The form given in Schedule 1 to this Act may be used with necessary modifications, and if used shall be sufficient.

95   Dividend warrants may be crossed
The provisions of this Act as to crossed cheques shall apply to a warrant for payment of dividend. ...

97   Savings
(1)   The rules in bankruptcy relating to bills of exchange, promissory notes, and cheques, shall continue to apply thereto notwithstanding anything in this Act contained.

(2)   The rules of common law including the law merchant, save in so far as they are inconsistent with the express provisions of this Act, shall continue to apply to bills of exchange, promissory notes, and cheques.

(3)   Nothing in this Act or in any repeal effected thereby shall affect—
   (a)   Any law or enactment for the time being in force relating to the revenue:

(b) The provisions of the Companies Act 1862, or Acts amending it, or any Act relating to joint stock banks or companies:

(c) The provisions of any Act relating to or confirming the privileges of the Bank of England or the Bank of Ireland respectively:

(d) The validity of any usage relating to dividend warrants, or the indorsements thereof.

99 Construction with other Acts, etc

Where any Act or document refers to any enactment repealed by this Act, the Act or document shall be construed, and shall operate, as if it referred to the corresponding provisions of this Act.

SCHEDULES

FIRST SCHEDULE
Section 94

Form of protest which may be used when the services of a notary cannot be obtained.

Known all men that I, *A.B.* [householder], of   in the country of in the United Kingdom, at the request of *C.D.*, there being no notary public available, did on the   day of   188   at   demand payment [or acceptance] of this bill of exchange hereunder written, from *E.F.*, to which demand he made answer [state answer, if any] wherefore I now, in the presence of *G.H.* and *J.K.* do protest the said bill of exchange.

(Signed by witnesses) *A.B.*

G.H.

J.K.

N.B.—The bill itself should be annexed, or a copy of the bill and all that is written thereon should be underwritten.

Cheques Act 1957

1 Protection of bankers paying unindorsed or irregularly indorsed cheques, etc

(1) Where a banker in good faith and in the ordinary course of business pays a cheque drawn on him which is not indorsed or is irregularly indorsed, he does not, in doing so, incur any liability by reason only of the absence of, or irregularity in, indorsement and he is deemed to have paid it in due course.

(2) Where a banker in good faith and in the ordinary course of business pays any such instrument as the following, namely,—

(a) a document issued by a customer of his which, though not a bill of exchange, is intended to enable a person to obtain payment from him of the sum mentioned in the document;

(b) a draft payable on demand drawn by him upon himself, whether payable at the head office or some other office of his bank;

he does not, in doing so, incur any liability by reason only of the absence of, or irregularity in, indorsement, and the payment discharges the instrument.

2   Rights of bankers collecting cheques not indorsed by holders
A banker who gives value for, or has a lien on, a cheque payable to order which the holder delivers to him for collection without indorsing it, has such (if any) rights as he would have had if, upon delivery, the holder had indorsed it in blank.

3   Unindorsed cheques as evidence of payment
An unindorsed cheque which appears to have been paid by the banker on whom it is drawn is evidence of the receipt by the payee of the sum payable by the cheque.

4   Protection of bankers collecting payment of cheques, etc
(1)   Where a banker, in good faith and without negligence,—
(a)   receives payment for a customer of an instrument to which this section applies; or
(b)   having credited a customer's account with the amount of such an instrument, receives payment thereof for himself;
and the customer has no title, or a defective title, to the instrument, the banker does not incur any liability to the true owner of the instrument by reason only of having received payment thereof.
(2)   This section applies to the following instruments, namely,—
(a)   cheques (including cheques which under section 81A(1) of the Bills of Exchange Act 1882 or otherwise are not transferable);
(b)   any document issued by a customer of a banker which, though not a bill of exchange, is intended to enable a person to obtain payment from that banker of the sum mentioned in the document;
(c)   any document issued by a public officer which is intended to enable a person to obtain payment from the Paymaster General or the Queen's and Lord Treasurer's Remembrancer of the sum mentioned in the document but is not a bill of exchange;
(d)   any draft payable on demand drawn by a banker upon himself, whether payable at the head office or some other office of his bank.
(3)   A banker is not to be treated for the purposes of this section as having been negligent by reason only of his failure to concern himself with absence of, or irregularity in, indorsement of an instrument.

5   Application of certain provisions of Bills of Exchange Act 1882 to instruments not being bills of exchange
The provisions of the Bills of Exchange Act 1882 relating to crossed cheques shall, so far as applicable, have effect in relation to instruments (other than cheques) to which the last foregoing section applies as they have effect in relation to cheques.

6   Construction, saving and repeal
(1)   This Act shall be construed as one with the Bills of Exchange Act 1882.
(2)   The foregoing provisions of this Act do not make negotiable any instrument which, apart from them, is not negotiable.

7   Provisions as to Northern Ireland
This Act extends to Northern Ireland.

8   Short title and commencement
(1)   This Act may be cited as the Cheques Act 1957.
(2)   This Act shall come into operation at the expiration of a period of three months beginning with the day on which it is passed.

Security Interests in Goods

Bills of Sale Act 1878

1 ...

2 Commencement
This Act shall come into operation on the first day of January one thousand eight hundred and seventy-nine, which day is in this Act referred to as the commencement of this Act.

3 Application
This Act shall apply to every bill of sale executed on or after the first day of January one thousand eight hundred and seventy-nine (whether the same be absolute, or subject or not subject to any trust) whereby the holder or grantee has power, either with or without notice, and either immediately or at any future time, to seize or take possession of any personal chattels comprised in or made subject to such bill of sale.

4 Interpretation of terms
In this Act the following words and expressions shall have the meanings in this section assigned to them respectively, unless there be something in the subject or context repugnant to such construction; (that is to say),

The expression 'bill of sale' shall include bills of sale, assignments, transfers, declarations of trust without transfer, inventories of goods with receipt thereto attached, or receipts for purchase moneys of goods, and other assurances of personal chattels, and also powers of attorney, authorities, or licenses to take possession of personal chattels as security for any debt, and also any agreement, whether intended or not to be followed by the execution of any other instrument, by which a right in equity to any personal chattels, or to any charge or security thereon, shall be conferred, but shall not include the following documents; that is to say, assignments for the benefit of the creditors of the person making or giving the same, marriage settlements, transfers or assignments of any ship or vessel or any share thereof, transfers of goods in the ordinary course of business of any trade or calling, bills of sale of goods in foreign parts or at sea, bills of lading, India warrants, warehouse-keepers' certificates, warrants or orders for the delivery of goods, or any other documents used in the ordinary course of business as proof of the possession or control of goods, or authorising or purporting to authorise, either by indorsement or by delivery, the possessor of such document to transfer or receive goods thereby represented:

The expression 'personal chattels' shall mean goods, furniture, and other articles capable of complete transfer by delivery, and (when separately assigned or charged) fixtures and growing crops, but shall not include chattel interests in real estate, nor fixtures (except trade machinery as herein-after defined), when assigned together with a freehold or leasehold interest in any land or building to which they are affixed, nor growing crops when assigned together with any interest in the land on which they grow, nor shares or interests in the stock, funds, or securities of any government, or in the capital or property of incorporated or joint stock companies, nor choses in action, nor any stock or produce upon any farm or lands which by virtue of any covenant or agreement or of the custom of the country ought not to be removed from any farm where the same are at the time of making or giving of such bill of sale:

Personal chattels shall be deemed to be in the 'apparent possession' of the person making or giving a bill of sale, so long as they remain or are in or upon any house, mill, warehouse, building, works, yard, land, or other premises occupied by him, or are used and enjoyed by him in any place whatsoever, notwithstanding that formal possession thereof may have been taken by or given to any other person:

'Prescribed' means prescribed by rules made under the provisions of this Act.

5   Application of Act to trade machinery

From and after the commencement of this Act trade machinery shall, for the purposes of this Act, be deemed to be personal chattels, and any mode of disposition of trade machinery by the owner thereof which would be a bill of sale as to any other personal chattels shall be deemed to be a bill of sale within the meaning of this Act.

For the purposes of this Act—

'Trade machinery' means the machinery used in or attached to any factory or workshop;

1st.   Exclusive of the fixed motive-powers, such as the water-wheels and steam-engines, and the steam-boilers, donkey-engines, and other fixed appurtenances of the said motive-powers; and

2nd.   Exclusive of the fixed power machinery, such as the shafts, wheels, drums, and their fixed appurtenances, which transmit the action of the motive-powers to the other machinery, fixed and loose; and

3rd.   Exclusive of the pipes for steam gas and water in the factory or workshop.
The machinery or effects excluded by this section form the definition of trade machinery shall not be deemed to be personal chattels within the meaning of this Act.

'Factory or workshop' means any premises on which any manual labour is exercised by way of trade, or for purposes of gain, in or incidental to the following purposes or any of them; that is to say,

(a)   In or incidental to the making any article or part of any article; or

(b)   In or incidental to the altering repairing ornamenting finishing of any article; or

(c)   In or incidental to the adapting for sale any article.

6   Certain instruments giving powers of distress to be subject to this Act

Every attornment instrument or agreement, not being a mining lease, whereby a power of distress is given or agreed to be given by any person to any other person by way of security for any present future or contingent debt or advance, and whereby any rent is reserved or made payable as a mode of providing for the payment of interest on such debt or advance, or otherwise for the purpose of such security only, shall be deemed to be a bill of sale, within the meaning of this Act, of any personal chattels which may be seized or taken under such power of distress.

Provided, that nothing in this section shall extend to any mortgage of any estate or interest in any land tenement or hereditament which the mortgagee, being in possession, shall have demised to the mortgagor as his tenant at a fair and reasonable rent.

7   Fixtures or growing crops not to be deemed separately assigned when the land passes by the same instrument

No fixtures or growing crops shall be deemed, under this Act, to be separately assigned or charged by reason only that they are assigned by separate words, or that power is given to sever them from the land or building to which they are affixed, or from the land on which they grow, without otherwise taking possession of or dealing with such land or building, or land, if by the same instrument any freehold or leasehold interest in the land or building to which such fixtures are affixed, or in the land on which such crops grow, is also conveyed or assigned to the same persons or person.

The same rule of construction shall be applied to all deeds or instruments, including fixtures or growing crops, executed before the commencement of this Act, and then subsisting and in force, in all questions arising under any bankruptcy liquidation assignment for the benefit of creditors, or execution of any process of any court, which shall take place or be issued after the commencement of this Act.

8 Avoidance of unregistered bills of sale in certain cases

Every bill of sale to which this Act applies shall be duly attested and shall be registered under this Act, within seven days after the making or giving thereof, and shall set forth the consideration for which such bill of sale was given, otherwise such bill of sale, as against all trustees or assignees of the estate of the person whose chattels, or any of them, are comprised in such bill of sale under the law relating to bankruptcy or liquidation, or under any assignment for the benefit of the creditors of such person, and also as against all sheriffs officers and other persons seizing any chattels comprised in such bill of sale, in the execution of any process of any court authorising the seizure of the chattels of the person by whom or of whose chattels such bill has been made, and also as against every person on whose behalf such process shall have been issued, shall be deemed fraudulent and void so far as regards the property in or right to the possession of any chattels comprised in such bill of sale which, at or after the time of filing the petition for bankruptcy or liquidation, or of the execution of such assignment, or of executing such process (as the case may be), and after the expiration of such seven days are in the possession or apparent possession of the person making such bill of sale (or of any person against whom the process has issued under or in the execution of which such bill has been made or given, as the case may be).

9 Avoidance of certain duplicate bills of sale

Where a subsequent bill of sale is executed within or on the expiration of seven days after the execution of a prior unregistered bill of sale, and comprises all or any part of the personal chattels comprised in such prior bill of sale, then, if such subsequent bill of sale is given as a security for the same debt as is secured by the prior bill of sale, or for any part of such debt, it shall, to the extent to which it is a security for the same debt or part thereof, and so far as respects the personal chattels or part thereof comprised in the prior bill, be absolutely void, unless it is proved to the satisfaction of the court having cognizance of the case that the subsequent bill of sale was bona fide given for the purpose of correcting some material error in the prior bill of sale, and not for the purpose of evading this Act.

10 Mode of registering bills of sale

A bill of sale shall be attested and registered under this Act in the following manner:

(1) The execution of every bill of sale shall be attested by a solicitor of the Supreme Court, and the attestation shall state that before the execution of the bill of sale the effect thereof has been explained to the grantor by the attesting solicitor.

(2) Such bill, with every schedule or inventory thereto annexed or therein referred to, and also a true copy of such bill and of every such schedule or inventory, and of every attestation of the execution of such bill of sale, together with an affidavit of the time of such bill of sale being made or given, and of its due execution and attestation, and a description of the residence and occupation of the person making or giving the same (or in case the same is made or given by any person under or in the execution of any process, then a description of the residence and occupation of the person against whom such process issued), and of every attesting witness to such bill of sale, shall be presented to and the said copy and affidavit shall be files with the registrar within seven clear days after the making or giving of such bill of sale, in like manner as a warrant of attorney in any personal action given by a trader is now by law required to be filed:

(3) If the bill of sale is made or given subject to any defeasance or condition, or declaration of trust not contained in the body thereof, such defeasance, condition, or

declaration shall be deemed to be part of the bill, and shall be written on the same paper or parchment therewith before the registration, and shall be truly set forth in the copy filed under this Act therewith and as part thereof, otherwise the registration shall be void.

In case two or more bills of sale are given, comprising in whole or in part any of the same chattels, they shall have priority in the order of the date of their registration respectively as regards such chattels.

A transfer or assignment or a registered bill of sale need not be registered.

11   Renewal of registration

The registration of a bill of sale, whether executed before or after the commencement of this Act. must be renewed once at least every five years, and if a period of five years elapses from the registration or renewed registration of a bill of sale without a renewal or further renewal (as the case may be), the registration shall become void.

The renewal of a registration shall be effected by filing with the registrar an affidavit stating the date of the bill of sale and of the last registration thereof, and the names, residences, and occupations of the parties thereto as stated therein, and that the bill of sale is still a subsisting security.

Every such affidavit may be in the form set forth in the Schedule (A) to this Act annexed.

A renewal of registration shall not become necessary by reason only of a transfer or assignment of a bill of sale.

12   Form of register

The registrar shall keep a book (in this Act called 'the register') for the purposes of this Act, and shall, upon the filing of any bill of sale or copy under this Act, enter therein in the form set forth in the second schedule (B) to this Act annexed, or in any other prescribed form, the name residence and occupation of the person by whom the bill was made or given (or in the case the same was made or given by any person under or in the execution of process, then the name residence and occupation of the person against whom such process was issued, and also the name of the person or persons to whom or in whose favour the bill was given), and the other particulars shown in the said schedule or to be prescribed under this Act, and shall number all such bills registered in each year consecutively, according to the respective dates of their registration.

Upon the registration of any affidavit of renewal the like entry shall be made, with the addition of the date and number of the last previous entry relating to the same bill, and the bill of sale or copy originally filed shall be thereupon marked with the number affixed to such affidavit of renewal.

The registrar shall also keep an index of the names of the grantors of registered bills of sale with reference to entries in the register of the bills of sale given by each such grantor.

Such index shall be arranged in divisions corresponding with the letters of the alphabet, so that all grantors whose surnames begin with the same letter (and no others) shall be comprised in one division, but the arrangement within each such division need not be strictly alphabetical.

13   The registrar

The masters of the Supreme Court of Judicature attached to the Queen's Bench Division of the High Court of Justice, or such other officers as may for the time being be assigned for this purpose under the provisions of the Supreme Court of Judicature Acts 1873 and 1875, shall be the registrar for the purposes of this Act, and any one of the said masters may perform all or any of the duties of the registrar.

14   Rectification of register

Any judge of the High Court of Justice on being satisfied that the omission to register a bill of sale or an affidavit or renewal thereof within the time prescribed by this Act, or the omission or mis-statement of the name residence or occupation of any person, was accidental or due to inadvertence, may in his discretion order such omission or mis-statement to be rectified by the insertion in the register of the true name residence or occupation, or by extending the time for such registration on such terms and conditions(if any) as to security, notice by advertisement or otherwise, or as to any other matter, as he thinks fit to direct.

15 Entry of satisfaction

Subject to and in accordance with any rules to be made under and for the purposes of this Act, the registrar may order a memorandum of satisfaction to be written upon any registered copy of a bill of sale, upon the prescribed evidence being given that the debt (if any) for which such bill of sale was made or given has been satisfied or discharged.

16 Copies may be taken, etc

Any person shall be entitled to have an office copy or extract of any registered bill of sale, and affidavit of execution filed therewith, or copy thereof, and of any affidavit filed therewith, if any, or registered affidavit of renewal, upon paying for the same at the like rate as for office copies of judgements of the High Court of Justice, and any copy of a registered bill of sale, and affidavit purporting to be an office copy thereof, shall in all courts and before all arbitrators or other persons, be admitted as prima facie evidence thereof, and of the fact and date of registration as shown thereon . . .

17 Affidavits

Every affidavit required by or for the purposes of this Act may be sworn before a master of any division of the High Court of Justice, or before any commissioner empowered to take affidavits in the Supreme Court of Judicature. ...

19 Collection of fees under 38 & 39 Vict c 77 s 26

Section twenty-six of the Supreme Court of Judicature Act 1875, and any enactments for the time being in force amending or substitute for that section, shall apply to fees under this Act, and an order under that section may, if need be, be made in relation to such fees accordingly.

20 Order and disposition

Chattels comprised in a bill of sale which has been and continues to be duly registered under this Act shall not be deemed to be in the possession, order, or disposition of the grantor of the bill of sale within the meaning of the Bankruptcy Act 1869.

21 Rules

Rules for the purposes of this Act may be made and altered from time to time by the like persons and in the like manner in which rules and regulations may be made under and for the purposes of the Supreme Court of Judicature Acts 1873 and 1875.

22 Time for registration

When the time for registering a bill of sale expires on a Sunday, or other day on which the registrar's office is closed, the registration shall be valid if made on the next following day on which the office is open.

23 As to bills of sale and under repealed Acts

Except as herein expressly mentioned with respect to construction and with respect to renewal of registration, nothing in this Act shall affect any bill of sale executed before the commencement of this Act, and as regards bills of sale so executed the Acts hereby repealed shall continue in force.

Any renewal after the commencement of this Act of the registration of a bill of sale executed before the commencement of this Act, and registered under the Acts hereby repealed, shall be made under this Act in the same manner as the renewal of a registration made under this Act.

24   Extent of Act
This Act shall not extend to Scotland or to Ireland.

SCHEDULE (A)
Section 11

I   [*A.B.*]   of   do swear that a bill of sale, bearing date the
              day of   18   [*insert the date of the bill*], and made be-
tween [*insert the names and descriptions of the parties in the original bill of sale*] and
which said bill of sale [*or, and a copy of which said bill of sale, as the case may be*]
was registered on the   day of   18   [*insert date of registration*], is still a subsisting security.
      Sworn, &c.

SCHEDULE (B)

...

Bills of Sale Act (1878) Amendment Act 1882

1   Short title
The Act may be cited for all purposes as the Bills of Sale Act (1878) Amendment Act
1882; and this Act and the Bills of Sale Act 1878 may be cited together as the Bills of
Sale Acts 1878 and 1882.

2   Commencement of Act
The Act shall come into operation on the first day of November one thousand eight
hundred and eighty-two, which date is herein-after referred to as the commencement
of this Act.

3   Construction of Act
The Bills of Sale Act 1878 is herein-after referred to as 'the Principal Act', and this
Act shall, so far as is consistent with the tenor thereof, be construed as one with the
principal Act; but unless the context otherwise requires shall not apply to any bill of
sale duly registered before the commencement of this Act so long as the registration
thereof is not avoided by non-renewal or otherwise.
      The expression 'bill of sale', and other expressions in this Act, have the same
meaning as in the principal Act, except as to bills of sale or other documents mentioned in section four of the principal Act, which may be given otherwise than by way
of security for the payment of money, to which last-mentioned bills of sale and other
documents this Act shall not apply.

4   Bill of sale to have schedule of property attached thereto
Every bill of sale shall have annexed thereto or written thereon a schedule containing
an inventory of the personal chattels comprised in the bill of sale; and such bill of
sale, save as herein-after mentioned, shall have effect only in respect of the personal
chattels specifically described in the said schedule; and shall be void, except as against
the grantor, in respect of any personal chattels not so specifically described.

5   Bill of sale not to affect after acquired property
Save as herein-after mentioned, a bill of sale shall be void, except as against the gran-

tor, in respect of any personal chattels specifically described in the schedule thereto of which the grantor was not the true owner at the time of the execution of the bill of sale.

6 Exception as to certain things

Nothing contained in the foregoing sections of this Act shall render a bill of sale void in respect of any of the following things; (that is to say,)

(1) Any growing crops separately assigned or charged where such crops were actually growing at the time when the bill of sale was executed.

(2) Any fixtures separately assigned or charged, and any plant, or trade machinery where such fixtures, plant, or trade machinery are used in, attached to, or brought upon any land, farm, factory, workshop, shop, house, warehouse, or other place in substitution for any of the like fixtures, plant, or trade machinery specifically described in the schedule to such bill of sale.

7 Bill of sale with power to seize except in certain events to be void

Personal chattels assigned under a bill of sale shall not be liable to be seized or taken possession of by the grantee for any other than the following causes:,—

(1) If the grantor shall make default in payment of the sum or sums of money thereby secured at the time therein provided for payment, or in the performance of any covenant or agreement contained in the bill of sale and necessary for maintaining the security;

(2) If the grantor shall become a bankrupt, or suffer the said goods or any of them to be distrained for rent, rates, or taxes;

(3) If the grantor shall fraudulently either remove or suffer the said goods, or any of them, to be removed from the premises;

(4) If the grantor shall not, without reasonable excuse, upon demand in writing by the grantee, produce to him his last receipts for rent, rates, and taxes;

(5) If execution shall have been levied against the goods of the grantor under any judgment at law:

Provided that the grantor may within five days from the seizure or taking possession of any chattels on account of any of the above-mentioned causes, apply to the High Court, or to a judge thereof in chambers, and such court or judge, if satisfied that by payment of money or otherwise the said cause of seizure no longer exists, may restrain the grantee from removing or selling the said chattels, or may make such other order as may seem just.

7A Defaults under consumer credit agreements

(1) Paragraph (1) of section 7 of this Act does not apply to a default relating to a bill of sale given by way of security for the payment of money under a regulated agreement to which section 87(1) of the Consumer Credit Act 1974 applies—

(a) unless the restriction imposed by section 88(2) of that Act has ceased to apply to the bill of sale; or

(b) if, by virtue of section 89 of that Act, the default is to be treated as not having occurred.

(2) Where paragraph (1) of section 7 of this Act does apply in relation to a bill of sale such as is mentioned in subsection (1) of this section, the proviso to that section shall have effect with the substitution of 'county court' for 'High Court'.

8 Bill of sale to be void unless attested and registered

Every bill of sale shall be duly attested, and shall be registered under the principal Act within seven clear days after the execution thereof, or if it is executed in any place out of England then within seven clear days after the time at which it would in the ordinary course of post arrive in England if posted immediately after the execution thereof; and shall truly set forth the consideration for which it was given; otherwise such bill of sale shall be void in respect of the personal chattels comprised therein.

9 Form of bill of sale
A bill of sale made or given by way of security for the payment of money by the grantor thereof shall be void unless made in accordance with the form in the schedule to this Act annexed.

10 Attestation
The execution of every bill of sale by the grantor shall be attested by one or more credible witness or witnesses, not being a party or parties thereto ...

11 Local registration of contents of bills of sale
Where the affidavit (which under section ten of the principal Act is required to accompany a bill of sale when presented for registration) described the residence of the person making or giving the same or of the person against whom the process is issued to be in some place outside the London insolvency district or where the bill of sale describes the chattels enumerated therein as being in some place outside the London insolvency district, the registrar under the principal Act shall forthwith and within three clear days after registration in the principal registry, and in accordance with the prescribed directions, transmit an abstract in the prescribed form of the contents of such bill of sale to the county court registrar in whose district such places are situate, and if such places are in the districts of different registrars to each such registrar.
Every abstract so transmitted shall be filed, kept, and indexed by the registrar of the county court in the prescribed manner, and any person may search, inspect, make extracts from, and obtain copies of the abstract so registered in the like manner and upon the like terms as to payment or otherwise as near as may be as in the case of bills of sale registered by the registrar under the principal Act.

12 Bill of sale under £30 to be void
Every bill of sale made or given in consideration of any sum under thirty pounds shall be void.

13 Chattels not to be removed or sold
All personal chattels seized or of which possession is taken under or by virtue of any bill of sale (whether registered before or after the commencement of this Act), shall remain on the premises where they were so seized or so taken possession of, and shall not be removed or sold until after the expiration of five clear days from the day they were so seized or so taken possession of.

14 Bill of sale not to protect chattels against poor and parochial rates
A bill of sale to which this Act applies shall be no protection in respect of personal chattels included in such a bill of sale which but for such bill of sale would have been liable to distress under a warrant for the recovery of taxes and poor and other parochial rates.

15 Repeal of part of Bills of Sale Act 1878
All enactments contained in the principal Act which are inconsistent with this Act are repealed.

16 Inspection of registered bills of sale
Any person shall be entitled at all reasonable times to search the register, on payment of a fee of one shilling, or such other fee as may be prescribed, and subject to such regulations as may be prescribed, and shall be entitled at all reasonable times to inspect, examine, and make extracts from any and every registered bill of sale without being required to make a written application, or to specify any particulars in reference thereto, upon payment of one shilling for each bill of sale inspected, and such payment shall be made by a judicature stamp. Provided that the said extracts shall be limited to the dates of execution, registration, renewal of registration, and satisfaction, to the names, addresses, and occupations of the parties, to the amount of the

consideration, and to any further prescribed particulars.

17 Debentures to which Act not to apply
Nothing in this Act shall apply to any debentures issued by any mortgage, loan, or other incorporated company, and secured upon the capital stock or goods, chattels, and effects of such company.

18 Extent of Act
This Act shall not extend to Scotland or Ireland.

SCHEDULE
FORM OF BILL OF SALE
Section 9

This Indenture made the   day of   between *A.B.* of   of the one part, and *C.D.* of   of the other part, witnesseth that in consideration of the sum of £   now paid to *A.B.* by *C.D.*, the receipt of which the said A.B. hereby acknowledges [*or whatever else the consideration may be*], he the said *A.B.* doth hereby assign unto *C.D.*, his executors, administrators, and assigns, all and singular the several chattels and things specifically described in the schedule hereto annexed by way of security for the payment of the sum of £ and interest thereon at the rate of   per cent per annum [*or whatever else may be the rate*]. And the said *A.B.* doth further agree and declare that he will duly pay to the said *C.D.* the principal sum aforesaid, together with the interest then due, by equal payments of £   on the   day of   [*or whatever else may be the stipulated times or time of payment*]. And the said *A.B.* doth also agree with the said *C.D.* that he will [*here insert terms as to insurance, payment of rent, or otherwise, which the parties may agree to for the maintenance or defeasance of the security*].

Provided always, that the chattels hereby assigned shall not be liable to seizure or to be taken possession of by the said *C.D.* for any cause other than those specified in section seven of the Bills of Sale Act (1878) Amendment Act 1882.

In witness, &c.

Signed and sealed by the said *A.B.* in the presence of me *E.F.* [*add witness' name, address, and description*].

Bills of Sale Act 1890

1 Exemption of letter of hypothecation of imported goods from 41 & 42 Vict c 31, and 45 & 46 Vict c 43, s 9
An instrument charging or creating any security on or declaring trusts of imported goods given or executed at any time prior to their deposit in a warehouse, factory, or store, or to their being reshipped for export, or delivered to a purchaser not being the person giving or executing such instrument, shall not be deemed a bill of sale within the meaning of the Bills of Sale Acts 1878 and 1882.

2 Saving of 46 & 47 Vict c 52, s 44
Nothing in this Act shall affect the operation of section forty-four of the Bankruptcy Act 1883 in respect of any goods comprised in any such instrument as is hereinbefore described, if such goods would but for this Act be goods within the meaning of subsection three of that section.

3 Short title
This Act may be cited as the Bills of Sale Act 1890.

Companies Act 1985

PART XII REGISTRATION OF CHARGES

Chapter 1 Registration of Charges (England and Wales)

395 Certain charges void if not registered
(1) Subject to the provisions of this Chapter, a charge created by a company registered in England and Wales and being a charge to which this section applies is, so far as any security on the company's property or undertaking is conferred by the charge, void against the liquidator [or administrator] and any creditor of the company, unless the prescribed particulars of the charge together with the instrument (if any) by which the charge is created or evidence, are delivered to or received by the registrar of companies for registration in the manner required by this Chapter within 21 days after the date of the charge's creation.

(2) Subsection (1) is without prejudice to any contract or obligation for repayment of the money secured by the charge; and when a charge becomes void under this section, the money secured by it immediately becomes payable.

396 Charges which have to be registered
(1) Section 395 applies to the following charges—
(a) a charge for the purpose of securing any issue of debentures,
(b) a charge on uncalled share capital of the company,
(c) a charge created or evidenced by an instrument which, if executed by an individual, would require registration as a bill of sale,
(d) a charge on land (wherever situated) or any interest in it, but not including a charge for any rent or other periodical sum issuing out of the land,
(e) a charge on book debts of the company,
(f) a floating charge on the company's undertaking or property,
(g) a charge on calls made but not paid,
(h) a charge on a ship or aircraft, or any share in a ship,
(j) a charge on goodwill, or on any intellectual property.
(2) Where a negotiable instrument has been given to secure the payment of any book debts of a company, the deposit of the instrument for the purpose of securing an advance to the company is not, for purposes of section 395, to be treated as a charge on those book debts.

(3) The holding of debentures entitling the holder to a charge on land is not for purposes of this section deemed to be an interest in land.

(3A) The following are 'intellectual property' for the purposes of this section—
(a) any patent, trade mark, service mark, registered design, copyright or design right;
(b) any licence under or in respect of any such right.
(4) In this Chapter, 'charge' includes mortgage.

397 Formalities of registration (debentures)
(1) Where a series of debentures containing, or giving by reference to another instrument, any charge to the benefit of which the debenture holders of that series are entitled pari passu is created by a company, it is for purposes of section 395 sufficient if there are delivered to or received by the registrar, within 21 days after the execution of the deed containing the charge (or, if there is no such deed, after the execution of

any debentures of the series), the following particulars in the prescribed form—

    (a)   the total amount secured by the whole series, and

    (b)   the dates of the resolutions authorising the issue of the series and the date of the covering deed (if any) by which the security is created or defined, and

    (c)   a general description of the property charged, and

    (d)   the names of the trustees (if any) for the debenture holders,

    together with the deed containing the charge or, if there is no such deed, one of the debentures of the series:

Provided that there shall be sent to the registrar of companies, for entry in the register, particulars in the prescribed form of the date and amount of each issue of debentures of the series, but any omission to do this does not affect the validity of any of those debentures.

    (2)   Where any commission, allowance, or discount has been paid or made either directly or indirectly by a company to a person in consideration of his—

    (a)   subscribing or agreeing to subscribe, whether absolutely or conditionally, for debentures of the company, or

    (b)   procuring or agreeing to procure subscriptions, whether absolute or conditional, for such debentures,

    the particulars required to be sent for registration under section 395 shall include particulars as to the amount or rate per cent of the commission, discount or allowance so paid or made, but omission to do this does not affect the validity of the debentures issued.

    (3)   The deposit of debentures as security for a debt of the company is not, for the purposes of subsection (2), treated as the issue of the debentures at a discount.

398   Verification of charge on property outside United Kingdom

    (1)   In the case of a charge created out of the United Kingdom comprising property situated outside the United Kingdom, the delivery to and the receipt by the registrar of companies of a copy (verified in the prescribed manner) of the instrument by which the charge is created or evidenced has the same effect for purposes of sections 395 to 398 as the delivery and receipt of the instrument itself.

    (2)   In that case, 21 days after the date on which the instrument or copy could, in due course of post (and if despatched with due diligence), have been received in the United Kingdom are substituted for the 21 days mentioned in section 395(2) (or as the case may be, section 397(1)) as the time within which the particulars and instrument or copy are to be delivered to the registrar.

    (3)   Where a charge is created in the United Kingdom but comprises property outside the United Kingdom, the instrument creating or purporting to create the charge may be sent for registration under section 395 notwithstanding that further proceedings may be necessary to make the charge valid or effectual according to the law of the country in which the property is situated.

    (4)   Where a charge comprises property situated in Scotland or Northern Ireland and registration in the country where the property is situated is necessary to make the charge valid or effectual according to the law of that country, the delivery to and receipt by the registrar of a copy (verified in the prescribed manner) of the instrument by which the charge is created or evidenced, together with a certificate in the prescribed form stating that the charge was presented for registration in Scotland or Northern Ireland (as the case may be) on the date on which it was so presented has, for purposes of sections 395 to 398, the same effect as the delivery and receipt of the instrument itself.

399   Company's duty to register charges it creates

    (1)   It is a company's duty to send to the registrar of companies for registration the particulars of every charge created by the company and of the issues of debentures

of a series requiring registration under sections 395 to 398; but registration of any such charge may be effected on the application of any person interested in it.

(2) Where registration is effected on the application of some person other than the company, that person is entitled to recover from the company the amount of any fees properly paid by him to the registrar on the registration.

(3) If a company fails to comply with subsection (1), then, unless the registration has been effected on the application of some other person, the company and every officer of it who is in default is liable to a fine and, for continued contravention, to a daily default fine.

400 Charges existing on property acquired

(1) This section applies where a company registered in England and Wales acquires property which is subject to a charge of any such kind as would, if it had been created by the company after the acquisition of the property, have been required to be registered under this Chapter.

(2) The company shall cause the prescribed particulars of the charge, together with a copy (certified in the prescribed manner to be a correct copy) of the instrument (if any) by which the charge was created or is evidenced, to be delivered to the registrar of companies for registration in manner required by this Chapter within 21 days after the date on which the acquisition is completed.

(3) However, if the property is situated and the charge was created outside Great Britain, 21 days after the date on which the copy of the instrument could in due course of post, and if despatched with due diligence, have been received in the United Kingdom is substituted for the 21 days above-mentioned as the time within which the particulars and copy of the instrument are to be delivered to the registrar.

(4) If default is made in complying with this section, the company and every officer of it who is in default is liable to a fine and, for continued contravention, to a daily default fine.

401 Register of charges to be kept by registrar of companies

(1) The registrar of companies shall keep, with respect to each company, a register in the prescribed form of all the charges requiring registration under this Chapter; and he shall enter in the register with respect to such charges the following particulars—

(a) in the case of a charge to the benefit of which the holders of a series of debentures are entitled, the particulars specified in section 397(1).

(b) in the case of any other charge—
   (i) if it is a charge created by the company, the date of its creation, and if it is a charge which was existing on property acquired by the company, the date of the acquisition of the property, and
   (ii) the amount secured by the charge, and
   (iii) short particulars of the property charged, and
   (iv) the persons entitled to the charge.

(2) The registrar shall give a certificate of the registration of any charge registered in pursuance of this Chapter, stating the amount secured by the charge.

The certificate—

(a) shall be either signed by the registrar, or authenticated by his official seal, and

(b) is conclusive evidence that the requirements of this Chapter as to registration have been satisfied.

(3) The register kept in pursuance of this section shall be open to inspection by any person.

402 Endorsement of certificate on debentures

(1) The company shall cause a copy of every certificate of registration given

under section 401 to be endorsed on every debenture or certificate of debenture stock which is issued by the company, and the payment of which is secured by the charge so registered.

(2)   But this does not require a company to cause a certificate of registration of any charge so given to be endorsed or any debenture or certificate of debenture stock issued by the company before the charge was created.

(3)   If a person knowingly and wilfully authorises or permits the delivery of a debenture or certificate of debenture stock which under this section is required to have endorsed on it a copy of a certificate of registration, without the copy being so endorsed upon it, he is liable (without prejudice to any other liability) to a fine.

403   Entries of satisfaction and release

(1)   The registrar of companies, on receipt of a statutory declaration in the prescribed form verifying, with respect to a registered charge,—

(a)   that the debt for which the charge was given has been paid or satisfied in whole or in part, or

(b)   that part of the property or undertaking charged has been released from the charge or has ceased to form part of the company's property or undertaking,

may enter on the register a memorandum of satisfaction in whole or in part, or of the fact that part of the property or undertaking has been released from the charge or has ceased to form part of the company's property or undertaking (as the case may be).

(2)   Where the registrar enters a memorandum of satisfaction in whole, he shall if required furnish the company with a copy of it.

404   Rectification of register of charges

(1)   The following applies if the court is satisfied that the omission to register a charge within the time required by this Chapter or that the omission or mis-statement of any particular with respect to any such charge or in a memorandum of satisfaction was accidental, or due to inadvertence or to some other sufficient cause, or is not of a nature to prejudice the position of creditors or shareholders of the company, or that on other grounds it is just and equitable to grant relief.

(2)   The court may, on the application of the company or a person interested, and on such terms and conditions as seem to the court just and expedient, order that the time for registration shall be extended or, as the case may be, that the omission or mis-statement shall be rectified.

405   Registration of enforcement of security

(1)   If a person obtains an order for the apportionment of a receiver or manager of a company's property, or appoints such a receiver or manager under powers contained in an instrument, he shall within 7 days of the order or of the appointment under those powers, give notice of the fact to the registrar of companies; and the registrar shall enter the fact in the register of charges.

(2)   Where a person appointed receiver or manager of a company's property under powers contained in an instrument ceases to act as such receiver or manager, he shall, on so ceasing, give the registrar notice to that effect, and the registrar shall enter the fact in the register of charges.

(3)   A notice under this section shall be in the prescribed form.

(4)   If a person makes default in complying with the requirements of this section, he is liable to a fine and, for continued contravention, to a daily default fine.

406   Companies to keep copies of instruments creating charges

(1)   Every company shall cause a copy of every instrument creating a charge requiring registration under this Chapter to be kept at its registered office.

(2)   In the case of a series of uniform debentures, a copy of one debenture of the series is sufficient.

407   Company's register of charges

(1)   Every limited company shall keep at its registered office a register of charges and enter in it all charges specifically affecting property of the company and all floating charges on the company's undertaking or any of its property.

(2)   The entry shall in each case give a short description of the property charged, the amount of the charge and, except in the case of securities to bearer, the names of the persons entitled to it.

(3)   If an officer of the company knowingly and wilfully authorises or permits the omission of an entry required to be made in pursuance of this section, he is liable to a fine.

408   Right to inspect instruments which create charges, etc

(1)   The copies of instruments creating any charge requiring registration under this Chapter with the registrar of companies, and the register of charges kept in pursuance of section 407, shall be open during business hours (but subject to such reasonable restrictions as the company in general meeting may impose, so that not less than 2 hours in each day be allowed for inspection) to the inspection of any creditor or member of the company without fee.

(2)   The register of charges shall also be open to the inspection of any other person on payment of such fee, not exceeding 5 pence, for each inspection, as the company may prescribe.

(3)   If inspection of the copies referred to, or of the register, is refused, every officer of the company who is in default is liable to a fine and, for continued contravention, to a daily default fine.

(4)   If such a refusal occurs in relation to a company registered in England and Wales, the court may by order compel an immediate inspection of the copies or register.

409   Charges on property in England and Wales created by oversea company

(1)   This Chapter extends to charges on property in England and Wales which are created, and to charges on property in England and Wales which is acquired, by a company (whether a company within the meaning of this Act or not) incorporated outside Great Britain which has an established place of business in England and Wales.

(2)   In relation to such a company, sections 406 and 407 apply with the substitution, for the reference to the company's registered office, of a reference to its principal place of business in England and Wales.

Appendix 3

Remedies

Torts (Interference with Goods) Act 1977

Preliminary

1 Definition of 'wrongful interference with goods'

In this Act 'wrongful interference', or 'wrongful interference with goods', means—

(a) conversion of goods (also called trover),

(b) trespass to goods,

(c) negligence so far as it results in damage to goods or to an interest in goods,

(d) subject to section 2, any other tort so far as it results in damage to goods or to an interest in goods

and reference in this Act (however worded) to proceedings for wrongful interference or to a claim or right to claim for wrongful interference shall include references to proceedings by virtue of Part I of the Consumer Protection Act 1987 or Part II of the Consumer Protection (Northern Ireland) Order 1987 (product liability) in respect of any damage to goods or to an interest in goods or, as the case may be, to a claim or right to claim by virtue of that Part in respect of any such damage.

Detention of goods

2 Abolition of detinue

(1) Detinue is abolished.

(2) An action lies in conversion for loss or destruction of goods which a bailee has allowed to happen in breach of his duty to his bailor (that is to say it lies in a case which is not otherwise conversion, but would have been detinue before detinue was abolished).

3 Form of judgment where goods are detained

(1) In proceedings for wrongful interference against a person who is in possession or in control of the goods relief may be given in accordance with this section, so far as appropriate.

(2) The relief is—

(a) an order for delivery of the goods, and for payment of any consequential damages, or

(b) an order for delivery of the goods, but giving the defendant the alternative of paying damages by reference to the value of the goods, together in either alternative with payment of any consequential damages, or

(c) damages.

(3) Subject to rules of court—

(a) relief shall be given under only one of paragraph (a), (b) and (c) of subsection (2).

(b) relief under paragraph (a) of subsection (2) is at the discretion of the court, and the claimant may choose between the others.

(4) If it is shown to the satisfaction of the court that an order under subsection (2)(a) has not been complied with, the court may—

(a) revoke the order, or the relevant part of it, and

(b) make an order for payment of damages by reference to the value of the goods.

(5)   Where an order is made under subsection (2)(b) the defendant may satisfy the order by returning the goods at any time before execution of judgment, but without prejudice to liability to pay any consequential damages.

(6)   An order for delivery of the goods under subsection (2)(a) or (b) may impose such conditions as may be determined by the court, or pursuant to rules of court, and in particular, where damages by reference to the value of the goods would not be the whole of the value of the goods, may require an allowance to be made by the claimant to reflect the difference.

For example, a bailor's action against the bailee may be one in which the measure of damages is not the full value of the goods, and then the court may order delivery of the goods, but require the bailor to pay the bailee a sum reflecting the difference.

(7)   Where under subsection (1) or subsection (2) of section 6 an allowance is to be made in respect of an improvement of the goods, and an order is made under subsection (2)(a) or (b), the court may assess the allowance to be made in respect of the improvement, and by the order require, as a condition for delivery of the goods, that allowance to be made by the claimant.

(8)   This section is without prejudice—

(a)   to the remedies afforded by section 133 of the Consumer Credit Act 1974, or

(b)   to the remedies afforded by sections 35, 42 and 44 of the Hire-Purchase Act 1965, or to those sections of the Hire-Purchase Act (Northern Ireland) 1966 (so long as those sections respectively remain in force), or

(c)   to any jurisdiction to afford ancillary or incidental relief.

4   Interlocutory relief where goods are detained

(1)   In this section 'proceedings' means proceedings for wrongful interference.

(2)   On the application of any person in accordance with rules of court, the High Court shall, in such circumstances as may be specified in the rules, have power to make an order providing for the delivery up of any goods which are or may become the subject matter of subsequent proceedings in the court, or as to which any question may arise in proceedings.

(3)   Delivery shall be, as the order may provide, to the claimant or to a person appointed by the court for the purpose, and shall be on such terms and conditions as may be specified in the order.

(4)   The power to make rules of court under section 84 of the Supreme Court Act 1981 or under section 7 of the Northern Ireland Act 1962 shall include power to make rules of court as to the manner in which an application for such an order can be made, and as to the circumstances in which such an order can be made; and any such rules may include such incidental, supplementary and consequential provisions as the authority making the rules may consider necessary or expedient.

(5)   The preceding provisions of this section shall have effect in relation to county courts as they have effect in relation to the High Court, and as if in those provisions references to rules of court and to section 84 of the said Act of 1981 or section 7 of the Northern Ireland Act 1962 included references to county court rules and to section 75 of the County Courts Act 1984 or Article 47 of the County Courts (Northern Ireland) Order 1980.

Damages

5   Extinction of title on satisfaction of claim for damages

(1)   Where damages for wrongful interference are, or would fall to be, assessed on the footing that the claimant is being compensated—

(a)   for the whole of his interest in the goods, or

(b)   for the whole of his interest in the goods subject to a reduction for contributory negligence,

payment of the assessed damages (under all heads), or as the case may be settlement of a claim for damages for the wrong (under all heads), extinguishes the claimant's title to that interest.

(2) In subsection (1) the reference to the settlement of the claim includes—

(a) where the claim is made in court proceedings, and the defendant has paid a sum into court to meet the whole claim, the taking of that sum by the claimant, and

(b) where the claim is made in court proceedings, and the proceedings are settled or compromised, the payment of what is due in accordance with the settlement or compromise, and

(c) where the claim is made out of court and is settled or compromised, the payment of what is due in accordance with the settlement or compromise.

(3) It is hereby declared that subsection (1) does not apply where damages are assessed on the footing that the claimant is being compensated for the whole of his interest in the goods, but the damages paid are limited to some lesser amount by virtue of any enactment or rule of law.

(4) Where under section 7(3) the claimant accounts over to another person (the 'third party') so as to compensate (under all heads) the third party for the whole of his interest in the goods, the third party's title to that interest is extinguished.

(5) This section has effect subject to any agreement varying the respective rights of the parties to the agreement, and where the claim is made in court proceedings has effect subject to any order of the court.

6 Allowance for improvement of the goods

(1) If in proceedings for wrongful interference against a person (the 'improver') who has improved the goods, it is shown that the improver acted in the mistaken but honest belief that he had a good title to them, an allowance shall be made for the extent to which, at the time as at which the goods fall to be valued in assessing damages, the value of the goods is attributable to the improvement.

(2) If, in proceedings for wrongful interference against a person ('the purchaser') who has purported to purchase the goods—

(a) from the improver, or

(b) where after such a purported sale of goods passed by a further purported sale on one or more occasions, on any such occasion,

it is shown that the purchaser acted in good faith, an allowance shall be made on the principle set out in subsection (1).

For example, where a person in good faith buys a stolen car from the improver and is sued in conversion by the true owner the damages may be reduced to reflect the improvement, but if the person who bought the stolen car from the improver sues the improver for failure of consideration, and the improver acted in good faith, subsection (3) below will ordinarily make a comparable reduction in the damages he recovers from the improver.

(3) If in a case within subsection (2) the person purporting to sell the goods acted in good faith, then in proceedings by the purchaser for recovery of the purchase price because of failure of consideration, or in any other proceedings founded on that failure of consideration, an allowance shall, where appropriate, be made on the principle set out in subsection (1).

(4) This section applies, with the necessary modifications, to a purported bailment or other disposition of goods as it applies to a purported sale of goods.

Liability to two or more claimants

7 Double liability

(1) In this section 'double liability' means the double liability of the wrongdoer which can arise—

(a) where one of two or more rights of action for wrongful interference is founded on a possessory title, or

(b)   where the measure of damages in an action for wrongful interference founded on a proprietary title is or includes the entire value of the goods, although the interest is one of two or more interests in the goods.

(2)   In proceedings to which any two or more claimants are parties, the relief shall be such as to avoid double liability of the wrongdoer as between those claimants.

(3)   On satisfaction, in whole or in part, of any claim for an amount exceeding that recoverable if subsection (2) applied, the claimant is liable to account over to the other person having a right to claim to such extent as will avoid double liability.

(4)   Where, as the result of enforcement of a double liability, any claimant is unjustly enriched to any extent, he shall be liable to reimburse the wrongdoer to that extent.

For example, is a converter of goods pays damages first to a finder of the goods, and then to the true owner, the finder is unjustly enriched unless he accounts over to the true owner under subsection (3); and then the true owner is unjustly enriched and becomes liable to reimburse the converter of the goods.

8   Competing rights to the goods

(1)   The defendant in an action for wrongful interference shall be entitled to show, in accordance with rules of court, that a third party has a better right than the plaintiff as respects all or any part of the interest claimed by the plaintiff, or in right of which he sues, and any rule of law (sometimes called jus tertii) to the contrary is abolished.

(2)   Rules of court relating to proceedings for wrongful interference may—

(a)   require the plaintiff to give particulars of his title,

(b)   require the plaintiff to identify any person who, to his knowledge, has or claims any interest in the goods,

(c)   authorise the defendant to apply for directions as to whether any person should be joined with a view to establishing whether he has a better right than the plaintiff, or has a claim as a result of which the defendant might be doubly liable,

(d)   where a party fails to appear on an application within paragraph (c), or to comply with any direction given by the court on such an application, authorise the court to deprive him of any right of action against the defendant for the wrong either unconditionally, or subject to such terms or conditions as may be specified.

(3)   Subsection (2) is without prejudice to any other power of making rules of court.

9   Concurrent actions

(1)   This section applies where goods are the subject of two or more claims for wrongful interference (whether or not the claims are founded on the same wrongful act, and whether or not any of the claims relates also to other goods).

(2)   Where goods are the subject of two or more claims under section 6 this section shall apply as if any claim under section 6(3) were a claim for wrongful interference.

(3)   If proceedings have been brought in a county court on one of those claims, county court rules may waive, or allow a court to waive, any limit (financial or territorial) on the jurisdiction of county courts in the County Courts Act 1984 or the County Courts (Northern Ireland) Order 1980 so as to allow another of those claims to be brought in the same county court.

(4)   If proceedings are brought on one of the claims in the High Court, and proceedings on any other are brought in a county court, whether prior to the High Court proceedings or not, the High Court may, on the application of the defendant, after notice has been given to the claimant in the county court proceedings—

(a)   order that the county court proceedings be transferred to the High Court, and

(b)   order security for costs or impose such other terms as the court thinks fit.

Conversion and trespass to goods

10   Co-owners

(1)   Co-ownership is no defence to an action founded on conversion or trespass to goods where the defendant without the authority of the other co-owner—

(a)   destroys the goods, or disposes of the goods in a way giving a good title to the entire property in the goods, or otherwise does anything equivalent to the destruction of the other's interest in the goods, or

(b)   purports to dispose of the goods in a way which would give a good title to the entire property in the goods if he was acting with the authority of all co-owners of the goods.

(2)   Subsection (1) shall not effect the law concerning execution or enforcement of judgments, or concerning any form of distress.

(3)   Subsection (1)(a) is by way of restatement of existing law so far as it relates to conversion.

11   Minor amendments

(1)   Contributory negligence is no good defence in proceedings founded on conversion, or on intentional trespass to goods.

(2)   Receipt of goods by way of pledge is conversion if the delivery of the goods is conversion.

(3)   Denial of title is not of itself conversion.

Uncollected goods

12   Bailee's power of sale

(1)   This section applies to goods in the possession or under the control of a bailee where—

(a)   the bailor is in breach of an obligation to take delivery of the goods or, if the terms of the bailment so provide, to give directions as to their delivery, or

(b)   the bailee could impose such an obligation by giving notice to the bailor, but is unable to trace or communicate with the bailor, or

(c)   the bailee can reasonably expect to be relieved of any duty to safeguard the goods on giving notice to the bailor, but is unable to trace or communicate with the bailor.

(2)   In the cases in Part I of Schedule 1 to this Act a bailee may, for the purposes of subsection (1), impose an obligation on the bailor to take delivery of the goods, or as the case may be to give directions as to their delivery, and in those cases the said Part I sets out the methods of notification.

(3)   If the bailee—

(a)   has in accordance with Part II of Schedule 1 to this Act given notice to the bailor of his intention to sell the goods under this subsection, or

(b)   has failed to trace or communicate with the bailor with a view to giving him such a notice, after having taken reasonable steps for the purpose.

and is reasonably satisfied that the bailor owns the goods, he shall be entitled, as against the bailor, to sell the goods.

(4)   Where subsection (3) applies but the bailor did not in fact own the goods, a sale under this section, or under section 13, shall not give a good title as against the owner, or as against a person claiming under the owner.

(5)   A bailee exercising his powers under subsection (3) shall be liable to account to the bailor for the proceeds of sale, less any costs of sale, and—

(a)   the account shall be taken on the footing that the bailee should have adopted the best method of sale reasonably available in the circumstances, and

(b)   where subsection (3)(a) applies, any sum payable in respect of the goods by the bailor to the bailee which accrued due before the bailee gave notice of intention to sell the goods shall be deductible from the proceeds of sale.

(6) A sale duly made under this section gives a good title to the purchaser as against the bailor.

(7) In this section, section 13, and Schedule 1 to the Act,

(a) 'bailor' and 'bailee' include their respective successors in title, and

(b) references to what is payable, paid or due to the bailee in respect of the goods include references to what would be payable by the bailor to the bailee as a condition of delivery of the goods at the relevant time.

(8) This section, and Schedule 1 to this Act, have effect subject to the terms of the bailment.

(9) This section shall not apply where the goods were bailed before the commencement of this Act.

13 Sale authorised by the court

(1) If a bailee of the goods to which section 12 applies satisfies the court that he is entitled to sell the goods under section 12, or that he would be so entitled if he had given any notice required in accordance with Schedule 1 to this Act, the court—

(a) may authorise the sale of the goods subject to such terms and conditions, if any, as may be specified in the order, and

(b) may authorise the bailee to deduct from the proceeds of sale any costs of sale and any amount due from the bailor to the bailee in respect of the goods, and

(c) may direct the payment into court of the net proceeds of sale, less any amount deducted under paragraph (b), to be held to the credit of the bailor.

(2) A decision of the court authorising a sale under this section shall, subject to any right of appeal, be conclusive, as against the bailor, of the bailee's entitlement to sell the goods, and gives a good title to the purchaser as against the bailor.

(3) In this section 'the court' means the High Court or a county court and a county court shall have jurisdiction in the proceedings save that, in Northern Ireland, a county court shall only have jurisdiction in proceedings if the value of the goods does not exceed the county court limit mentioned in Article 10(1) of the County Courts (Northern Ireland) Order 1980.

Supplemental

14 Interpretation

(1) In this Act, unless the context otherwise requires—

'enactment' includes an enactment contained in an Act of the Parliament of Northern Ireland or an Order in Council made under the Northern Ireland (Temporary Provisions) Act 1972, or in a Measure of the Northern Ireland Assembly,

'goods' includes all chattels personal other than things in action and money,

'High Court' includes the High Court of Justice of Northern Ireland.

(2) References in this Act to any enactment include references to that enactment as amended, extended or applied by or under that or any other enactment.

15 Repeal

(1) The Disposal of Uncollected Goods Act 1952 is hereby repealed.

(2) In England and Wales that repeal shall not affect goods bailed before the commencement of this Act.

(3) ...

16 Extent and application to the Crown

(1) ...

(2) This Act, except section 15, extends to Northern Ireland.

(3) This Act shall bind the Crown, but as regards the Crown's liability in tort shall not bind the Crown further than the Crown is made liable in tort by the Crown Proceedings Act 1947.

17 Short title, etc
(1) This Act may be cited as the Torts (Interference with Goods) Act 1977.
(2) This Act shall come into force on such day as the Lord Chancellor may by order contained in a statutory instrument appoint, and such an order may appoint different dates for different provisions or for different purposes.
(3) Schedule 2 to this Act contains transitional provisions.

SCHEDULE 1 UNCOLLECTED GOODS
Section 12

PART I POWER TO IMPOSE OBLIGATION TO COLLECT GOODS

1.—(1) For the purposes of section 12(1) a bailee may, in the circumstances specified in this Part of this Schedule, by notice given to the bailor impose on him an obligation to take delivery of the goods.
(2) The notice shall be in writing, and may be given either—
(a) by delivering it to the bailor, or
(b) by leaving it at his proper address, or
(c) by post.
(3) The notice shall—
(a) specify the name and address of the bailee, and give sufficient particulars of the goods and the address or place where they are held, and
(b) state that the goods are ready for delivery to the bailor, or where combined with a notice terminating the contract of bailment, will be ready for delivery when the contract is terminated, and
(c) specify the amount, if any, which is payable by the bailor to the bailee in respect of the goods and which became due before the giving of the notice.
(4) Where the notice is sent by post it may be combined with a notice under Part II of this Schedule if the notice is sent by post in a way complying with paragraph 6(4).
(5) References in this Part of this Schedule to taking delivery of the goods include, where the terms of the bailment admit, references to giving directions as to their delivery.
(6) This Part of this Schedule is without prejudice to the provisions of any contract requiring the bailor to take delivery of the goods.

Goods accepted for repair or other treatment
2. If a bailee has accepted goods for repair or other treatment on the terms (expressed or implied) that they will be re-delivered to the bailor when the repair or other treatment has been carried out, the notice may be given at any time after the repair or other treatment has been carried out.

Goods accepted for valuation or appraisal
3. If a bailee has accepted goods in order to value or appraise them, the notice may be given at any time after the bailee has carried out the valuation or appraisal.

Storage, warehousing, etc
4.—(1) If a bailee is in possession of goods which he has held as custodian, and his obligation as custodian has come to an end, the notice may be given at any time after the ending of the obligation, or may be combined with any notice terminating his obligation as custodian.
(2) This paragraph shall not apply to goods held by a person as mercantile agent, that is to say by a person having in the customary course of his business as a mercantile agent authority either to sell goods or to consign goods for the purpose of sale, or to buy goods, or to raise money on the security of goods.

Supplemental
5. Paragraphs 2,3 and 4 apply whether or not the bailor has paid any amount due to the bailee in respect of the goods, and whether or not the bailment is for reward, or in the course of business, or gratuitous.

PART II NOTICE OF INTENTION TO SELL GOODS

6.—(1)   A notice under section 12(3) shall
  (a) specify the name and address of the bailee, and give sufficient particulars of the goods and the address or place where they are held, and
  (b) specify the date on or after which the bailee proposes to sell the goods, and
  (c) specify the amount, if any, which is payable by the bailor to the bailee in respect of the goods, and which became due before the giving of the notice.
  (2)   The period between giving of the notice and the date specified in the notice as that on or after which the bailee proposes to exercise the power of sale shall be such as will afford the bailor a reasonable opportunity of taking delivery of the goods.
  (3)   If any amount is payable in respect of the goods by the bailor to the bailee, and became due before giving of the notice, the said period shall be not less than three months.
  (4)   The notice shall be in writing and shall be sent by post in a registered letter, or by the recorded delivery service.

7.—(1)   The bailee shall not give a notice under section 12(3), or exercise his right to sell the goods pursuant to such a notice, at a time when he has notice that, because of a dispute concerning the goods, the bailor is questioning or refusing to pay all or any part of what the bailee claims to be due to him in respect of the goods.
  (2)   This paragraph shall be left out of account in determining under section 13(1) whether a bailee of goods is entitled to sell the goods under section 12, or would be so entitled if he had given any notice required in accordance with this Schedule.

Supplemental
8.   For the purposes of this Schedule, and of section 26 of the Interpretation Act 1889 in its application to this Schedule, the proper address of the person to whom a notice is to be given shall be—
  (a) in the case of a body corporate, a registered or principal office of the body corporate, and
  (b) in any other case, the last known address of the person.

SCHEDULE 2 TRANSITIONAL
Section 17

1.   This Act shall not affect any action or arbitration brought before the commencement of this Act or any proceedings brought to enforce a decision in the action or arbitration.

2.   Subject to paragraph 1, this Act applies to acts or omissions before it comes into force as well as to later ones, and for the purposes of the Limitation Act 1939, the Statute of Limitations (Northern Ireland) 1958, or any other limitation enactment, the cause of action shall be treated as having accrued at the time of the act or omission even if proceedings could not have been brought before the commencement of this Act.

3.   For the purposes of this Schedule, any claim by way of set-off or counterclaim shall be deemed to be a separate action, and to have been brought on the same date as the action in which the set-off or counterclaim is pleaded.

Index